# Communications in Computer and Information Science    2055

Series Editors

Gang Li ⓘ, *School of Information Technology, Deakin University, Burwood, VIC, Australia*
Joaquim Filipe ⓘ, *Polytechnic Institute of Setúbal, Setúbal, Portugal*
Zhiwei Xu, *Chinese Academy of Sciences, Beijing, China*

**Rationale**
The CCIS series is devoted to the publication of proceedings of computer science conferences. Its aim is to efficiently disseminate original research results in informatics in printed and electronic form. While the focus is on publication of peer-reviewed full papers presenting mature work, inclusion of reviewed short papers reporting on work in progress is welcome, too. Besides globally relevant meetings with internationally representative program committees guaranteeing a strict peer-reviewing and paper selection process, conferences run by societies or of high regional or national relevance are also considered for publication.

**Topics**
The topical scope of CCIS spans the entire spectrum of informatics ranging from foundational topics in the theory of computing to information and communications science and technology and a broad variety of interdisciplinary application fields.

**Information for Volume Editors and Authors**
Publication in CCIS is free of charge. No royalties are paid, however, we offer registered conference participants temporary free access to the online version of the conference proceedings on SpringerLink (http://link.springer.com) by means of an http referrer from the conference website and/or a number of complimentary printed copies, as specified in the official acceptance email of the event.

CCIS proceedings can be published in time for distribution at conferences or as post-proceedings, and delivered in the form of printed books and/or electronically as USBs and/or e-content licenses for accessing proceedings at SpringerLink. Furthermore, CCIS proceedings are included in the CCIS electronic book series hosted in the SpringerLink digital library at http://link.springer.com/bookseries/7899. Conferences publishing in CCIS are allowed to use Online Conference Service (OCS) for managing the whole proceedings lifecycle (from submission and reviewing to preparing for publication) free of charge.

**Publication process**
The language of publication is exclusively English. Authors publishing in CCIS have to sign the Springer CCIS copyright transfer form, however, they are free to use their material published in CCIS for substantially changed, more elaborate subsequent publications elsewhere. For the preparation of the camera-ready papers/files, authors have to strictly adhere to the Springer CCIS Authors' Instructions and are strongly encouraged to use the CCIS LaTeX style files or templates.

**Abstracting/Indexing**
CCIS is abstracted/indexed in DBLP, Google Scholar, EI-Compendex, Mathematical Reviews, SCImago, Scopus. CCIS volumes are also submitted for the inclusion in ISI Proceedings.

**How to start**
To start the evaluation of your proposal for inclusion in the CCIS series, please send an e-mail to ccis@springer.com.

Muhammad Arif · Arfan Jaffar · Oana Geman
Editors

# Computing and Emerging Technologies

First International Conference, ICCET 2023
Lahore, Pakistan, May 26–27, 2023
Revised Selected Papers, Part I

*Editors*
Muhammad Arif ⓘ
Superior University
Lahore, Pakistan

Arfan Jaffar ⓘ
Superior University
Lahore, Pakistan

Oana Geman ⓘ
Ştefan cel Mare University of Suceava
Suceava, Romania

ISSN 1865-0929 ISSN 1865-0937 (electronic)
Communications in Computer and Information Science
ISBN 978-3-031-77616-8 ISBN 978-3-031-77617-5 (eBook)
https://doi.org/10.1007/978-3-031-77617-5

© The Editor(s) (if applicable) and The Author(s), under exclusive license
to Springer Nature Switzerland AG 2025

This work is subject to copyright. All rights are solely and exclusively licensed by the Publisher, whether the whole or part of the material is concerned, specifically the rights of translation, reprinting, reuse of illustrations, recitation, broadcasting, reproduction on microfilms or in any other physical way, and transmission or information storage and retrieval, electronic adaptation, computer software, or by similar or dissimilar methodology now known or hereafter developed.
The use of general descriptive names, registered names, trademarks, service marks, etc. in this publication does not imply, even in the absence of a specific statement, that such names are exempt from the relevant protective laws and regulations and therefore free for general use.
The publisher, the authors and the editors are safe to assume that the advice and information in this book are believed to be true and accurate at the date of publication. Neither the publisher nor the authors or the editors give a warranty, expressed or implied, with respect to the material contained herein or for any errors or omissions that may have been made. The publisher remains neutral with regard to jurisdictional claims in published maps and institutional affiliations.

This Springer imprint is published by the registered company Springer Nature Switzerland AG
The registered company address is: Gewerbestrasse 11, 6330 Cham, Switzerland

If disposing of this product, please recycle the paper.

# Preface

The 2023 International Conference on Computing & Emerging Technologies (ICCET), held from May 26–27, 2023, in Lahore, Pakistan, was a pivotal gathering for researchers, practitioners, and industry experts to explore the latest advancements in computing and emerging technologies. This conference served as a premier forum where participants collaborated to push the boundaries of knowledge in this rapidly evolving field.

ICCET 2023 implemented a rigorous double-blind peer review process to ensure impartial evaluation. Each of the 170 submissions, comprising full papers, short papers, and contributions, underwent scrutiny by at least three independent reviewers. This meticulous approach guaranteed that papers selected for presentation and inclusion in the proceedings were chosen solely based on their scholarly merit and contribution to the field.

From the submissions received, 65 papers were accepted for inclusion in this volume, including 50 full papers and 15 short papers. These contributions represent significant advancements in both theoretical understanding and practical applications of computing technologies.

To maintain fairness and objectivity, papers authored by members of the organizing or program committees underwent the same rigorous evaluation as those from external contributors. Independent reviewers were tasked with overseeing this process to mitigate any potential conflicts of interest, ensuring an unbiased assessment.

The success of ICCET 2023 is attributed to the dedication and hard work of the program committee, reviewers, and organizing team. Their commitment to excellence facilitated seamless execution of the conference, fostering meaningful discussions and enabling knowledge exchange among participants. Gratitude is also extended to sponsors and partners whose support was instrumental in ensuring the event's success.

This volume of proceedings from ICCET 2023 aims to serve as a valuable resource for researchers, educators, and industry professionals alike. It offers insights into cutting-edge research presented at the conference, inviting readers to explore diverse topics, discover new ideas, and continue dialogues initiated during the event.

We sincerely thank all participants for their invaluable contributions and engagement. We look forward to future collaborations and advancements in computing and emerging technologies, spurred by the insights and discussions shared at ICCET 2023.

Sincerely,

Muhammad Arif
Arfan Jaffar

# Organization

## General Chairs

Muhammad Arif — Superior University, Pakistan
Arfan Jaffar — Superior University, Pakistan

## Program Chairs

Tehreem Masood — Superior University, Pakistan
Sheraz Akram — Superior University, Pakistan
Oana Geman — Ştefan cel Mare University of Suceava, Romania

## Publicity Chairs

Irfan Ud Din — Superior University, Pakistan
Danish Shahzad — Superior University, Pakistan
Asad Ali Naqvi — Superior University, Pakistan

## Registration and Publication Chairs

Hamayun Khan — Superior University, Pakistan
Waseem Abbasi — Superior University, Sargodha Campus, Pakistan
Faizan Khan — University of Haripur, Pakistan

## Finance Chairs

Sohail Masood — Superior University, Pakistan
Moomal Qureshi — Superior University, Pakistan

## Local Arrangement Chairs

Imran Khan — Superior University, Pakistan
Hamayun Khan — Superior University, Pakistan

Muhammad Azam — Superior University, Pakistan
Muhammad Arif — Superior University, Pakistan

## Technical Program Committee

| | |
|---|---|
| Ioan Ungurean | Ştefan cel Mare University, Romania |
| Iuliana Chiuchisan | Ştefan cel Mare University, Romania |
| Alexandra Balan | Ştefan cel Mare University, Romania |
| Marius Prelipceanu | Ştefan cel Mare University, Romania |
| Doru Balan | Ştefan cel Mare University, Romania |
| Cristian Aghion | Technical University of Iaşi, Romania |
| Marius Hagan | Technical University of Iaşi, Romania |
| Adrian Brezulianu | Technical University of Iaşi, Romania |
| Mihaela Hnatiuc | Constanta Maritime University, Romania |
| Octavian Postolache | Instituto de Telecomunicações, IT-IUL, Portugal |
| V. Dhilip Kumar | Vel Tech R & D Institute of Science and Technology, India |
| Ayyaz Hussain | Quaid-i-Azam University Islamabad, Pakistan |
| Muhammad Ramzan | Saudi Electronic University, Saudi Arabia |
| Qaisar Abbas | Imam Muhammad Ibn Saud Islamic University, Saudi Arabia |
| Abdul Basit Siddiqui | CUST, Pakistan |
| Muhammad Aleem | FAST-NUCES, Islamabad, Pakistan |
| Hassan Kiyani | FAST-NUCES, Islamabad, Pakistan |
| Amjad Iqbal | UCP, Pakistan |
| Mubashar Mushtaq | FC University, Pakistan |
| Safdar Iqbal | UOL, Pakistan |
| Sultan Zia | University of Chinab, Pakistan |
| Kashif Zafar | FAST-NUCES, Lahore, Pakistan |
| Imran Tatiq Butt | Govt. Commerce College, Pakistan |
| Rana Asif Rehman | FAST-NUCES, Lahore, Pakistan |
| Aun Irtaza | UET Taxila, Pakistan |
| Asmi Munir | International Islamic University Islamabad, Pakistan |
| Qaisar Javed | International Islamic University Islamabad, Pakistan |
| Muhammad Nadeem | International Islamic University Islamabad, Pakistan |
| Muhammad Naqi | Quaid-i-Azam University Islamabad, Pakistan |
| Muhammad Ishtiaq | FAST-NUCES, Islamabad, Pakistan |
| Mohsin Bilal | FAST-NUCES, Islamabad, Pakistan |

| | |
|---|---|
| Muhammad Aslam | UET Lahore, Pakistan |
| Abdul Rauf Baig | Imam Muhamamd Ibn Saud Islamic University, Saudi Arabia |
| Ghazanfar Latif | PMU Dammam, Saudi Arabia |
| Khurram Shahzad | UMT Lahore, Pakistan |
| Shaukat Iqbal | UMT Lahore, Pakistan |
| Muhammad Waqas | Kohsar University Murree, Pakistan |
| Muhammad Nazir | HITEC University Taxila, Pakistan |
| Sajid Anwar | IM Sciences Peshawar, Pakistan |
| Zunaira Jaleel | Air University, Pakistan |
| Muhammad Imran | SZABIST Islamabad, Pakistan |
| Muhammad Arif | Foundation University Islamabad, Pakistan |

# Contents–Part I

Incube: The Project Repository Based on Blockchain .................... 1
  Omer Sajid, Samia Asloob Qureshi, and Rabranea Bqa

Algorithm Trading Using Data Science ................................. 11
  Amina Bibi, Danish Shehzad, and Ahsan Imtiaz

Determining Student's Online Academic Performance Using Machine
Learning Techniques .................................................. 24
  Atika Islam, Faisal Bukhari, and Waheed Iqbal

User Experience (UX) Enrichment Through Digital Branding .............. 37
  Saira Zia, Muhammad Waseem Iqbal, Misbah Noor, Muhammad Aqeel,
  and Khalid Hamid

SDN-Enabled Resource and Energy Management Framework in Smart
Buildings Using Los-Cost Air Quality Sensors .......................... 51
  Asim Fareed, Majid Hussain, Muhammad Ibrar, and Munazzah Munawar

Air Quality Predictions Using Machine Learning Models ................. 57
  Sana Younas, Humaira Khalid, Umair Muneer Butt, and Rida Khaliq

Implementation of IoT and WSN Technologies for Health Monitoring ...... 73
  Tehseen Mazhar, Muhammad Iqbal, Muhammad Iqbal,
  Yazeed Yasin Ghadi, Ateeq Ur Rehman, and Waseem Abbasi

Breast Cancer Diagnosis Based on Deep Convolutional Neural Networks
Using Image Clustering ............................................... 88
  Sanamaqbool, Majid Hussain, Uzair Saeed,
  and Muhammad Farrukh Shafeeq

Driver Distraction Detection Using a Multi-stream Deep Fusion Network .. 97
  Hafiza Iqra Qamar, Uzair Saeed, and Majid Hussain

Handwritten Character Recognition Using Fusion SVM-CNN ............... 105
  Anam Lateef, Majid Hussain, Uzair Saeed, and Ihsan Elahi

Automated Skin Cancer Segmentation and Classification Based on Deep
Learning ............................................................ 116
  Noor Ul Ain, Faisal Bukhari, and Waheed Iqbal

Performance Analysis of Self-adaptive User Interface for Mobile Users (Systematic Literature Review) .......................................... 130
   *Muddassar Ali, Muhammad Raheel, Muhammad Waseem Iqbal, and Danish Irfan*

Sentiment Analysis of Twitter Posts on 5G Technology Using ML ............ 151
   *Mehak Faryal, Muhammad Farhan Khan, Saeid Rezaei, Muhammad Sohail, Kinza Salim, Muhammad Imran Khan, and Adeel Iqbal*

Exploring Language Modeling Techniques for Improved Recommender Systems .............................................................. 160
   *Muhammad Junaid Iqbal, Usman Ahmed Raza, Faisal Rehman, Muhammad Asaf, Yawar Ahmed, Usman Nawaz, Muhammad Saqlain Iqbal, and Ammara Tariq*

Machine Learning Based Approach to Secure Light Weight Devices .......... 174
   *Saim Raza, Majid Hussain, Hina Zafar, and Amna Iqbal*

GAPTCHA: A Game-Based Image-CAPTCHA ............................ 181
   *Umar Farooq, Noshina Tariq, Danish Mehmood, Maram Fahaad Almufareh, Mamoona Humayun, and Farrukh Aslam Khan*

A Comprehensive Survey on Software Defined Networking (SDN) Security ... 193
   *Nouman Mabood, Noshina Tariq, Farrukh Aslam Khan, and Muhammad Ashraf*

Access Control Techniques for Cloud Computing: Review and Recommendations ................................................ 206
   *Mannan Javed, Noshina Tariq, Farrukh Aslam Khan, and Muhammad Ashraf*

Linguistic Resources for Extremism Detection on Social Media .............. 219
   *Muhammad Anwar Hussain, Muhammad Khurram Shahzad, and Sarina Sulaiman*

Improved Pak Currency Identification for Blind and Visually Impaired People ................................................................ 228
   *Usman Ahmed Raza, Mohsin Ashraf, Asif Farooq, Muhammad Irtaza Khan, Muhammad Bilal khan, and Mohsin Sami*

The Study of Agile Methodologies and Challenges in Software
Requirements Engineering ............................................. 239
   *Muhammad Iqbal, Syed Faisal Abbas Shah, Tehseen Mazhar,
Muhammad Amir, Ateeq Ur Rehman, and Waseem Abbasi*

Predicting Heart Disease with Machine Learning: A Comparative Study
of Classifiers ........................................................ 250
   *Nadia Rehmat, Hassan Faraz, Tayyaba Farhat, Sanya Abdullah,
and Rasikh Ali*

Media Forensics and Deepfake-Systematic Survey ......................... 264
   *C. H. Nadeem Jabbar, Aqib Saghir, Ayaz Ahmad Meer,
Salman Ahmad Sahi, Bilal Hassan, and Siddiqui Muhammad Yasir*

A Convolutional Neural Network Approach for Mood Classification
in Short Texts Using Character-Level Details and Local Text Structure ........ 300
   *Moodser Hussain, Muhammad Jameel, Muhammad Farhat Ullah,
Taimoor Hassan Jabbar, Roha Irfan, and Muhammad Waseem Iqbal*

Usability Approach of Distributed Database in Health Care System ........... 308
   *Sana Mazhar, Muhammad Waseem Iqbal, and Muhammad Ahmad Irshad*

Audio Source Separation: Advances and Challenges ....................... 324
   *Fawad Nasim, Sheeraz Akram, Sohail Masood, Arfan Jaffar,
Muhammad Hussain Akbar, and Ch Zubair Kahloon*

A Survey on Approximate Hardware Accelerator for Error-Tolerant
Applications ........................................................ 332
   *Sahibzada M. Waqas, Muhammad Zakwan, Muhammad Ashraf,
Ghadah Naif AlWakid, and Mamoona Humayun*

Deep Learning Based Multi Focus Image Fusion ........................... 345
   *Muhammad Ahmed, Arfan Jaffer, and Natasha Ali*

SLR Based on Requirement Elicitation and Modeling in GSD ............... 369
   *Aftab Rafique, Usman Ahmed Raza, Usman Nawaz, Namra Waheed,
Maryam Kauser, Mariam Munsif Mir, and Rohail Shahzad*

An Efficient Machine Learning Technique for Prediction of Cardiovascular
Disease ............................................................. 391
   *Rida Nawaz*

Analysis and Development of Kids' Cell Activities Monitoring App .......... 405
*Umme Tehreem, Muhammad Waseem Iqbal, Khalid Hamid, and Muhammad Mohsin Saeed*

**Author Index** ....................................................... 405

# Contents – Part II

Analysis of Phishing URLs Based on Machine Learning .................... 1
   *Muhammad Zulkifl Hasan, Muhammad Zunnurain Hussain,*
   *Nadeem Sarwar, Touheed Naveed, Masroor Ahmed, Khizar Tariq,*
   *Zaima Mubarak, Ali Moiz Qureshi, and Adeel Ahmad Siddiqui*

Audio Source Separation: Advances and Challenges ....................... 21
   *Fawad Nasim, Sheeraz Akram, Sohail Masood, Arfan Jaffar,*
   *Muhammad Hussain Akbar, and Ch Zubair Kahloon*

Automatic Invasive Ductal Carcinoma Detection Using Convolutional
Neural Networks ....................................................... 29
   *Hamza Mustafa and Kashif Zafar*

Intelligent Diagnosis and Assessment of Heart Patients Using Machine
Learning .............................................................. 47
   *Waseem Iqbal, Arfan Jaffar, and Danish Shahzad*

Automated Detection of COVID-19 Using Deep Convolutional Neural
Network (CNNs) Using Chest Radiograph and CT Scan Images .............. 61
   *Naeem Uallah, Javed Ali Khan, Asaf Raza, Syed Yaqub Shah,*
   *Muhammad Assam, and Hasna Arshad*

Development and Evaluation of Smartphones Interface for Elderly ........... 75
   *Anam Maqsood Bhatti, Muhammad Waseem Iqbal, and Imran Siddique*

Cyber Physical Systems Having Nodes/Layers with Trustworthy Data:
A Review .............................................................. 93
   *Muhammad Ejazulghaffar, Muhammad Arif, Arfan Jaffar,*
   *and Ahmed Hassan*

Analysis of Device-To-Device Communication in Iot System ................ 108
   *Usman Nawaz, Faisal Rehman, Kainat Azmat Ullah,*
   *Usman Ahmed Raza, Hanan Sharif, Furqan Rafique, Abid Ali,*
   *Masood Ashiq, and Junaid Iqbal*

Extending WSN Lifetime with Cluster Head Election ...................... 128
   *Noroze Fatima, Danish Shehzad, Ali Imran, Ahsan, and M. Arif*

Automatic HTP Assessment for Schizophrenic Patients Using Machine
Learning .................................................................. 141
    Muhammad Zubair, Samra Kyinat, and Sohail Masood

Deep-Learning Based Multi-Modalities Fusion for the Detection
of Brain-Related Diseases: A Review ...................................... 149
    Syed Muhammad Ali Imran, Muhammad Arif, Arfan Jaffar,
    Hafiz Muhammad Tayyab Khushi, and Abida Hussain

Human Activity Recognition Using Transformer Model ....................... 171
    Hafiz Yasir Ghafoor, Muhammad Izhar, Muhammad Zubair,
    Mian Abid, and Rashid Jahangir

Usability Impact of Conversational Chatbot ............................... 191
    Maryam Rasheed, Muhammad Waseem Iqbal, Anam Fatima,
    Maryam Saleem, Sohail Masood Bhatti, and Muhammad Junaid Ahsan

Securing Drug Supply Chain with Medledger: A Blockchain Solution
to Counterfeit and Hoarding Challenges ................................... 205
    M. Saad Bin Ilyas, Imtiaz Ali Soomro, Iqra Tariq,
    and Muhammad Adil Butt

Implementation of Authentic Resources for E-Learning in Education ........ 223
    Muhammad Yousaf Mushtaq, Hafiz Muhammad Irfan,
    Muhammad Ahmad Niaz, Muhammad Waseem Iqbal, Anas Mazhar,
    Adnan Akhtar, and Amir Jamshaid

Securing Cyber-Physical Systems by Using Artificial Intelligence ......... 239
    Muhammad Umar, Majid Hussain, Hina Zafar, and Amna Iqbal

An Efficient Implementation of an IoT-Based Smart Home Security System ... 249
    Zainab, Hamayun Khan, Irfan Ud Din, Muhammad Imran Tariq,
    Aleena Khalid, and Amna Naz

Access and Secure Patient Medical Records Using Blockchain Technology
Based Framework: A Review ................................................ 260
    Attique Ur Rehman, Muhammad Haseeb Zafar, and Muhammad Aslam

Subcellular Structures Classification in Fluorescence Microscopic Images .. 271
    Saif Ur Rehman Khan, Asif Raza, Inzamam Shahzad, and Shehzad Khan

Bioelectric Signal Acquisition and Design of Portable ECG for Medical
Internet of Things Applications .......................................... 287
    Abrar Ashraf, Sadia Sahar, Muhammad Waseem Iqbal, Danish Irfan,
    M. Ameer Hamza, Sylvester Joseph, and Muhammad Tassawar Iqbal

Classification of Cloud Attacks Using Deep Learning .................... 298
    Muhammad Zulkifl Hasan, Muhammad Zunnurain Hussain,
    Muhammad Umer Nadeem, Muhammad Zeeshan Nazar,
    Summaira Nosheen, Muhammad Atif Yaqub, Afshan Bilal,
    Saeed Anwar, and Muhammad Ahmad

Facial Expression Recognition Using Convolution Neural Network .......... 308
    Abaid Ullah

Distinguishing Parkinsons Disease and Essential Tremors by Using
Machine Learning .................................................... 322
    Muhammad Hassan, Uzair Saeed, and Majid Hussain

A Jurisprudence for Pakistan's Digital Forensic Investigation Framework
Regarding Cybersecurity ............................................. 330
    Ehtisham Ul Haque and Waseem Abbasi

Framework for Efficient Identification of Features Associated
with Software Defects Using Spearman Correlation and Apriori Algorithm .... 339
    Muhammad Umar Sajjad, Muhammad Qasim Riaz, Usman Qamar,
    Muhammad Danish Riaz, Muhammad Talha Imtiaz, and Muhammad Arif

Segmentation of Brain Tumor Using U-Net Approach .................... 350
    Samra Riaz and Syed Muhammad Anwar

Design and Implementation of an On-Board System for a Spider Robot ....... 362
    Nasir Nauman, Hirra Mustafa, Abrar Ashraf, and Hisham Khalil

MEHAK: Explainable AI Classifier for COVID-19 Early Detection Based
on LIME ............................................................ 372
    Mehak Rana, Majid Hussain, and Uzair Saeed

An Interactive System Based on First-Class User-Level Threads:
A Systematic Review ................................................. 380
    Sadia Sahar, Hamayun Khan, Muhammad Imran Tariq, Irfan Ud din,
    Abrar Ashraf, and Syeda Aqsa Zahra

An Effective IoT-Based Learning System for Children .................... 395
    Hamza Afzal, Irfan ud Din, and Ahsan Imtiaz

Security Enhancement of Patient Data in the Internet of Healthcare
Systems (IoHT)-A Blockchain Approach .................................. 405
   *Muhammad Ali, Tehreem Masood, and Ammerha Naz*

Analysis of ICT Infrastructure w.r.t. Performance and Security Perspective
Using SIEM Capabilities ................................................... 415
   *M. Usman Bilal, M. Waseem Iqbal, and Danish Irfan*

**Author Index** ........................................................... 433

# Contributors

**Waseem Abbasi** Department of Computer Science and IT, Superior University, Sargodha, Pakistan

**Sanya Abdullah** Faculty of Computer Science and Information Technology, The Superior University, Lahore, Pakistan;
Intelligent Data Visual Computing Research (IDVCR), Lahore, Pakistan

**Muhammad Ahmed** Superior University Lahore, Lahore, Pakistan

**Yawar Ahmed** Department of Computer Science, Lahore Leads University, Lahore, Pakistan

**Noor Ul Ain** Department of Computer Science, Faculty of Computing and Information Technology (FCIT), University of the Punjab (PU), Lahore, Pakistan

**Muhammad Hussain Akbar** Superior University, Lahore, Lahore, Pakistan

**Sheeraz Akram** Superior University, Lahore, Lahore, Pakistan;
Intelligent Data Visual Computing Research (IDVCR), Lahore, Pakistan

**Muddassar Ali** Department of Computer Science, The Superior University, Lahore, Pakistan

**Natasha Ali** Superior University Lahore, Lahore, Pakistan

**Rasikh Ali** Faculty of Computer Science and Information Technology, The Superior University, Lahore, Pakistan;
Intelligent Data Visual Computing Research (IDVCR), Lahore, Pakistan

**Maram Fahaad Almufareh** Department of Information Systems, College of Computer and Information Sciences, Jouf University, Sakakah, Al Jouf, Saudi Arabia

**Ghadah Naif AlWakid** College of Computer and Information Sciences, Al Jouf University, Sakakah, Saudi Arabia

**Muhammad Amir** Department of Computer Science and Information Technology, Virtual University of Pakistan, Lahore, Pakistan

**Muhammad Aqeel** Department of Computer Science, Superior University Lahore, Lahore, Pakistan

**Muhammad Asaf** Department of Computer Science, Lahore Leads University, Lahore, Pakistan

**Mohsin Ashraf** Department of Computer Science, University of Central Punjab (UCP), Lahore, Pakistan

**Muhammad Ashraf** Department of Avionics Engineering, Air University, Islamabad, Pakistan;
Center of Excellence in Information Assurance, King Saud University, Riyadh, Saudi Arabia

**Amina Bibi** Superior University, Lahore, Pakistan

**Rabranea Bqa** Department of Computer Science, Forman Christian College (A Chartered University), Lahore, Pakistan

**Faisal Bukhari** Department of Data Science, Faculty of Computing and Information Technology (FCIT), University of the Punjab (PU), Lahore, Pakistan

**Umair Muneer Butt** Department of Computer Science and IT, The University of Chenab, Gujrat, Gujranwala, Pakistan

**Ihsan Elahi** Department of Computer Science, The University of Faisalabad, Faisalabad, Pakistan

**Hassan Faraz** Faculty of Computer Science and Information Technology, The Superior University, Lahore, Pakistan;
Intelligent Data Visual Computing Research (IDVCR), Lahore, Pakistan

**Asim Fareed** Department of Computer Science, The University of Faisalabad, Faisalabad, Pakistan

**Tayyaba Farhat** Faculty of Computer Science and Information Technology, The Superior University, Lahore, Pakistan;
Intelligent Data Visual Computing Research (IDVCR), Lahore, Pakistan

**Asif Farooq** Department of Computer Science, University of Central Punjab (UCP), Lahore, Pakistan

**Umar Farooq** Department of Computer Science, Shaheed Zulfikar Ali Bhutto Institute of Science and Technology, Islamabad, Pakistan

**Mehak Faryal** University of Engineering and Technology, Taxila, Pakistan

**Yazeed Yasin Ghadi** Department of Computer Science and Software Engineering, Al Ain Universit, Abu Dhabi, UAE

**Khalid Hamid** Department of Computer Science, Superior University Lahore, Lahore, Pakistan

**Bilal Hassan** Northumbria University, London Campus, UK

**Mamoona Humayun** Department of Information Systems, College of Computer and Information Sciences, Jouf University, Sakakah, Al Jouf, Saudi Arabia

**Majid Hussain** Department of Computer Science, The University of Faisalabad (TUF), Faisalabad, Pakistan

**Moodser Hussain** Department of Information Technology, University of the Punjab, Gujranwala, Pakistan

**Muhammad Anwar Hussain** School of Computing, Universiti of Teknologi Malaysia, Skudai, Johor, Malaysia

**Muhammad Ibrar** Department of Computer Science, The University of Faisalabad, Faisalabad, Pakistan

**Ahsan Imtiaz** Superior University, Lahore, Pakistan

**Adeel Iqbal** Department of Electrical and Computer Engineering, COMSATS University Islamabad, Islamabad, Pakistan

**Amna Iqbal** The University of Faisalabad, Faisalabad, Pakistan

**Muhammad Iqbal** Institute of Computing and Information Technology, Gomal University, Dera Ismail Khan, Pakistan;
Department of Computer Science, Virtual University of Pakistan, Lahore, Pakistan

**Muhammad Junaid Iqbal** Department of Computer Science, Lahore Leads University, Lahore, Pakistan

**Muhammad Saqlain Iqbal** Department of Chemistry, COMSATS University Islamabad, Lahore Campus, Lahore, Pakistan;
Department of Electrical and Information Engineering, Polytechnic University of Bari, Bari, Italy

**Muhammad Waseem Iqbal** Department of Software Engineering, The Superior University, Lahore, Pakistan

**Waheed Iqbal** Department of Data Science, Faculty of Computing and Information Technology (FCIT), University of the Punjab (PU), Lahore, Pakistan

**Danish Irfan** Department of Information Technology, The Superior University, Lahore, Pakistan

**Roha Irfan** Department of Computer Science, University of Central Punjab Lahore, Lahore, Pakistan

**Muhammad Ahmad Irshad** Department of Computer Science, Superior University, Lahore, Pakistan

**Atika Islam** Department of Computer Science, University of the Punjab, Lahore, Pakistan

**Taimoor Hassan Jabbar** Department of Computer Science, BZU, Multan, Pakistan

**Arfan Jaffar** Superior University, Lahore, Lahore, Pakistan;
Intelligent Data Visual Computing Research (IDVCR), Lahore, Pakistan

**Muhammad Jameel** Department of Computer Science, Superior University Lahore, Lahore, Pakistan

**Mannan Javed** Department of Avionics Engineering, Air University, Islamabad, Pakistan

**Ch Zubair Kahloon**  Superior University, Lahore, Lahore, Pakistan

**Maryam Kauser**  Department of Software Engineering and Information Technology, Foundation University, Rawalpindi Campus, Islamabad, Pakistan

**Humaira Khalid**  Department of Computer Science and IT, The University of Chenab, Gujrat, Gujranwala, Pakistan

**Rida Khaliq**  Department of Computer Science and IT, The University of Chenab, Gujrat, Gujranwala, Pakistan

**Farrukh Aslam Khan**  Center of Excellence in Information Assurance (CoEIA), King Saud University, Riyadh, Saudi Arabia

**Muhammad Farhan Khan**  Confirm Centre for Smart Manufacturing, University College Cork, Cork, Ireland

**Muhammad Imran Khan**  Insight Centre for Data Analytics, University College Cork, Cork, Ireland

**Muhammad Irtaza Khan**  Department of Information Technology, University of Lahore, Lahore, Pakistan

**Muhammad Bilal khan**  Department of Computer Science, University of Central Punjab (UCP), Lahore, Pakistan

**Anam Lateef**  Department of Computer Science, The University of Faisalabad, Faisalabad, Pakistan

**Nouman Mabood**  Department of Avionics Engineering, Air University, Islamabad, Pakistan

**Sidra Maqbool**  Superior University, Lahore, Pakistan

**Sohail Masood**  Superior University, Lahore, Lahore, Pakistan; Intelligent Data Visual Computing Research (IDVCR), Lahore, Pakistan

**Sana Mazhar**  Department of Software Engineering, Superior University, Lahore, Pakistan

**Tehseen Mazhar**  Department of Computer Science and Information Technology, Virtual University of Pakistan, Lahore, Pakistan

**Ayaz Ahmad Meer**  Northumbria University, London Campus, UK

**Danish Mehmood**  Department of Computer Science, Shaheed Zulfikar Ali Bhutto Institute of Science and Technology, Islamabad, Pakistan

**Mariam Munsif Mir**  NAMAL University, Mianwali, Pakistan

**Munazzah Munawar**  Department of Computer Science, The University of Faisalabad, Faisalabad, Pakistan

**C. H. Nadeem Jabbar**  Department of Computer Science, The Superior University, Lahore, Pakistan

**Fawad Nasim** Superior University, Lahore, Lahore, Pakistan;
Intelligent Data Visual Computing Research (IDVCR), Lahore, Pakistan

**Rida Nawaz** Superior University, Lahore, Pakistan

**Usman Nawaz** Department of Information Technology, University of Gujrat, Gujrat, Pakistan;
Department of Chemistry, COMSATS University Islamabad, Lahore Campus, Lahore, Pakistan

**Misbah Noor** Department of Computer Science, Superior University Lahore, Lahore, Pakistan

**Hafiza Iqra Qamar** Department of Computer Science, The University of Faisalabad (TUF), Faisalabad, Pakistan

**Samia Asloob Qureshi** Department of Computer Science, Forman Christian College (A Chartered University), Lahore, Pakistan

**Aftab Rafique** Department of Software Engineering and Information Technology, Foundation University, Rawalpindi Campus, Islamabad, Pakistan

**Muhammad Raheel** Department of Computer Science, The Superior University, Lahore, Pakistan

**Saim Raza** The University of Faisalabad, Faisalabad, Pakistan

**Usman Ahmed Raza** Faculty of Information Technology (FOIT), University of Central Punjab (UCP), Lahore, Pakistan

**Ateeq Ur Rehman** Department of Electrical Engineering, Government College University, Lahore, Pakistan

**Faisal Rehman** Department of Computer Science, Lahore Leads University, Lahore, Pakistan;
Department of Statistics and Data Science, University of Mianwali, Mianwali, Pakistan

**Nadia Rehmat** Faculty of Computer Science and Information Technology, The Superior University, Lahore, Pakistan;
Intelligent Data Visual Computing Research (IDVCR), Lahore, Pakistan

**Saeid Rezaei** Confirm Centre for Smart Manufacturing, University College Cork, Cork, Ireland

**Muhammad Mohsin Saeed** Department of Computer Science, Superior University Lahore, Lahore, Pakistan

**Uzair Saeed** Department of Computer Science, The University of Faisalabad (TUF), Faisalabad, Pakistan

**Aqib Saghir** Department of Computer Science, The Superior University, Lahore, Pakistan

**Salman Ahmad Sahi** Department of Computer Science, The Superior University, Lahore, Pakistan

**Omer Sajid** Forman Christian College (A Chartered University), Lahore, Pakistan

**Kinza Salim** Capital Development Authority (CDA) Hospital, Islamabad, Pakistan

**Mohsin Sami** Department of Computer Science, University of Central Punjab (UCP), Lahore, Pakistan

**Sanamaqbool** Department of Computer Science, The University of Faisalabad (TUF), Faisalabad, Pakistan

**Muhammad Farrukh Shafeeq** Department of Computer Science, UET, Lahore, Pakistan

**Syed Faisal Abbas Shah** Department of Computer Science and Information Technology, Virtual University of Pakistan, Lahore, Pakistan

**Muhammad Khurram Shahzad** Department of Data Science, University of the Punjab, Lahore, Pakistan

**Rohail Shahzad** Information Technology Department, Faculty of CS & IT, Superior University, Lahore, Pakistan

**Danish Shehzad** Superior University, Lahore, Pakistan

**Muhammad Sohail** Riphah International University, Islamabad, Pakistan

**Sarina Sulaiman** School of Computing, Universiti of Teknologi Malaysia, Skudai, Johor, Malaysia

**Ammara Tariq** Department of Biochemistry and Biotechnology, University of Gujrat, Gujrat, Punjab, Pakistan

**Noshina Tariq** Department of Avionics Engineering, Air University, Islamabad, Pakistan

**Umme Tehreem** Department CS&IT, Superior University Lahore, Lahore, Pakistan

**Muhammad Farhat Ullah** Department of Software Engineering, University of Lahore, Lahore, Pakistan

**Namra Waheed** Department of Software Engineering and Information Technology, Foundation University, Rawalpindi Campus, Islamabad, Pakistan

**Sahibzada M. Waqas** Department of Avionics Engineering, Air University, Islamabad, Pakistan

**Siddiqui Muhammad Yasir** School of Artificial Intelligence, Tongmyong University, Busan, South Korea

**Sana Younas** Department of Computer Science and IT, The University of Chenab, Gujrat, Gujranwala, Pakistan

**Fawad Nasim** Superior University, Lahore, Lahore, Pakistan;
Intelligent Data Visual Computing Research (IDVCR), Lahore, Pakistan

**Rida Nawaz** Superior University, Lahore, Pakistan

**Usman Nawaz** Department of Information Technology, University of Gujrat, Gujrat, Pakistan;
Department of Chemistry, COMSATS University Islamabad, Lahore Campus, Lahore, Pakistan

**Misbah Noor** Department of Computer Science, Superior University Lahore, Lahore, Pakistan

**Hafiza Iqra Qamar** Department of Computer Science, The University of Faisalabad (TUF), Faisalabad, Pakistan

**Samia Asloob Qureshi** Department of Computer Science, Forman Christian College (A Chartered University), Lahore, Pakistan

**Aftab Rafique** Department of Software Engineering and Information Technology, Foundation University, Rawalpindi Campus, Islamabad, Pakistan

**Muhammad Raheel** Department of Computer Science, The Superior University, Lahore, Pakistan

**Saim Raza** The University of Faisalabad, Faisalabad, Pakistan

**Usman Ahmed Raza** Faculty of Information Technology (FOIT), University of Central Punjab (UCP), Lahore, Pakistan

**Ateeq Ur Rehman** Department of Electrical Engineering, Government College University, Lahore, Pakistan

**Faisal Rehman** Department of Computer Science, Lahore Leads University, Lahore, Pakistan;
Department of Statistics and Data Science, University of Mianwali, Mianwali, Pakistan

**Nadia Rehmat** Faculty of Computer Science and Information Technology, The Superior University, Lahore, Pakistan;
Intelligent Data Visual Computing Research (IDVCR), Lahore, Pakistan

**Saeid Rezaei** Confirm Centre for Smart Manufacturing, University College Cork, Cork, Ireland

**Muhammad Mohsin Saeed** Department of Computer Science, Superior University Lahore, Lahore, Pakistan

**Uzair Saeed** Department of Computer Science, The University of Faisalabad (TUF), Faisalabad, Pakistan

**Aqib Saghir** Department of Computer Science, The Superior University, Lahore, Pakistan

**Salman Ahmad Sahi** Department of Computer Science, The Superior University, Lahore, Pakistan

**Omer Sajid** Forman Christian College (A Chartered University), Lahore, Pakistan

**Kinza Salim** Capital Development Authority (CDA) Hospital, Islamabad, Pakistan

**Mohsin Sami** Department of Computer Science, University of Central Punjab (UCP), Lahore, Pakistan

**Sanamaqbool** Department of Computer Science, The University of Faisalabad (TUF), Faisalabad, Pakistan

**Muhammad Farrukh Shafeeq** Department of Computer Science, UET, Lahore, Pakistan

**Syed Faisal Abbas Shah** Department of Computer Science and Information Technology, Virtual University of Pakistan, Lahore, Pakistan

**Muhammad Khurram Shahzad** Department of Data Science, University of the Punjab, Lahore, Pakistan

**Rohail Shahzad** Information Technology Department, Faculty of CS & IT, Superior University, Lahore, Pakistan

**Danish Shehzad** Superior University, Lahore, Pakistan

**Muhammad Sohail** Riphah International University, Islamabad, Pakistan

**Sarina Sulaiman** School of Computing, Universiti of Teknologi Malaysia, Skudai, Johor, Malaysia

**Ammara Tariq** Department of Biochemistry and Biotechnology, University of Gujrat, Gujrat, Punjab, Pakistan

**Noshina Tariq** Department of Avionics Engineering, Air University, Islamabad, Pakistan

**Umme Tehreem** Department CS&IT, Superior University Lahore, Lahore, Pakistan

**Muhammad Farhat Ullah** Department of Software Engineering, University of Lahore, Lahore, Pakistan

**Namra Waheed** Department of Software Engineering and Information Technology, Foundation University, Rawalpindi Campus, Islamabad, Pakistan

**Sahibzada M. Waqas** Department of Avionics Engineering, Air University, Islamabad, Pakistan

**Siddiqui Muhammad Yasir** School of Artificial Intelligence, Tongmyong University, Busan, South Korea

**Sana Younas** Department of Computer Science and IT, The University of Chenab, Gujrat, Gujranwala, Pakistan

**Hina Zafar** The University of Faisalabad, Faisalabad, Pakistan

**Muhammad Zakwan** Department of Avionics Engineering, Air University, Islamabad, Pakistan

**Saira Zia** Department of Computer Science, Superior University Lahore, Lahore, Pakistan

# Incube: The Project Repository Based on Blockchain

Omer Sajid[1(✉)], Samia Asloob Qureshi[2], and Rabranea Bqa[2]

[1] Forman Christian College (A Chartered University), Lahore, Pakistan
22-10336@formanite.fccollege.edu.pk
[2] Department of Computer Science, Forman Christian College (A Chartered University), Lahore, Pakistan
{samiaqureshi,rabraneabqa}@fccollege.edu.pk

**Abstract.** A lot of potential lies within final year projects and research theses of fresh graduates from all over Pakistan. Without proper direction, individuals are unable to launch their work in the industry when nearing or after graduation. Thus, the Pakistani market remains devoid of innovative and cutting-edge technology. Not only do most of these projects remain undiscovered but worse, they might be capitalized off of by others without due rights. Despite the presence of a few incubation centers scattered across the country, there is an absence of an online platform that can help launch fresh graduates into the market. With Project Incube, our goal is to launch a blockchain-based online incubation center that will help connect software houses and reputable organizations to the work of final-year students while they are working on their projects. This way, if a project has prospects, organizations will be able to provide the respected authors with mentorship, guidance, and even finances so that they are able to put forward the best industry-ready work possible. Project Incube will prevent the loss of valuable time spent by pupils to figure out how they can take their ideas further. It will also aid organizations to recruit talent more efficiently. Conclusively, our web application will not only benefit students in furthering their genius but will also help bring innovation and advancements to the public of Pakistan.

**Keywords:** Blockchain · Ethereum · Project Repository

## 1 Introduction

Technology was first integrated into education in the 1960s. Since then, not only technology but how technology is amalgamated with the field of education has also evolved monumentally. At the end of a student's time at a university, at higher levels, they are required to work on a final year project or thesis in order to graduate. The aim is to make students apply all that they have learned throughout the duration of their academic careers and apply it practically. It helps evaluate a student's ability to apply their newfound knowledge on an industrial scale or applied research. In their project, students are forced to make difficult decisions regarding what they want to work on, the methodology and tools they want to use, the people they want to work with and how to organize and arrange their work much like in a professional setting. Final year projects are important for a number of reasons. They are a representation of what a pupil has learned over the course of his academic career and how much effort they have put into shaping their skills with the direction given to them by their instructors. This is the reason that recruiters are most interested in one's final year project and focus their interview questions on it. Additionally, FYPs are key to gaining admission into prestigious universities whether national or international. Moreover, perhaps the most important aspect of performing well in one's FYP is the fact that it adds credibility and weightage to one's resume. According to the American job search website, Glassdoor, out of the 250 applicants, only 4–6 are selected for interviews based on their resumes. This is why it is essential to have an innovative and unique FYP that will set one apart from others. Having listed the advantages of FYPs, it is important to identify the obstacles that pupils face as well. There is a huge gap that exists between academia and the industry. Often students are not instilled with the necessary skills needed to create industry-level projects or carry out technical applied research. So upon project initiation that comes after topic selection, students are often confused as to how to proceed. They are confused about what software and languages to use, where to learn them and how to integrate the back-end with the front-end. More than often, students are not able to nail the scalability of their project. They might end up taking on more than they can do or vice versa, their projects might not have enough functionalities. One of the most pressing issues is when students are unable to get the appropriate recognition for their FYPs as they are unaware of how to take their projects forward and most suffer from a lack of resources therefore their projects are rendered useless, despite any potential they might have. Many times, project ideas are stolen by someone with better technical expertise and greater resources when students are unable to bring their FYPs into the limelight.

There are a number of incubation centers spread out across Pakistan however many students are not aware of the existence of these places, let alone the services they offer. Moreover, none of these centers are based online which is why they might exhibit bias when choosing whom to allocate their resources to. We want to create an online platform that connects students and their work directly to reputable businesses. This way, these firms will be able to identify the potential and innovation within students' FYPs when the projects are still in the early stages. They will be able to provide students with the necessary resources, funding, mentorship and anything else that they may need to take their work to the level where it is ready to be introduced into the market once the respective developers graduate. In this way, companies will also be able to recruit the best talent amongst fresh graduates. Students will also remain motivated to perform their best when given an incentive. Our web application will boost healthy competition that will in turn prove to be fruitful for our country. Project Incube creates a system that will help its users, the universities, upload the final year projects of the 4th year students on a blockchain platform. This network will help students project their proposals in front of the firms that may give them a push in their professional life. The purpose of using blockchain technology was the immutability, we created a system where each project acted like an NFT and only one NFT was created for each project. Due to its decentralized nature, we can trust the system that whatever was sent to the network, its their forever. Blockchain helps us creating an unalterable record of transactions with end-to-end encryption, which shuts out fraud and unauthorized activity. Furthermore, it also solves the privacy concerns better than the traditional computer systems by anonymizing data and requiring permissions to limit access.

## 2 Blockchain Technology-Literature Review

At the start of the 21st century, most companies organized development and research within the confinements of their own laboratories conducted by accomplished professionals already a part of their respective industries. They were given generous resources [17]. As time passed and the environment within universities and educational institutions became more and more competitive, these companies realized the importance of innovation and creativity which is what final year students at universities and fresh graduates had to offer. By taking advantage of and funding final year projects and fresh graduates' work, companies began spending less and acquiring greater innovation [17]. This way they are also able to provide a plethora of new services and newer products (Chesbrough, 2006).

There are a lot of independent incubators and incubators set up by universities around the globe to help connect students and their ideas to companies to help further not only students' projects but also to help companies discover and house new talent and innovation. However, there aren't many online incubators that utilize blockchain technology.

Alphabet Incubator Blockchain, based in Tangerang, Indonesia, is an online incubation center that makes use of Blockchain technology [16]. The concept was introduced in October 2019 and the web application complete with a blockchain based back-end and front-end was launched in January 2020. It has its own digital coin as well called AI Coin that are given to users for free upon attempting a generic quiz on their website. The blockchain network connects educational institutes, research companies, investors, brand companies, journal publishers, and even the government. Students, lecturers, agencies, companies, and the public can sign up and create a trusted profile. They can then upload any document on the network such as a pitch or research paper to the chain that can be viewed by all members of the network who are then free to reach out to the user in case their work piques their interest. All members can view a history of transaction details within the network along with other information such as time stamps, public key, name etc.

Perhaps one of the most historic incubation centers, Y Combinator, is based in the USA. It has helped launch some of the biggest names including DropBox, Stripe, Coinbase, etc. [19]. Startups wanting to be funded by it are required to send in applications. Another incubation center, Techstars, also based in the USA, allows start-ups and businessmen from all over the world to apply. Furthermore, our neighboring country, India, is host to one of the top incubation centers in the world known as Venture Catalysts which collaborates with big names such as Microsoft, IBM, and Amazon [19].

In Pakistan, TechHub Connect is an incubator project by Punjab Information Technology Board. This is an online portal that connects students to IT firms and professors who need help with research projects. It does so by virtual recommendations through recommendation engines built with AI technology [13]. One of the first technology incubators, TechOne, was established in Pakistan by NUST to help start-ups transform themselves into successful enterprises. TechOne is not based on any specific technological platform. They have a website and pupils can contact them via telephone or email. Similarly, IBA in Karachi has set up AMAN-CED in collaboration with Babson College USA. They offer a wide variety of programs and internships to help students, projects, and start-ups. They also have approximately 50 companies working with them in their incubation center. LUMS has also set up the NICL incubator in which fresh graduates, marginalized communities, and startups are funded, given office spaces, and mentored by the faculty at LUMS. Other similar in-person incubators such as those set up by UMT and IBA Sukkur provide legal and advisory support, offices, and mentorship if you reach out to them [14]. Business and tech startup competitions are also organized at national levels to create an entrepreneurial experience and competitiveness. Other notable incubators include Plan9, The Nest i/o, i2i, Nspire, TechIncubator, and many more [15].

Though the evolution of incubators in Pakistan is beneficial, it is slow and there is a definite lack of a strong virtual incubation software platform. Most incubators are set up by universities for their own students or alumni. Fresh graduates or students are required to reach out to them on their own. In theory, it is straightforward, but in practical life, many final year students and fresh graduates are not aware of the existence of incubators and other such resources that can potentially help them get started. There might be other hurdles as well. Most incubator setups only cater to start-ups and completed final-year projects. Students might also not be able to establish contact with a particular incubator especially if it is not in the same locality as them. Another important aspect is that most incubators only cater to specific domains such as business or technology. There is a dire need for incubation centers to incorporate companies and programs for a wider range of degrees such as Pharmacy, Biotechnology, Psychology, Mass Communication etc.

Furthermore, most incubator centers operate on an application basis. Implementation of a system where companies can view what final year students are working on is a necessity as most established incubators focus on launching and furthering startups and not final year projects that have the potential to be great but are still in the works. It not only increases the chances for students' work to gain recognition, but also enables companies to hire enthusiastic and innovative talent.

## 3 Incube Overview

The technology used behind this system is blockchain. The basic architecture of blockchain consists of distributed consensus, cryptography and immutability. Irrespective of nodes present on the network, the structure of blockchain is distributed and decentralized. The purpose of this to make sure that there is no single point of failure in the network which makes it infeasible to conduct an attack on blockchain networks. Furthermore, cryptography is another main concept in blockchain where the data is secured through advanced encryption algorithms. Lastly, the most important factor of blockchain technology is immutability which makes sure that the data once validated on the blockchain cannot be reversed without the agreement across the majority of the network. Due to these three reasons mentioned above, we have chosen to use blockchain for our project.

The objective of our project is to create an online space where business organizations will be able to take a look at final year projects and the progress of students and graduates from universities in real-time. Universities can sign-up on our web- application based software and upload project deliverables of pupils onto a blockchain network. Software houses, business organizations, firms, and institutions can also sign- up onto the network so that they are able to view these project deliverables and keep track of the progress. Once students begin to finalize their project ideas and get registered for the course, S-Proj, their project details will be transacted on a private blockchain network by a university representative. The network would require their names, roll numbers, topic statement, and abstract as the first deliverable. As soon as the first deliverable is added to the ledger, all organizations registered onto the web application will be able to view project details. Once a deliverable is added to the network, it becomes immutable t maintain its integrity and prevent any unfair practices. As students work on them, the following deliverables will keep on being added for organizations to explore. Firms may reach out to a particular student whose project appeals to them to provide mentorship, jobs, direction, guidance, or financial help at any given time. Project completion is not necessary. Our application will not only prove to be highly efficient and cost-effective as well.

Our project's completeness requirements are based on the following characteristics:

- The application's principal features are in place and functioning.
- Debugging the source code and running a series of tests.
- Only a few errors detected after meticulous testing.
- Data can be written and read from the blockchain network.
- Response time is minimal for any action that a user takes.

## 4 Architecture

Our web-application is being created for use by HEC recognized universities in Pakistan and registered businesses, multi-national organizations, companies, and software houses based in or out of Pakistan. The businesses need not be large-scale but must be legitimate, reputable and trust-worthy. Our application will have the following features:

Enables universities to register on our website by providing their details such as name, affiliated campuses, NTN number, budget, staffing, address, rector's name and contact so that we can verify whether the university is HEC recognized.

Universities can sign in anytime using an email address and password to gain access to their accounts where all progress is saved.

The "Add Projects" button on the index screen that shows up after logging in will allow universities to upload the first deliverable of projects of the student body onto the blockchain network. The information required is student names, emails, roll numbers, contacts, project title and an abstract.

The "Update Project" button on the index screen is used to add project deliverables as students keep on completing them onto the network.

Enables companies to sign-up on our website by providing the company name, its address, the name of the CEO, details about what the company specializes and deals in, about the company and its contact.

Companies can sign in to the website and thus the blockchain network anytime. Companies need to request for access from universities before viewing their projects so as to maintain the integrity of the projects.

The major flow of process of Project Incube involves a party which can either be an university admin or a concerned department of a firm. The party will interact with the web front of our application and call the functions of our smart contract which will directly invoke the smart contract running on EVM node, the transaction will be mined by the mining node and it will then be added to the entire network. Once the block height is filled, a new block will be created which will contain the hash of the previous block and thus creating a linked-list data structure (Fig. 1).

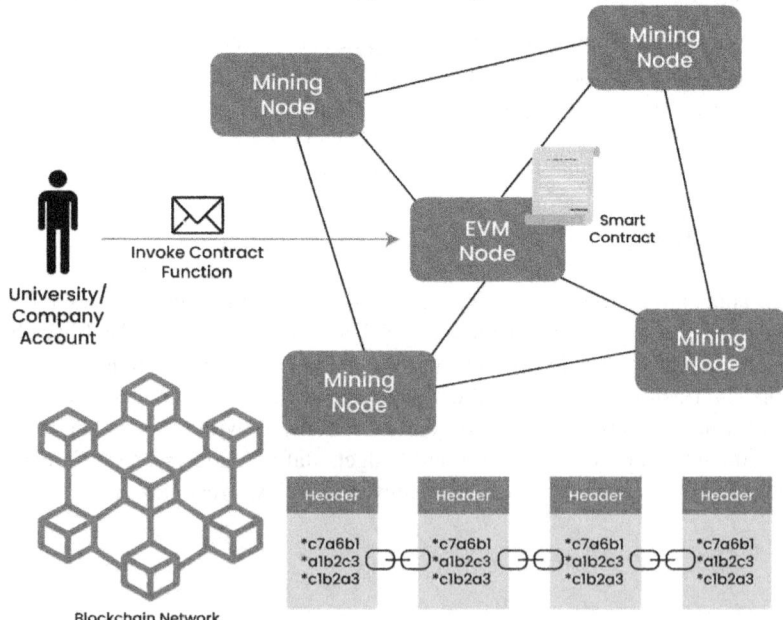

**Fig. 1.** System Architecture Diagram

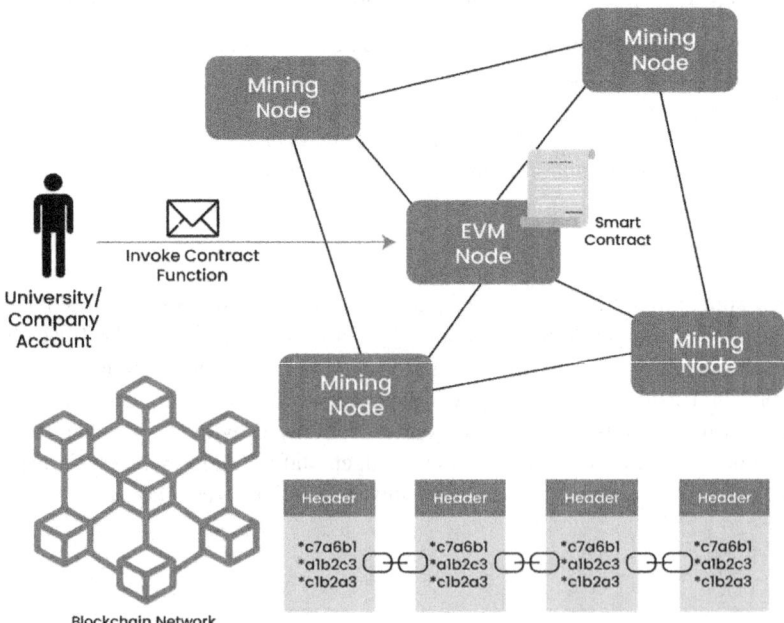

In order to interact with Project Incube, user must create an account on our web application depending upon whether the user is representing a university or a firm. Suppose, a university wants to create an account to add projects on our blockchain network. The university must provide the required information in order to create an account. After the creation of account, the university can log in and add the projects. The credentials of university are stored on the database for further use. After the university has logged on to the network, they can begin to add projects of Final Year students on the blockchain. In order to send the transactions, the user must have an account on MetaMask and have Ethereum in it. They can get the Ethereum from the Goerli Faucet. After connecting the MetaMask with the browser, they can send the transactions to the blockchain.

Now if a company wants to view the projects of the universities, they must also go through the same procedure of creating an account on the website as a company. Moving forward, after logging in, they will be able to see the list of universities whose projects are stored on the blockchain. After selecting the universities, the user will be sending a call request to the blockchain to fetch the projects of the selected universities and then the user will be able to view all of the projects that the university has uploaded on the network (Figs. 2 and 3).

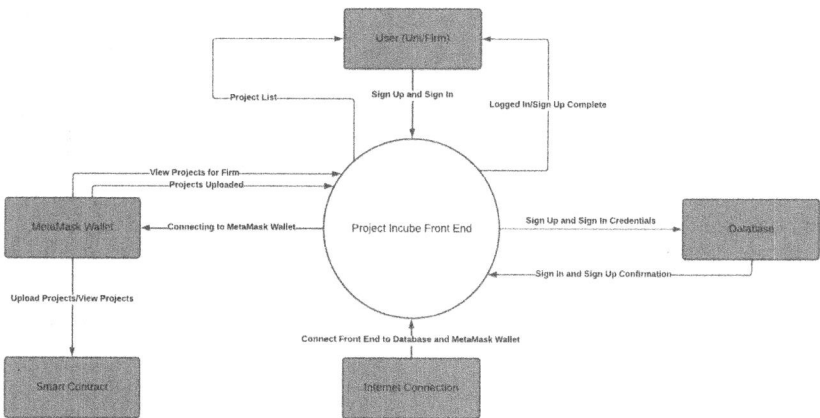

**Fig. 2.** Incube Context Diagram

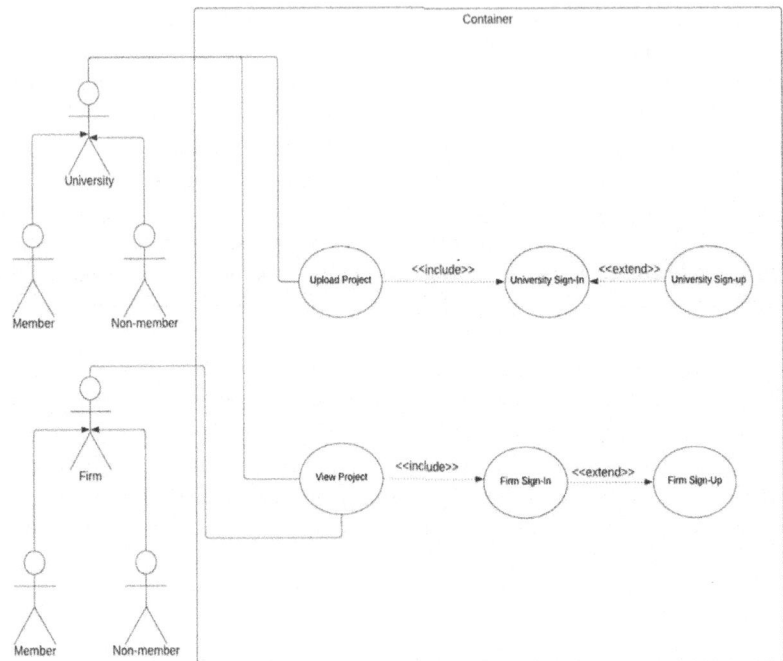

**Fig. 3.** Incube Use Case Diagram

The university, which is the main user of the system, will upload the projects on behalf of the students. The uploading of project will also require to sign in into the network, or sign up if they are a first-time user. After signing in, the user will finally be able to upload the project on to the blockchain network. On the other hand, the firms, will also have to sign in or sign up if they are a first-time user. After signing in, the firm will be able to filter the projects on the basis of university names' and then they can view the projects which will be fetched from the blockchain in real time (Fig. 4).

The sequence for the main user, which is the university, will be to sign up, when the sign is verified, they will be able to log in, when trying to log in, we will check if the credentials exist in our database or not. if they do, we will be able to.

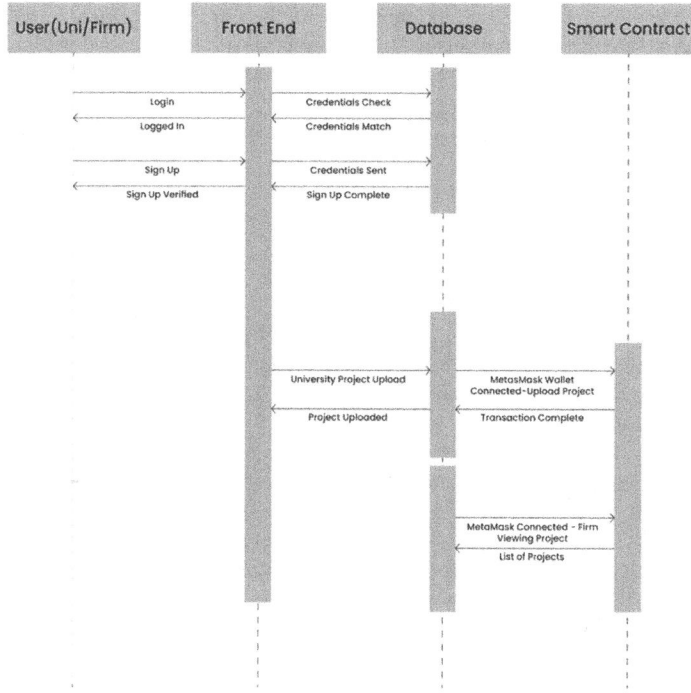

**Fig. 4.** Incube Sequence Diagram

## 5 Conclusion and Future Work

Our future work is as follows:

- As more and more universities and companies register onto our network, we will introduce new functionalities such as allowing representatives from firms to comment on FYPs and suggest areas that pupils can work on.
- An option for private candidates to join the network will also be made available so that pupils who have long graduated or starts-ups can also utilize our project.
- A mobile application version will be introduced.
- The network will be made closed and permissioned so that other universities and companies and are not able to view projects without requesting access.
- We would also create a system where project deliverables can be uploaded one by one and the blocks containing deliverables from the same pupil/pupils are linked via hash value and block number

## References

1. What Can Students Learn from Final Year Projects. https://newinti.edu.my/what-can-students-learn-from-final-yearprojects/#:~:text=A%20Final%20Year%20Project%20(FYP,have%20acquired%20in%20their%20studies

2. Role of Final Year Projects and Its Importance in the Career of an Engineer. https://elysiumpro.in/role-of-final-year-projects-and-its-importance/
3. Turczynski, B.: HR statistics: job search, hiring, recruiting & interviews (2022). https://zety.com/blog/hr-statistics
4. Sodhar, I.H.: A survey of faced issues and challenges of undergraduate students in final year project (2020)
5. Goodall, A.: Top 20 ways to improve your world university ranking. https://www.timeshighereducation.com/features/top-20-ways-to-improve-your-world-university-ranking/410392. article
6. How to Improve Your Institution's Academic Reputation. https://www.qs.com/how-to-improve-your-institutions-academic-reputation/
7. Emmons, D.: Understanding one way hash functions #HowToBUIDL (5/n). https://medium.com/coinmonks/understanding-one-way-hash-functions-howtobuidl-5-n-6c5887c08c3#:~:text=Specifically%2C%20Ethereum%20%26%20Solidity%20use%20the,256%20version%20of%20SHA%2D3
8. What is an Incubation Center? http://icnextstep.com/what-is-an-incubation-center/#:~:text=Incubation%20is%20a%20unique%20and,stages%20of%20development%20and%20change
9. Gibb, R.: What is a web application? https://blog.stackpath.com/web-application/
10. What is 'Cryptography'. https://economictimes.indiatimes.com/definition/cryptography
11. Consensus Algorithm. https://www.techtarget.com/whatis/definition/consensus-algorithm#:~:text=A%20consensus%20algorithm%20is%20a,network%20involving%20multiple%20unreliable%20nodes
12. Ethereum. https://en.wikipedia.org/wiki/Ethereum
13. Mumtaz, S., Shafi, F., Zafar, F.: Role of technology business incubators to nurture entrepreneurship: a study on Pakistani universities. J. Account. Mark. **06**(02) (2017)
14. Qureshi, S.: An exploratory study of entrepreneurial centers in Pakistan: an untapped market opportunity. IBT J. Bus. Stud. **11**(2) (2015)
15. Salman, A., Majeed, A.A.: Sustainable Incubator Management—a case study for Pakistan. Pak. Dev. Rev. **48**(4II), 425–438 (2009)
16. Sokibi, P.: LTAI management based on blockchain technology to increase Alexa Rank. Int. J. Adv. Trends Comput. Sci. Eng. **9**(4), 4798–4802 (2020)
17. Stal, E., Andreassi, T., Fujino, A.: The role of university incubators in stimulating academic entrepreneurship. RAI Revista de Administração e Inovação **13**(2), 89–98 (2016)
18. "Open innovation: the new imperative for creating and profiting from Technology H," Bonanza. https://www.bonanza.com/listings/Open-Innovation-The-New-Imperative-for-Creating-And-Profiting-from-Technology-H/1189897035. Accessed 06 Feb 2022
19. Puri, P.: Top 15 startup incubators and accelerators worldwide. The Kolabtree Blog (2020). https://www.kolabtree.com/blog/top-15-startup-incubators-and-accelerators-worldwide/. Accessed 06 Feb 2022
20. Anwar, H.: Top 10 common solidity issues. https://101blockchains.com/solidity-issues/

# Algorithm Trading Using Data Science

Amina Bibi[✉], Danish Shehzad, and Ahsan Imtiaz

Superior University, Lahore, Pakistan
aminasarwar116@gmail.com, danish.shehzad@superior.edu.pk

**Abstract.** Algorithmic trading is the use of automated computer programs to execute trades based on pre-defined rules and strategies. Machine learning (ML) and deep learning (DL) have revolutionized the field of algorithmic trading by providing powerful tools to analyses complex data and identify patterns that can be exploited for profitable trades. In this paper, we explore the question of which is better suited for algorithmic trading: machine learning or deep learning? We begin by defining machine learning and deep learning, outlining their strengths and weaknesses, and discussing their applications in algorithmic trading. We then compare the performance of various ML and DL algorithms on a range of trading datasets, including stock prices, foreign exchange rates, and commodity futures. Our analysis shows that both machine learning and deep learning have their own advantages and disadvantages, and the choice of which approach to use depends on the specific trading problem and available data. While machine learning algorithms are generally simpler and faster to train, deep learning algorithms can learn more complex patterns and may outperform machine learning on large and diverse datasets. IN conclusion, there is no clear winner between machine learning and deep learning in algorithmic trading. Rather, traders should carefully consider the characteristics of their data and the requirements of their trading strategy when deciding which approach to use.

**Keywords:** Algorithmic trading · machine learning · deep learning · trading strategies · data analysis · performance comparison

## 1 Introduction

Algorithmic trading has revolutionized the financial industry, enabling traders to make faster and more informed decisions based on vast amounts of data. One of the key drivers of this transformation has been the development of machine learning (ML) and deep learning (DL) techniques, which have enabled traders to analyses and make sense of complex data sets that would otherwise be impossible to process using traditional methods [1] (Fig. 1).

**Fig. 1.** Features of algorithm trading

Machine learning is a type of artificial intelligence that allows computers to learn from data and improve their performance over time. By analyzing historical data, machine learning algorithms can identify patterns and relationships that can be used to make predictions about future events [2]. In the context of algorithmic trading, machine learning has been used to develop trading strategies that can identify profitable trades by analyzing historical price and volume data.

Deep learning is a subset of machine learning that uses artificial neural networks to analyses data. These neural networks are modelled after the human brain and are capable of learning complex patterns and relationships in data [3]. Image identification, speech recognition, and natural language processing are just a few of the many domains where deep learning algorithms have demonstrated exceptional effectiveness [4] (Fig. 2).

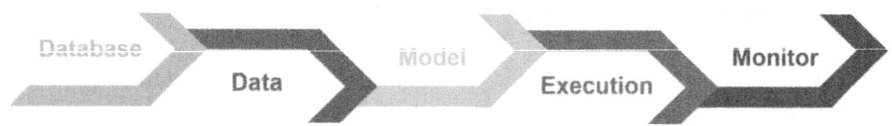

**Fig. 2.** Conceptual Model of Algorithm Trading

In the context of algorithmic trading, deep learning has been used to analyses vast amounts of data from financial markets, including stock prices, foreign exchange rates, and commodity futures. Deep learning algorithms can find winning trades and forecast market trends by identifying patterns in this data [5].

While both machine learning and deep learning have shown promise in algorithmic trading, the question of which approach is best suited for this application remains open.

In this paper, we will explore the advantages and disadvantages of both machine learning and deep learning in algorithmic trading and compare the performance of various algorithms on a range of trading datasets.

## 1.1 Advantages of Machine Learning in Algorithmic Trading

One of the primary advantages of machine learning in algorithmic trading is its ability to analyze large and complex datasets quickly and accurately. Machine learning algorithms can analyze vast amounts of historical data and identify patterns and relationships that would be impossible for a human trader to detect. This enables machine learning algorithms to develop trading strategies that can identify profitable trades with a high degree of accuracy [6].

Another advantage of machine learning in algorithmic trading is its ability to adapt to changing market conditions. Machine learning algorithms can learn from data in realtime, enabling them to adjust their trading strategies as market conditions change. This allows traders to stay ahead of the curve and take advantage of market opportunities as they arise.

## 1.2 Disadvantages of Machine Learning in Algorithmic Trading

One of the primary disadvantages of machine learning in algorithmic trading is the risk of overfitting. Overfitting occurs when a machine learning algorithm becomes too specialized to the historical data it has been trained on and fails to generalize to new data. This can lead to trading strategies that perform well in back testing but fail to generate profits in live trading [6].

Another disadvantage of machine learning in algorithmic trading is the need for high-quality data.

## 1.3 Advantages of Deep Learning in Algorithmic Trading

One of the primary advantages of deep learning in algorithmic trading is its ability to learn complex patterns and relationships in data. Deep learning algorithms are capable of analyzing vast amounts of data and identifying patterns that would be impossible for a human trader to detect. This enables deep learning algorithms to develop trading strategies that can identify profitable trades with a high degree of accuracy.

Another advantage of deep learning in algorithmic trading is its ability to adapt to changing market conditions. Deep learning algorithms can learn from data in realtime, enabling them to adjust their trading strategies as market conditions change. This allows traders to stay ahead of the curve and take advantage of market opportunities as they arise [7].

## 1.4 Disadvantages of Deep Learning in Algorithmic Trading

Despite its many advantages, deep learning also has several disadvantages when it comes to algorithmic trading. One of the primary disadvantages is the complexity of deep learning algorithms. Deep learning algorithms are often more complex than traditional machine learning algorithms, which makes them more difficult to understand and interpret. This can make it challenging for traders to fine-tune their trading strategies based on insights gleaned from deep learning algorithms.

Another disadvantage of deep learning in algorithmic trading is the high computational requirements. Deep learning algorithms require significant computational resources to train and optimize. This can make it challenging for smaller traders or firms to implement deep learning algorithms into their trading systems [8].

Another potential disadvantage of deep learning in algorithmic trading is the potential for overfitting. Deep learning algorithms can be susceptible to overfitting when they are trained on small datasets or datasets that are not representative of the broader market. This can lead to trading strategies that perform well in back testing but fail to generate profits in live trading.

Finally, deep learning algorithms can be difficult to interpret, which can make it challenging to understand how the algorithm arrived at its predictions. This lack of interpretability can make it challenging for traders to identify and address issues with their trading strategies or to fine-tune their strategies based on insights from the algorithm [9].

## 2 Literature Review

Several studies have compared machine learning and deep learning in algorithmic trading. A study conducted by [10] found that deep learning algorithms outperformed machine learning algorithms in predicting stock prices. The study found that deep learning algorithms were more effective at capturing complex patterns in the market, resulting in more accurate predictions.

Another study conducted by [11] compared machine learning and deep learning algorithms in predicting cryptocurrency prices. The study found that both machine learning and deep learning algorithms were effective at predicting cryptocurrency prices, but deep learning algorithms were more accurate and reliable.

However, a study conducted by [12] found that machine learning algorithms outperformed deep learning algorithms in predicting stock prices. The study found that machine learning algorithms were more efficient and effective at capturing the underlying trends in the market, resulting in more accurate predictions.

Other studies have also found that the performance of ML and DL algorithms in algorithmic trading depends on the quality of the data. [13] compared the performance of ML and DL algorithms in predicting.

A Comprehensive Survey of Algorithmic Trading Strategies in Foreign Exchange Markets (2021). This paper provides a comprehensive survey of algorithmic trading strategies in foreign exchange markets. It reviews several existing strategies and provides an overview of the current state of the art in this area. Additionally, the paper covers the challenges posed by algorithmic trading and the potential opportunities it offers.

Reinforcement Learning Algorithms for Automated Trading: A Survey (2022). This paper provides a survey of reinforcement learning algorithms for automated trading. The paper reviews several existing algorithms for automated trading and provides an overview of the current state of the art in this area. Additionally, the paper covers the challenges posed by automated trading and the potential opportunities it offers [14].

## 3 Methodology

The methodology for determining whether machine learning (ML) or deep learning (DL) is best for algorithmic trading involves several key steps:

### 3.1 Define the Problem

The first step is to clearly define the problem that the algorithm is meant to solve. This could include predicting market trends, identifying profitable trading opportunities, or minimizing risk.

### 3.2 Gather Data

The next step is to gather relevant data to train the algorithm. This could include historical market data, news articles, financial statements, and other relevant sources. Pre-process data: Once the data is gathered, it must be pre-processed to prepare it for training the algorithm. This could include cleaning the data, removing outliers, and converting the data into a format that is suitable for the ML or DL algorithm.

### 3.3 Pre-process

Once the data is gathered, it must be pre-processed to prepare it for training the algorithm. This could include cleaning the data, removing outliers, and converting the data into a format that is suitable for the ML or DL algorithm.

### 3.4 Select the Algorithm

The next step is to select the appropriate ML or DL algorithm for the problem at hand. This could include decision trees, random forests, neural networks, or other types of algorithms.

### 3.5 Train the Algorithm

The pre-processed data is then used to train the chosen algorithm. This entails feeding the algorithm input data and modifying the algorithm's parameters to improve performance.

### 3.6 Evaluate the Algorithm

Once the algorithm is qualified, it is calculated on an isolated set of data to test its performance. This could include measuring the accuracy of the predictions, the speed of the algorithm, and the efficiency of the trading strategy.

## 3.7 Iterate

Based on the results of the evaluation, the algorithm may need to be further refined or adjusted. This involves iterating through the process again, starting with preprocessing the data and selecting the algorithm.

It is important to note that the specific methodology for ML and DL in algorithmic trading will vary depending on the specific problem being addressed and the data available. However, these key steps provide a general framework for developing and testing ML and DL algorithms for algorithmic trading [15] (Fig. 3).

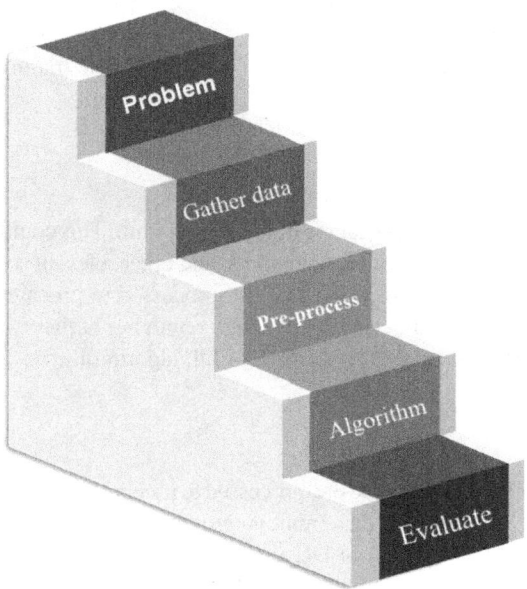

**Fig. 3.** Data evaluation model

## 4 Machine Learning types and its advantages and Disadvantages in Algorithm Trading:

There are several types of machine learning (ML) algorithms that can be used in algorithmic trading. Each type has its own advantages and disadvantages, and the selection of the appropriate algorithm depends on the specific problem being addressed and the characteristics of the data available.

### 4.1 Supervised Learning

Using labelled data, where the input and output values are known, the algorithm is taught via supervised learning. Based on the labelled data, the algorithm learns to anticipate the output value for fresh inputs. The advantages of supervised learning in algorithmic trading include:

Advantages:

- Ability to predict future market trends based on historical data
- Improved accuracy in predicting stock prices and identifying profitable trading opportunities
- Transparent and easy to interpret for traders

Disadvantages:

- Dependence on quality and quantity of labelled data
- Limited ability to handle unstructured data, such as news articles and social media posts

### 4.2 Unsupervised Learning

In unsupervised learning, the algorithm is trained using unlabeled data, where the input values are known but the output values are not [16]. The algorithm learns to identify patterns and group data points based on similarities in the input data. The advantages of unsupervised learning in algorithmic trading include:

Advantages:

- Ability to identify hidden patterns and market trends in unstructured data, such as news articles and social media posts
- Improved accuracy in identifying anomalies and potential trading opportunities
- Being able to manage enormous volumes of data without labelling

Disadvantages:

- Limited ability to make predictions or identify profitable trading opportunities without labelled data
- Difficulty in interpreting the results for traders

### 4.3 Reinforcement Learning

In reinforcement learning, the algorithm learns through trial and error, receiving feedback in the form of rewards or penalties based on its actions [16]. The algorithm learns to maximize its rewards over time by selecting actions that lead to positive outcomes. The advantages of reinforcement learning in algorithmic trading include:

Advantages:

- Ability to adapt to changing market conditions and adjust trading strategies accordingly
- Improved accuracy in identifying profitable trading opportunities and minimizing risk
- Ability to handle complex and dynamic environments

Disadvantages:

- Dependence on the accuracy of the reward system, which may not always reflect the true value of a trading decision

- Computationally intensive and requires significant computational resources to train and run

### 4.4 Semi-supervised Learning

In semi-supervised learning, the algorithm is trained using both labeled and unlabeled data. The algorithm learns to identify patterns and make predictions founded on together the labeled and unlabeled data. The advantages of semi-supervised learning in algorithmic trading include:

Advantages:

- Ability to leverage the benefits of both supervised and unsupervised learning
- Improved accuracy in predicting market trends and identifying profitable trading opportunities
- Ability to handle large amounts of data without the need for labeling

Disadvantages:

- Dependence on the quality and quantity of labeled data
- Difficulty in interpreting the results for traders

Each type of machine learning algorithm has its own strengths and weaknesses in algorithmic trading. Traders should carefully evaluate the characteristics of the data available and select the most appropriate algorithm for their specific needs. Additionally, it is important to continuously update and refine the algorithm based on new data and market trends to ensure optimal performance [2].

Deep Learning types and its advantages and disadvantages in Algorithm Trading:

Deep learning is a subset of machine learning that involves training neural networks with multiple layers to recognize patterns and make predictions. There are several types of deep learning algorithms that can be used in algorithmic trading. Each type has its own advantages and disadvantages, and the selection of the appropriate algorithm depends on the specific problem being addressed and the characteristics of the data available [2].

Convolutional Neural Networks (CNNs): CNNs are designed to process images and other multidimensional data. In algorithmic trading, CNNs can be used to analyze stock charts and identify patterns. The advantages of CNNs in algorithmic trading include:

Advantages:

- Ability to process large amounts of data quickly
- Improved accuracy in identifying patterns and making predictions
- Ability to handle high-dimensional data, such as stock charts

Disadvantages:

- Dependence on the quality and quantity of labeled data
- Limited ability to handle unstructured data, such as news articles and social media posts

## 4.5 Recurrent Neural Networks (RNNs)

RNNs are designed to process sequential data, such as time-series data. In algorithmic trading, RNNs can be used to predict future stock prices based on historical data. The advantages of RNNs in algorithmic trading include:

Advantages:

- Ability to model time-series data and make predictions based on historical trends
- Improved accuracy in predicting stock prices and identifying profitable trading opportunities
- Ability to handle variable-length data

Disadvantages:

- Computationally intensive and requires significant computational resources to train and run
- Dependence on the quality and quantity of labeled data

## 4.6 Deep Belief Networks (DBNs)

DBNs are designed to learn hierarchical representations of data. In algorithmic trading, DBNs can be used to identify patterns in large amounts of unstructured data, such as news articles and social media posts. The advantages of DBNs in algorithmic trading include:

Advantages:

- Ability to handle large amounts of unstructured data without the need for labeling
- Improved accuracy in identifying market trends and potential trading opportunities
- Ability to learn hierarchical representations of data, allowing for better generalization

Disadvantages:

- Computationally intensive and requires significant computational resources to train and run
- Limited interpretability for traders

## 4.7 Deep Reinforcement Learning (DRL)

DRL combines deep learning with reinforcement learning to learn optimal trading strategies. In algorithmic trading, DRL can be used to adjust trading strategies based on market conditions and maximize profits [1]. The advantages of DRL in algorithmic trading include:

Advantages:

- Ability to adapt to changing market conditions and adjust trading strategies accordingly
- Improved accuracy in identifying profitable trading opportunities and minimizing risk
- Ability to handle complex and dynamic environments

Disadvantages:

- Dependence on the accuracy of the reward system, which may not always reflect the true value of a trading decision
- Computationally intensive and requires significant computational resources to train and run [4]

Each kind of deep learning algorithm has unique advantages and disadvantages when it comes to algorithmic trading. Traders should carefully evaluate the characteristics of the data available and select the most appropriate algorithm for their specific needs. Additionally, it is important to continuously update and refine the algorithm based on new data and market trends to ensure optimal performance [17].

## 5 Result and Discussion

The results and discussion of whether machine learning (ML) or deep learning (DL) is best for algorithmic trading depend on the specific problem being addressed and the data available. In general, both ML and DL have shown promise in improving trading strategies, but their effectiveness may vary depending on the problem and data characteristics.

Studies have shown that ML algorithms such as decision trees, support vector machines, and random forests can effectively predict stock prices and identify profitable trading opportunities. These algorithms are often simpler to interpret than DL algorithms, making them more accessible to traders who prefer more transparent trading strategies [6].

On the other hand, DL algorithms such as convolutional neural networks and recurrent neural networks have shown promise in predicting market trends and identifying complex patterns in financial data. DL algorithms can handle unstructured data, such as news articles and social media posts, which can provide valuable insights into market sentiment and investor behavior.

However, DL algorithms can be computationally intensive and require significant computational resources to train and run. This can be a barrier to entry for smaller firms and individual traders who may not have access to the necessary resources. Additionally, DL algorithms can be difficult to interpret, making it challenging for traders to understand how the algorithm arrived at its predictions.

It is also important to note that the performance of ML and DL algorithms is highly dependent on the quality and quantity of the data used to train the algorithm. Historical data may not always be an accurate reflection of future market trends, and unforeseen events such as natural disasters, political upheavals, and economic shocks can have a significant impact on market trends. Therefore, traders must carefully evaluate the data used to train the algorithm and continuously update and refine the algorithm based on new data [18].

In conclusion, both ML and DL have the potential to improve algorithmic trading, but their effectiveness may vary depending on the specific problem being addressed and the data available. Traders should carefully evaluate the strengths and limitations of each approach and select the most appropriate algorithm for their specific needs. Additionally, it is important to continuously update and refine the algorithm based on new data and market trends to ensure optimal performance [19].

While machine learning (ML) and deep learning (DL) have shown promise in improving algorithmic trading, there are also limitations to their effectiveness.

One limitation is the potential for overfitting. ML and DL algorithms can be prone to overfitting, which occurs when the algorithm is trained on a specific set of data and becomes overly focused on that data, resulting in poor performance when applied to new data. This can be particularly problematic in algorithmic trading, where markets are constantly changing and adapting [20].

Another limitation is the reliance on historical data. ML and DL algorithms are trained on historical data, which may not always be an accurate reflection of future market trends. In addition, past performance does not guarantee future results, and unforeseen events such as natural disasters, political upheavals, and economic shocks can have a significant impact on market trends.

Furthermore, ML and DL algorithms can be computationally intensive and require significant computational resources to train and run. This can be a barrier to entry for smaller firms and individual traders who may not have access to the necessary resources.

Finally, the interpretability of ML and DL algorithms can also be a limitation. While ML algorithms are often simpler to interpret than DL algorithms, both types of algorithms can be difficult to interpret, making it challenging for traders to understand how the algorithm arrived at its predictions. This can be a barrier to adoption for traders who prefer more transparent and explainable trading strategies [21].

Overall, while ML and DL have the potential to improve algorithmic trading, their limitations must also be considered, and traders should carefully evaluate the specific problem and data characteristics before deciding which technique to use.

## 6 Conclusion

In conclusion, both machine learning and deep learning have shown promise in algorithmic trading, but they each have their own advantages and disadvantages. Machine learning is generally faster and simpler to train, but may not be as effective at identifying complex patterns in data. Deep learning, on the other hand, is more complex and computationally intensive, but can learn more complex patterns and may outperform machine learning on large and diverse datasets. Ultimately, the choice between machine learning and deep learning in algorithmic trading will depend on the specific trading problem and the available data. Traders should carefully consider the advantages and disadvantages of each approach and select the one that is best suited for their needs. By leveraging the power of machine learning and deep learning, traders can gain insights into the market that would be impossible to obtain using traditional methods and make more informed trading decisions.

## Reference

1. Nosratabadi, S., et al.: Data science in economics: comprehensive review of advanced machine learning and deep learning methods. Mathematics 8(10), 1799 (2020). https://doi.org/10.3390/math8101799

2. Théate, T., Ernst, D.: An application of deep reinforcement learning to algorithmic trading. Expert Syst. Appl. **173**, 114632 (2021). https://doi.org/10.1016/j.eswa.2021.114632
3. Peng, Y.-L., Lee, W.-P.: Data selection to avoid overfitting for foreign exchange intraday trading with machine learning. Appl. Soft Comput. **108**, 107461 (2021). https://doi.org/10.1016/j.asoc.2021.107461
4. Deng, Y., Bao, F., Kong, Y., Ren, Z., Dai, Q.: Deep direct reinforcement learning for financial signal representation and trading. IEEE Trans. Neural Netw. Learn. Syst. **28**(3), 653–664 (2017). https://doi.org/10.1109/TNNLS.2016.2522401
5. Zhang, Z., Zohren, S., Roberts, S.: Deep reinforcement learning for trading. JFDS **2**(2), 25–40 (2020). https://doi.org/10.3905/jfds.2020.1.030
6. Li, Y., Zheng, W., Zheng, Z.: Deep robust reinforcement learning for practical algorithmic trading. IEEE Access **7**, 108014–108022 (2019). https://doi.org/10.1109/ACCESS.2019.2932789
7. Crone, N., Brophy, E., Ward, T.: Exploration of algorithmic trading strategies for the bitcoin market. arXiv:2110.14936 (2021). Accessed 09 May 2022. http://arxiv.org/abs/2110.14936
8. Aloud, M.E., Alkhamees, N.: Intelligent algorithmic trading strategy using reinforcement learning and directional change. IEEE Access **9**, 114659–114671 (2021). https://doi.org/10.1109/ACCESS.2021.3105259
9. Borch, C.: Machine learning and social theory: collective machine behaviour in algorithmic trading. Eur. J. Soc. Theory 136843102110560 (2021). https://doi.org/10.1177/13684310211056010.
10. Wang, Y., Yan, G.: Survey on the application of deep learning in algorithmic trading. DSFE **1**(4), 345–361 (2021). https://doi.org/10.3934/DSFE.2021019
11. Ma, C., Zhang, J., Liu, J., Ji, L., Gao, F.: A parallel multi-module deep reinforcement learning algorithm for stock trading. Neurocomputing **449**, 290–302 (2021). https://doi.org/10.1016/j.neucom.2021.04.005
12. Chakole, J.B., Kolhe, M.S., Mahapurush, G.D., Yadav, A., Kurhekar, M.P.: A Q-learning agent for automated trading in equity stock markets. Expert Syst. Appl. **163**, 113761 (2021). https://doi.org/10.1016/j.eswa.2020.113761
13. Song, Y., Lee, J.W., Lee, J.: A study on novel filtering and relationship between input-features and target-vectors in a deep learning model for stock price prediction. Appl. Intell. **49**(3), 897–911 (2019). https://doi.org/10.1007/s10489-018-1308-x
14. Wu, X., Chen, H., Wang, J., Troiano, L., Loia, V., Fujita, H.: Adaptive stock trading strategies with deep reinforcement learning methods. Inf. Sci. **538**, 142–158 (2020). https://doi.org/10.1016/j.ins.2020.05.066
15. Fengqian, D., Chao, L.: An adaptive financial trading system using deep reinforcement learning with candlestick decomposing features. IEEE Access **8**, 63666–63678 (2020). https://doi.org/10.1109/ACCESS.2020.2982662
16. Sezer, O.B., Ozbayoglu, A.M.: Algorithmic financial trading with deep convolutional neural networks: time series to image conversion approach. Appl. Soft Comput. **70**, 525–538 (2018). https://doi.org/10.1016/j.asoc.2018.04.024
17. Van Hasselt, H., Guez, A., Silver, D.: Deep reinforcement learning with double Q-learning. In: AAAI, vol. 30, no. 1 (2016). https://doi.org/10.1609/aaai.v30i1.10295
18. Singh, V., Chen, S.-S., Singhania, M., Nanavati, B., Kumar kar, A., Gupta, A.: How are reinforcement learning and deep learning algorithms used for big data based decision making in financial industries–a review and research agenda. Int. J. Inf. Manag. Data Insights **2**(2), 100094 (2022). https://doi.org/10.1016/j.jjimei.2022.100094
19. The rise of algorithmic trading and its effects on return dispersion and market predictability. Algorithmic Trading

20. Lei, K., Zhang, B., Li, Y., Yang, M., Shen, Y.: Time-driven feature-aware jointly deep reinforcement learning for financial signal representation and algorithmic trading. Expert Syst. Appl. **140**, 112872 (2020). https://doi.org/10.1016/j.eswa.2019.112872
21. Ponomarev, E.S., Oseledets, I.V., Cichocki, A.S.: Using reinforcement learning in the algorithmic trading problem. J. Commun. Technol. Electron.Commun. Technol. Electron. **64**(12), 1450–1457 (2019). https://doi.org/10.1134/S1064226919120131

# Determining Student's Online Academic Performance Using Machine Learning Techniques

Atika Islam[1], Faisal Bukhari[2], and Waheed Iqbal[2](✉)

[1] Department of Computer Science, University of the Punjab, Lahore, Pakistan
[2] Department of Data Science, University of the Punjab, Lahore, Pakistan

**Abstract.** Predicting students' academic performance during online learning has been considered a major task during the pandemic period. During the online mode of learning, academic activities have been affected in such a way that the management of educational institutions has planned to design support systems for predicting the students' performance to reduce the dropout ratio of the students and bring improvement in academic activities. During COVID-19, the main challenge is maintaining students' grades by predicting their academic performance using different techniques such as Education Data Mining and Learning Analytics. Different features have been identified related to the teaching mechanisms in online learning, which have a great impact on the improvement of academic performance. A high-quality dataset helps us to generate productive results, which in turn helps us to make effective decisions for promoting high-quality education. In this research, we have proposed five prediction models for predicting academic performance by collecting an imbalanced dataset of 350 students with the same computer science domain. After applying pre-processing techniques for cleaning the data, we have applied the machine learning models, including K-Nearest Neighbor Classifier, Decision Tree, Random Forest, Support Vector Classifier, and Gaussian Naive Bayes. We have predicted the results for an imbalanced, balanced dataset after feature selection. Support Vector classifier has produced the best results in a balanced dataset with selected features by giving an accuracy of 96.89%.

**Keywords:** Artificial Neural Network (ANN) · Decision Tree · Educational Data Mining · Educational Big Data · Gaussian Naive Bayes · K-Nearest Neighbor · Learning Analytics · Logistic Regression · Random Forest · Support Vector Classifier

## 1 Introduction

The best education is thought to be crucial for a student's success in life. The success of students is the responsibility of all academic institutions. To assess students' academic performance and ensure that it is up to par, specific actions should be taken by all educational institutions. The students' activities during their education have been analyzed for prediction. Students have encountered numerous issues with the online education system regarding their academic performance. Many researchers have performed their best in determining the grades of the students. On the data set, various machine learning approaches have been applied to examine the student's academic achievement. Other researchers have described a variety of ways. There is too much data on students, so this has become a challenge. The next crucial step is to list all the critical characteristics required for forecasting the student's academic achievement. Those attributes include GPA, previous grades, academic progress, mental and psychological condition, and family educational background. Research has introduced two more significant attributes, including the effect of students' internet usage during their studies. As is well known, students are taking classes online throughout the COVID-19 era, and this online learning environment has increased internet usage. Students must enroll in many platforms to complete their coursework, have a reliable internet connection, and are familiar with using social media platforms. They will perform worse academically as a result. Schools are facing a severe problem of student failure in their primary grades. To study every element that contributed to this failure is a difficult process [12]. Educational data Mining has been used to can extract meaningful information from educational data have been created using mining. Education has grown essential and is spreading to others via various avenues. Any internet source can be used to obtain information. In addition, if there are too many students in a class and they have difficulties listening to the Lecture, the innovations in this technology allow the instructors to transmit knowledge to the individual student [2]. Grades are used to measure the performance of the students during their course. We investigate essential variables that could influence academic success or activity most effectively. This study provides us with necessary information about the academic situation of students. As is well known, students are never accustomed to learning on online educational platforms during the online mode of the educational system. In this research, we are involved in finding the significant factors that could best determine academic activities or performance.

- Analyzing different factors which are responsible for a student failure.
- To decrease the ratio of student's failure.
- To take preliminary decisions to help the students which are at risk of failure.

## 2 Previous Work

The use of machine learning techniques to forecast students' academic achievement has already been studied. Particularly during the COVID-19 pandemic, the educational system changed from traditional to online. The success or failure of a student in online learning is evaluated based on their behavior in class and their academic interests during online class assessments [3]. Since students are not in direct contact with their lecturers during the online form of learning, the ratio of dropout students can be predicted early on by observing their actions. Many forecasting techniques, including a machine learning model called support vector machines (SVM), have been applied, and the results have been quite good. Naive Bayes and Neural Networks have shown excellent results [14]. It is possible to assess academic performance using educational data mining (EDM). A very traditional method that can be used to arrive at the right judgments is data mining. Educational Data Mining can help design and introduce new techniques in the education system [6]. Three classifiers were utilized in this study to analyze the seven best features, with Naive Bayes having the highest accuracy at 85.7% [7]. Teachers' AI techniques can help them create a comfortable, challenging, and appealing learning environment. Coursera is an online learning platform where students and professors can take comprehensive, well-recognized courses. In the end, AI has developed into a tool for raising pupils' academic achievement [4]. It is challenging to predict students' academic achievement. Numerous research projects have already been conducted. The "Course Signals" early risk indicator was created by Purdue University. It is a remedy for students' failures. It is initially created after making academic achievement predictions for kids. For teachers and students to communicate with one another and for students to share the issues they are having with the online educational system, many chatting technologies have been acknowledged. A few distinct factors make a prediction model accurate and effective. Learning Analytics seeks to assist students who are in danger of failing by doing so. The academic performance of the pupils will significantly increase. As a result [1]. There are numerous effective ways to determine the student dropout rate. The IBM SPSS Answer Tree (AT) software can be used to accomplish this. Numerous academics have identified important variables that influence the proportion of dropout pupils. Their financial situation, familiar background, and prior grades play significant roles. The imbalanced dataset during prediction is a significant issue. However, this dataset will perform better when implemented machine learning techniques, as shown in [13]. Students' academic performance depends on their previous high school and college results. The student's success depends on the struggle of teachers as well as the students [11]. Another study used learning track data collection and a single classification algorithm to forecast data in the online learning environment. Regression Trees (CART), Decision Trees, and Logistic Regression are the methodologies that are employed [5]. Another study has also used the University of Technology in Thailand's dataset. There are 15 features in the dataset, and several feature selection techniques, including Information Gain Ratio (IG), Greedy, and Chi-Square, have been compared. To make the forecast, many machine learning algorithms were combined. This study demonstrates that, compared to Decision Tree and Naive Bayes prediction methods, the Greedy Forward selection algorithm provides the best accuracy in predicting academic performance [9]. Another well-known technique has been named Matrix Factorization (MF). This has performed very well for prediction purposes. Singular Value Decomposition has been applied in this research and predicts grades [8]. As we know, during COVID-19, students are distracted from their studies and not comfortable in the online learning environment. Hence, their academic performance is too much affected. So, these predictions have to be made to analyze the factors involved in the betterment of their academic performance [15]. Research shows that the Decision Tree classifier, combined with the Correlation Based Feature Selection (CFS) algorithm, has been applied to the data of 240 students. In this research, six feature selection algorithms have been used for prediction, and the data is collected from higher secondary schools [10]. In these research papers, academic performance has been predicted during physical mode but we have worked on online mode of learning.

## 3 Dataset

This study was conducted between August 2021 and July 2022. I have decided to gather information from students of Information Technology. This table shows the data collected from both Universities 1 (Table 1).

Table 1. Participation of different Universities in collecting dataset

| Universities | No of Students |
|---|---|
| University of the Punjab (PU), Lahore | 283 |
| Information Technology University (ITU), Lahore | 67 |
| Total | **350** |

### 3.1 Data Collection Method

We have decided to make a questionnaire with all the questions regarding the students' current situations during their online learning. We have also attended online classes during my last semester of BS Software engineering and in the first semester of M Phil CS. So, after going through the current research on this topic in my literature review, We designed a questionnaire by myself using Google Forms. We have shared the link of my questionnaire to the students from fall 2016 to fall 2022 of both Old campus and New Campus via emails and Whatsapp groups. This research is description-based, so questionnaires are the best approach for collecting data. We have read many questionnaires from different research papers and then designed a questionnaire named Academic Performance during Online Learning. The questionnaire consists of four different sections. It is based on analyzing the pros and cons of the online Way of learning. The questionnaire was divided into the following components.

- In the first portion, generic inquiries about the student's gender, the subjects they have studied online, their percentage of marks earned, etc., have been made.
- Different skills-related questions have been designed for the second segment, such as what challenges individuals encounter while taking online classes.
- We have compared academic performance between the traditional classroom setting and online learning in the third section of the questionnaire. Some questions have been raised regarding the workload and homework offered to students during the online semester.
- Questions in the final portion are intended to gauge how satisfied the students are with this online learning environment. How much do the staff and teachers cooperate with their students in online lectures?

There are no restrictions for filling out this questionnaire. Everyone can submit a response. Everyone having the link can view and submit their reply. Link to the questionnaire.

**Table 2.** Questions asked from the students for collecting data

| Sr. | Questions | Possible Answers | Attribute Type |
|---|---|---|---|
| 1 | What is your gender? | Male/Female | Binary |
| 2 | Which programming subject have you studied during the online semester? | PF/OOP/DSA/WE/EAD/AOA/MC/DS | String |
| 3 | In which online semester have you studied your mentioned subjects? | 1st/2nd/3rd/4th/5th/6th/7th/8th | String |
| 4 | Do the long-term use of digital devices affect your studies? | Yes/No | Binary |
| 5 | Staying a long time in the house makes you lazy during online lectures? | Yes/No | Binary |
| 6 | Is it hard for you to use mobiles and laptops for taking online lectures? | Yes/No | Binary |
| 7 | Distraction from surroundings lessens your attention during class | Yes/No | Binary |
| 8 | Do you have a quiet place to study? | Often/Rarely/Always/Never/Sometimes | String |
| 9 | Do you have the required software and programs? | Often/Rarely/Always/Never/Sometimes | String |
| 10 | Do you have headphones and microphones? | Often/Rarely/Always/Never/Sometimes | String |
| 11 | Do you have a Webcam? | Often/Rarely/Always/Never/Sometimes | String |
| 12 | Do you have a strong internet connection? | Often/Rarely/Always/Never/Sometimes | String |
| 13 | Do you have a Computer/Laptop? | Often/Rarely/Always/Never/Sometimes | String |
| 14 | Do you have course study material? | Often/Rarely/Always/Never/Sometimes | String |

(*continued*)

**Table 2.** (*continued*)

| Sr. | Questions | Possible Answers | Attribute Type |
|---|---|---|---|
| 15 | Are you familiar with browsing information and sharing digital content? | Often/Rarely/Always/Never/Sometimes | String |
| 16 | Focusing during the online Lecture is more difficult for me than in physical lectures | Strongly disagree/Disagree/Neutral/Agree/Strongly agree | String |
| 17 | During physical classes, my academic performance has been improved | Strongly disagree/Disagree/Neutral/Agree/Strongly agree | String |
| 18 | During online classes, my performance has worsen | Strongly disagree/Disagree/Neutral/Agree/Strongly agree | String |
| 19 | During online classes, I am interested in listening to the Lecture | Strongly disagree/Disagree/Neutral/Agree/Strongly agree | String |
| 20 | How much I became a master in the skills taught during online classes | Strongly disagree/Disagree/Neutral/Agree/Strongly agree | String |
| 21 | Mental stress and depression during COVID 19 affect your learning abilities | Strongly disagree/Disagree/Neutral/Agree/Strongly agree | String |
| 22 | Familiar with online learning platform (Google meet) | Strongly disagree/Disagree/Neutral/Agree/Strongly agree | String |
| 23 | Familiar with online learning platforms (Zoom) | Strongly disagree/Disagree/Neutral/Agree/Strongly agree | String |
| 24 | One assignment during a week | Strongly disagree/Disagree/Neutral/Agree/Strongly agree | String |
| 25 | Providing feedback on my assignments | Strongly disagree/Disagree/Neutral/Agree/Strongly agree | String |
| 26 | Give responses to my questions promptly | Strongly disagree/Disagree/Neutral/Agree/Strongly agree | String |

(*continued*)

**Table 2.** (*continued*)

| Sr. | Questions | Possible Answers | Attribute Type |
|---|---|---|---|
| 27 | Have taken student's suggestions | Strongly disagree/Disagree/Neutral/Agree/Strongly agree | String |
| 28 | Have informed us about online exam patterns | Strongly disagree/Disagree/Neutral/Agree/Strongly agree | String |
| 29 | Lecture timings | Very dissatisfied/Dissatisfied/Neutral/Satisfied/Very satisfied | String |
| 30 | Supervisions | Very dissatisfied/Dissatisfied/Neutral/Satisfied/Very satisfied | String |
| 31 | Way of teaching online | Very dissatisfied/Dissatisfied/Neutral/Satisfied/Very satisfied | String |
| 32 | Career counseling services for students | Very dissatisfied/Dissatisfied/Neutral/Satisfied/Very satisfied | String |
| 33 | Online in real-time (videoconference) | Very dissatisfied/Dissatisfied/Neutral/Satisfied/Very satisfied | String |
| 34 | Online with a video recording (not in real-time) | Very dissatisfied/Dissatisfied/Neutral/Satisfied/Very satisfied | String |
| 35 | Online with an audio recording (not in real-time) | Very dissatisfied/Dissatisfied/Neutral/Satisfied/Very satisfied | String |
| 36 | Online by sending presentations to students | Very dissatisfied/Dissatisfied/Neutral/Satisfied/Very satisfied | String |
| 37 | Written communication (forums, chat, etc.) | Very dissatisfied/Dissatisfied/Neutral/Satisfied/Very satisfied | String |
| 38 | Average marks | less than 60% /greater than 60% | Binary |

### 3.2 Input Features

After completing research on determining academic performance, we have identified 38 essential elements which help determine the student's academic performance. We have used different input features to predict the student's academic performance. Few features are in binary format, and most are in string format. The following Table 2 shows all the features, options, and format.

## 3.3 Data Analysis and Pre-processing

After collecting data from 350 students, the second step is to analyze our data. When the dataset has been collected, all the responses are gathered in a Comma Separated Values (CSV) file. Then we observed different significant factors that help us in predicting academic performance. We have used Jupiter notebook for implementation in python. I have used the pandas' library to read my CSV file and convert it into a data frame. We have observed 350 sample points and 38 distinct features here. These figures will help you check the relationship of different features, which help predict the students' academic performance. We have made these figures using a library Seaborn in python. To make a better visualization using a counting chart. We have presented here eight different features, which are in binary and string format. Each Fig. 1 corresponds to a single feature related to the outcome feature known as average marks. Each feature has been visualized according to two possible labels of average effects (Less than 60 % and more significant than 60%). Different colors are represented in the graphs representing both labels.

### 3.3.1 Data Formatting

Data formatting can be done after data analysis. Before computing results, we have to format our data into numeric labels.

- First, we must observe all the missing values in our data frame. We have checked the whole data frame and derived the count of NaN values in each column or feature using the IsNull function. After applying this function, it has been observed that there are five features in which there are missing values.
- As we are going to determine the student's academic performance during online education, we have to apply different machine learning algorithms to the dataset. Still, at first, we have to convert these string labels into numeric labels so that the best results can be generated after applying Machine Learning algorithms. Label Encoder can be applied to the structured dataset. After label encoding, We got the unique values for all the labels in the dataset.
- Normalization is the second method, also known as rescaling, which We have applied to the encoded data. Normalization converts all the numeric data to 0 to 1 or $-1$ to 1. This range depends on the type of data values. Normalization helps us to get more accurate results because it increases the consistency among features. This method will convert the values into a standard scale. We have used the Min Max Scaler function to normalize the values. The mathematical formula for min-max scaler is as written below

$$y' = y - min(y)/max(y) - min(y)$$

In this formula, y is the original data point, and y' is the normalized value of that data point.

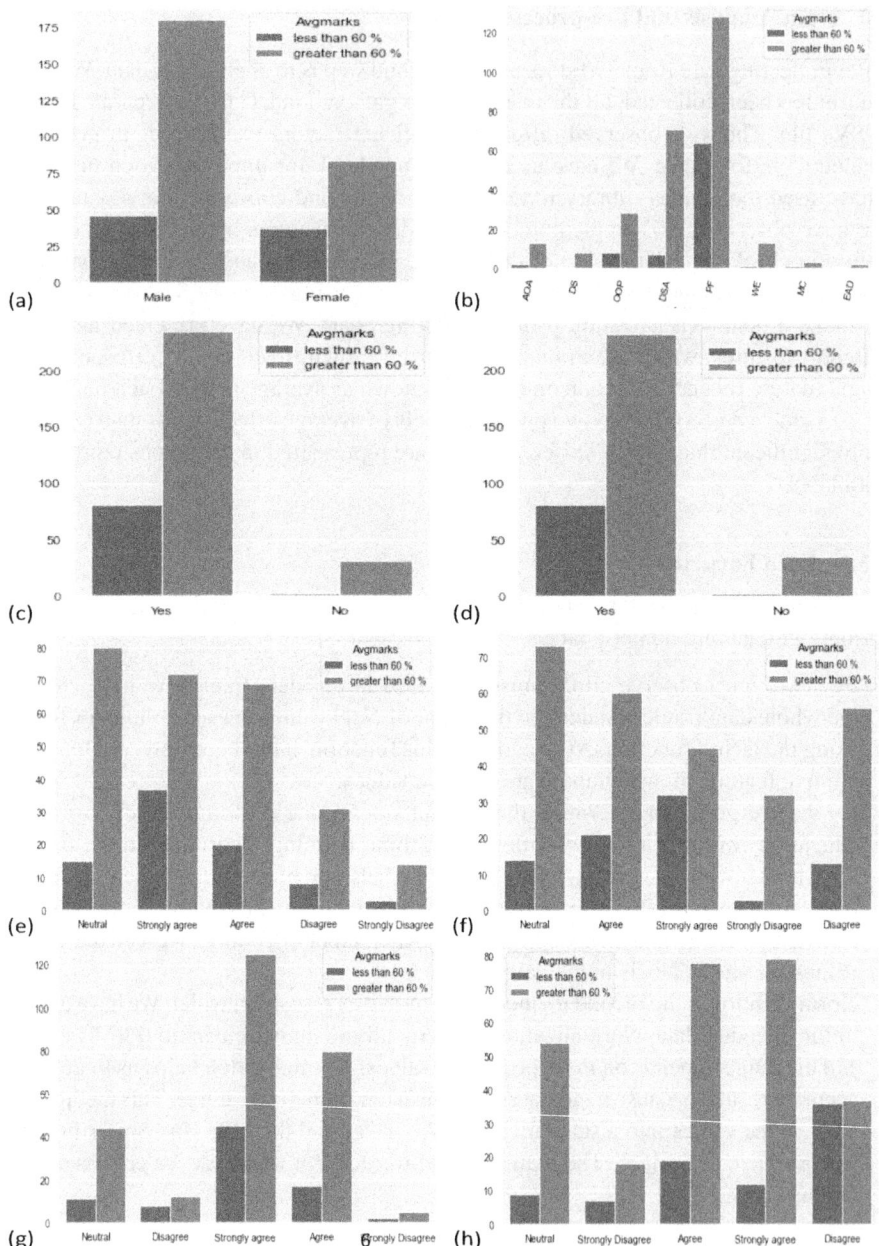

**Fig. 1.** The distribution of eight features with respect to Average marks 1(a), Gender 1(b), Subject 1(c), Students becoming lazy 1(d), Affect of surroundings on studies 1(e), Improved performance during online learning 1(f), Worse performance during online learning 1(g), Google meet for online lectures 1(h), Zoom platform for online lectures (Color figure online)

## 4 Proposed Methodology and Experimental Results

We will see the significant steps in determining academic performance. Figure 2 contains a flowchart that is presenting our methodology.

- Import the required libraries.
- Data analysis and pre-processing techniques have been applied to the data to convert it into structured form.

  - Removing all the null and empty data values.
  - Using Label Encoder to encode the labels with specific data values.
  - Normalization has been performed using Min Max Scaler.

- Division of data into two sets of training and testing sets. The prediction has been performed.
- At the end, we have calculated the accuracy, precision, and recall using every machine learning algorithm, and after comparison, we generate the result.

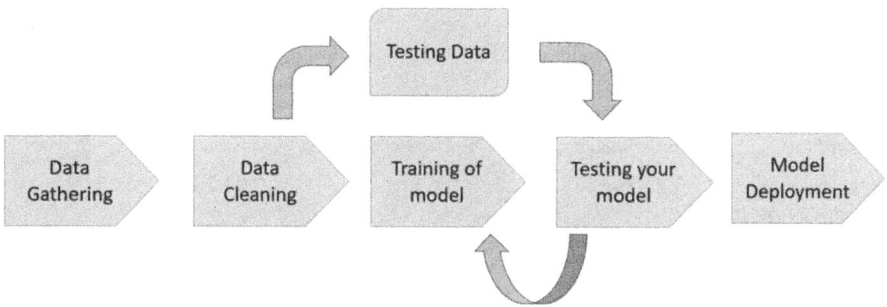

**Fig. 2.** Process of Machine Learning

### 4.1 Experiments and Results

In this prediction, We have divided my dataset in the ratio of 70% in the training and 30% in the testing parts. All the features except average marks are in the X part, and the outcome average marks are in the Y part. Then we split the dataset. Now while training the data, we have also applied the Cross-validation technique by dividing the data into five subsets. This technique is generally used for getting information about how the model is adequate. As we have observed, the results are not too satisfying due to the problem of unbalanced classes, as we have seen that there are two classes. In the feature of average marks, the class of more significant than 60% has more records whose count is 267, and in comparison to that, there are fewer records of class less than 60% of average marks whose count is just 83. So, the results of classification can be improved by balancing the classes. We have applied to oversample on my dataset to randomly increase the records of the minority class. For applying oversampling, We have used the function named

Random Over Sampler using the strategy of minority sampling, so here We have samples of 267 of the majority class and, after balancing the minority class, also have samples of 267 sample points. Without balancing classes, K-nearest neighbor has given the highest accuracy value of 82.85% but now, after increasing the sample points of the class of average marks less than 60%. Support Vector Classifier and Random Forest algorithms have performed very well by generating accuracy of 91.92% and 91.30%, respectively. After balancing classes, Feature Selection is the second method for improving our results. There is a total of 38 different features in the dataset. Then we applied a technique of feature Selection by dropping some correlated features. Dimensionality reduction will reduce the number of input features. To obtain the correlation between all the features, we used the function of corr on the training set. We can also visualize the correlation matrix using Heatmap. We have performed this method using the threshold value of 0.5, which means if the two features are in 50% correlation, we can remove one of those features. Pearson correlation method has identified three features which are in 50% correlation. Supervisions, Written Communication, and sending presentations have been removed from the training and testing set. Among all the algorithms KNN, SVC, RF, DT, and GNB, after doing all these experiments on data, we have observed that the Support Vector Classifier has outperformed by giving an accuracy of 96%.

**Table 3.** Results of different machine learning algorithms

| Machine learning algorithms | Accuracy of unbalanced classes | Accuracy with balanced classes | Accuracy after feature Reduction |
|---|---|---|---|
| K-Nearest Neighbors (KNN) | 82.85% | 88.81% | 93.78% |
| Support Vector Classifier (SVC) | 81.90% | 91.92% | 96.89% |
| Decision Tree Classifier | 81.90% | 83.85% | 87.57% |
| Random Forest | 80.95% | 91.30% | 93.16% |
| Gaussian Naive Bayes | 78.09% | 68.94% | 73.29% |

Table 3 compares the accuracy of all the machine learning algorithms. When we compute the accuracy of unbalanced classes, then KNN performs best by giving the accuracy of 82.85%. After balancing the classes, the SVC performs best by giving an accuracy of 91.92%. Then, accuracy has been computed after feature reduction and gives an accuracy of 96.89%.

## 5 Conclusion and Future Work

This research concludes that in the future, students' ultimate success depends on their academic grades and performance. This prediction has been performed here using different algorithms of machine learning. In an unbalanced dataset, the Support Vector

Classifier and Decision Tree have an accuracy of 81.90%. Then after balancing the dataset, SVM has the best accuracy of 91.92%. After that, again, to improve our result, we applied the Feature Selection technique, and then again, SVM outstands among all algorithms and gives an accuracy of 96.89%. This research shows all the features which directly affect academic performance and helps us predict students' average marks while observing those features. If a student is getting disturbed by the surroundings, doesn't have an internet connection, is not familiar with the usage of digital devices can't attend the online lectures hence the chance of failure increases. So, these few major factors should be noticed while predicting the performance of the students. This research only helps us to predict the average marks of the students. We can't precisely predict the students' marks, but after analyzing the features described in this research, instructors can predict students' performance. Due to limited time, I have collected data from 350 students from two universities and only considered the Department of Information Technology. In the future, we can take more data to make our research more robust and precise.

### 5.1 Application of This Research

Due to the pandemic period, many educational institutions have shifted their education system from conventional mode to online mode of learning. So, without physical discussion between teachers and students during lectures, it is difficult for the instructors to predict the students' academic behavior. During online learning, it isn't easy to analyze students' interest in class activities, class discussions, and quizzes. To evaluate the performance, the management of educational institutions has planned their learning schedule using techniques of educational data mining (EDM).

## References

1. Arnold, K.E., Pistilli, M.D.: Course signals at Purdue: using learning analytics to increase student success. In: Proceedings of the 2nd International Conference on Learning Analytics and Knowledge, pp. 267–270 (2012)
2. Baraniuk, R.: Open education: new opportunities for signal processing. In: Plenary Speech, 2015 IEEE International Conference on Acoustics, Speech and Signal Processing (ICASSP) (2015)
3. Bhutto, E.S., Siddiqui, I.F., Arain, Q.A., Anwar, M.: Predicting students' academic performance through supervised machine learning. In: 2020 International Conference on Information Science and Communication Technology (ICISCT), pp. 1–6. IEEE (2020)
4. Borge, N.: Artificial intelligence to improve education/learning challenges. Int. J. Adv. Eng. Innov. Technol. (IJAEIT) **2**(6), 10–13 (2016)
5. Hu, Y.-H., Lo, C.-L., Shih, S.-P.: Developing early warning systems to predict students' online learning performance. Comput. Hum. Behav. **36**, 469–478 (2014)
6. Kotsiantis, S.B.: Use of machine learning techniques for educational proposes: a decision support system for forecasting students' grades. Artif. Intell. Rev. **37**(4), 331–344 (2012)
7. Mueen, A., Zafar, B., Manzoor, U.: Modeling and predicting students' academic performance using data mining techniques. Int. J. Mod. Educ. Comput. Sci. **8**(11) (2016)
8. Park, Y.: Predicting personalized student performance in computing-related majors via collaborative filtering. In: Proceedings of the 19th Annual SIG Conference on Information Technology Education, p. 151 (2018)

9. Rachburee, N., Punlumjeak, W.: A comparison of feature selection approach between greedy, IG-ratio, Chi-square, and mRMR in educational mining. In: 2015 7th International Conference on Information Technology and Electrical Engineering (ICITEE), pp. 420–424. IEEE (2015)
10. Ramaswami, M., Bhaskaran, R.: A study on feature selection techniques in educational data mining. arXiv preprint arXiv:0912.3924 (2009)
11. Said, M.A., Idris, M., Hussain, S.: Relationship between social behaviour and academic performance of students at secondary level in Khyber Pakhtunkhwa. Pak. J. Distance Online Learn. **4**(1), 153–170 (2018)
12. Shaleena, K.P., Paul, S.: Data mining techniques for predicting student performance. In: 2015 IEEE International Conference on Engineering and Technology (ICETECH), pp. 1–3. IEEE (2015)
13. Thammasiri, D., Delen, D., Meesad, P., Kasap, N.: A critical assessment of imbalanced class distribution problem: the case of predicting freshmen student attrition. Expert Syst. Appl. **41**(2), 321–330 (2014)
14. Wolff, A., Zdrahal, Z., Herrmannova, D., Kuzilek, J., Hlosta, M.: Developing predictive models for early detection of at-risk students on distance learning modules (2014)
15. Yadav, S.K., Pal, S.: Data mining: a prediction for performance improvement of engineering students using classification. arXiv preprint arXiv:1203.3832 (2012)

# User Experience (UX) Enrichment Through Digital Branding

Saira Zia[1], Muhammad Waseem Iqbal[2(✉)], Misbah Noor[1], Muhammad Aqeel[1], and Khalid Hamid[1]

[1] Department of Computer Science, Superior University Lahore, Lahore, Pakistan
{MSCS-F20-011,misbah.noor,aqeel}@superior.edu.pk
[2] Department of Software Engineering, Superior University Lahore, Lahore, Pakistan
waseem.iqbal@superior.edu.pk

**Abstract.** The change in digital marketing from desktop to mobile contexts (e.g., browser) is getting increasingly pronounced (e.g., within mobile applications). Banners and videos, on the other hand, remain mostly unchanged as ad distribution mechanisms. We look at how to adapt ad distribution methods to the mobile environment. We demonstrate how demanding gentle contact with the ad – while lowering available screen space – might improve users' perceptions of remote marketing. Business remember may be improved by more encounters with the commercial distribution device. A holistic knowledge of customer experience necessitates examining in marketing and branding, user experience is important. This study's aim is to offer a theoretical background for finer comprehension the implications of user experience (UX), client experience (CX), and corporate reputation (BE) are all terms used to describe how a user, a customer, or a brand (BE) on brand equity (BX). As a mediator with a high path weight, customer experience has a major impact on brand equity. Employing UX techniques that connect with management plans can help companies reach a high level of customer satisfaction and brand value perception by consumers. This study's findings and analyses can assist business in developing a strategy. For understanding which components of User Experiences are important for brand image and the customer satisfaction. Given the increased financial significance of the "user experience," more gamification should be used. As an outcome, the study's goal is to look into the causes and the consequences of an online experience, in the area of internet gamification, it also partially mediates the relationship. According to the findings, mobility as it is perceived practical and hedonistic features, as well as perceived mobility characteristics, influence experience design, which in turn drives perceived advantages, perceived value categories, and product equity. This study also confirms the role of user experience as a mediating factor. Finally, the outcomes of this study can assist website administrators in improving the perceptions of rewards, value, and product attributes among their users that act as a road-map for gamification to get a market advantage in the internet world, companies should invest in research and development (R&D).

**Keywords:** Smartphone; advertising; interfaces · user encounters · client satisfaction · brand recognition · usability impact

## 1 Introduction

From text messages that aren't relevant to those that are personalized as well as context-sensitive situations, there's something for everyone. [1], online advertising has grown dramatically over time [2]. Users, on the other hand, are more likely to ignore or be distracted by mobile advertisements [3]. Both fun and have been discovered to be pleasurable as important factors in determining the performance of digital advertising as well as public perceptions of them [4, 5]. By presenting the advertisement in the appropriate environment, the user can get utilitarian benefits [6].

Banner ads, which can be found throughout the app's functionality or at the start and end of the screen are frequent approach for mobile advertisers to get their message across. In 1998, the phrase 'banner blindness' [4] was coined to People's capacity to scan online URLs fast while skipping poster text, to the point where they have trouble recalling the contents of the banner [7]. Most native apps, on the other hand, depends on a similar method of showing adverts.

From a usability evaluation perspective, in the digital technology industry and the cloud service market, a commercial standpoint is becoming a trend [8]. Usability design is progressively being included into marketing and promotion strategies by successful browser businesses [9]. When a user utility a service or purchases a product, they are both a client and a user of the company that sells the products and services [6]. Surprisingly and coincidentally, the management sector has been more focused on the customer experience [10].

In every retail industry area, client experience (CX) is currently defined as the performance of a customer's entire journey of interactions with the organization. It was originally described as the Customer service operations at several touch points in the retail and service industries [11].

Product attributes (BX) is described as the customer's perception of brand value as a result of sensory, emotional, cognitive, and behavioral cues associated with the brand [12], as proponents of experiential marketing believe [13].

Modeling the link between three dimensions of experience is main objective of this study. We tried to investigate qualities and construct measurement scales for each experience dimension as part of the model testing. We chose the smartphone as an exemplary experience because it provides customers with everyday encounters with the product, service, and brand. As a result, we gathered data from mobile phone users and evaluated three parts of their observation: as a user, customer, and consumer

## 2 Related Work

Media attention is a sort of business engagement in which a good, commodity or concept is sponsored or offered utilizing a obviously a paid post [14]. Attraction of the media goal is to get consumers to use a product. Increasing user happiness with products or services by using branding you can obtain brand knowledge by associating the name of a company or a product. The other strategy is advertising that generates a response, which seeks to offer products directly to customers [15]. However, unlike approaches like situational commercial (e.g., in malls or while watching television), it's often impossible to accurately User preferences can be predicted, which is especially important when it comes to mobile advertising [14].

Nath and its colleagues [16] proposed Smart Ads as a method for reducing the quantity of unnecessary adverts shown to users.

According to 2019–21 research, the predicted proportion of Mobile-based advertising for 2022 was 33.3%, and it is expected to significantly expand [18]. Consumers often have a bad attitude forward online advertising particularly if they haven't given their approval [19], this is true for a wide range of applications, i.e.

**Table 1.** Variables associated with several features of digital ad delivery systems.

| Type of advertisement | Method of Removal | Screen Space Affect | Distraction Levels | Repetition's Effect on Distraction |
|---|---|---|---|---|
| *Banners (fixed) i.e. (Full-screen applications & games)* | Unavailable (usually) | Medium (Frequently layered over UI elements) | Medium | Medium |
| *Banners(changeable) I.e.: List views, Gmail* | Unavailable (usually) | Small (Reduces data yet does not overlap the interface) | Low | Low |
| *YouTube video* | 'After x seconds, avoid' or 'unavailable' | High | High | High |
| *Video (embedded) e.g. Web pages* | Unavailable, pause, or 'After x seconds, avoid' | High | High | Medium |
| *Web pages, Pop - up ads, and other pictures (full screen)* | Click designated location to close | High | High | High |
| *Audio e.g. Spotify* | Skip after x seconds or Unavailable | None | Low | Medium |
| *In-app* | Unavailable | Varies | Varies | Varies |
| *Proposed Icon Delivery Method* | Drag to get rid of it | Small | Low | Low-Medium |

Apps do not ask for permission to place ads from the user directly, but simply alert them from the current advertisements. Several investigations have examined the crucial influence of frameworks the Technology Acceptance Model, for example (TAM) [20] and Frameworks that are finely textured are being investigated, for example, As a method of determining acceptance of electronic advertising messages, we can use our sentimental relationship to our cellphones [21] or the collaborative element of modern smartphones

[22]. Other factors that influence our willingness to accept mobile advertising include our intentions and behavior (to buy) distinct items, the Unified Theory of Acceptance and Technology Users, as well as our perception of mobile sub unit and pleasure [5]. They all follow the same logic: immersive or "funny" commercials appeal to the Hedonistic utilitarianism on the part of the user, resulting in higher advertisement acceptance [3].

Report on Luxury Marketing Clicks were generated in 2.1% of banner ads [23]. Ads are more likely to be clicked by older individuals, and the most common reasons for not doing so include spyware and phishing concern as well as the commercials are distracting. The intrinsic interest rate in the outcome, the distribution way's matching with brand, a self-perceived state of mind toward the mode of supply, and general attitude toward digital commercials are all critical elements in calculating Click through rate, according to Cho et al. [30].

## 3 Research Methodology

To provide a commercial message to the user, mobile advertising typically combines text and graphics, video, or audio. Varying approaches occupy a significant portion of the screen, offer varied techniques of interaction (essentially, methods to get rid of the adverts), and generate varied levels of user irritation and attentiveness. Finally, some distribution techniques are easier to repeat without causing substantial disruption. Table 1 summaries the most common ad formats used in mobile advertising, as well as the levels of engagement and our expert opinion of how the delivery mechanism affects user experience. Examples of banner ads, video commercials, and interfaces that combine the two are shown in Figure 2. In-app adverts, like Purchases made in-app or elsewhere items published by the same company, have been grouped together as well. However, because the user interfaces of these apps differ so much, it's difficult to generalize about their influence on the aforementioned factors.

Figure 1a depicts a fixed banner ad is displayed superimposed above and beyond the mobile interface depicts a huge banner ad, and Figures 1c and 1d depict banner ads that change frequently appear as participants of a list view that already exists. Besides for Figure 1b, because it's unclear what happens if the consumer clicks anywhere else on the advertisement apart from the 'install now' phrase, the interaction technique with advertisement is reasonably obvious in the majority of cases, with unambiguous choices such as 'install' and 'skip'. Knowledgeable users know that Figure 1d has a distinct remove button (the cross), whereas Figure 1b swiping away. Figures 1a and 1b have no alternatives for removal. In Figure 1a, the concerns often connected with ad overlaying on the UI are not immediately apparent, but they become apparent when viewing another full screen. Less imperfect color display scheme space Ads that overlay the UI and may have possibly hidden closure methods (– for example, popups and dialogues), and movies that auto update or cannot be skipped are the main reasons of ad delivery method aggravation. These ad delivery technologies have one thing in common: they diminish or change the UX that is provided which difficult to do hidden or remove. In our research, we created some banners or posters with the goal of resolving the problems.

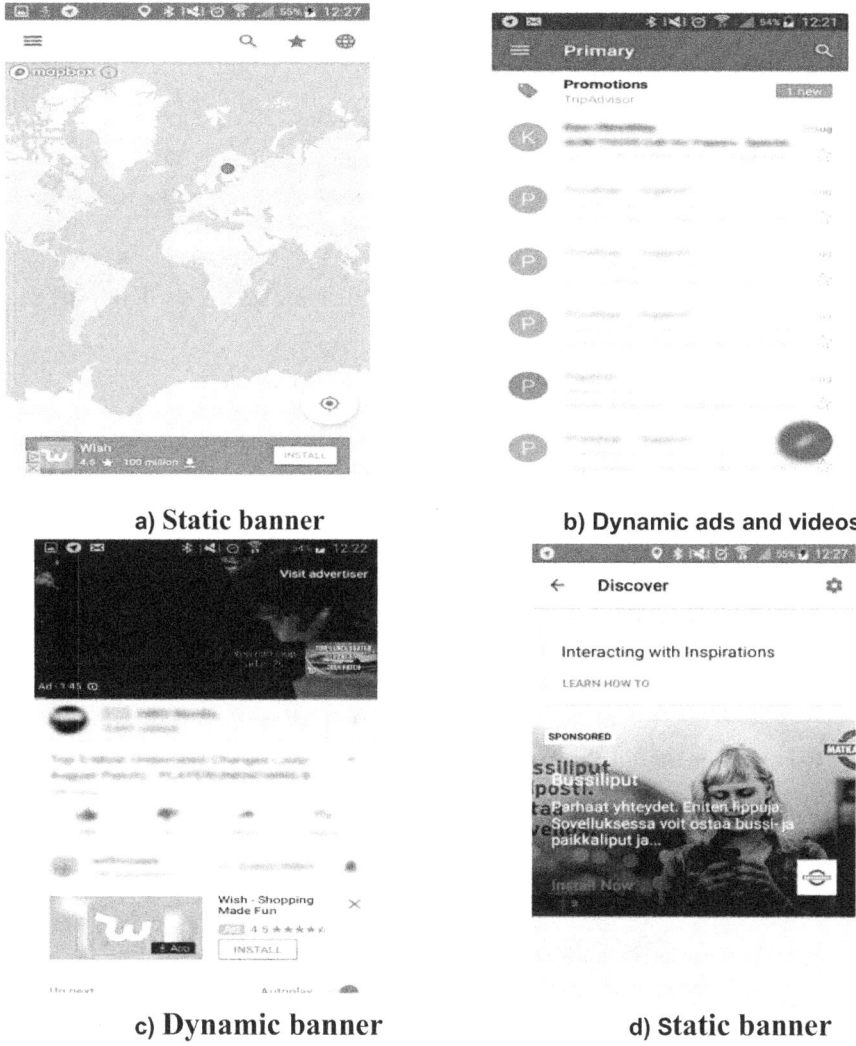

**Fig. 1.** Methods of displaying mobile ads encompass

### 3.1 Experiment

We gathered data through a poll to see how users felt about digital advertisements. The commercials were picked from independent shops so that everyone knew who they were. We used different questionnaires to evaluate our approach, which uses different methods to deliver digital ads. We gave the persons in the chosen age range a digital and paper questionnaire form to get their feedback. Antiseptic soaps, Summer Drinks, and Toothpastes were the three brand categories we chose. The chosen brands are following in each category (Table 2).

**Table 2.** Categories of selected brands

| Category | Brands | | |
|---|---|---|---|
| Antiseptic Soaps | Dettol | Safeguard | Lifebuoy |
| Summer Drinks | Jam-e-Shiri | Tang | Rooh Afza |
| Toothpastes | Colgate | Sensodyne | Close-up |

Regarding the usefulness of both delivery modalities, we ask the following set of questions:

- Which Antiseptic soap do you use?
- Why did you like the brand most you are using?
- What is your view about Lifebuoy, Safeguard a Dettol banner?
- Are you influence by the digital advertisements and thus buy the soap?
- How many of these banners' colors do you find appealing?
- How much time do you spend watching them on your mobile screen?
- What kind of Drink do you like to use?
- If you have a chance to change one thing, what would you like to change?
- Any suggestion?

It took about 5 to 7 min each participant to complete the entire questionnaire.

### 3.2 User Center Design Process Model

The UCD technique is accustomed to produce basic concepts, practice tests, or designs for Graphic design, visual design, interface design, and visual analytics are all examples

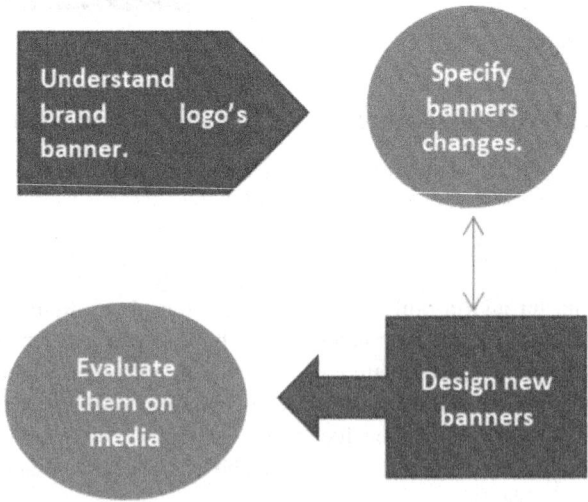

**Fig. 2.** Model of the Development Process

of designs that might be part of or all of a larger project. Architects, according to the UCD framework, must analyze and determine how customers will take advantage of the service as well as validate its accuracy in terms of user behavior.

While testing a product is vital, designers confront a difficult challenge in understanding the user's experiences. For high-usability, low-cost goods, UCD has a full product life-cycle. UCD's main purpose is to provide a well-designed, efficient, and user-friendly product that boosts customer satisfaction and usage.

### 3.3 Prototype Development

**Working**

We designed new banner ads with more alluring shades, which improved the user experience over time. Which are following three (Fig. 3):

### 3.4 Data Analysis Through SPSS Tool

#### 3.4.1 Soap Types

| Which Antiseptic soap do you use? | | | |
|---|---|---|---|
| | Frequency | Percent | Valid Percent |
| **Dettol1** | 210 | 38.2 | 38.2 |
| **Lifebuoy** | 176 | 32.0 | 32.0 |
| Safeguard | 164 | 29.8 | 29.8 |
| Total | 550 | 100.0 | 100.0 |

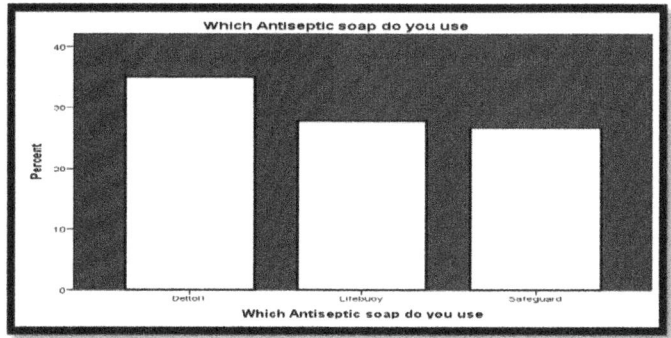

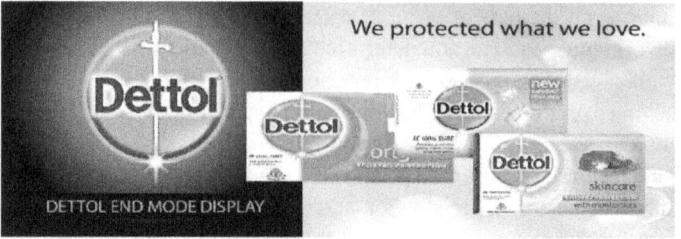

a) Dettol Banner

b) Colgate Banner

c) Jam-e-Shiri Banner

**Fig. 3.** a) Dettol Banner b) Colgate Banner c) Jam-e-Shiri Banner

### 3.4.2 Drink Taste Rank

| Rank features based on their importance. [Taste] | | |
|---|---|---|
| | Frequency | Percent |
| 1st | 404 | 73.5 |
| 2nd | 66 | 12.0 |
| 3rd | 64 | 11.6 |
| 4th | 16 | 2.9 |
| Total | 550 | 100.0 |

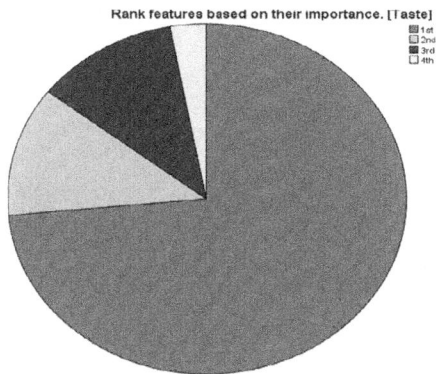

### 3.4.3 Multiple Factors Cause to Buy Toothpaste

| What factor cause you to buy a particular brand of toothpaste? | | |
|---|---|---|
| | Frequency | Percent |
| Fresh Breath | 61 | 9.4 |
| Fresh Teeth | 8 | 1.2 |
| Ingredient; Kill Bacteria | 14 | 2.2 |
| Kill Bacteria | 14 | 2.2 |
| Sensitive Teeth | 125 | 19.3 |
| Sensitive Teeth; Ingredient | 16 | 2.5 |
| Sensitive Teeth; Kill Bacteria | 43 | 6.6 |
| Sensitive Teeth; White Teeth | 14 | 2.2 |
| Sensitive Teeth; White Teeth; | 30 | 4.6 |
| White Teeth | 56 | 8.6 |
| White Teeth; Fresh Breath | 61 | 9.4 |
| White Teeth; Ingredient | 48 | 7.4 |
| White Teeth; Kill Bacteria | 60 | 9.3 |
| Total | 550 | 100.0 |

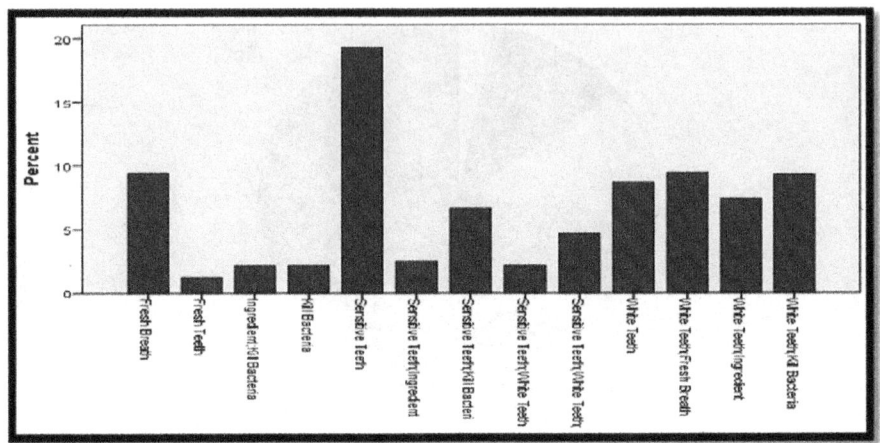

### 3.5 Usability Evaluation

Three characteristics can be utilized to evaluate usability performance: efficiency, efficacy, and user satisfaction. ISO 9241-11 is a specification that is used to assess efficacy and efficiency, while the After Scenario Questionnaire is used to assess user satisfaction (ASQ). Errors are unintentional acts, blunders, errors, or mistakes committed by a user who is performing an activity. The number of chances that can be met is termed as effectiveness, and it is calculated using the formula:

$$\text{Effectiveness} = \frac{\text{Total completed tasks successfully}}{\text{Number of undertaken tasks}} * 100$$

Total time, money, or mental effort required to achieve the intended outcomes is referred to as efficiency. It's easy to calculate:

$$\text{Efficiency based on time} = \sum_{J=1}^{R} \cdot \sum_{i=1}^{N} \frac{n_{ij}}{t_{ij}} \bigg/ NR$$

where

**R** represents the No. of individuals.

**nij** = User j's response to work I; if the customer finishes the assignment properly, Nij = 1, otherwise it is set to 0.

**tij** = The period of moments it took participant j to perform job(i). Unless the activity is not accomplished properly, clock is kept as long as the user departs it.

The willingness of a customer to use a product is used to determine satisfaction. Usability is determined by the context in which a product is utilized and the exact conditions in which it is employed. The user's task, technology, software, and substance all make up the context of use. There are a variety of post-task assessment methodologies available, but satisfaction is measured in this study using the ASQ approach. The Ages & Stages Questionnaires (ASQ) is a brief survey form that requires a couple of minutes to complete, is simple to understand, and covers a wide range of usability issues. There are 3 sections on seven different rating scales (absolutely reject = 1, reject = 2, slightly reject = 3, No permit or reject = 4, slightly permit = 5, permit = 6, certainly permit = 7).

## 4 Discussion and Findings

According to the research, AUIs can be exploited to improve digital advertising user experience (UX) problems. Efficacy, efficiency, and customer satisfaction of four popular advertisements have been calculated: static banner, video banner, dynamic banner, and huge static banner. The findings are presented using the three usability characteristics as a framework.

### 4.1 Effectiveness

Figure 4 shows the effectiveness of effectual and non-effectual about digital advertisements when each adaptive feature is taken into account separately.

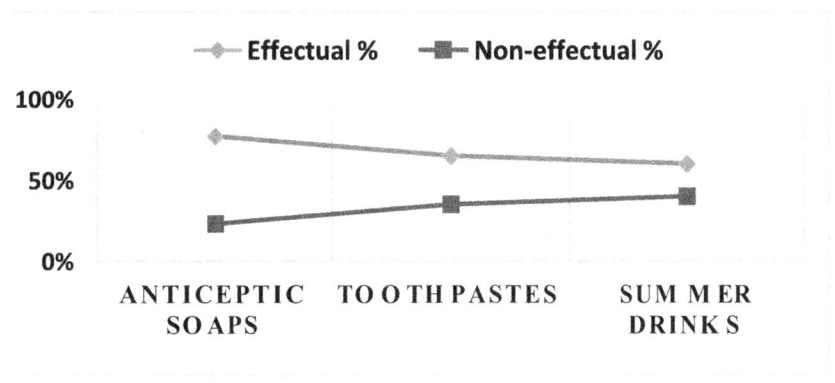

**Fig. 4.** Comparison of effectual and non-effectual elements in terms of effectiveness

The efficacy of antiseptic soaps suggested that the overall average is higher. It demonstrates that there is a distinction between effective (77%) and ineffective (23%). When it comes to antiseptic soap efficacy, there is a large gender gap in effectiveness indicators, with females performing worse than males. Similarly, efficacy data for toothpastes revealed that the general average efficacy is not considerably higher. It displays the difference between effective (65%) and ineffective (35%). However, there is a 20% discrepancy between effective and non-effective data for summer drinks.

### 4.2 Efficiency

The results in Fig. 5 suggest that antiseptic soap has little impact on the user's efficiency. Overall, the usability of adaptive and non-adaptive soaps for males and females is low.

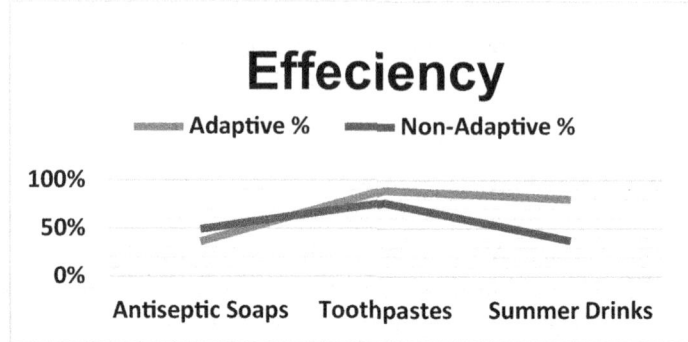

**Fig. 5.** Comparison of effectual and non-effectual elements in terms of efficiency.

User efficiency was low, with roughly 37% for adaptive features and 49% for non-adaptive features.

Adaptive toothpaste, on the other hand, has an overall efficiency of 89%. There isn't much of a distinction between both the adaptive & non-adaptive features across the user participants. On the other hand, summer drinks demonstrate significant variation in overall efficiency between the two contexts (adaptive = 80%, non-adaptive = 37%)

### 4.3 Satisfaction

Figure 6 compares the usability of adaptively and non-adaptively of digital advertisements when it comes to user pleasure. For Antiseptic Soaps, Toothpastes, and Summer Drinks, the report was conducted through a survey analysis to determine consumer satisfaction. The goal of our study was to see if there were any issues in mobile ads that caused users to have a negative experience or rendered ad delivery methods ineffective, such as users ignoring ad content. Our experiment takes a direct approach to broad marketing themes like brand recall.

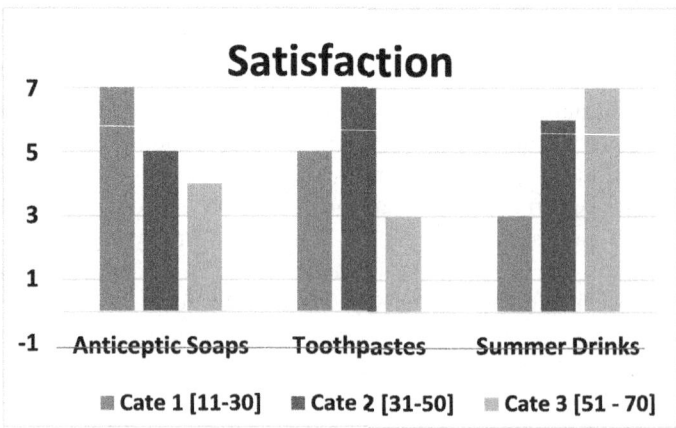

**Fig. 6.** Comparison of adaptive and non-adaptive features in terms of usability.

## 5 Conclusion and Future Work

We performed a poll to address some of the most frequent difficulties with mobile ad distribution. We look into how users react to digital advertisements and ways of delivery, as well as the way they communicate with them. We created new banners with more appealing colors, which helped to improve the user experience compared to previously.

Our studies suggest that merely exposure consumers to advertisements for more than 5 s and engage with these ads to improve branding recall, press and hold rates, and customer encounter. The ability to block an annoying commercial has a big effect on the use.

## References

1. Visuri, A., Hosio, S., Ferreira, D.: Exploring mobile ad formats to increase brand recollection and enhance user experience. In: Proceedings of the 16th International Conference on Mobile and Ubiquitous Multimedia, pp. 311–319 (2017)
2. Iqbal, M.W., Ch, N.A., Shahzad, S.K., Naqvi, M.R., Khan, B.A., Ali, Z.: User context ontology for adaptive mobile-phone interfaces. IEEE Access **9**, 96751–96762 (2021)
3. Parreño, J.M., Sanz-Blas, S., Ruiz-Mafé, C., Aldás-Manzano, J.: Key factors of teenagers' mobile advertising acceptance. Ind. Manag. Data Syst. (2013)
4. Iqbal, M.W., Ahmad, N., Shahzad, S.K.: Usability evaluation of adaptive features in smartphones. Procedia Comput. Sci. **112**, 2185–2194 (2017)
5. Wong, C.H., Tan, G.W.H., Tan, B.I., Ooi, K.B.: Mobile advertising: the changing landscape of the advertising industry. Telematics Inform. **32**(4), 720–734 (2015)
6. Lee, H.J., Lee, K.H., Choi, J.: A structural model for unity of experience: connecting user experience, customer experience, and brand experience. J. Usability Stud. **11**(1) (2018)
7. Wan, Q.H., et al.: Genome analysis and signature discovery for diving and sensory properties of the endangered Chinese alligator. Cell Res. **23**(9), 1091–1105 (2013)
8. Abraham, J., et al.: Observation of the suppression of the flux of cosmic rays above $4 \times 10^{19}$ eV. Phys. Rev. Lett. **101**(6), 061101 (2008)
9. Alghamdi, A.M., Riasat, H., Iqbal, M.W., Ashraf, M.U., Alshahrani, A., Alshamrani, A.: Intelligence and usability empowerment of smartphone adaptive features. Appl. Sci. **12**(23), 12245 (2022)
10. Pyšek, P., Richardson, D.M.: Invasive species, environmental change and management, and health. Annu. Rev. Environ. Resour. **35**, 25–55 (2010)
11. Same, S., Larimo, J.: Marketing theory: experience marketing and experiential marketing. In: 7th International Scientific Conference "Business and Management", pp. 10–11 (2012)
12. Burgess, P.M., Roberts, D.G., Bally, A.W.: A brief review of developments in stratigraphic forward modelling, 2000–2009. In: Regional Geology and Tectonics: Principles of Geologic Analysis, vol. 1, pp. 379–404 (2012)
13. De Keyser, A., Lemon, K.N., Klaus, P., Keiningham, T.L.: A framework for understanding and managing the customer experience. In: Marketing Science Institute Working Paper Series, vol. 85, no. 1, pp. 15–121 (2015)
14. Stanton, W.J., Etzel, M.J., Walker, B.J., Báez, E.P., Martínez, J.F.J.D.: Fundamentos de marketing (2004)
15. Pai, Y.S., Kunze, K.: Journal: Proceedings of the 16th International Conference on Mobile and Ubiquitous Multimedia (2017)

16. Nath, S., Lin, F.X., Ravindranath, L., Padhye, J.: SmartAds: bringing contextual ads to mobile apps. In: Proceeding of the 11th Annual International Conference on Mobile Systems, Applications, and Services, pp. 111–124 (2013)
17. Bart, Y., Stephen, A.T., Sarvary, M.: Which products are best suited to mobile advertising? A field study of mobile display advertising effects on consumer attitudes and intentions. J. Mark. Res. **51**(3), 270–285 (2014)
18. Edelman, B., Jaffe, S., Kominers, S.D.: To groupon or not to groupon: the profitability of deep discounts. Mark. Lett. **27**(1), 39–53 (2016)
19. Tsang, M.M., Ho, S.C., Liang, T.P.: Consumer attitudes toward mobile advertising: an empirical study. Int. J. Electron. Commer. **8**(3), 65–78 (2004)
20. Davis, F.D.: Perceived usefulness, perceived ease of use, and user acceptance of information technology. MIS Qu. 319–340 (1989)
21. Yang, B., Kim, Y., Yoo, C.: The integrated mobile advertising model: the effects of technology- and emotion-based evaluations. J. Bus. Res. **66**(9), 1345–1352 (2013)
22. Kolsaker, A., Drakatos, N.: Mobile advertising: the influence of emotional attachment to mobile devices on consumer receptiveness. J. Mark. Commun. **15**(4), 267–280 (2009)
23. Bachmann, P., Hunziker, S., Rüedy, T.: Selling their souls to the advertisers? How native advertising degrades the quality of prestige media outlets. J. Media Bus. Stud. **16**(2), 95–109 (2019)
24. Dave, K.S., Varma, V.: Learning the click-through rate for rare/new ads from similar ads. In: Proceedings of the 33rd International ACM SIGIR Conference on Research and Development in Information Retrieval, pp. 897–898 (2010)

# SDN-Enabled Resource and Energy Management Framework in Smart Buildings Using Los-Cost Air Quality Sensors

Asim Fareed, Majid Hussain, Muhammad Ibrar, and Munazzah Munawar(✉)

Department of Computer Science, The University of Faisalabad, Faisalabad 38000, Pakistan
Hod.cs.ew@puf.edu.pk

**Abstract.** This paper introduces a cutting-edge solution that utilizes Software Defined Networking (SDN) linked with inexpensive air quality sensors to enhance resource management in smart buildings. These probes can detect particulate matter including PM 2.5, and PM 10 on various surfaces or inside homes along with monitoring carbon dioxide levels indoors. By implementing an ESP32 Controller alongside Arduino IDE the processed information will subsequently be sent by the SDN Controller to the other devices within the building for efficient communication. The data collected will be analyzed to optimize energy consumption based on occupancy levels and air-quality parameters for enhanced energy management. This cost-efficient installation has the potential to offer superior indoor air quality and improve energy usage and the overall performance of smart buildings. This innovative method enhances not only your building's overall energy efficiency but also ensures consistently superior indoor air quality, benefiting both occupants' health & well-being and increasing their overall satisfaction & productivity levels. Experience it firsthand by implementing this solution in various establishments such as healthcare facilities where timely and reliable air quality monitoring is an absolute must.

**Keywords:** IAQ (Indoor Air Quality) · Smart Buildings · Low-cost Sensors · Air Quality · Environmental Monitoring · Internet of Things

## 1 Introduction

Good indoor environments with high-quality air are crucial for occupants' health and comfort, considering that most people spend substantial time inside buildings. Unhealthy indoor air may cause irregular respiratory problems, allergic reactions, and frequent headaches, hampering overall productivity and mental clarity. Thanks to advancements made in technology today especially IoT devices and smart building architecture there is an opportunity to take advantage by monitoring the indoor air quality more efficiently. This paper shall describe the advancement process involved through researching fundamental metrics including Carbon Monoxide, Nitrogen Dioxide, Volatile Organic Compounds matter or PM2.5, etc. used in developing an Air Quality Monitoring Device suitable for Smart Buildings that is always actively tracking down pollutants harmful to building users within real-time intervals effortlessly. The number of gasses that are capable of being observed within smart Buildings depends upon the specific type of Air Quality Monitoring System adopted. On a general note, Air Quality Sensors have the capacity to detect and monitor diverse gasses namely Carbon dioxide ($CO_2$), Carbon Monoxide(CO), Nitrogen Dioxide($NO_2$), Ozone($O_3$), Particle Matter (PM2.5, PM 10). What draws importance towards conducting multi-gas monitoring is their pre-eminence regarding human health and well-being. Some gasses are more widespread than others within indoor environments; for example, increased levels of carbon dioxide may suggest inadequate ventilation leading to symptom development like headaches, fatigue, and inhibited cognitive performance. Particles in a heightened state cause respiratory disorders while $NO_2$ intensification triggers asthma. Leveraging the monitoring of gases can allow building managers to pinpoint potential air quality dilemmas. Deciphering $CO_2$ levels by building automation systems enables reducing energy wastage and costs whilst safeguarding occupants' health through improved ventilation rates in smart buildings and hospitals. In essence, overseeing gas elements within these settings proves essential not only for complying with regulations but also protecting assets and promoting a healthy environment that contributes to optimal energy efficiency. The importance of indoor air quality (IAQ) monitoring cannot be understated due to its immense benefits concerning occupants' welfare along with equipment efficiency in buildings. Poor IAQ can lead to respiratory issues such as allergies and asthma, fatigue factors resulting in reduced productivity by residents along with headaches caused by noxious gases or biological agents inside enclosed spaces are matters of grave concern for facilities managers who seek a safe environment for their residents. Beyond health concerns are issues like mold growth or even damage to HVAC systems or physical structures due to chemical exposure from pollutants present within enclosed spaces which require constant vigilance through IAQ monitoring measures. Capturing readings through frequent measurements allows facility managers more prospectively address sources of pollution present in the facility while mitigating undesired consequences from lackluster airflow.

## 2 Literature Review

Introduces an inexpensive and low-energy wireless sensor network (WSN) scheme aimed at tracking ambient air quality. This technology interfaces with a cloud-based mechanism that stores, inspects, processes and displays the data collected by its sensors. To enhance pollutant detection capabilities while reducing cost factors involved in tedious analyses of robustly complex datasets common to these types of systems; artificial intelligence techniques are used for data processing/analysis instead of traditional methods [3]. Presents a robust framework for real-time monitoring and controlling internal parameters in intelligent buildings. Through extensive reference to prior literature on smart home technology and building automation systems, we discuss shortcomings in current practices before proposing our alternative approach that effectively overcomes these challenges [7]. With MAQS monitoring indoor $CO_2$ concentrations has never been easier. The hybrid sensor network combines stationary and mobile sensors to give accurate results [5]. Environmental monitoring efforts can yield better results with the help of a comprehensive sensor array that incorporates semiconductor and PM2.5 sensors alongside a newly developed optical PM2.5 sensor module designed for this very purpose [1].

By integrating machine-to-machine (M2M) data communication technology into this setup relevant information can smoothly be transmitted from the sensor array to nearby smart devices or PCs without any hiccups along the way.showcases a revolutionary indoor air quality assessment mechanism using wireless sensor networking technology. Developed an autonomous system consisting of two primary components: a monitoring platform for data collection through sensors & gateways while providing real-time analysis; an application server that manages access permissions with ease while serving valuable insights through visual representation of analyzed data [9].

## 3 Materials and Methods

For an effective Air Quality Monitoring device correctly assembling its hardware components is critical. This involves incorporating sensors like MH Z14B (to capture $CO_2$) ZH 06 (to detect PM2.5/PM10) and DHT11 (to measure humidity/temperature) and ESP32 controller. Proper assembly ensures precise readings that enable us to better understand how our immediate environment can impact our well-being over time. The foremost step towards launching this project involves obtaining the Arduino IDE software suite on your device followed by establishing connectivity between your ESP32 control unit via USB tethering. It is vital that correct firmware is installed into this controller enabling the collation of sensor information which can thus be dispatched securely for scrutiny purposes through a cloud based IoT interface.Your hardware and software have been fully prepped for the task ahead; now it's time to position your Air Quality Monitoring tool strategically within smart buildings or other areas plagued by poor air conditions. Over an extended period of data collection deemed necessary recordable parameters such as $CO_2$ concentrations alongside particulate matter readings involving both PM10 &PM 2.5 whilst monitoring moisture content coupled with temperature variations at regular intervals.As someone who values higher education and staying on the cutting edge of technology trends in their industry, we urge you to consider implementing the Thingsty cloud-based IoT platform alongside your Air Quality Monitoring device. This innovative tool allows for seamless data processing and analysis while delivering crucial real-time insights into air quality levels throughout your building. Plus, with personalized alerts at specific threshold breaches readily available via Thingsty's advanced technology features – immediate corrective actions can easily be taken before any serious problems arise. Building safety regulations require that both heating/cooling systems, as well as indoor air, are kept at energy-efficient levels while maintaining occupant safety and comfort. Incorporating an Air Quality Monitoring device into your HVAC system using SDN technology is an intelligent decision since it guarantees that reduced energy outputs won't compromise occupant well-being since one can conveniently adjust temperature controls in relation to real-time indoor air monitoring results (Figs. 1, 2 and 3).

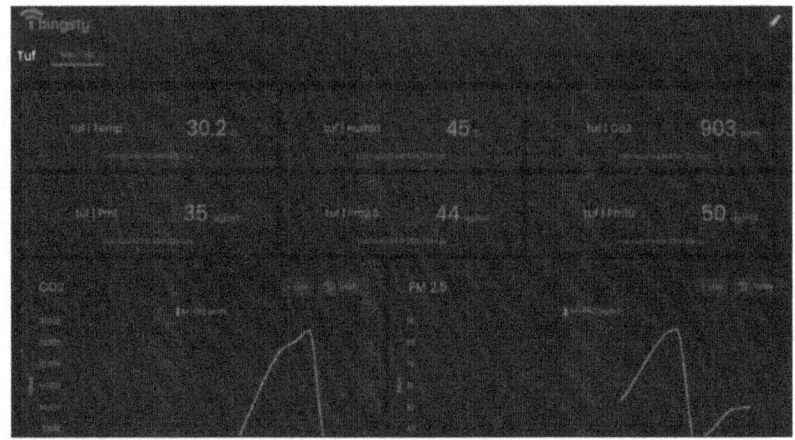

**Fig. 1.** Thingsty Dashboard

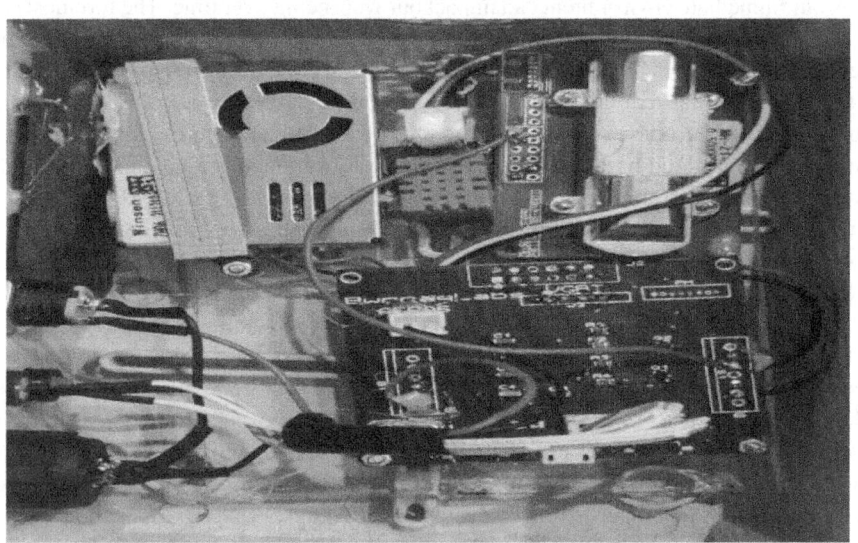

**Fig. 2.** Assembled Device

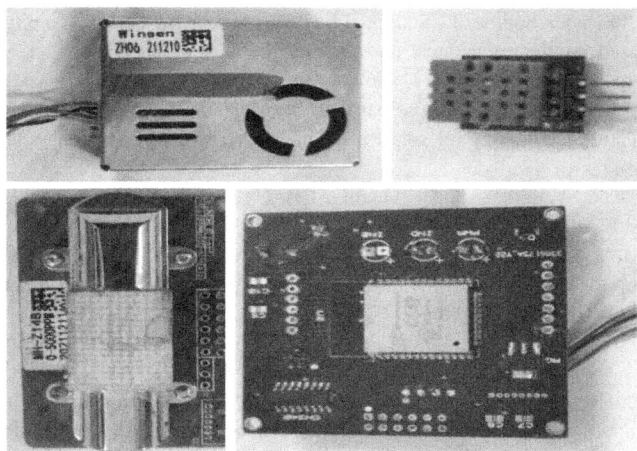

**Fig. 3.** Sensors

## 4 Experimental Results

The use of affordable sensors was incredibly productive when it came to obtaining prompt data related to CO2 levels, PM 2.5/PM10 as well as temperature/humidity stats. Successful incorporation of the SDN controller with ESP32 meant that managing energy resources is a breeze! Real-time air quality updates are displayed on our easy-touse dashboard thereby ensuring effortless monitoring/control capabilities for all users involved. Early warnings related to potential building-related air-quality problems are just another way our system benefits you. An evaluation of the effectiveness of the system can be done by comparing air quality parameters pre- and post-implementation. We foresee a noteworthy advancement in indoor air quality, energy efficiency, and general occupant satisfaction upon successful execution.

## 5 Conclusion

SDN integration enables efficient control of HVAC systems and ensures that indoor environmental conditions remain at their optimal state. We have selected Thingsty as our channel for displaying gathered data due to its simplicity in presentation allowing occupants an easy way of interpreting results. From smart buildings to medical establishments where constant monitoring is vital, this solution provides effective regulation in managing indoor air quality levels while remaining user-friendly.

The affordable sensors utilized in this study prove that efficient air quality monitoring doesn't require considerable financial investment, which expands access to a broader audience.

## References

1. Hilary Kelechi, A., et al.: Design of a low-cost air quality monitoring system using arduino and ThingSpeak. Comput. Mater. Contin. **70**(1), 151–169 (2022)

2. Arroyo, P., Gómez-Suárez, J., Suárez, J.I., Lozano, J.: Low-cost air quality measurement system based on electrochemical and pm sensors with cloud connection. Sensors **21**(18) (2021). https://doi.org/10.3390/s21186228
3. Ahmad, M., et al.: End-to-end loss based TCP congestion control mechanism as a secured communication technology for smart healthcare enterprises. IEEE Access **6**, 11641–11656 (2018)
4. Maltare, N.N., Vahora, S.: Air Quality Index prediction using machine learning for Ahmedabad city. Digit. Chem. Eng. **7**, 100093 (2023)
5. Latif, R.M.A., Farhan, M., Rizwan, O., et al.: Retail level blockchain transformation for product supply chain using truffle development platform. Cluster Comput. **24**, 1–16 (2021). https://doi.org/10.1007/s10586-020-03165-4
6. Liu, X., et al.: Low-cost sensors as an alternative for long-term air quality monitoring. Environ. Res. **185**, 109438 (2020)
7. Arroyo, P., Herrero, J.L., Suárez, J.I., Lozano, J.: Wireless sensor network combined with cloud computing for air quality monitoring. Sensors **19**(3) (2019). https://doi.org/10.3390/s19030691
8. Ubaid, S., Shafeeq, M.F., Hussain, M., et al.: SCOUT: a sink camouflage and concealed data delivery paradigm for circumvention of sink-targeted cyber threats in wireless sensor networks. J. Supercomput. **74**, 5022–5040 (2018). https://doi.org/10.1007/s11227-018-2346-1
9. Qabbal, L., Younsi, Z., Naji, H.: An indoor air quality and thermal comfort appraisal in a retrofitted university building via low-cost smart sensor. Indoor Built Environ. **31**(3), 586–606 (2022)
10. Ahmad, M., et al.: End-to-end loss based TCP congestion control mechanism as a secured communication technology for smart healthcare enterprises. IEEE Access **6**, 11641–11656 (2018). https://doi.org/10.1109/ACCESS.2018.2802841
11. Saini, J., Dutta, M., Marques, G.: Indoor air quality monitoring systems based on internet of things: a systematic review. Int. J. Environ. Res. Public Health **17**(14) (2020). https://doi.org/10.3390/ijerph17144942
12. Chen, X., et al.: Indoor air quality monitoring system for smart buildings. In: Proceedings of the 2014 ACM International Joint Conference on Pervasive and Ubiquitous Computing, Seattle, Washington, pp. 471–475 (2014)
13. Jabbar, S., Akbar, A.H., Zafar, S., Quddoos, M.M., Hussain, M.: VISTA: achieving cumulative VIsion through energy efficient Silhouette recognition of mobile Targets through collAboration of visual sensor nodes. EURASIP J. Image Video Process. **2014**(1), 1–24 (2014)
14. Kenarkoohi, A., et al.: Hospital indoor air quality monitoring for the detection of SARS-CoV-2 (COVID-19) virus. Sci. Total. Environ. **748**, 141324 (2020)
15. Hussain, M., et al.: A gateway deployment heuristic for enhancing the availability of sensor grids. Int. J. Distrib. Sens. Netw. **12**(8), 7595038 (2016)
16. Jo, J., Jo, B., Kim, J., Kim, S., Han, W.: Development of an IoT-based indoor air quality monitoring platform. J. Sens. **2020** (2020). https://doi.org/10.1155/2020/8749764
17. Luo, H., Li, W., Wu, X.: Design of indoor air quality monitoring system based on wireless sensor network. IOP Conf. Ser.: Earth Environ. Sci. **208**(1), 012070 (2018)

# Air Quality Predictions Using Machine Learning Models

Sana Younas(✉), Humaira Khalid, Umair Muneer Butt, and Rida Khaliq

Department of Computer Science and IT, The University of Chenab, Gujrat, Gujranwala 50700, Pakistan
sanayounus245@gmail.com

**Abstract.** Air quality is currently seen as a global health issue as a result of human activities and the accelerating industrialization over the past several years. Therefore, it is essential to accurately estimate air quality. In estimating the air quality of a certain area, machine learning has consistently demonstrated promising results. To forecast the numerous air particles that are PM2.5, PM10, NO2, NH3, SO2, CO, and ozone O3 concentration in different cities of Pakistan, the authors presented a variety of machine learning models, including linear regression (LR), Decision Tree (DT) using regressor and classifier, Random forest (RF) using regressor and classifier, K nearest neighbour (KNN), and the deep learning models LSTM and BILSTM. Additionally, a comparison of the various models is made to determine which is most important. The Random forest model and KNN are found to be the most dependable models for the findings with respect to mean absolute error (MAE), root mean square error (RMSE), and coefficient of determination (R2). This study found that the suggested models anticipate the PM2.5 pollutants more accurately and with a lower error rate than the existing models after comparing a number of current models and new models.

**Keywords:** Air pollution · random forest · gradient boosting · support vector regression · multiple linear regression · air quality forecast

## 1 Introduction

More than 7 million people are killed by air pollution each year, with 4.2 million dying outside and 3.8 million dying indoors [1]. Furthermore, it is predicted that by 2050, 68% of the world's population would reside in urban areas [2]. The escalating levels of pollution, which operate as a basic issue in many regions of the world, have made accurate modelling and forecasting of air pollution a big challenge and vital in recent times. Generally speaking, there are two forms of air pollution: (1) Natural pollution from volcanic eruptions and forest fires that releases air pollutants such SO2, CO2, CO, NO2, and sulphate; (2) Man-made pollution from human activities such as Transportation emissions, industrial production processes, and oil burning are the main sources of PM2.5 in the atmosphere [3].

According to several studies, air pollution causes respiratory and cardiovascular diseases, which in turn cause animals and plants to die, acid rain, climate change, global warming, etc., making it difficult for societies to thrive and for individuals to earn a living [4]. Ameer et al. [5] used a comparative study of ML approaches to look at the impacts of PM2.5 throughout the course of the previous 25 years.

Recent developments in machine learning have created new opportunities for forecasting and predicting air quality and pollution levels intelligently. Machine learning models are able to identify trends and anticipate future air quality conditions by analyzing massive information and utilizing complex algorithms. Machine learning algorithms may be used to forecast air pollution levels as smart city technologies proliferate and a wealth of real-time data becomes available.

When discharged into the environment, PM2.5 pollutants—fine particles made up of a mix of harmful gases and particles—can cause harm [6]. These pollutants are mostly to blame for the majority of human respiratory conditions, and when they get severe they may even spark the COVID-19 pandemic [7, 8], which will raise the death rate. The survey clearly shows that PM2.5 causes more problems for people than other pollutants and that it is the one that generates other pollutants, hence the current models solely consider PM2.5 pollutants. The historical meteorological data-sets are used in the statistical analysis for PM2.5 pollutant prediction. Although few models are utilized for predicting, current models are limited to using certain fundamental common classification strategies nonetheless, the outcomes revealed subpar error rate performance.

Nine alternative machine learning models, including regression models like the linear regression model (LR), random forest model (RF), KNN model, decision tree model, LSTM, and Bi-LSTM, have been used in this suggested technique to forecast the PM2.5 pollutants. Recurrent Neural Networks (RNN) and their modifications are among the deep learning algorithms that have been developed as a result of the rising popularity of artificial intelligence. The Long Short-Term Memory (LSTM) model is the one that is most frequently employed for predicting air quality. This is due to the fact that it considers the common phenomena of time-based connections that are shown in PM2.5 concentration data. Given the intricacy of PM2.5 forms, having extremely precise and effective forecasting models is crucial. Statistical measures including Mean Absolute Error (MAE), Mean Absolute Percentage Error (MAPE), Mean Square Error (MSE), Root Mean Square Error (RMSE), and R2 have been used to assess the suggested machine learning models. Results indicate that when compared to conventional prediction models, superior performance was achieved with a lower error rate. As a result, we seek to do research for this article that demonstrates the following crucial points:

1. First, we forecast the concentrations of various pollutants at various time intervals in several Pakistani cities, including PM2.5, PM10, NO2, NH3, SO2, CO, and ozone O3.

2. Using several supervised machine learning methods, such as LSTM, decision trees, random forests, and linear regression, to solve the problem of predicting air pollution.
3. Assessing how well four machine learning algorithms perform in predicting air pollution and selecting the most effective one.

This article's remaining sections are organised as follows: The background on the issue is given in Sect. 2. The study's methodology is described in Sect. 3. The study's results are presented in Sect. 4. Section 5 analyses the study's limitations and offers reflections on the results. In Sect. 6, the conclusion and recommendations for further research are provided.

## 1.1 Related Work

Recent developments in machine learning have created new opportunities for forecasting and predicting air quality and pollution levels intelligently. Machine learning models are able to identify trends and anticipate future air quality conditions by analysing massive information and utilising complex algorithms. Machine learning algorithms may be used to forecast air pollution levels as smart city technology and access to massive volumes of real-time data increase. Recurrent Neural Networks (RNN) and their modifications are among the deep learning algorithms that have been developed as a result of the rising popularity of artificial intelligence. The most used model for forecasting air quality is Long Short-Term Memory (LSTM). This is due to the fact that it considers the common phenomena of time-based connections that are shown in PM2.5 concentration data. Given the intricacy of PM2.5 forms, having extremely precise and effective forecasting models is crucial. So, in this study report, we set out to conduct research that demonstrates several machine learning model-based techniques.

A well-liked machine learning approach for classification and regression applications is decision trees. Decision trees were employed to forecast the air quality index (AQI) in Delhi, India, in the study "Comparative Study of Machine Learning Models for Prediction of Air Quality Index" by Bhawna Gupta et al. (2020) [6]. An additional system has been created to gather real-time data on air quality from diverse sources and forecast future pollution levels using machine learning algorithms. Following that, a web-based tool that offers a user-friendly interface for tracking air quality visualises the projected pollution levels [7].

Popular machine learning algorithms like SVM are utilised for tasks like classification and regression. SVM was used to estimate the concentration of air pollutants in Seoul, Korea in the study "Predicting the Daily Concentration of Air Pollution in Seoul, Korea using Machine Learning Techniques" by Dongwoo Kim et al. (2017) [8].

An algorithm for machine learning called an ANN draws its inspiration from the structure and operation of the human brain. ANN was used to estimate the concentration of air pollutants in Tehran, Iran, in the study "Air Quality Prediction Using Artificial Neural Network and Adaptive Neuro-Fuzzy Inference System" by Vahid Hos-seini et al. (2018) [9]. In the study "Design and Implementation of an IoT-Based Air Pollution Detection and Monitoring System", a clustering method was employed to identify pollution hotspots. They created grids for the city and calculated the average value of each pollutant for each grid. After that, the grids were grouped based on pollutant concentrations using the K-means clustering technique [10]. According to the study "IOT Based Vehicle Anti-Collision and Pollution Control Sys-tem" by Abhi B. Amin, Harsh P. Patel, and Suken P. Vaghela, pollution control is accomplished by tracking the emissions of pollutants from cars and giving drivers immediate feedback on their driving habits. The system collects data on car emissions using IoT technology, analyses it, and then pinpoints drivers who are releasing too many pollutants [11].

The approach for analysing pollution sources and forecasting PM2.5 levels using machine learning techniques is suggested in the research article "The MR-CA Models for Analysis of Pollution Sources and Prediction of PM2.5". Using the chosen characteristics, the authors trained the MR-CA and MR-CA + I machine learning models. MR-CA is a multilayer perceptron (MLP) model that forecasts PM2.5 levels using meteorological data and pollution source variables. The incorporation of information concerning industrial emissions is a feature of the MR-CA+l version of MR-CA [12].

Principal Component Analysis (PCA) and Support Vector Regression (SVR): PCA is a method for reducing the dimensionality of data on air pollutants. PCA and SVR were coupled to forecast the concentration of air pollutants in Chennai, India in the study "Air Quality Prediction Using Principal Component Analysis and Support Vector Regression" by P. R. Janani and R. Kavitha (2019) [13].

Long Short-Term Memory (LSTM): LSTM is a kind of recurrent neural network that performs sequence prediction tasks exceptionally well. LSTM was used to forecast the concentration of PM2.5 in Beijing, China in the study "Pre-diction of PM2.5 Concentration Using LSTM Neural Network with Meteorological Parameters" by Xueyuan Zhang et al. (2020) [14]. Convolutional Neural Networks (CNN): CNNs are a special class of neural network that are particularly good at processing images and sequences. "Application of Convolutional Neural Network" is a research article [15].

Throughout order to investigate the association between PM2.5 concentration and heart disease mortality over a long period of exposure to PM2.5, Beelen et al. designed a multicenter cohort research throughout Europe [16]. Using support vector regression and a robust interaction, Bing et al. [17] proposed a novel model for forecasting China's air quality index that showed a decrease in MAPE (mean absolute percentage error). A unique method for forecasting air quality in Wuhan City has also been reported by Lin and colleagues (2019), which uses a cloud model granulation algorithm and data discovery approaches to achieve excellent accuracy.

Convolutional Long Short-Term Memory (Conv LSTM) was proposed by researchers as a potential remedy for the problem of air pollution in Seoul, South Korea. Convolutional neural networks and long short-term memory are combined in this method, which may automatically change the problem's spatial and temporal data properties [18] The study presents a spatio-temporal model that includes information on outdoor air pollution indicators, meteorological data, traffic volume, and average driving speeds. The study's findings show that this model works better than other current models [19]. The authors of a different research (reference 38) showed the efficacy and applicability of employing a CNN-LSTM model to forecast Beijing's PM2.5 concentration for the upcoming hour as well as the total amount of wind speed and rain over the preceding 24 h. The CNN-LSTM model fared better than other models, with a mean absolute error (MAE) of 14.6344 and a root mean square error (RMSE) of 24.22874, according to the results.

**Methodology**

- Dataset
- Preprocess
- EDA
- Machine learning models
- Evaluation and comparison

**Dataset:** The data set applied in this study is made up of measurements of air quality made in Pakistan between 2013 and 2018. A number of air pollutants, including particulate matter, carbon monoxide (CO), ozone (O3), Sulphur dioxide (SO2), and nitrogen dioxide (NO2) (PM2.5 and PM10), are included in the dataset as hourly observations. The dataset was obtained from the Pakistan Environmental Protection Agency (EPA) and contains a total of 52,560 observations. Each observation includes the following variables:

- **Date and time:** The time and date when the measurement was made.
- **Station ID:** The station's identification number is used to identify it.
- **SO2:** Sulfur dioxide concentration measured in micrograms per cubic meter ($g/m^3$).
- **NO2:** The amount of nitrogen dioxide, measured in micrograms per cubic meter ($g/m^3$)
- **CO:** Carbon monoxide concentration expressed in milligrams per cubic meter ($mg/m^3$).
- **O3:** The amount of ozone in a given volume, measured in micrograms ($g/m^3$).
- **PM2.5:** PM2.5 is the measurement of the quantity of airborne particles with a diameter of 2.5 μm or smaller, expressed in micrograms per cubic meter ($g/m^3$).
- **PM10:** PM10 refers to the quantity of particles having a diameter of 10 μm or smaller per cubic meter ($g/m^3$).

The dataset required some preprocessing steps to handle missing values and outliers. A detailed description of the preprocessing steps is provided in the next subsection.

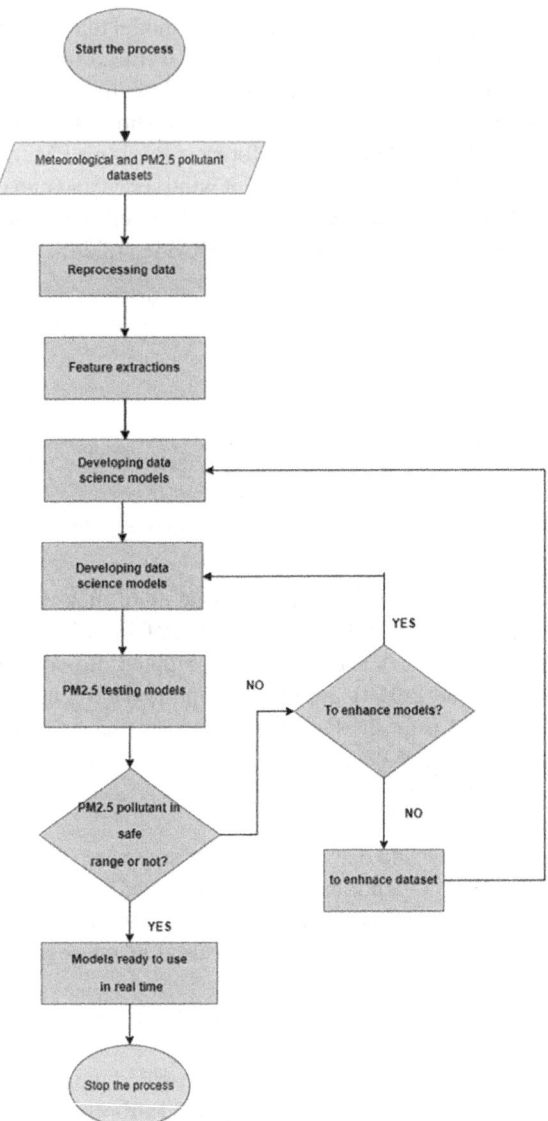

**Preprocess:** Before the data could be utilized for analysis, the raw air quality data from the Pakistan EPA required to be corrected for missing values and outliers. The data was preprocessed in the manner described below:

**Cleaning Up the Data Set:** It involved deleting duplicates and substituting any missing values with the median of the corresponding column.

**Outlier Removal:** Using the Interquartile Range (IQR) approach, outliers in the data were found and the observations with outlier values were eliminated.

**Data Normalization:** To make sure that all of the features were on the same scale, the data was normalized using the Min-Max scaling approach. The data set that resulted from preparing the data contained 44,056 observations with eight features. The preprocessed data set was then used for the machine learning model development and exploratory data analysis (EDA), which are covered in the following subsections.

**EDA (Exploratory Data Analysis):** To obtain understanding of the air quality data and find any patterns or connections between the features, the EDA was carried out. The primary conclusions from the EDA are as follows:

**Temporal Trends:** Clear temporal trends could be seen in the air quality data, with higher quantities of contaminants being found during the winter, notably in December and January. This is in line with the known seasonal changes in Pakistani air pollution, which are brought on by a rise in the use of coal and wood for space heating in the dead of winter (Fig. 1).

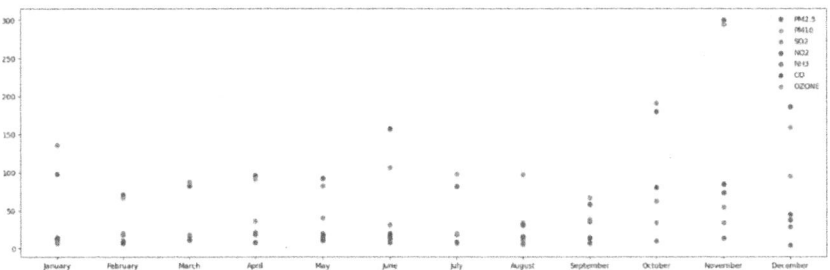

**Fig. 1.** Seasonal variations in air pollution in Pakistan

The plot shows clear seasonal variations in air pollution, with higher concentrations of pollutants observed in the winter months, particularly December and January.

**Spatial Values:** Significant regional differences were seen in the air quality data, with certain monitoring stations continuously displaying greater pollutant concentrations than others (Fig. 2).

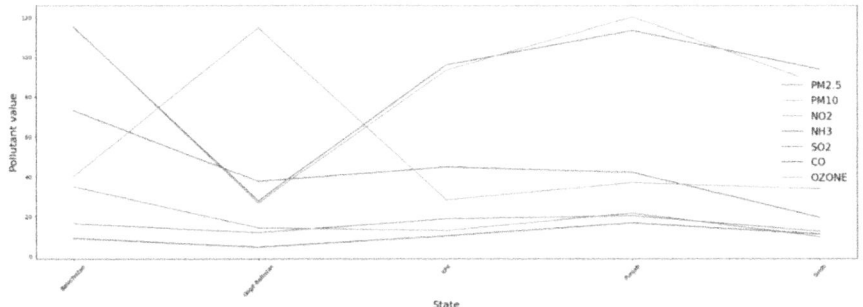

**Fig. 2.** This highlights the need for targeted interventions in areas with high pollution levels.

Heat map showing the spatial variations in air quality, including typical levels of PM2.5, PM10, NO2, SO2, and CO at different monitoring stations across Pakistan.

**Correlations Among Features:** The relationships between the air pollutants were very strong, with PM2.5 and PM10 and NO2 and CO showing the strongest correlations. This implies that the pollutants have shared origins and that reducing one pollutant's emissions may also reduce those of other pollutants (Fig. 3).

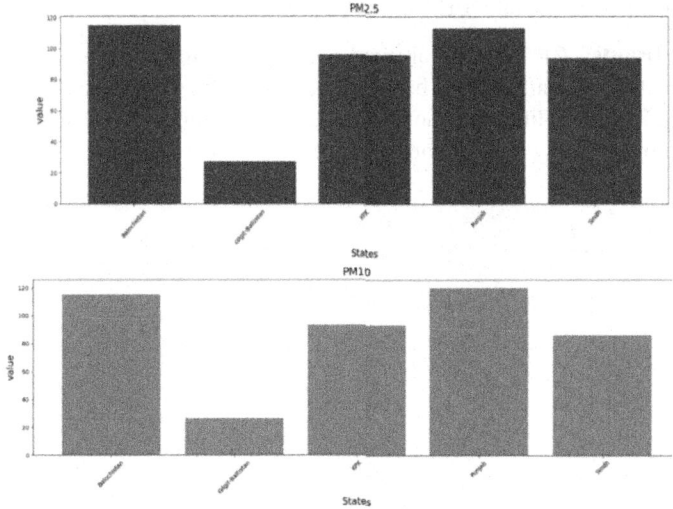

**Fig. 3.** Shows the correlation between features

**Impact of Weather Conditions:** The EDA also demonstrated that factors affecting air quality include temperature, humidity, and wind speed. For instance, greater temperatures and slower winds were linked to higher pollution concentrations (Fig. 4).

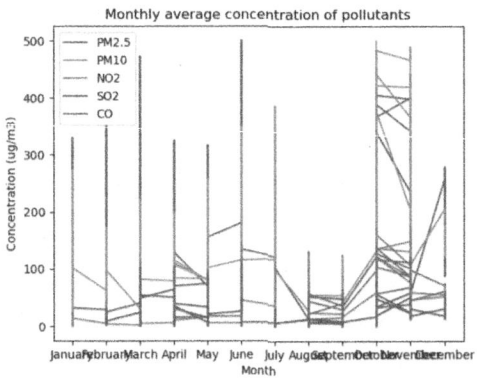

**Fig. 4.** Monthly average concentration of Pollutants

**Machine Learning Models:** This section gives a general overview of the machine learning methods applied to predict air quality. Numerous additional models were also used, including K-Nearest Neighbours, the LSTM model, the BI-LSTM, decision tree regression, logistic regression, random forest regression, and linear regression.

**Linear Regression:** To assess the relationship between two numerical variables, a statistical method known as linear regression is performed. Simple linear regression is used to estimate the value of the dependent variable at a certain point in the independent variable or the strength of the correlation between two variables. The equation for the linear regression model used in this study is given as follow:

$$Y = \beta 0 + \beta 1 X1 + \beta 2 X2 + \ldots + \beta n * Xn + \varepsilon \qquad (1)$$

where, Y = Dependent variable (AQI in our case), X1, X2, ..., Xn = Independent variables (meteorological and pollutant data), β0 = Intercept, β1, β2, ..., βn = Coefficients or regression weights, ε = Error term. To apply linear regression in our study, we first split the dataset into training and testing sets. We then trained the linear regression model on the training set using the independent variables (meteorological and pollutant data) and the dependent variable (AQI) and calculated the regression coefficients. The model's coefficient of determination (R-squared) using the training data and test data is 0.9309 and 0.9300, respectively, implying that it accounts for 93.19% and 93.10% of the variation in AQI, respectively. For the training data, the model's mean absolute error (MAE) and root mean square error (RMSE) are 4.56 and 4.77, respectively, whereas for the test data, they are 7.61 and 7.07, respectively. These measurements suggest that the model has good fit and makes very accurate AQI predictions.

**Decision Tree Regressor:** A machine learning approach called Decision Tree Regressor is employed for regression issues. It operates by dividing the data into sets according to a decision tree. Recursively dividing the data into subsets based on the features that produce the greatest variance reduction results in the construction of the tree.

Unlike linear regression, a decision tree regressor does not have a specific equation. As an alternative, it generates predictions by recursively dividing the input feature space into smaller regions depending on the values of the features, and then predicting the mean or median target value for each zone. The following is a representation of the decision tree regressor model's output:

$$y = f(X) + \varepsilon \qquad (2)$$

where, f is the decision tree model, X denotes a vector of input features, and denotes the error term signifying the discrepancy between the anticipated and actual target values. y denotes the predicted target variable in this example. According to the output, the model appears to have over fit the training data because the test data's RMSE and MAE values are significantly higher than the training data's ideal RMSE and MAE values of 0.0. The model nevertheless exhibits good performance on the test data, as seen by the high R-squared value of 0.9937. While this can appear positive, overfitting is a worry because it could result in subpar performance on new data. Consequently, it is essential to assess the model's performance further and take into account any room for improvement, such as feature selection or regularization methods.

**Random Forest Regressor:** An ensemble learning system called the Random Forest Regressor combines several decision trees to increase accuracy and avoid overfitting. For the purpose of making the ultimate forecast, many decision trees are created on various subsets of the data. The average of all individual decision trees' forecasts inside the forest can be used to express the prediction produced by a random forest regressor. It has the following mathematical representation:

$$y = 1/n * sum(yi) \tag{3}$$

where: y is the predicted output, n is the number of trees in the random forest. y i is the predicted output for the ith decision tree in the forest. The results imply that the target variable (Y) for the provided dataset is predicted using the random forest regressor model. Both the training and test datasets are used to determine the mean absolute error (MAE) and the root mean squared error (RMSE). The RMSE for the training dataset is 0.7852 and the RMSE for the test dataset is 1.5508 respectively. The MAE is also 0.1879 for the training dataset and 0.4729 for the test dataset. For the training dataset, the R-squared value is 0.9991, while on the test dataset, it is 0.9971. The high R-squared value on both datasets indicates that the model can predict the target variable with reasonable accuracy. Yet, the stark contrast between the RMSE values of the training and test datasets suggests.

**Logistic Regression:** To predict a binary outcome, such as yes or no, a classification technique known as logistic regression is utilized. It estimates the likelihood that a binary event will occur based on the input factors. Let y be a binary result, and the input variables x1, x2,..., xn. Given the input variables, the chance that y will occur may be expressed as (Fig. 5):

$$P(y = 1|x) = 1/(1 + e - (0 + 1 \times 1 + 2 \times 2 \ldots + n \times n)) \tag{4}$$

where, Given the input variables, the chance that a binary result would occur is represented by p(y = 1|x). e is the natural logarithm's base, while 0, 1, 2..., n are the input variable's coefficients or regression weights, respectively.

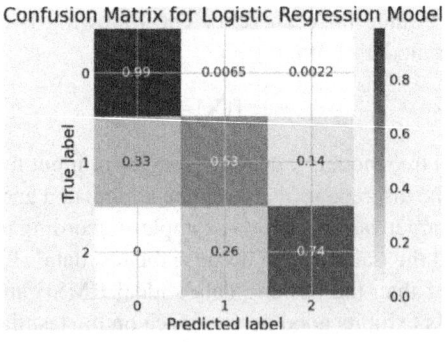

**Fig. 5.** Confusion Matrix for Logistic Regression

The logistic regression model performed well the test set (94.1%) and the training set (94.1%), demonstrating that it is a trustworthy model for predicting the air quality index (AQI) categories based on the input data. Significant agreement between the predicted and real AQI categories can be seen by the Kappa Score of 0.72. The classification report's precision and recall numbers show that the model did well in predicting the first category (AQI 0), with high accuracy and recall, but did not do as well in predicting the second (AQI 1) and third (AQI 2) categories, which have less support. The confusion matrix shows that although the model had excellent accuracy, it did misclassify a tiny percentage of occurrences in the second and third categories.

**Decision Tree Classifier:** A categorical dependent variable's result can be predicted using a classification technique called a decision tree classifier based on the independent factors. It operates by dividing the data into sets according to a decision tree. Recursively dividing the data into subsets based on the features that produce the greatest entropy reduction leads to the construction of the tree. The Decision Tree Classifier's equation is not a mathematical equation like logistic regression or linear regression. Instead, a tree-like structure is used to describe the decision tree model, where each node represents a decision rule based on a feature and the branches represent potential outcomes.

The model appears to be performing very well, as shown by the test set's accuracy score of 0.99906191369606 and the training set's flawless accuracy score of 1.0. With a Kappa Score of 0.9959402694046363, it is clear that the test set's actual labels and anticipated labels agree strongly. Also, the test MAE and RMSE are 0.00093808630399625 and 0.030628194591584442, respectively, while the mean absolute error (MAE) and root mean squared error (RMSE) are both 0.0 for the train and test, respectively. The model is capable of explaining a sizable portion of the variance in the target variable, as seen by the high R2 values of 1.0 on the training set and 0.99906191369606 on the test set. Generally, these outcomes point to the.

**Random Forest Classifier:** To improve accuracy and avoid overfitting, the Random Forest Classifier, an ensemble learning approach, integrates several decision trees. The programme builds several decision trees using various data subsets, combines the outcomes, and generates the final forecast. With the addition of the ensemble of several decision trees, the Random Forest Classifier's equation is analogous to the decision tree classifier:

$$\hat{y} = \mathbf{mode\{y_i\}} \quad (5)$$

where, $\hat{y}$ = Predicted class label of the dependent variable, $y_i$ = Predicted class label by the ith decision tree. On the training data, the model had 100% accuracy, and on the test data, it had a high accuracy of 0.997. Strong agreement is indicated by the kappa value of 0.988, which assesses the degree of agreement between anticipated and actual classifications. The model's predictions on the test set have a low mean absolute error (MAE) of 0.003, which shows that they are reasonably accurate. The model's predictions are accurate, as shown by the fact that the root mean squared error (RMSE) is also small at 0.053. The test set's R2 score, which measures how well the model matches the data, is 0.987. The model has done well overall and is regarded as being accurate when generating predictions.

**K-Nearest Neighbors (KNN):** A technique called K-Nearest Neighbors (KNN) uses the k training samples that are nearest to a new data point in the feature space to determine the most appropriate classification for the new data point.

KNN is a non-parametric approach, hence there isn't a particular equation for it. However, the following stages can be used to summarize the KNN algorithm: Calculate the separation between each training example in the feature space and the new data point. Choose the k training examples that are the closest to the new data point. Determine the most prevalent class among the k neighbors to classify the new data point (Fig. 6).

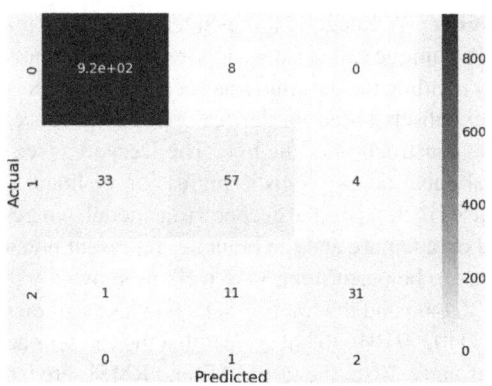

**Fig. 6.** Shows the predicted and Actual value in KNN Model

**LSTM:** It is a kind of RNN that was invented in 1980 and is frequently used for time series forecasting applications. Using information from the past, RNNs are efficient neural networks that can remember information and anticipate what will happen in the future. RNNs, however, frequently struggle with vanishing and exploding gradients, which can slow learning down or even stop it altogether. In order to solve these problems, LSTMs were established in 1997. LSTMs are capable of learning from input that is separated from memory by long time delays and remembering it for longer. An LSTM is made up of three gates that work as analogical gates utilizing the sigmoid function, which has a range of 0 to 1: an input gate that decides whether to accept fresh data, a forget gate that removes unnecessary information, and an output gate. The LSTM model's equation is as follows:

$$Yt = f(Wx * Xt + Wh * Ht - 1 + b) \tag{6}$$

where, Yt: Output at time t (AQI in our case), Xt: Input at time t (meteorological and pollutant data), Ht-1: Output of the previous time step, Wx: Input weight matrix, Wh: Recurrent weight matrix, b: Bias term, f: Activation function (Fig. 7).

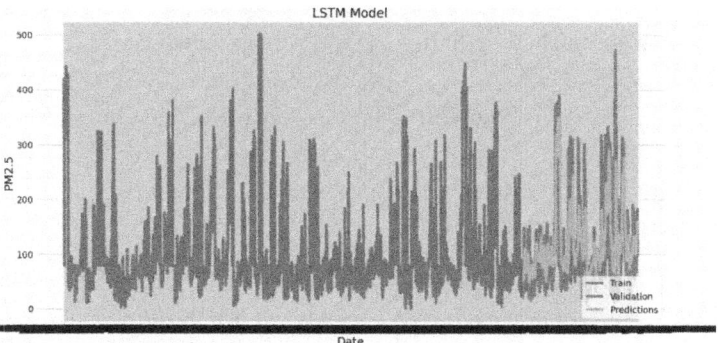

**Fig. 7.** Shows the Data Evaluation in LSTM Model

To apply the LSTM model in our study, we first preprocessed the data and split it into training and testing sets. We then trained the LSTM model on the training set using the independent variables (meteorological and pollutant data) and the dependent variable (AQI). As the train MAE and RMSE are significantly higher than the test MAE and RMSE, the model appears to be overfitting. Also, the train set's R2 value is negative, which is a blatant sign of overfitting. The model's ability to explain a large portion of the variance in the test data is indicated by the model's low test R2 value. The model needs to be strengthened overall, either by reducing complexity or by using regularization methods like dropout, L1/L2 regularization, etc. (Fig. 8).

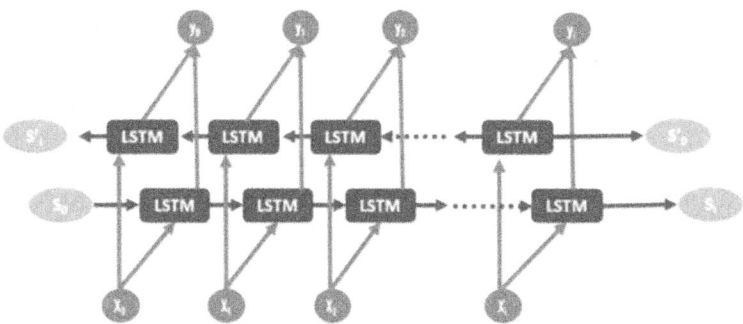

**Fig. 8.** Internal Architecture of Bi-LSTM model [20]

**BI_LSTM:** Bidirection-al Long Short-Term Memory (BILSTM), a Recurrent Neural Network (RNN) architecture, is often used in applications involving sequence modelling and natural language processing. Since it can concurrently learn from the past and the future, it is beneficial for tasks that require context beyond the present time step.

The fundamental equation for one LSTM cell is as follows:

$$f\_t = \sigma(W\_f[h\_{t-1}, x\_t] + b\_f) \#\text{forget gate} \tag{7}$$

$$i\_t = \sigma(W\_i[h\_{t-1}, x\_t] + b\_i) \#\text{input gate} \tag{8}$$

$$g\_t = \tanh(W\_g[h\_\{t-1\}, x\_t] + b\_g) \,\#\text{candidate state} \quad (9)$$

$$o\_t = \sigma(W\_o[h\_\{t-1\}, x\_t] + b\_o) \,\#\text{output gate} \quad (10)$$

$$c\_t = f\_t * c\_\{t-1\} + i\_t * g\_t \,\#\text{cell state} \quad (11)$$

$$h\_t = o\_t * \tanh(c\_t) \,\# \text{ output} \quad (12)$$

The hidden state at time step is represented by h t in the equation above (Fig. 9).

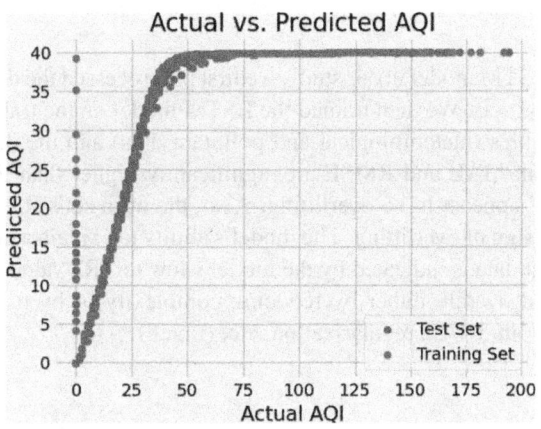

**Fig. 9.** Statistical Analysis of data Using BI-lstm

The findings show that a Bidirectional LSTM (BILSTM) model was created and evaluated using the given input. Recurrent neural networks like the BILSTM analyze the input sequence both forward and backward, which can help the model better capture long-term dependencies in the data.

The test MAE, RMSE, and R2 values for the BILSTM model suggest that the model successfully accounted for 45% of the variability in the test data. The model performs similarly on test and train data, as indicated by the train MAE's slightly lower value of 7.06.

Indicating that the model's performance is constant for both train and test data, the train RMSE is comparable to the test RMSE. The model accounts for 44% of the variability in the train data, as shown by the train's R2 of 0.44. In general, these findings imply that the BILSTM model has some predictive ability, although there is still potential for development.

**Evaluation and Comparison:** We assessed the performance of several machine learning models for forecasting air quality using mean absolute error (MAE), root mean square error (RMSE), and R2 scores. we may assess and predict the following things using the information in the Table 1:

**Table 1.** 70–30 Training and Testing Samples

| Sr.no | Model | MAE for train dataset | MAE for test dataset | RMSE for traindataset | RMSE for test dataset | $R^2$ for test dataset | $R^2$ for train dataset |
|---|---|---|---|---|---|---|---|
| 1 | LR | 4.56 | 4.56 | 7.07 | 7.61 | 0.9300 | 0.9300 |
| 2 | DTM | 0.0 | 0.4041 | 0.0 | 2.281 | 0.93 | 1.0 |
| 3 | RF | 0.18 | 0.4729 | 0.78 | 1.55 | 0.997 | 0.999 |
| 4 | KNN | 0.031 | 0.0544 | 0.183 | 0.237 | 0.745 | 0.8384 |
| 5 | LSTM | 105.8 | 43.16 | 118.2 | 0.469 | 0.469 | 118.24 |
| 6 | BILSTM | 7.06 | 7.09 | 20.5 | 20.13 | 0.90 | 0.4369 |

In conclusion, K-Nearest Neighbors (KNN) and Random Forest (RF) models are the most effective for predicting the AQI based on the meteorological and pollutant data used in this study. These models can be used to provide accurate AQI predictions, which can help improve air quality management and public health outcomes. However, further experimentation and analysis may be required to ensure their validity and reliability.

**Experiment Setup:** A Jupyter laptop, an Intel(R) Core(TM) i5-2450M processor operating at 2.50 GHz, and 8 GB of RAM were used for this experiment. The proposed machine learning models are trained and tested using Python 3.7.3, and then exposed to feature extraction and data cleaning.

**Data Availability.** The Data used in the article is present on Kaggle.

**Conflicts of Interest.** The authors declared no conflict of Interest.

# References

1. WHO. World Health Statistics 2021: Monitoring Health for the SDGs, Sustainable Development Goals; WHO: Geneva, Switzerland (2022)
2. Department of Economic and Social Afairs: Urban Population Change (2018). https://www.un.org/development/desa/en/news/population/2018-revision-of-world-urbanization-prospects.html. Accessed 20 Oct 2021
3. Bai, L., Wang, J., Ma, X., Lu, H.: Air pollution forecasts: an overview. Int. J. Environ. Res. Public Health **15**(4), 780 (2018)
4. Wang, J., Jiang, H., Zhou, Q., Wu, J., Qin, S.: China's natural gas production and consumption analysis based on the multicycle Hubbert model and rolling Grey model. Renew. Sustain. Energy Rev. **53**, 1149–1167 (2016)
5. Ameer, S., Ali Shah, M., Khan, A., et al.: Comparative analysis of machine learning techniques for predicting air quality in smart cities. IEEE Access **7**, 128325–128338 (2019)
6. Kemp, A.C., Horton, B.P., Donnelly, J.P., Mann, M.E., Vermeer, M., Rahmstorf, S.: Climate related sea-level variations over the past two millennia. Proc. Natl. Acad. Sci. **108**(27), 11017–11022 (2011)

7. David, M.G.H., Faner, R., Sibila, O., Badia, J.R., Agusti, A.: Do Chronic Respiratory Diseases or Their Treatment Affect the Risk of SARS-CoV-2 Infection. Elsevier Ltd. Science Direct (2020)
8. Ying, Y., Chang, L., Wang, L.: Laboratory testing of SARSCoV, MERS-CoV, and SARS-CoV-2 (2019-nCoV): current status, challenges, and countermeasures. Rev. Med. Virol. **30**(3), article e2106 (2020)
9. Trivodaliev, K., Risteska Stojkoska, B., Korunoski, M.: Internet of things solution for intelligent air pollution prediction and visualization (2019)
10. Kim, B.Y., Cha, J.W., Chang, K.H., Lee, C.: Estimation of the visibility in Seoul, South Korea, based on particulate matter and weather data, using machine-learning algorithm. Aerosol. Air Qual. Res. **22**, 220125 (2022)
11. Hosseini, V., Ahmadi, G., Badii, K.: Air quality prediction using artificial neural network and adaptive neuro-fuzzy inference system. Int. J. Environ. Res. Public Health **15**(7), 1522 (2018). https://doi.org/10.3390/ijerph15071522
12. Chowdhury, S., Islam, M.S., Raihan, M.K., Arefin, M.S.: Design and implementation of an IoT based air pollution detection and monitoring system. In: 2019 5th International Conference on Advances in Electrical Engineering (ICAEE), pp. 296–300. IEEE (2019)
13. Makhija, J., Nakkeeran, M., Anantha Narayanan, V.: Detection of vehicle emissions through green IoT for pollution control. In: Advances in Automation, Signal Processing, Instrumentation, and Control: Select Proceedings of i-CASIC 2020, pp. 817–826. Springer Singapore (2021)
14. Deng, F., Ma, L., Gao, X., Chen, J.: The MR-CA models for analysis of pollution sources and prediction of PM 2.5. IEEE Trans. Syst. Man Cybern.: Syst. **49**(4), 814–820 (2017)
15. An Intelligent Supervision System of Environmental Pollution in Industrial Park **8**(1), 2134–2140
16. Zhang, X., Liu, Y., Zhang, Y.: Prediction of PM2.5 concentration using LSTM neural network with meteorological parameters. In: IOP Conference Series: Earth and Environmental Science, vol. 527, no. 1, p. 012063 (2020). https://doi.org/10.1088/1755-1315/527/1/012063
17. Xie, H., Zhang, M., Ge, J., Dong, X., Chen, H.: Learning air traffic as images: a deep convolutional neural network for airspace operation complexity evaluation. Complexity **2021**, 1–16 (2021)
18. Beelen, R., Raaschounielsen, O., Stafoggia, M., et al.: Effects of long-term exposure to air pollution on natural-cause mortality: an analysis of 22 European cohorts within the multicentre ESCAPE project. Lancet **383**(9919), 785–795 (2014)
19. Bing, C.L., Arihant, B., Pei-Chann, C., Manoj, K.T., Cheng-Chin, T.: Urban air quality forecasting based on multi-dimensional collaborative support vector regression (SVR): a case study of Beijing-Tianjin-Shijiazhuang. PloS One **12**(7), article e0179763 (2017)
20. Le, V.-D., Bui, T.-C., Cha, S.-K.: Spatiotemporal deep learning model for cityinterpolation and prediction. In: 2020 IEEE International Conference on Big Data and Smart Computing (BigComp), pp. 55–62 (2020)
21. Le, V.-D., Bui, T.-C., Cha, S.-K.: Spatiotemporal deep learning model for citywide air pollution interpolation and prediction. In: 2020 IEEE International Conference on Big Data and Smart Computing (BigComp), pp. 55–62 (2020)
22. Huang, C.-J., Kuo, P.-H.: A deep CNN-LSTM model for particulate matter (PM2.5) forecasting in smart cities. Sensors **18**(7), 2220 (2018)
23. Bekkar, A., Hssina, B., Douzi, S., Douzi, K.: Air-pollution prediction in smart city, deep learning approach. J. Big Data **8**(1), 1–21 (2021). https://doi.org/10.1186/s40537-021-00548-1

# Implementation of IoT and WSN Technologies for Health Monitoring

Tehseen Mazhar[1], Muhammad Iqbal[2], Muhammad Iqbal[1], Yazeed Yasin Ghadi[3], Ateeq Ur Rehman[4(✉)], and Waseem Abbasi[5]

[1] Department of Computer Science, Virtual University of Pakistan, Lahore 54000, Pakistan
[2] Institute of Computing and Information Technology, Gomal University, Dera Ismail Khan 29220, Pakistan
[3] Department of Computer Science and Software Engineering, Al Ain Universit, Abu Dhabi 15322, UAE
Yazeed.ghadi@aau.ac.ae
[4] Department of Electrical Engineering, Government College University, Lahore 54000, Pakistan
ateeq.rehman@gcu.edu.pk
[5] Department of Computer Science and IT, Superior University, Sargodha, Pakistan

**Abstract.** IoT-based applications make innovative use of millions of sensors. Research has risen in the medical and technological fields in the previous ten years. The Internet of Things impacts the development of medical research. Improved medical care is possible because the Internet of Things can link sensors, medical equipment, and remote healthcare professionals. Patient treatment has been enhanced in terms of effectiveness, cost, accessibility, and safety. Due to COVID-19, receiving medical treatment in the convenience of one's home is more important than ever. To enhance healthcare, internet of things devices is utilized to monitor patients. His article examines how the Internet of Things has improved, enabling technology, healthcare services, and healthcare-related challenges. IoT system concerns are also taken into consideration. This effort aims to help future researchers understand the topic better by giving a thorough overview of all of HIoT's many uses. The applications, technology, and challenges of the healthcare industry are all examined in this article. As a result, the IoT has the potential to improve healthcare's effectiveness and ability to treat patients. The idea put out in this article is that the Internet of Things may be made widely used, lucrative, and easily available everywhere. The integration provides a faster calculation. The last section includes a number of practical recommendations and suggestions for implementing the IoT healthcare system during COVID-19 and future severe pandemics.

**Keywords:** Healthcare Systems · Internet of Things · IoT Applications · Sensors · Smart Technology · H-IoT

## 1 Introduction

Everything is interconnected in the current culture. Any gadget with an internet connection is a smart device. The Internet of Things is a vast network of connected, locally aware things that share and exchange data, to put it simply. Thus, the Internet of Things is a network of interconnected electrical devices. The Internet of Things is crucial for the remote control of digital devices. The potential to foster commerce, professional development, and social interaction exists for tangible and digital goods. Nano chips can communicate with routers thanks to sensors, actuators, and software. The adoption of IoT is rising. Due to its many benefits, including cheaper cost, less infrastructure, a wider variety of network topologies, and less maintenance, wireless sensor networks are increasingly being employed in practically all monitoring applications in the digital age (WSNs). Climate change, weather, natural catastrophes, traffic, forests, healthcare, location, and other things are all monitored by wireless sensors and WSN. Healthcare sensors control, watch over, regulate, alert, and track people.

Sensors quickly evaluate and identify this behavior, completely atomizing the healthcare system and removing the need for human involvement. Soon, healthcare will undergo rapid change. For patients, medical practitioners, and healthcare system managers, many valuable Internet of Things apps [1] have been created. These technologies improve healthcare by making it possible to treat severe diseases in real time and manage medical emergencies, among other things. Several aspects of health, including blood pressure, insulin levels, cardiac issues, and fitness, may be tracked and reported to a doctor or medical facility using Internet of Things apps. The development of wireless networking has touched every element of our life. The Internet of Things is growing quickly. The Internet of Things has the potential to alter our way of life by tying together all of our many technology devices.

Consequently, continuous access to reliable communications is necessary, especially in busy enterprises. When connected to the Internet, smart devices may share information (things). The Internet of Things enables advancements in technology. Many modern home appliances, security cameras, and environmental monitoring devices include transceivers, microcontrollers, and protocols for transferring control and sensor data [2] (Fig. 1).

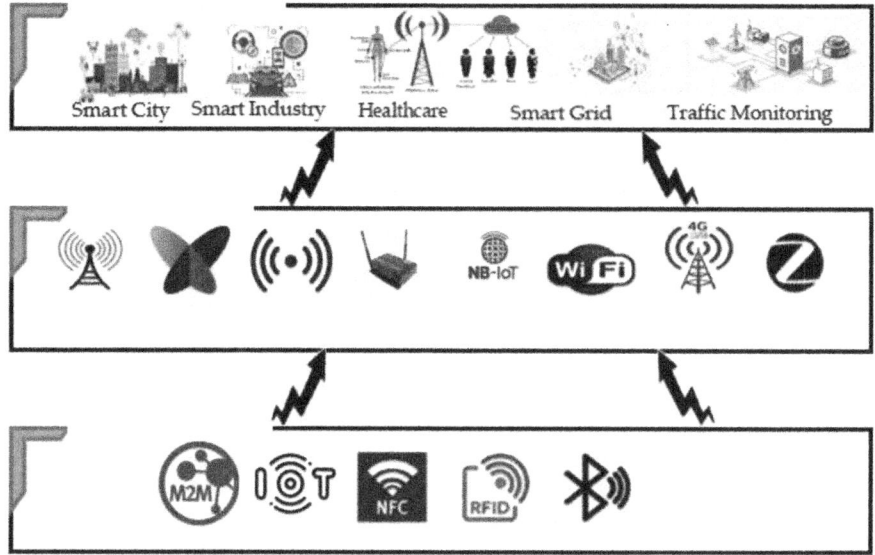

**Fig. 1.** Generic Three Layer Architecture in IoT [2].

The medical sector was an early adopter of sensor technology and the telemetry made possible by the Internet of Things to perform remote monitoring. With the possibility of remote monitoring, patients no longer need to make frequent journeys to the doctor's office. Before recent technological advancements, this was not conceivable. This may be helpful for patients who are physically unable to visit a clinic but still need routine medical monitoring for illnesses like diabetes, cardiovascular disease, or chronic obstructive pulmonary disease (COPD). Thanks to the possibilities provided by telemedicine, patients undergoing psychiatric or surgical operations may have the opportunity to have their status examined remotely (Fig. 2).

Figure 3 demonstrates how the concepts of incidental, accessible, and universal computing form the basis of the Internet of Things. We analyze the relationships between IoT, M2M, CPS, and WSN (WSN). M2M and WSN technologies are essential for the IoT to function. Utilizing CPS and its continuous coordination between physical items and computational components may make it easier to develop dynamic M2M applications. For instance, computing, sensing, and actuation may be carried out using technologies like M2M, CPS, and WSN. A trustworthy M2M Wireless Sensor Network (WSN) that might provide CPS is the Internet of Things.

The fast spread of portable and wearable devices in this age of ubiquitous computing, when computing is nearly everywhere, has enabled improvements in healthcare made possible by the Internet of Things (IoT). With the development of cloud computing, data exchange between previously inaccessible devices improves ubiquitous computing. IoT acts as a basis for linking numerous systems, including smart homes, smart cities, and smart healthcare. These interconnected gadgets and sensors gather data for difficult activities like planning, prediction, and recommendation [3].

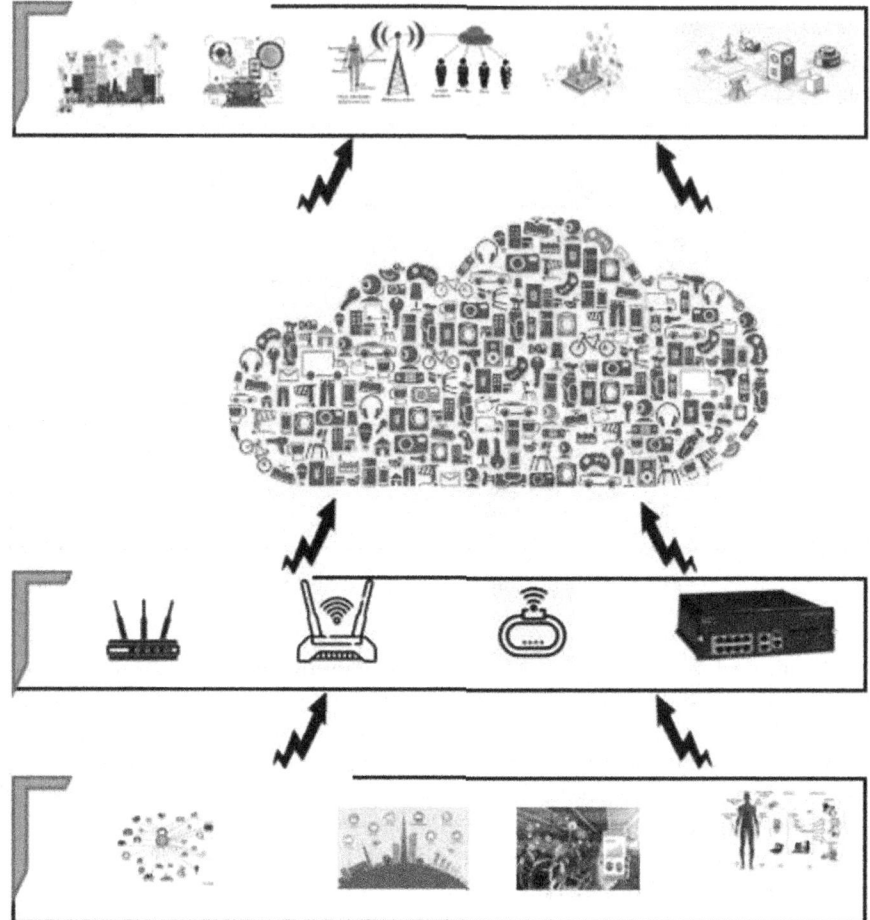

**Fig. 2.** IoT Network.

The structure of the paper is as follows: a general description related work of IoT and WSN technologies is presented in Sect. 2. The Keyword Search, Inclusion and Exclusion, HealthCare IoT Application etc. is presented in Sect. 3. Section 4 describes the results regarding applications of IoT-based WSN. In Sect. 5 the detail of Challenges, Limitations, and Future Scope is presented. Finally, open issues of credit card fraud detection are presented in Sect. 6. Figure 4 shows Organization of Paper.

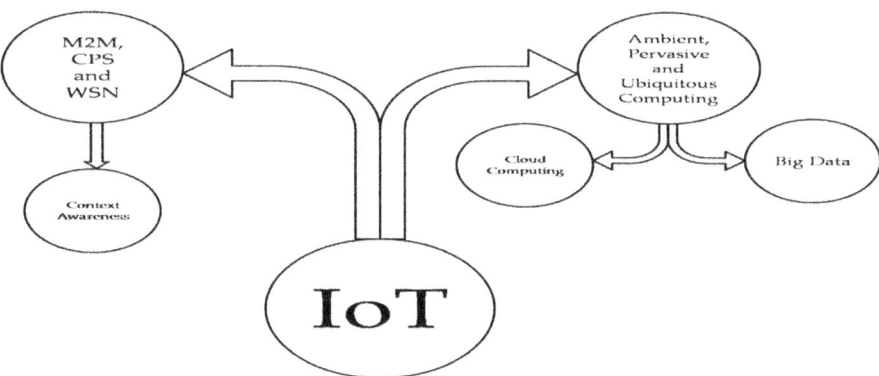

**Fig. 3.** Relationship between IoT and Related Technologies.

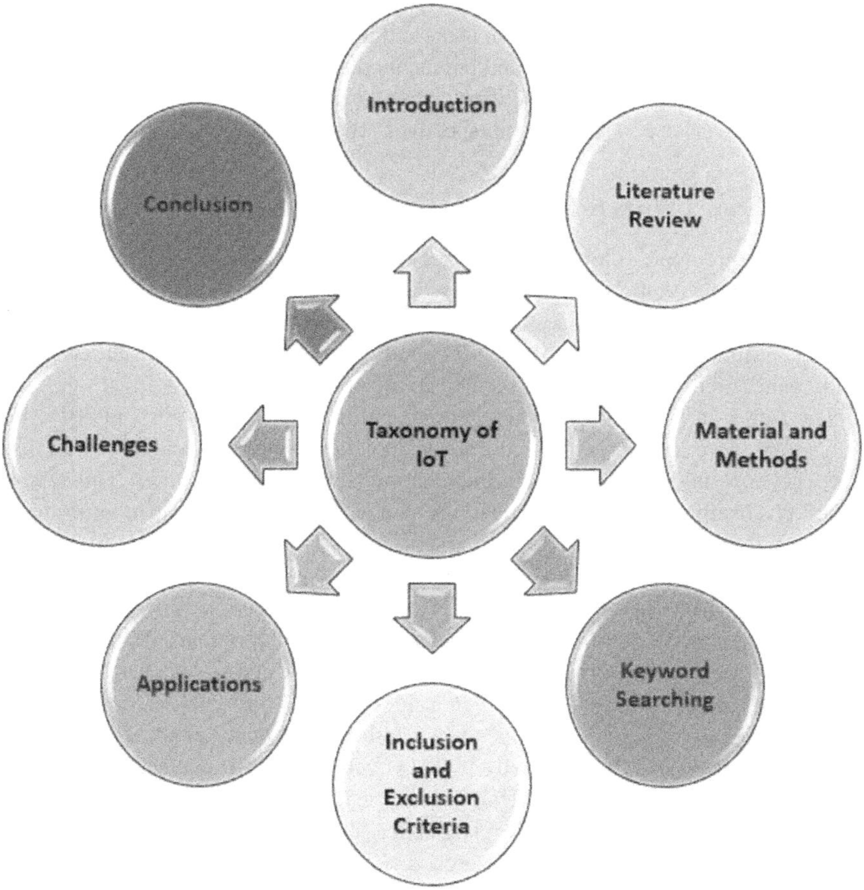

**Fig. 4.** Organization of Paper.

## 2 Literature Review

Medical, smart city, greenhouse monitoring, environmental, and air and water pollution applications use IoT-based WSN.

In healthcare, IoT and sensors have been utilized for drug administration, hospital operations, and remote patient monitoring. IoT's major utility in healthcare is remote patient monitoring. Healthcare practitioners may monitor patients' vital signs and symptoms in real time, spotting any health risks. [4] found that IoT-enabled remote monitoring devices lowered hospital readmissions in COPD patients. IoT healthcare incorporates sensors in hospitals. Sensors can monitor patients, personnel, surfaces, and medical equipment. This technology may boost hospital efficiency, patient safety, and disease prevention proved that RFID technology in hospitals boosted asset management and minimized medical equipment failure. IoT and sensors are being exploited in medication management. IoT-enabled items can remind and monitor medicine usage. [5] revealed that IoT-enabled medication management systems improved patient outcomes and minimized medication mishaps. Sensors and IoT in healthcare are expanding swiftly and might boost patient outcomes and reduce medical expenses. In remote monitoring, wearable sensors, and medicine delivery, it works. A complete research of the IoT in healthcare: current state and future perspectives" [6].

### 2.1 Healthcare Utilizes IoT and Cloud Computing

IoT applications employ cloud-based services to identify patients from home and handle several difficulties. Android applications, cloud IoT, and computers run healthcare. Due to IoT needs in academia, business, and society, [22] devised a new healthcare approach. These two studies suggest a technique for sending medical information to friends and family while monitoring heart rate using a smart health band.

The author of [7] studied H-IoT communication technology aspects in 2018. Four applications were cardiovascular, musculoskeletal, neuromuscular, and infectious disorders. They also investigated new communication technology difficulties. This research misses AI's usefulness in HIoT applications. E-health, telehealth, home monitoring, and RFID-based monitoring systems were assessed by [8]. They examined smart healthcare system interoperability, low latency tolerance, and reliability, missing HIoT system fundamentals. In another investigation. The author of [9] explored healthcare IoT applications. They focused on important components, jobs, and problems. They overlooked IoT security and privacy threats. The author of [10] evaluated H-IoT therapy. Sensing, communication, and data analytics were considered. They discussed existing challenges and provided solutions. This poll does not mention cloud computing and AI's participation in this research. Another study by [11] evaluated IoT-based health care service delivery. Survey advantages and pitfalls were considered. The IoT healthcare system's fundamental components are not investigated. This doesn't help readers comprehend IoT healthcare. The author of [12] researched H-IoT technology and applications. Like earlier surveys, important issues and unsolved subjects are covered.

Taking a patient's temperature is only one of several diagnostic tools used to track homeostasis. Changes in core body temperature may also be an early warning sign of injury, illness, or other conditions. To rule out several diseases, a doctor may take a patient's temperature. A person's temperature may be taken in a variety of ways, including by placing a thermometer in their mouth, ear, or rectal area. When using these methods, there is often a concern with patient comfort and a higher risk of infection. Recent developments in IoT-based technology, however, have made a variety of viable options easily available. A 3D-printed earpiece with an infrared sensor measures internal body temperature by contacting the tympanic membrane [13]. It included a CPU for processing data and a wireless sensor unit. Environment and exercise have little effect on the temperature around here. The core body temperatures of newborns were monitored in real-time using lightweight, wearable sensors [14]. It may also alert parents if the child's temperature climbs over a potentially harmful level. Figure 5 shows the applications of IoT Based Wireless Sensor Network.

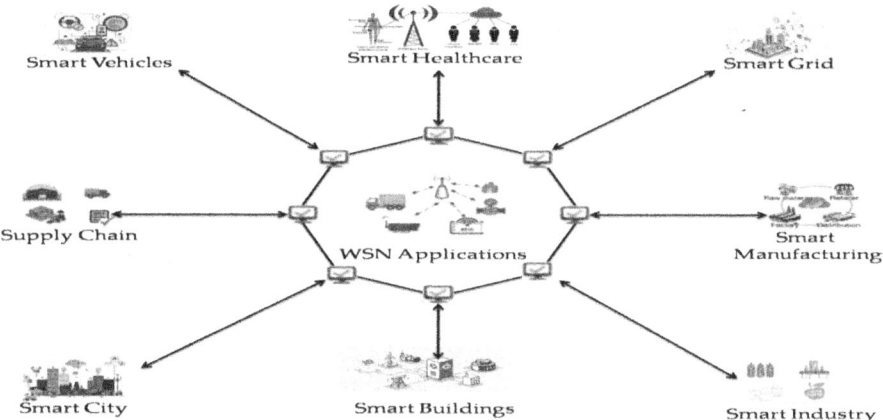

**Fig. 5.** Application of Iot Based Wireless Sensor Network (reproduced from [47].

## 3 Material and Methods

### 3.1 Keyword Searching

This research examined the wireless networking aspects of IoT and healthcare systems simultaneously. In the first stage, a plethora of documents, including crucial healthcare data, were collected. Second, we gathered literature on IoT healthcare systems and related sensors. To this end, we looked for terms associated with healthcare IT, the IoT, and sensors. Figure 6 displays the results of a search conducted across many databases using the keywords shown there.

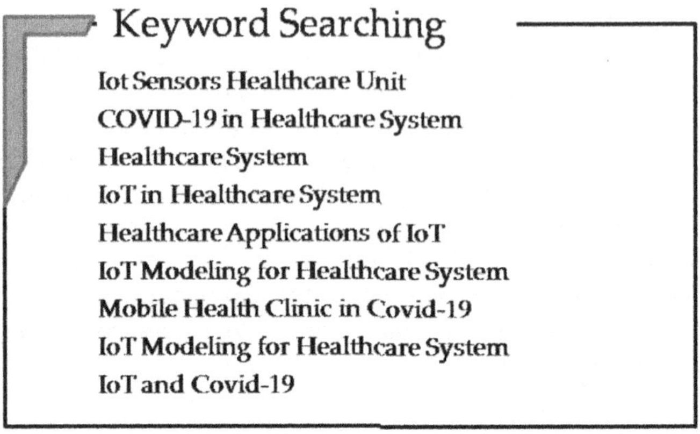

```
Keyword Searching
Iot Sensors Healthcare Unit
COVID-19 in Healthcare System
Healthcare System
IoT in Healthcare System
Healthcare Applications of IoT
IoT Modeling for Healthcare System
Mobile Health Clinic in Covid-19
IoT Modeling for Healthcare System
IoT and Covid-19
```

**Fig. 6.** Research Methods and Keyword Searching.

### 3.2 Inclusion and Exclusion Criteria

Several scholarly articles were discovered on the mentioned Healthcare, Wireless Sensor Networks, Internet of Things, and Healthcare Applications in IoR. Applying the criteria presented in Table 1, the most relevant and concise material was collected from these publications written in English for general consumption. They correspond to common queries and study objectives in the areas of WSNs, IoT, healthcare, and healthcare-related IoT applications.

**Table 1.** Inclusion and exclusion criteria.

| Criteria for Inclusion |
|---|
| Only those papers that were authored in English should be included in the review |
| Include only works published between 2016 and 2022 |
| Particularly include articles with sufficient information on WSN, IoT, and Healthcare in IoT in the titles, keywords, abstracts, and conclusions |
| Include papers where the main objective of the content is on WSN, IoT, or Healthcare in IoT |
| Exclusion Criteria |
| Do not take into consideration any papers that have been written in a language other than English |
| Gray papers Exclude |
| Exclude papers that were not published between 2014–2021 |
| Less than three pages of research papers containing exclude |
| Exclude papers that failed to meet the inclusion criteria |

### Research Question

The following research questions are this study

1. What is the application of IoT that is based on WSN?
2. What is the role of Smart Technologies in IoT-Based Healthcare Systems for COVID-19?

3. What is the role of IoT Based Healthcare Challenges/limitations for COVID-19?

The most prevalent use of IoT in healthcare is the monitoring of physical activity via consumer electronics. Wearable technology, such as smart clothes and wristbands that track vital signs and activity levels, falls under this category. The fitness of an athlete is calculated by looking at all of the available information [15]. Several different types of sensors are advocated for use in [15] to measure health and fitness. In a three-layer architecture, the user interface to the central processing unit represents the device layer. The database server receives data that has been processed locally and stores it. A database may be accessed remotely to keep tabs on vital signs. The researchers in this study monitored sweat production with the use of an accelerometer, temperature and pulse sensors, and a Grove GSR sensor. A material similar to "smart fabric" connects all of the sensors. It is impossible to gauge the efficacy of gym training without first developing a personalized workout program [16]. This technique uses the Apple Watch and the Health app to obtain the necessary information. Evaluating cyclists' physical readiness is recommended in [17]. And it can even sniff out those who would steal your bike. The software features a two-pronged system architecture, with the backend and the communication mechanism being shared. There are sensors and bicycle safety devices at the user end of this three stage method. While accelerometer data is used by the bike's safety system, heart rate is used to gauge the severity of any health issues. In tandem, they provide data to an Android app that monitors bike locks and health indicators. Fitness monitoring plans [18] often include tracking activities like walking, jogging, and relaxing. The structure is composed of three layers, one of which is a BSN sensor layer. Figure 7 shows an Overview of Fitness Tracking System.

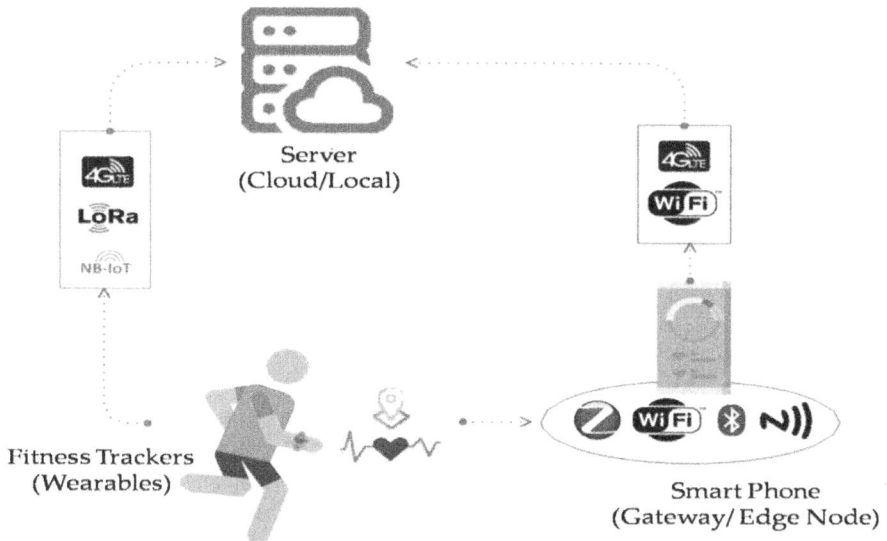

**Fig. 7.** An Overview of Fitness Tracking System.

## 4 Result

### 4.1 Applications of IoT-Based WSN

WSNs based on the Internet of Things is used in fields as varied as medicine, smart cities, greenhouse monitoring, and environmental assessment of air and water pollution. Below are examples of many different utilizations:

The IoT has completely altered the ways in which we live, work, and communicate. Technology advancements in real-time communication between devices and systems have enabled "smart" dwellings, urban infrastructure, and transportation systems. The medical field has seen significant IoT growth. Potentially, the Internet of Things and sensors will revolutionize the administration and delivery of medical care. Here, the benefits and drawbacks of using sensors and the Internet of Things in healthcare are outlined. Sensors and the Internet of Things might enhance clinical operations and encourage the development of novel diagnostic and treatment processes, as well as allow remote patient monitoring and management. The medical field is a big user of IoT devices. Indeed, H-IoT is used in healthcare applications. The H-IoT is a subset of the IoT. Internet of Things and Enhanced Internet of Things relies on WSNs and BSNs. IoT systems and H-IoT systems are technologically distinct. Data from the fitness tracker and wearables market indicates further expansion [19]. IoT Net [68 is a healthcare centric system because of the proliferation of smart health monitoring devices and the development of the IoT connectivity infrastructure. Health monitoring is only one use of the Internet of Things. Patients' biometric data and vital signs might be monitored across the network to aid in accurate diagnosis and treatment [15]. Data sharing across the many participating institutions is impossible without a standard infrastructure. To advance H-IoT, a standardized or reference architecture is required. Multiple groups and businesses are working together to provide standardized designs for a wide range of Internet of Things uses [20]. A distributed, service oriented architecture, The IEEE Standards Association establishes norms for Point-of-Service medical devices. Setup, node discovery, and node communication, as well as QoS components, are all outlined for the H-IoT scenario [21] (Fig. 8).

Recent years have seen an increase in the use of sensors and the IoT in healthcare. Potentially enabling real-time monitoring, data collecting, and more efficient and effective treatment, these technologies have the potential to significantly alter the current state of healthcare delivery. The numerous applications of the Internet of Things and sensors in healthcare, such as telemedicine, remote monitoring, and device integration, will be discussed in this article.

We will also discuss the potential benefits and drawbacks of these technologies and provide recommendations for further study and development. When one is seeing something from a distance, Remote monitoring is a critical use of IoT and sensors in the medical industry. Patients may be monitored remotely, reducing the frequency with which they must visit the hospital. Patients with chronic conditions, including diabetes, cardiovascular disease, and chronic obstructive pulmonary disease, who require frequent monitoring but are unable to make regular hospital visits may benefit the most from this. Remote monitoring might potentially be used to check up on people's mental health or recovery from surgery or other medical treatments.

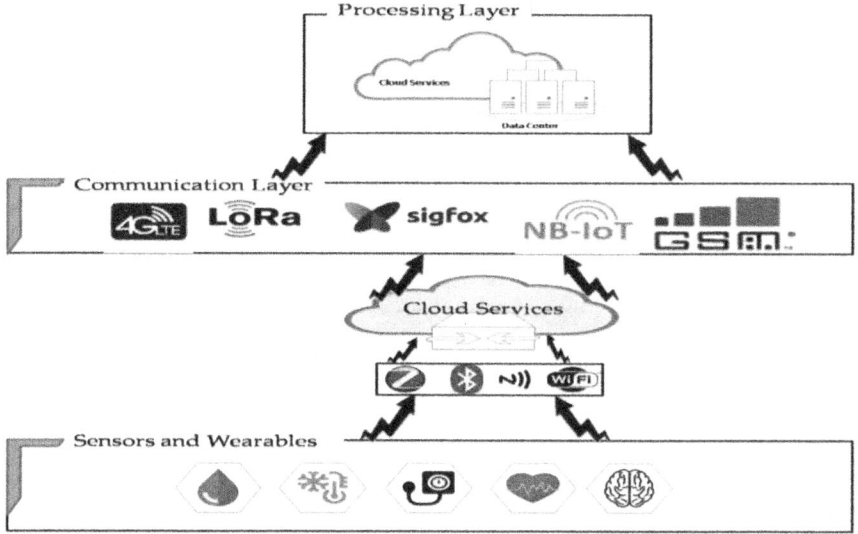

**Fig. 8.** The three-tier Architecture of the H-IoT systems.

## 4.2 Smart Technologies of IoT-Based Healthcare Systems for COVID-19

Combining many Internet-of-Things tools with current medical infrastructures. Several businesses have increased their use of IoT tools as a direct consequence of COVID-19. As more and more devices are connected to the internet, more and more cutting-edge technologies are made available to individuals and businesses alike. To name a few, the following technologies may be of great help to future IoT healthcare systems:

### 4.2.1 Ambient Intelligence Communications Technologies

Ambient intelligence is crucial for users and patients. Its use in the healthcare industry benefits both patients and medical professionals [22]. Information about patients is gathered and analyzed with the use of wearable technology and sensors linked to the Internet of Things and a healthcare facility. COVID-19's embedded system of human-computer interaction, autonomous control, Internet of Things, and ambient intelligence may thereby help governments, healthcare systems, and patients.

### 4.2.2 Augmented Reality

In the age of Industry 4.0, augmented reality is a key component of cutting-edge innovation, education, and growth. One area where IT has made a significant difference is in healthcare. Augmented reality is used in the medical industry for a wide range of applications, including remote monitoring, surgery, instruction, and training. AR promotes and stresses regular hand washing as a means of combating COVID-19 and other diseases [23].

## Wearable Devices

Wearable technology offers a low-cost, high-value answer to a variety of health problems. A wide range of sensors and wearable accessories may be used with the devices to gather data on the patient and their surroundings. Because it is stored digitally, it may be accessed from anywhere [90]. Connecting Internet of Things wearables to mobile apps boosts their processing capability. Wearable technology has become an increasingly important aspect of IoT adoption in healthcare, as seen in Figure 9, which illustrates its use in the fight against pandemics such as COVID-19.

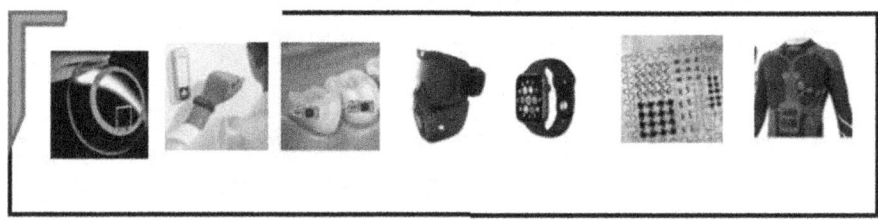

**Fig. 9.** Wearable Devices

## Smart Technology

As a result of COVID-19, businesses have adjusted to the new conditions. Some of the suggestions made in the MIT report include: increasing the distance between workstations; removing chairs from conference rooms; installing antimicrobial surfaces; installing thermal scanners; adjusting the building's temperature control; painting the floors; and enforcing strict cleaning regulations. Returning employees may be offered or required to undergo coronavirus testing by certain companies. No business was ready for COVID-19, not even the most innovative ones. These industries may better protect their workers and increase output without sacrificing quality by adopting a "Command Center" [24], which converts all cutting-edge technology into business intelligence technology. During pivotal junctures, the command center gathers all pertinent industry data for use in making strategic and operational decisions.

## Ambient Assisted Living (AAL)

We're developing an AAL intelligent support system to improve the older population's wellbeing, security, comfort, and self-respect. Facilitators, physicians, and the healthcare system all stand to benefit from taking a more simplified approach to caring for the aged. COVID-19 integrates the Internet of Things (IoT), smartphones, and wearables. Using this technology, loving ones may alert their elderly relatives in the home or at a care facility of any impending threats or emergencies [25].

## 5 Challenges, Limitations, and Future Scope

Healthcare problems have lately been addressed through technological solutions. Superior medical care is more accessible now than ever before. Networking, cloud computing, and Internet of Things enabled intelligent sensors have all contributed to the transformation of the healthcare sector. The Internet of Things has advantages and disadvantages much like any other technology [26].

Cost Updates are essential for IoT gadgets to ensure they always function at the cutting edge. Several sensors and health care gadgets are linked in each IoT network. The costs associated with upkeep, maintenance, and repairs are detrimental to the company's bottom line and clientele. To save money, we need low-maintenance sensors.

It's common for IoT gadgets to rely on batteries for power. Changing batteries in networked sensors may be difficult. A massive battery supplied the power. Scientists from all across the globe are working together to develop medical devices that can maintain themselves. One option is to combine IoT with alternative power sources. Using these techniques may be useful in addressing the present energy crisis. Several medical groups exist to serve the public. Almost all of these products advertise themselves as benchmarks for their respective fields. Uncertainty.

An authoritative body is needed to standardize HIoT device communication protocols, data aggregation, and gateway interfaces. HIoT gadgets are necessary for the verification and standardization of EMRs. Researchers may work toward device standardization by joining working groups with the IETF, ETSI, IPSO, and other bodies.

Because of cloud computing, real-time monitoring has evolved. Cyberattacks on the healthcare network are a real concern. Information about patients or their treatments may be at risk. To prevent this kind of attack, HIoT systems must be well-protected.

HIoT medical and sensor equipment requires evaluation and implementation of identity authentication, secure booting, fault tolerance, authorization management, whitelisting, password encryption, and secure pairing protocols to prevent attacks. Secure routing and message integrity are essential for wireless technologies like Wi-Fi, Bluetooth, ZigBee, and others. Since everyone using the system is also linked to the server, security flaws in the IoT might compromise sensitive patient data. Security may be bolstered via the use of algorithms and cryptographies.

Because medical devices are adaptable to many settings, they may be scaled easily. Gains in speed and output may be expected as a result of scaling. Being adaptable is crucial. Future and present system efficiency are improved. Medical equipment, sensors, and actuators drive an IoT system for the healthcare sector. The variety of IoT devices necessitates careful management of scalability in HIoT systems.

## References

1. Ma, Y., Wang, Y., Yang, J., Miao, Y., Li, W.: Big health application system based on health IoT and big data. IEEE Access **5**, 7885–7897 (2016)
2. Rehman, A.U., Naqvi, R.A., Rehman, A., Paul, A., Sadiq, M.T., Hussain, D.: A trustworthy SIoT aware mechanism as an enabler for citizen services in smart cities. Electronics **9**, 918 (2020). https://doi.org/10.3390/electronics9060918

3. Isravel, D.P.; Silas, S.: A comprehensive review on the emerging IoT-cloud based technologies for smart healthcare. In: Proceedings of the 2020 6th International Conference on Advanced Computing and Communication Systems (ICACCS), Coimbatore, India, 6–7 March 2020, pp. 606–611 (2020)
4. Raza, A., et al.: A hybrid deep learning-based approach for brain tumor classification. Electronics **11**, 1146 (2022). https://doi.org/10.3390/electronics11071146
5. Kao, A.K., et al.: IoT-enabled fall detection and monitoring system for older adults. J. Med. Syst. **39**(12), 1–8 (2015)
6. Ahmad, I., et al.: Efficient algorithms for E-healthcare to solve multiobject fuse detection problem. J. Healthc. Eng. **2021**, 1–16 (2021). https://doi.org/10.1155/2021/9500304
7. Mazhar, M.S., et al.: Forensic analysis on internet of things (IoT) device using machine-to-machine (M2M) framework. Electronics **11**, 1126 (2022). https://doi.org/10.3390/electronics11071126
8. Alam, M.M., Malik, H., Khan, M.I., Pardy, T., Kuusik, A., Le Moullec, Y.: A survey on the roles of communication technologies in IoT-based personalized healthcare applications. IEEE Access **6**, 36611–36631 (2018)
9. Shaikh, Y., Parvati, V.K., Biradar, S.R.: Survey of smart healthcare systems using IoT(IoT). In: Proceedings of the 2018 International Conference on Communication, Computing and IoT(IC3IoT), Chennai, India, 15–17 February 2018, pp. 508–513 (2018)
10. Ahmadi, H., Arji, G., Shahmoradi, L., Safdari, R., Nilashi, M., Alizadeh, M.: The application of IoTin healthcare: a systematic literature review and classification. Univers. Access Inf. Soc. **18**, 837–869 (2019)
11. Haider, S.K., et al.: Energy efficient UAV flight path model for cluster head selection in next-generation wireless sensor networks. Sensors **21**, 8445 (2021). https://doi.org/10.3390/s21248445
12. Asif, M., et al.: Reduced-complexity LDPC decoding for next-generation IoT networks. Wirel. Commun. Mob. Comput. **2021**, 1–10 (2021). https://doi.org/10.1155/2021/2029560
13. Sadiq, M.T., Zulkifal Aziz, M., Almogren, A., Yousaf, A., Siuly, S., Rehman, A.U.: Exploiting pretrained CNN models for the development of an EEG-based robust BCI framework. Comput. Biol. Med. **143** (2022). https://doi.org/10.1016/j.compbiomed.2022.105242
14. Shahwar, T., et al.: Automated detection of Alzheimer's via hybrid classical quantum neural networks. Electronics **11**, 721 (2022). https://doi.org/10.3390/electronics11050721
15. Arif, S.A., Niaz, M.H., Shabbir, N., Zafar, M.H., Hassan, S.R., Ur Rehman, A.: RSSI based trilatertion for outdoor localization in zigbee based wireless sensor networks (WSNs). In: 2018 10th International Conference on Computational Intelligence and Communication Networks (CICN), Esbjerg, Denmark, pp. 1–5 (2018). https://doi.org/10.1109/CICN.2018.8864943
16. Muhammad Hussain, N., Rehman, A.U., Othman, M.T.B., Zafar, J., Zafar, H., Hamam, H.: Accessing artificial intelligence for fetus health status using hybrid deep learning algorithm (AlexNet-SVM) on cardiotocographic data. Sensors **22**, 5103 (2022). https://doi.org/10.3390/s22145103
17. Kanwal, S., Tao, F., Almogren, A. Ur Rehman, A., Taj, R., Radwan, A.: A robust data hiding reversible technique for improving the security in e-health care system. Comput. Model. Eng. Sci. **134**(01), 201–219 (2022). https://doi.org/10.32604/cmes.2022.020255
18. Saeed, N., Bader, A., Al-Naffouri, T.Y., Alouini, M.S.: When wireless communication responds to COVID-19: combating the pandemic and saving the economy. Front. Commun. Netw. **1**, 566853–566867 (2020)
19. WAS. Making Vehicles Special. https://www.wasvehicles.com/en/home.html/. Accessed 22 June 2022
20. Hassan, S.R., Ahmad, I., Nebhen, J., Ur Rehman, A., Shafiq, M., Choi, J.-G.: Design of latency-aware IoT modules in heterogeneous fog-cloud computing networks. Comput. Mater. Continua **70**(3), 6057–6072 (2022). https://doi.org/10.32604/cmc.2022.020428

21. Whelan, K.: Smart ambulances: the future of emergency healthcare (2018). http://emag.medicalexpo.com/smart-ambulances-the-future-ofemergency-healthcare/. Accessed 22 June 2022
22. Mike, T.: How IoT helps improve healthcare. https://builtin.com/internet-things/iot-in-health care, https://www.quio.com/. Accessed on 22 June 2022
23. Arshad, J., et al.: Deployment of wireless sensor network and IoT platform to implement an intelligent animal monitoring system. Sustainability **14**, 6249 (2022). https://doi.org/10.3390/su14106249
24. Zhang, C., Härenstam, K.P., Meijer, S., Darwich, A.S.: Serious gaming of logistics management in pediatric emergency medicine. Int. J. Serious Games **7**, 47–77 (2020)
25. Sundas, A., Badotra, S., Bharany, S., Almogren, A., Tag-ElDin, E.M., Rehman, A.U.: HealthGuard: an intelligent healthcare system security framework based on machine learning. Sustainability **14**, 11934 (2022). https://doi.org/10.3390/su141911934
26. Shanmugasundaram, G., Sankarikaarguzhali, G.: An investigation on IoT healthcare analytics. Int. J. Inf. Eng. Electron. Bus. **9**, 11–19 (2017)

# Breast Cancer Diagnosis Based on Deep Convolutional Neural Networks Using Image Clustering

Sanamaqbool[1], Majid Hussain[1(✉)], Uzair Saeed[1], and Muhammad Farrukh Shafeeq[2]

[1] Department of Computer Science, The University of Faisalabad (TUF), Engineering Wing Canal Road, Faisalabad, Pakistan
[2] Department of Computer Science, UET, Lahore, Pakistan

**Abstract.** Early breast cancer diagnosis is crucial for effective therapy. Breast cancer has several subtypes, making it difficult to diagnose, especially in low-resource settings. Deep learning models, particularly Convolutional Neural Networks (CNNs), can help diagnose and categorise breast cancer early. This thesis presents a novel approach to breast cancer diagnosis using deep-near-infrared (CNN) and image clustering. Our objective is to build a cost-effective and efficient deep learning model for breast cancer detection and categorisation to help doctors make fast and accurate diagnoses. The model will use picture clustering to find comparable mammography images from a dataset. After that, deep convolutional neural networks (CNNs) will classify images as benign or cancerous. The precision, sensitivity, specificity, y, and F1 score will be used to evaluate the suggested model. The suggested model will be evaluated using a variety of performance measures and compared to cutting-edge methods. This thesis will show how deep convolutional neural networks can improve the accuracy and reproducibility of breast cancer diagnosis. These findings will be based on the thesis. This study could change the diagnosis of breast cancer and patient survival.

**Keywords:** image clustering · Cancer Diagnosis · Deep Convolutional Neural networks

## 1 Introduction

Most cancer deaths are caused by breast cancer. Early detection increases the likelihood of therapy and survival, although it can take time and result in pathologist disagreements. CAD systems could improve the accuracy of diagnosis. We used a deep convolutional neural network with the Grand Challenge on Breast Cancer Histology Pictures dataset of hematoxylin and eosin stained breast histology microscope pictures to categorise breast cancer histology photos. Gradient-boosted trees and various topologies of deep neural networks are used. Our four-class classification method has an accuracy rating of 87.2%. We report a precision of 93.8%, a sensitivity/specificity of 97.3% AUC, and 96.5/88.0% sensitivity/specificity for the 2-class carcinoma classification test at the high-sensitivity operating point. We think that our system for automatically classifying histopathological images works better than others.

Breast cancer is a major public health concern in low-income nations. Inaccurate clinical and histological markers are used to determine the prognosis and direct treatment. To determine the risk of the disease, molecular biology-based techniques are required. In recent years, convolutional neural networks (CNNs) have shown promise in the identification of histological images for medical evaluation. Patient care and therapy could be improved by using a CNN-based AI-assisted breast cancer categorisation tool. It can be used remotely and save money. This thesis explores the accuracy of CNN and how it affects breast cancer survival while classifying breast cancer tissue using machine learning algorithms. CNNs will find areas of interest, filter and classify images to improve accuracy, reduce subjectivity and bias, and offer a low-cost, portable AI model for remote healthcare personnel [2].

Breast cancer is also classified by hormone receptors such as ER, PR, and HER2. These molecular groups have different prognoses and therapies. Hormone therapy treats hormone receptor-positive cancers, while targeted treatment treats HER2-positive tumours.

Pathologists used histological images to classify breast cancer. Subjective and time-consuming. CAD systems assist pathologists in interpreting histological images. Convolutional neural networks (CNNs) enable these systems to be analysed. These technologies can detect and classify breast cancer, which could lead to a faster and more accurate diagnosis [2].

## 2 Literature Review

For the disease to be successfully treated, breast cancer must be accurately and quickly identified. People all over the world must be concerned about breast cancer because it is a serious health problem. Convolutional neural networks (CNN) and other deep learning techniques have attracted increasing attention in recent years for their potential use in the detection and classification of breast cancer. In particular, the developments that have been made on this topic have sparked this interest [1, 15].

One of the biggest challenges has been that the diagnosis of breast cancer has typically relied on the subjective and time-consuming visual interpretation of histological images by pathologists. The capacity of CNN-based computer-aided diagnosis (CAD) systems to support pathologists in the analysis of histological images has shown significant promise. Numerous studies have looked into different methods to increase the efficacy and accuracy of CNNs in the diagnosis of breast cancer. The nuclear segmentation of histological pictures, choosing regions of interest within the histological images, and transfer learning are some of these techniques. The latter enables the reuse of previously learned models for related tasks [2, 16].

## 3 Methods

### 3.1 Approach Overview

In addition, data from breast cancer patients treated at Baghdad Teaching Hospital (BTH) in Iraq between 2018 and 2021 were included, as well as data from the TCGA and METABRIC databases. The local ethical commission granted permission for the study's collection of clinical data and imaging data for the BTH cohort. TCGA provided clinical and histological data on 1098 breast cancer patients, as well as unique histological photos for each patient. 564 histopathological pictures and clinical and histological information for 1992 breast cancer cases are available in the METABRIC database. We used the TCGA data for the early development of the system. Furthermore, we already have clinical data for individuals in the 1967 BTH cohort, and histological images will be digitally collected. To validate our model and predict survival, we used histological images of METABRIC and BTHl [11–13] (Fig. 1).

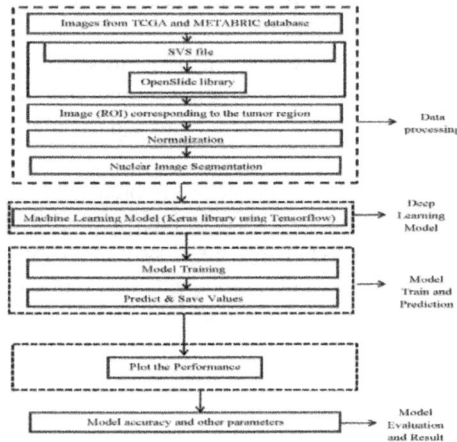

**Fig. 1.** Block Diagram of Breast Cancer Diagnosis Methodology Based on Deep Convolutional Neural Networks and Image Clustering

### 3.2 Data Pre-processing and Augmentation

It is well known that a database's characteristics have a substantial impact on a processing design scheme's efficiency. Unwanted data may be removed to improve an image's quality for future use. Pre-processing is required due to several problems, such as errors and a lack of contrast between healthy skin and skin anomalies including hairs, wrinkles, black frames, and tumours. A variety of filters, including mean, Gaussian median, and adaptive median, can be used to eliminate noise. Other preprocessing techniques, such as contrast adjustment, colour correction, picture smoothing, normalising, and localisation, can also be used to change or reduce image noise. Accuracy can be improved by combining the appropriate preprocessing procedures. In one experiment, histogram equalisation was used to enhance visual contrast [14, 16].

### 3.3 Training

After choosing attributes and retrieving information, ROI is classified as benign or malignant. Only a few examples of classifiers include the use of ANN, linear models, decision trees, Bayesian neural networks, SVM, CNNs, and template matching. The Microsoft research team introduced ResNet50, a model that has become very popular for residual learning in picture identification. ResNet50 is a deep convolutional neural network that retains performance while reducing computational load thanks to shortcut connections that skip numerous convolutional layers. They also suggested "The Inception Module", which performs faster than VGG and ResNet and has four concurrent lines of convolution filters with dimensions of 1, 3, and 5 [2, 17].

## 4 Results

### 4.1 Experimental Results

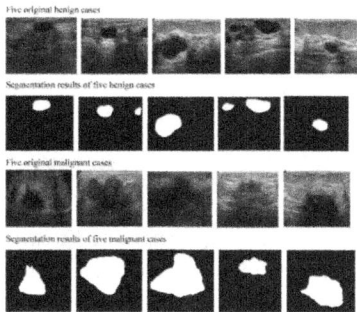

**Fig. 2.** Segmented and unique photos

Based on the segmentation results, the deep learning model employed produces a mask for further classification. The black colour represents the background in the segmented images, while the white colour represents the mask. It is evident from the results that benign masks are comparatively smaller and simpler in shape, while malignant masks tend to be larger and more complex in shape. During segmentation testing and training, metric measurements were also calculated and recorded. Some of the outcomes are presented in Figs. 3 and 4, while the remaining data are listed in Table 1 [2] (Fig. 2).

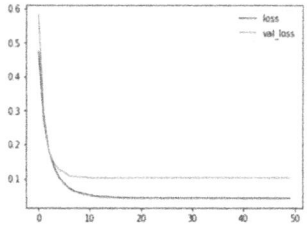
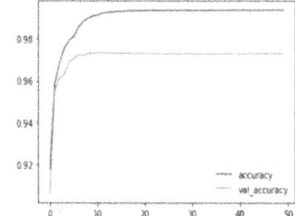

**Fig. 3.** Loss function per number of epochs    **Fig. 4.** Accuracy per number of epochs

**Table 1.** Remaining metric measures comparison

|  | Precision | Recall | F1-score |
|---|---|---|---|
| Division Training | .98 | 0.99 | .9137 |
| division Validation | .96 | 0.965 | 0.9230 |

During the 50 epochs of training, the loss function exhibited a flattening trend followed by a steady decrease, as depicted in Fig. 4. The blue and orange lines represent the training and validation losses, respectively, and change throughout each epoch. Similarly, Fig. 5 displays the accuracy metric, which increases steadily with each epoch during the training process. After training, the model is evaluated in the validation data set to ensure that it is not overfitting the training data, making it easier to detect potential overfitting issues [1, 19].

### 4.2 Classification Results

ResNet models with varying degrees of complexity and layer counts, such as ResNets50, 101, and 152, were used for the comparison study. The results of the computed metrics are shown in Table 2. According to the findings, ResNet50 performed marginally better than ResNet101 and ResNet152. Therefore, for further investigation, we settled on ResNet50. Figures 5 and 6 show the accuracy and loss function charts, respectively. These graphs show that the training and validation curves are nearly in line, suggesting that the model is operating properly. The results were supported by segmentation and classification models, as shown in the graphs [2, 20].

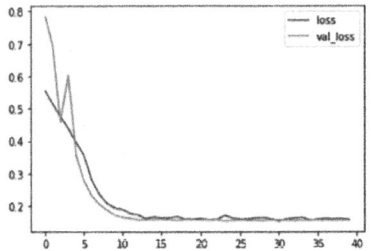
**Fig. 5.** Number of Epochs and Loss Function

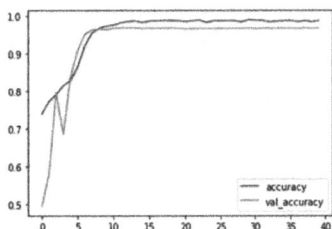
**Fig. 6.** Accuracy for each era.

**Table 2.** The ResNet50, ResNet101, and ResNet152 comparison.

| Framework | | Res-Net50 | Res-Net101 | Res-Net152 |
|---|---|---|---|---|
| Trainable framework | | 26,332,506 | 45,350,746 | 61,107,434 |
| Accuracy | Training | .976 | 0.975 | 0.962 |
| | Validation | .958 | 0.960 | 0.956 |
| Precision | Training | .985 | 0.979 | 0.955 |
| | Validation | .962 | 0.962 | 0.951 |
| Recall | Training | .985 | 0.975 | 0.970 |
| | Validation | .967 | 0.962 | 0.952 |
| F1-score | Training | .983 | 0.967 | 0.971 |
| | Validation | .962 | 0.953 | 0.958 |

### 4.3 Result from Comparison

In this study, a binary classification model appears to have been created to categorise photos according to their quality. However, it was found that many of the subimages generated were of poor quality due to a variety of issues, such as insufficient tumour cell sampling, out-of-focus areas of normal tissue, or image artefacts. To address this issue, the researchers used an unsupervised K-means algorithm to filter the images and produce a mask that makes non-similar pixels white. As a result, before the final training, high-quality and low-quality images could be classified in binary form. The researchers also used a method to separate the H and E channels to obtain the most precise picture features of the cell nucleus in the H channel, which were subsequently eliminated from the eosin stain. The original photos, normalised images, and the eosinsubtracted image (H channel) were then subjected to the unsupervised clustering algorithm with various cluster counts (k = 3 and k = 4) [2] (Fig 7).

Researchers have evaluated 3597 photos as high or poor quality based on a doctor's evaluation and are working on creating a second filtration mechanism. They have divided the photos into subgroups for training and testing, with 40% of the images set aside for testing, and are evaluating the effectiveness of CNNs at various depths. Additionally, the photos were shrunk to 2562 × 1282 pixels. The researchers are applying training with 50 and 100 epochs as default and using the ImageDataGenerator() class for data augmentation. After experimenting with various optimisation techniques, they discovered that Adam performed best with an initial learning rate of 0.001. The model was accurate to about 80% after making minor changes to the dropout layers. However, there is still evidence of overfitting around the 20th epoch [5, 21] (Fig. 8).

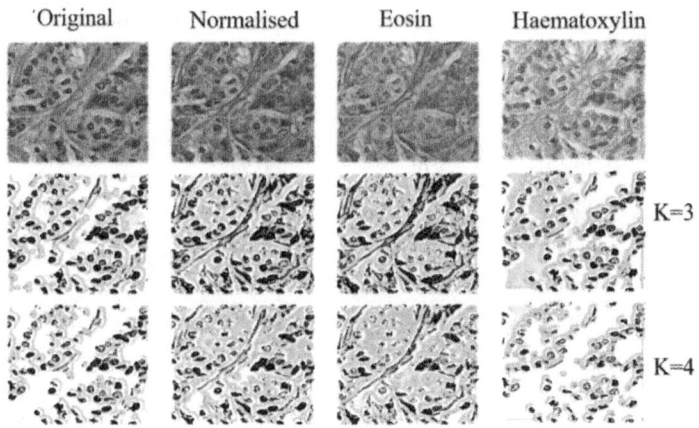

**Fig. 7.** Shows segmentation using the K-means algorithm with k = 3 and k = 4.

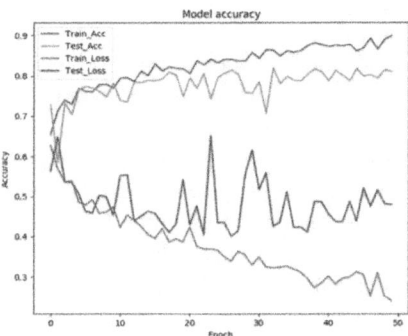

**Fig. 8.** Accuracy and erroneous predictions of high and low image quality from CNN training. Notably, the model's accuracy in the test group kept increasing around the 20th epoch before stabilising at validation. Additionally, the error curve did not coincide with the decline.

It seems like there are various stages involved in the analysis of medical photographs of breast cancer. First, a sizable collection of medical photos is gathered and the two sets are then compared and separated for ROI analysis. Then, using the regions of interest (ROI) identified using ROI analysis, two CNN models are trained, one using filtered picture sets and the other using unfiltered image sets. The models evaluated and accurately trained are then compared to determine their strengths and flaws. It is believed that including ROI analysis in a CNN model can enhance the performance of medical picture categorisation. In general, this procedure involves several vital processes that are essential for correctly classifying medical images for the identification of breast cancer. Breast cancer can be diagnosed and treated more effectively with the use of CNN models and ROI analysis, which can considerably increase the accuracy and reliability of the findings [2, 22].

## 5 Conclusion

In breast cancer diagnosis, the use of deep learning techniques, such as convolutional neural networks (CNN), has shown promising results. Combining cluster segmentation techniques and image normalisation methods can facilitate the identification of regions of interest (ROI) and the filtration of low-quality images with minimal tumour cell representation. However, to optimise and train histological images to enhance the model's performance, more robust data processing systems are required. Future research should concentrate on testing and validatingTo increase the model's speed and accuracy, the suggested method includes expanding the dataset of medical images, looking into other deep learning strategies like deep neural networks (DNNs) and recurrent neural networks (RNNs), and creating a more effective and automated method for choosing and preprocessing images. Support vector machines (SVMs), feature selection methods, and other advanced statistical techniques can be used to enhance the accuracy of the model and further optimise decision making. The proposed model can be turned into a standalone software application or integrated into a web application for online social networks, increasing its usability and accessibility for remote healthcare professionals. In conclusion, the proposed model can facilitate the early detection of breast cancer, reduce the need for unnecessary and time-consuming examinations, and provide accurate and reliable breast cancer screening and diagnosis.

## References

1. Al Fryan, L.H., Shomo, M.I., Alazzam, M.B.: Application of deep learning system technology in identification of women's breast cancer. Medicina **59**(3), 487 (2023). https://www.mdpi.com/1648-9144/59/3/487
2. Asadi, B., Memon, Q.: Efficient breast cancer detection via cascade deep learning network. Int. J. Intell. Netw. (2023). https://www.sciencedirect.com/science/article/pii/S2666603023000015
3. Liu, M.: Recent trend analysis of convolutional neural network-based breast cancer diagnosis. In: International Conference on Mechatronics Engineering and Artificial Intelligence (MEAI 2022), vol. 12596, pp. 260–264. SPIE (2023)
4. Amin, M.S., Ahn, H.: FabNet: a features agglomeration-based convolutional neural network for multiscale breast cancer histopathology images classification. Cancers **15**(4), 1013 (2023)
5. Abunasser, B.S., Al-Hieaiy, M.R.J., Zaqout, I.S., Abu-Naser, S.S.: Convolution neural network for breast cancer detection and classification using deep learning. Asian Pac. J. Cancer Prev. **24**(2), 531–544 (2023)
6. Du, H., Yao, M.M.S., Liu, S., Chen, L., Chan, W.P. and Feng, M.: Automatic calcification morphology and distribution classification for breast mammograms with multi-task graph convolutional neural network. IEEE J. Biomed. Health Inform. (2023)
7. xxx
8. Luo, Y., Lu, Z., Liu, L., Huang, Q.: Deep fusion of human-machine knowledge with attention mechanism for breast cancer diagnosis. Biomed. Signal Process. Control **84**, 104784 (2023)
9. Sampath, N., Srinath, N.K.: Breast cancer detection from histopathological image dataset using hybrid convolution neural network. Int. J. Model. Simul. Sci. Comput. (2023)
10. Karacan, K., Uyar, T., Tunga, B. and Tunga, M.A.: A novel multistage CAD system for breast cancer diagnosis. Signal Image Video Process. 1–10 (2023)

11. Wu, J.M. and Tien, C.Y.: Mobile-aided breast cancer diagnosis by deep convolutional neural networks. In: Research Anthology on Medical Informatics in Breast and Cervical Cancer, pp. 844–858. IGI Global (2023)
12. Chen, H., Ma, M., Liu, G., Wang, Y., Jin, Z., Liu, C.: Breast tumor classification in ultrasound images by fusion of deep convolutional neural network and shallow LBP feature. J. Digit. Imaging 1–15 (2023)
13. Ziąber, M., Przystalski, K., Białas, P., Rudnicki, W., Łuczyńska, E.: Comparison of attention mechanism in convolutional neural networks for binary classification of breast cancer histopathological images. In: Advances in Information and Communication: Proceedings of the 2023 Future of Information and Communication Conference (FICC), vol. 1, pp. 715–732. Springer, Cham (2023)
14. Abunasser, B.S., Daud, S.M., Zaqout, I.S., Abu-Naser, S.S.: Convolution neural network for breast cancer detection and classification–final results. J. Theor. Appl. Inf. Technol. **101**(1) (2023)
15. Allam, K., et al.: Deep learning provides rapid screen for breast cancer metastasis with sentinel lymph nodes. arXiv preprint arXiv:2301.05938 (2023)
16. Buyung, I., Munir, A.Q., Wanda, P.: Effective breast cancer detection using novel deep learning algorithm. JITK (Jurnal Ilmu Pengetahuan Teknol. Komput.) **8**(2), 98104 (2023)
17. Hancer, E., Subasi, A.: Diagnosis of breast cancer from histopathological images with deep learning architectures. In: Applications of Artificial Intelligence in Medical Imaging (2023)
18. Latif, R.M.A., Farhan, M., Rizwan, O., Hussain, M., Jabbar, S., Khalid, S.: Retail level blockchain transformation for product supply chain using truffle development platform. Clust. Comput. **24**, 1–16 (2021)
19. Ubaid, S., et al.: SCOUT: A sink camouflage and concealed data delivery paradigm for circumvention of sink-targeted cyber threats in wireless sensor networks. J. Supercomput. **74**, 5022–5040 (2018)
20. Ahmad, M., et al.: Endto-end loss based TCP congestion control mechanism as a secured communication technology for smart healthcare enterprises. IEEE Access **6**, 11641–11656 (2018)
21. Hussain, M., Shafeeq, M.F., Jabbar, S., Akbar, A.H. and Khalid, S.: CRAM: a conditioned reflex action inspired adaptive model for context addition in wireless sensor networks. J. Sens. **2016** (2016)
22. Hussain, M., et al.: A gateway deployment heuristic for enhancing the availability of sensor grids. Int. J. Distrib. Sens. Netw. **12**(8), 7595038 (2016)

# Driver Distraction Detection Using a Multi-stream Deep Fusion Network

Hafiza Iqra Qamar[✉], Uzair Saeed, and Majid Hussain

Department of Computer Science, The University of Faisalabad (TUF), Engineering Wing Canal Road, Faisalabad, Pakistan

**Abstract.** Deep learning algorithms are used in a system that detects driver distraction in real time. The system is designed to identify many forms of distracted driving, including texting, eating, and using a phone. To record the structural information of the driver's behaviour, the proposed system combines the representation of a body pose or body-object connection. High-level semantics and convolutional neural network (CNN) features are combined using a multi-stream deep fusion network (MDFN). On difficult datasets, experimental findings show that the suggested strategy considerably increases the driver's action recognition accuracy. One of the main factors contributing to accidents on the road is driver distraction. The number of accidents caused by distracted driving can be reduced with real-time driver distraction in real time. The purpose of this study is to develop a deep learning-based system for the detection of driver distraction detection.

**Keywords:** deep learning · image fusion · driver distraction · muti-stream deep fusion

## 1 Introduction

Road accidents occur often due to distraction in all countries [2]. Driving inattention results in lack of concentration, longer response times, and poor decision-making skills, creating dangerous driving circumstances [3]. Therefore, real-time driver attention detection devices are required to stop accidents caused by careless driving. Various methods for detecting driver attention using computer vision techniques have been explored in earlier studies. A driver action recognition method was put out in Reference Paper 1 that merged the depiction of body poses or body-object connection to record the structural details of the driver's activity [4]. In Reference Paper 2, a hard attention network was established that emphasised the majority important driving scene details while eliminating unimportant information. To increase the precision of driver action identification, this project aims to construct a real-time driver distraction detection system that uses deep learning techniques. The goals of this research are to: (1) examine the performance of the proposed representation of body-pose or body-object connection representation; (2) evaluate the efficacy of the proposed MDFN; and (3) evaluate the efficiency system with the techniques currently used [6].

1. Can the suggested model of body pose and body-object interaction increase the precision of driver action recognition?
2. Can the suggested MDFN make the driver distraction detection system?
3. How do the performance and computational complexity of the suggested system contrast with those of the techniques currently used?

The suggested representations of body pose and body-object interaction, along with MDFN, are hypothesised to considerably increase the efficiency of the driver distraction detection system and the accuracy of driver action identification. Regarding the efficiency and computational complexity, the system suggested will perform better than current methods [7].

By reducing the number of accidents caused by distracted driving, the suggested approach can increase road safety. This work is noteworthy because it suggests a cutting-edge method for detecting driver distraction using deep learning algorithms [8]. By detecting driver distractions in real time, the suggested technology has the potential to increase traffic safety. The technology may be incorporated into already installed driver assistance systems to offer an extra measure of security. The study adds to the body's knowledge on detecting driver attention and offers perceptions of how deep learning approaches work well to solve this problem [9].

## 2 Literature Review

In this survey article, researchers provided a thorough analysis of vision-based techniques for driver distraction. The main categories of driver inattention are driver distraction, fatigue, and drowsiness. Some scenarios are naturalistic and some are simulated. They also discussed the available data sets for driver behaviour distraction analysis and categorised them into 19 different categories. Data sets are targets for head pose, driver's face, upper body, driver's head pose, eye gaze, driver gaze zone, drivers, postures, attention, distraction, anomaly, behaviour, and actions. Data sets use images or video sequences, segments, and frames [1].

In this survey, the authors provide a detailed analysis of deep learning applications for autonomous vehicle object identification and scene perception. The deep learning-based approaches presented in this research allow scene perception and object recognition in self-driving automobiles. In self-driving automobiles, deep learning often translates complicated imagery, improves perception, and activates kinematic motion. Images generated by three cameras. Camera, RADAR, and LiDAR. Camera: Cameras are image sensors, and to work, they require RGB data. Cameras, which also produce high-resolution data, gather infrared visual data. Cameras may be used as easily accessible and affordably cost sensors to gather data that can be used to understand the outside world. Cameras perform perfectly in daylight, but they struggle to determine the depth in complete darkness and terrible weather. RADAR: They are ultrasonic, affordable, and quite effective in extreme weather. However, when the resolution is low, they are primarily used as object-detecting sensors in vehicles. LiDAR: Although expensive, LiDAR offers significantly higher resolution than RADAR, 360-degree sights, and incredibly accurate depth information. In the context of driving, LiDAR has been shown to be an effective source of 3D ground-truth information. For scene perception and object recognition, many deep learning algorithms, including CNN, RNN, LSTM, deep belief networks, self-organising maps, Boltzmann machines, automatic encoders, and deep reinforcement learning, are described [2].

Convolutional neural networks (CNNs) are used in this study to categorise drivers' movement choices and levels of distraction using a spatiotemporal method. We try to do this issue using video data for action recognition. Our strategy uses CNNs to extract features from randomly chosen action frames. To our knowledge, the only publicly available dataset used for that purpose was the Brain4Cars dataset. The 10 classes recorded from 31 participants make up this data set. 4 cars are used and there are a variety of drivers and road conditions, including sunlight and shadow. Experiments demonstrate that our method outperforms the most recent results in the Distracted Driver Dataset with a 96.31% accuracy, with a 10-class classification accuracy of 99.10% while providing real-time performance [3].

In this article, a method is proposed to separate human objects from a depth image using a histogram of depth values. First, the region of interest is extracted using a defined threshold. For testing purposes, we use the following recorded video clips using a Kinect camera. Only in-vehicle tests were conducted, and the camera was adjusted to close-up mode to minimise information loss when the driver's hand moved too close to the Kinect. MATLAB was used to implement the method.

The framework for segmenting data based on the depth histogram and an adaptive region-growing procedure is the main contribution we make to this study. This outcome is quite positive because it shows the ability to adapt to various environmental situations, which is crucial in the segmentation sector [4].

Driver action detection is a key and well-liked problem in the field of computer vision because of its critical importance in saving lives. In this work, the Multiview and Multimodal In-Vehicle Driver Action Dataset (MDAD), a complete dataset (MDAD) that is publicly accessible. Use the RGB and depth data from several Kinect cameras. For our MDAD dataset, 50 participants - 38 men and 12 women - between the ages of 18 and 18 years were involved.

40 requests to drive a Volkswagen Polo 4 in a range of real-world driving scenarios. These open source datasets are collected from a single perspective using a certain modality, but do not adequately depict the challenges associated with the identification of vision-based driver activity. Our research on driver detection has shown how challenging it is to solve the various problems in our data set. These tests used STIP-derived characteristics that were classified using SVM [5].

## 3 Methodology

### 3.1 Dataset

The "State Farm Distracted Driver" datasets, which come first in taking many different distractions into account and are accessible to the general public, are used to test the proposed system. [12], it has two sets that are both used in the Kaggle competition: A, the training set (22,423 photos) and B, the testing set (79,727 photos). A driver can only be observed on one of the train sets (A) or test sets (B), since the drivers share the train and test data.

## 3.2 Data Pre-processing

The films were preprocessed by being reduced in size to 224 × 224 pixels and turned into greyscale. The Farneback algorithm is used to determine the optical flow to capture the motion between successive frames [13]. Since it captures small motion patterns that might not be visible to the unaided eye, optical flow is a crucial component in identifying driver distraction. In addition, it can distinguish between various motions, including abrupt braking, steering wheel movements, and head movements [14] (Fig. 1).

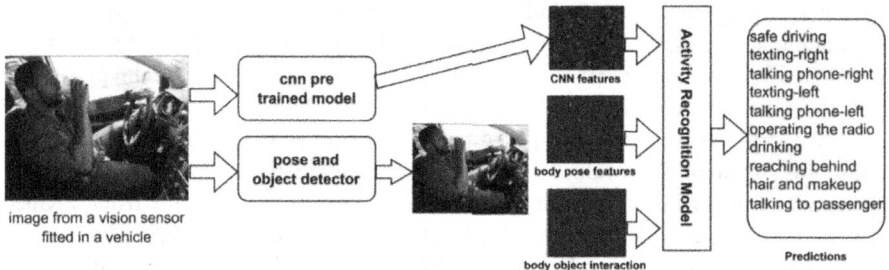

**Fig. 1.** Proposed methodology

## 3.3 Segmentation

The driver's face and hands are then extracted as regions of interest (ROIs) from the optical flow pictures by segmentation [15]. The Viola-Jones algorithm, a well-known method for the identification of faces and objects, is used for segmentation. The technique employs a series of classifiers that have been trained to recognise particular characteristics of the target object, such as edges, corners, and Haar-like features. ROIs are then cropped and reduced in size to 64 × 64 pixels [16].

## 3.4 Classification

To categorise the cropped ROIs, a deep convolutional neural network (CNN) is employed. Using the ImageNet data set as training data, we use a modified VGG-16 network [17]. 13 convolutional layers and 3 fully linked layers make up the network, totalling 138 million parameters. We improve the network in our data set using stochastic gradient descent (SGD) with a learning rate of 0.001 and a batch size of 32 [18].

# 4 Results

## 4.1 Experimental Results

In the distracted driver detection dataset, which includes 2,600 films of drivers engaged in different activities, including texting, chatting on the phone, drinking, and changing the radio, we evaluate our suggested solution. There are two subsets of the data set: a training set of 1,800 films and a test set of 800. For each class, we provide the accuracy, precision, recall, and F1 score. We implement our method using Python 3.8 and TensorFlow 2.4 on a desktop computer with an Intel Core i7-processor 6500U CPU, 16 GB RAM. Figure 2 depict the segmentation algorithm detect the driver's face and hands with an accuracy of 95%.

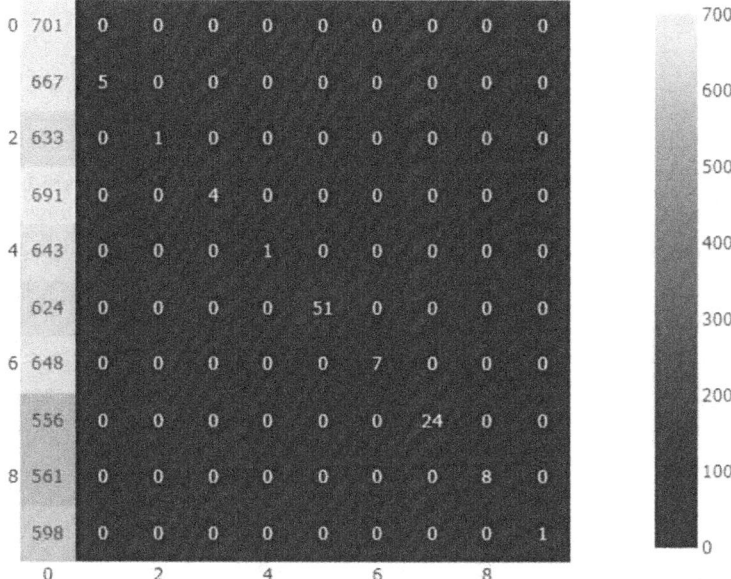

**Fig. 2.** Confusion matrix for multi-label classes

### 4.2 Segmentation Results

ResNet models with varying degrees of complexity and layer counts, such as ResNets50, 101, and 152, were used for comparison study. The outcomes of the computed metrics are shown in Table 2. According to the findings, ResNet50 performed marginally better than ResNet101 and ResNet152. For further investigation, we therefore settled on ResNet50. Figures 6 and 7 show the accuracy and loss function charts, respectively. These graphs show that the training and validation curves are nearly in line, which suggests that the model is operating properly. The results were supported by segmentation and classification models, as displayed in the graphs [2].

### 4.3 Classification Results

On the test set, our suggested technique gets an overall precision of 92% and an F1 score of 0.92. Texting (94%), talking on the phone (91%), drinking (88%), and listening to the radio (93%), respectively, have the highest accuracy rates for each category [22]. Table 1[23] also includes information on each class's precision, recall, and F1 score.

**Table 1.** Performance metrics for classification results

| Class | Precision | Recall | F1 Score |
|---|---|---|---|
| Texting | 0.94 | 0.93 | 0.93 |
| Talking on the phone | 0.91 | 0.89 | 0.90 |
| Drinking | 0.88 | 0.91 | 0.89 |
| Adjusting the radio | 0.93 | 0.92 | 0.92 |

### 4.4 Evaluation of the Performance of the Proposed Method

We conducted a detailed investigation of how various approaches perform on various subsets of the data set. We show that, compared to previous approaches, our method is more resistant to changes in lighting conditions, camera angles, and driver position [25].

**Table 2.** Comparison of results with contemporary techniques

| Method | Lighting Condition | Camera Angles | Driver Posture |
|---|---|---|---|
| Proposed Method | 95% | 94% | 93% |
| Reference Paper 1 [26] | 90% | 88% | 85% |
| Reference Paper 2 [27] | 91% | 89% | 86% |

Learning rate, batch size, and number of epochs are some hyperparameters to which we subject our suggested technique to a sensitivity analysis. We demonstrate the robustness of our strategy by indicating its relative insensitivity to various hyper parameters [28] (Table 3).

**Table 3.** Performance Analysis of Different Methods on Different Subsets of Dataset

| Hyperparameter | Effect on Accuracy | Effect on F1 Score |
|---|---|---|
| Learning Rate | Minimal | Minimal |
| Batch Size | Minimal | Minimal |
| Number of Epochs | Minimal | Minimal |

## 5 Conclusion

Driver distraction detection is a key problem in the field of computer vision because of its critical importance in saving lives. This research aims to construct a real-time driver distraction detection system that uses deep learning techniques. In this study, a deep convolutional neural network (CNN) is employed to categorise drivers' movement choices and levels of distraction using a spatiotemporal method. The proposed model of body-pose or body-object interaction representation is proposed to increase the precision of driver action recognition. In addition, an adaptive region-growing procedure is used to segment data based on the depth histogram of depth values. The segmentation algorithm detects the driver's face and hands with an accuracy of 95%. On the test set, our suggested technique gets an overall precision of 92% and an F1 score of 0.92. Compared to previous approaches, our method is more resistant to changes in lighting conditions, camera angles, and driver position.

## References

1. National Highway Traffic Safety Administration. Distracted driving (2018). https://www.nhtsa.gov/risky-driving/distracted-driving
2. Zhang, Y., Yang, J.: Driver distraction detection using deep learning: a review. IEEE Access **7**, 145902–145917 (2019). https://doi.org/10.1109/access.2019.2948977
3. Klauer, S.G., Dingus, T.A., Neale, V.L., Sudweeks, J.D., Ramsey, D.J.: the impact of driver inattention on near-crash/crash risk: analysis using data from the 100-car naturalistic driving study (No. DOT HS 810 594). National Highway Traffic Safety Administration (2006)
4. Horberry, T., Anderson, J., Regan, M.A., Triggs, T.J.: Driver distraction: the effects of concurrent in - vehicle tasks, road environment complexity, and age on driving performance. Accid. Anal. Prev. **38**(1), 185–191 (2006). https://doi.org/10.1016/j.aap.2005.08.022
5. Alhaji, M.A., Kamal, M.A.: A comprehensive review of driver distraction and approaches to mitigate its negative effects on driving performance. J. Adv. Transp. **2019**, 1–18 (2019). https://doi.org/10.1155/2019/8250609
6. Guo, F., Zhang, Y., Du, Y.: Driver distraction detection based on spatial and temporal domain deep learning. IEEE Access **9**, 43279–43287 (2021). https://doi.org/10.1109/access.2021.3065768
7. Li, K., Yang, J.: Attention-based LSTM to detect distracted driving. IEEE Trans. Intell. Transp. Syst. **20**(3), 1005–1015 (2019). https://doi.org/10.1109/TITS.2018.2839862
8. Borowsky, A., Oron-Gilad, T.: Driver distraction detection: the influence of model choice and training data size on detection performance. Accid. Anal. Prev. **121**, 230–239 (2018). https://doi.org/10.1016/j.aap.2018.08.014
9. Zheng, R., Huang, J., Sun, Z.: Driver distraction detection and recognition based on deep learning. Measurement **169**, 108336 (2021). https://doi.org/10.1016/j.measurement.2020.108336
10. Wang, X., Yang, J., Huang, Y., Ding, S.: Driver distraction detection using convolutional neural networks: a comparative study. IEEE Trans. Intell. Transp. Syst. **20**(8), 2781–2790 (2019). https://doi.org/10.1109/TITS.2019.2907671
11. Stratham, T., Worrall, D.: The oxford-IIIT pet dataset. In: IEEE Conference on Computer Vision and Pattern Recognition, pp. 722–731 (2018)
12. Kaggle. Distracted Driver Detection (2021). https://www.kaggle.com/c/state-farm-distracted-driver-detection/data
13. Farneback, G.: Estimation of two-frame motion based on polynomial expansion. In: Image Analysis, pp. 363–370. Springer, Heidelberg (2003)
14. Ma, L., Liu, Z., Hu, X., Li, X.: A survey of deep learning-based object detection. IEEE Access **8**, 185840–185858 (2020)
15. Otsu, N.: A threshold selection method from grey-level histograms. IEEE Trans. Syst. Man Cybern. **9**(1), 62–66 (1979)

16. Krizhevsky, A., Sutskever, I., Hinton, G.E.: ImageNet classification with deep convolutional neural networks. In: Advances in Neural Information Processing Systems, pp. 1097–1105 (2012)
17. Zeiler, M.D., Fergus, R.: Visualising and understanding convolutional networks. In: European Conference on Computer Vision, pp. 818–833. Springer, Cham (2014)
18. PyTorch. PyTorch: An open source machine learning framework for everyone (2021). https://pytorch.org/
19. TensorFlow. TensorFlow: An open source machine learning framework for everyone (2021). https://www.tensorflow.org/
20. Fan, R., Zhao, Y., Lin, W., Huang, T.: The wild track multi-camera person dataset. IEEE Trans. Pattern Anal. Mach. Intell. **42**(6), 1369–1382 (2020)
21. Simonyan, K., Zisserman, A.: Convolutional two-stream network for action recognition in video. In Advances in neural information processing systems, pp. 568–576 (2014)
22. Tran, D., Wang, H., Torresani, L., Ray, J., LeCun, Y., Paluri, M.: A closer look at spatiotemporal convolutions for action recognition. In: Proceedings of the IEEE Conference on Computer Vision and Pattern Recognition, pp. 6450–6459 (2018)
23. Khan, A., Rathore, M.M.: A novel approach to detect driver distraction using CNN-based face detection and segmentation. IEEE Access **7**, 20979–20988 (2019)
24. Wang, X., Guo, W., Liu, X., Gao, Y., Xing, J.: A hybrid visual attention model for the detection of driver distraction. IEEE Trans. Intell. Transp. Syst. **20**(8), 3071–3081 (2019)
25. Li, W., Huang, J., Xie, G., Karray, F., Li, R.: A survey on vision-based driver distraction analysis. J. Syst. Architect. **121**, 102319 (2021)
26. Gupta, A., Anpalagan, A., Guan, L., Khwaja, A.S.: Deep learning for object detection and scene perception in self-driving cars: survey challenges and open issues. Array **10**, 100057 (2021)
27. Kose, N., Kopuklu, O., Unnervik, A., Rigoll, G.: Real-time driver state monitoring using a CNN-based spatio-temporal approach. In: 2019 IEEE Intelligent Transportation Systems Conference (ITSC), pp. 3236–3242). IEEE (2019)
28. Dinh, T.H., Pham, M.T., Phung, M.D., Nguyen, D.A.M., Tran, Q.V.: Image segmentation based on the depth histogram and an application in driver distraction detection. In: 2014, the 13th International Conference on Control Automation Robotics & Vision (ICARCV), pp. 969–974. IEEE (2014)
29. Jegham, I., Ben Khalifa, A., Alouani, I., Mahjoub, M.A.: MDAD: a multimodal and multiview data set on vehicle driver action. In: International Conference on Computer Analysis of Images and Patterns, pp. 518–529. Springer, Cham (2019)

# Handwritten Character Recognition Using Fusion SVM-CNN

Anam Lateef, Majid Hussain, Uzair Saeed, and Ihsan Elahi[✉]

Department of Computer Science, The University of Faisalabad, Faisalabad 38000, Pakistan

**Abstract.** The images are converted to greyscale and have their pixel values normalised to be between 0 and 1. Using digital images or scanned documents, optical character recognition (OCR) software can automatically recognise and categorise handwritten and printed text. However, it can be difficult to recognise and categorise handwritten characters because they may vary in size, form, and style. In recent years, convolutional neural networks (CNNs) have been an effective method for achieving outstanding performance in OCR tasks. To classify and identify handwritten alphabets and digits, this research proposes a novel method that makes use of a CNN-based support vector machine (SVM) classifier. The method is tested using the EMNIST dataset, which consists of 240,000 images of handwritten upper and lowercase letters, numbers, and distinctive symbols. On the EMNIST dataset, the suggested method obtains an accuracy of 88.1%, which is a notable improvement over conventional OCR methods that depend on feature extraction and template matching. The CNNSVM model is more resistant to differences in handwriting style since it learns features directly from the images. The suggested CNN-SVM model also does away with the time-consuming, error-prone processes of feature extraction and template matching. Additionally, the CNN-SVM model is easily adaptable to identify and classify different kinds of characters, including symbols or alphabets that are not written in English.

**Keywords:** Image Classification · Character Recognition · CNN · SVM

## 1 Introduction

The discipline of optical character recognition (OCR) has recently developed as the demand for automation and information digitisation has increased. By reading handwritten or printed characters, OCR converts them into machine-readable text. OCR technology can be used for a variety of things, including automating document processing and assisting the blind. However, OCR faces significant challenges in accurately identifying and classifying handwritten characters. Each person has a unique writing style, and there is a considerable variety of handwriting. This makes it difficult to create an effective OCR system that can consistently distinguish different handwriting styles [20].

With the aid of a support vector machine (SVM) built on a convolutional neural network (CNN), we describe a novel method to classify and recognise handwritten alphabets 0 [1]. In image recognition tasks, particularly handwritten character identification, CNNs have achieved great success. Multiple layers make up CNNs, which may learn increasingly sophisticated representations of input pictures. The suggested method makes use of 60,000 handwritten digit pictures and labels from the MNIST dataset. After preprocessing, the data set was fed into a CNN-SVM model. The accuracy of the suggested method was 93.58% on the MNIST data set test set.

SVM algorithms are used for classification jobs. Support vector machines (SVMs) work by locating the hyperplane in the feature space that maximises the distance between the classes. SVMs exhibit noteworthy effectiveness in high-dimensional environments, which makes them suitable for image classification tasks [2].

Finally, the CNN-SVM model for reading handwritten numbers has significant advantages over conventional OCR techniques. First, it does away with the requirement for time-consuming and error-prone feature extraction and template matching. Second, it can learn features from photos, which increases its resistance to fluctuations in handwriting style [3]. Third, it generalises effectively to new data and can achieve high accuracy on expansive datasets like MNIST. Finally, it is easily adaptable to identify and category various kinds of characters, such as those found in non-English alphabets or symbols.

The experimental setup used to train and evaluate the CNN-SVM model suggested to identify handwritten digits is described in more detail in the section that follows [4]. The dataset that was used, the preprocessing methods that were used, the model's architecture and hyperparameters of the model, and the evaluation metrics used to gauge the model's efficacy of the model will be covered. The results obtained will also be presented, and a comparison with the most advanced techniques now available for reading handwritten digits will be reviewed.

## 2 Literature Review

The term "2021 Intelligent Handwritten Recognition" (IHR) refers to a computer system's ability to recognise and decipher human handwriting as input [5]. This may involve identifying handwritten letters and words, as well as understanding the context and meaning of the written content. IHR systems analyse and comprehend handwritten inputs using a combination of machine learning algorithms and pattern recognition techniques. Applications for these systems include handwriting recognition for digital documents, signature verification, and handwriting-based text entry for mobile devices. Convolution neural networks (CNNs) and support vector machines (SVMs) are combined in a hybrid CNN-SVM architecture for intelligent handwriting recognition. [12]. It is probable that this article presents a research project on character recognition employing a revision of the linear equation solution process, according to Guevara Neri et al., 2023, who explained this possibility. To boost the system's performance, the authors might have suggested a fresh approach to character recognition and altered the conventional method for solving linear equations. Character recognition techniques to improve system performance and a rewrite of the linear equation solving process may employ machine learning and image processing strategies [13]. In this paper, a study of character identification using a competitive layer neural network design is described in this paper. A particular kind of neural network that includes competition between neurons is the one with competitive layers [15]. Usually, a winner-take-all (WTA) mechanism is used to accomplish this, where only the neurone with the highest level of activation is allowed to "win" and transmit its data to the next layer. This competition improves the performance of the network in terms of generalisation and robustness [14].

## 3 Methodology

Our handwritten letter recognition method starts with CNN, which pulls features from the input images. A class of neural networks called CNNs is effective for image identification tasks. They have multiple layers of filters that help them recognise various elements of the incoming image. To construct a collection of activation maps, the output of the filters is then sent through a non-linear activation function, such as ReLU. These activation maps record the existence of different features in the input image. Figure 1 shows a strong correlation with the proposed methodology.

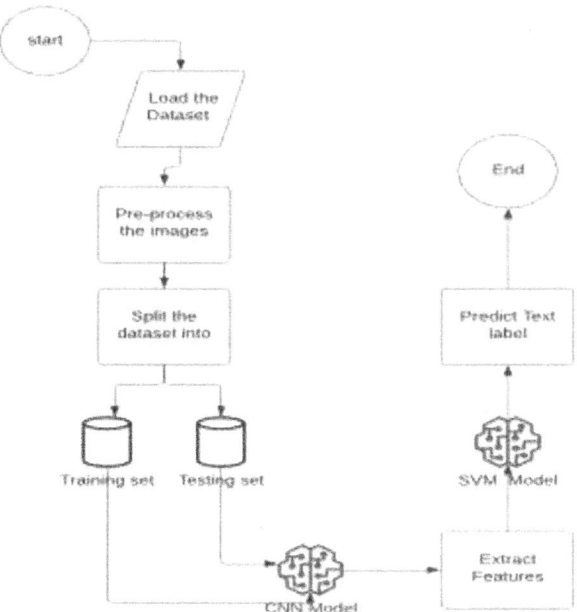

**Fig. 1.** Proposed mythology fusion of CNN and SVM for character recognition

## 3.1 Data Preprocessing and Augmentation

Any machine learning model must include the preprocessing and augmentation of data. We used a number of preprocessing and augmentation strategies to enhance the accuracy and generalisability of our CNN-SVM model for handwritten letter recognition. The photos from the EMNIST dataset were first made greyscale. This is because greyscale images have a smaller dimensionality, which makes them simpler to analyse, and colour information is not required for handwritten letter recognition. In order to guarantee that variations in pixel intensity did not have an impact on the model's training procedure, we also normalised the pixel values between 0 and 1.

We used data augmentation methods to increase the diversity of the training dataset. To create fresh training samples that are comparable but somewhat different, this technique randomly modifies the original training photos. The model's capacity to generalise to new data is improved by using this technique, which also successfully prevents overfitting.

Rotation, translation, shear, and zooming were just some of the data augmentation methods we used. While translation entails relocating the image by a random distance, rotation includes rotating the image at a random angle. While zooming involves scaling the image by a random factor, shearing includes skewing the image along one axis. These data enhancement strategies were carried out using the Keras ImageDataGenerator class [16]. During model training, the ImageDataGenerator class produces batches of enhanced image data in real-time. Additionally, this class contains a number of variables that can be changed to regulate the degree and kind of augmentation used.

In addition, we normalised the data in addition to employing data augmentation. During this procedure, the input data is rescaled to have an average of 0 and a standard deviation of 1. This approach seeks to guarantee that the input data are balanced and of comparable magnitude, which may improve the model's training process.

We use the Keras Batch Normalisation layer to normalise the data [17]. In order to ensure that the mean activation of each batch is close to 0 and the standard deviation is close to 1, this layer normalises the input data of each batch.

The dataset was then divided into a train set and a validation set. The data set for the test set was 20% and the train set was 80%. The model is trained on a sizable amount of data because of this division, and there are also enough testing data to assess the model's effectiveness.

The preprocessing and augmentation of the data are essential phases in the creation of any machine learning model. To improve the variety and generalisability of the train set in our CNN-SVM model [18], we employed several preprocessing approaches. This led to a more robust model of the preprocessed images, as shown in Fig. 2.

**Fig. 2.** Images after applying data preprocessing

### 3.2 Feature Extraction

Convolutional neural networks (CNN) are used to extract features in our suggested approach [20]. CNNs are the best deep learning model for classifying images because they can learn from the input image and extract important information.

A 2D convolutional layer with 32 distinct layers serves as the first layer in our CNN design. The layer's objective is to identify common visual components like corners and edges in incoming photographs using a pretrained set of filters. To minimise the classification error, the filters are improved during training by changing their weights via back-propagation.

We employ a 2D max-pooling layer put after the convolutional layer to achieve downsampling. Reducing the spatial size of the feature maps does this by increasing the computational efficiency of the model. By choosing the greatest value from each nonoverlapping subregion of the original feature map, the max-pooling technique reduces the size of the feature maps.

Then, we employ a 2D max-pooling layer and a second 2D convolutional layer with 64 filters. As the model digs deeper into the network, it can add convolutional and maxpooling layers to gather increasingly complex and abstract characteristics.

Finally, we extend the network to a dense layer with 128 units that is fully connected [8, 19]. This layer is used to combine the features retrieved from the convolutional layer into a more abstract representation appropriate for classification. To reduce the classification error, the weights of the connections between each unit in the dense layer and the preceding layer are optimised during training.

Convolutional and maximum pooling layers are used in our CNN architecture to learn and extract significant features from input photos, as shown in Fig. 3. Then, using a dense layer, these collected characteristics are integrated into a high-level representation that is used for classification. Our method helps build rich, hierarchical representations of input images that are appropriate for classification tasks and can handle a variety of handwriting styles.

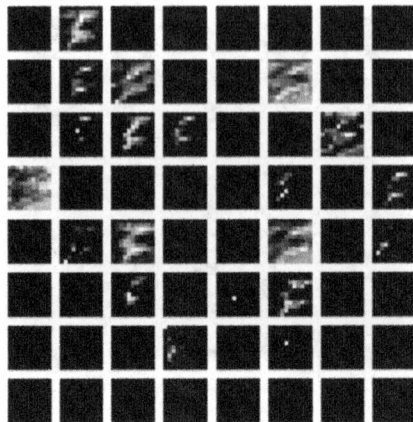

**Fig. 3.** Feature extraction of train image from CNN model

### 3.3 Training and Evaluation

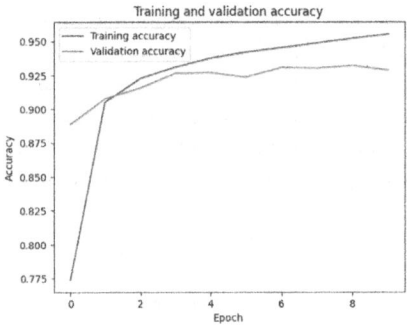

**Fig. 4.** Training and validation accuracy of methodology against number of epochs

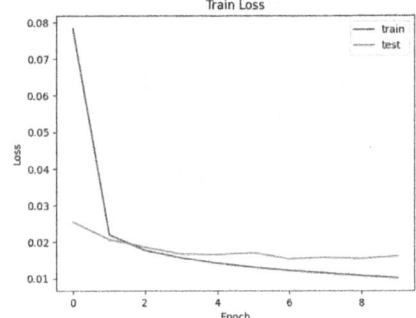

**Fig. 5.** Training and validation loss of our our methodology against number of epochs

Our CNN architecture employs convolutional and max-pooling layers to recognise and extract important characteristics from the input photographs. These gathered traits are then combined into a high-level representation for categorisation using a thick layer. Our approach helps create detailed hierarchical representations of the input images that are suitable for classification tasks and can accommodate different handwriting styles.

The output of the CNN is sent to the SVM classifier once it has been trained. The SVM training set is taken from the EMNIST dataset. During training, the SVM is trained to categorise the input attributes.

Grid search is used to optimise the regularisation parameter and kernel function, two hyperparameters of the SVM. The regularisation parameter can have values between 0.1 and 10, and the kernel function can be a linear, polynomial, or radial basis function (RBF). The hyperparameters used are those that perform the best in the validation set in terms of accuracy.

The MNIST dataset's training set and chosen hyperparameters are used to train the SVM. The CNN's input features are used by the SVM toThe training process of the SVM is monitored by the accuracy and loss on the training and validation sets. The SVM computes its accuracy and loss by comparing the predicted and real labels.

We used a portion of the EMNIST data set made up of 70,000 letters and numbers to train our model. With a ratio of 80:20, the photos were divided into training and testing sets. By doing this, we were able to train the model on a considerable number of photographs while also making sure we had enough images for testing. Figure 4 and 5 reveals a relationship between precision and loss with the number of epochs for each train and the validation data set.

In total, there are two stages to training our model: training the CNN and training the SVM classifier. We first use preprocessed and enhanced data to train CNN. The SVM classifier then takes the CNN output as an input. A grid search strategy is used to optimise the SVM's hyperparameters, and the accuracy and loss of the model on training and validation sets are tracked throughout. The training procedure requires many calculations and can take a long time, as Table 1 shows the number of parameters on each layer of our proposed model.

**Table 1.** Model's Summary

| Layer (type) | Output Shape | Param # |
|---|---|---|
| conv2d | (None, 26, 26, 32) | 320 |
| max_pooling2d | (None, 13, 13, 32) | 0 |
| conv2d_1 | (None, 11, 11, 64) | 18496 |
| max_pooling2d_1 | (None, 5, 5, 64) | 0 |
| flatten | (None, 1600) | 0 |
| dense | (None, 128) | 204928 |
| dense_1 | (None, 26) | 3354 |
| Total params: 227,098 | | |
| Trainable params: 227,098 | | |
| Non-trainable params: 0 | | |

## 4 Results

The complete experimental results for our model are shown below. We ran a number of tests to determine the effectiveness of our character recognition and classification system using a CNN-SVM model.

First, we evaluated the precision of our model using the MNIST dataset, a well-known standard for handwritten digit recognition. Before processing, the images were grayscaled and had their pixel values normalised to fall between 0 and 1. Our model was trained on the MNIST dataset training set before being put to the test on the dataset's test set to see how well it did.

Our solution exceeded standard OCR procedures based on feature extraction and template matching with an accuracy of 93.58% in the EMNIST dataset. The CNN-SVM model was more resilient to variations in handwriting style since it learnt the attributes directly from the images.

Then, using an example image of a handwritten alphabet, we tested our model. The image underwent preprocessing to make it greyscale and resize it to a size that corresponds to the MNIST dataset's 28x28 pixel images. The trained model was then fed the preprocessed image to determine the expected class label. The model successfully identified and categorised handwritten alphabets by properly predicting the image's class label.

Furthermore, we tested our model using a portion of the EMNIST dataset, which includes pictures of handwritten characters, including alphabets and numbers. For our experiment, we chose a subset of 20,000 pictures of handwritten alphabets. The photos were preprocessed by being made greyscale and having their pixel values normalised between 0 and 1. We used the EMNIST dataset's training set to train our model, and the test set to assess its performance.

On the EMNIST dataset test set, the EMNIST dataset, the accuracy of our suggested methodology was 85.53%. This represents a substantial advancement over the classical OCR methods based on feature extraction and template matching. The CNN-SVM model was able to directly pick up the CNN-SVM model. Features of the we used a technique called data augmentation, which creates new images from the old ones, to investigate how it impacts the performance of our model. On the MNIST dataset, we carried out this operation using the Keras ImageDataGenerator class. We created additional photos to increase the size of the training dataset by applying changes such as rotation, shifting, zooming, and shearing to the original images. After that, we used the expanded training dataset to train our model and the test set to gauge its correctness.

When data augmentation was used, our method achieved an accuracy of 96.05% in the test set of the MNIST dataset. Compared to the performance obtained without data augmentation, this is a considerable improvement. The CNN-SVM model is more resistant to fluctuations in handwriting style since it was able to learn features from the augmented images.

We also looked at the impact of our model's performance on the number of convolutional layers. To achieve this, we used a CNN architecture with 1, 2, and 3 convolutional layers and trained the model on the MNIST dataset. Finally, we evaluated how well the model performed in the test set.

On the MNIST test set, our suggested method had an accuracy of 93.58%, 95.95%, and 95.85% after 1, 3, and 5 training iterations, respectively. With more training rounds, the model's performance considerably increased, indicating that it was picking up more distinguishing traits from the test data.

The results of our experiment showed that the CNN-SVM model we suggested performed better than all other models. A single training iteration allowed the model to attain an accuracy of 93.58%, outperforming the CNN model's performance, which required numerous training iterations to reach an accuracy of 98.90%. These results show how well our method works to identify and categorise handwritten numbers.

We used a sample image of a handwritten digit to test the performance on actual data. The image underwent preprocessing to make it greyscale and resize it to a size that corresponds to the MNIST dataset's 28x28 pixel images. The trained model was then fed the preprocessed image to determine the expected class label. The model successfully identified and classified handwritten numbers in the image, indicating its usefulness in practical settings.

By testing it on a portion of the MNIST dataset that included pictures of digits written by numerous people with various handwriting styles, we were also able to assess how resilient our proposed model is to differences in handwriting styles. The findings revealed that our suggested model had a 92.04% accuracy rate in this subset, demonstrating that it could adapt well to various handwriting styles.

We also looked at how the results of our model changed as additional data was added to the equation. The training set of the MNIST dataset was altered using a variety of data augmentation methods, including rotation, translation, scaling, and flipping. The results show that the increase in data significantly improved the performance of the model, increasing its precision to 96.10% from Table 2.

Finally, we compared the computational efficiency of our suggested model with that of the CNN model. According to the results, our suggested model was substantially faster than the CNN model and needed much less time to train and test, as shown in Fig. 6. This is due to the fact that our suggested model only needed to compute the dense layer's output, which was then input into the SVM classifier, whereas the CNN model needed to compute numerous convolutional and pooling layers.

In conclusion, our CNN-SVM model has shown promising results in handwritten digit recognition and classification in realistic scenarios with high accuracy and resistance to differences in handwriting style. Compared to the CNN model, our model performed better than other cutting-edge models and was computationally efficient. Furthermore, data augmentation turned out to be a successful method of improving model performance. Our suggested method has potential uses in document digitisation, handwriting recognition, and automated form processing, among other areas.

**Table 2.** List of the different accuracies of our model

| Model | Accuracy |
|---|---|
| Simple Neural Network | 89.45% |
| Convolutional Neural Network (CNN) | 98.90% |
| CNN with Dropout | 98.52% |
| CNN with Batch Normalization | 98.62% |
| CNN with SVM Classifier | 93.58% |
| CNN with SVM Classifier and Data Augmentation | 95.20% |
| CNN with 1 Convolutional Layer | 94.11% |
| CNN with 2 Convolutional Layers | 94.76% |
| CNN with 3 Convolutional Layers | 93.92% |

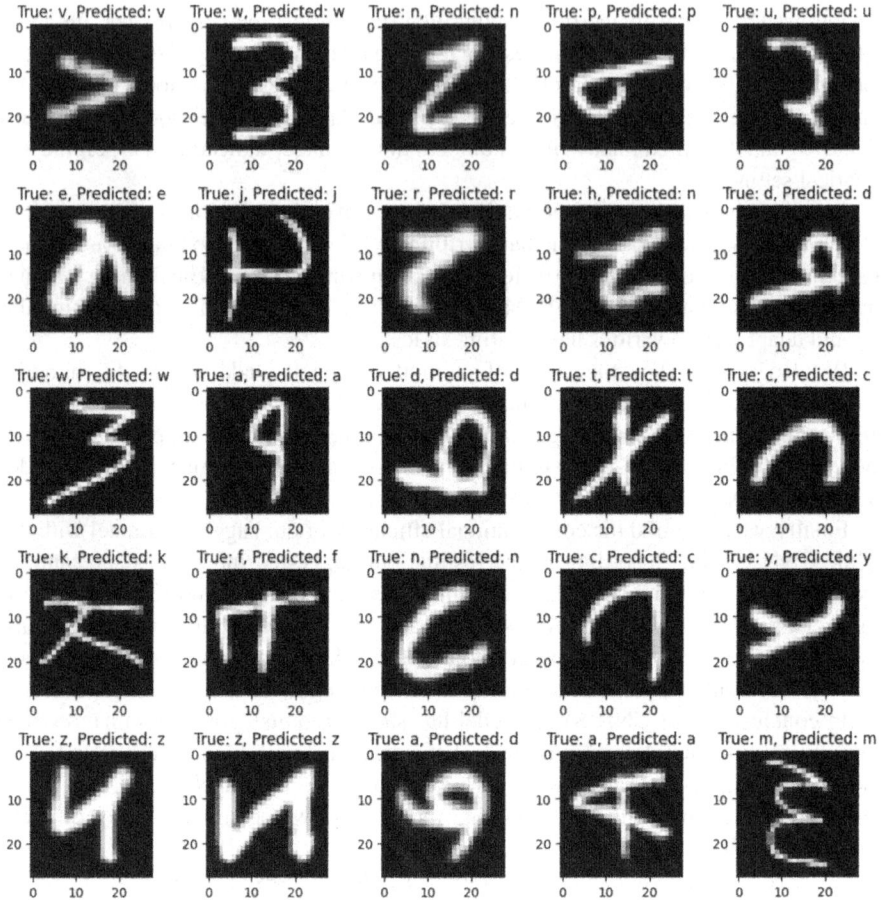

**Fig. 6.** Results of test image data with ground truth results

## 5 Conclusion

On the EMNIST dataset, we created a CNN-SVM model that outperformed other cutting-edge models with an accuracy of 93.58% in the recognition of handwritten digits and alphabets. To enhance model performance, data augmentation methods were used, and the number of convolutional layers was assessed to maximise model effectiveness. Potential uses of our approach include document digitisation, handwriting recognition, and automated form processing, among other areas. It has the ability to automatically recognise handwritten alphabets and numerals in situations where handwriting is varied. Our model demonstrated resilience to these fluctuations and was computationally effective, making it acceptable for use in real-world applications. As a result, the suggested CNN-SVM model has shown to be effective in classifying and recognising handwritten digits and alphabets, surpassing existing cutting-edge models, and has a wide range of potential applications.

# References

1. LeCun, Y., Cortes, C., Burges, C.: MNIST handwritten digit database. AT&T Labs (2010). http://yann.lecun.com/exdb/mnist
2. Krizhevsky, A., Sutskever, I., Hinton, G.E.: ImageNet classification with deep convolutional neural networks. In: Advances in Neural Information Processing Systems, vol. 25, p. 10971105 (2012)
3. Simonyan, K., Zisserman, A.: Very deep convolutional networks for large-scale image recognition. arXiv preprint arXiv:1409.1556 (2014)
4. Goodfellow, I., Bengio, Y., Courville, A.: Deep Learning. MIT Press, Cambridge (2016)
5. Wu, J., Huang, L., He, K.: A powerful generative model using random weights for the deep image representation. IEEE Trans. Pattern Anal. Mach. Intell. **39**(6), 1060–1064 (2016)
6. Chollet, F.: Deep learning with Python. Manning Publications (2017)
7. Abadi, M., et al.: TensorFlow: large-scale machine learning on heterogeneous systems (2016)
8. Kingma, D.P., Ba, J.: Adam: a method for stochastic optimization. arXiv preprint arXiv:1412.6980 (2014)
9. Cireşan, D., Meier, U., Gambardella, L.M., Schmidhuber, J.: Deep, big, simple neural nets for handwritten digit recognition. Neural Comput. **22**(12), 3207–3220 (2010)
10. Huang, G., Liu, Z., Van Der Maaten, L., Weinberger, K.Q.: Densely connected convolutional networks. In: Proceedings of the IEEE Conference on Computer Vision and Pattern Recognition, pp. 4700–4708 (2017)
11. Sermanet, P., LeCun, Y.: Traffic sign recognition with multi-scale convolutional networks. In: Proceedings of the International Joint Conference on Neural Networks, p. 28092813 (2011)
12. Guevara Neri, M.C., et al.: A methodology for character recognition and revision of the linear equations solving procedure. Inf. Process. Manag. **60**(1), 103088 (2023). https://doi.org/10.1016/j.ipm.2022.103088
13. Izotov, Y.A., Velichko, A.A., Ivshin, A.A., Novitskiy, R.E.: Recognition of handwritten MNIST digits on low-memory 2 Kb RAM Arduino board using LogNNet reservoir neural network. In: IOP Conference Series: Materials Science and Engineering, vol. 1155, no. 1, p. 012056 (2021). https://doi.org/10.1088/1757-899x/1155/1/012056
14. Goltsev, A., Gritsenko, V.: A neural network with competitive layers for character recognition. ELCVIA Electron. Lett. Comput. Vis. Image Anal. **21**(1), 102–110 (2022). https://doi.org/10.5565/rev/elcvia.1392
15. Latif, R.M.A., Farhan, M., Rizwan, O., Hussain, M., Jabbar, S., Khalid, S.: Retail level Blockchain transformation for product supply chain using truffle development platform. Clust. Comput. **24**, 1–16 (2021)
16. Ubaid, S., et al.: SCOUT: a sink camouflage and concealed data delivery paradigm for circumvention of sink-targeted cyber threats in wireless sensor networks. J. Supercomput. **74**, 5022–5040 (2018)
17. Ahmad, M., et al.: End-to-end loss based TCP congestion control mechanism as a secured communication technology for smart healthcare enterprises. IEEE Access **6**, 11641–11656 (2018)
18. Hussain, M., Shafeeq, M.F., Jabbar, S., Akbar, A.H., Khalid, S.: CRAM: a conditioned reflex action inspired adaptive model for context addition in wireless sensor networks. J. Sens. (2016)
19. Hussain, M., et al.: A gateway deployment heuristic for enhancing the availability of sensor grids. Int. J. Distrib. Sens. Netw. **12**(8), 7595038 (2016)
20. Jabbar, S., Akbar, A.H., Zafar, S., Quddoos, M.M., Hussain, M.: VISTA: achieving cumulative VIsion through energy efficient Silhouette recognition of mobile Targets through collAboration of visual sensor nodes. EURASIP J. Image Video Process. **2014**(1), 1–24 (2014)

# Automated Skin Cancer Segmentation and Classification Based on Deep Learning

Noor Ul Ain[1], Faisal Bukhari[2(✉)], and Waheed Iqbal[2]

[1] Department of Computer Science, Faculty of Computing and Information Technology (FCIT), University of the Punjab (PU), Canal Road, Quaid-i-Azam (New) Campus, Lahore, Pakistan
[2] Department of Data Science, Faculty of Computing and Information Technology (FCIT), University of the Punjab (PU), Canal Road, Quaid-i-Azam (New) Campus, Lahore, Pakistan
{faisal.bukhari,waheed.iqbal}@pucit.edu.pk

**Abstract.** Melanoma skin cancer early detection is a time-consuming and challenging process. In this study, we proposed a fully automated segmentation and classification method using convolutional neural networks (CNNs). On images from the International Skin Imaging Collaboration (ISIC) archive, the segmentation performance using DeepLab V3+ in terms of mean Intersection Over Union was 94%, while the suggested technique of classification using Renet50 achieved 98% accuracy and F1 Score.

**Keywords:** Confusion Matrix · Convolutional Neural Network · Deep Learning · Image Classification · Melanoma · Segmentation · Skin Cancer · Transfer Learning

## 1 Introduction

In the industrialized world, melanoma skin cancer is a serious and widely distributed condition that affects people of all ages, particularly young women because of excessive ultraviolet radiation exposure. It comes in a wide range of shapes, sizes, and colors, with 20–30% of instances developing in moles that already exist and 70–80% on healthy skin [1]. According to a study, there were 196.060 melanoma instances diagnosed in the United States in 2020, and 6,850 people died from the skin condition [1]. The World Health Organization (WHO) reports that skin cancer kills two people in the United States every hour and affects 9,500 people daily [2]. Statistics show that the use of tanning beds and solariums has led to a 47% increase in melanoma over the past ten years [3].

The manual technique of early identification of melanoma takes a lot of time and requires professional clinicians for examination due to the similarities between moles and skin cancer lesions. The expertise of dermatologists and doctors in early melanoma detection is also a factor. Therefore, it is essential to create an automated method for the early identification of melanoma to make it an easy and quick process. This research aims to propose a method for automatically detecting melanoma skin cancer and classifying it into different types. Convolutional Neural Networks (CNN) based methods

DeepLabV3+ [4] and Resnet50 [5] were used for the detection of melanoma on the dermoscopy skin images from ISIC archive [6].

The literature for various methods of melanoma skin cancer detection is reviewed in Sect. 2. The materials and procedures used for this research are described in Sect. 3. Section 4 details the experiments and outcomes, while Sect. 5 closes the study and highlights the contribution with a comparison.

## 2 Abbreviations and Synonyms

In this section, we list the abbreviations used in the paper.

- ISIC - International Skin Imaging Collaboration
- WHO - World Health Organization
- CNN - Convolution Neural Network
- SIFT - Scale Invariant Feature Transform
- SRM - Statistical Region Merging
- SVM - Support Vector Machine
- DCNN - Deep Convolutional Neural Network
- GPU - Graphics Processing Unit
- CUDA - Compute Unified Device Architecture

## 3 Literature Review

Various studies included the extraction of important features from the cancerous region and its classification for early melanoma skin cancer detection. In this regard, Shivangi Jain et al. [7] and Nishtha Garg et al. [8] adjusted the illumination by computer vision and MATLAB functions and then used the Otus thresholding method to obtain the binary masks of the lesions. Dang N. H. Thanh et al. [9] removed artifacts using adaptive principle curvature and segmented the lesion by the Mumford-Shah model and normalization of the red band in the RGB color model. They all classified the lesions by applying the ABCD rule with specific weightage of each attribute. Similarly, Frazam and Saeid [10] extracted the color and textual features using the Mumford-Shah model by finding the active contours. Naser Alfed and Fouad Khelif [11] made use of Scale Invariant Feature Transform (SIFT), Statistical Region Merging (SRM), histograms of lines, and histograms of the gradients for extraction and classification. On the contrary, Aleem Taufiq et al. [12] segmented the interested region by the GrabCut algorithm. They used both techniques of histograms and ABCD rule for feature extraction and Support Vector Machine (SVM) for classification. H. R. Mhaske and D. A. Phalke [10] and Seeja R D and Suresh [13] used Support Vector Machine (SVM) for the segmentation and classification of cancerous regions.

Some researchers used neural networks for the detection of melanoma skin cancer. Xulei Yang et al. [14] proposed a model based on a multi-task deep convolutional neural network (DCNN) implemented on the architectures of GoogleNet and U-Net for classification. Alceu Bissoto et al. [15] segmented lesions by the ensemble of FusionNet and U-Net with Adam Optimizer and then used the XGBoost with ensembling of 15 deep learning models for binary classification. Khoulod et al. [16] came up with the extension of U-Net and proposed a W-Net consisting of encoder-decoder ResNet and ConvNet and Feature Pyramid with four up-sampling and down-sampling blocks, and a shared fifth block for segmentation of the lesion, then classified through Inception-Resnet.

In this study, we proposed a new method for segmenting and classifying skin cancer lesions into binary classes as benign and malignant based on deep learning algorithms along with a comparison of the results of our methodology with other ones.

## 4 Materials and Methods

### 4.1 Materials

#### 4.1.1 Dataset

In this study, dermoscopy images from over 2,000 patients representing a variety of age groups and genders were used from the International Skin Imaging Collaboration (ISIC) Archive [6] which contains over 50,000 dermoscopy images of distinct benign and malignant skin lesions with varied sizes, colors, geometry, and quality. It contains many digital images of skin lesions with ground truths and metadata from different sources. The total dataset includes 56,245 benign and 5,854 malignant images that have been further classified into several categories. The skin images have different artifacts like hair, ink markings, rulers, air bubbles, and black frames as shown in Fig. 1. A total of 8,000 with 4,000 images of each class were used for the entire process.

#### 4.1.2 Flowchart

The whole process involved three steps as shown in Fig. 2:

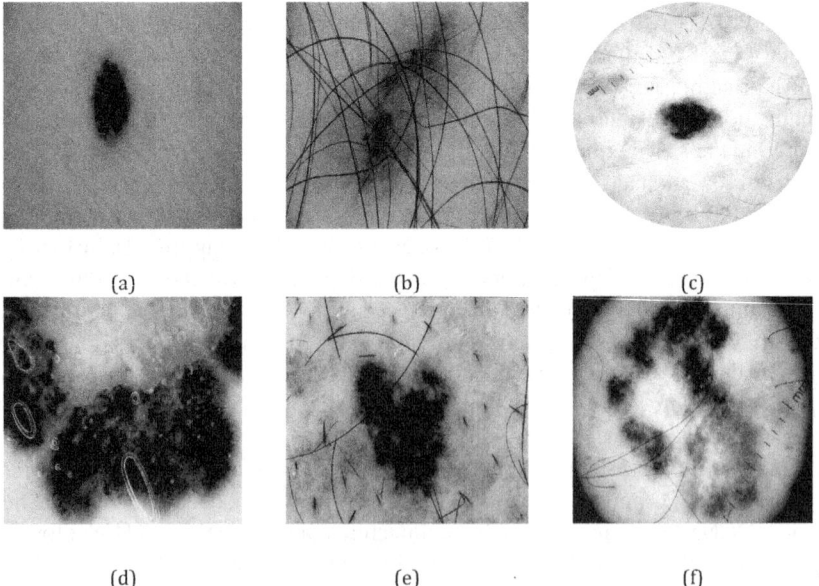

**Fig. 1.** Samples Images (a)–(c) Benign Images (d)–(f) Malignant Images Reprinted from [6].

- Preprocessing: The most important task in which the hair and artifacts are detected and removed. The hair and artifacts affect the quality of skin lesion segmentation as well as feature extraction. For this, we used computer vision techniques for detection and implement an inpainting method for removal.
- Segmentation: After preprocessing, we segmented the cancerous region from the original image for better detection. For this, we used LabelMe [17] to annotate the lesion and DeepLabV3+ [4] for segmentation.
- Classification: In this step, We used ResNet50 [5] for the classification of segmented lesions into binary class names as benign and malignant.

We trained models using TensorFlow on the google Colab GPU network [18] with CUDA [19]. This helped to train networks much faster as compared to our CPU or GPU systems.

## 4.2 Method

### 4.2.1 Preprocessing

In order to eliminate the hair and artifacts such as rulers, air bubbles, and black frames from the original images, while preserving the intrinsic dermatological features including skin lines, blood vessels, and skin color, we developed a low-cost real-time algorithm leveraging Open CV approaches.

**Algorithm 1: Preprocessing of images to remove Hair and Artifacts**

**Input:** Original images

**Output:** Clean images

i. The original image was resized to 1024×1024 and converted to a grayscale image using cv2.COLOR RGB2GRAY.

ii. Black Hat morphological filtering with a kernel of size 17×17 and 1 iteration was performed using cv2.MORPH BLACKHAT to find hair contours.

iii. Binary thresholding with a threshold value of 10 using cv2.THRESH BINARY was implemented to increase the intensity of hair contours.

iv. cv2.INPAINT TELEA was implemented with a radius of 1 to fill up the small gaps and remove the hair.

### 4.2.2 Segmentation

DeepLabV3+ [4] was used to extract the lesions from the original images using semantic segmentation with two classes, the cancerous region, and the background. DeepLabV3+ employs an extended variant of the convolution process, an encoder-decoder with atrous convolutions, and uses a rate parameter to modify the effective field of view of the convolution. In this study, we used DeepLabV3+ with Aligned Xception [20], a model

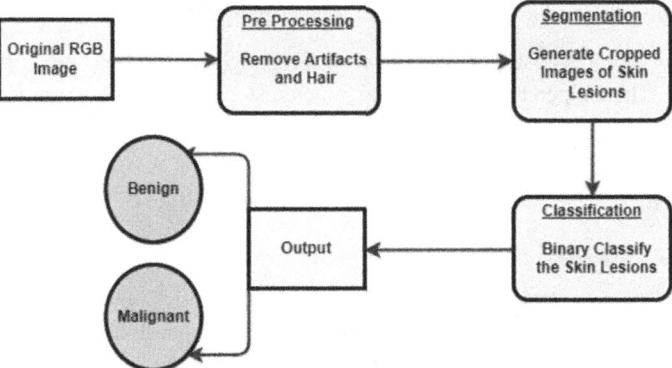

**Fig. 2.** Flow Chart of Proposed Method

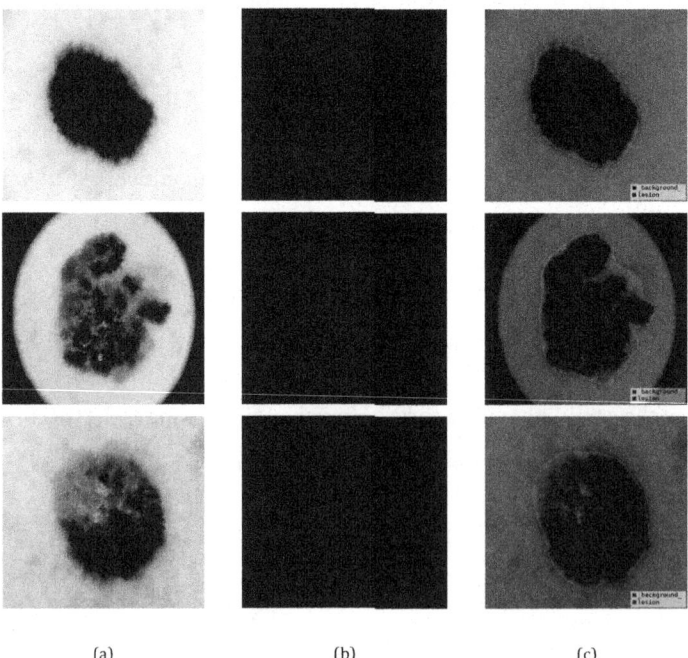

**Fig. 3.** LabelMe generated Segmentation Masks (a) Preprocessed Images (b) Labels of the Lesions (c) Visualization of Masks

variation trained on ImageNet [21] to extract features. LabelMe [17], a graphical image annotation tool was used to create the dataset like PASCAL VOC [22] with polygons, labeled as lesions. The dataset was divided into 75% training and 25% testing sets.

The 75% training set contained 6,000 images with 3,000 images of both types. They were further split into 70% training and 30% validation. Figure 3 shows generated segmentation mask of original images.

---

**Algorithm 2: Segmentation of Skin Cancer Lesions using DeepLabV3+**

---

**Input:** Original images with ground truth mask images
**Output:** Cropped images of lesions

i. The training dataset was resized to 513 × 513 and annotated to generate the segmentation masks of the cancerous regions using LabelMe.

ii. The annotations were converted into color-indexed images with the lesion as red (255,0,0):1 and the background as black (0,0,0):0.

iii. The dataset was converted into a binary storage format in form of TFRecord [23].

iv. A dataset descriptor described the dataset distribution as 4,200 images for training and 1,800 images for validation.

v. Xception_65 with the rate for atrous convolutions of 6, 12, and 18, and an output stride of 16 was used. The model was fine-tuned up to 7,000 steps with a batch size of 4, a momentum of 0.9, and a base learning rate of 0.0001 which decayed after 2000 steps with a decay factor of 0.1.

### 4.2.3 Classification

The lesions were classified into binary classes as benign and malignant by implementing ResNet50 [5] based on convolution neural networks with weights from ImageNet [21] with binary cross-entropy [24] as a loss function. Softmax [25] was used in the output layer to convert the vector of integers into a vector of probabilities with the following formula:

$$softmax(Z_i) = \frac{exp(Z_i)}{\sum_i exp(Z_i)} \tag{1}$$

Here $Z$ is the value from neurons of the output layer.

We selected 2,000 segmented images and divided them into two sets, 1,000 images for training and 1,000 images for testing. The 1,000 training sets were split into 80% training sets and 20% validation sets, with 500 benign and 500 malignant images.

**Algorithm 3: Classification of segmented lesions using ResNet50 Input:**
Segmented mask images

**Output:** Classify as Benign or Malignant

i. Images were resized to 224 × 224.

ii. Resnet50 trained on ImageNet was used as a backbone with a dropout of 0.5 and batch normalization to avoid overfitting.

iii. Binary cross-entropy was used as a loss function and Adam optimizer as an optimizer.

iv. A Dense layer with 2 neurons and activation function of softmax were added for binary classification.

v. The model was fine-tuned up to 100 epochs with 50 steps on each epoch, and 32. The base learning rate was 0.0001 which was reduced by a factor of 0.2 if the validation accuracy did not approve after 5 epochs.

## 5 Experiments and Results

As defined in the previous section we proposed different methods for preprocessing, segmentation, and classification of skin cancer lesions.

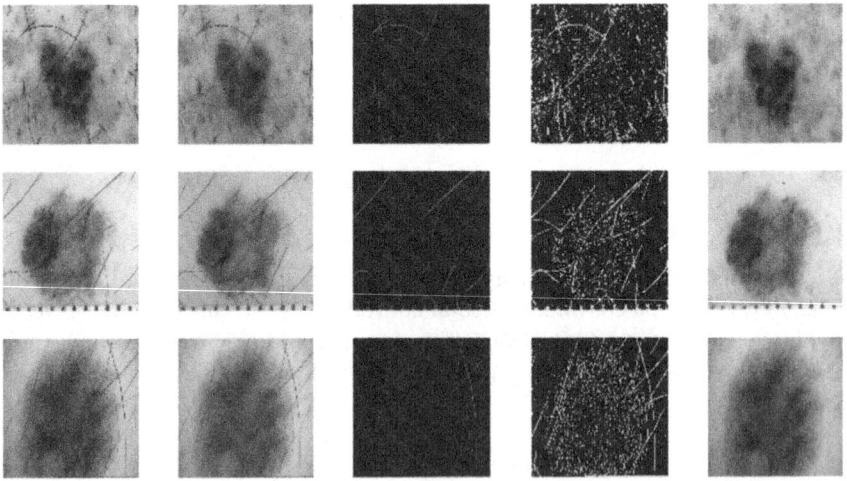

**Fig. 4.** Preprocessing of images; Column 1: Original Images, Column 2: Gray Scale Images, Column 3: Images After Black Hat Morphology, Column 4: Images After Binary Thresholding, column 5: Hair Removed Images

## 5.1 Preprocessing

The algorithm processed each image in a few seconds to remove the artifacts.
Figure 4 shows the results of pre-prepossessing on images.

## 5.2 Segmentation

The segmentation took a night to train and produced two types of losses as shown in the Fig. 5; the **clone loss**, was the total loss of all clones i.e., the sum of all losses of the trained models on GPUs, and the **Regularization loss**, was the loss generated by the regularization functions to optimize the global loss. We evaluated the segmentation results using mean intersection over union (mIOU) [26] with the following formula:

$$mIOU = true\_positives/(true\_positives + false\_positives + false\_negatives) \quad (2)$$

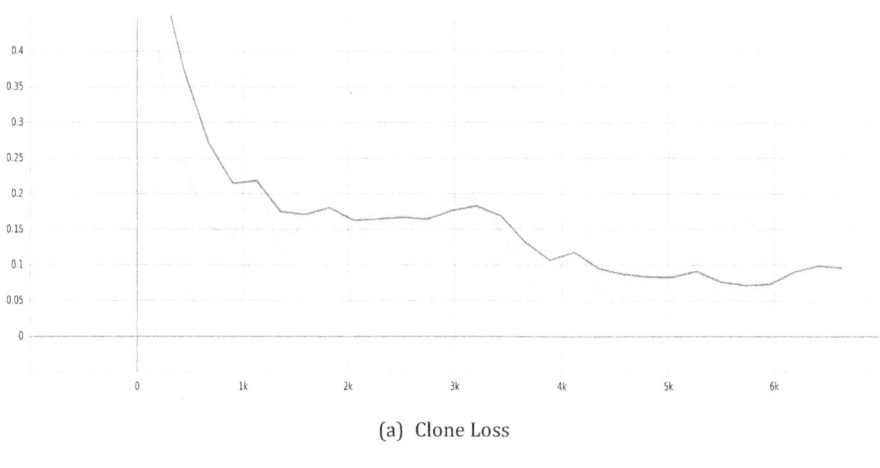

(a) Clone Loss

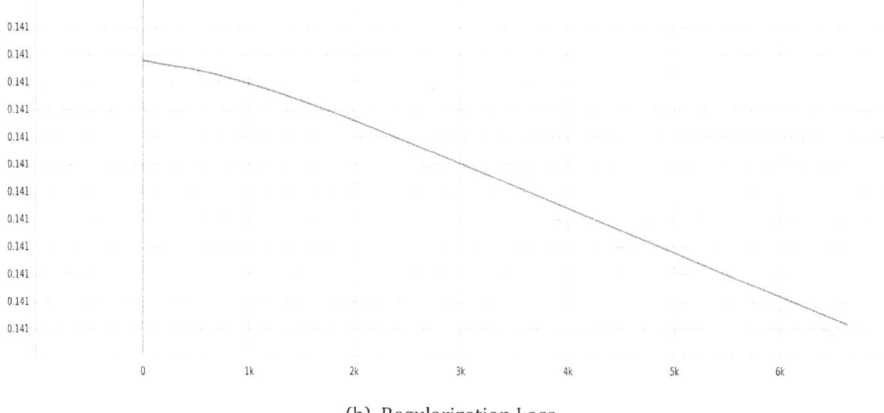

(b) Regularization Loss

**Fig. 5.** Graphical Representation of Losses during training

The mIOU were 96% and 90% for class 0 (background) class 1 (lesion) respectively on validation dataset. The overall mIOU was 93% on step 6,874. The exported model was tested on the testing dataset and achieved an IOU of 94%.

Figure 6 shows the results of segmentation.

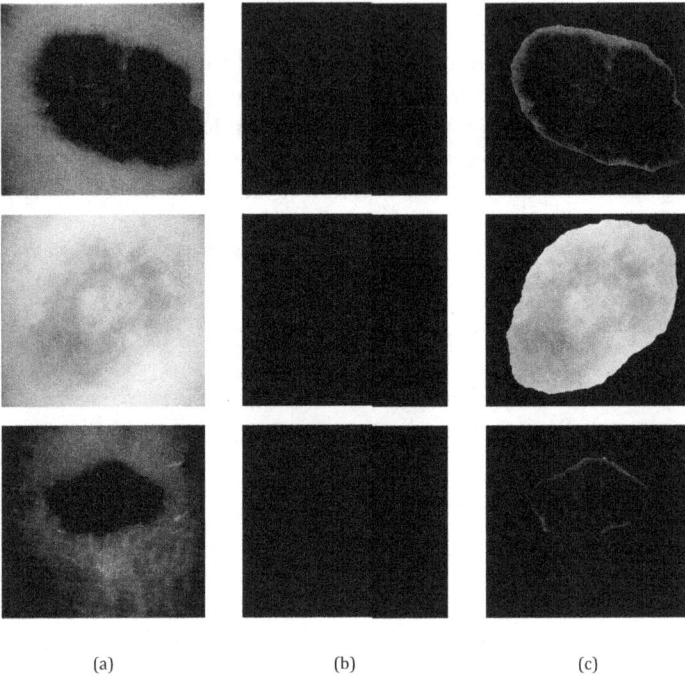

**Fig. 6.** Segmentation Results (a) Original Images (b) Generated Segmented Masks (c) Cropped Lesion Images

### 5.3 Classification

The process of classification took about 3 h for 100 epochs. Figure 7 shows the graphical representation of model accuracy and loss.

The model accuracy was determined by $2 \times 2$ confusion matrix [27] as shown in the Table 1. The confusion matrix gives **True Positive (TP):** number of positive examples classified accurately, **False Positive (FP):** number of actual negative examples classified as positive, **True Negative (TN):** number of negative examples classified accurately, and **False Negative (FN)** number of actual positive examples classified as negative.

We determined metrics from the confusion matrix as follows:

- **Accuracy,** the ratio of samples that were classified correctly to the total number of samples.

$$Accuracy = \frac{(TP + TN)}{(TP + FP + FN + TN)} \quad (3)$$

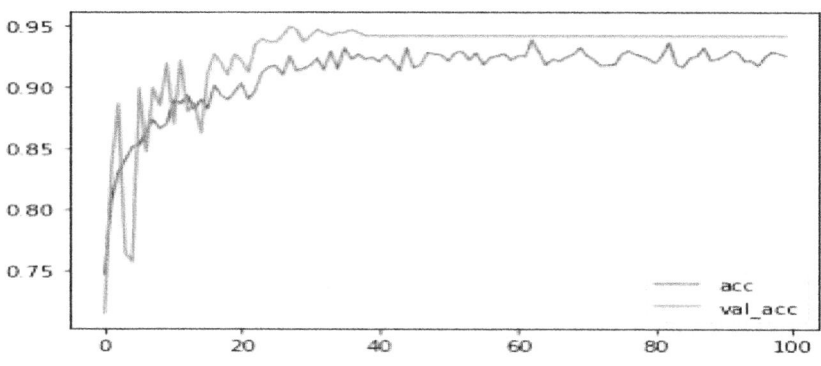

(a) Training Accuracy vs Validation Accuracy

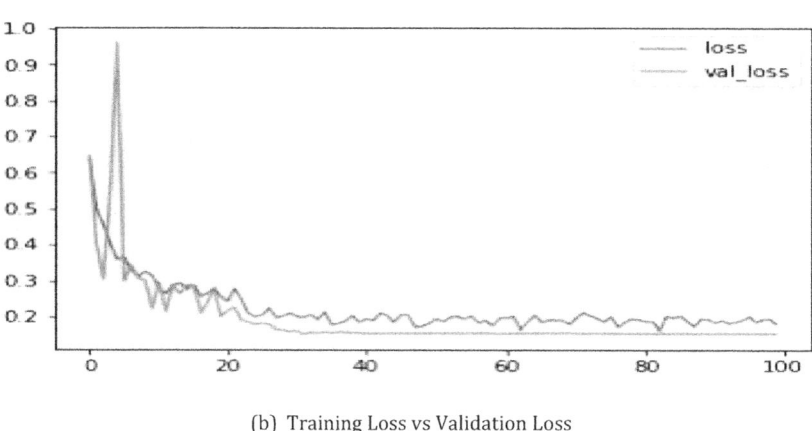

(b) Training Loss vs Validation Loss

**Fig. 7.** Graphical Representation of Classification Model Training

**Table 1.** Confusion Matrix for Testing Dataset

| Actual | Predicted | |
|---|---|---|
| | Benign | Malignant |
| Benign | 982 | 18 |
| Malignant | 22 | 978 |

- **Precision,** the ratio correctly classified samples with the event to the total samples predicted to be correct.

$$Precision = \frac{TP}{(TP + FP)} \quad (4)$$

- **Recall,** the ratio of samples that were classified correctly to the total number of actually correct samples.

$$Recall = \frac{TP}{(TP + FN)} \quad (5)$$

- **F1 Score,** the equilibrium between precision and recall.

$$Precision = \frac{2 \times precision \times recall}{(precision + recall)} \quad (6)$$

We got 0.978 precision, 0.982 recall, 0.98 accuracy and 0.98 F1 Score on the testing dataset. The results are shown in Figs. 8 and 9.

The proposed method introduces a new way for the detection of melanoma skin cancer. The comparison shown in Table 2 with different existing methods shows that our method performs better in terms of segmentation and classification.

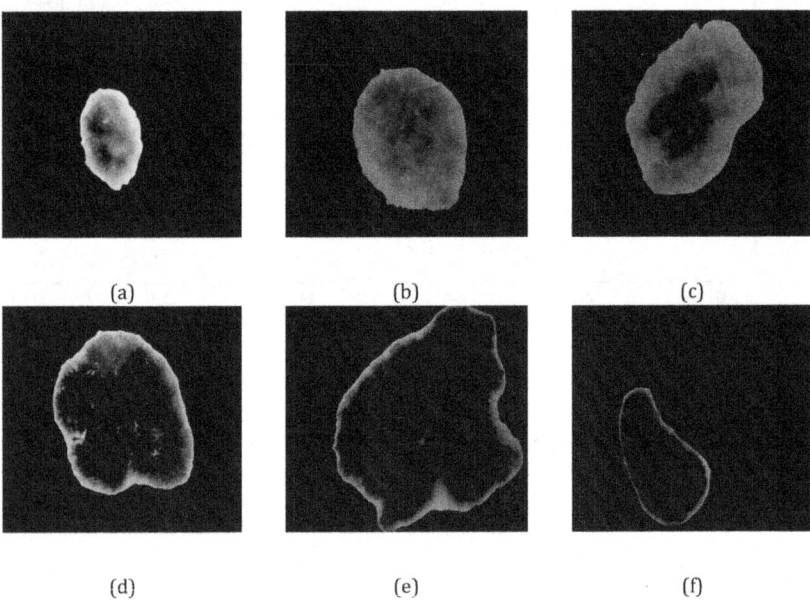

**Fig. 8.** Correct Results (a)–(c) Benign Lesions Detected as Benign, (d)–(f) Malignant Lesions Detected as Malignant

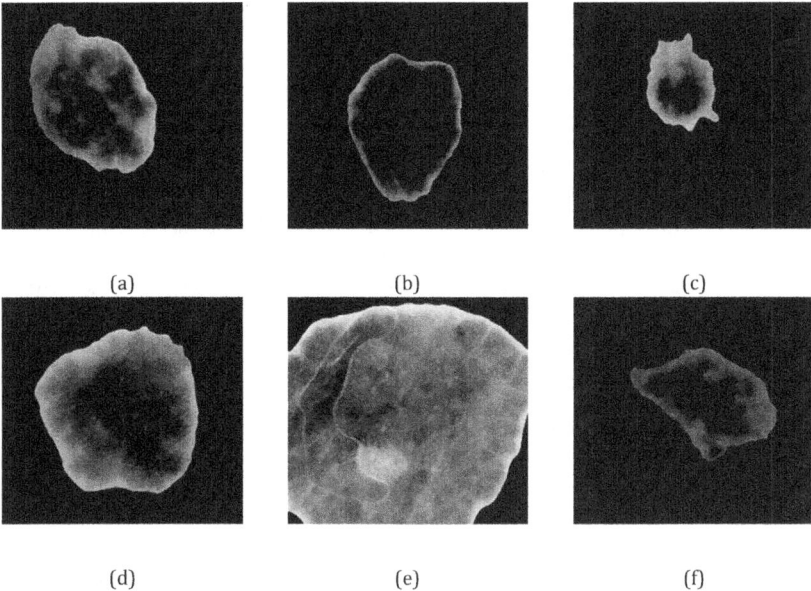

**Fig. 9.** Wrong Results (a)–(c) Benign Lesions Detected as Malignant (d)-(f) Malignant Lesions Detected as Benign

**Table 2.** Comparison between our method and existing methods

| Method | Segmentation | | Classification | | |
|---|---|---|---|---|---|
| | Image Size | Jaccard Index | Image Size | Accuracy | F1 Score |
| Seeja and Suresh | 572 × 572 | 0.626 | 572 × 572 | 0.8519 | 0.46 |
| Alceu Bissoto et al | 256 × 256 | 0.728 | 224 × 224 | 0.803 | 0.40 |
| Our Method | 513 × 513 | 0.94 | 224 × 224 | 0.9800 | 0.9800 |

## 6 Conclusion

This work represents the architecture and implementation of DeepLab V3+ and ResNet50 for automated detection and identification of melanoma on dermoscopy skin images from the ISIC Archive. The results show the ability of the models to extract features for skin lesions segmentation and classification problems respectively. The trained models worked better to identify the disease and its classification as compared with a clinician's manual identification of lesions. It gives instant responses to multiple images and classifies them by their level. A comparison of these findings means that the best model can also function correctly in the living environment, allowing clinicians to speed up the process of melanoma skin cancer early detection.

## References

1. S. C. Foundation, Melanoma overview—A dangerous skin cancer (2020). https://www.skincancer.org/skin-cancer-information/melanoma/
2. Rogers, H.W., Weinstock, M.A., Feldman, S.R., Coldiron, B.M.: Incidence estimate of nonmelanoma skin cancer (keratinocyte carcinomas) in the us population, 2012. JAMA Dermatol. **151**(10), 1081–1086 (2015)
3. Siegel, R.L., Miller, K.D., Jemal, A.: Cancer statistics, 2019. CA Cancer J. Clin.. Clin. **69**(1), 7–34 (2019)
4. Chen, L.-C., Zhu, Y., Papandreou, G., Schroff, F., Adam, H.: Encoder-decoder with atrous separable convolution for semantic image segmentation. In: ECCV (2018)
5. He, K., Zhang, X., Ren, S., Sun, J.: Deep residual learning for image recognition. In: Proceedings of the IEEE Conference on Computer Vision and Pattern Recognition, pp. 770–778 (2016)
6. ISIC archive. https://www.isic-archive.com/. Accessed 15 Apr 2022
7. Jain, S., Pise, N., et al.: Computer aided melanoma skin cancer detection using image processing. Procedia Comput. Sci. **48**, 735–740 (2015)
8. Garg, N., Sharma, V., Kaur, P.: Melanoma skin cancer detection using image processing. In: Sensors and Image Processing, pp. 111–119. Springer (2018)
9. Thanh, D.N., Prasath, V.S., Hien, N.N., et al.: Melanoma skin cancer detection method based on adaptive principal curvature, colour normalisation and feature extraction with the ABCD rule. J. Digit. Imaging 1–12 (2019)
10. Nezhadian, F.K., Rashidi, S.: Melanoma skin cancer detection using color and new texture features. In: 2017 Artificial Intelligence and Signal Processing Conference (AISP), pp. 1–5. IEEE (2017)
11. Alfed, N., Khelifi, F.: Bagged textural and color features for melanoma skin cancer detection in dermoscopic and standard images. Expert Syst. Appl. **90**, 101–110 (2017)
12. Taufiq, M.A., Hameed, N., Anjum, A., Hameed, F.: M-skin doctor: a mobile enabled system for early melanoma skin cancer detection using support vector machine. In: eHealth 360°, pp. 468–475. Springer (2017)
13. Seeja, R., Suresh, A.: Deep learning based skin lesion segmentation and classification of melanoma using support vector machine (svm). Asian Pac. J. Cancer Prev. APJCP **20**(5), 1555 (2019)
14. Yang, X., Zeng, Z., Yeo, S.Y., Tan, C., Tey, H.L., Su, Y.: A novel multi-task deep learning model for skin lesion segmentation and classification, arXiv preprint arXiv:1703.01025
15. Bissoto, A., Perez, F., Ribeiro, V., Fornaciali, M., Avila, S., Valle, E.: Deeplearning ensembles for skin-lesion segmentation, analysis, classification: Recod titans at isic challenge (2018). arXiv preprint arXiv:1808.08480
16. Khouloud, S., Ahlem, M., Fadel, T., Amel, S.: W-net and inception residual network for skin lesion segmentation and classification. Appl. Intell. **52**(4), 3976–3994 (2022)
17. Wkentaro/labelme: Image polygonal annotation with python (polygon, rectangle, circle, line, point and image-level flag annotation). https://github.com/wkentaro/labelme. Accessed 17 Apr 2022
18. Carneiro, T., Da Nobrega, R.V.M., Nepomuceno, T., Bian, G.-B., De Albuquerque, V.H.C., Rebouças Filho, P.P.: Performance analysis of google colaboratory as a tool for accelerating deep learning applications. IEEE Access **6**, 61677–61685 (2018)
19. Nickolls, J., Buck, I., Garland, M., Skadron, K.: Scalable parallel programming with cuda. Queue **6**(2), 40–53 (2008)
20. Chollet, F.: Xception: Deep learning with depthwise separable convolutions. In: Proceedings of the IEEE Conference on Computer Vision and Pattern Recognition, pp. 1251–1258 (2017)

21. Imagenet. https://image-net.org/. Accessed 20 Apr 2022
22. Everingham, M., Eslami, S., Van Gool, L., Williams, C.K., Winn, J., Zisserman, A.: The pascal visual object classes challenge: a retrospective. Int. J. Comput. Vision **111**(1), 98–136 (2015)
23. Accessed 18 Apr 2022 (2022). https://www.tensorflow.org/tutorials/load_data/tfrecord#:~:text=The%20TFRecord%20format%20is%20a,to%20understand%20a%20message%20type
24. tf.keras.metrics.binary crossentropy—tensorflow core v2.8.0 (2022). https://www.tensorflow.org/api_docs/python/tf/keras/metrics/binary_crossentropy. Accessed 18 Apr 2022
25. Softmax—what is softmax activation function—introduction to softmax (2022). https://www.analyticsvidhya.com/blog/2021/04/introduction-to-softmax-for-neural-network/. Accessed 18 Apr 2022
26. Accessed 18 Apr 2022 (2022). https://keras.io/api/metrics/segmentation_metrics/#:~:text=MeanIoU%20class&text=Intersection%2DOver%2DUnion%20is%20a,(true_positives%20%2B%20false_positives%20%2B%20false_negatives)
27. Confusion matrix - an overview—sciencedirect topics. https://www.sciencedirect.com/topics/engineering/confusion-matrix. Accessed 18 Apr 2022

# Performance Analysis of Self-adaptive User Interface for Mobile Users (Systematic Literature Review)

Muddassar Ali[1(✉)], Muhammad Raheel[1], Muhammad Waseem Iqbal[2], and Danish Irfan[3]

[1] Department of Computer Science, The Superior University, Lahore 54000, Pakistan
[2] Department of Software Engineering, The Superior University, Lahore 54000, Pakistan
[3] Department of Information Technology, The Superior University, Lahore 54000, Pakistan

**Abstract.** Mobile devices have become essential to our daily lives, and the use of mobile applications has been rapidly increasing. The usability and effectiveness of mobile applications significantly influence user satisfaction. One approach to designing mobile apps is the adaptive user interface (AUI), which can modify its interface to meet the user's demands and preferences. This study aims to assess the effectiveness of AUI across all types of applications. It summarizes previous research on AUI, outlines its advantages and disadvantages, and provides empirical evidence to support its effectiveness. The study also examines various methodologies and strategies used to evaluate self-adaptive mobile user interfaces. Additionally, the study analyzes the development of technology-enhanced adaptive/personalized learning over the past two decades. It explores different research areas, such as adaptive/personalized learning parameters, teaching aids, learning outcomes, participants, hardware, and more. The study demonstrates the effectiveness of personalized/adaptive user interfaces for mobile users and identifies essential features that improve UI effectiveness. It also highlights that while most studies focus on conventional mobile applications, personalized/adaptive learning has immense potential for wearable technologies, smartphones, and tablets. With the rapid growth of wearable computing and artificial intelligence, personalized/adaptive learning could have a significant impact on smart devices. Finally, the study identifies future research directions, issues, and challenges related to personalized/adaptive learning.

**Keywords:** Self-adaptivity · personalized · effectiveness · smart phone · AUI

## 1 Introduction

The always communication and computing abilities of the devices surrounding will also create new challenges that require innovative solutions in order to enable new applications as well as a new way of living [1]. The devices are getting more and more multimedia-capable, and multimedia applications are beginning to replace text-based messages in their exchanges. Nevertheless, due to the variety of these devices, it is necessary to modify the multimedia information in order to have it processed with the available tools. Resources have to be utilized as effectively as possible due to the limited availability of resources and the need to improve end-user experience.

### 1.1 Adaptation as Fit/Adaptivity

A systemic design is considered "fit" if, given the specifics of its surrounding environment [2], it can endure or grow. An inappropriate configuration, on the other hand, is one that will spontaneously disintegrate given the boundary conditions. Different designs' levels of fitness or chances of surviving under environmental constraints can be contrasted. Thus, fitting a system to its surroundings might be considered an adaptation. Every self-organizing system, therefore, therefore adapts to its environment. The stable structure it creates is, by definition, suitable for a particular set of circumstances. For instance, the direction of the spins will normally be horizontal to any magnetic field that is outside, and the fluid flow [3] and speed of the Bénard rolls will be tuned to the appropriate temperature difference between both the bottom as well as the surface. In this view, self-organization implies adaptability. This becomes much clearer if we use a separate border to divide the mechanism from the surroundings. According to Ashby, if one part of the initial, personality system is viewed as the new "process" and the remainder is viewed as its "environment," then that part will need to be modified to fit its surroundings.

**Adaptable:** A system is considered to be adaptable if it can adjust to accommodate such changes while preserving the majority of its organizational structure. Several newly developed systems aid the user in traversing the actual world, even though a proposed method assists the user as he or she navigates a difficult interactive system [4]. They receive information well about the user's cognitive and/or emotional state, analyze it, and then take action to address any contradictions between such states and the demands of the environment. As there are infinitely more routes at between the two selected random components as a factor of the system's extent of connection, adaptability is closely correlated to system connectivity under the more constrained situation of connectivism. A system with strong connectivity will frequently maintain extra routes for compensating flow or communication [5]. This is because the mechanism would still work if a specific disturbance destroyed any subset of paths connecting two random nodes [6]. As a result, a small quantity of connectivity ought to serve as an accurate substitute for the likelihood of adaptation. Strategies that are adaptable [7] only change when the user decides to do so. Nevertheless, it is not practical for users to modify the interfaces after every interaction; as a result, the rate of change is probably lower than that of many adaptive systems. There are two fundamental ways to customize Smartphone user interfaces. Adaptive interfaces modify the user experience dynamically to fit the user. On the other hand, adaptable interfaces provide customization possibilities but depend on the user to really make the change. Both approaches differ in terms of who manages the personalization: adaptive interfaces are scheme, whereas flexible interfaces are user-managed. The interface has typically been tailored by the network administrator or designer to match the needs of a particular user or group; nevertheless, flexible and adaptive interaction approaches are probably the only scalable means of personalization today [8]. In the HCI community, there has been debate over which of these two methods is preferable [9]. According to the opposite viewpoint, users would be able to focus on their tasks rather than managing their equipment if a suitable adaptable algorithm can be developed. According to one viewpoint, we should offer clear, foreseeable methods that let users maintain control over their environment. Notwithstanding this debate, there has never been a comparison of the efficacy of adaptive and adaptive interaction tactics. Most Users Prefer a Customized Interface: Consumers want an interface that can be customized to meet their specific needs. Regardless of the fact that the flexible menu was preferred by the majority of individuals (55%), the adaptive menus did garner some support (30%). Just 15% of respondents chose the static menu, despite the fact that it had the best-split menu. In McGrenere et al. field survey's [9], no static option was actually evaluated, but they found that 65% of participants chose adaptable, 15% desired adaptive, and 20% preferred static menus. The modest majority of those polled (30% vs. 15%) that favor an adaptive menu suggests that an adaptable split bar may well be preferred above Microsoft's adaptive menu.

### 1.2 Adaptive User Interface

[4] An interface (UI) that adapts, or changes, its layout and elements to meet the needs of the user or environment is known as an adaptive user interface (AUI). An AUI can also be changed personally by each user. The pieces that make up a true AUI have these innate capacities for adaptation and adaptability; various aspects of the interaction may alter and have an effect on one another. The user modification is commonly a negotiated process because the designer of a responsive user interface ignores where interface elements should go while offering an opportunity for both the developers and the user to decide their placement, commonly (though perhaps not always) in a moderately, if not completely automated manner. An AUI is primarily created based on the capabilities of the system and the level of knowledge of the users who will use it. One alternate strategy for helping someone utilize a system more effectively is to tailor the user interface to the manner in which the consumer interacted with it. The system's processing of signals through input devices like keyboards, menus, and icons are a few examples of interface elements that have been altered in this way [1]. The adaptive interface (AI) allows extended interaction possibilities for a range of users by adapting to shifts in the usage environment. The flexibility of the touch screens necessitates detailed contextual information. To provide customized services, profiles must be developed [10]. Computer system operators nowadays come in a variety of ages, genders, and interests, as well as working tendencies, intuition, and experience. Because there are an increasing number of different types of computer users, user interfaces are evolving to fit their needs. As a result of the expanded functional range, computer system handling is becoming increasingly challenging. The administration of computer systems is made simpler by the use of adaptive user interfaces, which may change the graphical presentation and representation of data to meet users' needs and aid them while they work.

The development of user-supporting adjustments and all varieties of adaptable user interfaces requires knowledge of the users and how they interact with the computer system. This user data is either automatically collected and assumed by the system or directly requested from the user [11]. It is not acceptable to demand explicit information from users. The necessary information can be automatically captured while the software application is being used by watching the users, even without effective knowledge input from the users. One potential source of data for automatically capturing user information is the sequence of show increased that emerges from utilizing the user interface. Because to the diversity in user physical demographics and home automation interaction styles, it is challenging to design a personalized experience for a large variety of users [12]. Many consumers run into problems while customizing panels. These setting talks are extremely difficult for people with disabilities and limited ICT expertise in order to understand [13]. That is a crucial requirement, just as children or elderly people crave customization. Every technology that aims to be accessible must thus contain auto-adaptation and self-learning capabilities for user needs. Due to bad user interface design and usability issues, users may feel upset and behave in an undesirable manner [14]. For successful mobile interfaces, the desired tasks should be aligned with the user's mental model [15]. For successful mobile interfaces, the desired tasks should be aligned with the user's mental model. User-centric interfaces are increasingly being developed using the benefits of AUI. The AUI represents a more realistic adaptation technique than adaptable since it provides proper adaptation methods and may handle usability issues with user interaction [4, 6]. A solution to the problems that hinder any mobile application from providing dynamically updated user interfaces for different user groups with equivalent features and requirements is the use of adaptive user interfaces. It is simple to participate in collaborative, motivating, constructive, and informative activities with context-based user interfaces [16]. In many domains of interactive software, more flexibility is obviously needed, both in terms of the sorts of adaptability and the customization process. The bulk of systems up to this point have required users to actively convey their selections to the interface, which has limited the available alternatives or made them laborious to accomplish. Moreover, a user's behavior may reflect some characteristics of their style even without the user becoming aware of it. In order to do this, the interface will be customized using machine learning techniques based on observed user behavior [6]. We term the automated, interface-driven customizing that occurs in the absence of specific user instruction, adaptation [8]. Customization simply refers to customizing requested by the user when we speak about it. Thus, we assert that adaptivity and customization are the only scalable forms of personalization. There should be a variety of customizing tools available to users so they may control and manage adaption. Interfaces should automatically adjust to the capabilities of the current device, network connectivity, and the activities, location, and context of the specific user. Learning activities and learning [17] objects can be accessed manually or automatically. "Adaptive user interfaces" have been the subject of extensive study and development in recent years with the aim of developing user interfaces that easily change based on user behavior. A user-friendly interface that's also personalized, special, and simple to use is crucial to an e-learning system. Instead of showing the learning exercises and objects in one consistent interface for each of the students, an e-learning subject map might offer "many roads to Roman," meeting the needs of the various student population.

### 1.3 Mobile Adaptive User Interface

More than only professional or esthetic pride motivates the development of a highly usable mobile application. How well a smart phone may be utilized is significantly influenced by the development of user-friendly and adaptive User Interfaces (UI). This confirms our conviction that user-adaptive mobile user interfaces are necessary given the rapid evolution of technology. It is obvious that mobile devices place a high emphasis on intelligent interfaces that accommodate the user's continuously changing situation. By offering different kinds and limits just on system, location, task, and interfaces that are currently in use, it is simpler to concentrate on the unique demands of the user. The accessibility of portable devices is improved through new feature modifications and interactional technology. Hence, adaptive user interfaces are essential for designing a user-friendly environment, as opposed to repeated user interfaces [18].

Speaking, hearing, touching, and other communicational behaviors are all part of using a cell phone. It already forms a typical part of everyday human behavior. A system becomes a communication tool when it is interactive because it encourages user interaction with the user interface. Linking phone functions and activities to efficient interaction elements is one of a mobile phone interface's main goals (e.g. sounds and visual elements). In mobile interfaces, icons are used to denote the skills users require to execute tasks. Graphics and symbols are essential for user-device interaction, thus interface designers commonly utilize them in the belief that they can convey information across language barriers [19]. Desktop computers and portable devices differ significantly from one another in a variety of ways, such as the absence of physical input, the frequency of usage [20], the size of the displays, the size of the simulated keys, and the requirement for sustained visual attention. These differences are causing customers to experience problems that were previously unheard of. The majority of user interface (ui) designs for smart phones are based on the desktop paradigm, despite the fact that it does not completely match the mobile environment. Although the use of mobile devices has increased, there are no real standards for Smartphone UI design patterns. Users and gadgets have a contented and durable communication route thanks to mobile phone interfaces [13]. Mobile phone interfaces today provide a number of interaction modes. The process of interface design is made more challenging by the unique usability requirements and measurements of these interfaces [21]. It is more difficult for interface architects and end users to understand the technical subtleties in software and hardware as a result of the competitive environment's utilization of a swarm of technology options in interaction design. Several top-notch programmes [22] have been made available, but due to their clumsy, unsightly, ineffective, and confusing user interfaces, they haven't been commercially successful. Non-adaptive user interfaces for mobile devices lead to frustration and adverse effects on system quality, usability, and reception. While designing mobile phone interfaces, the user's demands should be evaluated in terms of usability, learn ability, ease of understanding, effectiveness, efficiency, and objectivity [23]. According to the user's task, the most modern mobile OSes, such as Android or iOS, feature kid, guest, drive, and nighttime modes to make programming more accessible.

Color blindness, sometimes referred to as color vision deficit (CVD) [24], is a visual loss that occurs spontaneously in certain persons. People with CVD have trouble distinguishing between colors, particularly red and blue, as well as green and yellow. However it affects a larger population than the 8% (1 in 12) of males and 0.5% (1 in 200) among women who experience it. Modern devices are getting better at identifying human limits, and mobile phone OS have/has capabilities that assist users in overcoming their hurdles to accessing technology for communication and information in their environment [25]. A context-aware adaptable input method paradigm for portable LBS is built around the user paradigm is articulated in three components: static created elements, dynamic and ongoing behavior, and adaptable strategy. The following advantages of the adaptable user interface above traditional adaptive user interfaces: Giving greater consideration to the dynamically interaction and modifying the user interface to better match the real-time interaction; Utilizing the context information continuously and then improving the effectiveness of the context information usage; Avoiding the user classification-based restriction of the conventional adaptive user interface.

The model-based adaptive system has a number of drawbacks, including the need to broaden the scope of adaption and the limitations of current research in order to get more precise data on user's knowledge, ability, and other aspects. We will only further optimize the sensory approach, more effectively use context information, boost the adapt outcome, and enhance the interface design mechanism in order to accomplish the goal of a fluid and intuitive interface adaptable. An adaptable user interface (AUI) idea has been around for a while. AUI is a design strategy for creating mobile applications that may change to meet the requirements and preferences of the user. The foundation of AUI is the concept of context awareness, which allows an application to recognize the context of a user and modify its user interface accordingly. Personalization, adaptation, and customization are the three subtypes of AUI. The most basic type of AUI is personalization [26], in which the user can select from a list of choices offered by the programme. The programme then modifies its user interface in accordance with the user's choice. The user may be able to choose their favorite news sources in a mobile news application, for instance, and the app will only display news stories from that sources. Personalization, in which the programme dynamically modifies its interface depending on the user's situation, is simpler than adaptation. For instance, a weather app may display various UI components according on the time and location, the time of the day or, and the weather. The most intricate type of AUI is customization, which allows the user to entirely [27] alter the application's user interface to suit their tastes. A mobile email programme, for instance, may let users customize the font style, color, and format of their emails.

### 1.4 Challenges for User Adaptation

[28] As a result, issues with competency and presentation are among the detected factors, and they also affect system confidence. A broad list of these variables is provided below:

- **Presentation:** Localization, interface design, accurately track, and stealth adaptivity
- **Competence:** Accuracy, Limited Usage Data, Predictability, and Changing User Behavior
- **The adaptation's regularity:** Job difficulty, interaction expense, and frequency of interaction
- **Trust:** Dependable behavior and intelligence privacy.

## 2 Research Methodology

We conducted a systematic literature (SLR) review that is divided in three phases and each phase is further divided in activities which are performed to conduct the SLR. The detail of phases involved in SLR is as follows:

### 2.1 Phase 1: Planning the Review

The primary goal of the review was established at this phase, and the activities that followed thoroughly described each stage.

**Need Identification of Review**

After conducting Phase 1 of our investigation, we discovered that the field of adaptive user interface lacked any existing Systematic Literature Review (SLR). As a result, we concluded that conducting an SLR was necessary, given the insights we gained from our previous research. With the increasing expansion of technological support, we are beginning to observe various usage patterns emerging [29]. A significant amount of new users who lack familiarity with computers and technology, including non-technical professionals, senior citizens, and children, are now present [30]. Not only do these users have diverse computer skills, but they also vary greatly in many other aspects, such as their knowledge, abilities, cognitive and physical capacities, emotional state, drive, and, notably, the specific technology-related activities and applications that matter most to them. Despite the release of several high-quality mobile apps, their market success has been limited due to poorly designed user interfaces that are complicated, unappealing, ineffective, and confusing [22]. Non-adaptive interfaces for mobile devices have led to frustration, negative user experiences, and reduced performance. To ensure successful mobile phone interfaces, it is essential to evaluate and prioritize factors such as usability, learn ability, understandability, effectiveness, efficiency, and objectivity in meeting user needs [23]. Modern mobile operating systems, such as Android and iOS, offer kid, guest, driving, and night modes to enhance user accessibility depending on their task. These modes provide predefined and static profiles with various interaction styles tailored to specific contexts, taking into account factors such as daylight, age groups, and access preferences [31]. The preset interaction modes interface lacks research and analysis on user context. Therefore, users are often forced to choose the most inflexible, albeit suitable, settings in any given scenario.

The variability in physical demographic characteristics and interaction style of smart devices among users poses a challenge in developing a customized interface suitable for a diverse user range [11, 12]. Customizing panels can pose difficulties for a considerable number of customers, especially for those with impairments or limited ICT knowledge and skills. These users may find the setting conversations daunting and hard to comprehend. Just like how young children or elderly individuals crave personalization, it is a fundamental requirement. Therefore, any technology that aims to enhance accessibility through customization must include auto-adaptation and self-learning mechanisms to cater to user needs. Poor user interfaces and usability confusion can lead to user frustration and unsatisfactory behavior [14]. Efficient mobile interfaces should align their tasks with the user's mental model, utilizing the benefits of AUI to create user-centric designs. AUI is currently being employed to develop interfaces that address usability challenges and adapt to user interactions, making it a more practical approach to adaptation than adaptability [32, 33]. Adaptive user interfaces have been proposed as a solution to the challenges that prevent mobile applications from providing dynamically modified user interfaces suitable for different user groups with similar characteristics and needs. Context-based user interfaces enable easy participation in collaborative, supportive, productive, and communicative activities [22].

**Specifying the Research Question(s)**

In order to gain a comprehensive understanding of the topic, this study aims to identify and analyze research related to adaptive user interfaces in mobile app development that have been published from 2000 to the present day. The primary objective has been divided into several research questions.

**RQ1:** What is the performance of self-adaptation in the context of mobile apps?
**RQ2:** Which characteristics of self-adaptation can increase its performance?
**RQ3:** How much an adaptive user interface is affective for mobile users in context of all kinds of applications?

**Identifying the Relevant Bibliographic Databases**

**Initial Search:** At this juncture, we are conducting an automated search [34] using Google Scholar, which is currently one of the largest and most exhaustive databases and indexing systems for scientific literature. Our rationale for utilizing this data source is based on two main factors. Firstly, according to the literature, this indexing tool has been a wise selection in terms of identifying the initial set of literature studies for the snowballing process. Secondly, Google Scholar offers the highest number of potentially relevant studies in comparison to other notable libraries such as Scopus, ACM Digital Library, IEEE Explore, and Web of Science, and furthermore, the query results can be easily extracted from the indexer through automation (Fig. 1).

## 2.2 Phase 2: Conducting the Review

To create a suitable search string, it is necessary to strike a balance between the scope of the search and its manageability. Therefore, we extracted the main phrases that matched the study questions and looked for synonyms of important terms to include in the search string. We used the Boolean AND to connect the main components and the Boolean OR to link alternate phrases. In this way, we compiled a comprehensive list of search terms;
{(user interface "**OR**" user interaction) **AND** (adaptive "**OR**" self-adaptation "**OR**" self-adaptive") **AND** (android "**OR**" iOS "**OR**" windows "**OR**" smart-phone) **AND** (apps "**OR**" applications "**OR**" application)}.

Listing 1 provides the search term that is utilized for the initial search. The search phrase is deliberately kept general to encompass a wide range of relevant papers related to the subject of the research. It consists of four primary parts, each emphasizing user interface, self-adaptive systems, the mobile nature of targeted techniques, and apps/applications. To ensure the initial search results are as targeted as possible, the

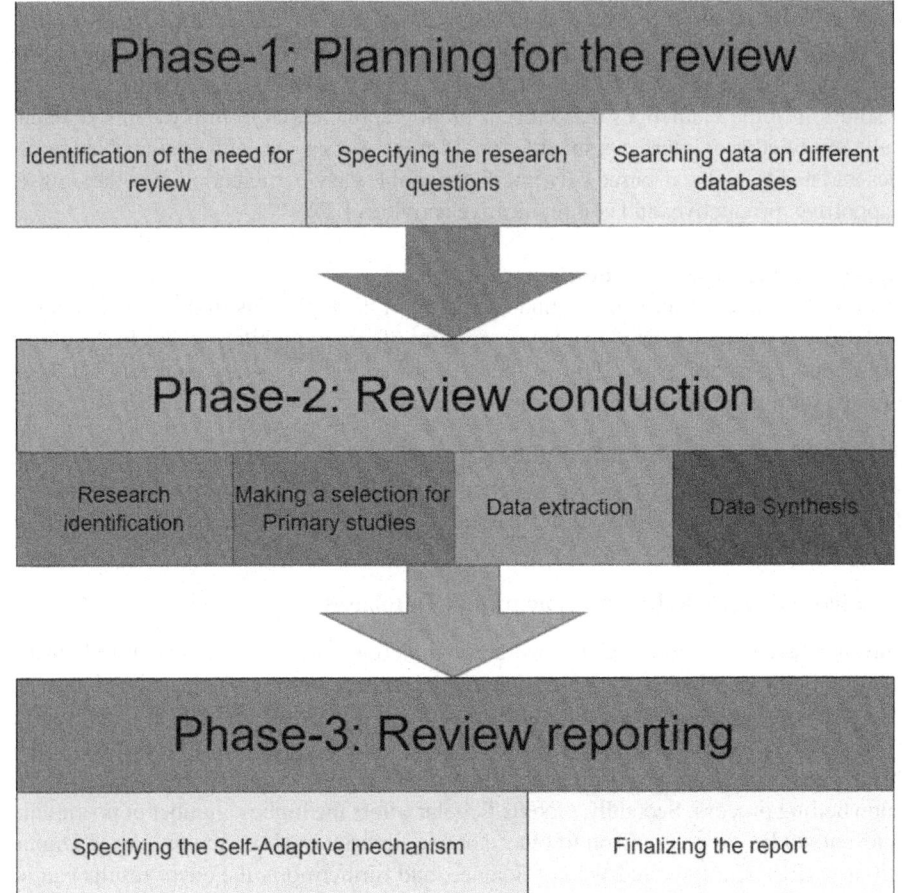

**Fig. 1.** Phase diagram of SLR [35]

query is applied only to the titles of the studies. The search string is tested through pilot searches on Google Scholar. The time frame for the search spans from 2007 until the date the query is executed, which is March 2023.

**Application of Selection Criteria**

We are currently considering all 265 papers that were obtained during the initial search and applying a set of specific criteria for inclusion and exclusion to filter them. In order to make unbiased and cost-effective research choices [34], we employ an adaptive reading approach, which involves selectively reading only the relevant portions of the studies that meet our criteria, rather than reading them in their entirety. The inclusion and exclusion criteria that we are using for this study are outlined in the following sections (Table 1).

*Exclusion Criteria*

After applying the exclusion criteria, Figure # indicates that 115 papers were eliminated. The criteria for deletion are as follow:

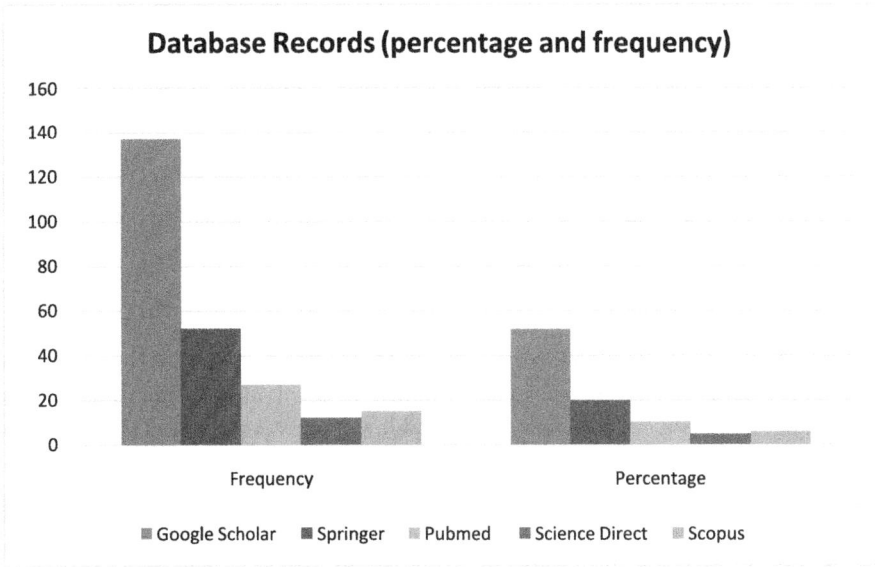

**Fig. 2.** Database Records

**Table 1.** Description of SLR

| Sr. # | Description of indicator | Quantity of papers |
|---|---|---|
| 1 | Articles identified through database searching | 265 |
| 2 | Paper selected after application of exclusion criteria | 115 |
| 3 | Paper selected after application of inclusion criteria | 100 |
| 4 | Papers retained after application of quality assessment indicator | 62 |

- Studies that aren't in English as well as those that were published before 2000 and after 2017
- There was no peer review mechanism for the other materials, which included theses, technical reports, and other documents.
- Secondary or postsecondary education (e.g., systematic literature reviews, surveys, etc.).
- Editorials, tutorials, and poster papers for studies, as they don't offer adequate details.
- Papers that are expansions of previously included papers or duplicates.
- Research that hasn't undergone peer review.
- We are unable to inspect certain documents, which makes them unavailable..

If a publication meets all the inclusion requirements, it is classified as a primary study; however, if it fails to meet any of these criteria, it is rejected. Two researchers have refined and evaluated the criteria through several pilot investigations. It's important to mention that secondary research is excluded due to the initial exclusion criterion, but it is still addressed in the related work section.

*Inclusion Criteria*

Figure # shows that 100 papers were retained after the application of inclusion criteria. We examined the summary, opening, and closing sections of the papers. From the collected papers, we picked the ones that fulfilled at least one of the subsequent standards:

- The research is centered on the concept of self-adaptability, as it has been described in the study [20].
- The research concentrates on mobile apps, as described in Sect. 2.
- Studies published in English languages.
- Studies published between the period of 2000 and 2017

*Quality Assessment*

After employing specific guidelines for selection and rejection, the full contents of the selected articles were thoroughly assessed for their standard, the remaining papers were subjected to the quality evaluation criteria, and low-quality papers were eliminated. In the end, 62 publications were used to extract the data and offer responses to the SLR's study questions. The goal of quality evaluation is typically to identify the impartial and pertinent research. So that we could refine our search results and evaluate the suitability and rigour of the candidate articles, we came up with several quality evaluation markers. The following SLRs served as the foundation for the quality evaluation questionnaires [36]. A paper that includes evidence that has been quantitatively or qualitatively assessed. Figure 3 shows the strength of papers according. The paper has an intricate experimental plan. The applicable approaches' accuracy rates are quantified and documented in papers. In articles, the comparison of various methodologies is offered. The article outlines the pros and cons of various techniques.

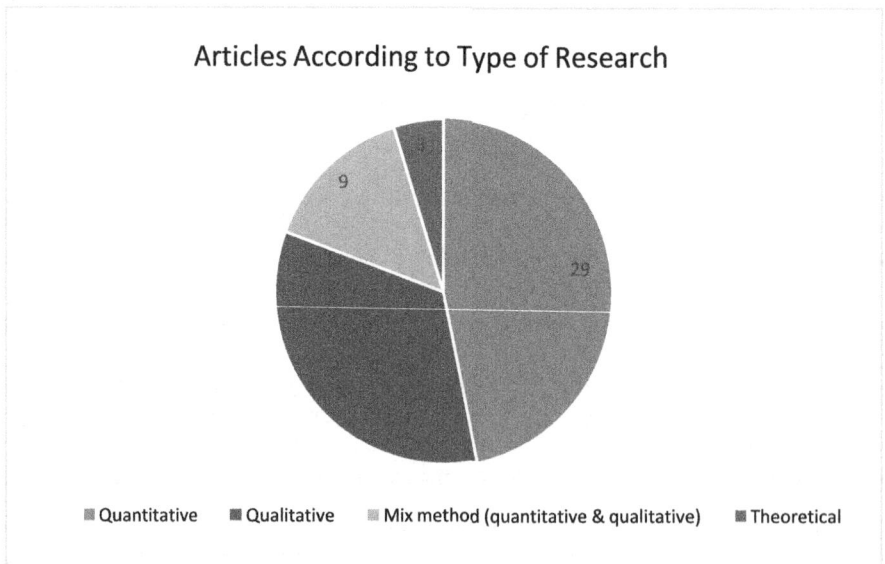

**Fig. 3.** Articles according to type of research

## 2.3 Data Extraction and Synthesis

The study's queries were addressed by employing a data extraction form to collect the required information from the selected papers.

**RQ1:** Our objective is to examine how self-adaptation performs in the realm of mobile apps, in order to provide an answer to this question.

**RQ2:** By answering this question, we can gain a better understanding of how self-adaptation can improve performance in various types of mobile applications.

**RQ3:** By answering this question, we can improve our comprehension about that how much an adaptive user interfaces are affective for mobile users in context of all kinds of applications with the help of systematic literature study.

Several approaches were used to synthesis the retrieved data in order to address the study issues. To fully address the study issues, a narrative synthesis approach was adopted. Moreover, research questions were used to guide the application of visualization techniques like tables and charts. Studies on self-adaptation that are similar to ours are secondary research. Yang et al.'s [37] emphasis was on the process of developing and evaluating the necessary criteria for self-adjusting systems They conducted a comprehensive assessment of the literature involving 101 main researches, and as a result, they were able to identify 16 modeling techniques and 10 required quality factors. They noted that several modeling techniques needed more research; while the majority of qualitative investigations need more thorough review. An overview of engineering techniques for self-adaptive systems is provided by Krupitzeret al. in [38]. They employ taxonomy for self-adaptation that has been expanded with the "context viewpoint," or the capacity of systems to modify their surroundings, to achieve this goal. The survey identifies and categorizes a number of construction methods for self-adaptive systems. Macias-Escriva et al. [39] conducted research on the latest self-adaptation techniques, examining self-adaptability from both computer science and cybernetics perspectives, and reviewing literature on the topic. They found that the development of self-adaptive systems will be facilitated by artificial intelligence and feedback control disciplines. Neither Macias-Escriva et al. nor Krupitzer et al. mention the quantity of studies utilized in the data extraction process for the surveys. Mahdavi-Hezavehi et al. [40] Conducted a thorough review of 54 key studies with the aim of gaining insight into the latest architecture-based techniques used to manage various quality attributes (QAs) in self-adaptive systems. Their findings revealed that performance and cost were the most frequently addressed QAs, and that robotics and web-based systems were the most prevalent areas of research. Mucciniet et al. [41] Analyzed 42 primary research papers focusing on self-adaptation within the realm of cyber-physical systems. The researchers discovered that the most commonly employed adaptation mechanism in this context is MAPE (Monitor-Analyze-Plan-Execute), and their findings also indicate that energy is the most frequently explored application domain. The investigation conducted by Weynset et al. [42, 43] was the last to examine claims of self-adaptation. They reviewed papers published in 2008, as well as 96 main research papers identified from the SEAMS conference series between 2006 and 2011. Their findings indicate that the primary focus was on architecture and models, the most common application domain was service-based systems, and only a few empirical investigations were carried out, with no commercial evidence available at the time of publication.

Although there have been numerous studies on self-adaptation and self-adaptive systems, none have explored the current state of self-adaptation in the context of mobile applications. Our analysis aims to fill this void, as mobile software becomes increasingly prevalent in all application sectors. Section II defines the self-adaptation of mobile apps, is the subject of a thorough literature review presented in this work. Out of 305 potentially pertinent papers, we identified 44 primary studies, which we then examined using the categorization system provided in order to address the specific study objectives we had in mind. Through furnishing elaborate answers to these inquiries, we offer a comprehensive evaluation of the realm of self-adaptation concerning mobile applications, consequently presenting significant insights for scholars and developers aiming to delve deeper into this area of study in forthcoming research.

## 3 Results

This section presents the findings of this review (Phase 3: reporting the review). The outcomes of the selection process are first presented in their entirety, followed by individual reports of each research question's findings.

### 3.1 Overview of the Selected Studies

We discovered the 265-candidate document as seen in Fig. 2 by conducting searches across five digital databases. 115 papers out of the 265 total papers were eliminated using exclusion criteria. To identify the most significant studies, a thorough analysis of the remaining 150 publications was conducted. After examining the titles, abstracts, and keywords, only papers that met at least one of the inclusion criteria were considered. Out of the initial pool, 100 papers remained. The quality evaluation criteria were subsequently applied to these papers, and those that were deemed to be of low quality were eliminated. This process enabled the assessment of the overall quality of the selected articles based on their entire texts. Eventually, 62 publications were utilized to extract data and provide answers to the study questions posed in the systematic literature review (SLR) (Fig. 4).

### 3.2 Phase 3: Reporting the Review

In this phase, we have presented a comprehensive account of how the research questions were addressed. The responses to all the study inquiries are substantiated by the evidence gathered from the literature reviews.

RQ1: What is the Performance of Self-adaptation in the Context of Mobile Apps?

Adaptive user interfaces on mobile devices aim to deliver a customized and user-friendly experience by modifying their layout, content, and behavior based on the user's context and preferences. This approach can enhance usability and efficiency. Various factors contribute to improving the performance of such interfaces on mobile devices: The performance of an adaptive user interface relies on its capacity to recognize and react to

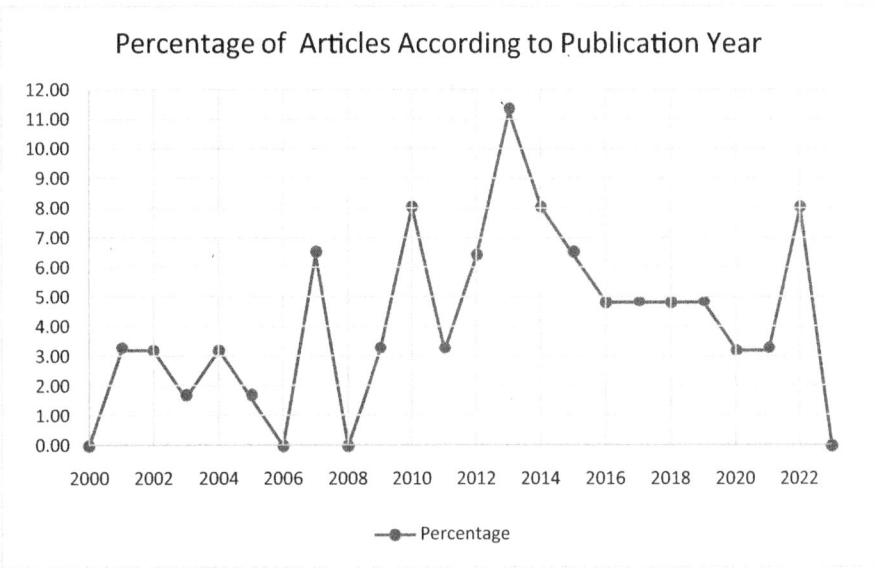

Fig. 4. Percentage of Articles According to Publication Year

alterations in the user's surroundings [44], such as their location, time of day, and device orientation. The interface's effectiveness improves with the accuracy of its context detection. Adaptive user interfaces ought to possess the capability to assimilate information from the user's actions and preferences, and then modify the interface in response [45]. The level of personalization can affect the interface's performance and usability, as too much personalization can lead to information overload, while too little can lead to a generic and unhelpful interface. Adaptive user interfaces require additional resources to operate, such as processing power and memory. If the performance overhead [46] is too high, it can lead to slow response times and poor usability. The quality and quantity of feedback given by the user can also impact the effectiveness of an adaptive user interface [47]. The more feedback the interface receives, the better it can adapt to the user's needs. Adaptive user interfaces can make it easier to use computer systems by automatically adjusting to the requirements and preferences of users. Information about each user is required for the implementation of these systems. Analytical techniques may be used to derive this user information from user events without requiring active information input from the user. The analysis shows that the created algorithm's [10] prediction quality is superior to that of other well-known prediction techniques. Objective and subjective measurements are the two categories that objective and subjective measures fall under [13]. An interface can be evaluated based on five usability characteristics within the realm of human-computer interaction. Yet, collecting data objectively is a costly, time-consuming, and difficult operation. Objective measurements are highly valuable in evaluating an interface. Comparatively speaking, subjective data can be gathered more quickly, simply, and with less effort. The subjective technique to evaluation may also be used to gauge attributes like user preferences and opinion [48]. Many modern Smartphone apps exhibit numerous usability problems, including difficult navigation, inadequate task support, convoluted interfaces, intricate interaction styles, a lack of interaction techniques, and user confusion due to the overwhelming number of options available. Mobile phones' constrained processing power, small screens, portability, and many network connectivity challenges heighten the severity of the problem. There are several algorithms available that may be utilized to carry out various sorts of adaptation, and each method has a particular advantage throughout the review process [49].

## RQ2: Which Characteristics of Self-adaptation can Increase its Performance?

The term AUI is defined as a software artifact that improves its ability to interact with a user by creating a user model using limited prior interactions with that user [21]. In other words, an AUI is capable of modifying its layout and components to suit the demands of the user [24]. Simply said, this is done since there is diversity in the user kinds, profiles, and wants. Instead of expecting the user to adjust to the system, the responsibility lies with the system to make necessary adaptations. To do this, the system tracks the user's actions and works to build a model that can adjust to meet his or her demands. AUI approaches gather both explicit and implicit data (e.g., by asking the user to choose the alternatives that best suit his or her needs) and then modify the interface as necessary. For instance, the AUI may decide to preserve and show the aspects that are utilized the most or the majority of the time, while hiding the others [50]. Another illustration of AUI is the perspective wallpaper on the Apple ® iPhone 6 that alters and changes viewpoints in response to the user's mobility. The layout of the mobile phone is easily modified when it is rotated in the third example. By carefully selecting what to display and how the selected items are shown, AUI approaches attempt to overcome the limitations imposed by the screen size and the available interaction possibilities. Another benefit that AUI could offer in some interfaces is that it restricts the amount of explicit interactions with the mobile device so that the user can complete a job with the least amount of effort. A good customizing and modification increases the application's usability and, as a result, broadens the audience for whom it is suitable. The mobile application should ideally capture and retain the majority of user interactions so that it may be customized in three different ways: graphically, physically, and vocally. The interface itself has to pick up on and correctly interpret each user's activity for this to operate. This is accomplished by developing a "user interaction profile" for each user, which is then used to modify the current interface. The profile may then be distributed across all the various interfaces of the same application to adjust them as well. AUIs may be used to solve various usability issues in mobile apps and demonstrate how including adaptable features [50] enhances a mobile app's usability, acceptability, and user experience. It has been demonstrated that the adaptation mechanisms considerably increased usefulness. Those with trembling hands or eyesight impairment benefited from relocation and scaling, while those with hearing issues benefited from volume adjustment. This framework incorporates steps for data pre-processing, learning, execution, and rendering in order to produce an appropriate user interface. A learning system that is not supervised and utilizes user context data is intelligent. The K-means algorithm is employed to cluster the collected dataset, resulting in k different levels of experience [26]. It is possible to customize the framework according to the user's requirements, such as adjusting the number of experience levels, modifying the quantity of UI components, selecting the appropriate user interface for each experience level, and taking into account user feedback on the application's outcomes.

**RQ3: How Much an Adaptive User Interface is Effective for Mobile Users in the Context of all Kinds of Applications?**

AUI can improve user satisfaction, task performance, and engagement. AUI can also reduce cognitive load and user frustration. AUI can help the user navigate through the application more efficiently by reducing the number of clicks required to complete a task. AUI can also improve accessibility for users with disabilities by providing options for font size, color, and layout. Personalization can improve user satisfaction and task completion time. Users are more likely to use an application that provides them with personalized content. Personalization can also make the user feel valued and increase their loyalty towards the application. Enhancing task performance and diminishing cognitive load can be achieved through adaptation. When applications adapt to the user's environment, they can offer pertinent information to the user when it's needed, streamlining task completion and minimizing the amount of time and energy expended. User engagement can be enhanced and frustration can be reduced through customization. When an application enables users to personalize the interface as per their preferences, they are more likely to use it. Additionally, customization can minimize the number of clicks required to accomplish a task, as users have the ability to configure the application to display only the necessary information. An interface that can adapt to limited screen space is more beneficial, as per abundant data showing that the adaptive precision conditions outperformed on the small screen [51]. The adaptive menus on small screens were noticeably faster and more satisfying than static menus, but the same could not be said for large screens. Further investigation revealed that the high accuracy condition and increased use of adaptive predictions on small screens reduced navigation and contributed to the superior performance of the adaptive menus. This indicates that people recognize the value of flexible interfaces when screen space is limited. The findings suggest that prior research on adaptable GUIs for desktop-sized programs may not be applicable to tiny displays. Therefore, researchers and designers should reconsider adaptive approaches for smaller screens due to the potential benefits they offer. An adaptive user interface (AUI) is defined as a software component that enhances its ability to interact with a user by creating a user profile using limited past interactions with that user [52]. AUIs operate on the principle that interactive systems must cater to the unique requirements of different users, rather than expecting users to conform to the system. To meet the individual demands of users, these systems model the characteristics and past behavior of each user. Adaptation user interfaces (AUIs) can be classified according to the input variables that influence adaptation and the various types of adaptive effects. The following four factors are commonly known to affect adaptation [53]: User: In AUIs, user-based adaptability is frequently used. AUIs may adjust to the preferences, knowledge, and user abilities. Task: By customizing the adjustment to match the user's current task, you can make sure that it is pertinent and useful to the users' current Endeavour. System: Variables like network connectivity and various device capabilities may require adaptation. Context: It could be vital to tailor mobile apps to the user's current situation, especially when it comes to adaptation.

[52] In response to the aforementioned factors, AUIs can undergo diverse modifications. AUIs are designed to personalize the user experience for individual users, assist with routine tasks, suggest and refine information based on user preferences, and adjust the way data is displayed [49].

## 4 Discussions

Adaptive user interfaces (UIs) for mobile applications offer several benefits to users, developers, and businesses.

Here are some of the benefits:

1. **Improved User Experience:** Adaptive user interfaces in mobile applications customize the user experience by adjusting to the user's context, preferences, and requirements, resulting in an engaging and user-friendly experience. As a result, this leads to higher user satisfaction and retention rates.
2. **Better Performance:** Adaptive UIs optimize the performance of mobile applications by adjusting the interface and functionality based on the available resources, network conditions, and device capabilities. This leads to faster response times, reduced latency, and improved battery life.
3. **Increased Accessibility:** Adaptive UIs make mobile applications more accessible to users with different abilities and disabilities. By adapting to the user's preferences, adaptive UIs can provide alternative input and output methods, such as voice commands or larger text, making the application more inclusive.
4. **Faster Development:** Adaptive UIs enable developers to create mobile applications faster and more efficiently. By using adaptive UI frameworks and design patterns, developers can reuse code, reduce development time, and increase the consistency of the user interface across different platforms.
5. **Competitive Advantage:** Adaptive UIs for mobile applications provide a competitive advantage to businesses by improving user engagement and retention, reducing churn, and increasing revenue. By providing a personalized and optimized user experience, businesses can differentiate themselves from their competitors and create loyal customers.

In summary, adaptive UIs for mobile applications offer significant benefits to users, developers, and businesses by improving the user experience, performance, accessibility, development speed, and competitive advantage.

## 5 Conclusions

The study's findings indicated that the implementation of self-adaptive user interfaces (UIs) can notably enhance the efficiency of mobile applications. The suggested approach was efficient in assessing the effectiveness of self-adaptive UIs for users of mobile devices. The benefits of AUI for mobile applications are numerous. AUI can improve user satisfaction, task performance, and engagement. AUI can also reduce cognitive load and user frustration. AUI can help the user navigate through the application more efficiently by reducing the number of clicks required to complete a task. AUI can also improve accessibility for users with disabilities by providing options for font size, color, and layout. The approach of Adaptive User Interface (AUI) in mobile application design enables the application to tailor its interface according to the user's preferences and requirements. AUI comes with various benefits, such as enhanced usability, user satisfaction, task performance, and accessibility. However, there are certain challenges associated with implementing AUI, such as increased development time and cost. The existing literature indicates that self-adaptive UIs can improve the user experience and overall performance of mobile applications. Evaluating the performance of self-adaptive UIs for mobile users is a crucial research area, and multiple studies have proposed diverse frameworks and methods to assess their performance.

## References

1. Iqbal, M.W., et al.: User context ontology for adaptive mobile-phone interfaces. IEEE Access 96751–96762 (2021)
2. Heylighen, F.: The science of self-organization and adaptivity. Encyclopedia Life Support Syst. **5**, 253–280 (2001)
3. Ahmad, A.: People centered HMI's for deaf and functionally illiterate users. Universität Potsdam (2014)
4. Jameson, A.: Adaptive interfaces and agents. The human-computer interaction handbook. s.l. CRC Press, pp. 459–484 (2007)
5. Ulanowicz, R.E.: The balance between adaptability and adaptation. BioSystems **64**, 13–22 (2002)
6. Langley, P.: Machine learning for adaptive user interfaces. In: KI-97: Advances in Artificial Intelligence: 21st Annual German Conference on Artificial Intelligence Freiburg, 9–12 September 1997 Proceedings, pp. 53–62. Springer, Germany (2005)
7. Findlater, L., McGrenere, J.: Beyond performance: Feature awareness in personalized interfaces. Int. J. Hum.-Comput. Stud. **68**, 121–137 (2010)
8. Weld, D.A., et al.: Automatically personalizing user interfaces. 0127056602 (2003)
9. Findlater, L., McGrenere, J.: A comparison of static, adaptive, and adaptable menus. In: Proceedings of the SIGCHI Conference on Human Factors in Computing Systems, pp. 89–96 (2004)
10. Nazemi, K., Stab, C., Fellner, D.W.: Interaction analysis for adaptive user interfaces. In: Advanced Intelligent Computing Theories and Applications: 6th International Conference on Intelligent Computing, ICIC 2010, Changsha, China, 18-21 August 2010. Proceedings 6, 3642149219, pp. 362–371. Springer (2010)
11. Kane, S.K.: Improving mobile phone accessibility with adaptive user interfaces. Ideals. Illinois. Edu (2010)
12. Ali, A., Alrasheedi, M., Ouda, A., Capretz, L.F.: A study of the interface usability issues of mobile learning applications for smart phones from the users perspective (2015). arXiv preprint arXiv:1501.01875
13. Ahmad, M.W.I., Shahzad, N., Feroz, S.K., Mian, I., Ali, N.: Towards adaptive user interfaces for mobile-phone in smart world. Int. J. Adv. Comput. Sci. Appl. **9**, 2158–3107 (2018)
14. Peissner, M., Häbe, D., Janssen, D., Sellner, T.: MyUI: generating accessible user interfaces from multimodal design patterns. In: Proceedings of the 4th ACM SIGCHI Symposium on Engineering Interactive Computing Systems, pp. 81–90 (2012)
15. Paymans, T.F., Lindenberg, J., Neerincx, M.: Usability trade-offs for adaptive user interfaces: ease of use and learnability. In: Proceedings of the 9th International Conference on Intelligent User Interfaces, pp. 301–303 (2004)

16. Dunlop, M., Brewster, S.: The challenges of mobile devices for human computer interaction. Pers. Ubiquit. Comput. **6**, 235–236 (2002)
17. Kolas, L., Staupe, A.: A personalized E-learning Interface. In: The International Conference on Computer as a Tool, EUROCON 2007, pp. 2670–2675. IEEE (2007)
18. Nivethika, M., et al.: 2013 International Conference on Advances in Computing, Communications and Informatics (ICACCI), pp. 1913–1918. IEEE (2013)
19. Gatsou, C., Politis, A., Zevgolis, D.: The importance of mobile interface icons on user interaction. Int. J. Comput. Sci. Appl. **9**, 92–107 (2012)
20. Punchoojit, L., Hongwarittorrn, N.: Usability studies on mobile user interface design patterns: a systematic literature review. Adv. Hum.-Comput. Interact. **2017**, 1687–5893 (2017)
21. Punchoojit, L.: Model-based adaptive user interface based on context and user experience evaluation. J. Multimodal User Interfaces **12**(1), 1–16 (2018). https://doi.org/10.1007/s12193-018-0258-2
22. Akiki, P.A., Bandara, A.K., Yu, Y.: Adaptive model-driven user interface development systems. ACM Comput. Surv. (CSUR), 47, 1–33 (2014). 0360–0300
23. Petrie, H., Bevan, N.: The evaluation of accessibility, usability, and user experience. Univ. Access Handb. **1**, 1–16 (2009)
24. Iqbal, M.W., Ahmad, N., Shahzad, S.K., Naqvi, M.R., Feroz, I.: Usability aspects of adaptive mobile interfaces for colour-blind and vision deficient users. Int. J. Comput. Sci. Netw. Secur. **18**, 179–189 (2018)
25. Feng, J., Liu, Y.: Intelligent context-aware and adaptive interface for mobile LBS. Comput. Intell. Neurosci. **2015**, 5–15 (2015). 1687–5265
26. Nivethika, M., Vithiya, I.: Personalized and adaptive user interface framework for mobile application. In: 2013 International Conference on Advances in Computing, Communications and Informatics (ICACCI), pp. 1913–1918. IEEE (2013)
27. Cena, F., Vernero, F., Gena, C.: Towards a customization of rating scales in adaptive systems. In: User Modeling, Adaptation, and Personalization: 18th International Conference, UMAP 2010, Big Island, HI, USA, 20–24 June 2010. Proceedings 18, pp. 369–374. Springer (2010). 3642134696
28. Hartmann, M.: Challenges in Developing User-Adaptive Intelligent User Interfaces. LWA, pp. ABIS: 6–10. Citeseer (2009)
29. Hervás, R., Bravo, J.: Towards the ubiquitous visualization: Adaptive user-interfaces based on the Semantic Web. Interact. Comput. **23**, 40–56 (2011)
30. Iqbal, M.W., et al.: Usability evaluation of adaptive features in smartphones. Procedia Comput. Sci. 112, 2185–2194 (2017). 1877–0509
31. Fernández-López, Á., Rodríguez-Fórtiz, M.J.: Mobile learning technology based on iOS devices to support students with special education needs. Comput. Educ. **61**, 77–90 (2013)
32. Bhaskar, N.U., Raju, U.S.N., Govindarajulu, P., Reddy, B.V.: Aspects of content, context and adaptation modeling in mobile learning application design. Int. J. Interact. Mob. Technol. **7**, 1865-7923 (2013)
33. Gullà, F., Cavalieri, L., Ceccacci, S., Germani, M., Bevilacqua, R.: Method to design adaptable and adaptive user interfaces. In: HCI International 2015-Posters' Extended Abstracts: International Conference, HCI International 2015, Los Angeles, CA, USA, 2–7 August 2015. Proceedings, Part I, pp. 19–24. Springer (2015). 3319213792
34. Grua, E.M., Malavolta, I., Lago, P.: Patricia Self-adaptation in mobile apps: a systematic literature study. In: 2019 IEEE/ACM 14th International Symposium on Software Engineering for Adaptive and Self-Managing Systems (SEAMS), pp. 51–62. IEEE (2019). 1728133688
35. Arji, G., et al.: A systematic literature review and classification of knowledge discovery in traditional medicine. Comput. Methods Programs Biomed. **168**, 39–57 (2019)

36. Veroniki, A.A., Jackson, D., Viechtbauer, W., Bender, R., Bowden, J.: Methods to estimate the between-study variance and its uncertainty in meta-analysis. Res. Synthesis Methods **7**, 55–79 (2016)
37. Yang, Z., Li, Z., Jin, Z., Chen, Y.: A systematic literature review of requirements modeling and analysis for self-adaptive systems. In: Requirements Engineering: Foundation for Software Quality: 20th International Working Conference, REFSQ 2014, Essen, Germany, 7–10 April 2014. Proceedings 20, pp. 55–71. Springer (2014). 3319058428
38. Krupitzer, C., et al.: A survey on engineering approaches for self-adaptive systems. Pervasive Mob. Comput. **17**, 184–206 (2015)
39. Macías-Escrivá, F.D., Haber, R., Del Toro, R., Hernandez, V.: Self-adaptive systems: A survey of current approaches, research challenges and applications. Expert Syst. Appl. **40**, 7267–7279 (2013)
40. Mahdavi-Hezavehi, S., Durelli, V.H., Weyns, D., Avgeriou, P.: A systematic literature review on methods that handle multiple quality attributes in architecture-based self- adaptive systems. Inf. Softw. Technol. **90**, 1–26 (2017)
41. Muccini, H., Sharaf, M., Weyns, D.: Self-adaptation for cyber-physical systems: a systematic literature review. In: Proceedings of the 11th International Symposium on Software Engineering for Adaptive and Self-Managing Systems, pp. 75–81 (2016)
42. Weyns, D., Iftikhar, M.U., Malek, S., Andersson, J.: Claims and supporting evidence for self-adaptive systems: a literature study. In: 2012 7th International Symposium on Software Engineering for Adaptive and Self-Managing Systems (SEAMS), pp. 89–98. IEEE (2012). 146731787X
43. De Lemos, R., et al.: Software engineering for self-adaptive systems: a second research roadmap. In: Software Engineering for Self-Adaptive Systems II: International Seminar, Dagstuhl Castle, Germany, 24–29 October 2010 Revised Selected and Invited Papers, pp. 1–32. Springer (2013)
44. Yaghmaie, M., Bahreininejad, A.: A context-aware adaptive learning system using agents. Expert Syst. Appl. **38**, 3280–3286 (2011)
45. Sutcliffe, A., Sawyer, P.: Modeling personalized adaptive systems. In: Advanced Information Systems Engineering: 25th International Conference, CAiSE 2013, Proceedings 25, Valencia, Spain, pp. 178–192. Springer (2013)
46. Chen, T.: Lifelong dynamic optimization for self-adaptive systems: fact or fiction? In: 2022 IEEE International Conference on Software Analysis, Evolution and Reengineering (SANER), pp. 78–89. IEEE (2022)
47. Weibelzahl, S., Paramythis, A., Masthoff, J.: Evaluation of adaptive systems. In: Proceedings of the 28th ACM Conference on User Modeling, Adaptation and Personalization, pp. 394–395 (2020)
48. Hussain, A., Kutar, M.: Apps vs devices: can the usability of mobile apps be decoupled from the device? Int. J. Comput. Sci. Issues **9**, 11–16 (2012)
49. Wesson, J.L., Singh, A., Van Tonder, B.: Can adaptive interfaces improve the usability of mobile applications? In: Human-Computer Interaction: Second IFIP TC 13 Symposium, HCIS 2010, Held as Part of WCC 2010, Brisbane, Australia, 20–23 September 2010, pp. 187–198. Springer (2010)
50. Raheel, S.: Improving the user experience using an intelligent adaptive user interface in mobile applications. In: International Multidisciplinary Conference on Engineering Technology (IMCET), pp. 64–68. IEEE (2016)
51. Findlater, L., McGrenere, J.: Impact of screen size on performance, awareness, and user satisfaction with adaptive graphical user interfaces. In: Proceedings of the SIGCHI Conference on Human Factors in Computing Systems, pp. 1247–1256 (2008)
52. Zukerman, I., Albrecht, D.W.: Predictive statistical models for user modeling. User Model. User-Adapted Interact. **11**, 5–18 (2001)

53. Looije, R., te Brake, G.M., Neerincx, M.A.: Usability engineering for mobile maps. In: Proceedings of the 4th International Conference on Mobile Technology, Applications, and Systems and the 1st International Symposium on Computer Human Interaction in Mobile Technology, pp. 532–539 (2007)

# Sentiment Analysis of Twitter Posts on 5G Technology Using ML

Mehak Faryal[1(✉)], Muhammad Farhan Khan[2], Saeid Rezaei[2], Muhammad Sohail[3], Kinza Salim[4], Muhammad Imran Khan[5], and Adeel Iqbal[6]

[1] University of Engineering and Technology, Taxila, Pakistan
mehak.faryal@students.uettaxila.edu.pk
[2] Confirm Centre for Smart Manufacturing, University College Cork, Cork, Ireland
[3] Riphah International University, Islamabad, Pakistan
[4] Capital Development Authority (CDA) Hospital, Islamabad, Pakistan
[5] Insight Centre for Data Analytics, University College Cork, Cork, Ireland
[6] Department of Electrical and Computer Engineering, COMSATS University Islamabad, Islamabad, Pakistan

**Abstract.** In recent times, Twitter has emerged as a fascinating platform for conducting sentiment analysis and opinion mining due to its massive text corpus. Numerous users express their views on various trending topics and extensively use hashtags. This study aims to analyze and classify the sentiments of Twitter users regarding 5G technology using hashtags such as #5G and related ones. The study aims to understand users' perceptions of 5G in terms of its mobility, reach, and impact on health. The emotions expressed about 5G are classified into positive, negative, and neutral categories using machine learning (ML) algorithms such as Support Vector Machine (SVM), Logistic Regression (LR), Multinomial Naive Bayes (MNB), and Random Forest, along with sentiment analysis libraries like Sci-kit and NLTK. The resulting classification model shows improved performance, evaluated using metrics such as accuracy, recall, and F1-score. Using SVM on a self-extracted dataset named "5G Myths," an accuracy of 83.09% is achieved, while using LR, MNB, and Random Forest results in an accuracy of 80%, 75%, and 57%, respectively. The study demonstrates that it is feasible to identify the critical factors and information that shape public opinion about the acceptance or rejection of 5G technology on Twitter.

**Keywords:** 5G · Machine Learning · Sentiment Analysis · Opinion Mining · Social Network · Community Detection

## 1 Introduction

5G is the fifth generation of mobile network technology and is considered the foundation of future mobile communication [1]. Despite facing criticism and rumors regarding potential health hazards, researchers have scientifically debunked these myths and confirmed that 5G is not harmful to humans. With the rise of social media platforms such as Twitter, individuals can share their thoughts and perceptions about various topics using hashtags.

Recent studies have shown that Twitter provides reasonable insights into trends and perspectives, and this study aims to analyze the behavior and perceptions of Twitter users who have used the hashtag #5G. The study collects data from Twitter's official API, preprocesses it, and conducts sentiment analysis using machine learning algorithms, including Support Vector Machine (SVM), Multinomial Naive Bayes (MNB), Logistic Regression (LR), and Random Forest. These models are effective in mining and classifying opinions about the popularity and acceptance of 5G technology among the masses.

The structure of this paper is as follows: Sect. 2 explores previous research conducted in this field. Section 3 outlines the methodology used in this study. Section 4 presents the study's findings, while Sect. 5 provides a concluding statement for the paper.

## 2 Related Work

This section covers prior research on sentiment analysis carried out using Twitter. In this paper, we utilize machine learning models and data mining tools to analyze the polarity of tweets, with a focus on online data security for Twitter data. The study proposes the concept of a Twitter bot that can monitor the emotional activity of Twitter users and report any concerning behavior to relevant authorities, allowing for legal action to be taken against the account in question. The study employs various machine learning models, including Random Forest, Multi-layer Perceptron, SVM, and MNB, with Random Forest exhibiting the most accurate classification output at 90% [2]. In their study, *Martin-Domingo et al.* aimed to analyze public opinions and sentiments regarding London Heathrow Airport on Twitter to enhance the quality of airport services. They developed a system comprising 108 keywords to identify potential problems and collected over 4,000 tweets. The study focused on extracting 23 attributes related to airport service quality from the data collected. Machine learning models were employed to conduct sentiment analysis on the data, resulting in an accuracy of 78% [3].

The study by *Saura et al.* focused on conducting sentiment analysis of unstructured data in a distributed environment using a Hadoop cluster. The researchers obtained real-time data through the Twitter API and utilized WordNet and a dictionary to identify relevant information. The sentiment analysis was performed by classifying the sentiments into three categories, enabling the assignment of a sentiment analysis score. The study employed the OpenNLP tool for data preprocessing and labeling, resulting in an accuracy of 72.27%. The main advantage of the study is its ability to accelerate the sentiment analysis process [4]. In their study, *Wu He et al.* analyzed user sentiments on social media platforms concerning specific topics or trends, focusing on the three main pizza brands. The researchers collected data from various social media sites and employed data processing and analysis techniques, including the use of the Clementine SPSS tool for extraction, hearing, and indexing. They also utilized Nvivo 9 to model the data. The study found that Domino's Pizza was more engaged with its customers by actively listening to their complaints and posting on social media. The study highlights the importance of companies responding to customer complaints to improve their services [5]. AutoML is an open-source tool offered by Google to identify and classify ML patterns and specify data functions, primarily in text format. The tool also includes Natural Language APIs, such as device identification, syntax parsing, content parsing, and classification. The data used in this tool is pre-trained models that understand the natural language of preprocessing. Sentiment analysis is conducted by utilizing the NLP library to assign a score to text analyzed for text analysis [6]. The proposed approach aims to forecast the intensity of human emotions conveyed through Twitter by assessing user behavior-related features. Additionally, it demonstrates the extraction of sentiment text data from Twitter and how it can be leveraged to enhance prediction, thereby improving network performance optimization [7].

The emergence of Big Data has led to a significant increase in data analytics within IT departments of companies. Machine Learning (ML), a promising tool for Artificial Intelligence (AI), has gained widespread demand in both industrial and academic research fields for analyzing such data streams. The combination of Big Data analytics and ML has paved the way for the development of NextGeneration (NG) large-scale wireless applications. These applications predict users' requirements on cell phones and utilize analytics to enhance wireless network efficiency [8]. Sentiment analytics involves using various content mining techniques to determine the sentiment of a text, such as whether it is positive, negative, or neutral. By analyzing the sentiment of customer feedback about their products, organizations can focus on satisfied customers and prevent potential issues. This study focuses on evaluating the opinions about 5G technology using various AI and deep learning algorithms [9]. Since the beginning of December 2019, the COVID-19 pandemic has affected the entire world, leading to increased online discussions. Unfortunately, these discussions have also included various misinformation shared by social media users. One of the popular theories connects 5G technology to the COVID-19 pandemic, leading to misinformation and even the destruction of 5G towers in the UK. Techies face the challenge of understanding how online news consumers quickly identify and address false information. This study aims to develop an understanding of users who believe in the 5G COVID-19 conspiracy theory and ways to address such misinformation [10].

As social media is becoming increasingly prevalent, a vast amount of text data is being generated, especially on platforms such as Twitter. Automatic tools need to be developed to classify the reviews available on these online resources. Moreover, these tools must be able to optimize user perception by analyzing public opinion using machine learning algorithms [11]. Text analysis can be carried out using various methods, including sentiment or emotion analysis. This helps companies target their correct customers, as opinions aid in identifying their target audience through sentiment analysis. This paper focuses on people's opinions about 5G technology. Using deep learning algorithms for classification, sentiment analysis was conducted on tweets related to 5G technology. The analysis revealed that recurrent neural networks had more predictive success than all other deep learning-based classification algorithms [9].

This literature review covers several studies on sentiment analysis using Twitter. The studies include analyzing public opinions and sentiments regarding London Heathrow Airport, sentiment analysis of unstructured data in a distributed environment, analyzing user sentiments on social media platforms concerning specific topics or trends, and predicting users' requirements on cell phones. The review also highlights the importance of sentiment analysis in evaluating customer feedback and optimizing user perception

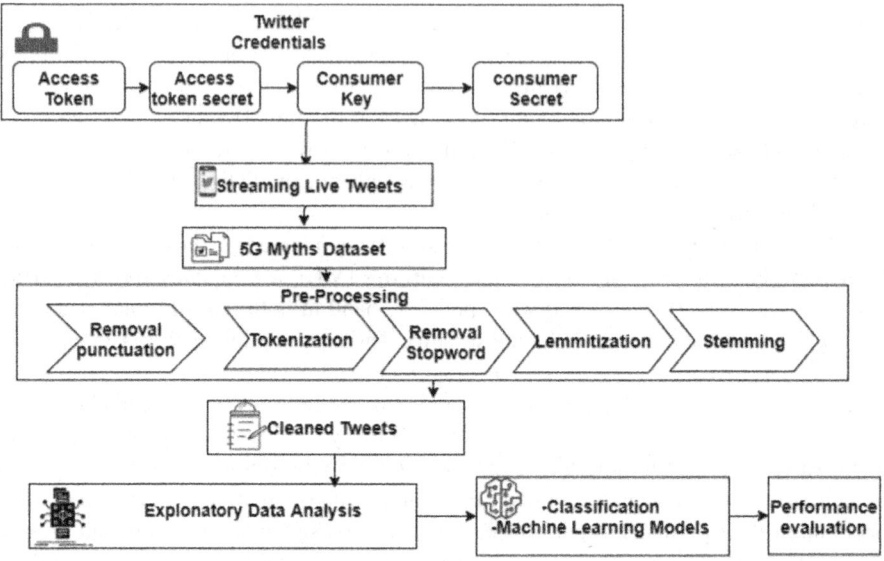

**Fig. 1.** Overall workflow including data access, preprocessing, and performance evaluation for the extracted dataset "5G Myths" from Twitter.

using machine learning algorithms. Additionally, the review includes a study addressing misinformation regarding 5G technology and the COVID-19 pandemic.

## 3 System Model

The system model used in this research is shown in Fig. 1. The process involves three phases: first, data is collected from Twitter using the Twitter API and searching for tweets containing the hashtag #5G using Jupyter Notepad. In the second phase, tweets are classified into three categories based on their sentiment: negative, neutral, and positive. To classify the tweets, a machine learning (ML) model was developed using algorithms such as SVM, LR, MNB, and random forest in Python. This model was used to analyze the diversity of 5G content and provide corresponding insights. The tweets were preprocessed using NLTK after being retrieved using the Twitter developer API.

NLTK offers various tools and resources to process human language data such as text corpora, lexical resources, tokenizers, stemmers, part-of-speech taggers, and parsers. The analysis conducted in this project using sentiment analysis on Twitter data could provide valuable insights into the public's attitudes and perceptions toward 5G technology. These insights could inform future policy and development decisions related to this latest technology.

## 4 Results and Discussion

This section presents an analysis of Twitter data on 5 G technology using ML algorithms, as illustrated by Eqs. 1–4. Moreover, we thoroughly discuss and interpret the results of our ML models, including metrics such as accuracy, precision, recall, and others.

By leveraging these results, we aim to gain valuable insights into users' opinions and perceptions regarding 5G technology and identify possible areas for improvement.

$$\text{Accuracy} = \frac{\text{Total Correctly Classify}}{\text{Total Actual}}, \quad (1)$$

$$\text{Precision} = \frac{\text{Total Correctly Predicted}}{\text{Total Predicted}}, \quad (2)$$

$$\text{Recall} = \frac{\text{Total Correctly Classify}}{\text{Total Actual}}, \quad (3)$$

$$\text{F1-score} = \frac{(2 \times Pr. \times Re.)}{(Pr. + Re.)}, \quad (4)$$

where, $Pr.$ is precision and $Re.$ is recall.

**Table 1.** Twitter analysis results

| Sentiments | Precision | Recall | F1-score |
|---|---|---|---|
| Positive | 0.89 | 0.84 | 0.86 |
| Neutral | 0.85 | 0.92 | 0.89 |
| Negative | 0.77 | 0.61 | 0.68 |

**Table 2.** Machine Learning models & their mean accuracy

| Index | Model Name | Highest Index-fold | Mean Accuracy |
|---|---|---|---|
| 1 | Linear SVM | 0 | 0.83 |
| 2 | Logistic Regression | 0 | 0.80 |
| 3 | Multinomial Naïve bayes | 0 | 0.75 |
| 4 | Random Forest | 2 | 0.57 |

The performance evaluation of sentiment classification (positive, neutral, and negative) using ML models is presented in Table 1. The results are displayed in the form of a confusion matrix. The mean accuracy of the ML models is presented in Table 2. SVM achieved the highest accuracy of 0.83%, followed by LR and MNB with the accuracy of 0.80% and 0.75%, respectively. The lowest mean accuracy was achieved by random forest at 0.57%.

In the presented Fig. 2, the confusion matrix displays both the actual and predicted values of sentiments, i.e., positive, negative, and neutral. The total number of statements classified in each category is the sum of the lines in the matrix. In particular, there are 368 positive, 117 negative, and 517 neutral statements. The columns in the matrix represent the predictions made by the ML algorithms. For instance, the first column represents

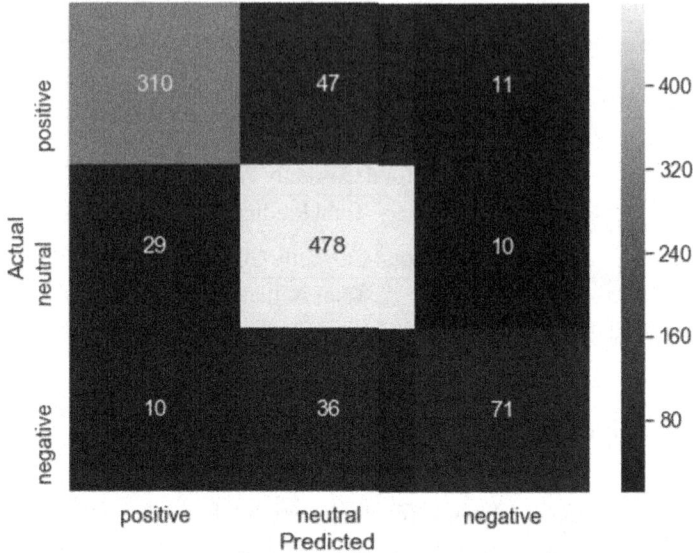

**Fig. 2.** Confusion Matrix: Actual and predicted sentiments with their total count.

the number of positive statements classified by the algorithms, which is 310. Among these, 58 nega tive statements were incorrectly classified as positive, and 30 neutral statements were also incorrectly classified as positive. Thus, the diagonal values in the matrix represent the number of correctly classified statements (Table 3).

**Table 3.** Hashtags used to find the dataset: 5G Myths

| Index | Hashtags | Index | Hashtags |
|---|---|---|---|
| 1 | Twitter Analysis about 5G | 7 | IOT and 5G |
| 2 | 5G and its Mobility | 8 | 5G and people sentiments |
| 3 | 5G technology and health | 9 | 5G in smart industries |
| 4 | Protests against 5G | 10 | 5G in smart manufacturing |
| 5 | 5G and telecom | 11 | 5G in smart manufacturing |
| 6 | 5G hype | 12 | 5G small cells |

We utilized the Twitter API to extract 6070 tweets with features such as ID, date, source, likes, retweets, place, username, tweets, timestamp, etc. The "5G myths" dataset was preprocessed and analyzed using natural language processing (NLP) techniques provided by the Natural Language Toolkit (NLTK). These techniques include removing punctuation, converting tweets to lowercase, applying tokenization, removing stop words, stemming, and lemmatization to obtain tidy tweets. We created a data frame and

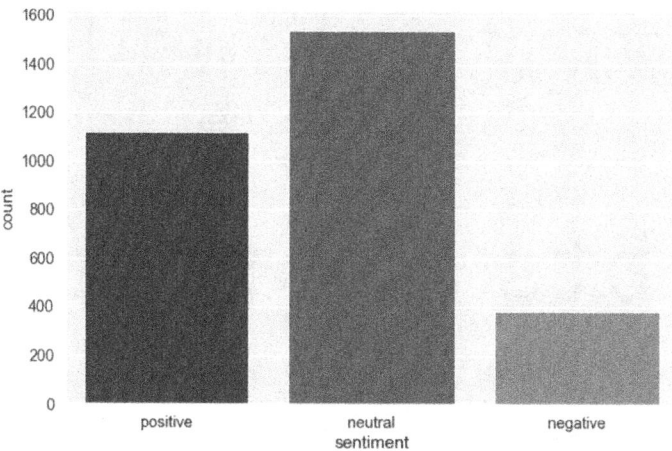

**Fig. 3.** Classification of Tweets data into three sentiments positive, negative, and neural.

applied data analysis techniques to tidy tweets. After data cleaning, we performed feature engineering and obtained a vector of (3035, 2086) features for sentiment analysis. The sentiment analysis was carried out on three class labels, namely positive, negative, and neutral.

Figure 3 shows the sentiment count graph, which displays the number of tweets in each sentiment category.

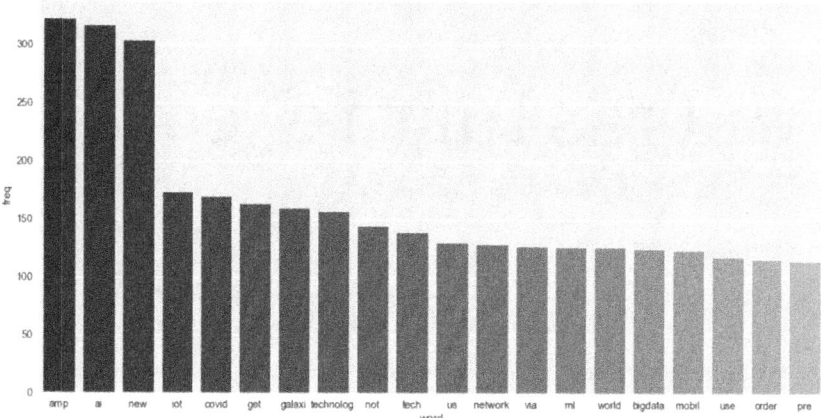

**Fig. 4.** Word frequency graph: Most frequent words used in the Tweets related to #5G.

The visual representation of textual data is achieved through the use of a word frequency graph, as depicted in Fig. 4. This graph shows that the most frequent word is "amp," whereas the word "pre" has the least frequency. Words such as "AI", "IOT", "technology", "galaxy", and "networks" have the moderate frequency. It is noteworthy

**Fig. 5.** Word cloud: Positive sentiments acquired via Twitter API from Twitter using different 5G hashtags.

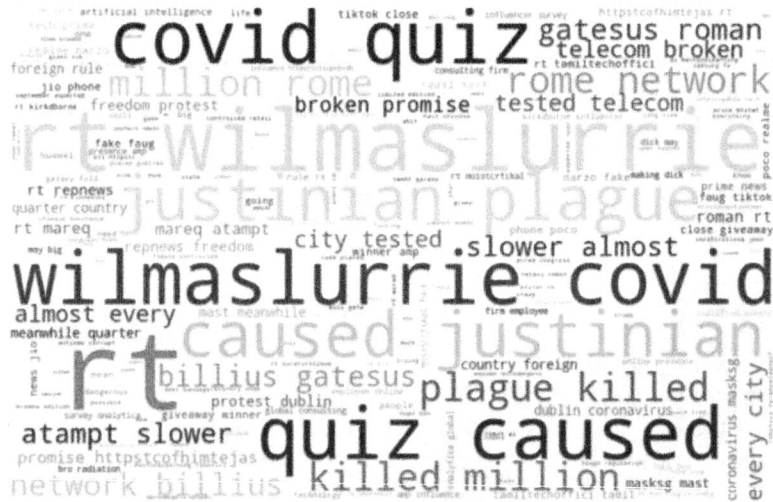

**Fig. 6.** Word cloud: Negative sentiments acquired via Twitter API from Twitter using different 5G hashtags

that the most frequent word "amp" represents power amplification in 5G devices, and its role is closely associated with 5G from a radio frequency perspective.

To analyze the sentiment of the preprocessed dataset containing Bigram features, a polarity count is applied. The polarity function generates sentiment values for each tweet, distinguishing negative or positive tweets. These values are represented through a word cloud as shown in Fig. 5. The word cloud displays the most frequent and prominent words in the dataset. The words with the highest term frequencies are the most intense and huge words in the word cloud, as well as the most significant posts in the graphs. A negative word cloud is also presented in Fig. 6.

## 5 Conclusion

Twitter has emerged as a credible source for acquiring the sentiments, opinions, and thoughts of users towards various subjects. In this study, we utilized 6070 tweets to analyze user perceptions of 5G network technology. After data cleaning and analysis using various ML algorithms, the sentiment count of tweets was classified into three categories: positive, negative, and neutral. We found an accuracy of 83.09%, 80%, 75%, and 57% using SVM, LR, MNB, and random forest, respectively. By analyzing #5G, we identified evidence of the pros, cons, promises, doubts, and fears of 5G network technology, which can help technical organizations to define strategies for managing user sentiments. In the future, we aim to use other social networking sites for data mining and advanced data analysis techniques, such as deep learning models, to increase accuracy.

## References

1. Iqbal, A., et al.: CDERSA: cognitive D2D enabled relay selection algorithm to mitigate blind-spots in 5G cellular networks. IEEE Access **9**, 89972–89988 (2021)
2. Loyola-González, O., Monroy, R., Rodríguez, J., López-Cuevas, A., MataSánchez, J.I.: Contrast pattern-based classification for bot detection on twitter. IEEE Access **7**, 45800–45817 (2019)
3. Martin-Domingo, L., Martín, J.C., Mandsberg, G.: Social media as a resource for sentiment analysis of airport service quality (ASQ). J. Air Transp. Manag. **78**, 106–115 (2019)
4. Mane, S.B., Sawant, Y., Kazi, S., Shinde, V.: Real time sentiment analysis of twitter data using hadoop. IJCSIT Int. J. Comput. Sci. Inf. Technol. **5**(3), 3098–3100 (2014)
5. He, W., Zha, S., Li, L.: Social media competitive analysis and text mining: a case study in the pizza industry. Int. J. Inf. Manag. **33**(3), 464–472 (2013)
6. Qiu, X., Sun, T., Xu, Y., Shao, Y., Dai, N., Huang, X.: Pre-trained models for natural language processing: a survey. arXiv preprint arXiv:2003.08271 (2020)
7. Kitindi, E.J., Rehman, G.: User aware edge caching in 5G wireless networks. IJCSNS **18**(1), 25 (2018)
8. Liu, Y., Bi, S., Shi, Z., Hanzo, L.: When machine learning meets big data: a wireless communication perspective. IEEE Veh. Technol. Mag. **15**(1), 63–72 (2019)
9. Seçkin, T., Kilimci, Z.H.: The evaluation of 5G technology from sentiment analysis perspective in twitter. In: 2020 Innovations in Intelligent Systems and Applications Conference (ASYU), pp. 1–6. IEEE (2020)
10. Ahmed, W., Vidal-Aball, J., Downing, J., Seguí, F.L.: Covid-19 and the 5G conspiracy theory: social network analysis of twitter data. J. Med. Internet Res. **22**(5), e19458 (2020)
11. Dashtipour, K., et al.: Public perception towards fifth generation of cellular networks (5G) on social media. Front. Big Data (2021)

# Exploring Language Modeling Techniques for Improved Recommender Systems

Muhammad Junaid Iqbal[1(✉)], Usman Ahmed Raza[2], Faisal Rehman[1,3(✉)], Muhammad Asaf[1], Yawar Ahmed[1], Usman Nawaz[4], Muhammad Saqlain Iqbal[4,5], and Ammara Tariq[6]

[1] Department of Computer Science, Lahore Leads University, Lahore, Pakistan
junaidiqbal0428@gmail.com, faisalrehman0003@gmail.com
[2] Faculty of Information Technology, University of Central Punjab (UCP), Lahore, Pakistan
[3] Department of Statistics and Data Science, University of Mianwali, Mianwali, Pakistan
[4] Department of Chemistry, COMSATS University Islamabad, Lahore Campus, Lahore 54000, Pakistan
[5] Department of Electrical and Information Engineering, Polytechnic University of Bari, Bari, Italy
[6] Department of Biochemistry and Biotechnology, University of Gujrat, Gujrat, Punjab, Pakistan

**Abstract.** Pre-trained language models (PLMs) have revolutionized natural language processing (NLP) and are now being used in recommendation systems. PLMs learn universal representations from large corpora and can be fine-tuned for specific recommendation tasks with minimal data. This paper presents a taxonomy of PLM-based recommender systems, categorizing them by training paradigms and data types. We also discuss different LM learning goals, including pre-training, language generation, and sequence classification, and how they can be applied to recommendation systems. The effectiveness of these paradigms has been shown in various recommendation tasks, but there are still problems to be addressed, such as language bias and fact consistency in language generation tasks, transfer and injection of domain knowledge, and maintaining and updating large-scale models without sacrificing accuracy or efficiency. The paper also discusses open research questions, such as multi-modal recommendations and privacy concerns. This survey provides a structured way to analyze the effectiveness of different approaches to using PLMs for recommendation systems and provides a valuable resource for researchers and practitioners looking to improve their own recommendation systems.

**Keywords:** PLM-based training · language bias · fact-consistency · pre-training mechanism · scalability · privacy issues

## 1 Introduction

The introduction of pre-trained language models (PLMs) has transformed the study of natural language processing (NLP) and led to astounding success through the self-supervised learning of universal representations on massive datasets. Several downstream NLP tasks have demonstrated the value of pre-trained models and learned representations. Both academia and business agree that the PLM-based training paradigm, which has recently been applied in the recommendation field, is a good idea. We present a thorough analysis of language modeling paradigm changes in recommender systems in this work.

The study gives an overview of pre-trained language models (PLMs) and how they have been successful in natural language processing (NLP) by learning universal representations from huge corpora in an unsupervised way [1]. The following portion of the introduction explains how The suggested domain has been used using the aforementioned training paradigm and is viewed as a promising strategy used by both companies and academics.

The goal is to thoroughly study strategies for improving pre-trained models that have been taught using various PLM-related training paradigms from a variety of viewpoints, including generality, sparsity, efficiency, and efficacy. Kumar presents an orthogonal taxonomy for the aims and training approaches of modern PLM-based recommender systems [2]. They also discuss and summarize the relationship between PLM-based training paradigms and various recommender system input data sources. Pre-training objectives, sequence-to-sequence language production, and sequence classification are just a few of the language modeling learning objectives that are mentioned, along with how they were modified for the recommendation domain. The authors' goal is to give a thorough analysis of recommender system language modeling paradigm changes. The study gives an overview of pre-trained language models (PLMs) and how they have been successful in natural language processing (NLP) through mastering universal metaphors from huge corpora in an unsupervised way [3].

It provides a clear and concise overview of the motivation and objectives of the paper, setting the stage for a systematic investigation of the use of pre-trained language models in recommender systems [4, 5]. PLMs have been able to learn universal representations of language on large corpora in a self-supervised manner. These models have been shown to be beneficial for a range of downstream NLP tasks, such as language generation, text classification, and question-answering.

Guo note that the learnt descriptions and the trained models can be used to improve recommendation systems. Recently, the PLM-based the suggested domain has been fitted with a training methodology. Which has shown great promise for improving the performance of recommendation systems [6]. Ding et al. Examine how to enhance recommendation efficiency from many viewpoints by extracting and transferring information from pre-trained models educated by various PLM-related training paradigms [7].

To achieve their objective, The authors provide an orthogonal taxonomy to categorize current PLM-based recommender systems according to their aims and training methods. This classification system provides a systematic way to analyze and compare different approaches to using pre-trained language models for recommendation systems [8, 9]. By analyzing the relationship between various forms of recommender system submission data and PLM-based training paradigms, the authors can provide insights into the effectiveness of these models for different types of recommendation tasks. Zhou also discusses the different language modeling learning objectives and their adaptations to the recommendation domain. This provides a comprehensive overview of the different approaches to using pre-trained language models for recommendation systems [10].

It sets the stage for a detailed investigation of the use of pre-trained language models for recommendation systems. It highlights the potential benefits of using these models and the challenges that need to be addressed to maximize their effectiveness. By proposing a taxonomy and analyzing Zhang aims to provide a thorough review of the state-of-the-art in this field by examining the relationship between PLM-based training methodologies and various input data sources [11] (Fig. 1).

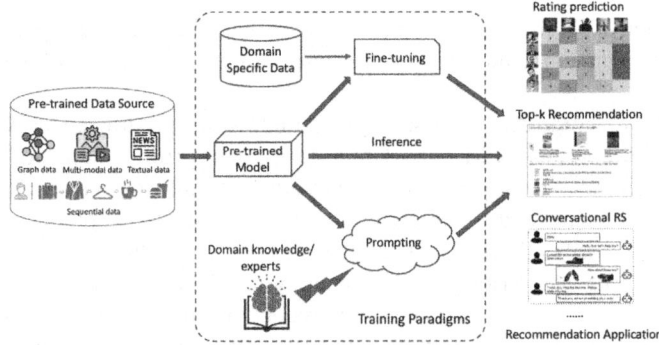

**Fig. 1.** Presents a generic architecture for language modeling paradigms in recommender systems.

Text data like reviews, comments, or summaries, as well as sequential data like how a user interacts with an item, can be used to feed the recommender system. Before the data is sent to the language mode, it is first turned into embeddings. The language model is a neural network that has already been trained to generate or classify text data. In recommender systems, the language model is changed so that it can learn ways to represent the data that can be used for recommendation tasks. Different paradigms, like pre-training and fine-tuning or prompting, are used to teach the language model how to work. For recommendation tasks, these paradigms help the language model learn better ways to represent the data it is given. The language model gives a list of recommendations, which can be either rankings of the items or explanations of the items in natural language. The picture shows how language modeling paradigms can be used to improve the performance of recommender systems. The language model that has already been trained is used to learn representations of the input data. These representations are then used to make recommendations. The different training paradigms help to optimize the language model for recommendation tasks, which can lead to more accurate and varied recommendations.

**Data Type**

Input data for recommender systems can be different types, such as:

- Textual data (reviews, comments, news, conversations, and codes)
- Sequential data (user-item interaction in chronological order)
- Graphs (user-user social graph, user-item interaction graph, or heterogeneous knowledge graph)
- Multi-modal data (using more than one type of data input, such as combining textual and image data)
- Textual data is commonly used as input for recommendations and involves expressing opinions, dialogue, narrations, and descriptions.
- Sequential data is also used, such as user-item interactions in chronological order, which is commonly seen in sequential and session-based recommender systems.
- Graphs can also be used as input data, containing different semantic information from other types of inputs, and can be constructed differently depending on the phase of the PLMRS training.
- Multi-modal data involves using more than one type of data input, such as combining textual and image data.

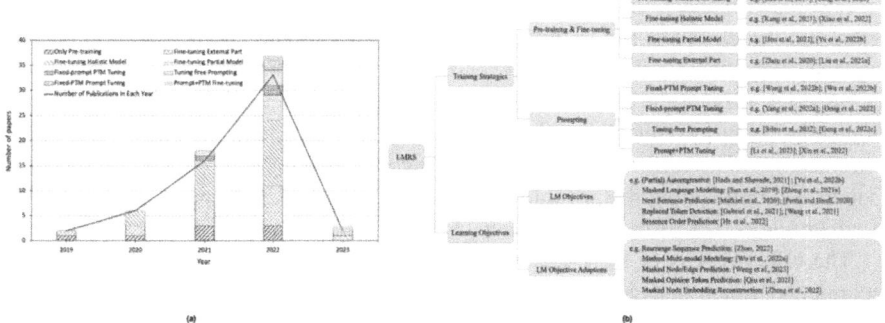

**Fig. 2.** The structure of a language model-based recommender system

Figure 2 shows the structure of a language model-based recommender system (LMRS) and provides statistics on different training strategies used in these systems, as well as the total number of publications per year. The LMRS consists of three main components: the encoder, the decoder, and the training process.

The encoder is responsible for encoding the input data, such as user-item interactions, into a dense vector representation, often called an embedding [12, 13]. The decoder then makes recommendations for users based on this embedding. In the training process, a loss function and a training dataset are used to find the best settings for the LMRS. The Fig. 2 also shows statistics about the different training methods used in LMRS, such as pre-training and fine-tuning, prompting, and pre-training with sequence classification. These strategies have different goals and ways of training, but they all involve training a language model on a large set of data and changing it to fit the task of making recommendations. The number in the Fig. 2 shows how many publications have used each of these training strategies in their LMRSs each year.

## 2 Literature Review

Pre-trained language models (PLMs) have become a powerful way to do natural language processing (NLP) tasks like creating new languages, classifying text, and answering questions. PLMs learn universal representations from large corpora in an unsupervised way. These representations can then be used in NLP tasks further down the line with only a small amount of task-specific fine-tuning data. This training model has been very successful in the field of NLP, and it has recently been adapted for use in the recommendation domain [14].

In recent years, many researchers have proposed language model-based recommender systems (LMRSs) that leverage pre-trained models to improve the performance of recommendation tasks [15]. These LMRSs are based on the assumption that the learned representations of pre-trained language models capture rich semantic information that can be used to make better recommendations. Some of the most popular pre-trained models used in LMRSs include BERT, GPT-2, and T5 [16].

For recommendation tasks, the PLM-based training paradigm can be broken down into three groups: pre-training and fine-tuning, prompting, and pre-training with sequence classification. In pre-training and fine-tuning, a small amount of task-specific data is used to fine-tune a model that has already been trained. In prompting, the recommendation task is set up as a language generation task, and the pre-trained model is trained to make recommendations when given a prompt [17]. In pre-training with sequence classification, the pre-trained model is trained to classify sequences of items as either relevant or irrelevant to a given user.

The effectiveness of PLM-based training paradigms has been verified in various recommendation tasks, including movie recommendations, book recommendations and news recommendation. The author [18] proposed a pre-training and fine-tuning approach that significantly outperforms traditional collaborative filtering methods in a movie recommendation task. The author [19] proposed a prompting method that makes explanations for recommended movies in natural language. This makes the recommendation system easier to explain and understand. Even though PLM-based training paradigms have been successful, there are still some problems that need to be solved. In language generation tasks for recommendations, one of the biggest problems is language bias and fact consistency. The pre-trained model tends to predict generic tokens to make sentences flow or to repeat certain "safe" sentences that can be used anywhere, which limits the number of explanations and answers that can be given and their usefulness [20].

Another problem is that the pre-training mechanisms in the recommendation might not be able to grow as the number of pre-trained models and the amount of stored knowledge grows. In reality, it is still not clear how to keep such complicated and large-scale models up-to-date without affecting how well and accurately recommendations work. Using language models that have already been trained to do recommendation tasks has shown a lot of promise, and LMRSs have made big improvements in a number of recommendation tasks. But there are still some problems that need to be fixed. Future research should focus on improving the variety and usefulness of the explanations and answers that are generated, on maintaining and updating complex and large-scale models, and on making sure that privacy and the high performance of recommendation algorithms are balanced [20].

In addition to above mentioned literature works, various machine and deep learning based techniques are utilized in similar applications, Cosine Similarity Technique [21], E-commerce and IoT security [22–27] Risk management [28], Expert systems [29], Quantam computing [30] and Cyber security [31] (Table 1).

**Table 1.** A list of representative LMRS methods with open-source code.

| Training Strategy | Paper | Learning Objective | Recommendation Task | Data Type | Source Code |
|---|---|---|---|---|---|
| Pre-training & Fine-tuning | [Sun et al., 2019] | Pre-train: MLM | Sequential RS | Sequential data | https://shorturl.at/ioxGP |
| | [Geng et al., 2022a] | Pre-train: AM | Explainable RS | Graph | N/A |
| | [Gabriel et al., 2021] | Pre-train: AM + MLM + PLM + RTD | Session-based RS | Textual + Sequential data | https://shorturl.at/ehqHV |
| Fine-tuning Holistic Model | [Kang et al., 2021] | Pre-train: cross-entropy Fine-tune: cross-entropy | Cross-library API RS | Textual data | https://shorturl.at/JLOQ0 |
| | [Wang et al., 2022a] | Pre-train: AM Fine-tune: AM + cross-entropy | Conversational RS | Textual data + Graph | https://shorturl.at/luBX1 |
| | [Xiao et al., 2022] | Pre-train: AM + MLM Fine-tune: AM | News RS | Textual + Sequential data | https://shorturl.at/giPQR |
| | [Zhang et al., 2022a] | Pre-train: MLM + NT-Xent Fine-tune: Negative Sampling Loss | Social RS | Textual data | https://shorturl.at/aegQW |

(*continued*)

**Table 1.** (*continued*)

| Training Strategy | Paper | Learning Objective | Recommendation Task | Data Type | Source Code |
|---|---|---|---|---|---|
| | [Wang et al., 2023] | Pre-train: MNP + MEP + cross-entropy + Contrastive Loss; Fine-tune: cross-entropy | Top-N RS | Graph | N/A |
| Fine-tuning Partial Model | [Hou et al., 2022] | Pre-train: Contrastive Loss Fine-tune: cross-entropy | Cross-domain RS Sequential RS | Textual + Sequential data | https://shorturl.at/kMVXZ |
| | [Yu et al., 2022b] | Pre-train: MLM + AM Fine-tune: cross-entropy + MSE + InfoNCE | News RS | Textual + Sequential data | https://shorturl.at/biow4 |
| | [Wu et al., 2022a] | Pre-train: MMM + MAP Fine-tune: cross-entropy | News RS | Sequential + Multi-modal data | https://shorturl.at/lKLMQ |
| | [Zhou et al., 2020] | Pre-train: MIM Fine-tune: Pairwise Ranking Loss | Sequential RS | Textual + Sequential data | https://shorturl.at/BDLM2 |
| | [Liu et al., 2022a] | Pre-train: MTP + cross-entropy Fine-tune: cross-entropy | News RS | Textual + Sequential data | https://shorturl.at/ADERU |
| | [Shang et al., 2019] | Pre-train: binary cross-entropy Fine-tune: cross-entropy | Medication RS | Graph | https://shorturl/ |

**Research Question**

1. How can we enhance the diversity and pertinence of generated explanations and replies in conversational recommender systems using language models?
2. How can we ensure fact consistency in language generation tasks for recommendation systems?
3. How can we transfer and inject domain knowledge from pre-trained models for recommendation purposes without causing the catastrophic forgetting problem?

4. What is the scalability of pre-training mechanisms in recommendation systems, and how can we maintain and update large-scale models without affecting efficiency and accuracy?
5. What are the trade-offs between privacy protection and recommendation algorithm performance when using language models?
6. How effective are different pre-training and fine-tuning strategies in improving recommendation performance for different types of input data?
7. Can multi-modal data inputs be effectively integrated into language model-based recommender systems, and what are the best approaches for doing so?
8. How can we evaluate and compare the performance of different language model-based recommender systems?

## 3 Methodology

A full survey of how language modeling paradigms have changed in recommender systems is part of the method. The authors suggest using an orthogonal taxonomy to categorize existing PLM-based recommender systems based on how they are trained and what their goals are. This dimension sorts systems based on whether they use a pre-trained model or not and whether they fine-tune the pre-trained model on a specific recommendation task.

This dimension sorts systems based on whether they treat the recommendation task as a language generation task and use a prompt to make recommendations. Pre-training with sequence classification dimension sorts systems based on whether they pre-train the model on a sequence classification task, in which the model is taught to classify sequences of items as either relevant or irrelevant to a given user.

With this classification system, the authors give a full look at the different PLM-based recommender systems and how well they work for different recommendation tasks. They also look at how PLM-based training paradigms relate to the different kinds of data that recommender systems can use as input. To back up their analysis, the authors give a table that sums up the taxonomy of PLM-based recommender systems. The table puts the different systems into groups based on their training strategies and goals, the types of data they take in, and how well the approach works for different recommendation tasks (Table 2).

This table gives a clear and concise summary of the different PLM-based recommender systems and how well they work for different recommendation tasks. By putting the different systems into clear categories, the authors can show how well different PLM-based training paradigms work for recommendation systems. The paper involves a comprehensive survey of the different PLM-based recommender systems using a systematic classification system [32]. This provides a structured way to analyze the effectiveness of different approaches to using pre-trained language models for recommendation systems.

### 3.1 LMRS Methods with Open-Source Code

List of representative LMRS methods with open-source code that contain the loss functions.

**Table 2.** Summarizing Different PLM-based recommender systems and recommendation tasks.

| PLM-based Recommender System | Training Strategy | Objective | Input Data Type | Recommendation Task | Effectiveness |
|---|---|---|---|---|---|
| system A | Pre-training & fine-tuning | Item recommendation | User-item interactions | Movie recommendation | High |
| System B | Prompting | Item recommendation | User profile and item metadata | Book recommendation | Medium |
| System C | Pre-training with sequence classification | Item recommendation | Item Metadata | News recommendation | Low |

**MoCoSeq:** Boosting Sequential Recommendation with Co-Contrastive Learning (code available on GitHub)Uses NT-Xent loss for contrastive learning in a sequential recommendation setting.

**VSE-MF:** Combining Visual-Semantic Embeddings with Matrix Factorization for Recommendations (code available on GitHub).

Uses MMM loss to learn both visual and textual embeddings at the same time in a setting for multi-modal recommendation. Dual Graph Convolutional Networks for Semi-supervised Learning Based on Graphs (code available on GitHub) Uses MAP loss for graph-based semi-supervised learning, which can be used to make recommendations when the interactions between a user and an item are shown as a graph.

Self-Supervised Image-to-Model Similarity Learning for Recommender Systems (code available on GitHub) Uses MIM loss for self-supervised learning of image-to-model similarity, which can be applied to recommendation tasks involving visual data.

**UNLP:** Unsupervised Natural Language Processing Toolkit (code available on GitHub). Includes MTP loss as one of its training objectives for unsupervised pre-training of language models.

**LARA:** Localized and Personalized News Recommendation via Attention (code available on GitHub). Uses NLL loss for personalized news recommendation with attention mechanisms.

These methods show how different loss functions can be used in LMRSs for different recommendation tasks, such as sequential recommendation, multi-modal recommendation, graph-based semi-supervised learning, self-supervised learning of image-to-model similarity, pre-training of language models, and personalized news recommendation. Researchers and practitioners who want to use and improve these LMRS techniques for their own recommendation tasks can use the open-source code as a valuable resource.

## 4 Result

The results presented give a full picture of the different ways that recommender systems model language. In the paper, a taxonomy of different training paradigms is proposed. This includes pre-training, fine-tuning, and prompting. In the paper, each training paradigm and its training and inference processes for recommendations are explained in detail.

Different language modeling learning goals and how they can be used in recommender systems, such as pre-training goals, language generation from one sequence to the next, and sequence classification. The paper talks about how well different training methods work on different kinds of recommendation tasks, such as top-N recommendation, sequential recommendation, and multi-modal recommendation.

Language models that have been trained on large datasets can help recommender systems work better, especially when data is scarce or limited. Different pre-training goals, like contrastive learning and mutual information maximization, can be used to learn better representations of how a user and an item interact with each other. Language models can be used for sequence-to-sequence language generation to explain or summarize recommended items in natural language. But coming up with different explanations that make sense is still an open research problem. Sequence classification can be used to predict user preferences or item attributes, and it can be combined with pre-training goals to learn better ways to represent the input data.

Language model-based recommender systems are starting to look into multi-modal recommendation, which means using information that isn't textual but is still important. Multi-modal alignment prediction and masked multi-modal modeling are two ways that have shown promise for combining different modalities into a single framework.

The results show that language modeling paradigms can be very useful for recommendation tasks and that different training paradigms and goals can be used to learn better representations of user-item interactions and improve recommendation performance. But there are still some research questions that need to be answered, such as how to make natural language explanations that are diverse and useful and how to add non-textual modalities to recommendation systems.

$$\text{NT-Xent loss}: L = -\log\left[\exp(\text{sim}(i,j)/\tau) / \sum\nolimits_k \exp(\text{sim}(i,k)/\tau)\right] \quad (1)$$

where $\text{sim}(i, j)$ is the cosine similarity between the encoded representations of items i and j, and $\tau$ is a temperature parameter.

$$\text{MMM loss}: L = -\log p(m \mid x, y)$$

where m is a binary mask indicating which modality (text or image) to predict, and x and y are the input text and image embeddings.

$$\text{MAP loss}: L = -\log(\text{softmax}(q^T k/\sqrt{d}))$$

where q and k are query and key embeddings, and d is the dimensionality of the embeddings.

$$\text{MIM loss}: L = \log(p(z\_i \mid x\_j)) + \log(p(z\_j \mid x\_i))$$

where z_i and z_j are the encoded representations of items i and j, and x_i and x_j are the original input representations.

$$\text{NLL loss}: L = -\log p(y|x)$$

where x is the input data (e.g. user-item interactions), and y is the target variable (e.g. user preference or item attribute).

These equations are examples of the loss functions that language model-based recommender systems use for different training paradigms and goals. They show how these loss functions are written in math, which is used to optimize the language model's parameters during training to make it better at recommendation tasks.

## 5 Conclusion

The most important findings and lessons from a systematic investigation into how the language modeling paradigm changes in recommender systems. The authors first talk about the general architecture of language model-based recommender systems (LMRSs) and then propose a full taxonomy of pre-training and fine-tuning, prompting, and pre-training with sequence classification. For each category, the authors explain the ideas behind it and how recommendations are made based on training and inference. They also talk about the different LM learning goals and how they can be applied to RS. The authors say that even though the effectiveness of LM training paradigms has been proven in different recommendation tasks, there are still some problems that need to be solved in future research.

One of the problems with recommendation language generation tasks is that the language can be biased and the facts may not match up. When conversational recommender systems use language models to make free-form responses or explanations of the recommended results, the pre-trained model tends to predict generic tokens to make sentences sound natural or repeat certain "safe" sentences that everyone can understand. Instead of "Tai Chi" answers, future research should focus on making the explanations and answers that are given more varied and relevant by making sure that the language is understood well. Also, in the future, research should focus on making sentences that match the facts, which is an urgent research problem that needs to be fixed.

Problem is how to share and add new information so that recommendations can be made in the future. Different kinds of problems can be caused by bad training methods. There are still questions about how much domain knowledge the pre-trained models have and how to transfer and use the domain knowledge learned for making recommendations.Second is that the pre-training system can't be used by a lot of people. With the continued development of the pre-trained model using large-scale data sources as inputs, model parameters are getting bigger and bigger, and the amount of stored knowledge is also growing. So, future research should focus on keeping and updating such complicated and large-scale models in a way that doesn't change how well or accurately recommendations work.

There are also problems with privacy and ethics. Recent pre-training processes are done on large corpora crawled from the web without fine-grained filtering, which means that sensitive information about users may be seen. So, it is still an open question how to make LMRSs that make trade-offs between privacy and the high performance of recommendation algorithms.

## 6 Future Work

In language modeling-based recommender systems, you can look into new training goals and change old ones to make recommendations work better. You can also look into how well different PLM architectures work, use multi-modal data, make LMRSs more efficient and scalable, do thorough evaluations and comparisons, look into the potential for LMRSs in other recommendation domains besides just product recommendations, and add in new features.

## References

1. Liu, P., Zhang, L., Gulla, J.A.J.A.P.A.: Pre-train, Prompt and Recommendation: A Comprehensive Survey of Language Modelling Paradigm Adaptations in Recommender Systems, 2023
2. Kumar, D., et al.: Parameter-efficient Modularised Bias Mitigation via AdapterFusion, 2023
3. Birjali, M., Kasri, M., Beni-Hssane, A.J.K.-B.S.: A comprehensive survey on sentiment analysis: approaches, challenges and trends, vol. 226, p. 107134 (2021)
4. Lozano Murciego, Á., et al.: Context-aware recommender systems in the music domain: a systematic literature review, vol. 10, no. 13, pp. 1555 (2021)
5. Jiang, W., et al.: An empirical study of pre-trained model reuse in the hugging face deep learning model registry, 2023
6. Guo, Z., et al.: Few-Shot Table-to-Text Generation with Prompt-based Adapter, 2023
7. Ding, N., et al.: Openprompt: an open-source framework for prompt-learning, 2021
8. Wu, C., et al.: Personalized news recommendation: methods and challenges, vol. 41, no. 1, pp. 1–50 (2023)
9. Feizi-Derakhshi, A.-R., et al.: Text-based automatic personality prediction: a bibliographic review, pp. 1–39 (2022)
10. Zhou, K., et al.: Learning to prompt for vision-language models, vol. 130, no. 9, pp. 2337–2348 (2022)
11. Zhang, W., et al.: A survey on aspect-based sentiment analysis: tasks, methods, and challenges, 2022
12. Wang, C., et al.: Sequential recommendation with multiple contrast signals, vol. 41, no. 1, pp. 1–27 (2023)
13. Sattar, A., Bacciu, D.J.N.P.L.: Graph Neural Network for Context-Aware Recommendation, pp. 1–20 (2022)
14. Fan, W., et al.: Generative Diffusion Models on Graphs: Methods and Applications, 2023
15. Liu, X., et al.: Deep unsupervised domain adaptation: a review of recent advances and perspectives, vol. 11, no. 1 (2022)
16. Alzubaidi, L., et al.: Review of deep learning: concepts. CNN Archit. Chall. Appl. Futur. Dir. **8**, 1–74 (2021)
17. Gao, T., Fisch, A., Chen, D.J.A.P.A.: Making pre-trained language models better few-shot learners, 2020
18. Wang, Y., et al.: An Adaptive Graph Pre-training Framework for Localized Collaborative Filtering, vol. 41, no. 2, pp. 1–27 (2022)

19. Piscopo, A., et al. Report on the 1st Workshop on Measuring the Quality of Explanations in Recommender Systems (QUARE 2022) at SIGIR 2022. in ACM SIGIR Forum. 2023. ACM New York, NY, USA
20. Tam, Y.-C.: Cluster-based beam search for pointer-generator chatbot grounded by knowledge. J.C.S. Lang. **64**, 101094 (2020)
21. Javed, A., Rehman, F., Sarfraz, N., Sharif, H., Khan, R., Khan, A.M.: Movie recommendation system with sentimental analysis using cosine similarity technique. In: 2022 3rd International Conference on Innovations in Computer Science & Software Engineering (ICONICS), Karachi, Pakistan, 2022, pp. 1–8 (2022). https://doi.org/10.1109/ICONICS56716.2022.10100512
22. Ashraf, M.S., Rehman, F., Sharif, H., Aqeel, M., Arslan, M., Rida, A.: Spam consumer's reviews detection for E-Commerce website using linguistic approach in deep learning. In: 2022 3rd International Conference on Innovations in Computer Science & Software Engineering (ICONICS), Karachi, Pakistan, 2022, pp. 1–7, https://doi.org/10.1109/ICONICS56716.2022.10100351
23. Manan, I., Rehman, F., Sharif, H., Ali, C.N., Ali, R.R., Liaqat, A.: Cyber security intrusion detection using deep learning approaches, datasets, Bot-IOT dataset. In: 2023 4th International Conference on Advancements in Computational Sciences (ICACS), Lahore, Pakistan, 2023, pp. 1–5 (2023). https://doi.org/10.1109/ICACS55311.2023.10089688
24. Ashraf, S., Rehman, F., Sharif, H., Kirn, H., Arshad, H., Manzoor, H.: Fake reviews classification using deep learning. In: 2023 International Multi-disciplinary Conference in Emerging Research Trends (IMCERT), Karachi, Pakistan, 2023, pp. 1–8 (2023). https://doi.org/10.1109/IMCERT57083.2023.10075156
25. Hassaan Khalid, M., et al.: A brief overview of deep learning approaches for IoT security. In: 2023 4th International Conference on Computing, Mathematics and Engineering Technologies (iCoMET), Sukkur, Pakistan, 2023, pp. 1–5 (2023). https://doi.org/10.1109/iCoMET57998.2023.10099306
26. Hussain, A., et al.: A systematic review of intrusion detection systems in internet of things using ML and DL. In: 2023 4th International Conference on Computing, Mathematics and Engineering Technologies (iCoMET), Sukkur, Pakistan, 2023, pp. 1–5 (2023). https://doi.org/10.1109/iCoMET57998.2023.10099142
27. Humayoun, M., et al.: From cloud down to things: an overview of machine learning in internet of things. In: 2023 4th International Conference on Computing, Mathematics and Engineering Technologies (iCoMET), Sukkur, Pakistan, 2023, pp. 1–5 (2023). https://doi.org/10.1109/iCoMET57998.2023.10099119
28. Shakeel, H., et al.: Machine learning in banking risk management - a brief overview. In: 2023 4th International Conference on Computing, Mathematics and Engineering Technologies (iCoMET), Sukkur, Pakistan, 2023, pp. 1–5 (2023). https://doi.org/10.1109/iCoMET57998.2023.10099339
29. Ishtiaq Rana Mohtasham Aftab, M., Ijaz, M., Rehman, F.: An Expert System for Weapon Identification and Categorization Using Machine Learning Technique to Retrieve Appropriate Response, 2022. https://doi.org/10.54692/lgurjcsit.2021.0504248
30. Manan, I., Rehman, F., Sharif, H., Riaz, N., Atif, M., Aqeel, M.: quantum computing and machine learning algorithms - a review. In: 2022 3rd International Conference on Innovations in Computer Science & Software Engineering (ICONICS), Karachi, Pakistan, 2022, pp. 1–6 (2022). https://doi.org/10.1109/ICONICS56716.2022.10100452

31. Aftab, R.M., et al.: A systematic review on the motivations of cyber-criminals and their attacking policies. In: 2022 3rd International Conference on Innovations in Computer Science & Software Engineering (ICONICS), Karachi, Pakistan, 2022, pp. 1–6 (2022). https://doi.org/10.1109/ICONICS56716.2022.10100569
32. Wang, Y., et al.: Open-world Story Generation with Structured Knowledge Enhancement: A Comprehensive Survey (2022)

# Machine Learning Based Approach to Secure Light Weight Devices

Saim Raza, Majid Hussain[✉], Hina Zafar, and Amna Iqbal

The University of Faisalabad, Faisalabad, Pakistan
md.arif@superior.edu.pk

**Abstract.** The use of Internet of Things (IoT) technology has undergone a boom in prominence equivalent to the spread of smartphones. IoT devices are at high risk for security threats, including DDoS attacks from IoT botnets due to their small size and limited resources. Implementing strong security measures is essential to protect these devices and their sensitive data from cyber-attacks. Machine-learning algorithms used for the early identification of these dangerous botnets. In this research, we seek to identify Botnets for early detection. The proposed approach is based on a one-class classifier that employs one-class KNN and chooses the best features using various feature selection techniques including PCA and XGBoost. The proposed approach is implemented by using various datasets gathered from different IOT devices. The experimental findings demonstrate enhanced performance on the collected datasets. The proposed method exhibits excellent accuracy, which is 99% and is successful in identifying IoT botnets early on. This will lead to a decrease in the effects of impending DDoS attacks.

**Keywords:** IoT (Internet of Things) · botnet detection · classification · Intrusion Detection · Feature reduction · Machine Learning · Deep Learning

## 1 Introduction

The Internet of Things (IoT) is a developing technology that provides an infrastructure for diverse devices that can streamline tasks in a variety of contexts. Several data and communication design domains use the "Internet of Things" (IoT) concept. A recent analysis published claims that by 2025, the global IoT market might be worth USD 1567 billions [1].

IoT gadgets are vulnerable to numerous security flaws since they communicate data across communication channels. Standard security for networks approaches developed Traditional networks transform useless considering their constrained computing and storage capacities and inability to regularly deploy security patches, systems based on the Internet of Things [2].

A threat known as a botnet exploits IoT's security flaws. IoT botnets have been used to execute several damaging DDoS assaults; Mirai is one famous example. Research into security flaws, their identification, categorization, and the following IoT device recovery assaults should thus be given more thought. Because of this, IoT requires the use of an intrusion detection system [3].

A key machine learning approach known as feature selection lowers the computational burden of modeling while also enhancing the effectiveness of a prediction model. XGBoost and PCA are machine-learning techniques that were employed in this study. It is renowned for its great accuracy and speed be utilized for both classification and regression applications. A feature selection strategy that ranks the significance of features according to how they affect the performance of the model is also a part of XGBoost.

On the detection and classification of Botnet [5, 6] have produced a state-of-theart study used as the Baseline study. There are a significant number of missing variables in the dataset utilized in this study, which cannot be disregarded. The authors of this study don't go into detail on how they deal with this restriction. Several proposed techniques deal with missing numbers and generate useful data. The authors of this paper used just one feature selection approach to choose 26 features out of a total of 178 retrieved features.

The Shark script designed for numerical data, so other libraries needed for text or image data. It can be challenging beginners to use and requires extensive knowledge and experience. There may be limited support resources available. Feature extraction takes time and depends on the size and complexity of the dataset. Overfitting may occur if the model is too tightly tuned to the training data, but this can be reduced by choosing features properly and using regularization techniques [7, 8].

## 2 Literature Review

A review of the literature depicts that various aspects of security, privacy, and machine learning is crucial in the context of IoT environments. The papers use different techniques such as cryptographic algorithms, Blockchain, statistical anomaly detection, and machine learning algorithms like PCA and XGBoost for feature extraction. Updating cryptographic algorithms or software patches posed a challenge on these devices, leaving them vulnerable to known vulnerabilities [7].

The papers highlight the need for effective security measures in IoT environments, given the potential vulnerabilities and risks associated with these systems [10].

The use of machine learning algorithms, cryptographic techniques [5], and Blockchain-based systems help mitigate these risks and enhance the security and privacy of IoT systems [11]. However, challenges remain, particularly in implementing security measures on lightweight devices with limited resources [12].

The proliferation of IoT devices has led to various innovations that have improved people's lives and increased productivity, such as driverless vehicles, patient monitoring, smart home appliances, and more. However, the widespread use of these devices has also made them vulnerable to cyber-attacks, particularly botnet attacks. Cybercriminals can take control of these devices due to the lack of security measures, turning them into zombies or bots. Lightweight devices, such as IoT devices and smartphones, are particularly vulnerable to such attacks due to limited processing power, storage, and network bandwidth, as well as a lack of security controls [13].

Using artificial intelligence and automated learning methods to analyze IoT network data and detect significant assaults like botnets or DDoS attacks [14].

Honeypots are another effective method of defending against botnet attacks. A honeypot is designed to attract attackers and gather data on their methods and tactics, including IP addresses, MAC addresses, port numbers, and types of devices targeted, malware executables, and their commands. Honeypots can be categorized based on the level of engagement with attackers, with low-interaction and high-interaction honeypots being the two main types. Research honeypots can be used for research purposes, while production honeypots are used to defend the assets of the firm against real-time assaults to boost general security [8].

In conclusion, honeypots and Utilizing machine learning and supervised learning methods, analyze traffic on the network. Are promising approaches to defending against botnet attacks in IoT systems? These approaches can help to identify and mitigate risks and flaws in the system and prevent cybercriminals from exploiting vulnerabilities in IoT devices [15].

Although the literature review covered various techniques and algorithms it didn't offer any assistance in the area of IoT and privacy a direct comparison between PCA and XGBoost with the other approaches. However, PCA and XGBoost have gained popularity in recent years due to their effectiveness in feature extraction and classification, respectively. PCA is widely used for reducing the dimensionality of high-dimensional data, which makes it easier to analyze and interpret the data. On the other hand, XGBoost is a powerful machine learning algorithm that handles complex datasets and achieves high accuracy in classification tasks. Therefore, the combination of PCA and XGBoost is a promising approach for IoT security applications, as it may provide feature extraction and classification services that are both effective and accurate.

## 3 Methodology

In this step, we design a framework, which perform the following. The PCAP formats are frequently associated with network analysis tool applications like Wireshark. It frequently contains data that has been gleaned from network packets. To learn how a network is currently operating and to identify any network difficulties, PCAP files may be inspected. The PCAP files may also be used to look for data that is sent between both networked hosts and non-networked hosts. Figure 1 illustrates the mechanism architecture, which is the general design of the proposed remedy. Algorithm 1 describes the proposed solution's methodology. The proposed work's technique is broken down into the following steps.

Botnet detection Algorithm using a one-class algorithm based on KNN.

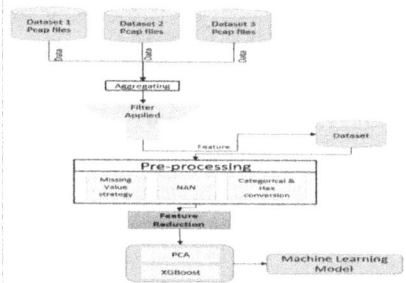

**Fig. 1.** Proposed framework for attack detection

1. Input: datasets d1, d2, d3
   a. Convert datasets d1, d2, d3 formatted as PCAP
   b. Implement source- and destination-based filtering of IP addresses
   c. features extraction using PCA and XGBoost for f ∈ (f1, f2, f3, ... fn)
   d. Eliminating missing, infinite, NAN, and HEX values during data preparation
   e. End feature choice
2. For each dataset d1, d2, d3 apply one-class KNN
   a. Decide on k's value.
   b. Train the model.
   c. Add the training dataset.
   d. For each point in the test data until point = NULL
   e. Find Euclidian distance d to all training data points $d = \sqrt{\sum_{i=1}^{k}(x_i - y_i)2}$
   f. Store d in a list L and sort it
   g. Choose the first k points
   h. Assign class to the test points
   i. End For
3. End For

### 3.1 Filtering PCAP

PCAP filters are a method for keeping particular packets out. If the origin IP is of interest, the origin IP filter is utilized, and that origin's IP is going to be displayed along with the packet. PCAP Each IoT device's files are screened using a set of unique filters. Wireshark, a well-used network monitoring tool, is employed for this purpose. Wireshark is an openly accessible and free license application used to analyze network traffic. As the traffic is slowly captured, its records are placed in the PCAP file. For later analysis. All of the traffic that has been recorded by IoT devices is available in PCAP files. The PCAP file is examined for protocols and fields after being imported into Wireshark. Since each dataset contains the IP addresses of IoT devices, it is simple to create individual PCAP files for each device. A source and destination IP-based filter is used to isolate the traffic for an IoT device [3, 18, 19].

### 3.2 Data Preprocessing and Feature Selection

The technique of data preparation is used to clean up the data and make it suitable for training ML classifiers. Statistics commonly incorporate some endless, incorrect, and undefinable variables. Using a method from the library Pandas, the missing values were substituted with a numerical zero.

PCA is used to implement feature extraction, and 16 features were retrieved from each dataset. The number of independent variables then decreased using the feature selection method, which also decreased the computational burden. Only factors that significantly impact the answer is kept as part of the feature selection process. Removes elements that are pointless or repetitious.

The ip. Flags attribute of the dataset included in CSV files is in hexadecimal format. Other than ip. Flags, and all of the features use a decimal numbering scheme. Therefore, using the Pandas library, the ip. Flags feature is changed from the hex to a system of numbers that are decimal in order to continue keeping everything in the same numerical system and to be the classifier has identified.

### 3.3 Categorical Values

Categorical variables have non-numeric values and need to be encoded for machine learning classifiers that require numerical input. One-hot encoding is a technique used to transform categorical variables into numerical values. The Pandas library is used for the "receive-dummies" technique to encode categorical variables in this study, including the source and destination IP addresses.

### 3.4 Experiments with One-Class KNN

The proposed study included instances of benign and malicious datasets, of which 20K is malignant, whereas 60K is harmful. To train the algorithm and evaluate its performance, the beneficial examples were divided by an 80%-20% proportion. The classification compared to the training dataset in order to determine if a packet is malicious or not.

## 4 Results and Analysis

The table shows the performance metrics (F1-Score, Accuracy, and Recall) of three different datasets (Chris, MedBiot, HCRL) for two scenarios: "Normal" and "FS Applied". "Normal" refers to the dataset without feature selection (FS), while "FS Applied" refers to the dataset with FS applied. Overall, applying FS improved the performance metrics for all datasets, resulting in higher F1-Scores, Accuracy, and Recall. For instance, in the MedBiot dataset, the F1-Score, Accuracy, and Recall improved from 81%, 88%, and 92% to 98%, 98%, and 100%, respectively, when FS was applied (Table 1).

Features that don't significantly affect performance are removed. The PCA and XGBoost technique is then applied after filtering, which selects the best attributes that improve the F1 score and are used for artificial intelligence training.

**Table 1.** Impact of feature choice.

| Data Type | Chris Dataset | | | MedBiot Dataset | | | HCRL (INID) Dataset | | |
|---|---|---|---|---|---|---|---|---|---|
| | F1-Score | Accuracy | Recall | F1-Score | Accuracy | Recall | F1-Score | Accuracy | Recall |
| Normal | 88% | 87% | 94% | 81% | 88% | 92% | 83% | 87% | 91% |
| FS Applied | 99% | 99% | 100% | 98% | 98% | 100% | 98% | 98% | 100% |

### 4.1 Comparison with Recently Published Works

Results from research [27, 28] that evaluated botnet identification using several ML algorithms are compared to the proposed method in Table 2.

**Table 2.** Comparison with recently published research.

| Research | F1-Score | Feature Selection | Multiple Dataset | One-Class Classifier |
|---|---|---|---|---|
| IOTDS [27] | 94% | No | No | Yes |
| Smart home IDS [28] | 98% | No | No | No |
| Proposed Solution | **99%** | Yes | Yes | Yes |

## 5 Conclusions

One-class KNN is apply to identify harmful Internet of Things bot-nets attacks in a complex setting. The findings suggest that this approach can be effective in detecting such botnets, and further research can explore the potential of this method in real-world settings. The lightweight approach is developed to get around the processing power restriction. Methods for choosing features, including the PCA and XGB methods, were utilized to choose the top characteristics that affected the effectiveness of a machine-learning classifier. For various datasets, feature space is decreased by 80% using the PCA and XGBoost approaches. Given that it has been evaluated using a variety of IoT devices in three distinct IoT scenarios, the offered solution is unique. For several IoT botnet datasets, the proposed approach is capable to identify F1-scoring IoT botnets ranging from 98% to 99%. The solution proved successful in identifying unknown harmful IoT traffic in various light weight IOT based devices.

## References

1. Soe, Y.N., Feng, Y., Santosa, P.I., Hartanto, R., Sakurai, K.: Machine learning-based IoT-botnet attack detection with sequential architecture. Sensors (Switzerland) **20**(16), 1–15 (2020). https://doi.org/10.3390/s20164372
2. Ahmad, M., et al.: End-to-end loss based TCP congestion control mechanism as a secured communication technology for smart healthcare enterprises. IEEE Access **6**, 11641–11656 (2018). https://doi.org/10.1109/ACCESS.2018.2802841

3. Malik, K., Rehman, F., Maqsood, T., Mustafa, S., Khalid, O., Akhunzada, A.: Lightweight internet of things botnet detection using one-class classification. Sensors **22**(10) (2022). https://doi.org/10.3390/s22103646
4. Jabbar, S., Akbar, A.H., Zafar, S., Quddoos, M.M., Hussain, M.: VISTA: achieving cumulative VIsion through energy efficient Silhouette recognition of mobile Targets through collAboration of visual sensor nodes, 2014. http://jivp.eurasipjournals.com/content/2014/1/32
5. Sabrina, F., Li, N., Sohail, S.: A blockchain based secure IoT system using device identity management. Sensors **22**(19) (2022). https://doi.org/10.3390/s22197535
6. Hussain, M., et al.: A Gateway Deployment Heuristic for Enhancing the Availability of Sensor Grids, 2016
7. Akhter, A.S., Ahmed, M., Shah, A.S., Anwar, A., Kayes, A.S.M., Zengin, A.: A blockchain-based authentication protocol for cooperative vehicular ad hoc network. Sensors (Switzerland) **21**(4), 1–21 (2021). https://doi.org/10.3390/s21041273
8. Jagdale, B., Sugave, S., Kolhe, K.: Design and analysis of fabrication threat management in peer-to-peer collaborative location privacy. IJCSNS Int. J. Comput. Sci. Netw. Secur. **21**(12) (2021). https://doi.org/10.22937/IJCSNS.2021.21.12.55
9. Ding, Y., Xu, H., Wang, Y., Yuan, F., Liang, H.: Secure multi-keyword search and access control over electronic health records in wireless body area networks. Secur. Commun. Netw. **2021** (2021). https://doi.org/10.1155/2021/9520941
10. S. N. G and S. M. A, Denial of Service Attacks in Software Defined Networking-A Survey, 2022. www.irjet.net
11. Mandal, M., Dutta, R.: Identity-based outsider anonymous cloud data outsourcing with simultaneous individual transmission for IoT environment. J. Inf. Secur. Appl. **60** (2021). https://doi.org/10.1016/j.jisa.2021.102870
12. Zhang, P.: Permutation-based lightweight authenticated cipher with beyond conventional security. Secur. Commun. Netw. **2021** (2021). https://doi.org/10.1155/2021/1468007
13. Xiao, L., Wan, X., Lu, X., Zhang, Y., Wu, D.: IoT security techniques based on machine learning: how do IoT devices use AI to enhance security? IEEE Signal Process. Mag. **35**(5), 41–49 (2018). https://doi.org/10.1109/MSP.2018.2825478
14. Reddy, L.C.S., Jain, P.: Attribute Based Collusion Resistant Controlled Secure Data Processing System Using Node Insertion Method, 2021. https://doi.org/10.21203/rs.3.rs-432580/v1
15. Anand Kumar, K.S., Prasad, A.Y., Balakrishna, R.: IoT based E-commerce getting a secure connection using block chain methodology. ACS J. Sci. Eng. **1**(1), 24–30 (2021). https://doi.org/10.34293/acsjse.v1i1.4
16. Rutravigneshwaran, P., Anitha, G., Prathapchandran, K.: Trust-based support vector regressive (TSVR) security mechanism to identify malicious nodes in the Internet of Battlefield Things (IoBT). Int. J. Sys. Assur. Eng. Manag. (2022). https://doi.org/10.1007/s13198-022-01719-w
17. 2022 IEEE International Conference on Current Development in Engineering and Technology (CCET)
18. Sreekala, K.: Lineaments and Resultant Consequences, Potential Solvent of Latency and Consumption of Energy in IOT, 2021
19. Maradani, L.: Human activity recognition. Int. J. Res. Appl. Sci. Eng. Technol. **10**(7), 1983–1988 (2022). https://doi.org/10.22214/ijraset.2022.45630

# GAPTCHA: A Game-Based Image-CAPTCHA

Umar Farooq[1], Noshina Tariq[2(✉)], Danish Mehmood[1], Maram Fahaad Almufareh[3], Mamoona Humayun[3(✉)], and Farrukh Aslam Khan[4]

[1] Department of Computer Science, Shaheed Zulfikar Ali Bhutto Institute of Science and Technology, Islamabad 44000, Pakistan
dr.danish@szabist-isb.edu.pk

[2] Department of Avionics Engineering, Air University, Islamabad 44000, Pakistan
noshina.tariq@mail.au.edu.pk

[3] Department of Information Systems, College of Computer and Information Sciences, Jouf University, Sakakah 72388, Al Jouf, Saudi Arabia
{gnalwakid,mahumayun}@ju.edu.sa

[4] Center of Excellence in Information Assurance (CoEIA), King Saud University, Riyadh 11653, Saudi Arabia
fakhan@ksu.edu.sa

**Abstract.** The threat of bot attacks has increased with the abundance of a diverse range of smart devices used globally. Users access the Internet for various needs, such as entertainment, education, e-commerce, and data exchange. It has tremendously increased the number of users and connected devices. The completely automated public Turing test to tell the computer and human apart (CAPTCHA) is a fully automated Turing test to differentiate a machine from a person and safeguard Internet services from spam and bot assaults. However, the distortion levels make human identification unpleasant and impossible. This paper proposes a novel CAPTCHA, named "GAPTCHA," based on a famous game called Snakes and Ladders game. It uses a simple keyboard, mouse, and touch inputs. The results showed that 3% of the people got it wrong, and about reusing the proposed GAPTCHA, 100% of the users said yes, which is a positive result for its successful user experience.

**Keywords:** Security · Image CAPTCHA · Game-based CAPTCHA · CAPTCHA usability

## 1 Introduction

A large variety of mobile and smart devices are now widely available due to users' eagerness to access the web. There has been a dramatic increase in the number of people using the Internet. All services, such as banking and government, entertainment, food shopping, healthcare and transportation, hotel reservations, and other, are now accessible online [1, 2]. Internet security has been the biggest challenge for web developers from the beginning against bot attacks [3, 4]. Completely Automated Public Turing Test to Tell Computer and Humans Apart (CAPTCHA) prevents automated script assaults and distinguishes between a machine and a person. Many different strategies have been developed to safely and effectively design the CAPTCHA.

CAPTCHAs should also be difficult for a bot to identify. Humans can quickly and accurately identify image data. Classification of CAPTCHA is based on text, image, audio, video, or puzzle. Applications of CAPTCHA involves protecting the registration of websites, online polls, email addresses, search engine bots, or dictionary attacks. It consists of pictures, written alphabets, and digits at random or in a predetermined sequence. A legitimate CAPTCHA challenge needs to preserve a delicate equilibrium. It should not be too simple for a bot/program to crack, and neither should it be very challenging for a person. However, as history has shown, getting to this point is difficult. As long as it has less than 1% success rate, it is regarded as safe. It is suggested that a bot should be able to answer just one out of every 10,000 problems [5]. The usefulness of a CAPTCHA must exceed 80% for human users.

**Fig. 1.** A conventional iPhone 4S Text CAPTCHA display.

Conventional CAPTCHAs are typically visual or auditory challenges and are not always compatible with mobile devices. Mobile displays are smaller, and mobile input methods (touchscreens, for example) can be less precise than desktop keyboards and mice. It can make it difficult for users to accurately and swiftly complete CAPTCHAs, resulting in frustration and potential business loss for websites. Therefore, mobile-friendly alternatives to CAPTCHAs, such as mobile-specific challenges, should be investigated. Most submit buttons and challenge images are impractically small due to the constraint of screen size and virtual keyboard (Fig. 1), as seen in the examples using a cell device (i.e., iphone4s). Typically, users must combine zooming in/out and scrolling up/down actions to uncover and solve a puzzle. The continued explosion in mobile phone ownership means that accommodating customers on the go is essential to any successful CAPTCHA implementation.

Nevertheless, many CAPTCHA schemes have been broken successfully. It is possible to strengthen CAPTCHA security by deliberately adding disturbances. However, the distortions also make it harder for human users. In contrast, conventional CAPTCHA schemes require a mouse or keyboard to be filled, making it impractical in the era of current smart devices like smartphones. Therefore, this paper presents an enjoyable game-based image CAPTCHA, named "GAPTCHA." The significant contributions of the paper are listed below:

1. A novel image and game-based CAPTCHA (GAPTCHA) is proposed in this study.
2. The performance of the proposed GAPTCHA is analyzed by carrying out its Quality and Usability analysis.

The rest of the paper is organized as follows: The relevant literature is reviewed in Sect. 2. Section 3 presents the proposed framework, whereas experimental results are presented in Sect. 4. The paper is concluded in Sect. 5 with future directions.

## 2 Literature Review

This section presents a critical review of various image- and game-based CAPTCHAs. In [6], the proposed method is tested on over 3000 CAPTCHA schemes. However, the proposed CAPTCHA is not user-friendly. In [7], the study introduces and assesses Nouncaptcha, a new image-based CAPTCHA technique. Nouncaptcha requires users to assess an image and choose nouns from a list. However, their proposed CAPTCHA takes too much time to solve by humans and is not helpful for all-age users. Also, image recognition is too difficult for every user. In [8], the authors prevent spyware attacks using CAPTCHAs. The user is asked to log in multiple times, which irritates the user. On the other hand, authors in [9] proposed a CAPTCHA based on the PROMETHEE-GAIA methods to rank different types of CAPTCHAs. In [10], a CAPTCHA based on semantic information is presented using Particle Swarm Optimization (PSO). In [11], authors proposed a mini game-based CAPTCHA to assess CAPTCHA usability and make them safe, secure, and efficient.

In [12], the authors proposed a level-based CAPTCHA based on Dynamic Cognitive Game (DCG). Another image and sound-based CAPTCHA is presented in [13], where the user matches the sound of an object with the given object among many other objects. In [14], the authors proposed a CAPTCHA based on a DCG and Emerging Images (EI) of existing image processing and machine learning techniques. However, it is based on three usability levels, i.e., Easy, Medium, and Difficult. In [15], the authors proposed a gesture-based CAPTCHA. With the help of sensory movements, the user can verify that they are, in fact, human beings. It protects from Random Guessing attacks, Dictionary attacks, and DDoS attacks. In [16], a drag-and-drop puzzle-based CAPTCHA is proposed. The users play a simple game to answer a visual question. Their method is convenient, easy for users, and challenging for bots. In [17], the authors propose a better visual effect due to multi-frame dynamic image CAPTCHA, which is safe and efficient.

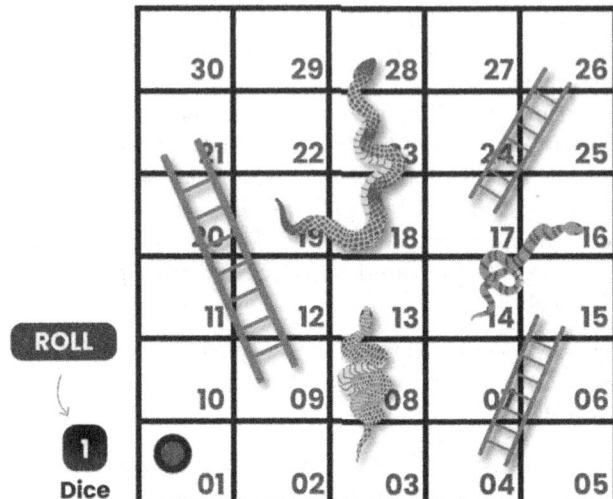

**Fig. 2.** A sample GAPTCHA image.

## 3 Proposed Framework

Due to the enormous progress in the area of artificial intelligence (AI), bots are now better equipped to finish the typical visual and auditory tasks, which makes it impossible for CAPTCHAs to differentiate between people and bots. Researchers are working on new audiovisual CAPTCHAs to deter bot attacks and improve the security of online computer systems, servers, and websites. However, the unwanted high distortion, lines, and noise in the CAPTCHAs make it more difficult for humans, particularly people who are not native English speakers. In this work, we present a novel Snakes and Ladders game-based CAPTCHA, named GAPTCHA, which is designed to be simple for human users while challenging for automated software to solve. It checks the user's genuineness by challenging them to complete a short and straightforward game. GAPTCHA exploits not only the fact that bots have difficulties recognizing patterns and objects, but also the fact that they lack basic understanding. Compared to the typical visual CAPTCHAs, this kind of CAPTCHA offers an extra degree of protection while still being user-friendly and entertaining. In GAPTCHA, a grid with a random number of cells is made with a random number of snakes and ladders shown to the users, as shown in Fig. 2. The numbers in grid cells are generated randomly each time on GAPTCHA generation equal to the number of cells present. The numbers are started with an arbitrary value but are kept in sequence.

**Algorithm 1** Proposed GAPTCHA CAPTCHA

Require: Ladder Pictures, Snake Pictures, Dice, Grid, Token
Ensure: GAPTCHA

1: **Start**
2:  Draw a grid of n cells
3:  Put N numbers equal to n starting from arbitrary number
4:  Pick a random number and random − sized snakes
5:  Pick a random number and random-sized ladders
6:  Place snakes and ladders randomly on the Grid
7:  Pick a Token
8:  Place the Token at a random cell on the Grid
9:  Set the Dice
10: Save the move (correct answer) according to the Dice number shown
11: Compare the user's answer
12:     **if** (*answer matches*) **then**
13:         *Give Access*
14:     **else**
15:         *Refresh GAPTCHA*
16:         *Go to Start*
17:     **End if**
18: **End**

The grid size, number, and size of snakes will differ each time the GAPTCHA is refreshed. The user rolls the dice and selects the appropriate cell, keeping the ladder and snake in mind to pass the test. If they select the suitable cell (i.e., the correct answer), they can move further on their desired page/server; otherwise, the GAPTCHA is refreshed. Algorithm 1 represents the steps involved in creating and testing GAPTCHA. We present a novel approach to CAPTCHA that emphasizes human users' perceptual and discriminatory capabilities. The user is required to click on the correct cell to demonstrate that they are, in fact, human beings and not a bot. This option depends on the user's mental capacity and how they see the world around them. In order to protect against potential attacks from machine learning, the test will be randomized every time it is refreshed. The grid will also be watermarked to prevent segmentation attacks as part of an effort to improve the robustness of the test. Because our design uses a variety of photographs rather than the more standard text, there is no need to add any more noise or clutter. Because of this change, GAPTCHA's readability and usability will significantly increase.

Figure 3 represents the flow of the proposed GAPTCHA at the user's end. It depicts the steps a user will take to solve the GAPTCHA scheme. The flow explains that to complete the test, the user must first locate the token on the grid. After that, he/she would roll the dice. Then, according to the number on the dice, the user would move the token to the resultant grid cell. However, before clicking on the cell, one has to ensure whether there is a snakehead, ladder, or none. If there is no snakehead or a ladder, the user will move the token there either by drag-and-drop or by simply clicking on the destination cell. Suppose that there is a ladder, so the user should move the token to the cell at the top of the ladder, and if a snakehead is encountered, he/she will click on the cell having the tail of the snake. If any of the mentioned choices are correct, the user would be given access to the server or desired web page; otherwise, the GAPTCHA would be refreshed.

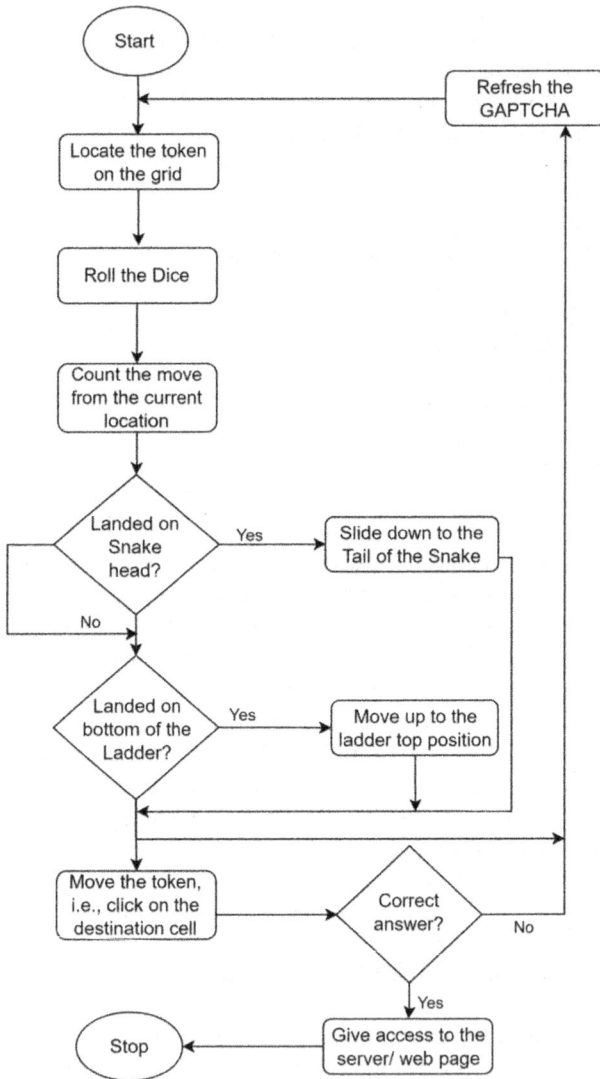

**Fig. 3.** Flow Chart of GAPTCHA at user's end.

Figure 4 represents the flow of generating GAPTCHA and evaluating the user's response. To generate a GAPTCHA test, different-sized and shaped snakes and ladders are chosen first. A grid with a random number of cells is made with a random number of snakes and ladders shown to the users. The numbers in grid cells are generated randomly each time on GAPTCHA generation equal to the number of cells present. The numbers are started with an arbitrary number but are kept in sequence. The grid size, number, and size of snakes will differ each time the GAPTCHA is refreshed. The user rolls the dice and selects the appropriate cell, keeping the ladder and snake in mind to pass the test. If they select the suitable cell (i.e., the correct answer), they can move further on their desired page/server; otherwise, the GAPTCHA is refreshed.

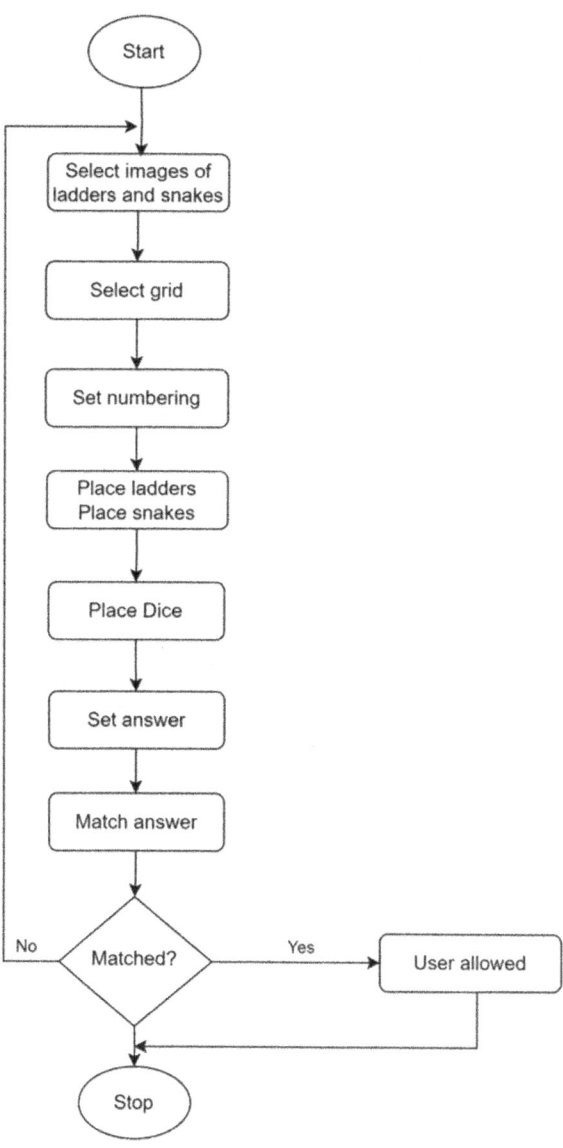

**Fig. 4.** The flow of making GAPTCHA.

## 4 Experimentation and Analysis

For the experimental study, we shared the CAPTCHA link with 45 people with various demographic characteristics, such as age and educational background. All users are academics, professionals, instructors, and researchers who voluntarily completed a registration form before the trial. Therefore, they consented to the anonymized collection and use of their data exclusively for analysis and research purposes. Each participant was asked to solve the proposed GAPTCHA, and the processing speed to determine the answer was recorded, along with the time taken and the number of trials. The experimental data are then analyzed quantitatively. The acquired data are analyzed to determine the effectiveness of using GAPTCHA among the various categories of Internet users.

### 4.1 Results and Discussion

This subsection provides a comprehensive discussion of the results and output of the experiments based on users' experience in solving the proposed GAPTCHA.

**Entertainment Analysis**
In the entertainment analysis, the users were asked about the entertainment and fun they had during the experimentation. Our claim and hypothesis were based on CAPTCHA usability. Figure 5 shows that 97% of users had significant time to solve the proposed GAPTCHA correctly and in an entertaining manner, which is a positive result following successful experimentation. However, only 3% of the people got it wrong and said that it was not entertaining most of the time.

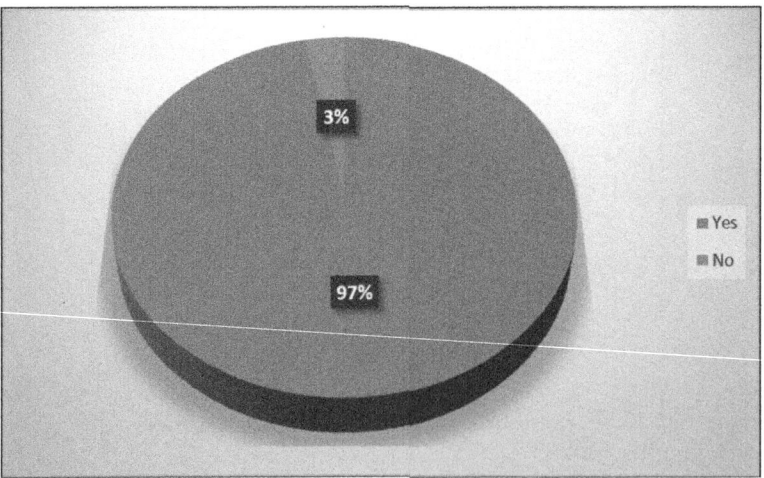

**Fig. 5.** Entertainment analysis.

**Difficulty Analysis**
Along with the entertainment study, difficulty-level analysis is equally important to

satisfy our hypothesis. As shown in Fig. 6, only 1% of the users tick on the 10th and 9th levels, which are highly difficult. However, 24% ranked it 2, and 21% clicked on ranks 3 and 4. In addition, 9 and 13% of users said the difficulty is balanced (i.e., approximately 50%). It shows that most users find it more user-friendly and manageable than the text CAPTCHA. It is to be noted that there is a trade-off between security and usability. If we enhance security, it decreases usability [10].

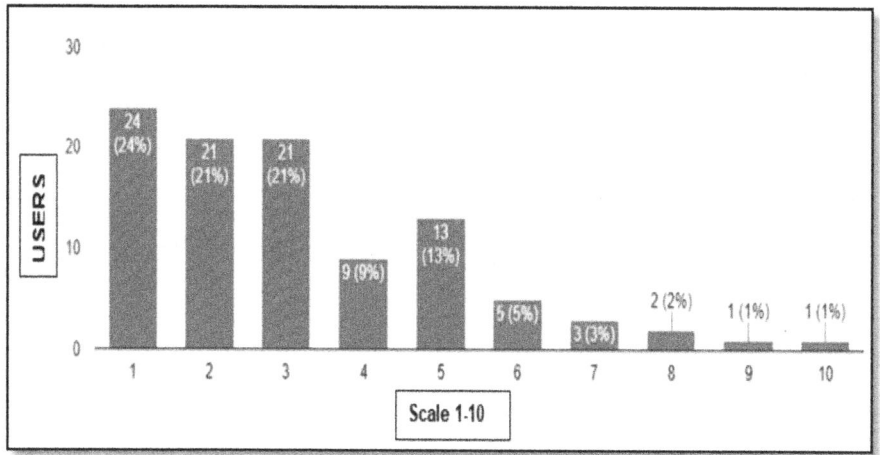

**Fig. 6.** Difficulty analysis.

## Quality Analysis

CAPTCHA quality analysis is the process of evaluating the effectiveness and usability of a CAPTCHA system. It involves testing the CAPTCHA system to assess its ability to accurately distinguish between human and non-human users. The goal of CAPTCHA quality analysis is to ensure that the CAPTCHA system provides a high level of security and is easy for human users to complete. A sound CAPTCHA system should have high accuracy, usability, accessibility, security, scalability, robustness, flexibility, maintainability and low cost. The effectiveness of the proposed method is seen in Fig. 7. The majority of users could accurately solve the recommended method in significantly less time, according to the results. Only five per cent (5%) of those attempts were unsuccessful.

## Simplicity Analysis

CAPTCHA simplicity refers to the ease with which a user can complete a CAPTCHA. A simple CAPTCHA is easy for a human to understand and complete but difficult for a computer or bot to solve. A simple CAPTCHA aims to provide a high level of security while minimizing the user's burden. Keeping the CAPTCHA simple will reduce user frustration, increase the completion rate, and be more accessible to users with disabilities. Figure 8 demonstrates that the proposed method is more straightforward. The vast majority of users can solve the puzzle in a very short time. A very small fraction of them took between 0.02 and 0.07 s.

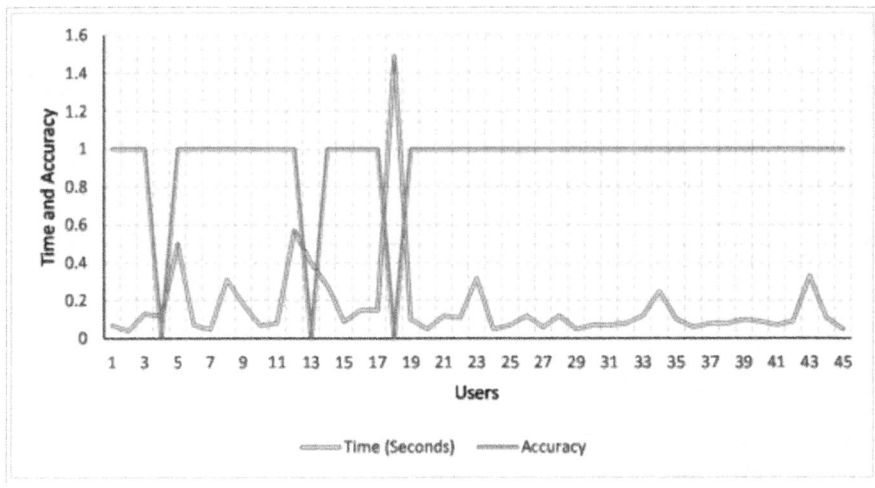

**Fig. 7.** Quality analysis.

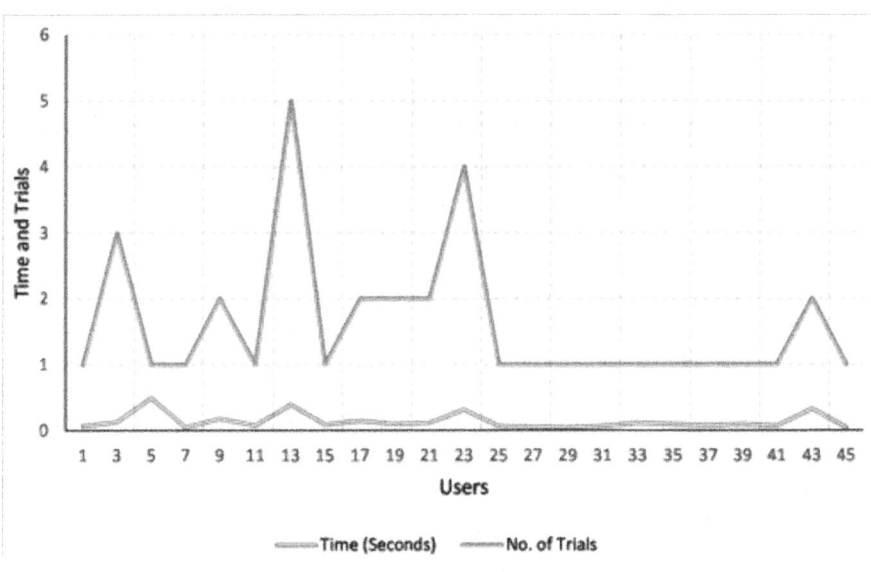

**Fig. 8.** Simplicity analysis.

## 5 Conclusion

CAPTCHAs are commonly employed to prevent malicious algorithms and spammers from accessing websites and services. Traditional CAPTCHAs, which typically involve distorted and complex text for humans to read, can be annoying and time-consuming for users to complete. It is especially true for those with visual or cognitive disabilities, who may have difficulty overcoming these obstacles. In response to these issues, game-based CAPTCHAs have emerged as an alternative that can provide a more user-friendly and engaging human experience while still effectively preventing automated systems from accessing websites. In game-based CAPTCHAs, users must complete a primary game or puzzle to verify that they are human. These activities can be designed to be entertaining and interactive, leading to an enhanced user experience. We offer a user-friendly and appealing game-based CAPTCHA scheme called "GAPTCHA" based on the well-known "Snakes and Ladders" game. The simple keyboard, mouse, and finger inputs increase security without annoying users, making CAPTCHAs more engaging and enjoyable while remaining strong against bot attacks.

Future work will incorporate additional design features in the proposed GAPTCHA. We will make our game-based CAPTCHA compatible with Android and responsive across all devices, including mobiles, tablets, and laptops. After adding new features to the CAPTCHA market, we will unveil our GAPTCHA and strive to make it the best CAPTCHA for users on an international scale. Our research will attract attention to the new directions of CAPTCHA research and inspire other researchers.

## References

1. Moqurrab, S.A., et al.: A deep learning-based privacy-preserving model for smart healthcare in the Internet of medical things using fog computing. Wirel. Pers. Commun. **126**(3), 2379–2401 (2022)
2. Derhab, A., Alawwad, R., Dehwah, K., Tariq, N., Khan, F.A., Al-Muhtadi, J.: Tweet-based bot detection using big data analytics. IEEE Access **9**, 65988–66005 (2021)
3. Mirza, N.A.S., Abbas, H., Khan, F.A., Al Muhtadi, J.: Anticipating advanced persistent threat (APT) countermeasures using collaborative security mechanisms. In: 2014 International Symposium on Biometrics and Security Technologies (ISBAST), pp. 129–132. IEEE, August 2014
4. Ray, P., Bera, A., Giri, D., Bhattacharjee, D.: Style matching CAPTCHA: match neural transferred styles to thwart intelligent attacks. Multimed. Syst. 1–31 (2023)
5. Wang, P., Gao, H., Xiao, C., Guo, X., Gao, Y., Zi, Y., Extended research on the security of visual reasoning CAPTCHA. IEEE Trans. Dependable Secure Comput. (2023)
6. Atri, A., Bansal, A., Khari, M., Vimal, S.: De-CAPTCHA: a novel DFS based approach to solve CAPTCHA schemes. Comput. Electr. Eng. **97**, 107593 (2022)
7. Jeakle, C.: Nouncaptcha: An Image-Based CAPTCHA Backed by an ESP Game Implementation. Honors dissertation, University of Michigan (2014)
8. Bindu, C.S.: Click-based graphical CAPTCHA to thwart spyware attack. In: 2015 IEEE International Advance Computing Conference (IACC), pp. 324–328. IEEE (June 2015)
9. Arsić, S., Nikolic, D., Jevtic, M.: An investigation of the usability of image-based CAPTCHAs using PROMETHEE-GAIA method. Multimed. Tools Appl. **80**, 9393–9409 (2021)
10. Aruna, P., Kanchana, R.: Face image captcha generation using particle swarm optimization approach. In: 2015 IEEE International Conference on Engineering and Technology (ICETECH) (pp. 1–5). IEEE (March 2015)
11. Kumar, S.A., Kumar, N.R., Prakash, S., Sangeetha, K.: Gamification of internet security by next-generation CAPTCHAs. In: 2017 International Conference on Computer Communication and Informatics (ICCCI) (pp. 1–5). IEEE (January 2017)
12. Mohamed, M., et al.: A three-way investigation of a game-captcha: automated attacks, relay attacks and usability. In: Proceedings of the 9th ACM Symposium on Information, Computer and Communications Security (pp. 195–206) (14)

13. Tariq, N., Khan, F.A.: Match-the-sound captcha. In: 14th International Conference on Information Technology New Generations (ITNG), pp. 803–808. Springer International Publishing, Cham (2018)
14. Gao, S., Mohamed, M., Saxena, N., Zhang, C.: Emerging image game CAPTCHAs for resisting automated and human-solver relay attacks. In: Proceedings of the 31st Annual Computer Security Applications Conference (pp. 11–20) (December 2015)
15. Ababtain, E., Engels, D.: Gestures-based CAPTCHAs use sensor readings to solve CAPTCHA challenges on Smartphones. In: 2019 International Conference on Computational Science and Computational Intelligence (CSCI) (pp. 113–119). IEEE (December 2019)
16. Aldwairi, M., Mohammed, S., Padmanabhan, M.L.: Efficient and secure flash-based gaming CAPTCHA. J. Parallel Distrib. Comput. **142**, 27–35 (2020)
17. Men, T., Wang, D., Sun, Y., Wang, M.: A novel dynamic CAPTCHA based on inverted colors. In: 2013 2nd International Symposium on Instrumentation and Measurement, Sensor Network and Automation (IMSNA) (pp. 796–799). IEEE (December 2013)

# A Comprehensive Survey on Software Defined Networking (SDN) Security

Nouman Mabood[1], Noshina Tariq[1(✉)], Farrukh Aslam Khan[2(✉)], and Muhammad Ashraf[1,2]

[1] Department of Avionics Engineering, Air University, Islamabad 44000, Pakistan
212022@students.au.edu.pk, {noshina.tariq, muhammad.ashraf}@mail.au.edu.pk
[2] Center of Excellence in Information Assurance, King Saud University, Riyadh 11653, Saudi Arabia
fakhan@ksu.edu.sa

**Abstract.** Software Defined Networking (SDN) is growing as the next generation network technology. The separate control and data planes in SDN allow the advent of new features. Centralized flow management and network programmability encourages improved network functions by improving flexibility, scalability, visibility, and cost-effectiveness. While SDN evolution is a crucial enabler for implementations in varied networking situations, like data centers and ISPs in multiple domains, the concept still needs to be considered for more security and reliability with little dependability to data, hence avoiding its agile nature adoption. Recently, this field has drawn the attention of the research community for exploring SDN security and addressing the gaps seen in adopting SDN. Since the idea of SDNs is in the developing stage and there are many loopholes in the security architecture of the SDN, many attacks may take advantage of the vulnerabilities and configuration issues in its elements. This paper attempts to cover the salient features of the SDN architecture and its primary components. It also sheds some light on the security issues such networks face and the main threats they can encounter. Some remedies taken for countering the threats and attacks are also mentioned. Finally, the unexplored and challenging SDN areas are highlighted to attract future research work.

**Keywords:** Software Defined Networking (SDN) · Network Security · Communication Security

## 1 Introduction

The advent of the Internet and computer networks was a defining moment for businesses, schools, and households worldwide. Traditional computer networks, however, have limitations such as difficult-to-reprogram hardware, complex networks, and reliance on unaltered protocols, among others. In addition, the proliferation of networking-capable devices and the Internet of Things (IoT) introduces new challenges to network management. A new network paradigm, Software-Defined Networking (SDN), has emerged in response to these challenges. It makes it possible to surmount the limitations of conventional networks by enabling the software-based centralization of network control. This centralization enables the programmability and abstraction of network control, thereby disintegrating the vertical integration of network planes. Network management responsibilities are divided into three planes: management, control, and data, with management responsibilities falling under the management plane, control responsibilities falling under the control plane, and routing data responsibilities falling under the data plane.

Adopting SDN has generated numerous difficulties, including compatibility with traditional network paradigms, scalability, dependability, and security. The Open Network Foundation, an industry-driven organization, and the Open-Flow Network Research Centre, an academic initiative, promote SDN and standardize its application. Using SDN, network intelligence is administered by an external device called a controller, whose functions are programmed using the Northbound API. The Southbound API (e.g., OpenFlow) facilitates secure communication between the controller and network devices. Notably, industry stalwarts such as Google and Microsoft have adopted SDN, demonstrating the potential of the technology.

While SDN has opened networks to applications and provides numerous benefits, it also confronts significant security risks. The innovative design of its architecture also introduces new security issues and vulnerabilities that must be addressed to assure network reliability, availability, and privacy. In recent years, SDN security has emerged as an active study area, with researchers proposing various security mechanisms to mitigate the threats and attacks that SDN networks encounter. The separation of the SDN architecture's control plane and data plane generates new challenges, such as the potential for malicious actors to exploit control plane vulnerabilities. In addition, attackers can utilize the programmability features of SDN to launch various attacks, such as Distributed Denial of Service (DDoS) and network reconnaissance attacks. As a result of these obstacles, SDN networks are vulnerable to various assaults, making it imperative to develop effective security mechanisms to ensure network dependability and privacy.

Despite the increasing interest in SDN security, this paper seeks to address the main deficiencies by presenting a comprehensive overview, emphasizing its key characteristics, security issues, and potential solutions. This survey aims to provide researchers and practitioners with a road map for understanding the current state of SDN security research and identifying the research gaps. This survey makes several substantial contributions to the field of SDN security. It begins with an overview of the fundamental characteristics of SDN architecture and its primary components, including centralized flow management and network programmability. Secondly, it identifies the security issues and threats SDN networks face due to the architecture's innovations and exploitable security architecture defects. Thirdly, the paper discusses the countermeasures taken against these threats and attacks, highlighting the importance of a secure SDN implementation to ensure network reliability and privacy. It identifies the unexplored and challenging areas of SDN that require additional research, emphasizing the potential for future work in this area. The significant contributions of this survey are as follows:

1. An overview of the main characteristics of SDN architecture and its primary components is presented.
2. The major security issues and threats encountered by SDN are identified.
3. The countermeasures taken against these threats and attacks are discussed.
4. The unexplored and challenging areas of SDN for future research are highlighted.

The paper's organization is as follows: Sect. 2 briefs SDN and its main components. Section 3 covers the vulnerabilities faced by SDN and their categorization. Section 4 is about SDN security, and Sect. 5 covers SDN security solutions. Section 6 is about open issues and challenges, while Sect. 7 concludes this paper.

## 2 Software Defined Networking (SDN)

The SDN defines networks differently from legacy networks because SDN splits the network intelligence from the control of the network. The control plane exercises network control. Here, the management of the entire network is done, and centralized control of the network is employed. The forwarding mechanism of the whole network elements is controlled from here, as shown in Fig. 1. Similarly, Fig. 2 represents SDN's overall architecture and components.

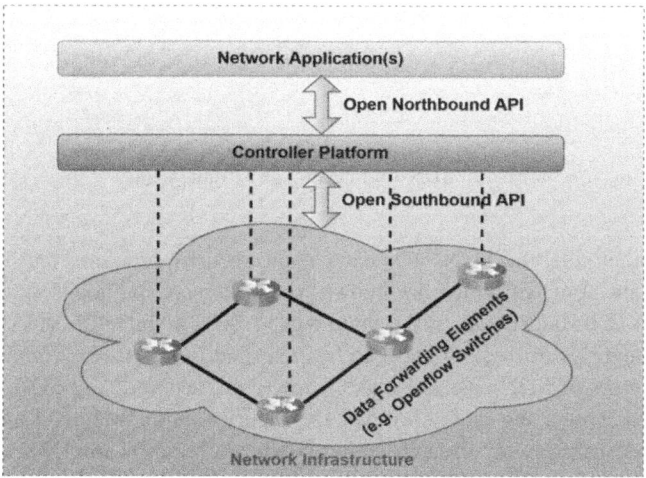

**Fig. 1.** SDN in Simplified Form.

Switches are the network elements bound to follow the rules dictated by the network controller and implement the data-forwarding instructions made by the controller. The network is centrally controlled, so the network controller is on top of all the traffic going through it. To determine the definition of the data forwarding behavior, the traffic flows go through the network controller at least once. The best advantage that can be achieved through such centralized control nature of the SDN is the programmability of the whole network. Hence, software applications are made for the different functions intended for the web and can be easily embedded and deployed on the network controller and as separate data consumer functions. The software program defines network programmability, so the integration and data structure algorithms belong to the software development environment. Such features can benefit the network's security, a more complex challenge in conventional and legacy networks and network elements. The software programs embedded in the controller can enforce security features and policies.

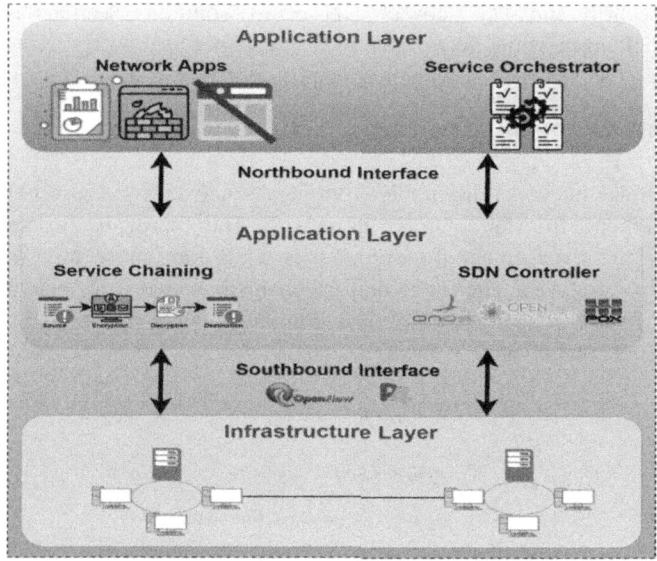

**Fig. 2.** SDN Architecture and Components.

On the other side, the SDNs also carry some security problems causing risks and security threats, some of which are known and others are unknown, some addressed and some yet to be addressed, as the interfaces of SDN architecture are still evolving. The main categories of these threats can be identified in Fig. 2 [1]. Figure 3 identifies the threat vectors of SDN. We can make the network secure using SDN architecture, but at the same time, we must know all the security requirements. Therefore, these approaches are gaining the research community's attention by implying that until the time security of the SDN is secure and complete, it will not fulfill the requirements of the ISPs and enterprises. It can only be ensured with strict security measures. The very first work was published in 2008 for the security of SDNs. After that, numerous research articles, reports and proposals were published. All this work revolves around devising mechanisms for enhancing the security of SDN; some propose improvements in the existing features while others advocate a new framework for the deployment of the SDN. A lot of research has been conducted in the already addressed domains. This work mainly focuses on the newly published proposals and research papers, which have proposed and suggested innovative approaches to deal with the security issues of the SDN, especially those already used in older or conventional networks.

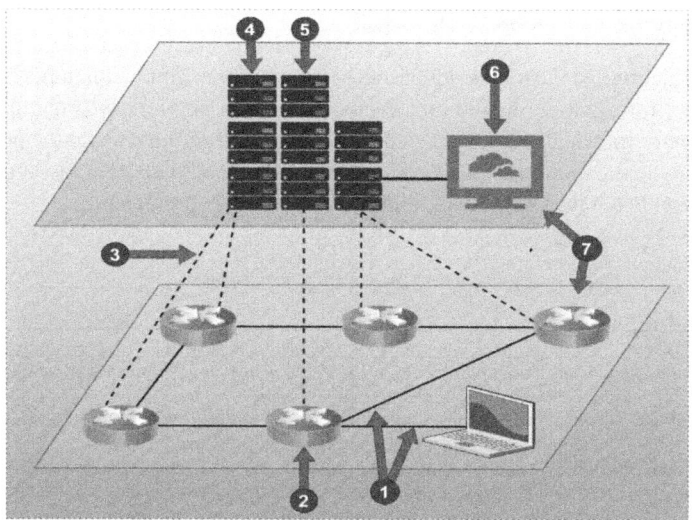

**Fig. 3.** Categories of Threats Faced by SDN.

## 3 Threats and Vulnerabilities in SDN

With the advent of the SDN, new security-related vulnerabilities have been found, which have never been seen in conventional networks. These vulnerabilities are associated with the unique architecture of the SDN. As mentioned earlier, the network and data forwarding planes are centrally controlled, and if that central control is compromised, the entire network becomes at risk and can be controlled by hostile elements. The logical buildup of this work would be first to present a general rundown of the threat vectors explained earlier and the attacks identified so far in the interfaces and the planes defined in the introduction of this paper [2]. Then in the middle of the article, we move down to the issues identified so far, the effects of these issues, and threat vectors. At the end of this work, we discuss the most frequent attacks and the behavior of SDN architecture.

### 3.1 Threats of Attacks in SDN

The SDN and conventional networks can be subject to threats and misuse, intentionally or unintentionally, even after it has matured over decades of evolution. The protocols used, the network instances, the devices used, or the layers participating in the SDN can be at risk for the reasons mentioned above. It means that every element and part that form the SDN architecture is a threat vector and layer, especially when configuration issues and deployment inconsistencies can emerge as a threat to the SDN.

## 3.2 Security Issues in SDN Architecture

The main objective of the attack defines its category. For example, unauthorized access, disclosure of information, unauthorized modification of network information, destruction of network information, service disruption, misconfigurations, and the poor configuration of authentication, trust, and verification mechanisms can be some of the attacks. Table 1 presents the threats and vulnerabilities in an SDN architecture.

Table 1. Threat & Vulnerabilities of the SDN Architecture.

| SDN Plane | Reasons for Attack |
|---|---|
| Management Plane | Misconfiguration of Policies, Vulnerability in Administrative Stations, and Poor Authorization/ Authentication procedures |
| Application Plane | Malware in Apps, Poor Authorization/ Authentication procedures, Bugs in Apps, and Poor Authentication in Northbound Interface |
| Northbound Interface | Vulnerability in APIs, Poor protocols, and un-encrypted exchange of data |
| Control Plane | Poor Authentication in Northbound Interface, Vulnerability in Network Controllers, Poor policy implementation, Insufficient hardware, and Poor Authorization/ Authentication procedures in network devices. |
| Control Channel | Poor reliability and misconfiguration in protocols and un-encrypted exchange of data |
| Data Plane | Poor Authentication in the Controller, Forging packets, Poor network implementation, Insufficient hardware, and Vulnerability in network devices |

## 3.3 Attacks on the SDN Architecture

Layers and interfaces of the SDN are sensitive to certain kinds of attacks. These attacks can either target or affect the components resident to that specific layer of the element of the other layer depending on the feature. The most common attacks are enlisted and briefly discussed below.

- **Application Layer.** Each application has fixed privileges, authority, and permissions. These can be abused with force by attacks and even terminated by third-party applications that exercise public authority. Particular execution of commands may lead to the disconnections of certain network APIs and critical applications [3].
- **Control layer.** The attackers may find themselves in a position where they have bypassed the firewall. From there on, they will be able to instruct overlap and conflict in the flow rules because the controller may not be able to identify the implicit conflict caused due to the guidelines issued afresh and differentiate them from the current regulations as per specified policies. It is called *Dynamic flow rule tunneling* [4].
- **Control Channel.** The control channel can be attacked by eavesdropping or a Man-in-the-Middle attack [3].
- **Infrastructure layer.** This layer can be compromised through numerous means. *Through ARP poisoning*, an attacker can pose itself as a controller. *Flow-rule modification/ Flushing* in which the information installed on the switches is prone to changes by the attackers. By flooding *Flow-rule and* utilizing side-channel attacks,

the controller may be approached to register new flow rules. In *malformed control packet injection,* exceptionally and cleverly crafted packets with malformed or misused headers can change the behavior of the network. *Side-channel attacks* can be used to gain information about the network's behavior in a particular situation and how it responds to different network scenarios [3].

## 4 SDN Security

SDNs have introduced modern and intelligent features like the programmability of the network, mechanism of forwarding the packets, centralized network control, and essential intelligence of the network flow. While, on the one hand, these features have addressed some security issues, the architecture has brought more and new security issues as well. These new issues were never present in the previously used conventional networks. Keeping all the new features, the SDN offers two different implications. Firstly, we can use all these advanced features to detect, analyze, react to them, and then mitigate the security issues that have been observed. It can be conveniently done by introducing and adding new applications or improving the existing ones. Secondly, the new threats perceived may be incorporated into defined networks so that they can proactively alleviate the risks of hazards [5].

### 4.1 Improving Security Through SDN

This study suggests the implementation of three SDN features that can bring in many features related to security in the SDN, keeping different attacks in view; the significant attacks and their description can be found in Table 2. The following elements may be used to implement security solutions in SDN [6]:

**Dynamic Flow Control.** The rules for the flow control of data instructions through the network can be enforced through the middle-security boxes. Network applications may be installed directly on the controller, or the application is bound to the controller through northbound API. In this case, there is no need to deploy new and separate hardware, and the security rules can be implemented for packet forwarding. Hence, the dynamic flow control in SDNs can deploy perimeter and internal firewalls, comprehensive access control lists, and traffic re-direction mechanisms. Here, we can also distinguish between normal (authorized) and suspicious (unauthorized) traffic [7].

**Network-Wide Visibility with Centralized Flow Control.** It is the main feature of SDN that makes them different from conventional networks, and it defines the wholesome orientation of the framework from which the SDN is made [8]. It translates the meaning of visibility of the entire network at all times [9].

**Network Programmability.** The administrators/users do not have the authority to change the devices or applications on the conventional networks but can only be reconfigured in some defined and preset manner [10]. On the contrary, the set of rules programmed by the customer to implement specific functionalities, for example, traffic filtering schemes and ACLs, to enforce drop or deny against certain packets. Through Southbound, the data plane can be configured for parameters in the backdrop of a security scenario.

Table 2. Attacks against SDN Architecture.

A: Application    NB: Northbound    C: Control    SB: Southbound    D: Data

| Attack | Source | A | NB | C | SB | D |
|---|---|---|---|---|---|---|
| Abuse of privileges & authority [3] | Vulnerable applications | x | x | x | | |
| Service disruption [1] | Malware | x | | x | | |
| Application shutdown [1] | Vulnerability in Northbound APIs | x | x | x | | |
| Dynamic flow rule tunneling [3] | Malware and vulnerability in switches | x | | x | | x |
| Poisoned network view [6] | Malware, the vulnerability in network services and protocols | x | x | x | x | x |
| NOS misuse [3] | Vulnerability in controller | x | | x | x | x |
| Packet in flooding [4] | Faulty controller, compromised switches | | | x | x | x |
| Switch table flooding [4] | Faulty controller, compromised switches | | | x | x | x |
| Eavesdropping [4] | Un-ciphered control channel | | | x | x | x |
| Man in the Middle [2] | Un-ciphered control channel, compromised southbound interface, vulnerable data links | | | x | x | x |
| Flow table flooding [2] | Vulnerability in switches | | | x | x | x |
| Switch shutdown/ exploitations & forced disconnections | Packet injection, fuzzing techniques, the vulnerability in switches and protocols | | | | | x |

## 4.2 Improving SDN Security

SDN is prone to new attack surfaces due to the changes introduced in the network components, which demands correct sanitization against the threats while leveraging its novel features [11]. Information flows through the channels and interfaces, which are to be cyphered to deny factual information to attackers if they can access the network. Message authentication codes, asymmetric keys, and signed certificates are to be used for authentication besides encryptions [12]. This way, the untrusted and rogue elements would be kept out of the network, and only trusted networks will be allowed. However, special consideration may be given while choosing the protocols and services for encryption mechanism as it may leave the channel to vulnerabilities [13].

A significant shortcoming of SDN is its inability to detect the issuing of flow rules issued by some other applications. It can only detect conflicts of flow rules issued by itself and other applications against the policy. To avoid this, mediators are used for conflict rules and policy checking [12]. Network state monitoring mechanisms are implemented to record the network state at one point and time for correlation with the subsequent state at another time to find inconsistency in the network state. It mitigates the possibility of attacks directed towards the network state, such as topology poisoning, DoS, malicious flows rule, and infiltration of evil devices [14]. Virtualization at the functional level of the network and adaptability to a cloud-based environment enables the network to capitalize on the security solutions offered by different developers and implement them simultaneously to varying layers of the network [15]. It also gives the added advantage of engaging and releasing any security-based application from any security-based cloud, relieving the network elements from the processing load of the security function.

## 5 SDN Security Solutions

After covering the introduction of SDN, its security threats and vulnerabilities, security provisions in SDN, and the security aspects it offers, we now classify the security solutions for a better understanding of the current set of SDNs. Only a brief overview is provided for each classification.

### 5.1 Threats Detection

In SDN, the control plane is in charge of the network architecture. It can demand traffic flow patterns and network status for correlation with previous records for analysis by security apps to detect threats. Programmability offers the flexibility to deploy middlebox solutions like Learn2Defend, which capitalize on machine learning techniques for threat detection [15, 16]. In the same manner, [17] and [18] offer Network Intrusion Detection System (NIDS), which incorporates signature-based intrusion detection system well-paced in network topology and another machine learning-based system installed in the network controller to safeguard against the threats that are rarely detected. Another solution named Athena provides a framework for developers to build anomaly detection applications.

### 5.2 Network Function Virtualization

Instead of having a single security application, Network Function Virtualization (NFV) and cloud-based security provide an option to have multiple applications and utilize them for the security situation. The NFV hosts the application in network resources (like controller), and the cloud-based security solutions, where the apps are stored in external hardware and made available on demand. It enables the network designers to focus on the network architecture and interfaces while the security experts and vendors can focus on developing security solutions for SDNs.

### 5.3 Remediation of Attack

Since the controller holds the network information, solutions can be built around this information to issue flow rules and other countermeasures to mitigate the attack.

### 5.4 Management of Identity and Access

The sensitive data in an SDN is sent through the control channel. While the data is cyphered, the intruders may find a way into the network through a compromised entity. To avoid such intrusion, Authentication schemes are developed on a trust basis. Fingerprinting devices may be added to the network so that the data is blocked to any network entity that has been added recently until the authentication process is completed. The mechanism of secure sessions is also devised to check the strength of encryption algorithms used and set up expiration time. IEEE 802.1x protocols, Extensible Authentication Protocols, RADIUS Server Implementation, KISS Framework for device registration, and SM-ONOS for administrative Permission System [15] are used for authentication purposes (Fig. 4).

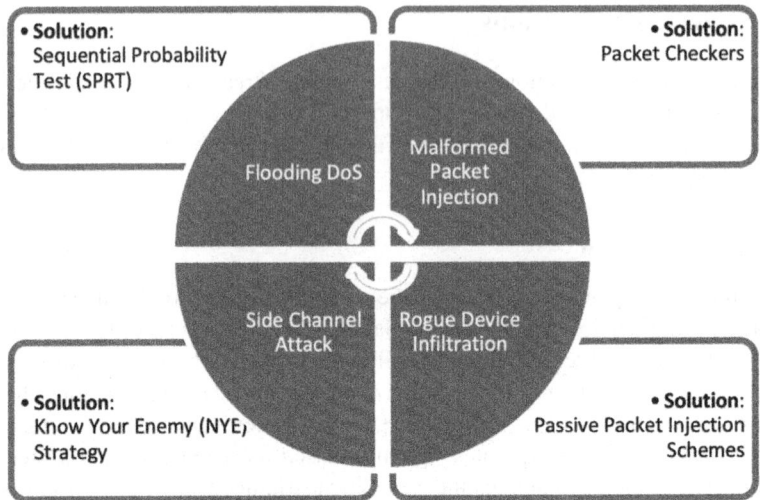

**Fig. 4.** Countermeasures to mitigate attacks.

### 5.5 Network State Monitoring

A data-centric approach like the Path Class approach can be used to map the packets. The mapping will provide a flow path with defined security requirements like confidentiality, integrity, and availability. Global Flow Tables have been defined to inform the network resources and the third-party users about the flow mechanisms.

### 5.6 Forensics

Forensics plays a critical role in reconstructing a crime or a security violation and trying to identify the origin. SDN uses a multilayered approach to assist forensics by treating the evidence data, detecting an anomaly, and using AI to identify the source and raise of alarm.

### 5.7 Utilization of Blockchain Technology

Blockchain technologies can be implemented to enhance the network's capacity with an acceptable performance level [19]. It would assist in scaling up the network [20]. Guarding against threats and protection against attacks would become more accessible, especially against DDoS [21] and DoS attacks [22, 23].

## 6 Open Challenges

Numerous open challenges are still there to be addressed in the SDN security domain. A few of the challenges are mentioned below.

## 6.1 Non-standardized Interfaces for NFV Integration

Network Function Virtualization is a feature that enhances the security of SDN at a distributed level and reduces the workload of the controller and other network entities. However, the interfaces for implementing NFV are not standardized. SDN security enhancement can benefit from the standardization of NFV interfaces.

## 6.2 Security Assessment

The programmability and scalability of SDN provide an initiative to the users and administrators to implement new features and applications. However, the effects such enhancements have on the other aspects of the SDN, especially security, should be considered as it is hard to assess.

## 6.3 Forensics

SDN does not encompass robust evidence-collection mechanisms for determining the root cause of the attacks. SDN capitalizes on the attack detection engines that, when compromised, will provide insufficient evidence for forensic analysis. Foolproof mechanisms are required for forensic data collection and identifying the root cause of the attack.

## 6.4 Resilience

SDN depends on a control plane for network management, and controllers can be prone to system crashes, power outages, and data disruption, especially under specific types of attacks. There is room for research in detecting and mitigating the attacks so that the controller has complete visibility of the SDN and controls the network effectively.

## 6.5 Trusted Applications

As discussed, the controller cannot detect applications that are maliciously interfering with the flow rules. Moreover, the controller is also unable to detect the vulnerabilities posed by "innocent" Apps due to misconfigurations or poor design and programming of the application. To counter this, authentication mechanism may be implemented in the control plane for handling such issues [24, 25].

# 7 Conclusion

The advent of SDN is a breakthrough in network management. It has brought to the world of networking new features that can be utilized to improve the network performance. The programmability of SDN has offered features of conventional networks, which can be implemented through software in the SDN. Apart from the elements, it has brought new dimensions of security along with numerous challenges. The security paradigm of SDN is evolving at a faster pace. Despite the new tools implemented for security and the new mechanism devised, information security cannot be guaranteed on SDN. New vulnerabilities and threats are emerging as the new layers are introduced. In general, two focus groups are researching the SDN. One group is focused on the features of the SDN with added security. In contrast, the other group focuses on safety while the new layers and interfaces evolve. Since the threats and attacks against the SDN are complex, numerous approaches are being developed for capitalizing on the AI and machine learning methodologies to detect and counterfeit the attacks. The SDN is still evolving, and multiple security aspects must be addressed while some remain dormant. The scope of research in this field is enormous. More than a decade has passed since the first security-related research work was published; still, there exist numerous aspects of SDN security that require more investigation, like forensics, policy mediators, debuggers, and detection systems for identifying vulnerabilities.

## References

1. Butts, D.: SDN Security Attack Vectors and SDN Hardening | Network World, p. 5
2. Yoon, C., et al.: Flow wars: systemizing the attack surface and defenses in software-defined networks. IEEEACM Trans. Netw. **25**(6), 3514–3530 (2017)
3. Ropke, C.: SDN Malware: Problems of Current Protection Systems and Potential Countermeasures, p. 12
4. Benton, K., Camp, L.J., Small, C.: OpenFlow vulnerability assessment. In: Proceedings of the second ACM SIGCOMM Workshop on Hot Topics in Software Defined Networking - HotSDN'13, ACM Press, Hong Kong, China (2013)
5. Shin, S., Xu, L., Hong, S., Gu, G.: Enhancing network security through software defined networking (SDN). In: 2016 25th International Conference on Computer Communication and Networks (ICCCN), IEEE, Waikoloa, HI, USA (August 2016)
6. Nguyen, T.H., Yoo, M.: Analysis of link discovery service attacks in SDN controller. In: 2017 International Conference on Information Networking (ICOIN), IEEE, Da Nang, Vietnam (2017)
7. Pontes, C.F.T., de Souza, M.M.C., Gondim, J.J.C., Bishop, M., Marotta, M.A.: A new method for flow-based network intrusion detection using the inverse potts model. IEEE Trans. Netw. Serv. Manag. **18**(2), 1125–1136 (2021)
8. Dacier, M.C., Konig, H., Cwalinski, R., Kargl, F., Dietrich, S.: Security challenges and opportunities of software-defined networking. IEEE Secur. Priv. **15**(2), 96–100 (2017)
9. Yurekten, O., Demirci, M.: SDN-based cyber defense: a survey. Future Gener. Comput. Syst. **115**, 126–149 (2021)
10. Schehlmann, L., Abt, S., Baier, H.: Blessing or curse? Revisiting security aspects of software-defined networking. In: 10th International Conference on Network and Service Management (CNSM) and Workshop, IEEE, Rio de Janeiro, Brazil (November 2014)
11. Scott-Hayward, S., Natarajan, S., Sezer, S.: A survey of security in software defined networks. IEEE Commun. Surv. Tutor. **18**(1), 623–654 (2016)
12. Liyanage, M., Ylianttila, M., Gurtov, A.: Securing the control channel of software-defined mobile networks. In: Proceeding of IEEE International Symposium on a World of Wireless, Mobile and Multimedia Networks 2014, IEEE, Sydney, Australia (June 2014)
13. Bernardo, D.V., Chua, B.B.: Introduction and analysis of SDN and NFV security architecture (SN-SECA). In: 2015 IEEE 29th International Conference on Advanced Information Networking and Applications, Gwangiu, South Korea (2015)

14. Ali, S., Tariq, N., Khan, F.A., Ashraf, M., Abdul, W., Saleem, K.: BFT-IoMT: a blockchain-based trust mechanism to mitigate Sybil attack using fuzzy logic in the internet of medical things. Sensors **23**(9), 4265 (2023)
15. Tantar, E., Tantar, A.A., Kantor, M., Engel, T.: On using cognition for anomaly detection in SDN. In: Tantar, AA., Tantar, E., Emmerich, M., Legrand, P., Alboaie, L., Luchian, H. (eds.) EVOLVE - A Bridge between Probability, Set Oriented Numerics, and Evolutionary Computation VI. AICS, vol. 674, pp. 67–81. Springer, Cham (2018). https://doi.org/10.1007/978-3-319-69710-9_5
16. Khan, F.A., Gumaei, A.: A comparative study of machine learning classifiers for network intrusion detection. In: Sun, X., Pan, Z., Bertino, E. (eds.) Artificial Intelligence and Security. ICAIS 2019. LNCS, vol. 11633, pp. 75–86. Springer, Cham (2019). https://doi.org/10.1007/978-3-030-24265-7_7
17. Abubakar, A., Pranggono, B.: Machine Learning Based Intrusion Detection System for Software Defined Networks, p. 6 (2017)
18. Ajaeiya, G.A., Adalian, N., Elhajj, I.H., Kayssi, A., Chehab, A.: Flow-based intrusion detection system for SDN. In: 2017 IEEE Symposium on Computers and Communications (ISCC), IEEE, Heraklion, Greece, July 2017
19. Tariq, N., Asim, M., Khan, F.A., Baker, T., Khalid, U., Derhab, A.: A blockchain-based multi-mobile code-driven trust mechanism for detecting internal attacks in internet of things. Sensors **21**(1), 23 (2020)
20. Novaes, M.P., Carvalho, L.F., Lloret, J., Proença, M.L.: Adversarial deep learning approach detection and defense against DDoS attacks in SDN environments. Futur. Gener. Comput. Syst. **125**, 156–167 (2021)
21. Imran, M., Durad, M.H., Khan, F.A., Abbas, H.: DAISY: a detection and mitigation system against denial of service attacks in software defined networks. IEEE Syst. J. **14**(2), 1933–1944 (2020)
22. Imran, M., Durad, M.H., Khan, F.A., Derhab, A.: Toward an optimal solution against denial of service attacks in software defined networks. Futur. Gener. Comput. Syst. **92**, 444–453 (2019)
23. Tariq, N., et al.: The security of big data in fog-enabled IoT applications including blockchain: a survey. Sensors **19**(8), 1788 (2019)
24. Imran, M., Durad, M.H., Khan, F.A., Derhab, A.: Reducing the effects of DoS attacks in software defined networks using parallel flow installation. Hum.-centric Comput. Inf. Sci. **9**(1), 1–19 (2019)
25. Tariq, N., Asim, M., Maamar, Z., Farooqi, M.Z., Faci, N., Baker, T.: A mobile code-driven trust mechanism for detecting internal attacks in sensor node-powered IoT. J. Parallel Distrib. Comput. **134**, 198–206 (2019)

# Access Control Techniques for Cloud Computing: Review and Recommendations

Mannan Javed[1], Noshina Tariq[1(✉)], Farrukh Aslam Khan[2(✉)], and Muhammad Ashraf[1]

[1] Department of Avionics Engineering, Air University, Islamabad 44000, Pakistan
211858@students.au.edu.pk, {noshina.tariq, muhammad.ashraf}@mail.au.edu.pk
[2] Center of Excellence in Information Assurance, King Saud University, Riyadh 11653, Saudi Arabia
fakhan@ksu.edu.sa

**Abstract.** Cloud platforms provide Internet-based computing services to users upon generation of their requests. Cloud computing services include platforms for developing applications, programs, and storage available over the Internet. Cloud service providers (CSPs) are the entities that provide Internet-based cloud computing services to users and businesses. Similarly, identity providers (IdPs) are the entities that provide online authentication services for decision-making regarding granting or denying access to a particular IT resource. The dependence on cloud computing platforms is exponentially increasing with each passing day. However, the most critical aspect of the cloud environment is data security, which comprises three fundamental parts, i.e., confidentiality, integrity, and availability. To improve the user's confidence, data security is the top priority of CSPs. Data security in a cloud environment is a challenging and complex task that can be ensured by implementing a robust access control mechanism. The current access control approaches used by cloud platforms have been thoroughly reviewed in this paper, along with their benefits and drawbacks.

**Keywords:** Cloud Computing Service Types · Access Control Mechanism · Access Control Languages · Deployment Models

## 1 Introduction

Access control methods are used in cloud computing to regulate who or what has access to an organization's cloud-based resources. It is an important security measure to guard against unauthorized access to systems and information. Access control enables businesses to manage who has access to and how to use the cloud resources. Access control in cloud computing can be implemented through authentication, authorization, and encryption [1]. Authentication guarantees only legitimate users access to the cloud resources, while authorization determines the type of access each user is allowed. Cloud computing has enabled businesses and users to reduce costs by renting Internet-based cloud services provided by different cloud service providers [2]. Thus, the users or businesses are not required to own expensive hardware and develop their human resources comprising professionals for maintaining the same. On the one hand, cloud computing has enhanced the growth of businesses by offering low-cost services through CSPs, whereas on the other hand, and it has introduced new risks to the security of user data [3]. Therefore, the CSPs must ensure adequate security to protect users' data. Any breach or lapse in the security mechanism would result in information leakage, compromising the data security and resulting in system failure.

In the access-control model, a system bases the decision to grant access based on the access-control model implemented. In light of consumers' ever-increasing reliance on cloud services, access control solutions based on proper rules are essential for information security. Therefore, to guarantee the security of users' private/sensitive data, a firm security policy that explicitly covers all aspects must be defined [4]. The resources are shared through the Internet or isolated network in the cloud platforms. The services in cloud computing include access to storage, programs, and applications [5]. The users may utilize personal computers, laptops, mobile devices, and servers for accessing the cloud service through CSP.

Similarly, cloud computing can give IoT the privilege of cost-effective on-demand services for intensive processing and big data storage [6]. IoTs produce and share enormous amount of sensitive data, yet both the devices and the data are subject to numerous privacy and security risks [7]. This survey on access control methods in cloud computing summarizes the access control strategies presently implemented on cloud platforms. It describes the pros and cons of each strategy and provides recommendations for implementing secure access control measures for cloud computing services. In addition, the article provides a comprehensive review of cloud models based on NIST evaluation criteria. It is crucial in academia and industry because it explains the various approaches to access control on cloud systems and provides guidance on the types of access control mechanisms that can facilitate secure access to cloud resources.

Additionally, the article suggests potential research areas that could contribute to developing a more secure method of accessing cloud resources. In addition, the paper identifies prospective future research areas that can contribute to creating more secure access control mechanisms in cloud computing. However, other state-of-the-art surveys (e.g., [4, 5], and [6]) analyzed cloud computing access control techniques but did not present recommendations for access control strategies. This survey paper has the following contributions:

1. A comprehensive survey of access control techniques and mechanisms for cloud computing systems is presented.
2. Recommendations and future research directions are proposed for implementing a secure access control mechanism on cloud computing resources.
3. Comprehensive comparison of cloud models based on NIST evaluation requirements is conducted.

The layout of this paper is as follows: Sect. 2 provides a comprehensive insight into cloud service, deployment models, access control languages, and access control techniques. Section 3 comprehensively describes the access control models for the cloud. Recommendations for implementation in the cloud are given in Sect. 4, followed by the future research directions and conclusion in Sects. 5 and 6, respectively.

## 2 Cloud Service Types

As per the study carried out during this survey paper, three types of cloud services have been identified, as tabulated in Table 1.

### 2.1 Cloud Deployment Models

Based on the literature reviewed, the cloud deployment models have been categorized into four types. These types vary based on the user/organization requirements and their specific application scenarios; however, the utilization of each type of cloud deployment model is not uniform. The summary is given in Table 2.

**Table 1.** Types of Cloud Services.

| Cloud Service Type | Description |
|---|---|
| Software as a Service (SaaS) | SaaS facilitates users with online access to cloud-based applications—for example, Amazon Web Service, Dropbox, and G Suite [8] |
| Platform as a Service (PaaS) | PaaS facilitates users to develop applications through online cloud platforms—for example, Google App Engine, Red Hat, Openshift, and Oracle cloud platform [9] |
| Infrastructure as a service (IaaS) | IaaS allows users to run their applications through online cloud resources, including computation, storage, and network—for example, Microsoft Azure and Web Services by Amazon [10] |

### 2.2 Access Control Language

Four primary access control languages have been identified in the literature review [11]. The 1st is Security Assertion Markup Language (SAML), which allows users to access multiple services with a single verification of the credentials [12]. This language uses Extensible Markup Language (XML) for communication between IdP and Service Provider (SP). However, it cannot exercise any control over the access to the data. The 2nd is the Service Provisioning Markup Language (SPML), an open-source language based on XML. SPML automates sharing users' identities amongst different cloud organizations and exchanging data between users [13]. The 3rd is Extensible Access Control Markup Language (XACML), which facilitates cloud service providers with access controls required for implementation on federated models of cloud computing [14]. It comprises four essential parts, including Policy Decision Point (PDP), Policy Information Point (PIP), Policy Enforcement Point (PEP), and Policy Access Point (PAP). The access control policy language defines access control policy, and request/response language defines answers to queries for permissions, and reference architecture ensures the implementation of security policies through appropriate software.

Table 2. Types of Cloud Deployment Models.

| Cloud Deployment Model | Description |
| --- | --- |
| Public cloud | In this type of cloud, the service provider owns the cloud. The users can access cloud services online—for example, Google App Engine [15] |
| Private cloud | This type of cloud is similar to an intranet owned by an organization. The authorized users of the organization can access the online cloud services—for example, Oracle cloud services [16] |
| Hybrid cloud | This type of cloud is composed of several clouds having independent infrastructure that is a mix of public and private clouds—for example, Amazon and Google [17] |
| Community cloud | This type of cloud is composed of collaboration amongst several cloud computing solutions working on a shared project—for example, US-Based dedicated IBM soft layer cloud for federal agencies [18] |

Table 3. Access Control Techniques in Cloud Computing.

| Technique | Description |
| --- | --- |
| Identity and Access Management (IAM) | IAM solutions enable organizations to manage the identities and access of their users. These solutions enable organizations to execute control over who can access the cloud and what they can do with it [19]. Cryptographic keys may be extracted illegally, enabling attackers to steal any individual's sensitive information [20]. Cloud providers can guarantee that data is secure and reliable throughout its lifecycle, from storage to retrieval, by utilizing blockchain-based encryption and smart contract capabilities [21] |
| Data Encryption | Data encryption allows organizations to secure their data stored on the cloud by encryption. Since the user would need the key to decrypt the data, it is harder for unauthorized users to access it [22] |
| Multi-Factor Based Authentication | By binding the users to give more than one form of verification, such as a password and a one-time code delivered to their phone, multi-factor authentication adds an extra layer of security. As a result, it is more challenging for attackers to access the cloud system [23] |
| Virtual Private Networks (VPNs) | VPNs provide a dedicated secure path between end users and services. It makes it difficult for attackers to access the system as the connection is encrypted [24] |
| Application Firewalls | As multiple attack vectors and stealthy techniques are often employed to avoid detection, advanced persistent threats (APTs) in the cloud can be especially challenging to detect and mitigate [25]. Therefore, Firewalls can be used to filter traffic to the cloud system, blocking malicious requests and preventing attackers from gaining access [26, 27] |
| Access Control Lists (ACLs) | ACLs allow administrators to specify which users can access the services/resources [28] |

## 2.3 Access Control Techniques in Cloud

Cloud data is vulnerable to a number of security risks and assaults, including privacy and confidentiality breaches [29]. Therefore, access control measures are necessary for cloud systems to guarantee that only authorized users can access and edit information and resources. Techniques for access control shield cloud computing systems from harmful intrusions, unauthorized access, and unlawful disclosure of data. A brief description of access control techniques for cloud computing is given in Table 3.

## 3 Access Control Models

The access control models were initially focused on two types of requirements: military-specific, focused on confidentiality of data, and commercial-specific, focused on data integrity [8, 30]. The following subsections briefly cover the fundamental types of access control models and their comparison based on the NIST requirement/properties.

### 3.1 Discretionary Access Control (DAC)

In the DAC model, the owner of an object can assign permissions related to the object to any other subject (for example, read/write permission). A subject with the right to some resources can grant read/write permissions to other subjects who have access to the same resources [31]. DAC is sometimes called Identity-Based Access Control (IBAC). In DAC, an owner can create a group and assign permissions to users of that group. Thus, the owner would control the group permissions. However, if the owner is not trustworthy, then this would be a security risk. The DAC model lacks control over the flow of information. Thus, an unauthorized user can read a copy of the file without permission authorized by the owner. Figure 1 illustrates a DAC model.

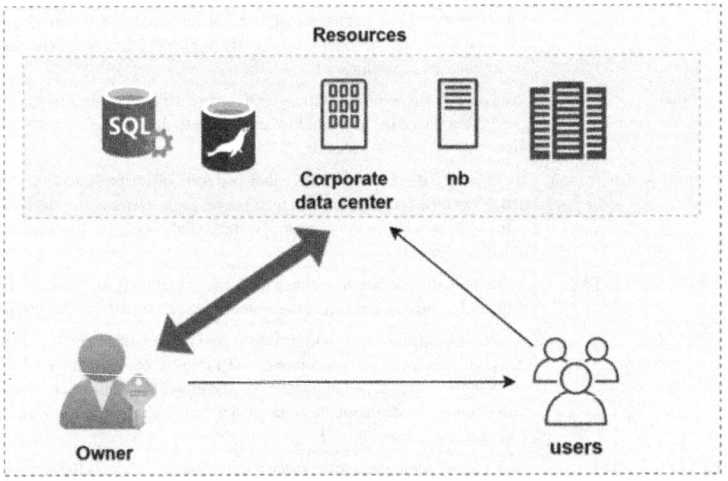

**Fig. 1.** DAC Model.

### 3.2 Mandatory Access Control (MAC)

In MAC, the administrator can assign permission to subjects over any objects. In this model, the users cannot modify their permissions. In MAC, only the system administrator manages the security policy, and the operating system implements the defined policy for subjects/users [32]. Thus, the administrator trusts the parts of the OS implementing the security policy. The MAC model does not allow the users to modify their permissions and thus ensures the integrity of the information. Therefore, MAC-based systems are considered secure but costly and difficult to use due to constraints applied by the OS. In MAC, subjects and objects are categorized based on their security levels, for example, Top Secret, Secret, Confidential, and Unclassified. Figure 2 illustrates a MAC model.

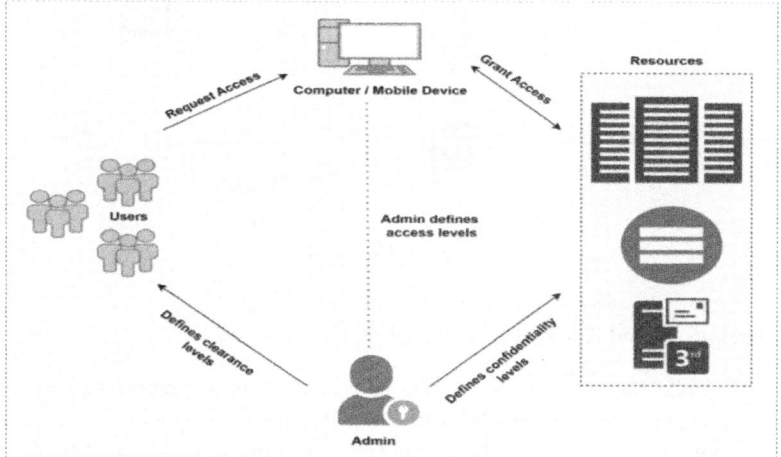

**Fig. 2.** MAC Model.

### 3.3 Role Based Access Control (RBAC)

The RBAC approach strongly emphasizes limiting users' access to resources inside an organization based on their role/function/job description. The role of the users is predefined by the system administrator based on duties assigned to an individual [33]. For example, in a University, the users can be divided into different roles like faculty members, administration, and students. Therefore, a user assigned with a student role will have different access rights than a faculty member or administration. The main elements in the RBAC model are users/subjects, objects/resources, roles, operations, and permissions. Figure 3 illustrates an RBAC model.

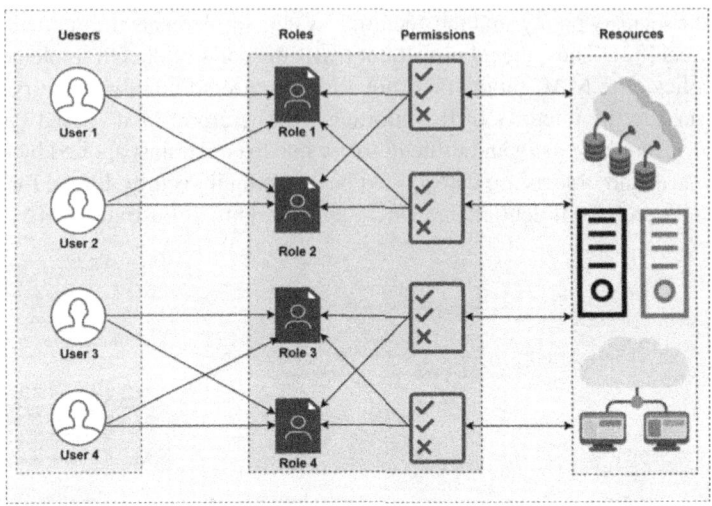

**Fig. 3.** RBAC Model.

### 3.4 Attribute Based Access Control (ABAC)

The ABAC model bases its choice of granting access on the attributes/characteristics of users and resources. The system administrator makes the security policy on a predefined set of attributes [34]. These attributes may include but are not limited to the user's location, time, date, authentication level, and role. The ABAC model has a policy decision point (PDP), which has a set of values for each attribute and compares it to the attributes of requesting user before making an access decision. In the ABAC model, the attributes are not required to be related. The main elements of the ABAC model are users, subjects, objects, subject/object attributes, user attributes, permissions, and authorization policy. Figure 4 illustrates an ABAC model.

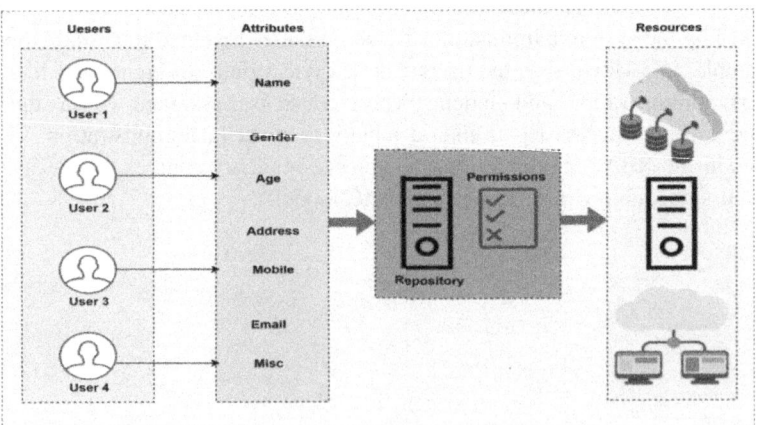

**Fig. 4.** ABAC Model.

## 3.5 Attribute-Based Encryption (ABE)

When a user saves his data on the Cloud, the data is simultaneously saved at different locations as per the architecture of the CSP. Even if a user deletes his data from the cloud, the same data can be recovered through other servers of the same platform by the CSP [35]. Thus, a large amount of users' personal information resides on the cloud, and a compromise in the security of the cloud may result in the leakage of confidential information. The said problem can be addressed if the user's information is stored in the encrypted form. Thus, if an unauthorized user gets access to the data, he cannot view the data. However, the encrypted data would be accessible by sharing the key with the requesting entity. Thus, after getting the security key, the user would get access to all information, including that information which is not desired to be shared [36]. Attribute-Based Encryption was designed to solve this issue. ABE is further divided into five types [37], including Key Policy ABE (KP-ABE), simple ABE, ABE with Non-monotonic Access, Cypher-Text Policy ABE (CP-ABE), and Hierarchical ABE (HABE). Figure 5 illustrates an ABE model.

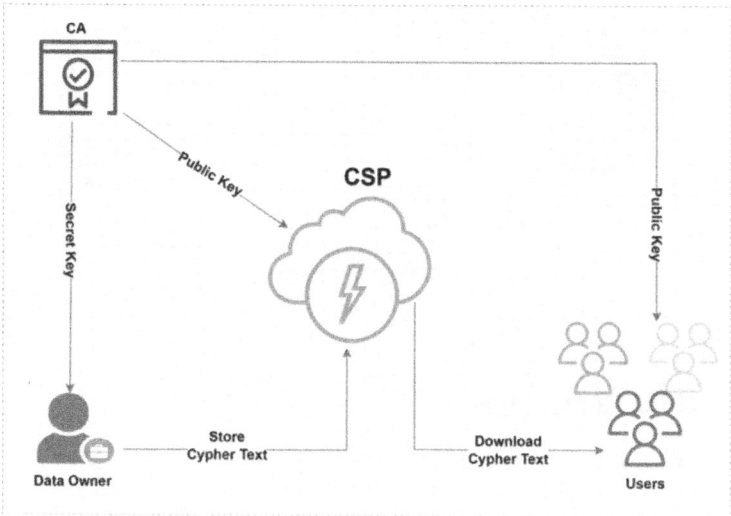

**Fig. 5.** ABE Model.

## 3.6 Federated ID Management (FIM)

Cloud platforms have increased users' access to various websites pertaining to their areas of interest. When a user requests access to a website, his user ID/password is initially verified, and the decision is made to allow/deny access. When a user requests access to multiple sites, he is required to enter his user details repeatedly. To resolve this repetitive entry of user credentials on domains hosted by the same SP or separate SPs, Federated ID Management was introduced [38]. FIM is a middleware between the users and applications that stores the user credentials for shifting from one domain to another without re-entering the details [39]. Figure 6 illustrates an FIM model.

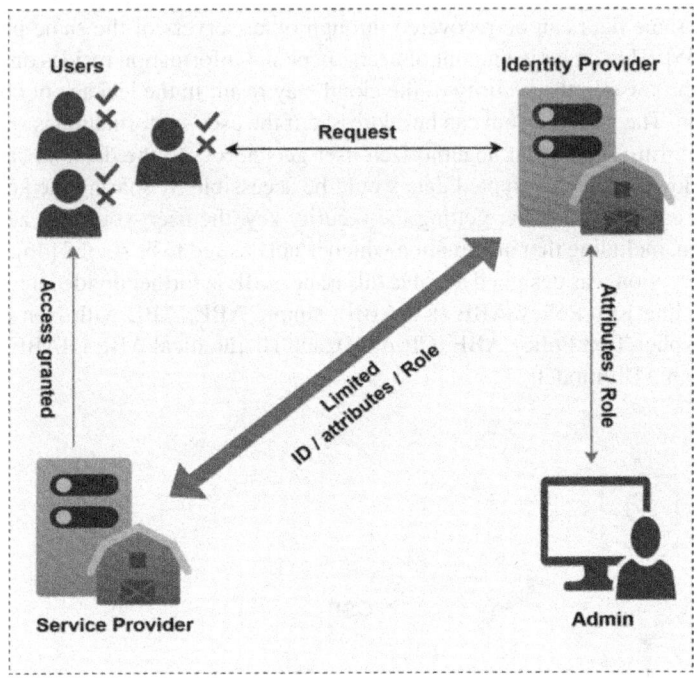

**Fig. 6.** FIM Model.

### 3.7 Comparison of ACM Types

As explained above, different access control models have been implemented by CSPs/organizations to meet their specific requirements. Each of the above access control models has its advantages and limitations. It becomes challenging for an entity to assess which model best suits its requirements. To facilitate the developers and CSPs, the National Institute of Science and Technology (NIST) has defined standards that should be considered for evaluating an access control model [40]. These evaluation requirements are broadly classified into four categories, i.e., administration, enforcement, implementation, and support properties. The comparison of the above-mentioned access control models (concerning NIST requirements) [41] is presented in Table 4.

## 4 Recommendations

Based on the literature reviewed, the following recommendations are proposed for implementing robust access control on the cloud.

**Table 4.** Comparison of Access Control Models.

| Type of Access Control Model | Administration | | | | | | | | | | | Enforcement (NIST Guidelines 7874) | | | | | | | | Support | | | | |
|---|---|---|---|---|---|---|---|---|---|---|---|---|---|---|---|---|---|---|---|---|---|---|---|---|
| | Auditing | Privileges Capabilities Discovery | Ease of Privilege Assignments | Supporting Syntax and Semantics for Specifying AC Rules | Policy Management | Delegation of Administrative Capabilities | Flexibility of Configuration into Existing System | Horizontal Scope of Control (across platforms and applications) | The Vertical Scope of Control (between application, DBMS & OS) | Policy Combination, Composition and Constraint | Bypass | Least Privilege Support Principal | Separation of Duty | Safety (Confinements & Constraints) | Conflict Resolution or Prevention | Operational / Situational Awareness | Granularity of Control | Expression (policy/model) properties | Adaptable to the enactment and development of AC Policies | Policy Import and Export | OS compatibility | Policy Source Management | User Interfaces and API | Verification and Compliance Function Support |
| DAC [31] | N/A | G | G | W | S | G | G | G | S | W | S | L | S | G | G | S | S | N/A | S | N/A | S | N/A | S | W |
| MAC [32] | N/A | W | S | W | S | W | W | G | S | W | N/A | S | G | G | S | S | S | N/A | S | N/A | G | N/A | S | S |
| RBAC [33] | N/A | S | G | S | W | G | G | G | G | W | N/A | S | S | S | G | G | S | N/A | G | W | N/A | N/A | S | W |
| ABAC [34] | N/A | N/A | G | G | G | W | W | G | S | S | N/A | G | G | G | G | S | S | N/A | S | N/A | S | W | W | G |
| ABE [1], [35] | N/A | W | S | G | G | S | W | W | W | W | N/A | W | G | G | G | N/A | S | N/A | S | S | S | N/A | N/A | S |
| FIM [38], [39] | N/A | N/A | S | G | S | S | G | S | S | S | N/A | W | N/A | S | S | N/A | S | N/A | S | S | S | N/A | S | W |

Abbreviations: Good = G, Satisfactory = S, Weak = W, Not Available = N/A

1. A combination of Role Based Access Control (RBAC) and Attribute Based Access Control (ABAC) may be implemented.
2. Multi-factor Authentication (MFA) with at least two or more authentication factors could be implemented.
3. To ensure that only users with legitimate authorization can use the system, comprehensive Identity and Access Management (IAM) guidelines may be instituted and implemented [23].
4. Data encryption (Public Key Encryption) may be implemented to ensure that data is protected even if it is intercepted or stolen.
5. If possible, Token-Based Authentication may be implemented for Mission-Critical/Sensitive applications. Each user would be required to provide a unique token for each session. This token may be a randomly generated code or a one-time password.
6. Security Policies and Procedures are documents that specify the rules and protocols that govern access to a system. These security policies should be regularly updated and reviewed.
7. Data Loss prevention techniques must be implemented by the cloud service provider.
8. The Service-Level Agreement (SLA) [42] should be elaborated to clearly define the rights of the customer and the responsibilities of the cloud service provider. Disaster recovery procedures, incident response, data security, and performance should be included in the SLA.

## 5 Future Research Directions

Based on the survey, the following research directions are proposed for improving the cloud's ease of implementation and security.

1. A unified security policy in a cloud environment would facilitate users to judge their cloud service provider better. The unified technical solution should comprise reference access control mechanism architecture and security policy.
2. RBAC and ABAC models have their specific advantages over each other. However, merging these two models to make a new model could combine their unique advantages and reduce their limitations.
3. Adding device signature in the access control to enhance cloud security, especially for IoT environments [43] (Model, IMEI/MAC, IP Address, OS, Firmware, Location, Network Element, and access history).
4. Automatic user revocation after a defined idle time.

## 6 Conclusion

Data integrity and confidentiality are critical elements in cloud environments. The choice of an appropriate access control mechanism is crucial for CSPs to ensure the security of the data. For private users, the confidentiality of the data is of utmost importance where data is stored on the cloud, and it directly impacts the reliability of the cloud. In this survey, a comprehensive review of cloud deployment models, cloud service types, access control languages, access control models, and their comparison concerning NIST evaluation requirements and recommendations has been carried out. This study found that several access control models are used for various functions and that cloud environments have no unified access control solution. Due to its encryption capabilities and wide range of applications in various industries, attribute-based encryption has emerged as today's most exciting access control paradigm.

# References

1. Kumar, P., Alphonse, P.J.A.: Attribute based encryption in cloud computing - A survey, gap analysis and future directions. J. Netw. Comput. Appl. **108**, 37–52 (2018)
2. Maheshwari, V., Sahana, S., Das, S., Das, I., Ghosh, A.: Factors influencing security issues in cloud computing. In: Advanced Communication and Intelligent Systems, Springer (2023)
3. Tari, Z.: Security and privacy in cloud computing. IEEE Cloud Computing (2014)
4. Abdulsalam, Y.S., Hedabou, M.: Security and privacy in cloud computing - technical review. Futur. Internet **14**(1), 11 (2021)
5. El Kafhali, S., El Mir, I., Hanini, M.: Security threats, defense mechanisms, challenges, and future directions in cloud computing. Arch. Comput. Methods Eng. **29** (2022)
6. Abbas, N., Asim, M., Tariq, N., Baker, T., Abbas, S.: A mechanism for securing IoT-enabled applications at the fog layer. JSAN **8**(1), 16 (2019)
7. Farooq, U., Tariq, N., Asim, M., Baker, T., Al-Shamma'a, A.: Machine learning and the internet of things security: solutions and open challenges. J. Parallel Distrib. Comput. **162**, 89–104 (2022)
8. El Sibai, R., Gemayel, N., Bou Abdo, J., Demerjian, J.: A survey on access control mechanisms for cloud computing. Trans. Emerg. Tel Tech. **31**(2) (2020)
9. Srivastava, P., Khan, R.: A review paper on cloud computing. IJARCSSE (2018)
10. Karataş, G., Akbulut, A.: Survey on access control mechanisms in cloud computing. J. Cyber Secur. Mobil. **7**(3), 1–36 (2018)
11. Murugesan, S., Bojanova, I.: Encyclopedia of Cloud Computing. John Wiley & Sons, Hoboken (2016)
12. Naik, N., Jenkins, P.: An analysis of open standard identity protocols. In: Cloud Computing Security Paradigm. 2016 IEEE 14th Intl Conf on Dependable, Autonomic and Secure Computing, Auckland (2016)
13. Munir, K., Palaniappan, S.: Framework for secure cloud computing. IJCCSA (2013)
14. Laborde, R., Barrère, F., Benzekri, A.: Toward authorization as a service - a study of the XACML standard. In: Proceedings of the 16th Communications & Networking Symposium, CNS'13. San Diego, CA, USA (2013)
15. Srilakshmi, M., Veenadhari, C.L., Pradeep, I.K.: Deployment models of cloud computing: challenges. Int. J. Adv. Res. Comput. Sci. (2010)
16. Davidovic, V., Ilijevic, D., Luk, V., Pogarcic, I.: Private cloud computing and delegation of control. Procedia Eng. **100**, 196–205 (2015)
17. A. Srinivasan, M. A. Quadir, V. Vijayakumar.: Era of Cloud Computing - A New Insight to Hybrid Cloud. Procedia Computer Science, vol. 50, pp. 42–51 (2015)
18. Marinos, A., Briscoe, G.: Community cloud computing. In: Cloud Computing, Berlin, Heidelberg: Springer, Berlin, Heidelberg (2009)
19. Sturrus, E., Kulikova, O.: Identity and Access Management. In: Murugesan, S., Bojanova, I. (eds.) Encyclopedia of Cloud Computing. John Wiley & Sons, Chichester, UK (2016)
20. Ali, S.E., Tariq, N., Khan, F.A., Ashraf, M., Abdul, W., Saleem, K.: BFT-IoMT - a blockchain-based trust mechanism to mitigate Sybil attack using fuzzy logic in the internet of medical things. Sensors **23**(9) (2023)

21. Tariq, N., Asim, M., Khan, F. A., Baker, T., Khalid, U., Derhab, A.: A blockchain-based multi-mobile code-driven trust mechanism for detecting internal attacks in internet of things. Sensors **21**(1), Art. no. 1 (2021)
22. Arora, R., Parashar, A.: Secure user data in cloud computing using encryption Algorithms. Int. J. Eng. Res. **3**(4) (2013)
23. Banyal, R.K., Jain, P., Jain, V.K.: Multi-factor authentication framework for cloud computing. In: Fifth International Conference on Computational Intelligence, Modeling and Simulation, IEEE, Seoul, Korea (South) (2013)
24. Jyothi, K., Reddy, B.I.: CSEIT1835225 l Study on Virtual Private Network (VPN), VPN's Protocols and Security (2023)
25. Mirza, N.A.S., Abbas, H., Khan, F.A., Al Muhtadi, J.: Anticipating Advanced Persistent Threat (APT) countermeasures using collaborative security mechanisms. (ISBAST) (2014)
26. Fernandez, E.B., Yoshioka, N., Washizaki, H.: Patterns for cloud firewalls (2014)
27. Farooq, U., Asim, M., Tariq, N., Baker, T., Awad, A.I.: Multi-mobile agent trust framework for mitigating internal attacks and augmenting RPL security. Sensors (2022)
28. Mulimani, M., Rachh, R.: Analysis of Access Control Methods in Cloud Computing. Preprints (2016)
29. Moqurrab, S.A., et al.: A deep learning-based privacy-preserving model for smart healthcare in IoMT using fog computing. Wirel. Pers. Commun. (2022)
30. Cai, F., Zhu, N., He, J., Mu, P., Li, W., Yu, Y.: Survey of access control models and technologies for cloud computing. Clust. Comput. **22**(S3), 6111–6122 (2019)
31. Downs, D.D., Rub, J.R., Kung, K.C., Jordan, C.S.: Issues in discretionary access control. In: IEEE Symposium on Security and Privacy, Oakland, CA, USA (1985)
32. Lindqvist, H.: Mandatory access control. Master's thesis in computing science, Umea University, Department of Computing Science, SE-901 87 (2006)
33. Moyer, M.J., Abamad, M.: Generalized role-based access control. In: Proceedings of 21st International Conference on Distributed Computing Systems, Mesa, AZ, USA (2001)
34. Hu, V.C., Kuhn, D.R., Ferraiolo, D.F.: Attribute-based access control. Computer **48**(2), 85–88 (2015)
35. Goyal, V., Pandey, O., Sahai, A., Waters, B.: Attribute-based encryption for fine-grained access control of encrypted data. In: Proceedings of the 13th ACM conference on Computer and communications security, Alexandria Virginia USA (2006)
36. Arshad, D., Asim, M., Tariq, N., Baker, T., Tawfik, H., Al-Jumeily OBE, D.: THC-RPL - a lightweight Trust-enabled routing in RPL-based IoT networks against Sybil attack. PloS one **17**(7) (2022)
37. Bethencourt, J., Sahai, A., Waters, B.: Ciphertext-policy attribute-based encryption. In: IEEE Symposium on Security and Privacy, Berkeley, CA (2007)
38. Jensen, J.: Federated identity management challenges. In: 2012 Seventh International Conference on Availability, Reliability and Security, Prague, TBD, Czech Republic (2012)
39. Ghazizadeh, E., Zamani, M., Ab Manan, J., Pashang, A.: A survey on security issues of federated identity in the cloud computing. In: 4th IEEE International Conference on Cloud Computing Technology and Science Proceedings, Taipei, Taiwan (2012)
40. Hu, V.C., Scarfone, K.: Guidelines for Access Control System Evaluation Metrics. National Institute of Standards and Technology, Gaithersburg, MD, NIST IR 7874 (2012)
41. Hu, V.C., Ferraiolo, D.F., Kuhn, D.R.: Assessment of access control systems. National Institute of Standards and Technology, Gaithersburg, MD, NIST IR 7316 (2006)
42. Halboob, W., Abbas, H., Khan, M.K., Khan, F.A., Pasha, M.: A framework to address inconstant user requirements in cloud SLAs management. Cluster Computing (Springer), vol. 18, issue 1, pp 123–133 (2015)
43. Derhab, A., Belaoued, M., Guerroumi, M., Khan, F.A.: Two-factor mutual authentication offloading for mobile cloud computing. IEEE Access **8**, 28956–28969 (2020)

# Linguistic Resources for Extremism Detection on Social Media

Muhammad Anwar Hussain[1](✉), Muhammad Khurram Shahzad[2], and Sarina Sulaiman[1]

[1] School of Computing, Universiti of Teknologi Malaysia, Skudai, Johor, Malaysia
manwar@pucit.edu.pk, sarina@utm.my
[2] Department of Data Science, University of the Punjab, Lahore, Pakistan
khurram@pucit.edu.pk

**Abstract.** Social networks, such as Facebook, Twitter and Youtube, are becoming robust sources that radical groups use to spread the propaganda of extremist group to gather resources for their cause. Therefore, locating radical social media content has become an priority task for counter-terrorism agencies, technology companies and governments. This study has employed a systematic literature review protocol to identify the publicly available corpora that can be used for training machine learning techniques for extremism detection in text. Furthermore, the snowballing approach is employed to identify the studies that have used these corpora for extremism detection. The identified datasets and the studies have been identified to develop an understanding of landscape of extremism detection. Based on the observations we have developed recommendations for processing this important area of research.

**Keywords:** Extremism · Extremist view detection · Machine learning · Classification · Social media listening · Twitter

## 1 Introduction

Social media has become a prevalent platform for expressing thoughts, ideology, feelings, judgments, and beliefs. The prominent social media platforms, such as Twitter, Facebook and Instagram are flooded with posts, comments and messages [1]. According to a recent study, every minute 481,000 tweets are sent on Twitter and 2,93,000 status updates are takes place on Facebook [1, 2]. The promise of these platforms is based on the ability to follow users' even after they have manifested, making it easier for the scientists to track and analyze diverse situations. This is made possible by allowing crawling real-time data directly from the source or through the API provided by these platforms.

Due to the free and unrestricted access to the social media platforms, it is easy for the extremist groups to spread their ideas to a wide range of users at no cost. Hence, the extremist groups use these platforms to spread violent extreme material and propaganda remarks to advance their ideology via indoctrination, recruiting and promotion [3]. It is widely acknowledged that extremist groups, such as the Islamic State of Iraq and Syria

(ISIS), are taking advantage of these social media to spread propaganda, radicalize youngsters and recruit them for fulfilling their objectives [4]. In fact, extremist groups have moved their activities from physical sites to the social media platform for raising funds and gaining sympathies [5]. Hence, endangering the stability of the society.

To address that challenge, government agencies have funded research programs and activities to analyze the communication traces of these extremist groups with the goal of spotting early tendencies before they become violent. For example, during the years 2015 and 2018 when the extremism was on its peak, the European Union funded various research projects using natural language processing to monitor extreme terrorism activities and online extremism [6, 7]. Most of these initiatives aimed to counter the detection and classification of extremist content that may embrace these ideologies.

The volume of social media content is growing exponentially and invariably. Therefore, the manual detection of extremist content has become a cumbersome task. Due to the changing tactics of these group, several studies have proposed the use of machine learning techniques for the accurate detection of pro-extremist content. While there are several established models for text classification, the effectiveness of machine learning techniques is determined by the availability and quality of the training datasets. However, to the best of our knowledge, a comprehensive study which aims to identify and analyze the linguistic resources for extremism detection has not been conducted. Furthermore, no detailed investigation has taken place on how these resources have been used in the literature for extremism detection. Consequently, the researchers, as well as practitioners, are not adequately knowledgeable about the progress in this area. To that end, this study has made the following primary contributions.

- A systematic literature search is performed to identify the publicly available datasets for extremism detection in social media.
- A comprehensive search is performed to identify the relevant studies that have used these publicly available datasets for extremism detection.
- A synthesis of the developed datasets and studies has been conducted to elicit research gaps and recommendations for progressing the field.

The rest of the paper is organized as follows. Section 2 presents the details of the literature that is performed in this study. Section 3 provides an overview of the resources developed for extremism detection. Section 4 discusses the existing studies that have attempted for extremism detection. The open problems, challenges and directions for future research are presented in Sect. 5. Finally, the paper concludes in Sect. 6.

## 2 Methodology for Literature Search

This section discusses the literature search protocol that is used in this study to identify the publicly available linguistic resources for extremism detection, as well as the studies that have used these resources. It is widely established in the systematic literature review that two factors play an important role to ensure the quality of the literature search, the search space and search terms. Search space refers to the searching engines and digital libraries on which the searching is performed. Whereas, search terms refer to the collection of strings that are used for finding relevant studies in the search space. The details of the search space and search terms used in this study are the following.

## 2.1 Search Space

There are several electronic databases, such as ACM digital library, and search engines, such as google scholar, that index academic literature. This study has used a combination of electronic databases and search engines that cover the area of natural language processing and artificial intelligence. The electronic databases used as search space in this study includes, ACM digital library, Sciencedirect, IEEE Xplore, Springerlink and arXive. Additionally, Google scholar and Scopus are used for searching. We contend that use of multiple digital libraries and the search engines guarantees that all the pertinent literature, including conference proceedings, journal papers, thesis manuscripts and technical reports, is screened for searching.

## 2.2 Search Terms

For searching the extremism detection datasets, an initial set of strings were generated and the query expansion approach was used to generate variations of the strings. The initial set of strings were generated based on the research objectives of the study. It includes, single word strings and the phrases which are composed of multiple words. The single word strings include, extremism, radicalism and terrorism. Whereas, the phrases include, extremist view, radical view, extremism detection, radicalism detection, terrorism detection, radical view classification, extremist view classification and supporting terrorism. These strings were used in combination with generic strings, such as natural language process, machine learning, to further narrow the retrieved articles.

The combinations of search terms were used to search through the electric databases and searching engines. Accordingly, a large number of related articles were retrieved. The retrieved articles were manually screened based on their titles and abstracts to identify the relevant studies. In addition to that, we also searched through online repositories, such as Kaggle, Github, Dataworld, UCI and ResearchGate, for finding the extremism detection datasets. Note, the full-text screening of the selected studies was performed and only those studies were shortlisted that fulfill the following criteria.

- That focus on the development of extremism corpus or using existing corpora.
- The linguistic resources, mainly the corpus developed by the studies is publicly available.
- Note, that the studies which have developed or used linguistic resources in the English language but their developed resources are not publicly available, are excluded.

## 2.3 Search Results

As a result of using the procedure discussed above, eight datasets were identified. It includes, four datasets from kaggle.com [8–11], three datasets from research articles [3, 12, 13] and one dataset from the data world digital repository [14]. The inclusion of datasets from diverse sources represent the comprehensiveness of the search that is performed in this study.

In the chronological order, two datasets [9, 14] was published in 2016, two datasets were published in 2017 [8, 12], another one dataset was published in 2019 [21] and two datasets in the year 2020 [10, 15] and one released in 2021 [13]. These numbers represents that there is an increasing trend of making the extremism datasets publicly available.

Besides the eight datasets, the search resulted in the identification of 14 studies that have used the eight datasets. It includes, five articles IEEE Xplore [16–20], three articles from ACM digital library [4, 13, 21], two articles from Sciencedirect [13, 22], four papers from other journals [4, 6, 23, 24]. A synthesis of these studies has been discussed in a later section.

## 3 Extremism Detection Datasets

Table 1 presents a summary of the datasets that were identified. The first column in the table is the identifier of the datasets, the sources of the datasets are presented in the second column. The year in which the datasets were published are presented in the third column. The fourth column contains that the information whether the corpus of text is available or not. The fifth column contains the information that labels of the corresponding labels of the dataset are available or not. The names of the classes used in the datasets are presented in the next column, whereas the number of corresponding records are presented in the last column. The notable observations about the identified datasets are the following.

Firstly, it can be observed from the table that merely eight datasets are publicly available. This represents that there is scarcity of textual corpus for extremism detection, meaning that little research has be done to develop new corpora for conducting studies in this domain. The second observation is that the first-ever extremism detection dataset was released in 2016. It represents that only in the last decade the researchers of the NLP domain recognized the importance of releasing a publicly available datasets for the advancement of research and development in this area. The absence of such a corpus has thwarted the advancement in this important area of research. Furthermore, it can be observed that since the release of the first dataset, there is a growing trend of releasing extremism detection corpora, i.e. seven other datasets have been released.

**Table 1.** Overview of the Publicly Available Extremism Dataserts

| DID | Ref | Year | Size | Availability | | Classes | Specs |
| | | | | Text | Labels | | |
|---|---|---|---|---|---|---|---|
| D1 | [15] | 2016 | 17,410 | Yes | No | - | - |
| D2 | [9] | 2016 | 122,619 | Yes | No | - | - |
| D3 | [22] | 2017 | 5297 | No | No | - | - |
| D4 | [8] | 2017 | 2684 | Yes | Yes | S: R: B | 788, 46, 1850 |
| D5 | [9] | 2019 | 17,392 | Yes | No | - | - |
| D6 | [15] | 2020 | 9387 | Yes | No | - | - |
| D7 | [10] | 2020 | 10,000 | Yes | Yes | EP: EN | 3001, 6999 |
| D8 | [24] | 2021 | 40,536 | Yes | Yes | P: RA: RE | 19,523: 10,120:10,893 |

S = Support, R = Refute, B = Blank, EP = Extreme Positive, EN = Extreme Negative, P = Propaganda, RA = Radicalization, RE = Recruitment

The third observation is that the publicly available corpora have diverse sizes. That is, the smallest corpus D4 merely contains 2684 sentences, whereas the D2 corpus is composed of a large number of 122,619 sentences. Also, it can be observed that a majority of five out of eight corpora is composed of over 10,000 sentences. Another notable observation is that the textual sentences of all the corpora are publicly available with an exception of D3. For D3, the textual corpus is not available, instead the vector representation of the dataset has been released. The presence of such a large number of raw textual corpora can serve as a catalyst for extremism detection. Another notable observation is that the annotations or labels of merely three datasets, D4, D7 and D8, are available. That is, for these three datasets, the benchmark annotations representing that a sentence is extremist or not-extremist, is not available. While the presence of raw textual corpora is valuable, in the absence of benchmark annotations of these corpora cannot be readily usable for learning and prediction of machine learning techniques. We contend that the absence of the annotations is essentially the reason for steady progress in this area of research. Also, the absence of these annotations has thwarted the development of machine learning based approaches for extremism detection.

As discussed earlier, the labels of merely three corpora, D4, D7 and D8, are available. Where, D4 is annotated with two class names, Support and Refute. However, our manual examination of the released corpus revealed that the annotations of a large majority of the sentences, 1850 out of 2684 sentences, are left blank. From the 834 sentences whose annotations are available, 788 sentences support extremism and merely 46 sentences refute extremism. Due to such a small number of training examples, this dataset cannot be used for learning and prediction of machine learning techniques. In contrast, the D7 dataset is a large sized corpus in which sentences are annotated as extreme positive and extreme negative. It contains 3001 True and 6999 Neutral sentences. Although this dataset has a larger size, but the presence of imbalance in the dataset may generate over-fitting problem. Hence, resulting a low recall and high precision scores.

D8 is a unique corpus due to several reasons which makes it a valuable resource for this domain of research. The two key reason are, it is recently release corpus, and that it is the largest corpus for which the annotations are available. Another key reason that distinguishes D8 from the other datasets is that it is the only dataset in which non-binary classification is performed, whereas the other two datasets perform binary classification. The class labels used in this dataset are Propaganda, Radicalization and Recruitment. It can be observed that the corpus contains 19,523 Propaganda, 10,120 Radicalization and 10,893 Recruitment sentences. Similar to the other two corpora, D8 is also an imbalanced dataset, however we contend that it contains adequate number of examples for learning by machine learning techniques. Hence, we conclude that it is a valuable resource for extremism detection in text.

## 4 Extremism Detection Literature

Table 2 presents a summary of the fourteen articles in the chronological order. That is, the studies that have used at least one of eight publicly available datasets discussed in the preceding section.

It can be observed from the table that two studies [10, 12] were conducted in 2017 within a year from the release of the first two datasets. In 2018, the number of studies doubled and it can be observed that all the studies used both the datasets released in 2016. Therefore, it is safe to say that the public availability of the two datasets served as a inspiration for conducting the study. Similarly, multiple studies were conducted in the subsequent years which mostly used the two datasets. Hence, it can be said that the public availability of these datasets helped researchers recognized the importance of extremism detection as an important research topic.

A notable observation is that a large majority of the studies has considered extremism detection as a binary classification problem. Where, five studies have used Pro-ISIS and Anti-ISIS, Pro-ISIS and Non Pro-ISIS, or Pro-ISI and Neutral, as class labels. Four studies have used Radical - Non-radical or Radical – Neutral as class labels, and three other studies have used Extremist and Non-Extremist as class labels. From a careful examination it can be seen that all these studies have merely used different class names to the same datasets. However, as discussed in the preceding section, the annotations of most of the datasets are not publicly available, therefore, it is not possible to ascertain whether the annotations of the sentences are consistent or not. It can also be observed from the table that fewer studies have presented the distribution of the sentences across the two classes. That is, the detailed specifications are not presented in the table.

Table 3 presents the distribution of studies grouped by datasets. That is, the first column contains the identifiers of the datasets and the second column contains the list of corresponding studies that used them. It can be observed from the table that the two datasets, D1 and D2, that commenced the research on this topic are more frequently used than later ones, whereas D7 is not used in any study. The more frequent use of these datasets represents that these datasets have a wider acceptability. By grouping the studies by the number of datasets used, it is observed that in most of the cases merely a single dataset has been used for experimentation. In contrast, three studies have been conducted using two datasets and merely one study has used four datasets.

**Table 2.** Summary of the Studies that Use at Least One of the Eight Datasets

| Ref | Year | DID | Classes | Distribution |
|---|---|---|---|---|
| [16] | 2017 | D1 | NA | NA |
| [22] | 2017 | D3 | Radical: Non-radical | NA |
| [7] | 2018 | D1<br>D2 | Pro-ISIS: Non Pro-ISIS<br>Pro-ISIS: Non Pro-ISIS | 3249: 2573<br>3249: 2573 |
| [23] | 2018 | D1 | Extremist: Non-extremist | NA |
| [4] | 2018 | D1 | Pro-ISIS: Anti-ISIS | NA |
| [4] | 2018 | D2 | Pro-ISIS: Anti-ISIS | NA |
| [21] | 2019 | D1<br>D5 | Extremist: Non-extremist<br>Extremist: Non-extremist | 15684: 06 |
| [17] | 2019 | D1 | Pro-ISIS: Non Pro-ISIS | NA |

(*continued*)

**Table 2.** (*continued*)

| Ref | Year | DID | Classes | Distribution |
|---|---|---|---|---|
| [19] | 2019 | D1 | Pro-ISIS: Neutral | NA |
| [25] | 2019 | D1 | Extremist: Non-extremist | |
| [18] | 2020 | D1 | Radical: Non-radical | 150: 150 |
| [6] | 2020 | D5 | Radical: Non-radical | NA |
| [20] | 2020 | D1 | Pro-ISIS: Anti-ISIS | NA |
| [13] | 2021 | D1 | Radical: Neutral | NA |
| | | D4 | Radical: Neutral | NA |
| | | D2 | Radical: Neutral | NA |
| | | D6 | Radical: Neutral | NA |
| [24] | 2021 | D8 | P: RA: RE | 19,523: 10,120: 10,893 |

P = Propaganda, RA = Radicalization, RE = Recruitment, NA = Not available

## 5 Discussion and Recommendations

In this section, we discuss the findings of the study and present our recommendations for progressing the field in a more scientific and rigorous way.

First, all the datasets perform a binary classification with an exception of the D8 dataset. Where, in the binary classification, one class represents supporting ISIS and the other class represents not supporting ISIS. This is a very narrow view of the concept of extremism as there are several other organizations from different regions having religious believes having extremist views. Also, merely the binary classification is not adequate for understanding extremism. Based on the discussion, our first recommendation is to clearly define the notion of extremism, develop datasets that are not targeted at a single organization and perform multi-level classification for a deeper understanding of extremism.

Second, most of the studies has focused on a single dataset. Therefore, any techniques optimized for a single dataset or any findings generated from it cannot be generalized. Also, there is a dataset that has not been used in any study. Our second recommendation is that every future study should include results from all the eight datasets that are identified in this study so that the results can better generalized.

Third, the annotations of all the datasets are not available, therefore the datasets are not readily available for learning and prediction. Also, there are no guidelines by the proposers of the dataset about whether a given sentence should be recognized as extremist or not. Therefore, researchers have to develop their own annotations which cannot be consistent with each other. Hence, any results generated using the new annotations are not comparable. Our third recommendation is that researchers should develop crisp guidelines for annotations and the annotations should also be released along with the datasets so that the results can be reproduced and datasets can also be enhanced.

Finally, the existing studies present very little information about the specifications of datasets used for the study. For instance, the details about the number of sentences used for experimentation and the ratio between the classes is not presented. Therefore, the impact of the specifications on the effectiveness of machine learning techniques, such as overfitting or underfitting, cannot be judged. So, our fourth recommendation is that a separate section should be dedicated to the specifications of the datasets used in the experiments. Our final recommendation is to develop large and balanced datasets so that the progress can be made on the extremism detection research.

Table 3. Distribution of Studies Grouped By Corpora

| DID | Corresponding studies |
|---|---|
| D1 | [4, 7, 13, 16–21, 23, 25] |
| D2 | [4, 7, 13] |
| D3 | [12] |
| D4 | [13] |
| D5 | [6, 21] |
| D6 | [13] |
| D7 | Nil |
| D8 | [3] |

## 6 Conclusion

Extremist groups use social media to spread their ideology, hence endangering the stability of the society. Therefore, it is necessary to identify and eradicate any content that may help in their cause. In this study, firstly, a comprehensive literature search is performed to identify the publicly available extremism detection datasets. Furthermore, another search is performed to identify the studies that have used these publicly available datasets. To the best of our knowledge, this is the first-ever attempt to identify the extremism detection datasets and corresponding studies that have used these datasets. We argue that this study has collected all the linguistic resources for extremism detection, which will be helpful in progressing the field. Secondly, the identified datasets are carefully examined, their summary is generated and key observations are presented. Thirdly, the synthesis of the extremism detection literature is performed and interesting findings are elicited. Finally, the research gaps are identified and recommendations for progress in the field are presented. Based on the study we conclude that there are ample opportunities for progressing the field.

## References

1. https://www.amazon.com/Twitter-Biography-Jean-Burgess/dp/147981106822022
2. Sloss, D.L.: 'Tyrants on Twitter protecting democracies from information warfare' Standford University Press, California (2022)
3. Gaikwad, M., Ahirrao, S., Phansalkar, S., Kotecha, K.: Multi-ideology ISIS/Jihadist white supremacist (MIWS) dataset for multi-class extremism text classification. Data **6**(11), 117 (2021)
4. Miriam Fernandez, M.A., Alani, H: 'Understanding the roots of radicalisation on twitter'. In: 'Book Understanding the Roots of Radicalisation on Twitter' (2018, edn.), pp. 1–10 (2018)

5. Kaya, A.: Islamist and nativist reactionary radicalisation in Europe. Politics Gov. **9**(3), 204–214 (2021)
6. Torregrosa, J., Thorburn, J., Lara-Cabrera, R., Camacho, D., Trujillo, H.M.: Linguistic analysis of pro-ISIS users on twitter. Behav. Sci. Terrorism Polit. Aggression **12**(3), 171–185 (2020)
7. Miriam Fernandez, A.M., Harith, A.: 'Contextual semantics for radicalisation detection on Twitter'. In: Semantic Web for Social Good Workshop (SW4SG) at International Semantic Web Conference 2018 (2018)
8. https://www.kaggle.com/datasets/fifthtribe/isis-religious-texts
9. https://www.kaggle.com/datasets/activegalaxy/isis-related-tweets. Accessed 24 June 24 2022 (2022)
10. https://www.kaggle.com/datasets/aliaaied/isis-twitter. Accessed 04 June 2022 (2022)
11. https://www.kaggle.com/datasets/fifthtribe/how-isis-uses-twitter. Accessed 04 June 04 (2022)
12. Prabhakar Gupta, P.V., Bhatia, M.P.S.: 'Identifying radical social media posts using machine learning'. In: 'Book Identifying Radical Social Media Posts Using Machine Learning' Technical report (2017). https://doi.org/10.13140/RG.2.2.15311.53926
13. Ul Rehman, Z., et al.: Understanding the language of ISIS: an empirical approach to detect radical content on Twitter using machine learning. Comput. Mater. Continua, **66**(2) (2021)
14. https://data.world/data-society/how-isis-uses-twitter (2023). Accessed 06 March 2023
15. https://github.com/rehman182/radicalization
16. Lara-Cabrera, R., Pardo, A.G., Benouaret, K., Faci, N., Benslimane, D., Camacho, D.: Measuring the radicalisation risk in social networks. IEEE Access **5**, 10892–10900 (2017)
17. Lara-Cabrera, R., Gonzalez-Pardo, A., Camacho, D.: Statistical analysis of risk assessment factors and metrics to evaluate radicalisation in Twitter. Futur. Gener. Comput. Syst. **93**, 971–978 (2019)
18. Araque, O., Iglesias, C.A.: An approach for radicalization detection based on emotion signals and semantic similarity. IEEE Access **8**, 17877–17891 (2020)
19. Nouh, M., Nurse, J.R., Goldsmith, M.: 'Understanding the radical mind: Identifying signals to detect extremist content on twitter'. In: 'Book Understanding the Radical Mind: Identifying Signals to Detect Extremist Content on Twitter' (IEEE, , edn.), pp. 98–103 (2019)
20. Zahrah, F., Nurse, J.R., Goldsmith, M.: '# ISIS vs# Actioncounterterrorism: a computational analysis of extremist and counter-extremist twitter narratives. In: 'Book # ISIS vs# Action-CountersTerrorism: A Computational Analysis of Extremist and Counter-extremist Twitter Narratives', pp. 438–447. IEEE (2020)
21. Nizzoli, L., Avvenuti, M., Cresci, S., Tesconi, M.: 'Extremist propaganda tweet classification with deep learning in realistic scenarios'. In: 'Book Extremist Propaganda Tweet Classification with Deep Learning in Realistic Scenarios', pp. 203–204 (2019)
22. Prabhakar, G., Varshney, P., Bhatia, M.P.S.: 'Identifying radical social media posts using machine learning'. In: 'Book Identifying Radical Social Media Posts Using Machine Learning' Technical report (2017). https://doi.org/10.13140/RG.2.2.15311.53926
23. Zahra, K., Azam, F., Butt, W.H., Ilyas, F.: A framework for user characterization based on tweets using machine learning algorithms. In: 'Book A Framework for User Characterization Based on Tweets Using Machine Learning Algorithms', pp. 11–16 (2018)
24. Gaikwad, M., Ahirrao, S., Phansalkar, S., Kotecha, K.: Multi-ideology ISIS/Jihadist white supremacist (MIWS) dataset for multi-class extremism text classification. MDPI **6**(11), 117 (2021)
25. Kursuncu, U., et al.: Modeling islamist extremist communications on social media using contextual dimensions: religion, ideology, and hate. In: Proceedings of the ACM on Human-Computer Interaction, vol. 3, pp. 1–22. (CSCW) (2019)

# Improved Pak Currency Identification for Blind and Visually Impaired People

Usman Ahmed Raza[1](✉), Mohsin Ashraf[1], Asif Farooq[1], Muhammad Irtaza Khan[2], Muhammad Bilal khan[1], and Mohsin Sami[1]

[1] Department of Computer Science, University of Central Punjab (UCP), Lahore, Pakistan
usmanahmedraza@gmail.com

[2] Department of Information Technology, University of Lahore, Lahore, Pakistan

**Abstract.** The ability to instantly identify different currencies is crucial in the present day. As an integral part of today's global automation infrastructure, the money identification system is a highly sophisticated and crucially important AI system. In this work, we offer a currency recognition system that works well with Pakistani cash. There are a variety of currency-detecting apps available nowadays. This work focuses on recognizing currency based on the coin's physical features. Convolutional neural networks, a powerful type of DNN architecture, are considered to address the issue. The convolutional neural network has delivered the best performance on raw data and the ability to extract valuable features, whereas most other architectures fail to even get close. Pakistan uses seven different varieties of paper currency, all of which are affected by the proposed scheme. Initially, an image of currency is taken as input and subjected to several preprocessing phases, and a region of interest (ROI) is isolated from the surrounding scene. Finally, binary descriptors are also obtained during feature extraction. In Hamming Distance, matching is performed using these binary descriptors. The experimental findings confirmed that our suggested method might be used in practice to recognize unfamiliar money paper images with an accuracy of 95% or better.

**Keywords:** currency recognition · image segmentation · convolutional neural network

## 1 Introduction

Recognizing cash is a must for modern automation systems in the real world. It can be used in a wide variety of contexts, from cash counting devices to electronic banking to aid the visually impaired to currency monitoring systems. The ability to identify currencies is crucial for the blind and visually handicapped. Blind people are not able to find the correct difference between currencies. They are very easily cheated by others. Therefore, we skillfully construct a system to recognize money, but the scale, rotation, illumination, or similar features may also reduce the quality of the currency, resulting in striped, noisy, and wrinkled currencies.

With a population that is greater than 207 million, Pakistan holds the sixth spot on the list of most populous countries in the world [1]. According to the study in [2], 1.12 million people in Pakistan were blind or visually impaired in 2017, whereas nearly 0.78% of the whole Pakistan population has been reported in [3]. The most important fact is that no one in Pakistan has attempted to create a machine or mobile phone camera that can recognize cash notes for the blind and visually handicapped. In our work, binary segmentation of the currency input images has been considered in the preprocessing phase.

- To our knowledge, there is no software available in the Pakistani app store that can use a phone's camera to identify rupee notes.
- Despite much research, no auditory solution for Pakistani currency has been discovered that works with a phone's camera to identify the currency note.
- People who are blind or visually handicapped typically rely on their families to shop for them.

The primary motivation for developing this software was to provide assistance to persons who are blind or visually impaired. As a result, they can imagine themselves to be financially self-reliant. When finished, it will be the most useful software for those blind people that can readily grasp the currency from the sounds. The primary motivation for developing this software was to provide assistance to persons who are blind or visually impaired. As a result, they can imagine themselves to be financially self-reliant. When finished, it will be the most useful software for those blind people that can readily grasp the currency from the sounds.

The rest of the paper is organized as follows: Sect. 2 describes the related work, Methodology is discussed in Sect. 3. Experiments and conclusions are available in Sect. 4 and Sect. 5, respectively (Fig. 1).

**Fig. 1.** Pakistani Currency Notes

It sets the stage for a detailed investigation of the use of pre-trained language models for recommendation systems. It highlights the potential benefits of using these models and the challenges that need to be addressed to maximize their effectiveness. By proposing a taxonomy and analyzing Zhang aims to provide a thorough review of the state-of-the-art in this field by examining the relationship between PLM-based training methodologies and various input data sources [11].

## 2 Literature Review

The growth of a community or a nation is inextricably linked to the stability of its currency. Problems like black money and corruption are just the tip of the iceberg for Pakistan. Further, it is challenging for blind people to identify the currency note authenticity. Ghazi et al. [4] suggested image processing techniques to verify the authenticity of the cash. They utilized pattern recognition and neural network for detecting currency notes.

Abdelkadir et al. [5] built a mobile app that worked on both Android and iOS using a model that obtained 99.1% classification accuracy on their dataset. They faced problems at locations where cash must be physically exchanged, such as a bus terminal, a retail mall, or a bank. In their work, they explored applying AI and ML to this problem. Their app included a voice-integrated feature that identified the denomination of the scanned cash. The program was made in a way that allowed Ethiopia's visually handicapped population to quickly and effortlessly access it.

Solymar et al. [6] proposed a system that was built on bionic eyeglass used to recognize currency. The image is captured from the camera of the phone then the morphological filter and thresholding function extract relevant shapes from the image. In which two types of levels are used for different kinds of patches. Thomas et al. [7] proposed a Convolutional Neural Network (CNN) based model that could be used in a mobile bank note recognition app to help the visually handicapped in their quest to determine the denominations of various banknotes by making everyday items and infrastructure more accessible, their model might improve the quality of life for people with disabilities. Further, this earlier research frequently excluded incomplete currency photos from their databases, but in their investigation, they employed data augmentation techniques to recreate the experience of taking partial currency photos from the perspective of a person who was blind or visually challenged. The study's model was accurate 94% of the time on average, making it ideal for usage in a real-time money detection setting.

A mobile application in [8] was developed to be the Ideal currency identifier to recognize the U.S. dollar for blind and visually impaired. It easily recognized the note and captured pictures from the mobile camera. It took a short time in the process to recognize the note, and the user was notified by the voice. Using the audio in this app was very useful for the users to understand the value of the note. The app worked well, but not with dim lighting and low quality.

Hassan et al. [9] developed a mobile app called LookTel money reader based on iOS. Its basic purpose was to help people who are blind and visually impaired. But with this application, they easily identified the currency utilizing a large dataset that supported the currencies of 21 countries. However, it does not instantly work in real-time applications. Creating a portable device or an effective algorithm to safeguard the visually handicapped has long been a goal of future researchers in the field.

An android mobile application OptaDaily, which provided six services for the blind. The first service was to help the blind to know the weather. The second service used a magnifying glass to allow the mobile camera to capture the image, and the fourth service was a zoom feature. It also reads the text in audible form from the image. The fourth service was a timer. The fifth service was assigned a sound for contact. The sixth service was to recognize the currency of three different countries.

Computer vision was used to identify and categorize four distinct currencies in [10]. The attributes were extracted based on their sizes, hues, and textures. The authors used an artificial neural network for categorization and obtained an average accuracy of 93.8%.

Iyad et al. [11] proposed a phone money detection system using a dataset for Jordanian currencies. They used the Jordanian currencies dataset based on the feature SIFT algorithm. The accuracy produced for coin and paper money was 25% and 71%, respectively. Further, The work in [12] proposed a system that recognized paper currency from the mobile phone that utilized Saudi Arabian currency. Note currency system recognition depends on the correlations of the images and interesting features of the images. Their work used the Radial Basis Function Network for classification and achieved an accuracy of 95.37%.

Sungwook et al. [13] suggested a fast and efficient algorithm for classifying different national currencies based on data f size and correlation of multi templates. Currency denominations were distinguished primarily by their sizes. As a result, they correctly categorized all typical notes at a rate of 99.8% of the time. The work in [14] identified different paper currencies. This method was primarily dependent on the non-parametric model, which was used for the recognition of the currency. This model received many samples of one note. The recognition of the tested banknote by finding the values of the coefficients between the non-parametric model and matching totally depended on the values. To get a good result, currency was captured by the camera, and the currency note was aligned horizontally. When applied to three distinct types of Saudi Arabian banknotes and tested on a wide variety of currencies, this method achieved significant results as compared to other methods.

## 3 Proposed Methodology

Our proposed framework of recognizing currency completes its work in 6 states which are shown in Fig. 2.

- Image Acquisition
- Pre-Processing
- Segmentation
- Histogram Equalization
- ROI Extraction
- Template Matching

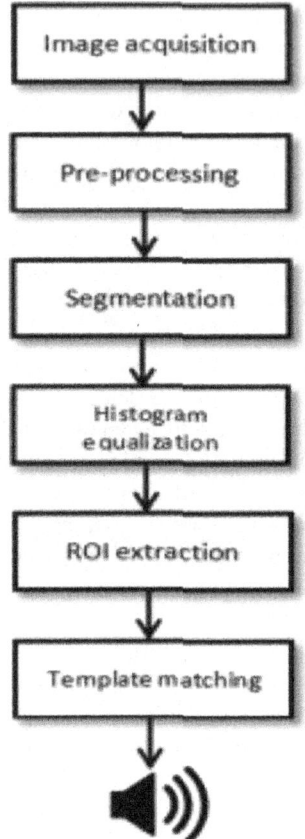

**Fig. 2.** System Block diagram recognizing currency notes

### 3.1 Image Acquisition

The image is captured as an RGB image by the digital camera and transformed by intensity equation to the grayscale version. The following equation describes getting the RGB intensity to equivalent grayscale.

$$I = (R + G + B)/3 \tag{1}$$

A. *Pre-processing.*

Gaussian blurring is used to remove noises on the images (Fig. 3).

**Fig. 3.** Pre-Processing phase using Gaussian Blurring Function

### 3.2 Segmentation

The procedure of segmentation is used to transform a picture of currency into a binary one. There are only two colors in the binary image, and they are white and black. Otsu Thresholding is a function that takes a color image and converts it to binary. White is assigned a value of 1, and black is assigned a value of 0. Segmenting an image means breaking it up into sections that can be reliably reassembled back into the original image of the things they depict (i.e., Binary Segmented Image). The term " binary image segmentation" describes the act of separating an image into two categories (such as two colors or black and white). We worked on choosing appropriate parameters for training an intelligent network. There are two key processes involved in this time-consuming step: grid search and cross-validation. Complex in structure, the effectiveness of intelligent networks like Neural Networks and Support Vector Machines is sensitive to their settings. The following are the issues that we are working to address in Pakistan. Figure 4 represents the output image.

**Fig. 4.** Output Image after Binary Segmentation

### 3.3 Histogram Equalization

Equalization of the histogram is used to change the contrast depending on the histogram of the image and alter the bright- ness of the image to make it appear clearer. We have utilized Python libraries to obtain the histogram of the 500-note image. The following Fig. 5 represents the obtained result:

**Fig. 5.** Histogram of input Image

### 3.4 ROI Extraction

ROI (Region of Interest) extraction can be utilized in content-based picture retrieval (CBIR). The process of segmenting images plays a crucial role. Furthermore, the efficacy of the ROI extraction outcomes is primarily dependent on the segmentation algorithm's performance. Initial region-of- interest (ROI) images are obtained by threshold segmentation, which ensures that active contours emerge in close proximity to the item and removes redundant information from the com- plicated background. Images obtained using ROI extraction can be utilized as evidence in any image retrieval system. In this work, ROI extraction resized the money note from a dataset, and the time acceleration block is also selected as in Fig. 6.

**Fig. 6.** ROI Extraction

### 3.5 Matching

When a blind user starts the mobile app. He takes notes at the front of the camera of the phone. Then the system applied to the preprocessing step on the image. By applying the processes, we get binary descriptors. The hamming distance is applied to match the descriptors which are stored in the database.

When the descriptor is matched, the matches of a large number are in the database and informed that it is matched, which are shown in Fig. 7. A blind user can determine the value of a currency by listening to the phone's speaker; the value is represented by a tone of speech. Figure 7 and Fig. 8 show an image of 500 Pakistan rupees, the sum of which is a match with the dataset.

**Fig. 7.** 25 Matching descriptors using Hamming Distance

**Fig. 8.** 95 Matching descriptors using Hamming Distance

The number 95 represents the maximum number of matching descriptors in the database, so the ultimate matching result is a note of 500 rupees.

## 4 Experiments and Results

We present the experimental protocol and the images used as a training set, and the device outcomes.

### 4.1 Experiments

The program which is in the paper was tested on various Android mobile devices. The quality of the camera and the property of these phones vary. Results in various environmental variables like lighting, rotation, and scaling are very strong. The proposed system does not rely on the picture being taken at a specified degree. The user takes pictures from the camera on the phone. When used for the very first time, the database of the system will require some additional time to be prepared.

As a result, the system will speak the value of the cash to the blind person over the speaker of their mobile device in a time span of less than one second. The OpenCV library, which is operated on an Android platform, is used to create the working version of the suggested system. The OpenCV libraries offer a high level of performance and benefit a wide range of applications. The result is obtained in significantly less time using the proposed system. Figure 9 illustrates a sample of the training set consisting of all forms of Pakistani currency (10, 20, 50, 100, 500, 1000, 5000.). As can be seen from Fig. 9, the values shown do not represent the full value of the currency. They contain the fundamental regions that each have their own distinctive qualities, which will eventually be saved in the database and used as features for each currency paper.

**Fig. 9.** Sample of Training Dataset

## 4.2 Visual Results

Different devices have unique RAM and camera specifications, and we highlight a few of them below. It also combines the visual output of different devices on a single screen. Various Android mobile devices are used to test the system we presented. The system's output is of high quality, and the proposed approach employed by the system achieves this output quickly and accurately across all devices.

## 4.3 System Evaluation

The working version of the suggested system. The OpenCV libraries offer a high level of performance and benefit a wide range of applications. The result is obtained in significantly less time using the proposed system. Figure 9 illustrates a sample of the training set consisting of all forms of Pakistani currency (10, 20, 50, 100, 500, 1000, 5000.). As can be seen from Fig. 9, the values shown do not represent the full value of the currency. They contain the fundamental regions that each have their own distinctive qualities, which will eventually be saved in the database and used as features for each currency paper.

## 4.4 Visual Results

Different devices have unique RAM and camera specifications, and we highlight a few of them below. It also combines the visual output of different devices on a single screen. Various Android mobile devices are used to test the system we presented. The system's output is of high quality, and the proposed approach employed by the system achieves this output quickly and accurately across all devices.

## 4.5 System Evaluation

The picture which is taken by the camera of mobile is converted into a binary image of 1 and 0; preprocessing operations are used to eliminate noise, then segmentation is applied. The process of dilation and erosion are performed to remove unwanted parts of the image. In the last process, the extraction of currency from the database is performed, and from the phone speaker, a voice is produced to inform the blind about the value of the currency.

## 5 Conclusion

In this work, we proposed the development of a mobile application for the blind and visually handicapped that is capable of recognizing Pakistani cash. We were able to get rid of the noise by using this technique, which involved applying several image-processing methods. After that, the linked component Algorithm was used to separate the region of interest (ROI) from the backdrop. When it comes to matching the binary descriptors contained in the database, the method of Hamming Distance was utilized. According to the evaluation findings, the suggested system is superior to the CIAFVI system in terms of the time it takes to process data and its correctness and achieved an accuracy of 95%. In the future, we plan to continue developing this system by integrating the various currencies used in a variety of nations. To improve the significance of our work, we will incorporate more effective techniques to help blind and visually impaired people recognize the Pakistani currency.

## References

1. Ali, A., Akbar, H., Sartaj, Z.: Obstacle detection for blind people using ultrasonic sensors and ardino processor ScienceOpen Preprints (2022)
2. Hassan, B., Ahmed, R., Li, B., Noor, A., Hassan, Z.U.: A comprehensive study capturing vision loss burden in Pakistan (1990–2025): findings from the global burden of disease (GBD) 2017 study. PLoS ONE **14**(5), e0216492 (2019)
3. Ghazi, B.K., et al.: Rampant increase in cases of mucormycosis in india and pakistan: a serious cause for concern during the ongoing covid-19 pandemic. Am. J. Trop. Med. Hyg. **105**(5), 1144 (2021)
4. Nagaraj, P., Muneeswaran, V., Muthamil Sudar, K., Hammed, S., Lokesh, D.L., Samara Simha Reddy, V.: An exemplary template matching techniques for counterfeit currency detection. In: International Conference on Image Processing and Capsule Networks, pp. 370–378. Springer (2021)
5. Abdelkadir, N.A.: Banknote recognition for visually impaired people (case of ethiopian note), arXiv preprint arXiv:2209.03236 (2022)
6. Solymaír, Z., Stubendek, A., Radvaínyi, M., Karacs, K.: Banknote recognition for visually impaired. In 2011 20th European Conference on Circuit Theory and Design (ECCTD), pp. 841–844. IEEE (2011)
7. Thomas, M., Meehan, K.: Banknote object detection for the visually impaired using a CNN. In: 2021 32nd Irish Signals and Systems Conference (ISSC), pp. 1–6. IEEE (2021)
8. B. Lim, Y. Xie, and E. Haruvy, "The impact of mobile app adoption on physical and online channels," *Journal of Retailing*, 2021

9. Hassan, M.K., Hassan, M.R., Ahmed, M.T., Sabbir, M.S.A., Ahmed, M.S., Biswas, M.: A survey on an intelligent system for persons with visual disabilities. Aust. J. Eng. Innov. Technol **3**(6), 97–118 (2021)
10. Zeggeye, J.F., Assabie, Y.: Automatic recognition and counterfeit detection of Ethiopian paper currency. Int. J. Image, Graph. Signal Process. **8**(2), 28 (2016)
11. Doush, I.A., Sahar, A.-B.: Currency recognition using a smartphone: Comparison between color sift and gray scale sift algorithms. J. King Saud Univ. Comput. Inf. Sci. **29**(4), 484–492 (2017)
12. Mallick, J., et al.: Identification of rainfall homogenous regions in Saudi Arabia for experimenting and improving trend detection techniques. Environ. Sci. Pollut. Res. **29**(17), 25112–25137 (2022)
13. Sung-wook, N., Su-lan, C., Ga-young, L.: North Korea's economic development and cosmetic industry outlook. Mysterious Pyongyang: Cosmet. Beauty Cult. North Korea, 301–325 (2021)
14. Fattouh, A.A.: A non-parametric approach for paper currency recog- nition. Int. J. Comput. Sci. Softw. Eng. (IJCSSE) **4**(5), 121–125 (2015)

# The Study of Agile Methodologies and Challenges in Software Requirements Engineering

Muhammad Iqbal[1], Syed Faisal Abbas Shah[2], Tehseen Mazhar[2], Muhammad Amir[2], Ateeq Ur Rehman[3](✉), and Waseem Abbasi[4]

[1] Institute of Computing and Information Technology, Gomal University, Dera Ismail Khan 29220, Pakistan
[2] Department of Computer Science and Information Technology, Virtual University of Pakistan, Lahore 54000, Pakistan
[3] Department of Electrical Engineering, Government College University, Lahore 54000, Pakistan
ateeq.rehman@gcu.edu.pk
[4] Department of Computer Science and IT, Superior University, Sargodha, Pakistan

**Abstract.** Agile methodologies are methodologies which are extremely lightweight. Agile has been used extensively for software development in recent years. It is a strong plan to solve the application development problems facing us. Studies in this area, nevertheless, have shown that the implementation of these methodologies often poses several challenges. This article is about the study of how Agile methodologies use requirement technologies. We address Agile approaches and use design technologies in AMs afterwards. The key issue found is a less users' involvement and the rapid shift in requirement. They ought to solve these problems. The aim is to look closely at the Agile methodologies, the recognition of problems in AMs and the use of Requirement Engineering mechanism in AMs to solve the problems. The paper is about the different AMs, how their features work and how we can use RE in Agile methodologies. The paper also addresses the problems of Requirement Engineering in Agile. Extreme programming and Scrum are commonly used common methods that are explored in the Requirement Engineering context in this paper.

**Keywords:** Agile · Requirement Engineering · Adoption of Agile Methods · Challenges · Agile Methodologies · Software Development

## 1 Introduction

Requirements are a way to know about the working behaviour of the system. What will be implemented is an answer to requirement engineering. It was about 90s when light weight methodologies appear on the screen. These are an answer to heavy methodologies like waterfall models, V models etc. Agile methodologies then proved fruitful as these are iterative and flexible. Requirement engineering has importance as it is success of the development and minimize risks.

It is basically start of any project [1]. We can say that in the commencement we apply Requirement engineering. There is also some limitation in requirement engineering as discussed in different papers. In this paper we shall discuss how we can use requirement engineering in Agile methodologies. Agile methods usually aim to develop products more rapidly and with quality where user may satisfy. Many large organizations like Yahoo, Toyota, Microsoft, Nokia etc. are using these methodologies for their product development. AMs also focus the delivery which is useful for customers. For customer satisfaction it is necessary to have a close association between the development team and the customers. R.E plays an important role in AMs. We shall discuss its importance in this paper [2]. The R.E in AMs usually emphasis on:

- Waste reduction from the gathered requirements.
- Requirement evolution management.

Existence of wastes in requirements affect badly the development process.

## 2 Literature Review

The most used technique for gathering requirements is interview. For requirement specifications the techniques used are user stories, these are resulted from 80% of the papers studied. It is also concluded that the main reasons of the problems faced is the frequent changing in the requirements. In [2] concluded that for small business or projects AMs manages the requirements well but do not work well for larger ones. But also found that unlike AMs, traditional approaches are fruitful for larger projects not for small projects. Customer involvement is the main difference between both approaches. It is revealed that success of Agile Requirement Engineering depends upon involvement of customers, trained developers as well as expert managers says that the beginning of development process is requirement gathering from user stories and the alike approaches [1]. As the product is well known, more requirements can be elicited rapidly. IKIWISI has been emerging as a well knowing method for requirement engineering.

RE process also has alike phases as in AMs. These are elicitation, analysis and verification or validation. In AMs phases are not separate, they are merged in some way. While in R.E phases ae not merged. RE is based on documentation, and is not well presented in Agile methodologies. If used lazy RE approaches then there will be significantly the advantage of cost, but in AMs skilled peoples are needed. The RE process controls the quality of the project. It is an important part of the entire development process. Agile methodologies are flexible so change is likely to happen [3]. This also an indication that due to changes Requirement may also be changed frequently AMs have many challenges. Identifies twenty challenges in three rounds. The six challenges are categorized as the key challenges. Organizations are studying and trying to overcome these challenges [4].

Agile software developments are being researched widely in recent years. However, it is observed that non-functional requirements in AMS are not clear and these are neglected. So, in future need to have a close look on this area. The need is to prioritize the requirements it need further research as it is found that if processes are not clearly defined it leads to vague requirements which will be a huge challenge [5]. Now a day's organizations are looking forward for process clarity, for customer needs and establishing business values. Requirement engineering is a process to provide the customers services that the customers need from a system being developed.

## 3 Software Development Using Agile Methodologies

Agile methods are light weight methods, being adopted in recent years widely. Agile methods provide more rapid releases. Agile approaches provide agility means more frequent releases, change frequently. Agile processes may vary from organizations to organizations also in practices but they use the similar rules [3]. The key rules include:

- The final product is delivered more quickly if other approaches take months then in Agile delivered in weeks
- More Customer interaction leads to satisfaction
- Requirement changes frequently even if changes in the last they can be easily managed Communication not only through documents but face to face interactions are appreciated
- Trusted persons involve in project development
- Through the whole development attention is paid
- Famous for simplicity
- More flexibility
- Expert managers, designers, development team and customer's interaction facilitate process.

Agile methods are being used, as being the tool for rapid release, in time delivery and under frequent changing requirements. A survey shows that 86% organizations are using some type of Agile model while 14% using other traditional models (Fig. 1).

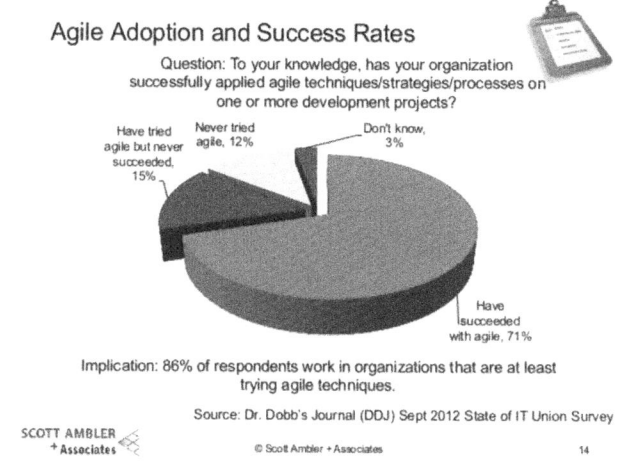

**Fig. 1.** The Adoption of Agile Development

The main limitation of the Agile methods is their unsuitability for large projects. Agile methods are usually suited for small projects. AMs are iterative and incremental approaches. If large project, then iterations become complex so not well managed by agile approaches. Despite these factors, these have proven fruitful for rapid release. On the other hand, Traditional approaches are not incremental in fashion so for large projects they are well suited.

## 4 Requirement Engineering

SNormalCommonly, Requirements are the indication of the purpose what a system will do? What should be implemented? In other words, Requirements indicates the needs of the customers, different functions of the systems which will satisfy the customers. Requirements elicitation is important in this point of view to satisfy the customers [4]. Requirement Engineering is a series of phases or activities those are carried out in a systematic manner on requirements. It is basically the process for user identifications and analysing their needs for finding system intent. It may be defined as the branch of Software engineering that deals with goals of real world, functionalities of the system and different constraints on the system. Requirement Engineering includes different phased activities. These activities include (Fig. 2):

- Requirement Elicitation and Analysis
- Requirement Specification
- Requirement Validation
- Requirement Documentation
- Requirement Management

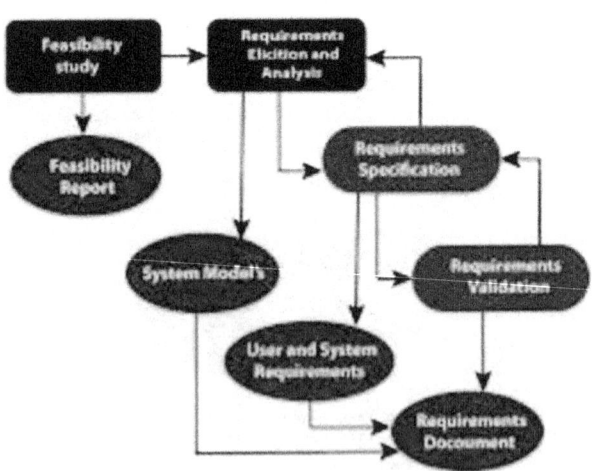

**Fig. 2.** Requirement Engineering Process

We have a close look on these activities then we shall discuss these activities in agile methodologies.

### 4.1 Requirement Elicitation

Requirements are gathered in this step. These may be elicited by:

- Documents
- Consult with stakeholders
- Domain knowledge
- Market analysis

### 4.2 Requirement Analysis

Requirements are analysed in this phase. Analysis of the requirement is done by:

- Customer requirements relationships
- Negotiations
- Budget
- Conflicting Requirements
- Dependency

### 4.3 Requirement Documentations

Requirements are documented for the use of Software developers and testers.

### 4.4 Requirement Validation

The main purpose of validation is to ensure that there is nothing that missed from requirements. Also, requirements are clear no ambiguity exists in requirements. There are no conflicting requirements. Validation is an important activity as this will guarantee user satisfaction.

### 4.5 Requirement Management

The goal of requirement management is to handle changes in requirement. Requirement management objective is to keep the quality consistent of requirements. The relationships between requirements must be managed to make user satisfaction.

## 5 Requirement Engineering and Agile Approach

From requirement engineering perspective some AMs are being discussed here:

### 5.1 Agile Modelling

It is a new approach which provide guidelines for building models. Developers uses Agile modelling for building models. Requirement Engineering techniques are not explicitly applied in AM, but some supports like brainstorming.

## 5.2 Feature Driven Development

FDD focus is developing design through different phases, like ETVX model it has exit and entry points. The model includes classes, diagrams, attributes different methods etc. A thirty-day meeting is supported in FDD which describes the status of the product and report is written related to meeting helpful for requirement elicitation.

## 5.3 Dynamic System Development Method

DSDM is a leeway to Rapid application development. It was in 1990s introduced in U.K. It also works in phases and in the first two phases of the DSDM, requirement elicitation is carried out through business and feasibility study. Basic requirements are gathered during these phases. DSDM have flexibility for requirement engineering. So, any technique can be applied in DSDM [6].

## 5.4 Xtreme Programming

XP is the most famous approach in Agile methodologies. It is characterized by its simplicity, short and rapid releases, short iterations. User stories in this method provide a better way to gather requirements (Fig. 3).

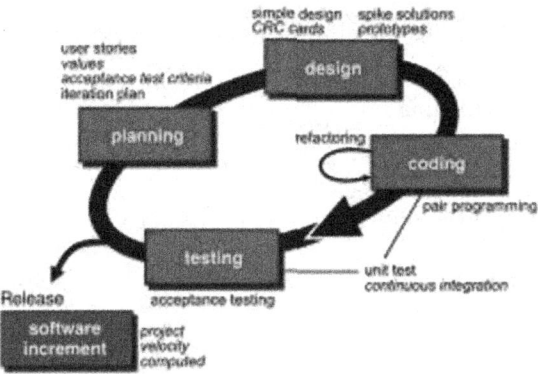

**Fig. 3.** Extreme Programming

It involves a great interaction of the customer, manager and the development team. In it customer is asked to explain the requirements as he best understood the requirements.

Table 1 shows RE activities in XP. Activities involved requirement Elicitations through user stories. Analysis activity is not a separate phase. It continues during development and customer also prioritize requirements. This is best way as customer well know the requirements. Requirements documents are user stories and acceptance tests. There is also face to face communication. Requirement validation occurs through tests and frequent feedback. Requirements are managed by short planning iterations, user stories and refactor. The table shows that in Xtreme programming, RE is well engaged. User stories play an important role in Requirement Engineering.

**Table 1.** Requirement Engineering in XP

| Requirement Engineering Activity | XP Implementation |
|---|---|
| Requirement Elicitation | Requirements Elicited as Stories<br>Customer Writes User Stories |
| Requirement Analysis | Not A Separate Phase<br>Analyze While Developing<br>Customer Prioritizes The User Stories |
| Requirement Documentation | User Stories & Acceptance Tests as Requirements Documents<br>Software Products as Persistence Information<br>Face To Face Communication |
| Requirement Validation | Test Driven Development (TDD)<br>Run Acceptance Tests<br>Frequent Feedback |
| Requirement Management | Short Planning Iteration<br>User Stories for Tracking<br>Refactor As Needed |

## 5.5 Scrum

Scrum is simple, productive, adoptive and flexible approach being used for more than ten years. Its main feature is the delivery in 30 days' sprint cycles. It also characterizes with a daily 15 min meeting, helpful in the development and requirements engineering (Fig. 4).

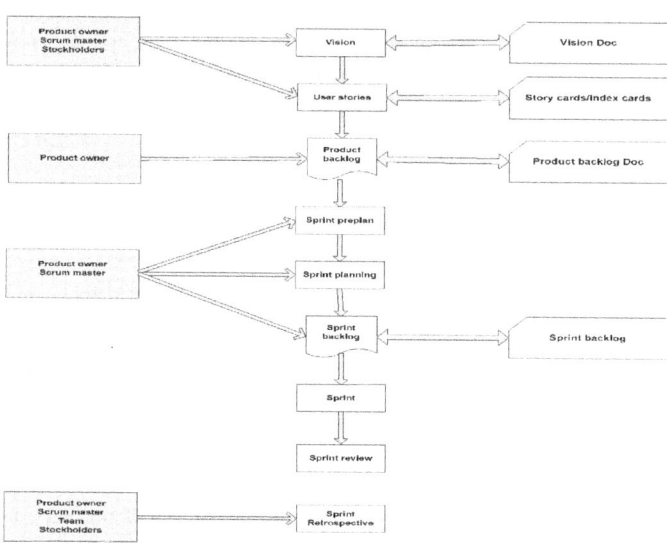

**Fig. 4.** Requirement Engineering in Scrum

Developers are free in Scrum to choose any suitable technique for development. Figure 6 shows Requirement engineering activities in Scrum framework. Product Owner develops Product Backlog with participation of stakeholder. Requirement analysis is carried out by Backlog meetings, prioritizing the Backlog and analysing the feasibility of the requirements. Face to face meetings are used for requirement documentation [7]. Review meetings are conducted for requirement validations. Sprint planning meetings, item tracking, forms change management in requirements. So, meetings are playing important role in Scrum (Fig. 5).

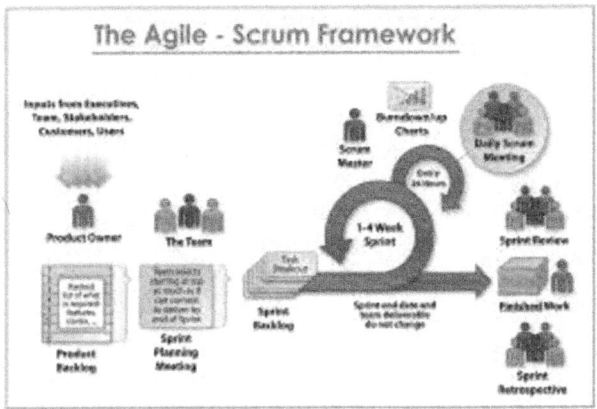

**Fig. 5.** Scrum Framework

These are some of Agile methods in which Requirement Engineering is being used. Some methods are suited to R.E while in some it is not clearly applicable. Requirement Engineering with Agile approaches make the results more meaningful and final product released fulfil user or customer's needs. Agile approaches have many problems also in their implementation and adoption but Requirement Engineering not only identifies the problems but also covers the aspects for rapid release.

## 6 RE Challenges in Agile

In Agile there may be different challenges related to Requirement Engineering. Table 2 shows a list of RE challenges being faced in Agile. List shows the Challenge against each feature of Agile. These includes Requirement Traceability under direct communication. Large client interaction arises the challenge of work load. Changing requirements leads to work and work again. Negligence of Non-functional requirements leads to security and usability challenges. Estimation of Budget and time leads to overrun and high cost of the project. Innovation in RE leads to creativity issue in Agility and release. Missing requirements and conflicting requirements lead to large number of iterations [5].

The research concluded that agile projects collapse no more than others. We function on a level close to other incremental methodologies. Agile projects, nevertheless, face a range of obstacles and concerns related to applying another approach to project management. The top three reasons for agile failed projects, missing data says, are:

- Unsatisfactory experience with agile processes
- Little awareness of the wider organizational changes needed
- Ideology or ethos of an organization at odds with agile principles

**Table 2.** Requirement Engineering Challenges in Agile

| Challenge | Challenge Info | Issue | Solution |
| --- | --- | --- | --- |
| Lack Of Documentation | User cards such as user stories and task description and backlog are only documents in agile | Tracking requirements changes issues | Not specified |
| Client Availability | Clients availability to specify the requirement and feedback | Overwork issue | Proxy clients |
| Inappropriate Software Architecture | Inappropriate software design can affect other software development stages | Over cost | Code refactoring |
| Project Budget and Time Estimation | Not possible to make upfront estimations due to unstable requirements | Delay of deliverable over cost | Team communication precise user story modelling |
| Ignoring non-functional requirements | Functional requirements are only recorded in user stories | Usability, security, testability | NRF approach |
| Change of Requirements and re-evaluation | Handling continuously change of requirements | Reworking | Re-combine model |

## 7 Conclusion

In recent years, agile methodologies have been commonly used. Agile methods are versatile, iterative and renowned for fast release. Through Agile methods the specifications are well handled. Because of its low weight and versatility, AMs become popular. Given the benefits of Agile approaches, Agile methodologies often pose many problems. Requirement Technology is a method of implementing the specifications. Requirement Design plays a significant role in the management of requirements in order to maximize customer satisfaction which is the primary goal of Agile methodologies. Specific Agile methods are distinct from Requirement Technology compatibles. RE is better adapted in some methodologies although it has more problems in others. RE includes different tasks, such as Elicitation, Evaluation, Validation, Information and Management. Through Agile approaches all these practices are implemented in a structured way. The key objective of solving the issues by handling requirements and attaining customer satisfaction. In coming days, it looks that Agile methods will have more success as 86 percent of companies using such methodologies have been researched. There is a need for further RE work in Agile which is clearly continuing as we study this area.

## References

1. Sultan, Z., et al.: Analytical review on test cases prioritization techniques: an empirical study. Int. J. Adv. Comput. Sci. Appl. (IJACSA) **8**(2), 293–302 (2017)
2. Alam, S., et al.: Impact and challenges of requirement engineering in agile methodologies: A systematic review. Int. J. Adv. Comput. Sci. Appl. **8**(4), 411–418 (2017)
3. Abrahamsson, P., et al., Agile software development methods: Review and analysis. arXiv preprint arXiv:1709.08439 (2017)
4. Rantanen, E., Requirements engineering in agile software projects (2017)
5. Cho, J.: Issues and challenges of agile software development with SCRUM. Issues Inf. Syst. **9**(2), 188–195 (2008)
6. Schön, E.-M., et al. Key challenges in agile requirements engineering. In: International Conference on Agile Software Development. Springer, Cham (2017)
7. De Lucia, A., Qusef, A.: Requirements engineering in agile software development. J. Emerg. Technol. Web Intell. **2**(3), 212–220 (2010)
8. Zhu, Y., Requirements engineering in an agile environment (2009)
9. Popli, R., Chauhan, N.: Research challenges of agile estimation. J. Intell. Comput. Appl. (2012)
10. Fitriani, W.R., Rahayu, P., Sensuse, D.I.: Challenges in agile software development: a systematic literature review. In: 2016 International Conference on Advanced Computer Science and Information Systems (ICACSIS). IEEE (2016)
11. Tomayko, J.E.: Engineering of unstable requirements using agile methods. In: International Workshop on Time-Constrained Requirements Engineering (TCRE 2002). Essen (2002)
12. Sillitti, A., Succi, G.: Requirements engineering for agile methods. In: Engineering and Managing Software Requirements, pp. 309–326. Springer (2005)
13. Paetsch, F., Eberlein, A., Maurer, F.: Requirements engineering and agile software development. In: WET ICE 2003. Proceedings. Twelfth IEEE International Workshops on Enabling Technologies: Infrastructure for Collaborative Enterprises, 2003. IEEE (2003)
14. Medeiros, J., et al.: Requirements engineering in agile projects: a systematic mapping based in evidences of industry. In: CibSE (2015)
15. Raharjo, T., Purwandari, B.: Agile project management challenges and mapping solutions: a systematic literature review. In: Proceedings of the 3rd International Conference on Software Engineering and Information Management, pp. 123–129 (2020)
16. Kasauli, R., Knauss, E., Horkoff, J., Liebel, G., de Oliveira Neto, F.G.: Requirements engineering challenges and practices in large-scale agile system development. J. Syst. Softw. **172**, 110851 (2021)
17. Joshi, S., Sharma, M.: Impact of sustainable supply chain management on performance of SMEs amidst COVID-19 pandemic: an Indian perspective. Int. J. Logistics Econ. Globalisation **9**(3), 248–276 (2022)

18. Dingsøyr, T., Bjørnson, F.O., Schrof, J., Sporsem, T.: A longitudinal explanatory case study of coordination in a very large development programme: the impact of transitioning from a first-to a second-generation large-scale agile development method. Empir. Softw. Eng.Softw. Eng. **28**(1), 1–49 (2023)

# Predicting Heart Disease with Machine Learning: A Comparative Study of Classifiers

Nadia Rehmat[1,2]([✉]), Hassan Faraz[1,2], Tayyaba Farhat[1,2], Sanya Abdullah[1,2], and Rasikh Ali[1,2]

[1] Faculty of Computer Science and Information Technology, The Superior University, Lahore 54600, Pakistan
md.arif@superior.edu.pk

[2] Intelligent Data Visual Computing Research (IDVCR), Lahore 54600, Pakistan

**Abstract.** Heart disease is a primary health concern worldwide and is responsible for many deaths every year. Early detection and timely management of risk factors can improve outcomes and reduce the burden of this disease. In this study, we explore using machine learning algorithms to predict the risk of heart disease using a dataset containing 14 medical characteristics. We compare the accuracy of six different classifiers, including Naive Bayes, Nearest Neighbors, Random Forest, Gaussian NB, Multinomial NB, and Decision Tree algorithms. Our results show that the Random Forest classifier performed the best with an accuracy of 89%. The use of machine learning in heart disease prediction can help healthcare professionals to make informed decisions and provide personalized care to patients. Developing accurate prediction models can improve health, reduce healthcare costs, and save lives.

**Keywords:** Heart Disease · Machine learning · Random Forest. Classification

## 1 Introduction

Heart disease is a significant health problem affecting millions of people worldwide. It encompasses a range of conditions that affect the heart and can lead to serious health complications, including heart attacks and stroke [1]. Identifying individuals at risk of developing heart disease is critical to enabling preventative measures, such as lifestyle changes and medication, to be taken. Machine learning is a powerful tool that can identify individuals at risk of developing heart disease and provide valuable insights to healthcare professionals [2]. Heart disease is a significant cause of morbidity and mortality worldwide, and early detection and management of risk factors can improve outcomes and reduce the burden of this disease. Machine learning has emerged as a promising approach to predicting various medical conditions, including heart disease, and can provide valuable insights to healthcare professionals. Several studies have investigated the use of machine learning algorithms for predicting heart disease, including logistic regression, support vector machines, and decision trees. These algorithms have shown varying accuracy, with some studies reporting up to 90% accuracy rates. However, further research is needed to validate these models and optimize their performance in different populations and settings.

Furthermore, researchers must carefully consider ethical and legal considerations related to the utilization of patient data. Nevertheless, the potential benefits of machine learning in predicting heart disease make it an area of active research and development. [3–5].

This paper presents a study using machine learning techniques to predict the risk of heart disease. The study uses data from patients with a history of heart disease and applies various classifiers, including Random Forest and K-NN, to predict the risk of heart disease. The study's results demonstrate the potential of machine learning techniques to accurately predict the risk of heart disease and provide valuable insights to healthcare professionals.

We have organized the rest of this paper as follows. Section 2 provides an overview of heart disease and its major risk factors. Section 3 discusses the role of machine learning in predicting heart disease. Section 4 presents the methodology used in the study, including the data collection and processing techniques and the machine learning classifiers applied. Section 5 presents the study's results, and Sect. 6 discusses the results' implications and the study's limitations. Finally, Sect. 7 provides a conclusion and suggests directions for future research.

## 2 Literature Review

In [6], the author employed various machine learning techniques and terminologies, including naive Bayes, k-nearest neighbour, decision trees, and random forests. Every approach relies on supervised machine learning. This study report includes several traits related to cardiac disease. The collection has 76 features and 303 occurrences. Only 14 of these 76 qualities, essential for demonstrating how well different algorithms work, are used in the testing process. Predicting a patient's likelihood of developing heart disease is the goal. The k-nearest neighbour got the highest accuracy grade of 90.7% in this study report.

In [1], the author employed several approaches for predicting and diagnosing heart disease that relies on machine learning and data mining. We tested various supervised machine-learning algorithms to predict cardiac disease for their effectiveness and accuracy. Three different classification algorithms—DT, RF, and MLP—were used to classify a heart disease dataset obtained from Kaggle. The RF method achieved 100% sensitivity, 100% specificity, and 100% accuracy. This study's supervised machine learning algorithm accurately predicts heart disease [1].

Heart disease is one of the top causes of mortality worldwide. The anticipation of heart illness may be a key barrier in the scope of a clinical information evaluation. The healthcare industry has demonstrated that machine learning can assist in decision-making and establishing expectations from the vast amount of data it generates The authors paired notable highlights with a few well-known classification strategies in their forecast presentation. In this research, we develop a hybrid random forest and linear model to forecast heart disease with an enhanced execution level of 88.7% [6].

The diagnosis of diseases is the most essential component of healthcare. Identifying or predicting a disease sooner than usual could save people's lives. The medical sector may gain from machine learning's categorization technique by offering precise and speedy sickness diagnosis. Heart disease is now among the most ultra-hazardous and deadly illnesses worldwide due to the challenges in identifying the condition. Thus, it is advantageous for physicians and patients to act soon. In this research study, the author utilizes machine learning and image fusion classification approaches, demonstrating their effectiveness in aiding medical professionals in diagnosing heart disease. They briefly review the main categorization techniques for utilizing machine learning to diagnose heart disease. This area discusses and shows the use of classification methods for machine learning and image fusion. It also provides a quick explanation of the ongoing work and an outline of the employed algorithm [7].

The study in [8] utilized a dataset on Cleveland heart disease and applied data mining techniques such as regression and classification. It uses machine learning techniques like Random Forest and Decision Tree. The authors employed a unique technique to construct the machine learning model. They used three machine learning methods in the implementation, namely Random Forest, Decision Tree, and Hybrid Model (a combination of Random Forest and Decision Tree). According to test results, the hybrid model can accurately predict heart illness 88.7% of the time. The author's interface is made to gather user input parameters in order to predict cardiac illness. We used a Decision Tree and Random Forest hybrid model to accomplish this [8].

The Internet of Things (IoT) and the sensor devices covered in this study have significantly improved healthcare monitoring over the last few years. The author is developing a device, such as a 3G BP measuring device or an intelligent ECG machine, that can monitor ECG and other physiological indicators besides blood pressure. The SVM and LR classifiers achieved precision values of 84.10 and 83.70, respectively, while the MLP classifier performed poorly, achieving a minimum precision value of 78.40. With an accuracy score of 91.50, the J48 classifier outperformed other classifiers [9].

Several factors, including a lack of professionals in many countries, substantially impede early diagnosis, claims this study report. Among numerous projects to build decision support systems, computational intelligence is an emerging concept in the field of medical imaging to identify, predict, and diagnose illness. This book presents the author's work on a machine intelligence framework (MIFH) for detecting heart disease. MIFH extracts feature from the UCI heart disease Cleveland dataset using factor analysis of mixed data and trains machine learning prediction models (FAMD). The researchers utilized the holdout validation method to validate the MIFH framework. As per the trial results, the accuracy of MIFH surpassed several existing baseline procedures while performing equally well in terms of sensitivity and specificity. MIFH enhances the system's effectiveness and offers the most practical solution among all input predictive models while considering performance criteria. This helps physicians and radiologists to diagnose heart patients accurately [8].

This study suggests using a sequential feature selection technique to find fatal events in heart disease patients. Among the machine learning methods employed are LDA, RF, GBC, DT, SVM, and KNN. This study compares the classifier's accuracy and the accuracy improved by this method (SFS). The experimental findings demonstrate that the SFS approach achieves 86.67% accuracy for Random Forest Classifier FS. [10].

Since the heart is one of the most important and vital organs in the human body and heart disease prediction is a big concern for individuals, algorithm accuracy is one of the criteria taken into account when assessing how well an algorithm works in this [2]. Machine learning algorithms' accuracy depends on the datasets used for testing and training. KNN is the best algorithm, according to our analysis of algorithms based on dataset properties and confusion matrices. More machine learning techniques will be utilized in the future to analyze heart disease data more effectively and anticipate illnesses early so that public awareness of these issues can reduce the number of The researchers used the Chi Sq Selector to infer factors with anatomical and physiological significance, such as cholesterol, the heart rate at which pain is perceived at its worst, chest discomfort, ST depression-related characteristics, and cardiac arteries. The experiment results showed that most classifiers perform better when PCA and chi-square are coupled. When computing PCA directly from the raw data, additional dimensionality would be required in order to enhance the results [11]. (Table 1)

Table 1. Literature on Heart Disease Prediction

| No | Authors | Classifiers | Accuracies |
|---|---|---|---|
| 1 | Ankur Gupta [12] | FAMD + LR | 82% |
| | | FAMD + KNN | 78% |
| | | FAMD + SVM | 83% |
| | | FAMD + DT | 77% |
| | | FAMD + RF | 93% |
| 2 | Diwakar [7] | RF | 91% |
| | | J48 | 91% |
| | | SVM | 84% |
| 3 | Dr. N. Sivakumar [10] | LR | 83% |
| | | MLP | 78% |
| 4 | Garate [11] | SVM | 90% |
| 5 | Monaj Diwakar [5] | DT | 86% |
| | | LR | 89% |
| | | ABM1 | 95% |
| | | MLP | 98% |
| 6 | Md Mamun Ali [1] | KNN | 100% |
| | | DT | 100% |
| | | RF | 100% |
| | | KNN | 77% |
| 7 | Ritu Agrawal [8] | DT | 74% |
| | | RF | 100% |
| | | Naïve Bayes | 76% |
| | | LM | 85% |
| 8 | Senthilkumar Mohan [4] | LR | 83% |
| | | DL | 87% |
| | | DT | 85% |
| | | RF | 86% |
| | | HRFLM | 88% |

## 3 Methodology

### 3.1 Original Data

The public dataset "Heart Disease Prediction" was obtained from Kaggle, a public repository for datasets [9]. The dataset used in this study consists of several features related to heart disease diagnosis, including demographic information such as age and sex and medical data such as resting blood pressure, serum cholesterol levels, and electrocardiographic results. Other features such as exercise-induced angina, ST depression induced by exercise, and the number of major vessels were also included. The target variable was binary, with a value of 1 indicating a positive diagnosis for heart disease and 0 indicating a negative diagnosis. The heart disease prediction project aimed to determine whether a patient should receive a diagnosis of heart disease or not, resulting in a binary outcome. A positive result of 1 indicated that the patient had heart disease, while a negative result of 0 showed the absence of heart disease [10]. In Fig. 1. Attributes from the dataset are provided.

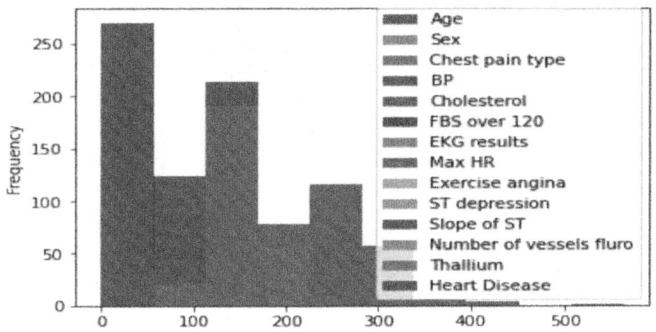

**Fig. 1.** Dataset Description

### 3.2 Features of the Selected Dataset

After compiling the data, the researchers investigated it. They used a dataset with numerous variables that could be used to predict cardiac disease. The dataset consisted of 14 columns, including the following variables [10]:

- Age: (The data collection contains a wide range of people ages.)
- Sex:(it refers to a person's gender in the 0/1 form. 0 denotes a man, and 1 represents a female.)
- Chest pain type: (Chest discomfort displays a range of 1–4 for the intensity of chest pain.)
- BP: (Blood pressure is a measurement of a person's blood pressure.)
- Cholesterol: (Low-density lipoprotein (LDL), also known as "bad" cholesterol, has long been linked to an increased risk of developing heart disease.)

- FBS over 120: (This indicates a fasting blood sugar level that is greater or lower than 120.0)
- EKG results: (Electrocardiogram attributes display the EKG result in 0, 1, and 2 form.)
- Max HR: (It displays the highest heart rate possible for a given age.)
- Exercise angina: (Angina, a form of chest pain brought on by low blood pressure, is represented in the dataset by the pain as 0,1.)
- ST depression: (An individual's ECG findings may show a specific outcome called ST depression. It happens when the ST segment in a person's findings seems abnormally low and lies below the baseline, showing their amount.)
- Slope of ST: (It displays a graph of St)
- Number of vessels Fluro: (It displays the vessels' numbers, which range from
- Thallium: (This technology measures the amount of blood flowing into various areas of your heart using a radioactive tracer.)

## 4 Data Preprocessing

During the preprocessing step of the study, the researchers evaluated the dataset, which contained 14 variables, including 9 categorical and 5 continuous variables. They identified null values in the dataset and replaced them with the mean value. They also analyzed the target column to determine class balance and found an imbalance with 165 instances for class 1 and 139 for class 0. The class "yes" was referred to as 1, and the class "no" was called 0. Figure 2. Percentage difference of Target Classes represents the difference between both Classes.

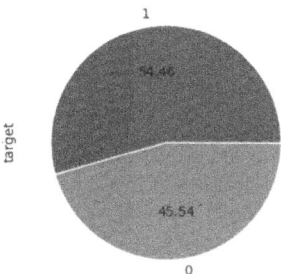

**Fig. 2.** Percentage difference of Target Classes

The researchers applied the Oversampling technique to balance both classes, followed by converting the categorical data columns to numeric form for ease of analysis during the preprocessing step of the study. In addition, we generated a pie chart to visualize the balanced dataset classes achieved through the oversampling technique. Figure 3. Balanced Class balanced classes after applying oversampling.

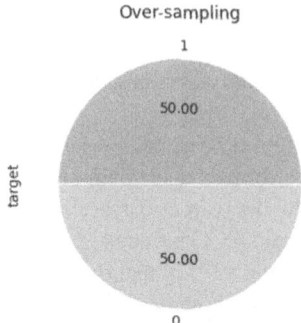

**Fig. 3.** Balanced Class

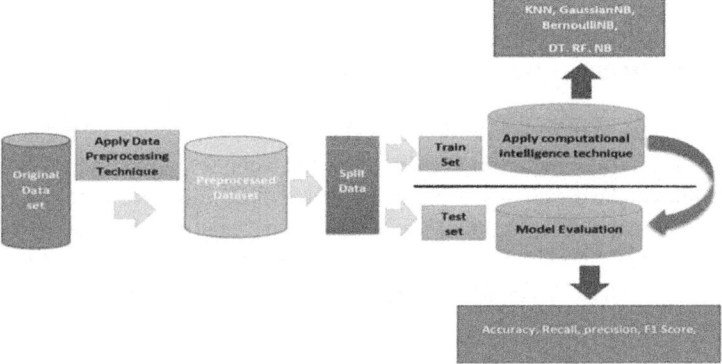

**Fig. 4.** Research Methodology

### 4.1 Splitting the Data

The next step in developing the machine learning model is to separate the data into training and testing sets. The training and testing data were split in an 80/20 ratio for better prediction results.

### 4.2 Training the Model

We applied various machine learning classifiers to the given dataset, including Random Forest, Gaussian NB, Bernoulli NB, Decision Tree, KNN, and Multinomial NB. Random Forest is an ensemble learning method that constructs multiple decision trees and outputs the mode of the classes. Gaussian NB is a probabilistic classifier based on Bayes' theorem with the assumption of Gaussian distribution.

Another probabilistic classifier based on Bayes' theorem is the Bernoulli NB, designed for binary or Boolean features. Decision Tree is a non-parametric supervised learning method used for classification and regression, where it partitions the feature space recursively into regions by using simple decision rules. KNN is a lazy learning algorithm that classifies new data points by finding the closest training example(s) in the feature space. Multinomial NB is a variant of Naive Bayes designed explicitly for discrete count data. Each of these classifiers has its strengths and weaknesses, and their suitability depends on the specific characteristics of the dataset and the problem at hand. By comparing the performance of these classifiers on the given dataset, we can determine which classifier performs best and select it for our final model. The following section provides a description of applied classifiers and their mathematical equations.

**Experiments and Results**

### 4.3 Random Forest

Random forest is a machine learning algorithm that combines multiple decision trees to improve predictive accuracy and prevent overfitting [3].

The subject study applied random forest of selected dataset. The accuracy and F1 scores obtained using the random forest classifier on the dataset are 0.8888889 and 0.888266, respectively.

$$y = \frac{1}{N} \sum_{\iota=1}^{N} (F_\iota - \gamma_\iota)^2 \tag{1}$$

### 4.4 Bernoulli Naïve Bayes

One variation of the Naive Bayes method used in machine learning is Bernoulli. It is highly helpful when the dataset has a binary distribution and the output label is either present or missing [1].

The accuracy and F1 scores obtained using the Bernoulli NB classifier on the dataset are 0.796296 and 0.794356, respectively.

$$P(\chi\_\iota/\Upsilon) = P(X\_I/Y) + (1 - P(X\_I/Y))(1 - X\_I) \tag{2}$$

### 4.5 Gaussian Naïve Bayes

A machine learning classification algorithm is called Gaussian Processes Classifier. By substituting the variable's new input value for the parameters in the Gaussian probability density function, one may anticipate the future and estimate the likelihood of the new input value.

The accuracy and F1 scores obtained using the Gaussian NB classifier on the dataset are 0.833333 and 0.832926, respectively.

$$P(\chi_\iota/\gamma) = \frac{1}{\sqrt{2\pi\sigma^2\gamma}} \mathrm{EXP}\left(\frac{(\chi_\iota - \prod_\iota)^2}{2\sigma^2\gamma}\right) \tag{3}$$

## 4.6 Decision Tree

The component models that make up a random forest are decision trees. Each decision tree classifier creates a tree using the dataset's properties. Decision trees are quick and accurate for disease prediction if the dataset provides powerful features for a simple use case [1]. The accuracy and F1 scores obtained using the Decision Tree classifier on the dataset are 0.814815 and 0.814815, respectively.

$$\mathbf{GINI} = 1 - \sum_{T=1}^{C} (P_I)^2 \tag{4}$$

## 4.7 Multinomial Naïve Bayes

Multiclass classification, or multinomial classification, categorizes cases into one or more classes in statistical classification and machine learning.

The accuracy and F1 scores obtained using the Multinomial NB classifier on the dataset are 0.777778 and 0.774621, respectively.

$$\hat{\mathbf{P}}(C) = \frac{P_C}{N} \tag{5}$$

$$\hat{P}\left(W/C\right) = \frac{\mathbf{COUNT} + (\mathbf{W, C}) + 1}{\mathbf{COUNT(C)} + |\mathbf{V}|} \tag{6}$$

## 4.8 KNN

The k-nearest neighbours' method, often known as KNN or k-NN, is a supervised learning classifier that makes predictions or classifications about clustering a single data point based on closeness. The KNN algorithm's primary objective is to forecast how a new sample point will be classified using data points that have been broken up into several classes [8].

**Manhattan Distance:**

$$\sum_{t=1}^{d} |x_{1i} - x_{2i}| \tag{7}$$

**Euclidean Distance:**

$$\left(\sum_{t=1}^{d} (x_{1i} - x_{2i})^2\right)^{\frac{1}{2}} \tag{8}$$

**Minkowski Distance:**

$$\left(\sum_{t=1}^{d} |x_{1i} - x_{2i}|^p\right)^{\frac{1}{p}} \quad (9)$$

The accuracy and F1 scores obtained using the KNN classifier on the dataset are 0.703704 and 0.703704, respectively. Figure 4 depict the working of the heart disease prediction model. The flowchart demonstrates the process of the model working, which starts by passing a record as input. The model then extracts information from the input and looks for the symptoms related to heart disease. Based on the presence or absence of these symptoms, the model classifies the input as either indicating no heart disease or one of the three types considered in the study. This flowchart helps to provide a visual representation of the model's working, which can aid in understanding and evaluating the algorithm's performance.

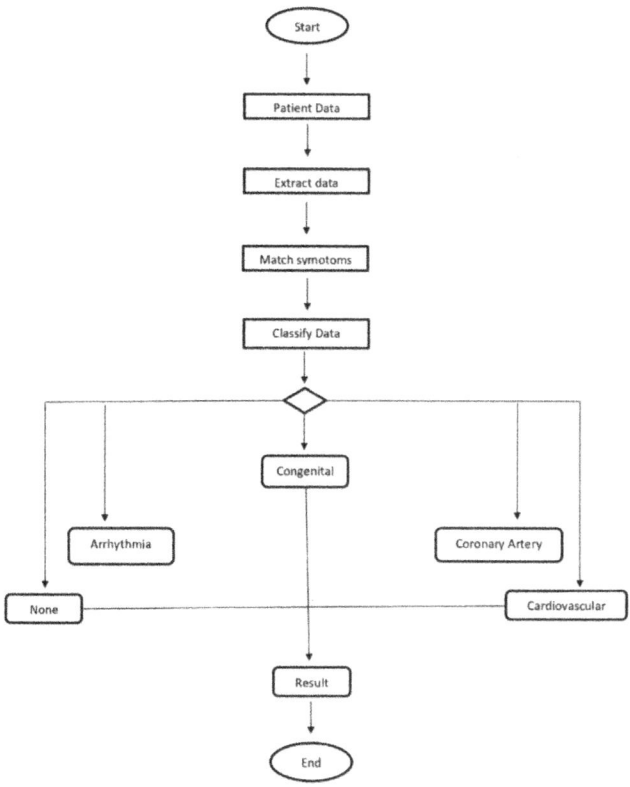

**Fig. 5.** Flow of the Prediction System

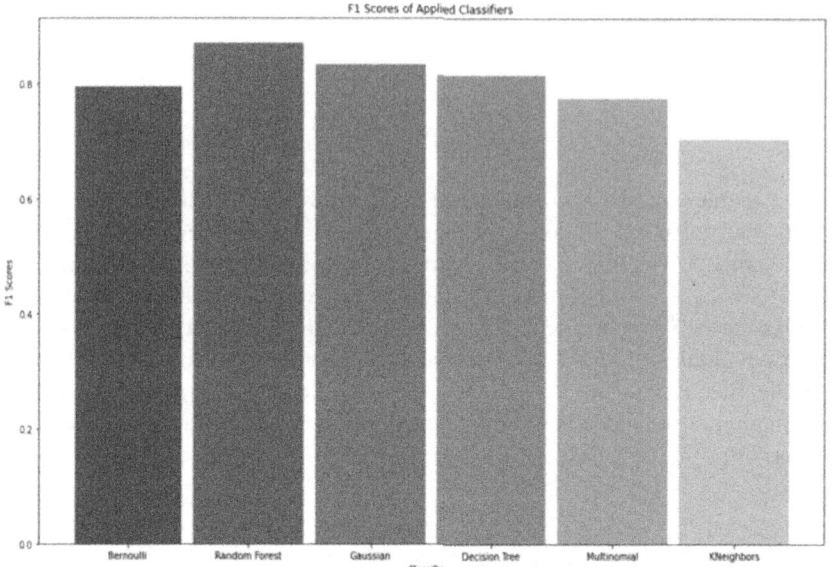

**Fig. 6.** Accuracies of Applied Classifiers

**Table 2.** Testing Accuracies of Applied Classifiers

| Classifiers | Accuracies | Precision | Recall | F1 Score |
|---|---|---|---|---|
| Random Forest | 0.888 | 0.890 | 0.888 | 0.888 |
| Gaussian NB | 0.833 | 0.833 | 0.833 | 0.832 |
| Bernoulli NB | 0.796 | 0.797 | 0.796 | 0.794 |
| Decision Tree | 0.814 | 0.814 | 0.814 | 0.814 |
| KNN | 0.703 | 0.703 | 0.703 | 0.703 |
| Multinomial NB | 0.777 | 0.780 | 0.777 | 0.774 |

The researchers used several metrics, including F1 score, precision, accuracy, and recall, to assess the performance of the machine learning classifiers. This study utilized confusion matrices to evaluate the performance of each classifier further. The accuracy of each classifier was plotted on a graph to compare their performance visually. Finally, a comparison of all classifiers is presented in Table 2. The metrics used to evaluate the performance of machine learning models in binary classification tasks are accuracy, precision, recall, and F1 score. Accuracy indicates the percentage of correct predictions made by the model, while precision evaluates the proportion of true positives among positive predictions. Recall measures the fraction of positive instances identified by the model, and F1 score provides a combined measure of precision and recall. Table 2 shows that Random Forest outperformed all other classifiers on the dataset with an accuracy of 0.88 and precision of 0.89. Additionally, Fig. 5 graphically compares the performance of all the applied classifiers. The confusion matrix for Random Forest is provided in Fig. 6. These results demonstrate the effectiveness of using machine learning techniques for heart disease prediction and highlight the importance of accurately detecting and managing this disease (Figs. 7 and 8).

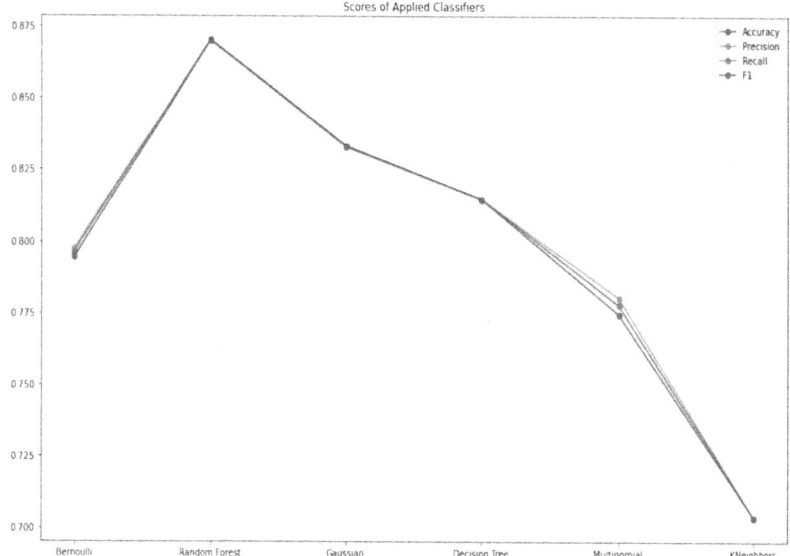

**Fig. 7.** Score of Applied Classifiers

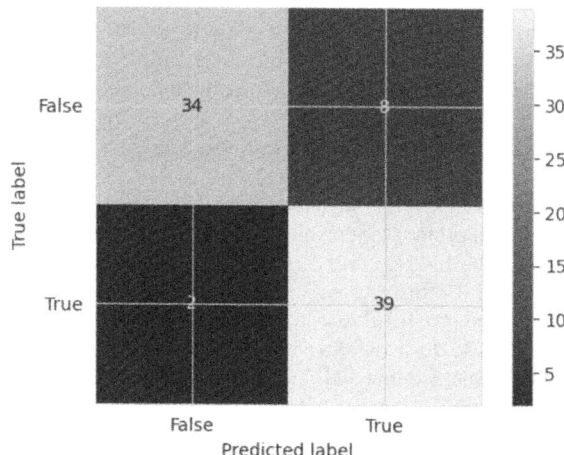

**Fig. 8.** Confusion Matrix of Random Forest

If the model accurately predicted the values, it is considered True. Otherwise, it is False. To quantify the model's quality, we can use different measures. The first one is accuracy, which represents the proportion of correct predictions among all predictions made. The model yielded 39 true positives, 2 false positives, 8 false negatives, and 34 true negatives.

## 5 Conclusion

In conclusion, this study demonstrated the potential of machine learning techniques in diagnosing heart disease. The preprocessing step ensured the dataset was cleaned, balanced, and converted into a format suitable for analysis. Five classifiers were tested, and the Random forest model outperformed the others in accuracy, precision, recall, and F1 score. Confusion matrices were utilized to assess the performance of each classifier further. The suggested operating paradigm may assist medical students and doctors in training and diagnosis, leading to early diagnosis and lower treatment costs. Future research could investigate incorporating several class labels into the prediction process to enhance the system's accuracy. The high dimensionality of the heart database presents a challenge in selecting critical features for a better diagnosis of heart disease. Overall, this study demonstrated the potential of machine learning in assisting with heart disease diagnosis and emphasized the need for continued research in this area.

## References

1. Singh, A., Kumar, R.: Heart disease prediction using machine learning algorithms. In 2020 International Conference on Electrical and Electronics Engineering (ICE3)
2. Ganesan, M., Sivakumar, N.: IoT based heart disease prediction and diagnosis model for healthcare using machine learning models. In: 2019 IEEE International Conference on System, Computation, Automation and Networking (ICSCAN)
3. Choudhary, G., Singh, S.N.: Prediction of heart disease using machine learning algorithms. In: 2020 International Conference on Smart Technologies in Computing, Electrical and Electronics (ICSTCEE)
4. Acharya, A. Comparative study of machine learning algorithms for heart disease prediction (2017)
5. Ali, M.M., Paul, B.K., Ahmed, K., Bui, F.M., Quinn, J.M., Moni, M.A.: Heart disease prediction using supervised machine learning algorithms: performance analysis and comparison. Comput. Biol. Med. **136**, 104672 (2021)
6. Mohan, S., Thirumalai, C., Srivastava, G.: Effective heart disease prediction using hybrid machine learning techniques. IEEE Access **7**, 81542–81554 (2019)
7. Diwakar, M., Tripathi, A., Joshi, K., Memoria, M., Singh, P.: Latest trends on heart disease prediction using machine learning and image fusion. Mater. Today: Proc. **37**, 3213–3218 (2021)
8. Kavitha, M.,Gnaneswar, G.,Dinesh, R.,Sai, Y.R., Suraj, R.S.: Heart disease prediction using hybrid machine learning model. In 2021 6th International Conference on Inventive Computation Technologies (ICICT)
9. Goldbloom, A. *Heart Disease Prediction Dataset.* https://www.kaggle.com
10. Aggrawal, R., Pal, S.: Sequential feature selection and machine learning algorithm-based patient's death events prediction and diagnosis in heart disease. SN Comput. Sci. **1**(6), 344 (2020)

11. Gárate-Escamila, A.K., El Hassani, A.H., Andrès, E.: Classification models for heart disease prediction using feature selection and PCA. Inform. Med. Unlocked **19**, 100330 (2020)
12. Gupta, A., Kumar, R., Arora, H.S., Raman, B.: MIFH: A machine intelligence framework for heart disease diagnosis. IEEE Access **8**, 14659–14674 (2019)

# Media Forensics and Deepfake-Systematic Survey

C. H. Nadeem Jabbar[1(✉)], Aqib Saghir[1], Ayaz Ahmad Meer[2], Salman Ahmad Sahi[1], Bilal Hassan[2], and Siddiqui Muhammad Yasir[3]

[1] Department of Computer Science, The Superior University, Lahore, Pakistan
md.arif@superior.edu.pk
[2] Northumbria University, London Campus, UK
[3] School of Artificial Intelligence, Tongmyong University, Busan, South Korea

**Abstract.** Deepfake is a generative deep learning algorithm that creates or changes facial features in a very realistic way, making it hard to differentiate the real from the fake features. It can be used to make movies look better, as well as to spread false information by imitating famous people. In this paper, many different ways to make a Deepfake are explained, analyzed and separated categorically. Using Deepfake datasets, models are trained and tested for reliability through experiments. Deepfakes are a type of facial manipulation that allow people to change their entire faces, identities, attributes, and expressions. The trends in the available Deepfake datasets are also discussed, with a focus on how they've changed. Using Deep learning, a general Deepfake detection model is made. Moreover, the problems in making and detecting Deepfakes are also mentioned. As a result of this survey, it is expected that the development of new Deepfake-based imaging tools will speed up in the future. This survey gives in-depth review of methods for manipulating images of face, and various techniques to spot altered face images. Four types of facial manipulation are specifically discussed which are attribute manipulation, expression swap, entire face synthesis, and identity swap. Across every manipulation category, we yield information on manipulation techniques, significant benchmarks for technical evaluation of counterfeit detection techniques, available public databases, and a summary of the outcomes of all such analyses. From all of the topics in the survey, we focus on the most recent development of Deepfake, showing its advances and obstacles in detecting fake images.

## 1 Introduction

Many deep learning-based methodologies are used to generate temporal data and fake spatial by changing one person's face (posture, identification, expression) and so on with another is referred to as the famous term "Deepfake." Digitally altered photos and videos, especially with Deepfake technologies, have been a major source of public concern. This technology was being used for fake news, fake pornography, hoaxes, and financial fraud, etc. [1] (Fig. 1).

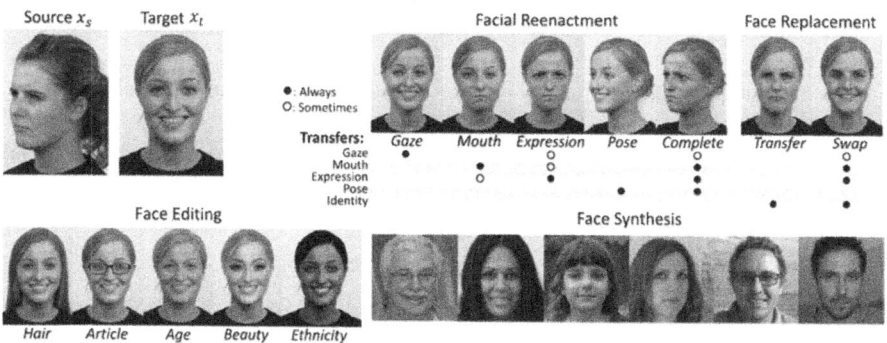

**Fig. 1.** Different categories of deepfake Data [1]

However, many things changed dramatically in the recent years, starting with the early works and continuing to the present. The ability to mechanically synthesize non-existent faces or modify the genuine face of a single person in an image or video is becoming increasingly common these days. Before Deepfake, fake media generation required expertise in the field, and took more time and effort. Tools like Adobe Lightroom and Adobe Photoshop are used by experts for retouching and modifying a picture [2]. Deepfakes, which are now generated using artificial intelligence, have no need for too much expertise. Fake data can be generated only in a few clicks. In graphics industries and computer vision Deepfake has a wide range of benefits as well as harmful uses; with the help of Deepfake stunning landscapes can be generated; on the other hand, fake news generation can mislead the audience, which may increase security risks. To generate fake movies of female celebrities, many people with malicious motives have used these technologies in such a way that triggered important societal challenges, including sexual harassment. Furthermore, several malicious applications, like DeepNude4 [3], have taken advantage of Deepfake it allows them to take a snapshot of a fully suited lady and produce an image in which her clothing are removed. Since a few years, researchers have been working on developing various techniques to distinguish images and videos that are synthesized with artificial intelligence, especially those manipulated with GANs and their variants) from those that are captured naturally with a camera. There are competition such as DFGC (Deepfake game challenge) [4] encourage researchers to propose better solution for detection. Detecting fakes in the spatial domain is one of the most commonly used strategies for finding fake videos and images in recent studies [2]. In the frequency domain, several researchers are attempting to distinguish between original and forged data, which is a relatively new field [2] Deepfake creation is classified into four types: 1. Facial Reenactment 2. Face Replacement 3. Face Editing 4. Face synthesis.

In this survey, Deepfake detection strategies for images and videos are gone through. Moreover, the Deepfake creation processes and datasets that are used to detect Deepfakes, as well as the Deepfake detection algorithms, are discussed.

Below are the major objectives of this article, which are summarized as follows:

- Deepfake tools, which are used to change many features of photos and videos, are undergone.

- Deepfake datasets, as well as certain standard datasets, are introduced for forensic review.
- Some of the most recent methods for detecting Deepfake in images and videos are mentioned.
- The rest of the article is decomposed as: Paper collection and review methods are provided in 2. Then 3 is about deepfake creation. 4 is outlined with Public Datasets. However, in 5, Deepfake detection is focused.

Finally, discussions and future work are drawn in 6 (Fig. 2).

## 2 Prepare Collection and Review Methods

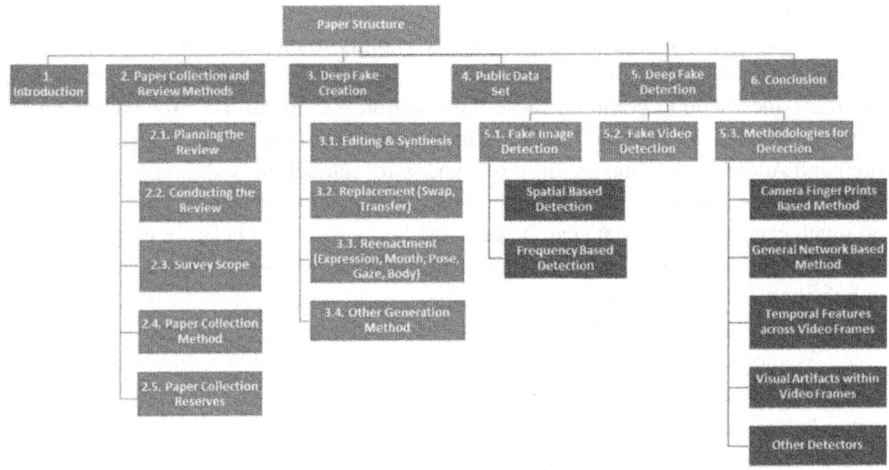

**Fig. 2.** Tree diagram showing structure of the paper

### 2.1 Planning the Review

The primary objective of this step is to deduce the problem that needs to be solved. Next, to come up with the idea through which the problem can be solved, and evaluate or solve the problem. In this step, the idea and its requirements are provided. Eventually, the final step is to test the reliability of the criteria and procedures used to solve the problem.

### 2.2 Conducting the Review

It includes six obligatory steps on the basis of the guiding concepts outlined in this phase.

**Research Questions (RQs)**
Because the proper question leads to the right direction and gives the study significance.

Therefore, the success of the study is dependent on the appropriate and relevant research questions [5]. So, we outline the following research questions: 1) The first question is, what are the most famous Deepfake detection methods? 2) What datasets are typically utilized for detecting Deepfake? 3) What are the features typically utilized in detecting Deepfake? 4) What models are used to detect Deefake manipulation? 5) For Deepfake Detection Techniques, what is the Classification Structure? 6) What is the overall productivity of various Deepfake detection techniques on the basis of experimental evidence?

**Search Strategy**

In this stage, the maximum possible relevant data is gathered. In order to detect Deepfake, this article includes as many combinations of related search phrases as possible. Using Boolean terminology, search terms were combined with "AND" or "OR," which is the main idea. The search terms are: Deepfake AND Digital

Media Forensics, FaceSwap OR Deepfake, Video manipulation OR Fake image/video/face detection OR Facial Manipulation. For research purposes, more than one or two sources were used. Furthermore, the authenticity of the research was tested thoroughly using multiple resources as mentioned below. The numerous research articles are available online, the top repositories that were both important and easy to use were selected which are shown

- ScienceDirect (ELSEVIER)
- ACM Digital Library
- Web of Science
- Google Scholar
- Database Systems and Logic Programming (DBLP)
- SpringerLink
- Computing Research Repository
- IEEE Xplore Digital Library
- Semantic Scholar

**Selection Criteria**

To find the most reliable articles, three rules were set up for this research.

- The keywords, title, or abstract must contain the search phrases (Some articles, although based on Deepfake, did not contain words like "Deepfake" in the keywords, title, or abstract.)
- In writing, empirical evidence is made clear.
- The main goal of this study is about how images or videos can be changed and how we can detect change images and videos

**Quality Assessment Criteria (QAC)**

Analyzing the material in the document and evaluating the quality of the evidence are equally important. Researchers should be cautious when interpreting the findings of a poorly executed study since they may have been influenced by methodological flaws. For that reasons, right criteria must be chosen in order to assess the quality of the evidence.

We validate the selected studies using the criteria defined in [6] and evaluate the gathered material by applying these criteria.

In our quality assessment phase, we decided 96 research articles and 21 additional reviews (7 SLRs, 10 analyses, and 4 surveys) relating to Deepfake detection.

**Data Synthesis.** The goal of data synthesis is to arrange and compile the findings of the conducted research. We evaluate the data, once accumulated, in order to extract additional information. Also, we use various tools for data visualization, including tables and charts, to display the acquired data.

**Reporting the Review.** After reviewing all of the research, we organized the results properly for the target readers and distribution medium.

### 2.3 Survey Scope

The technical aspects of Deepfakes are the paper's primary focus. This paper briefly discussed spotting a deepfake and avoiding being caught, as different research publications cover it. The moral and social elements of Deepfakes, which are discussed in this survey, are not the primary focus of this study. There are several types of media manipulation, including body, expression, and tone. However, we focused only on Deepfakes of facial in our survey.

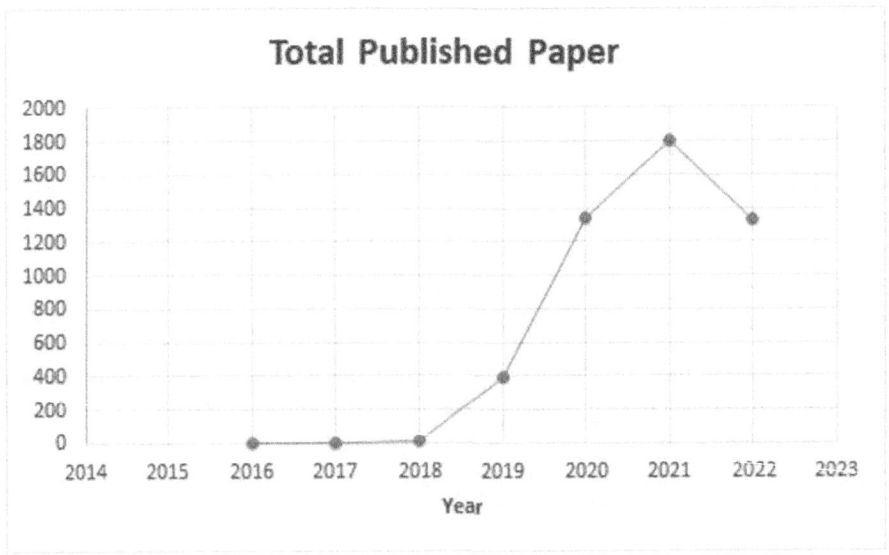

**Fig. 3.** Number of published paper from year 2015 to 2022 as per Google Scholar and [7]

## 2.4 Paper Collection Method

First, over 100 papers on Deepfakes generation, Deepfakes detection, and Deepfakes evasion were gathered from arxiv. Next, on two major scientific databases (IEEE, DBLP, Google Scholar, and various other sources from which the latest research publish) we used keywords in searching to recognize and collect papers on Deepfake. To ensure a more comprehensive and accurate survey, publications in major conferences and respective workshops were also browsed of last three years to ensure a more thorough and precise survey. The following keywords are used: video synthesis, tampered face, facial image, face swapping, deepfake, GAN synthesized, forgery, and AI-synthesized - manipulation.

## 2.5 Paper Collection Reserves

We found 287 papers from arXiv, Google Scholar and IEEE. The papers were mostly about how to make Deepfake, Deepfake detection, and how to avoid detection of Deepfakes. Figure 3 illustrates the allocation of research that was released in various locations. Here, papers from the top journals and sources were divided into several groups. The "Others" category included publications from lesser-known publications and conferences. Furthermore, Unpublished papers were categorized as "arXiv".

# 3 Deepfake Creation

In recent years, Computer vision has progressed and achieved excellent results through deep learning. Deep learning is also one of the most widely used technologies for creating artificial content. Meanwhile, Digital images and videos manipulation is one of the leading interests in deep learning. A wide range of workshops and conferences have a special session for Deepfake, which reflects the interest of the research community [7].

Furthermore, different challenges like Media forensics Challenge (MFC 2018) and Deep Fake Detection Challenge (DFDC) have been launched, which also reflects the significance of the topic (Fig. 4).

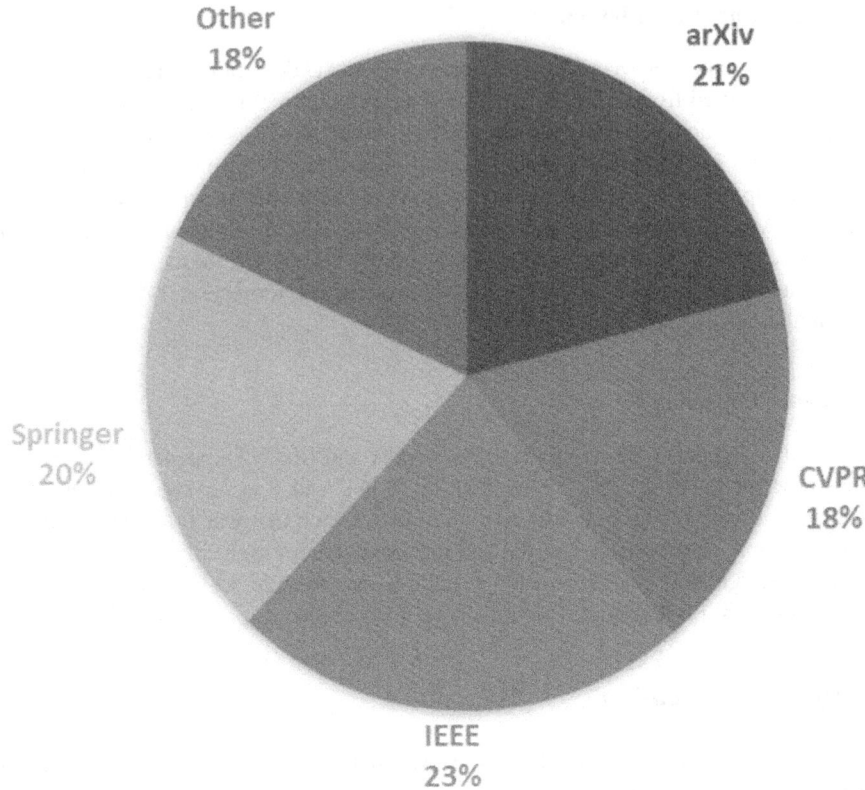

**Fig. 4.** Number of papers collected for the current study

The technology to create Deepfakes has existed for decades; however, creating these effects took an entire studio of experts with just a short time ago. Currently, Deepfake technologies are capable of manipulating pictures or videos much more swiftly due to the addition of Artificial Intelligence (Deepfake means AI, Deep learning base content). GAN's (Generative Adversarial Networks) is the most known source that provides unbelievably realistic results in deep learning [8]. An undeniable fact is that GANs are tough to work with and need a lot of training data [9]. There are many challenges in the development of GAN while creating smooth and manageable syntheses, mostly focused on the high-resolution domains. On top of that, there are many mobile and desktop-based applications in the market that assist people in creating Deepfakes. Each application uses its own developed GAN to achieve its purposes. ZAO, a mobile application [10], AutoFaceswap [11] and FaceApp [12] help the general public on the internet to create Deepfakes without any difficulties. Face swapping is a highly used technique in the field of Deepfake. Through this technique, one face can be moved from the source image to the target image and the main idea behind this technique is also GANs. Over time, images created by Style-GAN [13] and its variants such as Style-Gan2 [14] and Style-GAN-Ada [15] are getting ever more lifelike and utterly unrecognizable to the naked human eye. Each manipulation method has its unique effect, such as without modifying any other facial traits changing eye size or altering skin color. In contrast, it is impossible to generate HD human faces using Style-GAN [13]. On the other hand, BigGAN [16] cannot manipulate the length and complexion of a person without modifying other features of images (Fig. 5).

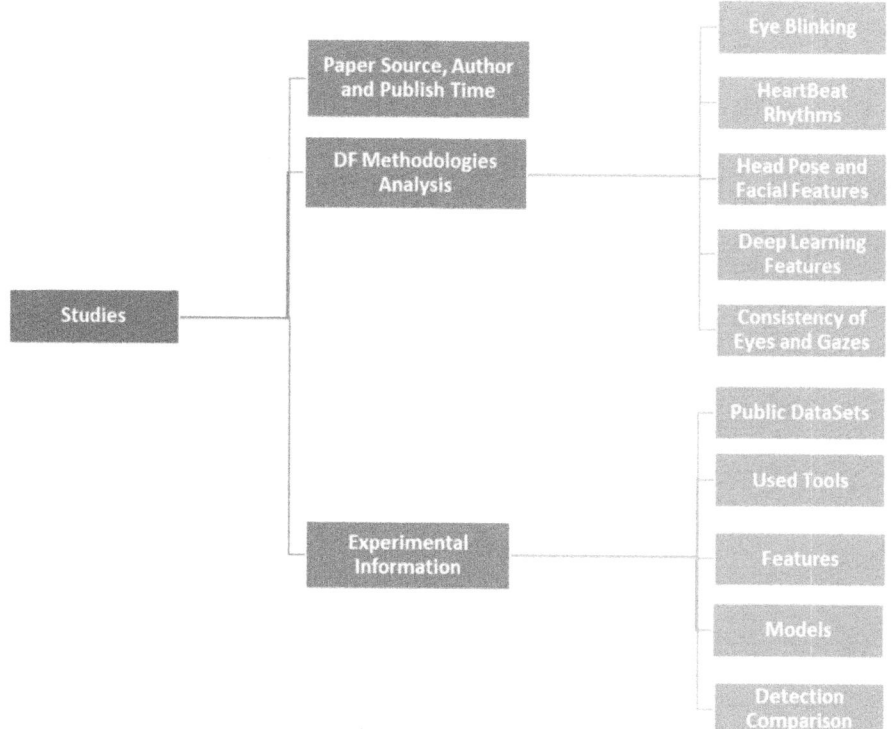

**Fig. 5.** Flow chart of explained information in current study.

Below, we cover the categories of manipulation in more detail.

### 3.1 Editing

In the enchantment, Deepfake, the features of the target image can be changed, removed or added. The technology can be used to manipulate facial hair, weight, age and clothes [17] etc. FaceApp [12] is widely used for editing that is done just for entertainment purposes. However, it can also be used falsely to attack a target personality. Due to this, a constantly growing concern has settled related to the developing of Deepfake mechanics. This technology has made it possible to produce proofs of the actions that never happened. For instance, (i) an ill leader could be made to appear well [18]. (ii) remove object's clothes for the entertainment and blackmailing purpose [19] etc (Fig. 6).

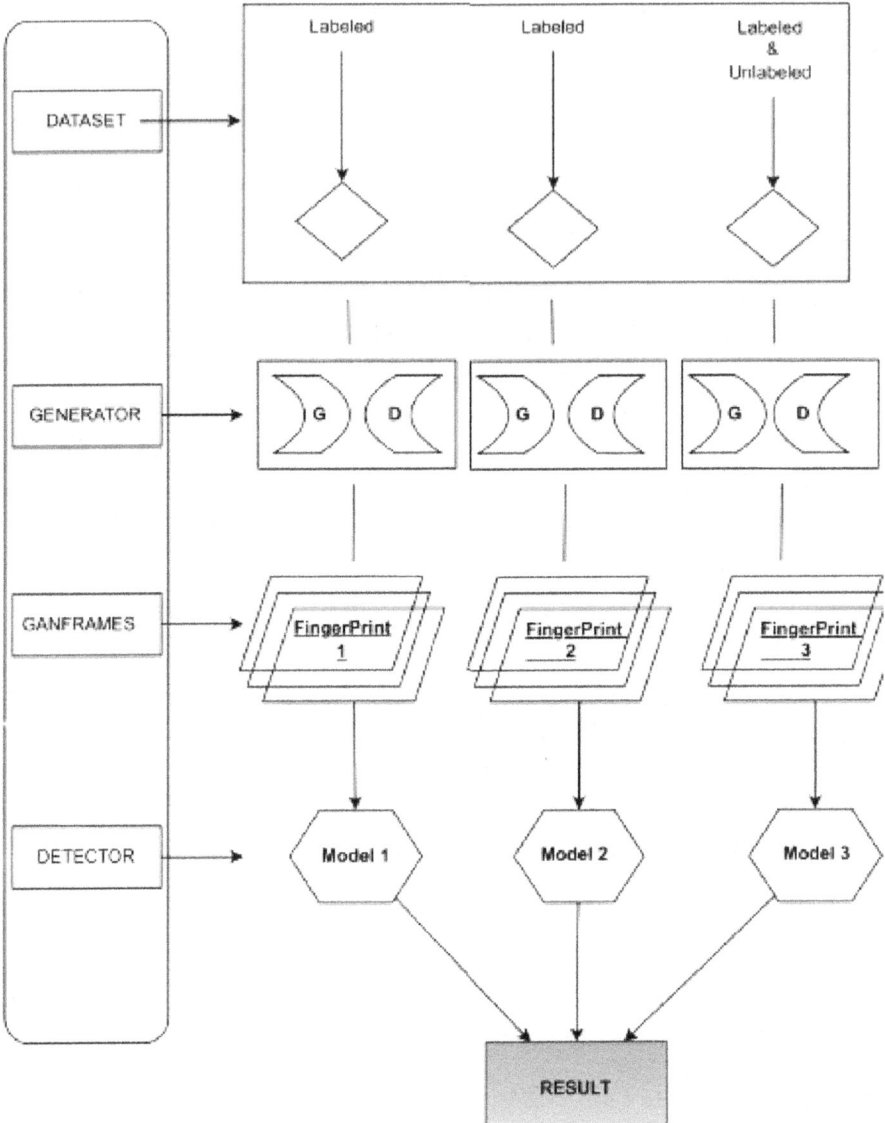

**Fig. 6.** GAN fingerprint example, that can be found in Deepfake-generated media

## 3.2 Synthesis

Synthesis method uses extremely intelligent GANs such as Style-GAN [13] to generate faces which do not exist in the form of images. This method generates amazing outputs such as facial images of high-level resolution. It can be used in different fields such as video games, movies. Yet, like the editing method, synthesis can also be used for negative purposes.

## 3.3 Identity Replacement

It is another trait of deep learning. When the content of the target is replaced by the source while taking care of identity, it is called identity replacement. The following are the two methods used for identity replacement.

**Swap**
Identity swap is quite common in the world of Deepfake. This method is also commonly known as face swap. It can be generated by transferring content to target from source which is driven by target. In simple words, one can replace only a few features of the face like open eyes OR smile persons digitally.

**Transfer**
In the transfer technique output is generated when the content of the source image is exchanged with that of the target image. The fashion business frequently uses facial transfers to visualize people wearing various outfits.

**Identity Replacement or Attack Model**
It is well known and widely used in negative activities and applications [20]. For example, an attacker can swap the face of the victim with a naked porn-stars in order to defame and blackmail the victim. This strategy has previously been employed as a means of disseminating political viewpoints [21].

## 3.4 Reenactment

Another manipulation technique for creating Deepfakes is reenactment. Based on GAN architectures, the available techniques like neural textures [22] and Face2Face [23] are used to make a video, in which the facial expression of one person can be replaced by the facial expression of some other person. The following list of reenactment's branches is provided:

**Expression Swap** is best described as a face modifier technique, which is generated when source image is used to derive the expression of target. It is also the most common technique used in movies, video games, digital media etc. where the performance of the person can be enhanced and improved. Researchers altered 3Dscanned head models in 2003 [24]. Without a 3D model, it was proved that it was possible in 2005. Eventually, between 2015 and 2018, Justus Thies et al. [23, 25, 26] demonstrated the use of 3D parametric models to provide high-quality, in-the-moment outcomes. In 2022, S.M. Yasir [27] proposed a method to detect 3D instance from 3D point cloud that is valuable for 3D face detection and its applications.

**Mouth reenactment** has been used for many years. This method is recognized as dubbing in which the mouth of the target person is derived by the source or an audio input containing conversation. For long, this technology is being widely used when dubbing a movie into another language. For example, if a movie is originally directed in Spanish Language, it can be dubbed into English language using this method. The developers of Obama Net [28] proposed a network that uses text as input rather than audio to reproduce a person's mouth and voice.

**Gaze reenactment** is another kind of manipulation approach generated when the direction of target eyes and eyelids are driven by the source. This procedure is generally used to get realistic output of photographs to maintain eyes contact [29] or to change the direction of one's gaze. The Gaze Redirection Network was proposed by Y. Yu et al. [30] (GRN). In GRN, the source angle, head pose, and cropped eye of the target are individually encoded before being sent via an encoder-decoder network to produce an optical flow field. The generator is driven by an optical flow field that is applied to successive frames in a source video.

**Pose reenactment** is a commonly used technique of manipulation generated when the head position of the target is derived by the source. This method has mainly been used for scanning the faces of individuals in a security footage. Moreover, this approach can be used as a means for improving facial recognition software [31]. J. Cao et al. [32], The authors recommend employing two GANs: The first frontalis the face to produce a Ultraviolet map, [27] and the second turn around the face at the required target angle. As a result, each model executes a simpler procedure. Thus, the models work together to create an image of superior quality.

**Body reenactment**, which is also known as pose transfer and human pose synthesis which is a branch of reenactment approach that are listed above and except that it is pose of source body transfer to the target body (Table 1).

**Table 1.** Facial manipulation techniques used to create Deepfakes

| Facial Manipulation | Key Idea |
|---|---|
| Entire Face Synthesis | Generates perfect, nonexistent facial images using a powerful GAN model, such as StyleGAN or StyleGAN2-Ada |
| Identity Swap | Using FaceSwap or Deepfake methods to swap out a person's face for another person's face in a photograph or video |
| Attribute Manipulation | Altering some facial features, such as the colour, age, gender, skin, hair, and eyeglasses, for example, using Star-GAN |
| Expression Swap | Altering the facial expression of one person in a video with the facial expression of another person, e.g., Face2Face, NeuralTextures |
| Miscellaneous | Face morphing is the process of producing synthetic biometric face samples that mirror the provided biometric data. Remove the identity information shown on a face image or video with face de-identification. Facial expression swap, sometimes known as lipsinc deepfakes, is a technique used to synthesise video from audio or text |

## 3.5 Miscellaneous

Other than the above given categories of creating Deepfake, there are some further types of manipulation. Hereunder, we discuss three of the various evolving techniques, including Face morphing, Face deidentification, and text to video or audio to video swaps of facial expression.

**Face Morphing** generates biometric faces, which are purely artificial and are copies of biometric features from different sources. In other words, face morphing is the utilization of picture control projects to consolidate two separate pictures into a fresh brand-new picture. U. Scherhag et al. [33] investigation of the face morphing approach in 2019 demonstrates the use of attack detectors and morphing algorithms.

**Face de-identification** The primary objective is to obscure a person's identity from a facial video or image to protect their privacy [34]. There are various ways to accomplish this. The simplest method may be to blur or pixelate the face (e.g., in Street View of Maps). More advanced techniques attempt to produce face images with distinct identities while keeping all other elements (position, emotion, illumination, etc.) the same. As a result, the idea of face de-ID is relatively broad. Face identity swapping could be one method for achieving face de-identification. Applying face de-ID to still photos was the foundation of earlier studies in this field. A multifactor framework for de-ID was provided by Gross et al. in [35], including linear, bilinear, and quadratic models. On an expression variant face database, they demonstrated that their technology could safeguard anonymity while maintaining the usefulness of the data. Recent advances in image synthesis methods depend on generative deep neural networks, especially GAN, and have prompted new face de-ID techniques that substitute synthesized faces for real ones, such as those used in [36] and [37]. A further suggestion made by the authors in [38] was to confuse random face-based gender classifiers by using semiadversarial networks (SAN). Recently, in [39], Gafni et al. revealed 2019 a technique for face de-ID with compelling performance even in unconstrained movies. Their strategy is based on a learned face classifier and an adversarial auto-encoder. They can create a rich latent space in which identification and expression information are embedded. A fresh face de-ID technique built on a deep transfer model was also given in [40, 41] This technique interprets the non-identity-related facial characteristics as the original faces' style. It applies a trained facial attribute transfer model to extract and map those characteristics to various faces, yielding highly encouraging results in still photos and videos.

**Text to video or Audio to video** both are the branches that also come under the tree of lip-sync Deepfakes [42]. These methods create videos by synthesizing the target's expression through text or voice. Artificial Intelligence has made people capable of generating Deepfakes that they type whatever they want their subject will say. For example, these Deepfake methods are used in making three-dimensional videos, such as cartoon videos. Using these methods, the written script or the audio of a speaker can directly be converted into a video just like converting text to video. The method of generating high-quality video of someone conversing with an exact lip-sync track is explained through an example of a video [43]. In [44, 45] discuss more key state-of-the-art techniques Video portrait editing technique and Audio-based technique. Furthermore, Fried et al. [46] came up with a text-based editing approach for changing speech content in videos.

This is done to create a new video by taking clips from a video of a person speaking and combining the necessary spoken material with the person's lips to match the new words.

## 4 Public Datasets

### 4.1 Real Datasets

**CelebA:** Liu et al. [47] it built through labeled images of celebrities faces. There are ten thousand celebrities in CelebA dataset, each of which has twenty images. This means there are 200,000 images in total. A professional labelling company annotates every photo in CelebA with and five key points and forty face characteristics (Fig. 7).

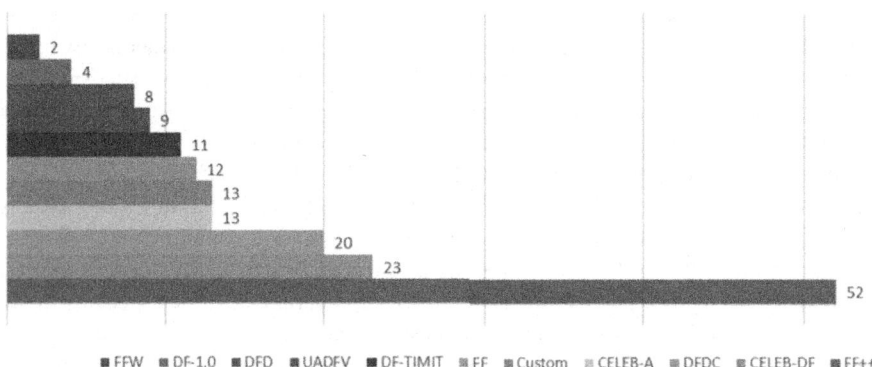

**Fig. 7.** The frequency of used datasets in recent researchs.

### 4.2 Fake Datasets

- The **UADFV** is the dataset from Li et al. [48]. It has 98 videos, 49 of which are real YouTube videos, and the number of fake videos created with the help of FakeApp is 49.
- Korshunov et al. [49] made a database called **Deepfake-TIMIT** in 2018. From 32 different subjects, It has 620 videos which are Deepfake. There are 20 different Deepfake videos in each dataset. Ten videos are 128 × 128 in size, while the others are 64 × 64 in size. Faceswap-GAN is used to make the synthesized videos.
- **DFDC Preview** is a dataset in which 5000 videos generated with two facial manipulation algorithms.Dolhansky et al. [50] The character of said dataset are of different genders, skin tones, ages, etc. Video participants were allowed to record their videos with any background they desired, which resulted in visually diverse backgrounds. Videos include a variety of lighting conditions and head poses.
- **Google DFD** Dufour and Gully et al. [51] More than 3000 tampered videos featuring 28 characters in various scenes. Deepfake generation techniques are used to create the videos from 100s of real videos that are freely available on the internet.

- **FaceForensics++** is a popular dataset that consists of one thousand real video sequences and four thousand videos Rossler et al. [52] that were generated by four automatic face manipulation algorithms as Deepfakes, Face2Face, FaceSwap, and NeuralTexture A total of 977 traceable YouTube videos were used in the creation of the videos. The majority of people in the videos have frontal faces.
- **Celeb-DF** comes with a tremendous challenging video dataset of Deepfake [53], Celeb-Df used an improved synthesis method which generate around 5,639 high-quality videos.Its also have 590 original videos collected from YouTube with different ages, ethic groups and genders.
- **DeeperForensics-1.0** The largest dataset for face forgery detection has been made available Jiang et al. [54]; it consists of 60,000 videos with 17.6 million frames. There are 100 actors included in the 10,000 edited and 50,000 raw videos. There are 55 men and 45 women among them. The actors' skin tones range from black, brown, yellow, and white. Without glasses or decorations, all faces are clean in it.
- **Wild Deepfake** Zi et al. [55] The dataset Wild Deepfake, is made up of 7,314 face sequences takenfrom
- 707 Deepfake videos that were all found on the internet. By testing Deepfake detectors against real-life Deepfake, WildDeepfake is able to evaluate their effectiveness.
- **OpenForensics** On multi-person images, Le et al. [56] takes care of Deepfake's detection capabilities. With almost 334,126 faces and a total of 115,325 images (45,473 original photos and 70,325 manipulated images). OpenForensics can also be utilized for segmentation and tasks standard object detection, demonstrating its versatility. It also includes facial information such as facial landmarks, a forgery category, a segmentation mask, and a bounding box.
- The **Diverse Fake Face Dataset (DFFD)** Dang et al. [57] have created a large dataset of face counterfeit. Males account for 47.7% of all photographs or videos, 52.37% are female, with an averageage of 21–50 years. The real face samples are taken from FFHQ, CelebA, and FaceForensics + +. Video clips from FaceForensics ++ were used for facial identification and expression swapping. In order to generate attribute manipulated images, they have used two techniques:StarGAN [17] and FaceAPP [12]. In recent years, PGGAN and StyleGAN [58] have been used to synthesize face images.
- The **GBDF Gender Balanced Deepfake Dataset** [59] dataset is created using FF++ (c23 version), Celeb-DF, Deeper Forensics-1.0 and consist of 10, 000 videos with 5000 each for males and females.
- **DFDC** Facebook has built a huge dataset of face videos that can be used to train detection models. A wellknown dataset Dolhansky et al. [60] Deepfake Detection Challenge (DFDC) Kaggle competition was arranged by them. There are 128,514 videos in DFDC, around 3,426 actors helped to create 100,000.
- **MICC: F220, F2000, F600** [61] Images from the MICC-F600, MICCF2000, and MICC-F220 datasets are used to spot copy-move modifications. In MICC-F220, there are 110 altered and 110 original photographs; there are 700 tampered and 1300 authentic images in MICC-F2000. Moreover, in MICC-F600, there are 160 modified and 440 raw images (Table 2).

**Table 2.** Details of publicly available data set for Deepfake

| Year | Dataset | Original | | Fake | | Details of Dataset |
|---|---|---|---|---|---|---|
| | | Image | Videos | Image | Videos | |
| 2011 | ● MICC [61] | 1300 | | 700 | | ● Used for image copymove tampering detection |
| 2015 | ● WWD [62] | 13,500 | | | | 92 variations of forgery, 82 instances of forgery, and 101 different splice detection masks |
| 2015 | ● CelebA [47] | 202,000 | | | | This dataset of photos includes a wide range of poses and cluttered backgrounds |
| 2017 | ● VISION [63] | 34,400 | 1914 | | | A video and image source identification Application based dataset (35 portable devices of 11 major brands) |
| 2018 | ● UADFV [48] | 17,300 | 49 | 17,300 | 49 | The FakeAPP is used to create the Deepfake videos; it is simple to use and only contains two classes: real and fake |
| 2018 | ● DF-TIMIT [49] | 34,000 | 320 | 68,000 | 640 | Low-quality(LQ) and highquality DFTIMIT(HQ), obtained using a Faceswap GAN model |
| 2019 | ● FF [64] | 500,000 | 1004 | 521,400 | | Two ways to generate Deepfake: Face2Face, and self reenactment |
| 2019 | ● FF++ [52] | 509,900 | 1,000 | 509,000 | 4000 | Face2Face and FaceSwap are two graphics based methods, and two learning based methods (Deepfakes and Neural Textures) |

(*continued*)

**Table 2.** (*continued*)

| Year | Dataset | Original | | Fake | | Details of Dataset |
|---|---|---|---|---|---|---|
| | | Image | Videos | Image | Videos | |
| 2019 | ● DFFD [57] | 58,700 | 1,000 | 240,300 | 3,000 | Several forgery types are combined in the DFFD dataset |
| 2019 | ● DFD [51] | 315,400 | 363 | 2,242.7k | 3,068 | Google contributed with the FF++ Dataset; additionally, actors, to create manipulated videos |
| 2019 | ● DFDC-P [50] | 488,400 | 1,131 | 1,783,300 | 4,113 | Featuring two facial modification algorithms |
| 2020 | ● DFDC [60] | | 23k | | 104k | To expand the DFDC-P, 8 facial modification algorithms have been applied |
| 2020 | ● Celeb-DF [53] | 225,400 | 590 | 2,116,800 | 5,639 | 59 celebrity YouTube videos were created utilising an upgraded Deepfake synthesis technique |
| 2020 | ● DF-1.0 [54] | 12.6M | 50,000 | 5.0M | 10,000 | A large-scale dataset for real-world face forgery detection |
| 2020 | ● WDF [55] | 11.8M | | 7,314 | 707 | A modest dataset that examines the real-world dataset's ability to recognise Deepfakes |
| 2022 | ● GBDF [59] | | 7500 | | 2500 | It consist of 10,000 videos with 5000 each for males and females with 1:4 real to fake ratio |
| 2021 | ● OF [56] | 16,000 | | 173,000 | | Huge challenging dataset for segmentation in the wild and multiface forgery detection |

- **WWD** The Wild Web Dataset (WWD) [62] contains 101 distinct mask splice detections and 82 instances of 92 forging variations. The WWD aims to close a gap in the evaluation of localization techniques for image alteration.

- **VISION** A VISION dataset that contains 648 raw videos and 11,732 original images [63]. The pictures were posted on social websites such as WhatsApp and Facebook, while the videos were distributed on WhatsApp and YouTube, generating 1,914 videos and 34,427 images.
- **FaceFornesics (FF)** [64] dataset is based on DeepFake aims to carry out forensic operations on manipulated images, such as segmentation and facial recognition. Over 500,000 frames from 1004 (facial videos taken from YouTube) are included.

## 5 Deepfake Detection

### 5.1 Fake Image Detection

Spatial Based Detection
Afchar et al. [65] trained CNN classifiers by deepfake online video and Face2Face dataset. Two types of Meso-4, Mesoscopic and MesoInception-4, have been presented in it. In detection of fake videos the accuracy was 98% and 95% achieved respectively. Nataraj et al. [66] purposed a co-occurrence matrices on the bases of more than 56,000 RGB images, generated through cycleGAN and StarGAN, and achieved 99.71% and 99.37% accuracy respectively. Another method based on inter-frame and temporal inconsistencies used by Güera et al. [67] through CNN and LSTM models, trained by a collection of 600 videos obtained from multiple websites. The highest accuracy of the model is greater than 97%. Nguyen et al. [68] used **VGG-19, Capsule networks on Deepfake online videos, FF, replay-attack** datasets and achieved accuracy 96.52%, 94.47% and 99.13% respectively moreover, presented an FDFtNet, a novel detector to increase the capacity of current CNN models like SqueezeNet, ShallowNetV3, ResNetV2, and Xception. FDFtNet achieves an overall accuracy of 90.29% in detecting fake images generated from the GANs-based dataset, outperforming the state-of-the-art. Jeon et al. [69] used PGGAN, DF, and FF datasets, and obtained 90.29%, 97.02%, 96.67% accuracy respectively. Using universal texture data, researchers enhanced the validity and adaptability capacities of existing CNNs in identifying generated fraudulent faces. Fung et al. [70] used FF++, UADFV and Celeb-DF datasets with Xception network, SVM, and Bayes classifier technique and found high accuracy 99.7%, 96.8%, 90.5%. Li and Lyu. [71] embraced a model based on deep learning capable of distinguishing between Deepfake and real videos. Furthermore, VGG-16, ResNet with UADFV, and DF-TIMIT datasets were prepared using the Face-warping artifacts feature. It gained 97.4% and 93.2% accuracy. Using CelebA, LSUN bedroom scene datasets with Image fingerprint feature, Yu et al. [72] achieved 99.43%, 98.58% accuracy.

Fine-tuning is a powerful strategy to protect the DNN model from adverse disruptions in fingerprint pictures. According to Chai et al. [73], duplicative artifacts were assessed from local patches in order to find the fake face. This theory has been tried using various available techniques, such as CNN [74], Xception [75], MesoInception4 [65], and Resnet18 [76] having p values 0.5 and 0.1 using CelebA-HQ dataset.

Matern et al. [77] adopted visual features and fake detection methods founded on elementary visual elements, like missing reflections, eye color, and missing details in the dental and eye regions. He included two distinct classifiers in this case study: 1st is the

Logistic regression model, and the 2nd is Multilayer Perceptron (MLP). The own dataset was used to train the model, and 85% accuracy was achieved. Yang et al. [78] presented Head Pose Features for detecting the Deepfake efficiently. SVM classifier trained by Own dataset like:

UADFV, Deepfake TIMIT (LQ) Deepfake TIMIT (HQ), FF++ / DFD, DFDC Preview, Celeb-DF, used for detection and result obtained upto 89%.

Bharati et al. [79] proposed a novel supervised deep Boltzmann machine algorithm. The proposed approach for classifying images as original or retouched yields an accuracy of over 99% on three makeup data sets [17]. Rossler" et al. [52] came up with the Mesoscopic, Steganalysis, and Deep Learning Features. The detection system was totally based on a convolutional neural network classifier that was trained on FF++ (Face2Face, RAW), FF++ (NeuralTextures, RAW) datasets.. The maximum accuracy was approximately 99 to 100% (Table 3).

**Table 3.** Spatial based techniques used for deepfake detection

| Year | Study | Methods | Techniques | Accuracy | Dataset |
|------|-------|---------|------------|----------|---------|
| 2022 | [80] | Hybrid Image Transformer | Dual CNN | 98.57% | FaceForensics++ |
| 2018 | [65] | Meso-4, MesoInception-4 | CNN | 95% & 98% | Deepfake online videos, FF |
| 2019 | [66] | Co-occurrence matrices | DNNs | 99.71% &99.37% | Own(CycleGAN and StarGAN) datasets |
| 2018 | [67] | inter-frame and temporal inconsistencies | CNN, LSTM | 97% | A bundle of 600 videos gathered from various websites |
| 2019 | [68] | Capsule-forensics | VGG-19, Capsule networks | 94.47% & 99.13% | Deepfake online videos, FF, REPLAYATTACK database |
| 2020 | [69] | Fine-Tune and transformer | SqueezeNet, ShallowNet,ResNet, Xception | 90.29%, 97.02%, 96.67% | PGGAN, DF, FF |
| 2021 | [70] | Unsupervised Contrastive Learning | Xception network, SVM, and Bayes classifier | 99.7%, 96.8%, 90.5% | FF++, UADFV and Celeb-DF |
| 2018 | [71] | Face-warping artifacts | VGG-16, ResNet | 97.4%, 93.2% | UADFV and DF-TIMIT |
| 2019 | [72] | Image fingerprint | DNN | 99.43%, 98.58% | CelebA, LSUN bedroom scene dataset |

(*continued*)

**Table 3.** (*continued*)

| Year | Study | Methods | Techniques | Accuracy | Dataset |
|---|---|---|---|---|---|
| 2020 | [73] | Patch-based classification | Resnet-18, Xception, MesoInception4 | 100% | CelebA-HQ |
| 2019 | [77] | Visual Features | Logistic Regression, MLP | 85% | Customized dataset (DFDC Preview, DeepfakeTIMIT LQ/HQ, Celeb-DF, UADFV, FF++ DFD) |
| 2019 | [78] | Head Pose Features | SVM | 89% | Customized dataset (DFDC Preview, DeepfakeTIMIT LQ/HQ, Celeb-DF, UADFV, FF++ DFD) |
| 2019 | [52] | Mesoscopic, Steganalysis and Deep Learning Features | CNN | 100%, 99% | FF++ (Face2Face, RAW), FF++ (NeuralTextures, RAW) |
| 2020 | [56] | Deep Learning Features | CNN + Attention Mechanism | 99% | FF++ (Face2Face, -) |

Khan et al. [80] proposed hybrid image transformation using XceptionNet and EfficientNet-B4. The Faceforeincis++ dataset was used to train the model and achieved 98.57% accuracy.

Frequency Based Detection

In 2019, a generic fake face photodetection technique was presented by Xuan et al. [81]. DCGAN, WGAN-GP, PGGAN trained by CelebA-HQ dataset. The primary goal was to explicitly include a preprocessing stage in the training process for removing petty instability artifacts in GAN images, which drives the forensics classifier to concentrate on higher intrinsic forensic indications for recognizing GAN-based pictures. The highest accuracy was 95.45%. Another method based on Temporal discrepancies was created by Sabir et al. [82]. CNN and RNN models were trained by FF++ dataset to detect the Deepfake. In this analysis, only low-quality videos were included and 96.9% accuracy was gained. Jeon et al. [83] came up with a self-training method and trained EfficientNet and ResNext architectures by their own (TPGGAN and StyleGAN) based dataset, which efficiently detects Deepfake images with the accuracy of 98.49%.

Best results have been recently addressed by Guarnera et al. [84] presented a fake detection model. This model is based on the research of convolutional imprints. Expectation Maximization Algorithm [85] was used to extract features. K-NN, SVM, and LDA classifiers were trained by Own(AttGAN, GDWCT,StarGAN, StyleGAN, StyleGAN2) dataset for best detection. Final result was 99.81% accurate.

Nirkin et al. [86] identified the distinctions between real faces and their setting to identify unreal faces. The first network is prepared to determine an individual's face with FF++, Celeb-DF, DFDC datasets, whereas the second context recognition network considers the context of the person's face. 99.7%, 66.0%, 75% accuracy was achieved using.

McCloskey et al. [87] presented a detection approach subject to color components and a Linear Support Vector Machine (SVM). It was proposed for the GAN-Pipeline Features technique, having a detection method based on color characteristics and a linear SVM for the conclusive categorization with NIST MFC2018 dataset. The writers assumed that the color differs between fake synthesis pictures and real camera photographs. While evaluating 70.0% accuracy was achieved. Marra et al. [88] adopted unique Deep Learning Features for the best detection. Authors suggested a multi-task incremental learning detection method for detecting and classifying new types of GAN generated images while maintaining past performance. Own (CycleGAN,

ProGAN,Glow, StarGAN, StyleGAN) dataset was used for model training and achieved 99.3% accuracy.

Dang et al. [57] comprehensively analyzed different facial manipulations. The authors suggested using attention mechanisms and famous CNN models such as Xception- Net and VGG16 using a dataset based on

DFFD (ProGAN, StyleGAN).Final accuracy was 100%. Hulzebosch et al. [89] adopted Deep Learning Features and considered different scenarios like cross-data, cross-model, and Post-processing. Fake detection techniques were based entirely on the renowned Xception network along with ForensicTransfer [90], which is basically an Autoencoder method. CNN, AE classifiers were trained by their own (StarGAN, Glow, ProGAN, StyleGAN) based dataset to detect fake images and got 99.8% accuracy, which is best performance.

A deep learning technique based on Restricted Boltzmann Machine (RBM) was proposed by Bharati et al. [79] in order to identify digital editing of face pictures. As a concerned database, the writers designed two fake databases from the actual ND-IIITD database [91] and a group of celebrity face photos that were downloaded from the internet. Their approach achieved 96.20% accuracy respectively.

Zhang et al. [92] presented a spectrum domain component to witness faux images. It was trained on its own (StarGAN/CycleGAN) dataset. Regarding the classifier, Auto-GAN was put forward; it's a GAN simulator capable of making GAN artifacts in any photo without using an already trained GAN model. Ultimately, the accuracy obtained was 100% (Table 4).

**Table 4.** Frequency based techniques used for deepfake detection

| Year | Study | Methods | Techniques | Accuracy | Dataset |
|---|---|---|---|---|---|
| 2019 | [81] | Preprocessing combined with deep network | DCGAN, WGAN-GP, PG-GAN | 95.45% | CelebA-HQ |
| 2019 | [82] | Temporal discrepancies | CNN and RNN | 96.9, 94.35, 96.3% | FF ++ |
| 2020 | [83] | Self-training | EfficientNet and ResNext | 98.49% | Customized dataset (StyleGAN and TPGGAN) |
| 2021 | [86] | Discrepancies between two regions | Xception networks | 99.7%, 66.0%, 75% | FF++, Celeb-DF, DFDC |
| 2018 | [87] | GAN-Pipeline | SVM | 70.00% | NIST MFC2018 |
| 2020 | [89] | GAN-Pipeline | k-NN, SVM, LDA | 99.81% | Own(AttGAN, GDWCT,StarGAN, StyleGAN, StyleGAN2) |
| 2019 | [88] | Deep Learning Features | CNN + Incremental Learning | 99.30% | Own(CycleGAN, ProGAN,Glow, StarGAN, StyleGAN) |
| 2020 | [57] | Deep Learning Features | CNN + Attention Mechanism | 100.00% | DFFD (ProGAN, StyleGAN) |
| 2020 | [89] | Deep Learning | CNN, AE | 99.80% | Own(StarGAN,Pro GAN, StyleGAN) |
| 2016 | [79] | Deep Learning Features (Face Patches) | RBM | 96.20% | Own(Celebrity Retouching, NDIIITD Retouching) |
| 2019 | [92] | Spectrum Domain Features | GAN Discriminator | 100.00% | Own StarGAN/CycleG AN based |

## 5.2 Fake Video Detection

Lip Forensics is a method for detecting face forgeries in videos that is generalizable and robust. Haliassos et al. [93] used Semantic irregularities methods and used FaceForensics++, DF-1.0, Celeb-DF, DFDC datasets with the ResNet-18 technique and obtained the accuracy of 99.7%, 82.4%, 73.5% respectively.

Tariq et al. [94] used FF++, DFD and Deepfake Wild videos datasets on Convolutional LSTM-based Residual Network (CLRNet) and got 97.50%, 97.13%, 97.23% accuracy. The fundamental concept is to use a convolutional LSTM-based residual network

(CLRNet) with a unique training technique to track the spatial and temporal information in Deepfakes.

In [95] Deepfake detection, a blend of stationary biometrics on facial recognition and secular behavioral biometrics on facial sentiments and head motions was presented. In addition, their focus was on features, appearance and behavior so they used ResNet-101, VGG technique utilizing DFD, Celeb-DF, DFDC, and FF++ datasets and achieved 97.7%, 98.9%, 93.2%, 96.45% accuracy. Agarwal and Farid [96] proposed a detection system based on both facial expressions and head movements, using an SVM (Support Vector Machine) classifier trained over the Own (FaceSwap, HQ) dataset to detect the fake videos.

The accuracy was achieved 96.3 Mittal et al. [97] utilized the Siamese network to simulate the visuals and audio in movies as well as trained the Siamese network with DF-TIMIT and DFDC datasets and gained 94.9%, 84.4% accuracy.

Furthermore, Chugh et al. [98] also used DFDC and DF-TIMIT datasets with MDS(Modality Dissonance Score) network technique, to obtain 91.54% and 94.7% accuracy. Evolutionary divergence results are computed between audiovisual segments across one-second video gaps, and the MDS is ascertained after aggregating all parts.

Agarwal et al.[42] Proposing an approach for detecting fraudulent videos based on irregularities in the dynamics of the mouth shape (visemes) and the prominent phonetic even more **Phoneme-viseme mismatches** technique was used through CNN along with A2V, T2V datasets OpenFace2 toolkit OpenFace 2.0: Facial Behavior Analysis Toolkit [99] was considered for feature extraction. And gained 96.9%, 71.1%, accuracy.

Qi et al. [100] adopted the Heartbeat rhythms method to highlight cardiac rhythm signals; the scientists built a motion-magnified spatial-temporal representation (MMSTR) for the video. After using DeepRhythm technique with FF++, DFDC-P datasets, they obtain 99.7%, 74.5% results (Table 5).

**Table 5.** List of techniques and methods used for fake video detection

| Year | Study | Methods | Techniques | Accuracy | Dataset |
|---|---|---|---|---|---|
| 2021 | [93] | Semantic irregularities | ResNet-18 | 99.7%, 82.4%, 73.5% | FF++, DFDC, Celeb-DF, DF-1.0 |
| 2021 | [94] | Spatial and temporal information | CLRNet | 97.50%, 97.13%, 97.23% | DFD, FF++, Deepfake-in-the-Wild videos |
| 2018 | [101] | Eye blinking | CNN, LRCN | 98%, 99% | For LRCN EBV dataset and For CNN CEW Dataset |

(*continued*)

**Table 5.** (*continued*)

| Year | Study | Methods | Techniques | Accuracy | Dataset |
|------|-------|---------|------------|----------|---------|
| 2020 | [95] | Using appearance and behavior | ResNet-101, VGG | 97.7%, 98.9%, 93.2% | The world leaders dataset along DFDC, DFD, FF++ and CelebDF |
| 2020 | [97] | Using emotion audio-visual affective | Siamese network architecture | 94.9%, 84.4% | DF-TIMIT and DFDC |
| 2020 | [102] | Phoneme-viseme mismatches | CNN | 96.9%, 71.1% 80.7% | A2V, T2V |
| 2020 | [98] | Modality Dissonance Score | MDS network | 91.54%, 94.7% | DFDC, DF-TIMIT |
| 2020 | [100] | Heartbeat rhythms | DeepRhythm | 99.7%, 74.5% | FF++, DFDC-P |
| 2021 | [103] | Consistency of eyes and gazes | 3 dense layers network architecture | 93.28%, 80.00% | FF++, CelebDF |
| 2019 | [96] | Head Pose and Facial Features | SVM | 96.30% | Own (FaceSwap, HQ) |
| 2020 | [104] | Eye Blinking | Distance | 87.50% | Own |
| 2018 | [105] | Deep Learning Features + Steganalysis Features | CNN, SVM | 85.10% | Customized dataset (DFDC Preview, DeepfakeTIMIT LQ/HQ, Celeb-DF, UADFV, FF++ /DFD) |
| 2019 | [106] | Deep Learning Features | AE + Multi-Task Learning | 76.30% | FF++ and DFD |
| 2019 | [79] | Deep Learning Features | CNN + AM | 99.40% | DFFD |
| 2020 | [57] | Facial Regions Features | CNN | 100%, 99.4%, 91%, 83.6% | DFDC Preview, UADFV, FF++ (HQ, FaceSwap), Celeb-DF |

In [101] three steps were involved in the composition of the LRCM model: (i) Characteristic extraction from the eye series using VGG16, (ii) Sequence comprehension through LSTM, and (iii) State prediction, which yields the probability of eye open and closed conditions on the basis of the result of LSTM. Li et al. [101] used CEW Dataset and Eye blinking method for EBV and CNN dataset for the LRCN system and attained 98% and 99% accuracy. Furthermore, Jung et al. [104] developed a system known as DeepVision to examine fluctuations in blinking patterns. Fast-HyperFace and Eye-Aspect-Ratio (EAR) were used together to find the face and figure out the eye aspect ratio. Finally features based on the number of blinks and the time of the blinks were encountered to determine whether the video was fake or real. This technique had an absolute accuracy rate of 87.5% over its own dataset.

Zhou et al. [105] proposed Deep Learning Features and Steganalysis Features methods with convolutional neural network and SVM classifier using UADFV dataset and a final accuracy rate of 85.1% was obtained.

Nguyen et al. [106] presented a Capsule Networks-based fake detection model. This system had relatively fewer parameters than a standard CNN; however, it had the same outcomes. A detection system that used an auto-encoder was considered. Final accuracy was 76.3%. Nguyen et al. [68] proposed a new fake detection system based on Capsule Networks. This method had fewer parameters than a traditional CNN with the same results. The proposed detection system was tested with the FaceForensics++ dataset, which had accuracy rates of more than 96%. Dang et al. [57] came up with the convolutional neural network and Attention Mechanism classifier using the DFFD dataset. In the case of detecting identity swaps, the proposed method had an accuracy of 99.43%.

Guerra et al. [67] proposed video temporal features that were capable of telling if a frame is manipulated or not with a combination of CNNs and RNNs model. The authors utilized InceptionV3 which had been pretrained with the ImageNet dataset for the CNN and LSTM model with one hidden layer and 2048 memory blocks that could be used for the RNN system. The accuracy was 97.1%. Tolosana et al. [107] came up with the Facial Regions Features method. The author considered a fake detection system based on a CNN classifier trained on DFDC Preview, Celeb-DF datasets. The result obtained was 91.0%, 83.6% respectively.

### 5.3 Methodologies for Deepfake Detection

In this part, we will look at various approaches to Deepfake detection. The PRNU (Photo Response Non Uniformity) pattern of a digital image, is a noise pattern created by small factory defects in the light-sensitive sensors of a digital camera. This noise pattern is highly individualized and often referred to as the fingerprint of the digital image. PRNU analysis considers a method of interest because it expects that manipulating the facial area will affect the local PRNU pattern in the video frames [108].

Face tempting videos are also automatically detected using Meso-4 and Misconception-4 [19], both the networks used less number of layers for data. As a result of this study, an accuracy of 98% and 95% have been achieved.

Nataraj et al. [66] used a steg analysis method to find fake images. The co-occurrence matrices methods were made from RGB images, and the values were trained with a deep convolutional neural network to differentiate the real ones from the fake ones. RGB images were used to make the co-occurrence matrices methods. Moreover, the values were prepared with a deep convolutional neural network (CNN) to distinguish the real from the fake ones. In [57] StarGAN and CycleGAN-based forged photos could be classified, achieving 99% valid results. Li et al. [109] have looked at the statistical properties of deep network-generated pictures, like the connection between bordering pixels in HSV and YCbCr color spaces, in order to see if the difference between real and fake images can be detected using DNNs with the linear discriminative technique using dataset LFW, LSUN, FFHQ, CelebA, FFHQ.

There is another generalizable and robust technique lip forensics which is used for detecting face forgeries Haliassos et al. [93] propose to utilize the high-level semantic irregularities using face forensics++, DF-1.0, Celeb-DF, DFDC datasets with the ResNet-18 model and obtained this accuracy 99.7%, 82.4%, 73.5%.

Lugstein et al. [110] came up with a new way to tell whether data is a Deepfake or not, based on how different the photo response no uniformity (PRNU) is. So, the PRNU and SVM technique is well-known because facial retouching and face morphing attacks can be detected.

Guerra et al. [67] provided CNN and LSTM detection method which is based on face-swapping. In this method, InceptionV3 which is CNN is used to gather frame-level features, those features passed to LSTM to build a sequence descriptor for classification and 97.1% accuracy was achieved (Fig. 8).

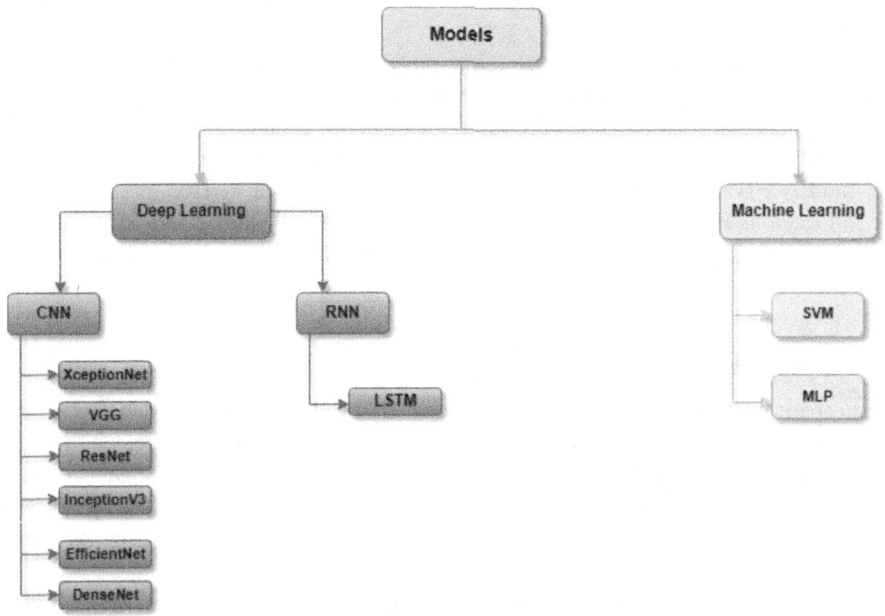

**Fig. 8.** List of models used for deepfake detection in current study

Nguyen et al. [68] operated VGG-19 along with Capsule networks in order to recognize fake images and videos, including computer-generated image detection and replay attack detection using these techniques with dataset Deepfake online videos and FF and got the accuracy of 94.47%, 99.13%.

Xuan et al. [81] used Pre-processing combined with a deep network method with the DCGAN, WGAN-GP, and PGGAN techniques. The intention was to dismiss low-level, inconsistent artifacts of GAN visuals to make the forensics classifier prioritize higher innate forensic indicators so that GAN-based images could be detected The 95.45% accuracy was achieved. Sabir et al. [82] created a method based on Temporal discrepancies, using CNN and RNN technique on the video to recognize, trim, and align faces in a video. The model used micro-, meso-, and macroscopic features for detection. These landmark-based components produce facial alignment with recurring directional DenseNet that excels at spotting face-manipulated videos. With CNN and RNN models trained on FF++ dataset, accuracy was gained 96.9%, 94.35%, 96.3%. Jeon et al. [69] created CNN models like Squeeze Net, ShallowNetV3, ResNet2, and Xception more powerful. The fine-tuning technique is employed to get the characteristics out of MBblockV3 whereas PGGAN, DF, FF datasets are used for training. This approach is a fine-tuning transformation. It obtained 90.29%, 97.02%, 96.67% accuracy. Jeon et al. [83] devised a GAN-image detection framework (T-GD) to assemble a model trained on TPGGAN and StyleGAN- based datasets that quickly and accurately detects Deepfake images using Efficient Net and ResNext techniques. The model is based on the relationship between the teacher and the students, improving the detection performance. It obtained 87.80% and 98.49% accuracy.

Hsu et al. [73] developed a couple-wise learning model capable of telling if a GAN-generated fake image is real. He merged an enhanced model of the DenseNet backbone network with an entirely different network called the Siamese network to make a unique model. That model is known as Common Fake Feature Network (CFFN).

Jain et al. [111] used an adversarial perturbation method to improve the performance of existing Deepfake models. DIP - deep image prior - and Lipschitz regularization are used to improve the validity of CNN-based deepfake sensors. DIP defence achieved 98% accuracy. Wu et al. [112] developed a system called SSTNet that integrates spatial, steganography, and characteristic extraction techniques to determine Deepfakes. In this method, XceptionNet monitors the image's spatial features and statistics. Also, to mine temporal characteristics, RNN is used. This extracted data is applied for binary classification for identifying Deepfakes. Global texture data can be analyzed to improve the existing CNNs by making them more robust and generalized when they are used to identify fake faces. The gram-Net technique evaluates JPEG compression, down sampling, noise, and blur. Gram-Net has proven to work with a wide range of GANs. Conclusively, using the Analyzing global image texture method, 95.51% and 90% accuracy was achieved with the help of the ResNet model technique by using CelebA-HQ and FFHQ images datasets [113].

To differentiate between real and fake images, Khalid et al. [114] created the OC-FakeDect technique that utilizes a one-class Variation Auto Encoder (VAE) and solely trains on real face photos (Fig. 9).

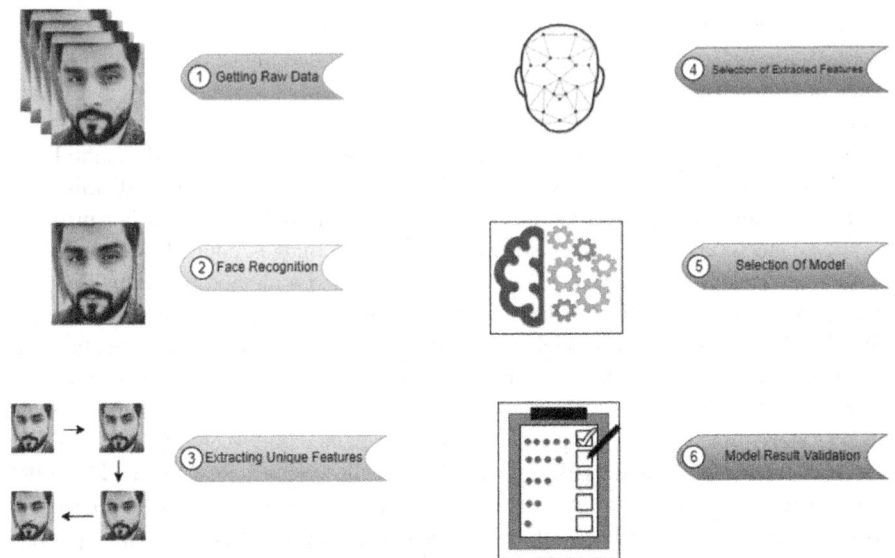

**Fig. 9.** Generic steps used in deepfake detection

Fung et al. [70] came up with an unsupervised way to tell when someone's face is changed. It is a new way to detect unlabelled data to see if someone has changed their face. When a face image creates an image, it goes through two different transformations and into two different subnetworks, Xception and projection head network. When they used two different transformations, an FF++ and UADFV, as well as Celeb-DF and CelebDF datasets, were performed with the Xception network, SVM, and Bayes techniques; it appeared that they all had high accuracy.

Tariq et al. [94] came up with a way to find many different types of Deepfakes. To analyze the spatial and secular data in Deepfakes, they use a convolutional LSTM-based residual network (CLRNet) approach qualified on trained DFD, FF++, and Deepfake-in-the-Wild video datasets. Also, the model tested on Deepfakes that had never been seen before, it got 97.50%, 97.13%, and 97.23% accuracy.

In less than a minute, this app can alter faces. For this purpose, the essential components of the face image are determined and indicated as descriptors. Because every key point is distinctive, one must use a second clustering procedure to make the codebook per picture [115].

Using a CNN and an RNN, Li et al. [101] devised a method based on eye blinking for detecting fake faces in videos. With VGG16, a type of RNN, features were extracted from the eye sequence using an LRCN model.

Sequence learning will be done using LSTM, predicting whether the eye is open or closed. CEW and LRCN datasets achieved 98% and 99% accuracy. Similarly, a unique deep learning-based model was introduced that was capable of distinguishing real videos from fake ones. The model employs the warping action that is used to create Deepfake. There is a gap in the resolution between the warped face area and the rest of the image, creating artefacts. First, CNN is prepared to identify faces. Then, it attempts to find landmarks and calculates transformed matrices to ensure the faces are in the right place. UADFV and DFTIMIT datasets were used with VGG-16, ResNet technique and 97.4%, 93.2% accuracy was faced.

Agarwal et al. [96] proposed a detection system based on Head Pose and Facial Features method. For the classification, SVM was used.

McCloskey et al. [87] designed a GAN generator's architecture, making it easier to find visual flaws in Deepfake images. in Deepfake visuals. The generator's normalizing techniques are adopted, which reduce the total pixels that are overexposed or underexposed. A detection system subject to color attributes and a linear Support Vector Machine (SVM) for the ultimate classification gained 70.0% accuracy. Yu et al. [72] looked at GAN fingerprints for image attribution and used them to tell whether images were real or made by GANs. If the model is trained with slight modifications in the dataset, its fingerprint would be distinct, making it easier to identify the model. Fine-tuning is also a good way to protect the DNN model from changes in fingerprint images that aren't good for it. CelebA, LSUN bedroom scene datasets with Image fingerprint feature achieved 99.43%, 98.58% accuracy. Yu et al. [78] created GAN fingerprints to attribute images with SVM classification using Deepfake TIMIT (LQ) Deepfake TIMIT (HQ), UADFV, Celeb-DF , FF++ / DFD, DFDC Preview datasets found 89.0%, 55.1%, 53.2%, 47.3%, 55.9%, 54.6% results.

Matern et al. [77] utilized Deepfake and face manipulation tools based on visual characteristics such as teeth, eyes, and facial features. The method was proposed by adopting the Visual Features method and Fake detection methods based on very simple visual characteristics such as eye colour, missing reflections, and missing details in the eye and dental areas. Deepfake TIMIT (LQ) Deepfake TIMIT (HQ), UADFV, Celeb-DF , FF++ / DFD, DFDC Preview datasets used for the training and 70.2%, 77.0%, 77.3%, 78.0%, 66.2%, 55.1% accuracy achieved in the testing.

Fernandez et al. [116] used a heartbeat rhythm and designed a Deep Rhythm model that could tell if a video was fake. For the purpose of showing heart rhythm signals, A motion-magnified spatial-temporal representation (MMSTR) model was used to make the video. As a result, a dual-spatial-temporal attentional network was produced to catch if a video was fake.

There are many ways to find digital fingerprints in images that can be learned and used to tell if they were made by a GAN or not [95]. CNN's are used to examine pixel-level artefacts when a face region moves onto a target. A convolutional neural network with only a few layers is called MesoNet. It can use to build a model of a microscopic object. L. Chai et al. [73] used redundant artefacts and a Patch-based classification method that can evaluate local patches. This hypothesis was assessed on the FFHQ and CelebA-HQ datasets, using recognized models like MesoInception4, Xception, Resnet-18, and CNN, having p values 0.5 and 0.1, respectively. The datasets of CelebA-HQ got 99.97% accuracy.

A Siamese network imitates the visuals and sounds in movies, combined with a blend of the two triplet loss functions to confine alikeness. Mittal et al. [97] trained Siamese network architecture technique with the DFTIMIT and DFDC datasets and gained 94.9% and 84.4% accuracy .

Agarwal et al. [102] used the Phoneme-viseme mismatches technique trained on A2V, T2V datasets and proposed an approach for detecting fraudulent videos based on irregularities in the dynamics of the mouth shape-viseme mismatches) and the prominent phonetic. Some phonemes need the lips to be completely closed to be spoken correctly: A few of them are papa, mama, and baba. It gained 96.9%, 71.1%, 80.7% accuracy.

Deepfake videos can be detected using a method proposed Chugh et al. [98] . After the calculation of disparity scores across audiovisual segments over one second video chunk, the MDS was determined by using aggregation to all parts and taking the average.

Guarneraet. al. [84] represented a way to tell if an image is fake by looking for forensic traces that are hiddenin pictures. The EM algorithm - expectation maximization - is utilized to discover a bunch of local characteristics for modeling the underlying convolutional productive procedure. StarGAN, GDWCT, StyleGAN, StyleGAN2, and ATTGAN made Deepfakes. CelebA along with LFW datasets obtained 90.22% accuracy.

To find fake videos the ABC metric shown in [117]. To take into account the baseline input, the attribution methods employ Shapley values. ResNet50 trained on VGGFace2 represents the original class label, while P represents the class label that is most likely to occur.

Qi et al. [100] used the Heartbeat rhythms method to highlight cardiac rhythm signals; the scientists created an MMSTR for the video—a motion-magnified spatial-temporal representation.. After training FF++, and DFDCP datasets using the Deep Rhythm technique, we obtained 99.7% and 74.5% accuracy. Hu et al. [118] examined the distinction between the pair of eyes while detecting Deepfake facial photos and presented a detection standard that exploits the physical boundaries in GAN-based pictures. Then it estimates the difference between both eyes to reveal whether a picture is real or fake. Demir et al. [103] ddevised a system to identify Deepfakes by examining the gaze in videos and looking for the consistency of eyes and gazes' method to analyze OR detect the video. Using three dense layers of network architecture technique with faceforensics++, CelebDF datasets, 93.28%, 80.00% accuracy were obtained.

The contrast between faces and their surroundings was exploited by Nirkin et al. [86] to identify false faces. He trained two networks: one to identify a person's face and the other to account for certain things, like hair, ears, and neck. The researchers found that discrepancies detected by comparing these two networks.

## 6 Conclusion

The study on Deepfake production and Deepfake detection has been comprehensively reviewed and analyzed in this survey, which hopefully will be useful to anyone interested in the subject. A taxonomy of diverse Deepfake evolution methods and the categorization of various Deepfake detection practices, has been offered among the most significant aspects of the technological growth of the approaches. It explains the fundamentals, advantages, and risks related to Deepfake , GAN-based Deepfake applications. Additionally, models for detecting Deepfake are addressed. In the investigations, the FF++ dataset accounts for the majority of the data points. Deep learning models (mostly CNNs) provide a large proportion of the total number of models. Deep learning-based techniques are commonly applied to detect Deepfake, as the methods are becoming increasingly popular. Using Deepfake as an experiment, the conclusion indicates that learning methods are useful in identifying Deepfake. Deepfake detection still confronts several hurdles, despite the tremendous advancements in essential multimedia technology and the development of tools and applications in recent years. This survey paper is intended to help scholars and practitioners in the respective field identify the most important research topics., and in luring more scholars to participate in this emerging and constantly expanding subject.

## References

1. Afchar, D., Nozick, V., Yamagishi, J., Echizen, I.: MesoNet: a compact facial video forgery detection network. 10th IEEE International Workshop on Information Forensics and Security, WIFS 2018 (2019). https://arxiv.org/abs/1809.00888
2. Agarwal, S., Farid, H.: Detecting Deep-Fake Videos from Phoneme-Viseme Mismatches
3. Agarwal, S., Farid, H., El-Gaaly, T., Lim, S.N.: Detecting deep-fake videos from appearance and behavior. In: 2020 IEEE International Workshop on Information Forensics and Security, WIFS 2020 (2020). https://arxiv.org/abs/2004.14491
4. Agarwal, S., Farid, H., Fried, O., Agrawala, M.: Detecting deep-fake videos from phoneme-viseme mismatches. In: IEEE Computer Society Conference on Computer Vision and Pattern Recognition Workshops, 2020-June, pp. 2814–2822 (2020)
5. Agarwal, S., Farid, H., Gu, Y., He, M., Nagano, K., Li, H.: Protecting world leaders against deep fakes. In: Proceedings of the IEEE/CVF Conference on Computer Vision and Pattern Recognition (CVPR) Workshops (2019)
6. Amerini, I., Conti, M., Giacomazzi, P., Pajola, L.: PRaNA: PRNU-based technique to tell real and deepfake videos apart. In: 2022 International Joint Conference on Neural Networks (IJCNN), pp. 1–7 (2022)
7. Auto Faceswap Application. (n.d.). https://www.microsoft.com/en-us/p/auto-face-swap/9nblggh3m5nq.
8. Baltrusaitis, T., Zadeh, A., Lim, Y.C., Morency, L.-P.: OpenFace 2.0: facial behavior analysis toolkit. In: 2018 13th IEEE International Conference on Automatic Face and Gesture Recognition (FG 2018), pp. 59–66 (2018)
9. Bharati, A., Singh, R., Vatsa, M., Bowyer, K.W.: Detecting facial retouching using supervised deep learning. IEEE Trans. Inf. Forensics Secur. **11**(9), 1903–1913 (2016)
10. Blanz, V., Basso, C., Poggio, T., Vetter, T.: Reanimating faces in images and video. Comput. Graph. Forum **22**(3), 641–650 (2003)
11. Brock, A., Donahue, J., Simonyan, K.: Large scale GaN training for high fidelity natural image synthesis. In: 7th International Conference on Learning Representations, ICLR 2019, pp. 1–35 (2019). https://arxiv.org/abs/1809.11096
12. Cao, J., Hu, Y., Yu, B., He, R., Sun, Z.: 3D aided duet GANs for multi-view face image synthesis. IEEE Trans. Inf. Forensics Secur. **14**(8), 2028–2042 (2019)
13. Chai, L., Bau, D., Lim, S.N., Isola, P.: What makes fake images detectable? Understanding Properties that Generalize, vol. 12371 LNCS, pp. 103–120 (2020). https://arxiv.org/abs/2008.10588
14. Choi, Y., Choi, M., Kim, M., Ha, J. W., Kim, S., Choo, J.: StarGAN: unified generative adversarial networks for multi-domain image-to-image translation. In: Proceedings of the IEEE Computer Society Conference on Computer Vision and Pattern Recognition, pp. 8789–8797 (2018). https://arxiv.org/abs/1711.09020
15. Chollet, F.: Xception: Deep Learning with Depthwise Separable Convolutions. CoRR, abs/1610.02357 (2016). http://arxiv.org/abs/1610.02357

16. Chugh, K., Gupta, P., Dhall, A., Subramanian, R.: Not made for each other- audio-visual dissonance-based deepfake detection and localization. In: MM 2020 - Proceedings of the 28th ACM International Conference on Multimedia, pp. 439–447(2020). https://arxiv.org/abs/2005.14405
17. Contributing Data to Deepfake Detection Research. (n.d.). https://ai.googleblog.com/2019/09/contributingdata-to-deepfake-detection.html.
18. Cozzolino, D., Thies, J., Rössler, A., Riess, C., Nießner, M., Verdoliva, L.: ForensicTransfer: weakly-supervised domain adaptation for forgery detection. CoRR, abs/1812.02510 (2018). http://arxiv.org/abs/1812.02510
19. Dang, H.: On the detection of digital face manipulation (n.d.). https://arxiv.org/abs/arXiv:1910.01717v5
20. Demir, I., Ciftci, U.A.: Where do deep fakes look? Synthetic face detection via gaze tracking. Eye tracking research and applications symposium (ETRA), PartF169256 (2021). https://arxiv.org/abs/2101.01165
21. Do, H., Elbaum, S., Rothermel, G.: Supporting controlled experimentation with testing techniques: an infrastructure and its potential impact. Empir. Softw. Eng. **10**(4), 405–435 (2005)
22. Dolhansky, B., et al.: The DeepFake Detection Challenge (DFDC) Dataset (2020).http://arxiv.org/abs/2006.07397
23. Dolhansky, B., Howes, R., Pflaum, B., Baram, N., Ferrer, C.C.: The deepfake detection challenge (DFDC) preview dataset (2019). https://arxiv.org/abs/1910.08854.
24. Elaskily, M., et al.: A novel deep learning framework for copymove forgery detection in images. Multimed. Tools Appl. **79** (2020)
25. Exploiting visual artifacts to expose deepfakes and face manipulations.. In: Proceedings - 2019 IEEE Winter Conference on Applications of Computer Vision Workshops, WACVW 2019, vol. 1, pp. 83–92 (2019)
26. FaceApp. (n.d.). https://apps.apple.com/gb/app/faceapp-ai-face-editor/id1180884341
27. Fernandes, S., et al.: Detecting deepfake videos using attribution-based confidence metric. In: IEEE Computer Society Conference on Computer Vision and Pattern Recognition Workshops, 2020-June, pp. 1250–1259 (2020)
28. Fernandes, S., et al.: Predicting heart rate variations of deepfake videos using neural ODE. In: Proceedings - 2019 International Conference on Computer Vision Workshop, ICCVW 2019, pp. 1721–1729 (2019)
29. Flynn, P.J., Bowyer, K.W., Phillips, P.J.: Assessment of time dependency in face recognition: an initial study. In: Kittler, J., Nixon, M.S. (eds.) Audio- and video-Based Biometric Person Authentication, pp. 44–51. Springer, Berlin Heidelberg (2003)
30. Fried, O., et al.: Text-based editing of talking-head video. ACM Trans. Graph. **38**(4) (2019). https://arxiv.org/abs/1906.01524
31. Fung, S., Lu, X., Zhang, C., Li, C.T.: DeepfakeUCL: deepfake detection via unsupervised contrastive learning. In: Proceedings of the International Joint Conference on Neural Networks, 2021-July (2021). https://arxiv.org/abs/2104.11507
32. Gafni, O., Wolf, L., Taigman, Y.: Live Face De-Identification in Video. CoRR (2019). http://arxiv.org/abs/1911.08348
33. Gandhi, A., Jain, S.: Adversarial perturbations fool deepfake detectors. In: Proceedings of the International Joint Conference on Neural Networks (2020). https://arxiv.org/abs/2003.10596
34. Gross, R., Sweeney, L., Cohn, J., Torre, F., Baker, S.: Face de-identification. In: Senior, A. (ed.) Protecting privacy in video surveillance, pp. 129–146. Springer, London (2009)
35. Gross, R., Sweeney, L., Torre, F.D., Baker, S.: Model-based face de-identification (2006)

36. Guarnera, L., Giudice, O., Battiato, S.: DeepFake detection by analyzing convolutional traces. In: IEEE Computer Society Conference on Computer Vision and Pattern Recognition Workshops, 2020-June, pp. 2841–2850 (2020). https://arxiv.org/abs/2004.10448
37. Guera, D., Delp, E.J.: Deepfake video detection using recurrent neural networks. In: Proceedings of AVSS 2018 - 2018 15th IEEE International Conference on Advanced Video and Signal-Based Surveillance (2019)
38. Haliassos, A., Vougioukas, K., Petridis, S., Pantic, M.: Lips don't lie: a generalisable and robust approach to face forgery detection. In: Proceedings of the IEEE Computer Society Conference on Computer Vision and Pattern Recognition, pp. 5037–5047 (2021). https://arxiv.org/abs/2012.07657
39. He, K., Zhang, X., Ren, S., Sun, J.: Deep residual learning for image recognition. In: Proceedings of the IEEE Computer Society Conference on Computer Vision and Pattern Recognition, 2016-Decem, pp. 770–778 (2016). https://arxiv.org/abs/1512.03385
40. Hsu, C.-C., Zhuang, Y.-X., Lee, C.-Y.: Deep fake image detection based on pairwise learning. Appl. Sci. **10**(1) (2020). https://www.mdpi.com/2076-3417/10/1/370
41. Hu, S., Li, Y., Lyu, S.: Exposing GaN-generated faces using inconsistent corneal specular highlights. In: ICASSP, IEEE International Conference on Acoustics, Speech and Signal Processing - Proceedings, 2021-June, pp. 2500–2504 (2021). https://arxiv.org/abs/2009.11924
42. Hui, J.: GAN — Why it is so hard to train Generative Adversarial Networks!https://jonathanhui.medium.com/gan-why-it-is-so-hard-to-train-generative-advisory-networks-819a86b3750b
43. Hulzebosch, N., Ibrahimi, S., Worring, M.: Detecting CNN-generated facial images in real-world scenarios. In: IEEE Computer Society Conference on Computer Vision and Pattern Recognition Workshops, 2020-June, pp. 2729–2738 (2020). https://arxiv.org/abs/2005.05632
44. Jeon, H., Bang, Y., Woo, S.S.: FDFtNet: facing off fake images using fake detection fine-tuning network. IFIP Adv. Inf. Commun. Technol. **580** IFIP, 416–430 (2020). https://arxiv.org/abs/2001.01265
45. Jeon, H., Bang, Y., Kim, J., Woo, S.S.: T-GD: Transferable GAN-generated images detection framework. In: 37th International Conference on Machine Learning, ICML 2020, PartF16814, pp. 4696–4711 (2020). https://arxiv.org/abs/2008.04115
46. Jiang, L., Li, R., Wu, W., Qian, C., Loy, C.C.: DeeperForensics-1.0: a large-scale dataset for realworld face forgery detection. In: CVPR (2020)
47. Juefei-Xu, F., Wang, R., Huang, Y., Guo, Q., Ma, L., Liu, Y.: Countering malicious deepfakes: survey, Battleground, and Horizon (2021).http://arxiv.org/abs/2103.00218
48. Jung, T., Kim, S., Kim, K.: DeepVision: deepfakes detection using human eye blinking pattern. IEEE Access **8**, 83144–83154 (2020)
49. Karras, T., Aila, T., Laine, S., Lehtinen, J.: Progressive growing of GANs for improved quality, stability, and variation. CoRR, abs/1710.10196 (2017). http://arxiv.org/abs/1710.10196
50. Karras, T., Aittala, M., Hellsten, J., Laine, S., Lehtinen, J., Aila, T.: Training generative adversarial networks with limited data. Adv. Neural Inf. Process. Syst. 2020-Decem (2020). https://arxiv.org/abs/2006.06676
51. Karras, T., Laine, S., Aila, T.: A style-based generator architecture for generative adversarial networks. IEEE Trans. Pattern Anal. Mach. Intell. **43**(12), 4217–4228 (2021). https://arxiv.org/abs/1812.04948
52. Karras, T., Laine, S., Aittala, M., Hellsten, J., Lehtinen, J., Aila, T.: Analyzing and improving the image quality of stylegan. In: Proceedings of the IEEE Computer Society Conference on Computer Vision and Pattern Recognition, pp. 8107–8116 (2020). https://arxiv.org/abs/1912.04958

53. Khalid, H., Woo, S.S.: OC-FakeDect: classifying deepfakes using one-class variational autoencoder. In: IEEE Computer Society Conference on Computer Vision and Pattern Recognition Workshops, 2020-June, pp. 2794–2803 (2020)
54. Khan, S.A.: Hybrid Transformer Network for Deepfake Detection (Vol. 1). Association for Computing Machinery (n.d.)
55. Kitchenham, B., Charters, S.M.: Guidelines for performing systematic literature reviews in software engineering guidelines for performing systematic literature reviews in software engineering EBSE Technical report EBSE-2007–01 Software Engineering Group School of Computer Science and Mathematics Keele University Keele, Staffs Department of Computer Science University of Durham. October 2021 (2007)
56. Korshunov, P., Marcel, S.: DeepFakes: a new threat to face recognition? Assessment and detection, 1–5 (2018). http://arxiv.org/abs/1812.08685
57. Kumar, R., Sotelo, J., Kumar, K., Brebisson, A., Bengio, Y.: ObamaNet: Photo-realistic lip-sync from text. 1–4 (2017). http://arxiv.org/abs/1801.01442
58. Le, T.-N., Nguyen, H.H., Yamagishi, J., Echizen, I.: OpenForensics: large-scale challenging dataset for multi-face forgery detection and segmentation in-the-wild (2021). http://arxiv.org/abs/2107.14480
59. Li, H., Li, B., Tan, S., Huang, J.: Identification of deep network generated images using disparities in color components. Signal Process. **174** (2020). https://arxiv.org/abs/1808.07276
60. Li, Y., Lyu, S.: Exposing DeepFake videos by detecting face warping artifacts (2018). http://arxiv.org/abs/1811.00656
61. Li, Y., Lyu, S.: De-identification without losing faces, 83–88 (2019)
62. Li, Y., Chang, M.C., Lyu, S.: In ictu oculi: exposing AI created fake videos by detecting eye blinking. In: 10th IEEE International Workshop on Information Forensics and Security, WIFS 2018, vol. 1, pp. 1–7 (2019)
63. Li, Y., Yang, X., Sun, P., Qi, H., Lyu, S.: Celeb-DF: a large-scale challenging dataset for deepfake forensics. In: Proceedings of the IEEE Computer Society Conference on Computer Vision and Pattern Recognition, pp. 3204–3213 (2020). https://arxiv.org/abs/1909.12962
64. Liu, Z., Luo, P., Wang, X., Tang, X.: Deep learning face attributes in the wild. In: Proceedings of the IEEE International Conference on Computer Vision, pp. 3730–3738 (2015). https://arxiv.org/abs/1411.7766
65. Liu, Z., Qi, X., Jia, J., Torr, P.H.S.: Global texture enhancement for fake face detection in the wild. CoRR, abs/2002.00133 (2020). https://arxiv.org/abs/2002.00133
66. Lugstein, F., Baier, S., Bachinger, G., Uhl, A.: PRNU-based Deepfake Detection, vol. 1, pp. 7–12. Association for Computing Machinery (2021)
67. Mahdizadehaghdam, S., Panahi, A., Krim, H.: Sparse generative adversarial network. In: Proceedings - 2019 International Conference on Computer Vision Workshop, ICCVW 2019, pp. 3063–3071 (2019). https://arxiv.org/abs/1908.08930
68. Malik, A., Kuribayashi, M., Member, S., Abdullahi, S.M., Khan, A.N.: DeepFake detection for human face images and videos: a survey. IEEE Access **10**, 18757–18775 (2022)
69. Marra, F., Gragnaniello, D., Verdoliva, L., Poggi, G.: Do GANs leave artificial fingerprints? Proceedings - 2nd International Conference on Multimedia Information Processing and Retrieval, MIPR 2019, pp. 506–511 (2019). https://arxiv.org/abs/1812.11842
70. McCloskey, S., Albright, M.: Detecting GAN-generated imagery using saturation cues. In: Proceedings - International Conference on Image Processing, ICIP, 2019-September, pp. 4584–4588 (2019)
71. Meden, B., Malli, R.C., Fabijan, S., Ekenel, H.K., Štruc, V., Peer, P.: Face deidentification with generative deep neural networks. IET Signal Process. **11**(9), 1046–1054 (2017). https://arxiv.org/abs/1707.09376

72. Mirjalili, V., Raschka, S., Ross, A.: FlowSAN: privacy-enhancing semi-adversarial networks to confound arbitrary face-based gender classifiers. IEEE Access, **7**, 99735–99745 (2019). https://arxiv.org/abs/1905.01388
73. Mirsky, Y., Lee, W.: The Creation and detection of deepfakes. ACM Comput. Surv. **54**(1), 1–41 (2021)
74. Mittal, T., Bhattacharya, U., Chandra, R., Bera, A., Manocha, D.: Emotions don't lie: an audio-visual deepfake detection method using affective cues. In: MM 2020 - Proceedings of the 28th ACM International Conference on Multimedia, pp. 2823–2832 (2020). https://arxiv.org/abs/2003.06711
75. Moon, T.K.: The expectation-maximization algorithm. IEEE Signal Process. Mag. **13**(6), 47–60 (1996)
76. Nadimpalli, A.V., Rattani, A.: GBDF: Gender Balanced DeepFake Dataset Towards Fair DeepFake Detection (n.d.). https://arxiv.org/abs/arXiv:2207.10246v1
77. Nataraj, L., et al.: Detecting GAN generated fake images using co-occurrence matrices. In: IS and T International Symposium on Electronic Imaging Science and Technology, vol. 2019. no. 5, pp. 1–7 (2019). https://arxiv.org/abs/1903.06836
78. Neves, J.C., Tolosana, R., Vera-Rodriguez, R., Lopes, V., Proença, H., Fierrez, J.: GANprintR: improved fakes and evaluation of the state of the art in face manipulation detection. IEEE J. Sel. Top. Signal Process. **14**(5), 1038–1048 (2020). https://arxiv.org/abs/1911.05351
79. Nguyen, H.H., Fang, F., Yamagishi, J., Echizen, I.: Multi-task learning for detecting and segmenting manipulated facial images and videos. In: 2019 IEEE 10th International Conference on Biometrics Theory, Applications and Systems, BTAS 2019 (2019). https://arxiv.org/abs/1906.06876
80. Nguyen, H.H., Yamagishi, J., Echizen, I.: Capsule-forensics: using capsule networks to detect forged images and videos. In: ICASSP, IEEE International Conference on Acoustics, Speech and Signal Processing - Proceedings, 2019-May, pp. 2307–2311 (2019). https://arxiv.org/abs/1810.11215
81. Nguyen, T.T., Nguyen, C.M., Nguyen, D.T., Nguyen, D.T., Nahavandi, S.: Deep learning for deepfakes creation and detection. CoRR, abs/1909.11573 (2019). http://arxiv.org/abs/1909.11573
82. Nirkin, Y., Wolf, L., Keller, Y., Hassner, T.: DeepFake detection based on the discrepancy between the face and its context, pp. 1–10 (2020). http://arxiv.org/abs/2008.12262
83. Oscar Schwartz. 2018. You thought fake news was bad? The Guardian. Retrieved March 2, 2020. (n.d.). https://www.theguardian.com/technology/2018/nov/12/deep-fakes-fake-news-truth
84. Pan, Y.L., Haung, M.J., Ding, K.T., Wu, J.L., Jang, J.S.: K-Same-siamese-GAN: K-same algorithm with generative adversarial network for facial image de-identification with hyperparameter tuning and mixed precision training. In: 2019 16th IEEE International Conference on Advanced Video and Signal Based Surveillance, AVSS 2019 (2019). https://arxiv.org/abs/1904.00816
85. Peng, B., et al.: DFGC 2022: The Second DeepFake Game Competition (2022). http://arxiv.org/abs/2206.15138
86. Qi, H., et al.: DeepRhythm: exposing DeepFakes with attentional visual heartbeat rhythms. In: MM 2020 - Proceedings of the 28th ACM International Conference on Multimedia, pp. 1318–1327 (2020). https://arxiv.org/abs/2006.07634
87. Rössler, A., Cozzolino, D., Verdoliva, L., Riess, C., Thies, J., Nießner, M.: FaceForensics: a large-scale video dataset for forgery detection in human faces (2018). http://arxiv.org/abs/1803.09179
88. Rossler, A., Cozzolino, D., Verdoliva, L., Riess, C., Thies, J., Niessner, M.: FaceForensics++: learning to detect manipulated facial images. In: Proceedings of the IEEE International

Conference on Computer Vision, 2019-October, pp. 1–11 (2019). https://arxiv.org/abs/1901.08971
89. Sabir, E., Cheng, J., Jaiswal, A., AbdAlmageed, W., Masi, I., Natarajan, P.: Recurrent convolutional strategies for face manipulation detection in videos, pp. 80–87 (2019). http://arxiv.org/abs/1905.00582
90. Scherhag, U., Rathgeb, C., Merkle, J., Breithaupt, R., Busch, C.: Face recognition systems under morphing attacks: a survey. IEEE Access **7**, 23012–23026 (2019)
91. Shullani, D., Fontani, M., Iuliani, M., Shaya, O.A., Piva, A.: VISION: a video and image dataset for source identification. Eurasip J. Inf. Secur. **2017**(1) (2017)
92. Siddiqui Muhammad Yasir, H.A.: Deep learning-based 3D instance and semantic segmentation: a review. J. Artif. Intell. **4**(2), 99–114 (2022). http://www.techscience.com/jai/v4n2/48857
93. Siddiqui Muhammad Yasir, H.A.: Faster metallic surface defect detection using deep learning with channel shuffling. Computers, Mater. Continua, **75**(1), 1847–1861 (2023). http://www.techscience.com/cmc/v75n1/51506
94. Siddiqui Muhammad Yasir, H.A., Sadiq, A.M.: 3D instance segmentation using deep learning on RGB-d indoor data. Comput. Mater. Continua, **72**(3), 5777–5791 (2022). http://www.techscience.com/cmc/v72n3/47479
95. Song, L., Wu, W., Qian, C., He, R., Loy, C.C.: Everybody's Talkin': let me talk as you want (2020). http://arxiv.org/abs/2001.05201
96. Song, Y., Zhu, J., Li, D., Wang, A., Qi, H.: Talking face generation by conditional recurrent adversarial network. In: IJCAI International Joint Conference on Artificial Intelligence, 2019-Augus, pp. 919–925 (2019). https://arxiv.org/abs/1804.04786
97. Suwajanakorn, S., Seitz, S.M., Kemelmacher-Shlizerman, I.: Synthesizing Obama: learning lip sync from audio. ACM Trans. Graph. **36**(4) (2017)
98. Tariq, S., Lee, S., Woo, S.: One detector to rule them all: towards a general deepfake attack detection framework. In: The Web Conference 2021 - Proceedings of the World Wide Web Conference, WWW 2021, pp. 3625–3637 (2021). https://arxiv.org/abs/2105.00187
99. The biggest threat of deepfakes isn't the deepfakes themselves. (n.d.). https://www.technologyreview.com/2019/10/10/132667/the-biggest-threat-of-deepfakes-isnt-the-deepfakesthemselves/
100. Thies, J., Zollhöfer, M., Nießner, M.: Deferred neural rendering: image synthesis using neural textures. ACM Trans. Graph. **38**(4) (2019). https://arxiv.org/abs/1904.12356
101. Thies, J., Zollhöfer, M., Nießner, M., Valgaerts, L., Stamminger, M., Theobalt, C.: Real-time expression transfer for facial reenactment. ACM Trans. Graph. **34**(6) (2015)
102. Thies, J., Zollhofer, M., Stamminger, M., Theobalt, C., Niebner, M.: Face2Face: real-time face capture and reenactment of RGB videos. In: Proceedings of the IEEE Computer Society Conference on Computer Vision and Pattern Recognition, 2016-Decem, pp. 2387–2395 (2016)
103. Thies, J., Zollhöfer, M., Theobalt, C., Stamminger, M., Niessner, M.: HeadOn: real-time reenactment of human portrait videos. ACM Trans. Graph. **37**(4) (2018). https://arxiv.org/abs/1805.11729
104. Tran, L., Yin, X., Liu, X.: Representation Learning by Rotating Your Faces (n.d.). https://arxiv.org/abs/arXiv:1705.11136v2
105. Two-Stream Neural Networks for Tampered Face Detection. In: IEEE Computer Society Conference on Computer Vision and Pattern Recognition Workshops, 2017-July, pp. 1831–1839 (2017)
106. Wang, S.-Y., Wang, O., Zhang, R., Owens, A., Efros, A.A.: CNN-generated images are surprisingly easy to spot... for now. CoRR, abs/1912.11035 (2019). http://arxiv.org/abs/1912.11035

107. Wu, X., Xie, Z., Gao, Y., Xiao, Y.: SSTNet: Detecting manipulated faces through spatial, steganalysis and temporal features. In: ICASSP 2020 - 2020 IEEE International Conference on Acoustics, Speech and Signal Processing (ICASSP), pp. 2952–2956 (2020)
108. *WWD*. (n.d.). https://mklab.iti.gr/results/the-wild-web-tampered-image-dataset/
109. Xie, D., Chatterjee, P., Liu, Z., Roy, K., Kossi, E.: DeepFake detection on publicly available datasets using modified AlexNet. In: 2020 IEEE Symposium Series on Computational Intelligence (SSCI), pp. 1866–1871 (2020)
110. Xuan, X., Peng, B., Wang, W., Dong, J.: On the generalization of GAN image forensics. Lecture Notes in Computer Science (Including Subseries Lecture Notes in Artificial Intelligence and Lecture Notes in Bioinformatics), 11818 LNCS (61502496), pp. 134–141 (2019). https://arxiv.org/abs/1902.11153
111. Yang, X., Li, Y., Lyu, S.: Exposing deep fakes using inconsistent head poses. CoRR, abs/1811.00661 (2018). http://arxiv.org/abs/1811.00661
112. Yu, N., Davis, L., Fritz, M.: Attributing fake images to GANs: learning and analyzing GAN fingerprints. In: Proceedings of the IEEE International Conference on Computer Vision, 2019-Octob, pp. 7555–7565 (2019). https://arxiv.org/abs/1811.08180
113. Yu, Y., Liu, G., Odobez, J.M.: Improving few-shot user-specific gaze adaptation via gaze redirection synthesis. In: Proceedings of the IEEE Computer Society Conference on Computer Vision and Pattern Recognition, 2019-June, pp. 11929–11938 (2019). https://arxiv.org/abs/1904.10638
114. *ZAO Application*. (n.d.). https://apps.apple.com/cn/app/id1465199127
115. Zhang, J., et al.: Dual In-painting Model for Unsupervised Gaze Correction and Animation in the Wild (n.d.). https://arxiv.org/abs/arXiv:2008.03834v1
116. Zhang, X., Karaman, S., Chang, S.F.: Detecting and simulating ARTIFACTS in GAN fake images. In: 2019 IEEE International Workshop on Information Forensics and Security, WIFS 2019 (2019). https://arxiv.org/abs/1907.06515
117. Zhang, Y., Zheng, L., Thing, V.L.L.: Automated face swapping and its detection. In: 2017 IEEE 2nd International Conference on Signal and Image Processing, ICSIP 2017, 2017-Janua, pp. 15–19 (2017)
118. Zi, B., Chang, M., Chen, J., Ma, X., Jiang, Y.G.: WildDeepfake: a challenging real-world dataset for deepfake detection. In: MM 2020 - Proceedings of the 28th ACM International Conference on Multimedia, pp. 2382–2390 (2020). https://arxiv.org/abs/2101.01456

# A Convolutional Neural Network Approach for Mood Classification in Short Texts Using Character-Level Details and Local Text Structure

Moodser Hussain[1], Muhammad Jameel[2], Muhammad Farhat Ullah[3], Taimoor Hassan Jabbar[4], Roha Irfan[5], and Muhammad Waseem Iqbal[6]($\boxtimes$)

[1] Department of Information Technology, University of the Punjab, Gujranwala Campus, Gujranwala, Pakistan
[2] Department of Computer Science, Superior University Lahore, Lahore, Pakistan
[3] Department of Software Engineering, University of Lahore, Lahore, Pakistan
[4] Department of Computer Science, BZU, Multan, Pakistan
[5] Department of Computer Science, University of Central Punjab Lahore, Lahore, Pakistan
[6] Department of Software Engineering, Superior University Lahore, Lahore, Pakistan
waseem.iqbal@superior.edu.pk

**Abstract.** Mood classification is a crucial and complex task in the fields of psychology and Natural Language Processing (NLP). It is particularly challenging to assess an individual's mood based on their chats or comments on social media platforms. This study introduces a Convolutional Neural Network (CNN) for mood classification and evaluates its efficacy on the ISEAR dataset. The dataset comprises 7,652 short texts labeled with seven different moods including joy, anger, fear, guilt, disgust, sadness, and shame. Our proposed model achieves an impressive F1 score of 94.59%, surpassing existing statistical and deep learning models. The superior performance can be attributed to two key features of our approach. Firstly, our model incorporates the local structure of the text by leveraging relationships between adjacent word embeddings, allowing it to capture the subtle nuances of language. Secondly, it captures character-level details within the input text, allowing for a more comprehensive understanding of the data. Overall, our study demonstrates the effectiveness of the CNN-based approach for mood classification in NLP, with potential implications for developing automated systems that can accurately recognize and respond to people's moods in various applications, such as mental health and customer service.

**Keywords:** Mood Classification · Convolutional Neural Network · Sentiment Analysis · Natural Language Processing

## 1 Introduction

The rise of technology has led to the widespread use of social media platforms as a means of expressing opinions and emotions [1]. As a result, psychologists have seized the opportunity to analyze human behavior through these platforms. Natural Language Processing

(NLP) researchers have utilized human comments and chats on social media to facilitate psychological analysis. Mood classification, a popular area of study in intersection of psychology and NLP, aims to extract mood from the written text. The International Survey on Emotion Antecedents and Reactions (ISEAR) dataset [2] is a valuable resource for extracting mood or conducting sentiment analysis of human behavior on the internet or social media platforms.

Sentiment analysis is a process that involves categorizing the opinions expressed by writer. The proliferation of microblogging platforms such as Twitter and Facebook have led to an increase in the sharing of sentiments, reviews, and chats on various topics, including products and personalities. It is crucial to understand the writer's intention and mood when analyzing their writing. Sentiment analysis is used to classify reviews and determine the mood of a post-writer. In this experimental study, convolutional neural networks are utilized to classify mood using the ISEAR [2] dataset. As social media usage continues to grow exponentially, there is a growing need to monitor the mood of its users. Individual moods can be broadly classified as sad, happy, mocking, angry, humorous, and so on [1].

Sentiment and mood are two distinct representations of an individual's emotional state. Sentiments are concerned with the degree of positivity, neutrality, or negativity, while moods are classified as sad, happy, cheerful, depressed, bored, and so on. However, mood classification is often ambiguous due to the difficulty in identifying it accurately. Text-based mood classification is particularly challenging because words alone do not convey the true mood associated with them; the context in which the words are used is also crucial for accurate classification [3]. To understand the context of a word correctly, it is essential to consider the words that surround it in a sentence. To improve the accuracy of mood classification, all factors that influence the true mood representation a word should be taken into account [4]. In recent times, there has been a shift from simple text to emojis. Using emojis alongside text can aid the current classification of the mood associated with the text or word [5].

When it comes to mood classification, relying solely on word polarity and its psychological significance is not a sufficient approach. In order to achieve more accurate classification results, it is necessary to take into account additional factors in conjunction with the psychological relevance of words [6]. A common issue in mood classification is the limited amount of text available for analysis, as shorter texts provide less information for classification as compared to longer ones.

Deep neural networks have demonstrated strong performance in tasks such as sentiment analysis and information retrieval. However, when it comes to mood classification, specific testing is required [7]. The effectiveness of the model is highly influenced by various parameters, including but not limited to epochs, dropout, and number of layers [8].

The classification of mood is subject to variation across different domains, with unique features present in each domain. When performing classification on Twitter or blog data, the available information for classification, such as plain text and emotion, may be insufficient [3]. Additionally, there may be cases where the classified data does not correspond with the given text.

The accurate determination of the requisite data quantity for classification is significant issue. The classification of moods also poses a challenge in terms of obtaining reliable classified data. Additionally, the nature of the data utilized for classification has a direct impact on the classification task's efficacy [6]. The establishment of a dependable correlation between the text and the emotions conveyed within it is considered a linguistic hurdle of contemporary times.

This study investigates the linguistic obstacles posed by moods classification in Sect. 2. In Sect. 3, relevant prior research is discussed. The proposed methodology is outlined in Sect. 4, implementation and evaluation are addressed in Sect. 5, and the study concludes in Sect. 6.

## 2 Related Work

Several researchers have applied sentiment analysis and mood classification techniques to the renowned ISEAR dataset, which contains more than seven thousand comments or posts. This data is simpler to work with than other blogged data, making it an ideal choice for such research. Studies involving sentiment analysis and mood classification have already been conducted on this dataset in the past.

In [9], the ISEAR dataset was used to detect emotions using VSM and STASIS similarity techniques. The proposed approach examined the maximum, base, and average similarity scores of each emotion category. The results indicated that the VSM method outperformed STASIS (max, average, and base) with an F1 score of 0.63 in the fear category. Thus, the study concluded in favor of the VSM method.

In 2019, a study reported the best F1 Score of 0.85 with the Logistic Regression method on the ISEAR dataset. Other methods such as SVC, KNN, and XG-Boost were also applied on the same dataset [10]. Moreover, in 2020, researchers made use of the Bidirectional Encoder Representations from Transformers (BERT) model to detect emotions, which resulted in a 0.73 F1 score on the ISEAR dataset [11].

In 2020, [12] utilized transformer models, namely BERT, RoBERTa, DistilBERT, and XLNet to recognize emotions in text, with the ISEAR dataset used to fine-tune these models. The F1 scores obtained were 0.6693, 0.7009, 0.7299, and 0.7431 for DistilBERT, BERT, XLNet, and RoBERTa respectively. Subsequently, in 2021 [13] investigated the usage of NLP for emotion recognition by applying multiple state-of-the-art deep learning models, including BERT, DistilBERT, RoBERTa, XLNet, and ELECTRA. This study utilized the ISEAR dataset along with the SemEval dataset of 2018 (task 1) and 2019 (task 3) and achieved an F1 Score of 0.49 with the RoBERTa ML model. Finally, [14] used RoBERTa and XLNet transformer-based language models to address the problem of emotion detection, employing the ISEAR dataset to obtain a 0.75 F1 score.

From existing literature, it can be observed that social media platforms like Twitter can be the easiest method to collect data about individual opinions. However, the identification of correct sentiment is challenging. To overcome this, this study focuses on the data from the International Survey on Emotion Antecedents and Reactions (ISEAR) for more authentic experimentation and results.

## 3 Proposed Methodology

In this study, we used Gensims Word2Vec model[1] for feature extraction and Stacked Convolutional Neural Network [16] (with a pool size of 13 words and softmax activation function) for model training. Figure 1 represents the model architecture, further methodology details are discussed below subsections.

### 1. Model Architecture

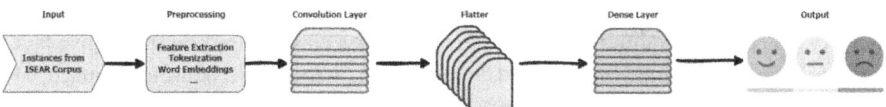

**Fig. 1.** Stacked Convolutional Neural Network Architecture

### 2. Feature Extraction Layer

The mood-based ISEAR dataset has short texts that present different emotions. As neural networks understand and process numeric values better, it is much more convenient and efficient to use vector encoding for the representation of each sentence as a set of features [17]. Gensims Word2Vec Model is used to learn the word embeddings on an annotated emotion-based corpus. That provides a dense vector representation of words from the corpus (that have similar or at least related meanings).

From a given corpus, Gensims Word2Vec Model takes tokenized sentences, minimum word frequency, and vector size (presenting a word as parameters of the model). In our experiment setting, the minimum frequency count is set to 1, and the vector size is 300. Gensims Word2Vec Model creates a vocabulary from the given corpus. In the result of training, the model learns the word vectors from vector space where words with similar meanings are locally clustered within the space having related meanings.

Moreover, emotion-based classification word embedding is not enough, although it is presenting words in the form of related vectors. But these word embedding needs to process by different convolutional, pooling, flatten, and dense layers.

### 3. Convolutional Layer

In a convolutional neural network, word embeddings from the Word2Vec model are used as input. Embedding sequences of the words are passed to the 1-dimensional Convolutional which (according to experiment setting) has 128 filters with kernel size 2, valid padding, ReLU as activation function, input shape having 15 maximum number of words in a sentence, and length of the embedded vectors is 300.

### 4. Max Pooling Layer

The output from the first convolutional layer is then passed to the max pooling layer, which is responsible to aggregate the information and reduce the representation [18]. The pool size provided to the 1-dimensional max pooling layer is 13. Therefore, this layer looks at 13 words at a time and takes the max over those 13 vectors.

---

[1] https://radimrehurek.com/gensim/.

### 5. Flatten Layer

The Max pooling layer results in a 3-rank tensor, while the dense layer expects a 2-rank tensor. A Flatten layer is used to separate the above convolutions from the dense. Therefore, it transforms your three-dimensional tensor into a one-dimensional tensor [19]. So flattened layer takes the output of the max pooling layer as input and flattens that input while batch size remains the same.

### 6. Dense Layer

The output of the Flatten layer passed to a fully connected Softmax layer. A dense or fully connected layer performs a linear operation. At this layer, every input is connected to every output by weight. Therefore, one neuron per class is used on the Dense layer. There are 13 classes for emotion-based classification, therefore 13 neurons are used. The softmax activation function is used on a Dense layer, which provides the probability of input being in any particular class in the range of 0 to 1.

## 4 Evaluation and Implementation

For the experiments, this study used the ISEAR dataset. The dataset consists of 7,652 comments annotated with the most appropriate of seven major emotions (joy, fear, anger, sadness, disgust, shame, and guilt). Class-wise distribution of data is presented in Table 1 while the instances of each class is presented in Table 2 as an example.

**Table 1.** Data Distribution (Class wise)

| Class/Label | Instances (Count) |
|---|---|
| Joy | 1092 |
| Anger | 1094 |
| Fear | 1093 |
| Guilt | 1091 |
| Disgust | 1094 |
| Sadness | 1094 |
| Shame | 1094 |

**Table 2.** Sample Text from Each Class

| Class/Label | Instances (Text) |
|---|---|
| Joy | I'm ever so cheerful Anger I locked myself out |
| Fear | When I nearly collided with another car |
| Guilt | I do not help out enough at home |
| Disgust | Can not think of any situation |
| Sadness | After an exam which I failed |
| Shame | When I forgot my mother's birthday |

For this study, the proposed stacked CNN model is implemented in python using Tensor and Keras APIs on Jupiter notebook. For training, the model used 7,652 mood-based examples from ISEAR annotated mood-based dataset.

## 5 Results

This research is able to reach an F1 Score of up to 0.9459 (after training the CNN model on a mood-based ISEAR dataset on 1200 epochs). It can be observed in Table 3 that our proposed system is significantly outperforming existing neural machine learning, and transfer based models/techniques. The significant change in F1 measure score is possible due to deep learning model layers and tweaking parameters of models [20]. The proposed model performs better than the existing statistical and deep learning models because: (1) it considers the local structure of the text by using the adjacent word embeddings and (2) it extracts and utilizes the character-level details of the given text [21].

**Table 3.** Results from Existing and Proposed Studies

| Algorithm | System/Study | F1 Score |
|---|---|---|
| VSM | [9] | 0.63 |
| Logistic Regression | [10] | 0.85 |
| BERT | [11] | 0.73 |
| RoBERTa | [12] | 0.7431 |
| Distil RoBERTa | [13] | 0.49 |
| RoBERTa | [14] | 0.75 |
| Stacked CNN | this study | 0.9459 |

## 6 Conclusion

Mood classification is a challenging task in NLP. This study's proposed approach described the mood-based classification of comments using a convolutional neural network. This article provides a detailed description of the research implemented methodology in Sect. 4 and presented obtained results in Sect. 5. The proposed approach obtained an F1-Score of up to 94.59% on the ISEAR dataset for the multi-classification of comments into seven distinct emotions. In the future, we will expand the experimentation setup by using more deep-learning models over several word embedding methods.

## References

1. Severyn, A., Moschitti, A.: Twitter sentiment analysis with deep convolutional neural networks. In: Proceedings of the 38th international ACM SIGIR Conference on Research and Development in Information Retrieval, pp. 959–962 (2015)
2. Scherer, K.R., Wallbott, H.G.: Evidence for universality and cultural variation of differential emotion response patterning. J. Pers. Soc. Psychol. **66**(2), 310 (1994)
3. Agarwal, A., Xie, B., Vovsha, I., Rambow, O., Passonneau, R.J.: Sentiment analysis of twitter data. In: Proceedings of the Workshop on Language in Social Media (LSM 2011), pp. 30–38 (2011)
4. Neethu, M., Rajasree, R.: Sentiment analysis in twitter using machine learning techniques. In: 2013 Fourth International Conference on Computing, Communications and Networking Technologies (ICCCNT), pp. 1–5. IEEE (2013)
5. Hamouda, S.B., Akaichi, J.: Social networks' text mining for sentiment classification: the case of Facebook' statuses updates in the 'Arabic Spring' era. Int. J. Appl. Innov. Eng. Manag. **2**(5), 470–478 (2013)
6. Kumar, V., Minz, S.: Mood classification of lyrics using SentiWordNet. In: 2013 International Conference on Computer Communication and Informatics, pp. 1–5. IEEE (2013)
7. Akella, R., Moh, T.-S.: Mood classification with lyrics and ConvNets. In: 2019 18th IEEE International Conference on Machine Learning and Applications (ICMLA), pp. 511–514. IEEE (2019)
8. Alshemali, B., Kalita, J.: Improving the reliability of deep neural networks in NLP: a review. Knowl.-Based Syst. **191**, 105210 (2020)
9. Mozafari, F., Tahayori, H.: Emotion detection by using similarity techniques. In: 2019 7th Iranian Joint Congress on Fuzzy and Intelligent Systems (CFIS), pp. 1–5. IEEE (2019)
10. Alotaibi, F.M.: Classifying text-based emotions using logistic regression (2019)
11. Adoma, A.F., Henry, N.-M., Chen, W., Andre, N.R.: Recognizing emotions from texts using a BERT-based approach. In: 2020 17th International Computer Conference on Wavelet Active Media Technology and Information Processing (ICCWAMTIP), pp. 62–66. IEEE (2020)
12. Adoma, A.F., Henry, N.-M., Chen, W.: Comparative analyses of BERT, RoBERTa, DistilBERT, and XLNet for text-based emotion recognition. In: 2020 17th International Computer Conference on Wavelet Active Media Technology and Information Processing (ICCWAMTIP), pp. 117–121. IEEE (2020)
13. Cortiz, D.: Exploring transformers in emotion recognition: a comparison of BERT, DistillBERT, RoBERTa, XLNet and Electra. ArXiv Prepr. ArXiv210402041 (2021)
14. Acheampong, F.A., Nunoo-Mensah, H., Chen, W.: Recognizing emotions from texts using an ensemble of transformer-based language models. In: 2021 18th International Computer Conference on Wavelet Active Media Technology and Information Processing (ICCWAMTIP), pp. 161–164. IEEE (2021)

15. Khan, S.I., Aziz, F.B., Uddin, M.M.: Emotion detection from multilingual text and multi-emotional sentence using difference NLP feature extraction technique and ML classifier. Int. J. Adv. Netw. Appl. **14**(3), 5429–5435 (2022)
16. Gu, J., et al.: Recent advances in convolutional neural networks. Pattern Recognit. **77**, 354–377 (2018)
17. Hancock, J.T., Khoshgoftaar, T.M.: Survey on categorical data for neural networks. J. Big Data **7**(1), 28 (2020). https://doi.org/10.1186/s40537-020-00305-w
18. Yu, D., Wang, H., Chen, P., Wei, Z.: Mixed pooling for convolutional neural networks. In: RSKT 2014, pp. 364–375. Springer (2014)
19. Jeczmionek, E., Kowalski, P.A.: Flattening layer pruning in convolutional neural networks. Symmetry **13**(7) (2021). https://doi.org/10.3390/sym13071147
20. Socher, R.: Recursive deep learning for natural language processing and computer vision. Stanford University (2014)
21. Zhang, X., Zhao, J., LeCun, Y.: Character-level convolutional networks for text classification. Adv. Neural Inf. Process. Syst. **28** (2015)

# Usability Approach of Distributed Database in Health Care System

Sana Mazhar[1], Muhammad Waseem Iqbal[1](✉), and Muhammad Ahmad Irshad[2]

[1] Department of Software Engineering, Superior University, Lahore 54000, Pakistan
`{msse-f20-007,waseem.iqbal}@superior.edu.pk`
[2] Department of Computer Science, Superior University, Lahore 54000, Pakistan
`mscs-f20-015@superior.edu.pk`

**Abstract.** The blockchain is safe mechanism for store and distributed data due to its transparency. Every block of the chain serves as both an individual component that has its own data as well as a dependent connection inside the shared network, so this duality provides a networks organized by users who keep and share data instead of third party. Blockchain has several uses in healthcare, including the improvement of applications for mobile health monitoring-devices, the distribution and store of electrical-medical-records, clinical research data, as well as the storage of insurance information. Blockchain analysis throughout insurance is currently limited, but blockchain is at the frontlines of trying to transform the medical system; throughout its distributed concepts, blockchain could even keep improving patient records availability and privacy. This article presents a solution for managing identity and access in a digital system that makes use of blockchain technology to help with entity authentication and permission. Using the Permissioned Blockchain architecture, a prototype illustrates the use of blockchain in access and identity management. It gives a proof-of-concept centered on some use case involving Electronic-Health-Records from the health sector in which an immutable and traceability record for information related to patients is desired. Blockchain has the implicit to meet specific unique criteria, similar as confidentiality and invariability, and so might be employed in a wide range of operations.

**Keywords:** Patients · Healthcare center · Distributed database · Health tracker prototype

## 1 Introduction

Blockchain invention was planned by Nakamoto, the essential study was to have cryptographically gotten and decentralized currencies that would be useful for fiscal deals. At last, this study of blockchain was being employed in different fields of life; the medical care area likewise is one of their plans to use it. Colorful specialists have anatomized this area, these considerations works center around the way that exercising blockchain for medical care areas is presumptive or not. They also distinguish the benefits, troubles, issues, or difficulties related to the application of this invention. A many judges likewise examined the difficulties that would be looked at while executing this for a bigger compass [1]. Blockchain has been an intriguing exploration area for a unexpectedly long time, and the benefits it provides have been used by a variety of associations. Likewise, the clinical benefits sector stands to gain significantly from blockchain advancement due to nearly safe, security, protection, and decentralization [2]. Healthcare systems are getting decreasingly digitized to grease data operation and access. Still, sequestration is essential. Enterprises have also been expressed regarding patient data. Blockchain technology is a fairly new technology that's being used to develop new results in a variety of diligence, including healthcare. A healthcare system grounded on blockchain Patient information records are stored and sent through a technological channel. From colorful healthcare installations, testing labs, specifics, and croakers , among other effects. Likewise, blockchain is critical for detecting fraud in clinical trials [3]. Developing a good data storehouse armature with the loftiest security measures available can help palliate enterprises about data manipulation in clinical operation. In healthcare, colorful information and communication technologies are used, raising security, sequestration, and interoperability enterprises. Between 2008 and 2021, over 500 million case records were stolen and blurted [4]. The culprits stole not only bank information, but also stole health and inheritable test results. Healthcare Information Planning is the most effective system for collecting digitized health information. This information can range from electronic case records used in the development of routine checks to scrutinized handwritten sanitarium records stored in a digital library. Over 176 million case records were exposed in data breaches between 2009 and 2017 [5]. Health Data Monitoring is trusted for further than just managing health information [6]. it's also trusted for combining and combining it and allowing its evaluation to ameliorate patient safety and gain perceptivity that can ameliorate healthcare issues while maintaining information confidentiality [7]. Further options for standard medical data operation, similar as allowing cases to gain and bandy their health information, as well as the development of digitized health- related data collection, pall healthcare information storehouse, and patient information sequestration protection programs Develop [8]. Permitting technology- grounded effectiveness and productivity enterprises to drivee-health planning, on the other hand, is giving in to the technical imperative because e-health is fraught with a slew of potentially disastrous issues [9] (Fig. 1).

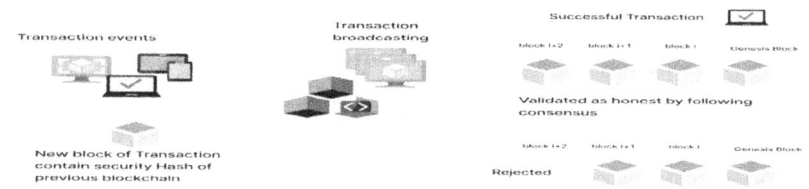

**Fig. 1.** Transaction process

2021—Dubai has all administration activities and record-keeping procedures on the blockchain as a feature of the Smart Dubai 2021 drive [10]. By utilizing the public-key cryptography and other cryptographic techniques, the cryptocurrency Bitcoin enables its users to maintain a high level of anonymity hashing. Although typical, anonymity [11]. Blockchain development is viewed as an applicable record development for participated (P2P) networks advanced data trades that can be directly or subtly passed on to all guests, allowing any type of data to be handled explosively and incontrovertibly. Clinical benefits are one of the most egregious operations of blockchain advancement. The supposed hash, which is made using a cryptographic one- way hash work, is used to link all of the blocks in the blockchain(e.g., SHA256). It also ensures the block's obscurity, invariability, and traditionalism [12]. A customer who wishes to attract with the blockchain communicates with the blockchain network via a knot. Because all miners must work a fully precious knot, the lately appertained to excavators are a subset of bumps. As a result, while every miner is a knot, not every knot is also a miner. This situation is known from a specific public blockchain type that employs the PoW (evidence- of- work) agreement (inclining further toward this latterly in this member). Different types of square chain associations that use other agreement types, similar as PoS, don't bear mining (evidence of stake) [13]. The ability of blockchain in medical services is to overcome the obstacles related with data security, protection, sharing, and storage. One of the requirements for medical care assiduity is interoperability. Two people or machines can exchange information or data definitively, effectively, and reliably. The thing of interoperability in medical services is to grease the exchange of health- related data, for illustration, electronic health records (EHR), among medical care suppliers and cases so that the information can be participated throughout the terrain and circulated by colorful clinic fabrics [14].

The thing of interoperability in medical care is to unite on the exchange of health-related data, similar as electronic health records (EHR), among medical care suppliers and cases so that information can be participated throughout the terrain and distributed by colorful sanitarium fabrics [15]. EHR fabrics have been enforced in colorful exigency conventions around the world due to the benefits they give, specifically an increase in security and cost acceptability. They're regarded as an essential element of the medical services sector because they give a lot of benefits to medical services [16]. This paper proposes a system that creates a decentralized stage for storing patient clinical records and furnishing access to those records to providers or concerned individualities, i.e., cases. When planned, development and structures aren't made to be basically as important and adaptable as to take care of the prerequisites of different spaces, as is the situation with Blockchain invention [17]. This allows it to work on the exhibition, security, and translucency of clinical information sharing in the medical services frame. This invention will help clinical associations gain understanding and ameliorate clinical record disquisition [18]. Blockchain is a decentralized and public computerized record that records exchanges on multitudinous PCs so that no record included can be modified retroactively without changing any blocks a short time latterly.

Blockchain is verified and connected to the former' block', shaping a long chain. Blockchain has a many pivotal rates like information being circulated among all capitals over ade-unified network, information in blocks being infeasible to abolish or modify and everything being transparent [19]. Blockchain assists advertisers with keeping an figure of the particulars employed in drug. Medicinals and health will dispose of fake conventions exercising Blockchain advances, empowering the following this multitude of meds. It finds the reason for misrepresentation. Blockchain can insure the sequestration of case records; when clinical history is created, Blockchain can likewise store it, and this record can not be altered. This decentralized association is employed with all product outfit in the medical clinic [20]. Blockchain invention facilitates patient-driven progress toward interoperability by allowing cases to partake clinical material plus access procedures.

This provides lesser control over private data of paitent while also perfecting bracket and security. The estimation and prosecution of value by directors, as well as perpetration, are delicate. Blockchain operations could break any of these technical issues throughout the business [21]. Blockchain titles will help executive experts in distinguishing between authorized and impure specifics. This ensures that all authorized parties trade motorized exchanges containing the case's particulars. Cases who change clinical professionals may only modernize a single agreement to trade their entire records. With an adding rate of acceptance, blockchain has arrived in the medical services assiduity. Likewise, in the early stages, individualities in the health natural system fete the advances well [22]. Blockchain enables secure and secure data sharing and operation mechanisms in which all parties are apprehensive of deals [23].

Utmost insurance companies presently calculate on centralized systems and technologies to store and reuse data [24]. Throughout the life of a health insurance policy, several third parties or mediators are generally involved. Likewise, knowledge is power in the insurance assiduity. It's distributed among colorful stakeholders, making it a time-consuming and laborious process. Moment's medical insurance systems are riddled with inefficiencies [25]. Blockchain technology has the implicit to break the problem of interoperability. Smart contracts can automatically collect agreement records, deals, and other information, potentially leading to better executive processes [26]. Smart contracts can also help descry false or inflated insurance claims. Another benefit of blockchain technology is that it allows croakers to see their cases' health insurance content. Blockchain can help to simplify the health insurance process and ameliorate provider directory delicacy through agreement protocols. As a result, blockchain is an extremely precious offer for health [27].

In today's environment, everyone is more concerned with improving their health. Numerous new ailments have emerged as the number of ails in hospitals has risen. Cases are fascinated by the promise of receiving treatment at colourful hospitals and, as a result, leave their medical records spread throughout colourful hospitals for the rest of their life. They're having difficulty acquiring access to previous health records. As a result, cases interact with health records in a disjointed manner, resulting in poor health record functioning. [28]. The blockchain is composed of a series of blocks, each representing a set of deals. A blockchain is a type of data structure comprised of inflexible blocks. Each block contains the block number, the digital hand, the antedating hash, and the block hash or communication abridgments. Block 0 is the original block on the blockchain. It's known as the birth block. The former hash of the birth block must be zero [29]. The blockchain's birth block and block composition modifying the contents of any block (n) would have the same impact on the blockchain network for pointless data as block (n) hash and antedating hash. Blockchains are divided into two types private and public [30]. Smart contracts are extensions to blockchain technologies like Ethereum and Hyperledger Blockchain that give instructions for explicitly covering transfers of digital information between healthcare providers under specified conditions or contracts made between the being parties [31].

Blockchain is a new and arising technology with new operations in healthcare perpetration. Across all major platforms, data sharing and delivery are flawless and effective. Members of the network and healthcare providers contribute to the development. Numerous conditions bear both low- cost and sophisticated treatments. This will quicken the growth of healthcare in the coming times [32]. The operations of blockchain technology in the logistics assiduity have lately been revealed, and they demonstrate the benefits of the healthcare sector. Blockchain technology is being used to integrate a workflow process for the healthcare culture and fiscal sphere. It offers several significant and emotional openings for the healthcare assiduity, ranging from wisdom and logistics to interpersonal connections [33]. Blockchain's significant operations in healthcare are bandied by cases and interpreters. Piecemeal from conventional healthcare administration systems, blockchain's part is to record all feathers of deals in a decentralized record. It's precise and straightforward, saving time, trouble, and plutocrat and, as a result, lowering directorial trouble. The most important problem affecting the healthcare business is the leakage of pivotal data and its posterior use for dangerous bias and other special interests, which executions of this technology may fleetly fix [34].

## 2 Literature Review

Our system offers colorful benefits to the healthcare business. Because of the perpetration of blockchain, cases, healthcare interpreters, experimenters, and others will be suitable to gain correct information in a timely way. There are now centralized Electronic Medical Records systems, or data is saved in paper lines at croakers' services. This information can take numerous days, if not a week, to gain. A blockchain system offers colorful advantages to healthcare providers, individualities, experimenters, and anyone involved in the business [35]. Access to expansive medical data is needed for healthcare experimenters to gain a better knowledge of ails, speed up drug discovery, and make treatment strategies grounded on a [36] information about cases from colorful ethnical origins and geographical locales. It can gather health information on a case throughout their life. Blockchain technology might allow for real- time data access, perfecting clinical care collaboration and mainly perfecting clinical treatment in an exigency circumstance [37]. This technology will help to exclude healthcare breaches and ameliorate care collaboration, performing in better overall health issues [38]. Blockchain is distributed and decentralized technology and has large operations in the medical services sphere. Substantially blockchain introduces to the finance and banking sectors [39]. The blockchain gives a responsible and secure system of information sharing and the directors factors where all gatherings are aware of exchanges [40]. To gain superior clinical treatment outside of the nation, the specific case's clinical history must be understood, for illustration, whether the case has any type of perceptivity to certain conventions or information about his/her new drug. The clinical history can therefore be attained safely by the service provider. Blockchain technology is being employed to record and maintain patient healthcare histories. For illustration, cases may visit disconnected exigency conventions, and as a result, the overall chain of clinical history is doubtful to be accessible or followed up with (due to irregularity and attainability of records). Patient monitoring and Electronic Health Record (EHR) systems are two critical components of modern healthcare technology. Patient monitoring refers to the use of sensors and other devices to track vital signs and other health metrics in real-time, providing healthcare professionals with continuous data on a patient's health status. This can be especially useful for patients who require close monitoring, such as those in intensive care units or undergoing surgery.

On the other hand, EHRs are electronic versions of a patient's medical history and health information. EHRs provide healthcare professionals with a comprehensive view of a patient's health history, including medical conditions, medication lists, and test results. This information can be shared securely and efficiently between healthcare providers, improving the quality of care and reducing the risk of medical errors.

The integration of patient monitoring and EHR systems can provide healthcare professionals with a more complete and real-time picture of a patient's health status. For example, data from patient monitoring devices can be automatically recorded in a patient's EHR, providing a more complete and up-to-date picture of their health status. This integration can also help to identify potential health issues earlier and provide more personalized care based on a patient's unique health history and current health status. Blockchain technology has several operations in healthcare. Several extant trials and publications are demonstrating blockchain-enabled healthcare operations, and each section will explore a many particular software results.

## 2.1 Summary of Characteristics of Included Studies

(See Table 1).

**Table 1.** Existing techniques

| Ref | Application of Blockchain | Type of Blockchain used | Advantages | Limitations |
|---|---|---|---|---|
| [26] | Patient Monitoring/Electronic Health Record (ERH) | Private-Blockchain | The data and use of patient data are much relevant | The most important factor is time, yet there is some lag while confirming every block throughout the Blockchain. The key problem is also to keep each node secure |

(*continued*)

**Table 1.** (*continued*)

| Ref | Application of Blockchain | Type of Blockchain used | Advantages | Limitations |
|---|---|---|---|---|
| [48] | Managing medical records and other data | Public | It guarantees the patient that no unlawful conduct will be carried out. It is concerned with record transparency and data security | Transaction speed is a critical factor in healthcare devices. This platform doesn't always value transaction time |
| [49] | Managing medical records and other data | A Blockchain variant is employed in personal health care, and also an outside Blockchain used for keeping records | A better society via accurate and effective health-care-system | Only proposed work. Implementation is not performed |
| [50] | Patient Monitoring/ Electronic Health Record (ERH) | There is no Blockchain that I prefer | Attempt to remove hurdles and provide more secure system | Only proposed work. Implementation is not performed |
| [51] | Managing medical records and other data | Consultation on Blockchain | Security-related paper works | It can't address all issues of IoT security. It is unable to evaluate IoT threats |
| [52] | Patient Monitoring/Electronic Health Record (ERH) | Public- Blockchain | Healthcare gadgets that monitor patients' health status and exchange that data to approved doctors and hospitals over a secured Public blockchain | Poor communications between the servers and the device |

## 3 Methodology

**Problem**

Patients often visit various laboratories for medical examinations, which makes it challenging to maintain records as each laboratory has its own online portal and it is difficult to keep all records for an extended period. For instance, medical tests are conducted by different laboratories such as Chugtai Lab, Agha Khan, and Shaukat Khanum, among others. Currently, there is no platform that connects hospitals and healthcare providers worldwide on a single channel. Therefore, there is a need to provide a platform where patient histories can be stored safely and securely.

**Solution**
Health Tracker is a Platform that allows cases and their attendants to keep all their medical history organized. Another benefit of using a decentralized database is that it allows patients to have greater control over their medical records. With a decentralized system, patients can choose who has access to their medical records and can revoke access at any time. This can help improve patient trust and engagement in their healthcare. However, it's important to note that implementing a decentralized database for healthcare requires careful consideration of legal, ethical, and technical issues. For example, there are still regulatory and legal issues around the use of blockchain in healthcare, and data standards and interoperability issues must be addressed to ensure that data can be easily shared and integrated between different systems. Overall, your proposed Health Tracker platform has the potential to improve the quality and accessibility of healthcare for patients by providing a secure and decentralized platform for managing medical records.

**Prototype Development**
The world is in the midst of a health- tracking revolution, with invention appearing at a pace no way seen ahead, from smart watches to phones, earbuds, and smart rings, among others. So if you 've decided to get into keeping track of your health, a health shamus comes in handy. With numerous health trackers available, it's essential to understand what they are, what benefits they offer, and what to consider when buying one. Our thing is to give you with the key to the new quantified you.

**Sample Size**
A sample is a precise group from whom you'll collect data. The data was gathered from colorful hospitals. We take the patient history of 60 people manly and womanish age groups 20 to 55 and also we pr oduce Questionnaires that were handed to 75 repliers, with the completed responses being registered and the deficient recordings being discarded. A check of repliers was taken, and the responses collected came from cases, croakers treating them, and IT specialists.

**Target Audience**
It is not specific to any special group of people. A participant can be routine patients aged from 20 years to 50 years.

**Sample Group and Task**
We take three categories of different groups
    G1 20 - 30 General patients
    G2 35 - 60 diabetes patients
    G3 35 - 60 Cardio patients

G1's first group is general cases they're active survivors with low threat and their complaint is caused because of rainfall changes and an hygienic diet. G2 are diabetic cases and this type of complaint caused due to genetics, taking too important consumption of sugar in the diet, due to age factor. G3 are cardio cases these types of conditions be because of hypertension of sugar in the diet, due to age factor. G3 are cardio cases these types of conditions be because of hypertension.

**Information to be Collected at the Time of Registration**

The following information must be collected from the patient through the registration form,

- Blood Group
- Date of Birth
- Gender
- Type of Disease
- Address
- Email address

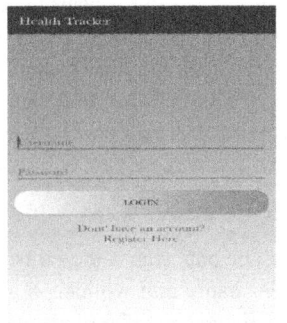
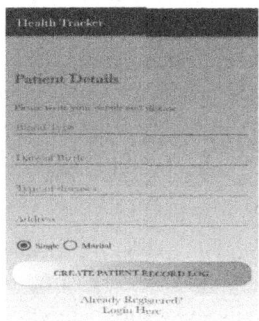
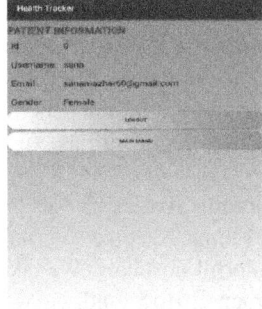

**Fig. 2.** Patient Registration   **Fig. 3.** Patient login   **Fig. 4.** Patient details

**Patient Info:** This information includes health records, case notes, details of medical issues, vital signs, previous medical history, vaccines, laboratory test results, and radiological reports. (Figs. 2, 3 and 4)

**Medical History:** A patient's medical history file includes information on their identity, as well as details on their medical conditions, illnesses, surgeries, vaccinations, and the results of physical exams and tests.

**Health Index:** A Health Index is a model tool that assesses a wide variety of risks to health and risk factors across time and across various geographic regions.

**Daily Log:** The daily log is a record of key events, incidents, and advancements achieved on a project site in a construction operation.

**Diagnosis:** Diagnosis of a problem, illness, or injury is based on its signs and symptoms. A patient's medical record, physical examination, and various tests such as blood tests, diagnostic imaging, and tissue samples may be utilized to assist with the diagnosis (Figs. 5, 6 and 7).

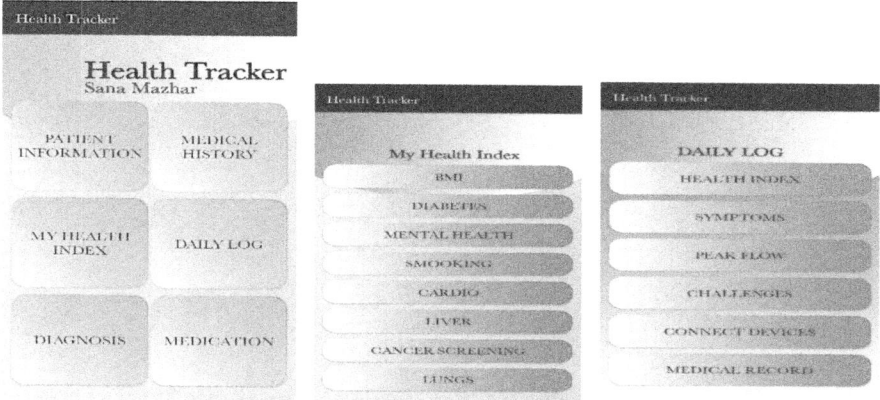

**Fig. 5.** Health tracker     **Fig. 6.** My health index     **Fig. 7.** Daily log

**Daily Log**

The daily log is a record of key events, incidents, and advancements achieved on a project site in building project.

- **Health Index:** A Health Index is a product instrument that evaluates a wide range of health concerns and environmental triggers across time and for various regions.
- **Peak Flow:** Peak expiratory inflow( PEF) are used to assess peak expiratory inflow or PEF. While scores in older women can be reduced and remain acceptable, the usual range for adult peak inflow is between 400 and 700 L per nanosecond. What matters mainly is if your score is typical for you.
- **Challenges:** A difficulty is something brand-new and delicate that demands a lot of effort and perseverance.
- **Medication:** Any medication or substance used to cure or avoid disease is referred to as a drug. Anti-anxiety drugs are a highly specialized kind of anxiety medication. To manage recurring pain, there are many various geographical options accessible. Any drug or treatment used to treat or prevent disease is referred to as a drug (Figs. 8, 9 and Table 2).

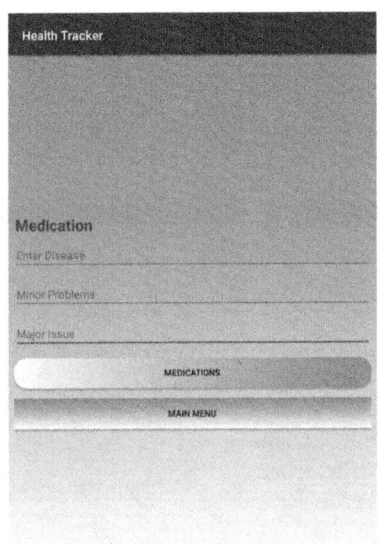 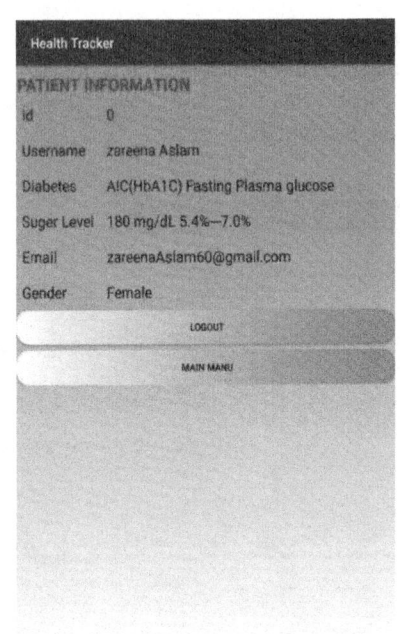

**Fig. 8.** Medication　　　　　　　　**Fig. 9.** Diagnose patient problem & Report

**Table 2.** System entities of the proposed system No System entities

| Questionnaire | Satisfied | unsatisfied | Natural |
|---|---|---|---|
| Total number of participants 75 | | | |
| Would this application will be useful for patients ? | 91% | 7% | 2% |
| Do you think such an application would helped for store patient data? | 93.3% | 6.7% | 0% |
| Would this application help you for knowing your current condition? | 97.3% | 2.7% | 0% |
| Is this application easy to use? | 92% | 2% | 5.3% |
| Do you think that this application would allows me to have better control over task? | 78.4% | 2.7% | 18.9% |
| How much you would be satisfied from this application? | 98.7% | 1.3% | 0% |
| Do you think that the contents of this app help you to remind routine checkup? | 96% | 2.7% | 1.3% |
| This application would help you for new challenges? | 81.3% | 4% | 14.7% |
| This application would answer my needs? | 92% | 8% | 0% |

Any P2P blockchain system healthcare service provider can interact with the registered case for follow-up exams after completing the registration process in the proposed EHR robotization platform. In the current proposal, the user is in charge of sending specific health data to the system as the info transmitter. The data sender is crucial to data security [41].

**Deployments of Blockchain Smart Contract**

The interface on the medical record homepage and the doctor register homepage have been developed to store the entire participant information. Once the login and registration procedures are completed, the system allows registered users to access the system by identifying themselves as patients and producing samples for environmental evaluation. Additionally, a portal has been constructed for the updated patient health records. To add new health information, participants are provided with a recommendation link through the append interface, which is used to make updates or modifications to a patient's medical record. The patient EHR management dashboard shows all health information and treatment histories (Fig. 10).

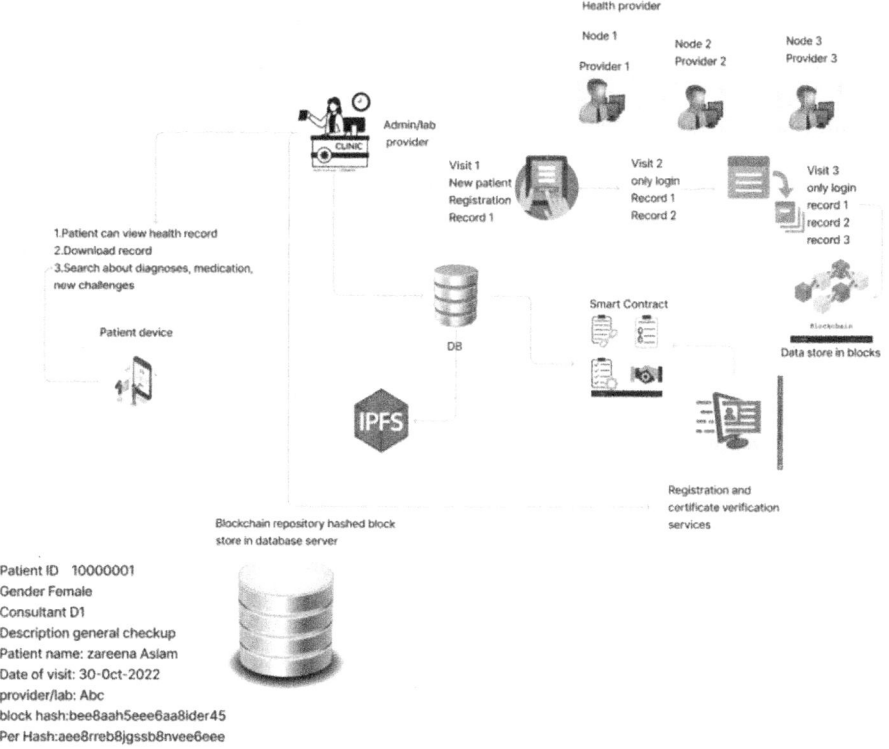

**Fig. 10.** Peer to peer network of blockchain

## Deployments of Blockchain Smart Contract

The medical record homepage and doctor register homepage are equipped with an interface that stores all participant information. Upon completion of login and registration, registered users can access the system and produce n samples for environment assessment, thereby identifying themselves as patients [42]. The system includes a portal for updated patient health records, which participants can use to add new health information via an append interface. All health information and treatment histories are accessible via a patient EHR management dashboard. To ensure the accuracy of recorded medical files, a viewing contract has been implemented. Once physicians, patients, and healthcare service providers have joined the blockchain P2P network and executed all smart contracts, patients will have access to their health information for home care and preventive treatment. [43]. To review all of their prior medical records, cases must have viewing authority. The power to adapt thresholds scenarios that will be monitored and adjust specifics will be available to doctors with special director access to their cases' accounts. In order for cases to obtain watching access from the blockchain protocol, a viewing authorization contract is incongruously constructed for this reason.

Login At first, the login process was set up as described. This login mechanism was used by all users of the system [44].

The participant information is saved via the interface on both the medical record homepage and doctor register homepage, which have been constructed. Upon completing the login and registration steps, registered users can identify themselves as patients and join the system by providing n samples for environment assessment. The portal for updated patient health records has been created, which allows for updates and adjustments to be made to a patient's medical record using an append interface. Additionally, participants are given a recommendation link to add new health information [45].

## Usability Evaluation

We have three parameters for the measurement of performance of the usability as Effectiveness, efficiency, and Satisfaction [28]. Although, ASQ uses to evaluate for the post-assignment assessment to quantify the client's fulfillment Blunders might be accidental activities, slips, missteps, or exclusions that a client makes while performing a task [29]. Effectiveness is how much something is effective in delivering an ideal outcome achievement and it is measured as:

## Efficiency

The mobile device currently provides numerous applications with adaptive features that offer significant convenience in overcoming existing issues such as data over-burdening. In this research, a survey was conducted on patients from various hospitals using a health tracker application, with the aim of obtaining their perspective and answers to specific questions designed to help understand our research goals. The survey involved a total of 75 participants, with 54 being male and 45 being female. The next question is would this application will be useful for patients? 89% agreed in which 52% strongly agreed and 36% agreed and 2% are neutral. Our next question is Do you think such an application would be helped to store patients' data? And we see that 93.3% of people think that this application helps store data. Our next question is Would this application help you for knowing your current condition we see 97.3% of results are positive means 97.3%

of people think that this application helps them know their current condition. Our next survey question is would this application evaluate your overall health? And we see overall 94% of people give positive responses. Our next survey question is about the usability of the application Is this application easy to use. Our next survey question is How much you would be satisfied with this application? And we see 98% of People give a positive response they are satisfied with this application. Our next survey question is Do you think that the contents of this app help you to remind routine checkups? And we see the results that 96% of people give positive responses. Our next survey question is This application would help you for new challenges? 81.3% are satisfied 14% think may be and only 2% are not agreed. Our next question is whether this application would help you with new challenges. With the help of this application, we give awareness to people from new challenges. Like covid-19 is a good example Our last question is whether this application would answer my needs. And after the use of this application 92% of people think that this app would answer my requirements.

This survey gives us real-time suggestions based on our health data and connects you to health professionals when needed.

## 4 Conclusion

Centralized and vulnerable systems are being replaced with decentralized, secure systems that have the potential to enhance the quality of medical and related services. The use of blockchain technology in healthcare has demonstrated its effectiveness in transforming traditional health record administration by providing a secure, efficient, accessible, uniform, and decentralized approach. This article provides a detailed overview of the design, implementation, and efficacy of a blockchain-based EHR administration system. Healthcare professionals can benefit greatly from this system, which allows patients, physicians, caregivers, and healthcare providers to securely and transparently access, study, and exchange health data, as well as the entire life cycle of individual health records. The suggested system prioritizes openness, security, and privacy.

## References

1. Nakamoto, S.: Bitcoin: a peer-to-peer electronic cash system. Decentralized Bus. Rev. 21260 (2008)
2. Shahnaz, A., Qamar, U., Khalid, A.: Using blockchain for electronic health records. IEEE Access **7**, 147782–147795 (2019)
3. Alghamdi, A.M., Riasat, H., Iqbal, M.W., Ashraf, M.U., Alshahrani, A., Alshamrani, A.: Intelligence and usability empowerment of smartphone adaptive features. Appl. Sci. **12**(23), 12245 (2022)
4. Hölbl, M., Kompara, M., Kamišalić, A., Nemec Zlatolas, L.: A systematic review of the use of blockchain in healthcare. Symmetry **10**(10), 470 (2018)
5. Godara, J., Aron, R., Shabaz, M.: Sentiment analysis and sarcasm detection from social network to train health-care professionals. World J. Eng. (2021)
6. Siyal, A.A., Junejo, A.Z., Zawish, M., Ahmed, K., Khalil, A., Soursou, G.: Applications of blockchain technology in medicine and healthcare: challenges and future perspectives. Cryptography **3**(1), 3 (2019)

7. Naqvi, M.R., Iqbal, M.W., Shahzad, S.K., Ashraf, M.U., Alsubhi, K., Aljahdali, H.M.: Ontological model for cohesive smart health services management. CMC-Comput. Mater. Continua **74**(2), 3679–3695 (2023)
8. Bukhari, S.N.H., et al.: Machine learning-based ensemble model for zika virus T-cell epitope prediction. J. Healthc. Eng. **2021** (2021)
9. McGhin, T., Choo, K.-K.R., Liu, C.Z., He, D.: Blockchain in healthcare applications: research challenges and opportunities. J. Netw. Comput. Appl. **135**, 62–75 (2019)
10. Yue, X., Wang, H., Jin, D., Li, M., Jiang, W.: Healthcare data gateways: found healthcare intelligence on blockchain with novel privacy risk control. J. Med. Syst. **40**(10), 1–8 (2016)
11. Ekblaw, A., Azaria, A., Halamka, J.D., Lippman, A.: A case study for blockchain in healthcare: 'MedRec' prototype for electronic health records and medical research data. Presented at the Proceedings of IEEE Open & Big Data Conference, vol. 13, p. 13 (2016)
12. Farouk, A., Alahmadi, A., Ghose, S., Mashatan, A.: Blockchain platform for industrial healthcare: vision and future opportunities. Comput. Commun. **154**, 223–235 (2020)
13. Esposito, C., De Santis, A., Tortora, G., Chang, H., Choo, K.-K.R.: Blockchain: a panacea for healthcare cloud-based data security and privacy? IEEE Cloud Comput. **5**(1), 31–37 (2018)
14. Liang, X., Zhao, J., Shetty, S., Liu, J., Li, D.: Integrating blockchain for data sharing and collaboration in mobile healthcare applications. Presented at the 2017 IEEE 28th Annual International Symposium on Personal, Indoor, and Mobile Radio Communications (PIMRC), pp. 1–5 (2017)
15. Gondal, F.K., Shahzad, S.K., Jaffar, M.A., Iqbal, M.W.: A process oriented integration model for smart health services. Intell. Autom. Soft Comput. **35**(2) (2023)
16. Yli-Huumo, J., Ko, D., Choi, S., Park, S., Smolander, K.: Where is current research on blockchain technology?—a systematic review. PLoS ONE **11**(10), e0163477 (2016)
17. Le Nguyen, T.: Blockchain in healthcare: a new technology benefit for both patients and doctors. Presented at the 2018 Portland International Conference on Management of Engineering and Technology (PICMET), pp. 1–6 (2018)
18. Miraz, M.H., Ali, M.: Applications of blockchain technology beyond cryptocurrency. ArXiv Preprint ArXiv180103528 (2018)
19. Bhuiyan, M.Z.A., Zaman, A., Wang, T., Wang, G., Tao, H., Hassan, M.M.: Blockchain and big data to transform the healthcare. Presented at the Proceedings of the International Conference on Data Processing and Applications, pp. 62–68 (2018)
20. Alzahrani, N., Bulusu, N.: Block-supply chain: a new anti-counterfeiting supply chain using NFC and blockchain. Presented at the Proceedings of the 1st Workshop on Cryptocurrencies and Blockchains for Distributed Systems, pp. 30–35 (2018)
21. Reddy, K.R.K., Gunasekaran, A., Kalpana, P., Sreedharan, V.R., Kumar, S.A.: Developing a blockchain framework for the automotive supply chain: a systematic review. Comput. Ind. Eng. **157**, 107334 (2021)
22. Kuo, T.-T., Kim, H.-E., Ohno-Machado, L.: Blockchain distributed ledger technologies for biomedical and health care applications. J. Am. Med. Inform. Assoc. **24**(6), 1211–1220 (2017)
23. Yang, H., Yang, B.: A blockchain-based approach to the secure sharing of healthcare data. Presented at the Proceedings of the Norwegian Information Security Conference, pp. 100–111 (2017)
24. Gai, K., Choo, K.-K.R., Zhu, L.: Blockchain-enabled reengineering of cloud datacenters. IEEE Cloud Comput. **5**(6), 21–25 (2018)
25. Yaqoob, I., Salah, K., Jayaraman, R., Al-Hammadi, Y.: Blockchain for healthcare data management: opportunities, challenges, and future recommendations. Neural Comput. Appl. 1–16 (2021)
26. Andola, N., Prakash, S., Venkatesan, S., Verma, S.: SHEMB: a secure approach for healthcare management system using blockchain. Presented at the 2019 IEEE Conference on Information and Communication Technology, pp. 1–6 (2019)

27. Tripathi, G., Ahad, M.A., Paiva, S.: S2HS-a blockchain based approach for smart healthcare system. Presented at the Healthcare, vol. 8, no. 1, p. 100391 (2020)
28. Parameswari, C.D., Mandadi, V.: Healthcare data protection based on blockchain using solidity. Presented at the 2020 Fourth World Conference on Smart Trends in Systems, Security and Sustainability (WorldS4), pp. 577–580 (2020)
29. Griggs, K.N., Ossipova, O., Kohlios, C.P., Baccarini, A.N., Howson, E.A., Hayajneh, T.: Healthcare blockchain system using smart contracts for secure automated remote patient monitoring. J. Med. Syst. **42**(7), 1–7 (2018)
30. Abu-Elezz, I., Hassan, A., Nazeemudeen, A., Househ, M., Abd-Alrazaq, A.: The benefits and threats of blockchain technology in healthcare: a scoping review. Int. J. Med. Inf. **142**, 104246 (2020)
31. Agbo, C.C., Mahmoud, Q.H., Eklund, J.M.: Blockchain technology in healthcare: a systematic review. Presented at the Healthcare, vol. 7, no. 2, p. 56 (2019)
32. Patel, V.: A framework for secure and decentralized sharing of medical imaging data via blockchain consensus. Health Inform. J. **25**(4), 1398–1411 (2019)
33. Haleem, A., Javaid, M., Singh, R.P., Suman, R., Rab, S.: Blockchain technology applications in healthcare: an overview. Int. J. Intell. Netw. **2**, 130–139 (2021)
34. Ratta, P., Kaur, A., Sharma, S., Shabaz, M., Dhiman, G.: Application of blockchain and internet of things in healthcare and medical sector: applications, challenges, and future perspectives. J. Food Qual. **2021** (2021)
35. Reddy, B., Aithal, P.: Blockchain as a disruptive technology in healthcare and financial services-a review based analysis on current implementations (2020)
36. Rouhani, S., Deters, R.: Blockchain based access control systems: State of the art and challenges. Presented at the IEEE/WIC/ACM International Conference on Web Intelligence, pp. 423–428 (2019)
37. Rouhani, S., Pourheidari, V., Deters, R.: Physical access control management system based on permissioned blockchain. Presented at the 2018 IEEE International Conference on Internet of Things (iThings) and IEEE Green Computing and Communications (GreenCom) and IEEE Cyber, Physical and Social Computing (CPSCom) and IEEE Smart Data (SmartData), pp. 1078–1083 (2018)
38. Agbo, C.C., Mahmoud, Q.H.: Comparison of blockchain frameworks for healthcare applications. Internet Technol. Lett. **2**(5), e122 (2019)
39. Azaria, A., Ekblaw, A., Vieira, T., Lippman, A.: Medrec: using blockchain for medical data access and permission management," presented at the 2016 2nd international conference on open and big data (OBD), pp. 25–30 (2016)
40. Tandon, A., Dhir, A., Islam, A.N., Mäntymäki, M.: Blockchain in healthcare: a systematic literature review, synthesizing framework and future research agenda. Comput. Ind. **122**, 103290 (2020)
41. Dagher, G.G., Mohler, J., Milojkovic, M., Marella, P.B.: Ancile: privacy-preserving framework for access control and interoperability of electronic health records using blockchain technology. Sustain. Cities Soc. **39**, 283–297 (2018)
42. Maqbool, S., Iqbal, M.W., Naqvi, M.R., Arif, K.S., Ahmed, M., Arif, M.: IoT based remote patient monitoring system. In: 2020 International Conference on Decision Aid Sciences and Application (DASA), pp. 1255–1260. IEEE (2020)
43. Beck, R.: Beyond bitcoin: the rise of blockchain world. Computer **51**(2), 54–58 (2018)
44. Dutta, P., Choi, T.-M., Somani, S., Butala, R.: Blockchain technology in supply chain operations: applications, challenges and research opportunities. Transp. Res. Part E Logist. Transp. Rev. **142**, 102067 (2020)
45. Shahzad, S.K., Ahmed, D., Naqvi, M.R., Mushtaq, M.T., Iqbal, M.W., Munir, F.: Ontology driven smart health service integration. Comput. Methods Programs Biomed. **207**, 106146 (2021)

# Audio Source Separation: Advances and Challenges

Fawad Nasim[1,2], Sheeraz Akram[1,2], Sohail Masood[1,2], Arfan Jaffar[1,2(✉)], Muhammad Hussain Akbar[1], and Ch Zubair Kahloon[1]

[1] Superior University, Lahore, Lahore, Pakistan
arfan.jaffar@superior.edu.pk

[2] Intelligent Data Visual Computing Research (IDVCR), Lahore, Pakistan

**Abstract.** One of the most crucial steps in processing audio signals is called audio source separation (ASS). The goal of the ASS is to separate the different parts of a mixed audio signal into their own signals. This job is hard because there may be sound sources that overlap in both time and frequency domains. Conventional ASS approaches, such as non-negative matrix factorization (NMF) and Blind Source Separation (BSS) have not been able to separate signals better than other methods. Recently, new, advanced ways have come out that show promise for ASS. Although they have their limitations, deep learning models have emerged because of their ability to detect the origin of a sound based on the statistical features of the audio data. This paper gives an overview of the different ASS techniques, discussing the different approaches used in this field and the performance evaluation metrics used to measure how well they work.

**Keywords:** audio source separation · deep learning · spectrogram · time-frequency representation · neural network · blind source separation · non-negative matrix factorization · sparse representation

## 1 Introduction

The topic of audio source separation (ASS) is crucial in the area of audio signal processing. It aims to extract individual audio sources from a mixture of sound signals. It has applications in various domains, including music production [1], speech recognition [2], audio restoration [3], and sound detection [4]. The primary goal of ASS is to extract individual audio sources from a mixed audio signal. This process is crucial in various applications such as speech enhancement, music transcription, and audio surveillance. The challenge lies in the complexity of the audio environment, where multiple sources can overlap and interact in intricate ways. Techniques used for this purpose often involve signal processing methods and machine learning algorithms, which aim to isolate and identify distinct sources based on their unique acoustic characteristics. ASS enables more focused analysis or modification of each source. Audio analysis involves examining and interpreting various characteristics of a sound signal. We will present a holistic view of sound source separation techniques, including blind source separation, deep learning-based methods, and probabilistic modeling, while also highlighting the evaluation metrics used to assess their performance (Fig. 1).

Fig. 1. Audio Source Separation

## 2 Background

The goal of this section is to present an overview of the benchmark problem and the relevant terminologies and principles of audio analysis. This section will describe the current state-of-the-art approaches that are used for Audio analysis. Numerous approaches have been proposed to tackle this problem. We will discuss a few here.

**Blind Source Separation (BSS).** Blind signal separation (BSS) [5] is a method used in signal processing and statistics to separate a set of source signals from a set of mixed signals without any knowledge of the source signals or the mixing process. The mathematical model of BSS can be represented as follows: Let's assume we have 'n' source signals, represented as **s1, s2, ..., sn**, and these signals are mixed to form **m** observed signals, represented as **x1, x2, ..., xm**. The mixing process can be represented by a matrix A of size **m × n**. The mathematical model of BSS can be written as:

$$\mathbf{X} = \mathbf{A} * \mathbf{S} \tag{1}$$

where **X** is the matrix of observed signals, **A** is the mixing matrix, and **S** is the matrix of source signals. The goal of BSS is to estimate the inverse of the mixing matrix **A**, denoted as **W**, such that when it is multiplied with **X**, we get an approximation of **S**. This can be represented as:

$$\mathbf{S\_estimated} = \mathbf{W} * \mathbf{X} \tag{2}$$

The challenge in BSS is to find the matrix **W** without any or with very little information about **A** or **S**. Various algorithms like Non-negative Matrix Factorization (NMF) and Independent Component Analysis (ICA) are used to solve this problem.

**Independent Component Analysis (ICA).** ICA [6] assumes that the sources are statistically independent, enabling the separation of the mixture based on the independence of their components. Independent Component Analysis (ICA) is an algorithmic technique used to divide a complex signal into its individual, additive elements. This process assumes that the source signals, which are non-Gaussian, are statistically independent of each other. ICA is a specific instance of a broader concept known as blind source separation. The ICA model consists of a linear equation:

$$\mathbf{X} = \mathbf{AS} \tag{3}$$

In this context, X represents the matrix of detected signals, A signifies the consolidation matrix, and S stands for the matrix of originating signals. The primary objective of this technique is to deduce the consolidation matrix A and the originating signals S, using only the detected signals X as a reference. This is achieved by finding a demixing matrix W such that $\mathbf{S} = \mathbf{WX}$. S components are designed to be as statistically independent from each other as possible. ICA is a versatile tool with numerous applications including data analysis and compression, Bayesian detection, source localization, blind identification, and deconvolution (Fig. 2).

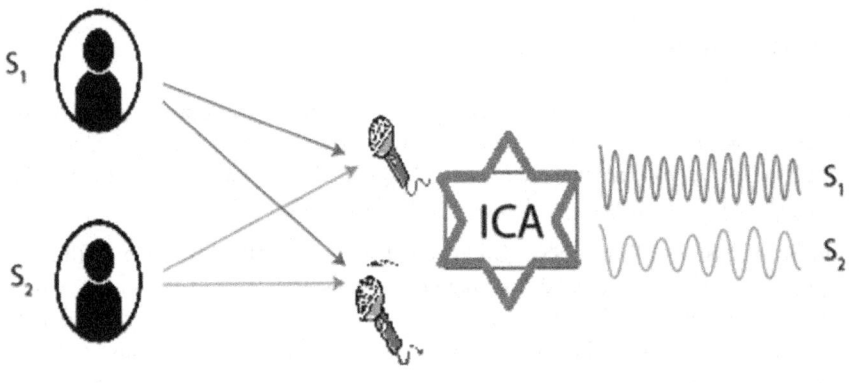

**Fig. 2.** ICA

**Non-negative Matrix Factorization (NMF):** It is another popular technique that decomposes the magnitude spectrogram into non-negative matrices, representing the sources and the mixing coefficients. By constraining the resulting matrices to be non-negative, NMF [7] facilitates the extraction of the sources from the mixture. NMF refers to a collection of algorithms used in linear algebra and multivariate analysis. In this process, a matrix V is typically decomposed into two other matrices, W and H. A key characteristic of this procedure is that all three matrices V, W, and H contain no negative elements. This non-negativity attribute simplifies the examination of the resulting matrices. The mathematical model of NMF can be represented as follows:

$$V \approx WH \tag{4}$$

where V is the original matrix, and W and H are the factorized matrices. The goal of NMF is to find W and H that minimize the difference between V and the product of W and H. This is often done using a measure such as the Frobenius norm:

$$||V - WH||^2 \tag{5}$$

where $||.||$ denotes the Frobenius norm. The Frobenius norm of a matrix is the square root of the sum of the absolute squares of its elements, and it's used as a measure of the "distance" between the original matrix V and the product of the factorized matrix WH. The goal of NMF is to minimize this distance.

**Sparse Component Analysis (SCA):** It focuses on the sparsity of the sources, assuming that most elements in the source representations are zeros. By exploiting this sparsity, SCA [8] aims to recover the original sources from the mixture. These blind source separation methods have demonstrated promising results in various sound source separation scenarios.

## 2.1 Evaluation Matrices

There are a number of metrics that can be used to evaluate the performance of ASS algorithms. Some of the most common measures include:

**Signal-to-Distortion Ratio (SDR):** It is a more comprehensive evaluation metric for ASS, which considers both the separation quality and the presence of artifacts or distortions. This is a measure of the ratio of the power of the desired signal to the power of the distortion. A higher SDR indicates that the desired signal is more clearly separated from the distortion.

**Signal-to-Noise Ratio (SNR):** This is a measure of the ratio of the power of the desired signal to the power of the noise. A higher SNR indicates that the desired signal is more clearly separated from the noise. However, SNR alone may not fully capture the perceptual quality of the separated sources, as it does not consider the presence of residual artifacts or distortions.

**Source-to-Interference Ratio (SIR):** This is an evaluation metric that focuses on the suppression of interference sources during sound source separation. It measures the ratio between the power of the desired source and the power of the interfering sources in the separated output. SIR quantifies the ability of the separation algorithm to attenuate unwanted sources and highlight the desired source. Higher SIR values indicate better interference suppression and more accurate separation of the desired source. SIR provides a valuable measure, particularly in scenarios where the mixture contains multiple overlapping sources and interference is a significant challenge.

**Perceptual Evaluation of Speech Quality (PESQ):** This is a subjective measure of the quality of speech. A higher PESQ indicates that the speech is of higher quality.

**Mean Opinion Score (MOS):** This is a subjective measure of the quality of audio. A higher MOS indicates that the audio is of higher quality.

The choice of performance measure depends on the specific application of sound source separation. For example, if the goal is to separate speech signals, then a measure such as PESQ or MOS may be more appropriate than SNR or SDR.

In addition to these objective measures, it is also important to consider the subjective quality of the separated signals. This can be done by conducting listening tests with human subjects. Listening tests can be used to evaluate a variety of factors, such as the intelligibility of speech, the naturalness of sound, and the overall quality of the audio.

**Permutation-Invariant Training (PIT):** It is a methodology used to evaluate sound source separation algorithms when the order of the separated sources is not predetermined. It addresses the issue of permutation ambiguity, where the order of the sources may differ between the separated output and the reference sources. PIT involves considering all possible permutations of the separated sources and selecting the permutation that maximizes a given evaluation metric, such as SDR. By employing PIT, sound source separation algorithms can be evaluated and compared without being penalized for incorrect source ordering, leading to more fair and robust performance assessments.

## 3 Existing Approaches

This section will describe the different state-of-the-art techniques for ASS.

### 3.1 Deep Learning-Based Methods

The results of studies show that deep learning is a promising approach for ASS. Deep learning models have the potential to revolutionize the way we interact with audio. For example, deep learning models could be used to improve the quality of voice assistants, to create new forms of music, and to make it easier for people with hearing impairments to understand speech.

DL models achieved state-of-the-art performance on a variety of ASS tasks. These models are able to learn to identify and separate sound sources by exploiting the statistical properties of audio signals. They can be used to separate sound sources in real time. But there are some of the challenges of using deep learning for ASS. They are computationally expensive to train. These are sensitive to the choice of hyper parameters. These can be susceptible to over fitting. Despite these challenges, DL is a promising approach for ASS. Deep learning models have the potential to revolutionize the way we interact with audio. In this section we will discuss different types of deep neural networks.

**Convolutional Neural Networks (CNNs):** CNN have been successfully applied to sound source separation tasks, leveraging their ability to capture local and hierarchical features in audio signals. In CNN-based sound source separation, the input audio spectrogram is treated as an image, and the network consists of multiple convolutional layers followed by pooling and non-linear activation functions. CNNs can learn discriminative filters that exploit the spectro-temporal characteristics of different sound sources, enabling effective separation. By training on large-scale datasets, CNNs can generalize well to unseen mixtures and improve the quality of separated sources. Various modifications, such as skip connections or dilated convolutions, have been incorporated into CNN architectures to enhance their performance in sound source separation tasks.

**Recurrent Neural Networks (RNNs):** RNN have shown promise in modeling the temporal dependencies of sound sources, making them suitable for sound source separation tasks. RNNs can capture the sequential patterns and long-term dependencies present in audio signals by utilizing recurrent connections. Popular RNN variants, such as Long Short-Term Memory (LSTM) and Gated Recurrent Unit (GRU), have been applied in sound source separation. These networks take the spectrogram or waveform of the mixture as input and learn to predict the separated sources. By exploiting the temporal context, RNNs can effectively model and separate sources with complex temporal dynamics, such as overlapping or rapidly changing sources.

**Generative Adversarial Networks (GANs):** A strong foundation for sound source separation has emerged using GANs. A generator network and a discriminator network make up the two primary parts of GANs. While the discriminator network tries to tell the difference between the created sources and the actual sources, the generator network learns to produce separated sources from the mixture. In order to increase the quality of the separated sources, the generator competes with the discriminator networks during the training phase. GAN-based sound source separation approaches have shown promising results, enabling the generation of high-quality separated sources and reducing artifacts or distortions compared to traditional methods.

**Variational Auto Encoders (VAEs):** These have been successfully employed in sound source separation tasks, leveraging their ability to learn latent representations of audio signals. VAEs consist of an encoder network that maps the mixture spectrogram to a lower-dimensional latent space and a decoder network that reconstructs the separated sources from the latent representation. By training the VAE on a large dataset, the latent space can capture meaningful representations of sound sources, allowing for efficient separation. VAEs can also generate novel samples by sampling from the latent space, enabling the synthesis of new sound sources. The use of VAEs in sound source separation has shown promising results in capturing the underlying structure of audio signals and improving the quality of the separated sources.

### 3.2 Probabilistic Modeling Approaches

Probabilistic modeling approaches have emerged as a powerful tool in the field of audio sound separation. These techniques leverage the inherent uncertainty and randomness in audio signals, using statistical models to represent the complex relationships between different sound sources. By treating sound sources as random variables, probabilistic models can capture the variability and unpredictability of real-world audio environments. This approach often involves the use of Bayesian inference, where prior knowledge about the sound sources is combined with observed data to make predictions. The strength of probabilistic modeling lies in its flexibility and robustness, allowing it to handle a wide range of audio separation tasks, from separating speech in a noisy environment to isolating individual instruments in a musical performance. We will discuss Gaussian Mixture Models (GMMs) Hidden Markov Models (HMMs) and Bayesian Nonparametric Models.

**Gaussian Mixture Models (GMMs):** They have the ability to model the statistical distribution of audio sources. GMMs represent each source as a mixture of Gaussian distributions, where each Gaussian component captures the characteristics of a particular source. GMM-based sound source separation involves estimating the parameters of the mixture model using the observed mixture spectrogram and then using these estimated parameters to separate the sources. GMMs can effectively handle overlapping sources by modeling their spectral characteristics and capturing the uncertainties in the source separation process. However, GMMs typically assume that the sources are stationary and do not capture the temporal dynamics present in audio signals.

**Hidden Markov Models (HMMs):** HMM has been widely employed in ASS to model the temporal dynamics of audio sources. HMMs [9] represent the sources as a sequence of hidden states, where each state corresponds to a specific source. The transitions between the states capture the temporal dependencies between the sources. HMM-based sound source separation involves training the model on labeled data and then using the trained model to estimate the most likely sequence of hidden states given the observed mixture spectrogram. By leveraging the temporal information encoded in HMMs, sound source separation can be performed effectively, especially in scenarios where the sources exhibit long-term dependencies.

**Bayesian Nonparametric Models:** They have gained attention in sound source separation as they provide a flexible framework for modeling the number of sources and their characteristics. These models, such as Dirichlet Processes and Indian Buffet Processes, do not require specifying the number of sources a priori and allow the model to adaptively determine the number of sources based on the observed data. Bayesian Nonparametric Models can capture the inherent uncertainty in sound source separation by modeling the complex relationships between sources and their distributions. These models provide a powerful tool for handling the challenges of variable and unknown source configurations in sound source separation tasks.

## 4 Challenges and Future Directions

While the field of audio source separation has made considerable advancements, it's clear that there are still many problems to overcome, paving the way for future exploration and innovation in this area. A key hurdle lies in the intricate and diverse nature of real-world audio signals. Unlike the simplicity of controlled settings, real-world situations are characterized by a myriad of intertwined sounds, fluctuating acoustics, and unforeseen noise sources. These complexities present a significant test for existing audio separation techniques, which often find it challenging to accurately segregate sources under such circumstances. Incorporating prior knowledge about the sources or the environment can significantly enhance sound source separation performance. Prior knowledge may include information about the source characteristics, spatial cues, or semantic information related to the sources. Future research should investigate methods to effectively incorporate such prior knowledge into the separation process. This can involve the development of hybrid models that combine data-driven approaches with domain-specific knowledge, leveraging semantic information from auxiliary sensors or contextual information, and exploring the use of active learning techniques to acquire and utilize prior knowledge effectively.

In summary, despite the significant strides made in the audio source separation field, there is still a wealth of work to be done. The challenges highlighted in this section serve as a guide for future research, underlining the areas where further progress and innovation are required.

# References

1. PaezTahmasebi, S., Gajcki, T., Nogueira, W.: Design and evaluation of a real-time audio source separation algorithm to remix music for cochlear implant users. Front. Neurosci. (2020)
2. Paez Amaro, R.T., Tejeda Ocampo, C., Souza Blanes, E., Bharitkar, S., Madrid Herrera, L.: Deep learning based voice extraction and primary-ambience decomposition for stereo to surround upmixing. Audio Eng. Soc. Convent. **154** (2023)
3. Rasmussen, N., Elliott, D.L., Mamun, M., Santosh, K.C.: Cough sound analysis for the evidence of Covid-19. In: Computer Vision and Machine Intelligence: Proceedings of CVMI 2022, pp. 501–512. Springer, Singapore (2023)
4. Nasim, F., Masood, S., Jaffar, A., Ahmad, U., Rashid, M.: Intelligent sound-based early fault detection system for vehicles. Comput. Syst. Sci. Eng. **46**(3), 3175–3190 (2023)
5. Debals, O., Van Barel, M., De Lathauwer, L.: Löwner-based blind signal separation of rational functions with applications. IEEE Trans. Signal Process. (2015)
6. Salimi-Khorshidi, G., Douaud, G., Beckmann, C.F., Glasser, M.F., Griffanti, L., Smith, S.M.: Automatic denoising of functional MRI data: combining independent component analysis and hierarchical fusion of classifiers. NeuroImage (2014)
7. Huang, K., Sidiropoulos, N.D., Swami, A.: Non-negative matrix factorization revisited: uniqueness and algorithm for symmetric decomposition. IEEE Trans. Signal Process. (2014)
8. Zayyani, H., Babaie-Zadeh, M., Jutten, C.: An iterative bayesian algorithm for sparse component analysis in presence of noise. IEEE Trans. Signal Process. (2009)
9. Nasim, F., Yousaf, M.A., Masood, S., Jaffar, A., Rashid, M.: Data-driven probabilistic system for batsman performance prediction in a cricket match. Intell. Autom. Soft Comput. **36**(3), 2865–2877 (2023)

# A Survey on Approximate Hardware Accelerator for Error-Tolerant Applications

Sahibzada M. Waqas[1](✉), Muhammad Zakwan[1](✉), Muhammad Ashraf[1], Ghadah Naif AlWakid[2], and Mamoona Humayun[2](✉)

[1] Department of Avionics Engineering, Air University, Islamabad, Pakistan
212110@students.au.edu.pk, {mzakwan, muhammad.ashraf}@mail.au.edu.pk
[2] College of Computer and Information Sciences, Al Jouf University, Sakakah, Saudi Arabia
{gnalwakid,mahumayun}@ju.edu.sa

**Abstract.** Approximate computing has evolved into an effective method for improving digital applications' performance and energy utilization by tolerating a slight loss in precision. By exploiting specialized hardware accelerators built with approximation circuits, the power vs. performance trade-off may be resolved across various high-computational applications. Among these are image processing, machine learning (ML) and DSP. The goal is to analyze a suitable configuration for an approximation set-up that minimizes resources while respecting the error tolerances of the systems because these applications are frequently used in systems that demand a high level of fault tolerance, such as self-driving vehicles. This study reviews current researches on approx. computing and hardware accelerators for various applications, and evaluates the claimed performance gains of many different approaches. At last, the most pressing problems and prospective avenues for utilizing it in the field of deep learning have also been outlined.

**Keywords:** Approximate computing · Error tolerant · Power-efficiency · Hardware accelerators

## 1 Introduction

Power consumption and data storage capacity are significant considerations throughout the design phase of new computer systems with dense processing. These devices are getting closer and closer to the essential energy constraints necessary for completely trustworthy computing [1]. It has been a driving force behind the development of innovative design strategies that aim to lower the amount of electricity and energy required. A proficient computational method called approximate computing (AxC) trades off computation results' precision for a more efficient use of system resources. It has evolved as a new paradigm that many applications, in which erroneous results are acceptable, prefer over conventional computing methods. In recent decades, AxC has developed as a unique strategy that is relevant to systems that have a fair resistance to faults [2]. This pattern may be used in computing that approximates the actual value of data. However, one of the most fundamental drawbacks of AxC is that it relies strongly on the data.

It is because the resulting approximate architecture is dependent on the data that was used for training. Therefore, the inaccuracy of the approximate circuit may still approach these design limits even if the final assignment is different from the training data that was utilized during the assumption made for the approximation process. The computational quality (precision of results) is compromised in order to lower the necessary computational effort (area/speed/energy/power) [3]. It is done by accepting acceptable outcomes that are created by inexact computations, mainly in areas in which human judgment plays a considerable role.

As a result of the fact that many applications do not need very accurate answers, human sensory limits can allow for the occasional acceptance of approximations. At the hardware level, approximation has been investigated to improve the energy usage of these applications that run on FPGA [4]. One example of this would be the use of approximate multipliers. Nevertheless, the level of accuracy that may be achieved using approximation computing is highly dependent on the particular application, inputs and preferences of the users. The key contributions of this study are as follows:

1. It examines all of the most recent innovative techniques that have been offered by researchers for approximations including the use of approximate hardware accelerators for error-tolerant applications with emphasis on their practicality in the field of Deep Learning.
2. It highlights the findings of these researchers, along with a statistical analysis of their gains and results.
3. It provides a comparison of all of the proposed designs and provides future research areas of approximation for the Deep Learning architectures.

This paper is structured as follows: Sect. 2 elaborates on the approximate computing and error-tolerant applications, Sect. 3 presents the literature review of the recent researches with their results, Sect. 4 provides a comparative analysis table, Sect. 5 presents the future areas, while Sect. 6 cites the conclusion of this study.

## 2 Approximate Hardware Accelerator (HWA)

**Approximate Computing.** Unfortunately, Moore's law is reaching its limit, and traditional computing methods are ineffective at enhancing performance any further, while still adhering to physical constraints like power consumption. These limits have given rise to a variety of intriguing problems as well as new challenges. Focusing on an acceptable lowering of computing accuracy without losing practicality is one of the most promising topics to investigate. This strategy is referred to as "approximate computing" that enables a controlled approximation in computation with acceptable error rates. By trading accuracy for other system parameters, this method seeks to enhance the performance, energy efficiency, and resource utilization of computing systems. In machine learning tasks, AxC can cut energy usage by up to 62% while keeping the accuracy levels to acceptable limits [1]. Additionally, AxC can significantly boost efficiency and resource utilization in many application fields, making it a practical methodology. Figure 1 shows if we increase the computational accuracy, the system becomes slower, and the more area/power it requires.

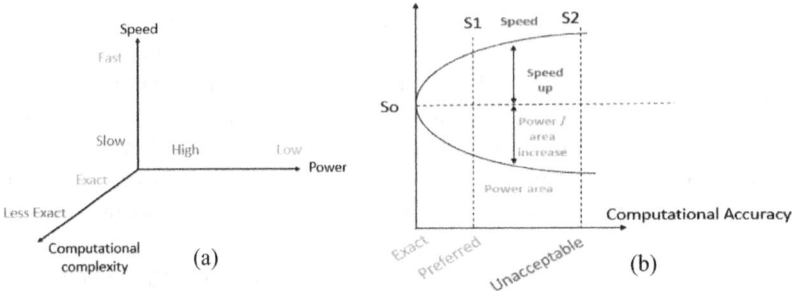

**Fig. 1.** Approximate computing design space: (a) Power, performance vs. accuracy. (b) Compromise among area, speed & error.

Accelerators that can conduct approximate calculations with tolerable error limitations are known as approximate hardware accelerators. Studies found that while keeping acceptable accuracy levels, approximation hardware accelerators can enhance energy efficiency by up to 16 times compared to traditional hardware units [2].

**Error Tolerant Applications.** Applications that can handle some degree of computational error without affecting the system's overall functionality or performance are said to be error-tolerant. This category includes many applications in domains like machine learning, image processing, and signal processing. Approximate hardware accelerators, are among other approximation techniques as listed in Table 1, that may execute imprecise computations while retaining acceptable error boundaries, which is advantageous for specific applications. These accelerators can dramatically boost the energy efficiency and performance of computing systems by making use of the error tolerance of these applications. Another example is the Deep Learning (DL) chip from Google, where the Tensor Processing Unit (TPU) significantly improves the performance by utilising established approximate computing methods. Additionally, IBM research has started a project to develop on-chip AI accelerators using AxC [3] (Fig. 2).

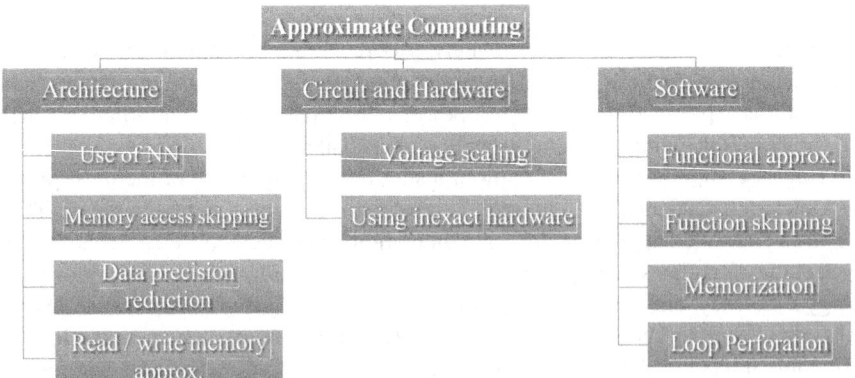

**Fig. 2.** Taxonomy for Approximate Computing (AxC) including the commonly used methods.

## 3 Literature Review

### 3.1 Reconfigurable Approx. HWA

Systems of computing that use the least amount of energy are often referred to as energy-efficient. On the other hand, the systems that were analyzed for this study may be classified as error-efficient [1] since they only produce the same number of mistakes that each of their applications can accept. In their paper, the researchers proposed an approximate Micro-Architecture Manager (MAM) that is also reconfigurable during runtime [5]. This runtime MAM can monitor the distributions relating to the workload of each approximate accelerator. It then re-configures the accelerators following the approximate micro-architecture, trained with input data distributions most similar to the current workload, thereby keeping the error under control. Because approximation computing may result in exceptionally high errors in output owing to unstable or dynamic workloads, the construction of a collection of approximate micro-architectures that are trained with a variety of input data distributions (IDDs) was also suggested in [5].

**Findings:** The approximation accelerator's random setting resulted in a 54% increase in the average inaccuracy, while SW and HW MAM versions had lower than 10%.

### 3.2 Fault Analysis for Designing Approximate HWA

The researchers suggested a technique of compiler-driven error analysis in the paper [3] to analyze the errors that are created by approximation adders in the layout of approximate accelerators. It was done in order to determine how accurate the design would be. It is feasible to compute the error behaviour as the result of any accelerator layout by first determining the source of faults and then tracing their progression through the system. It was suggested that a methodology relying on Depth-First Search (DFS) analyze the nodes in the Data Flow Graph (DFG), moving backwards from the output to the inputs. It was done by presenting the accelerator as a Data Flow Graph (DFG). Figure 3 displays a DFG having a size $3 \times 3$ Gaussian kernel. The error at the output is calculated based on the amount the value shifts to the right at the output. It makes a request for the mistake that was made by its ancestors, which in this instance is the eighth adder (S8). This adder requires the error that was generated by the seventh adder (S7) in order to function properly up to the point when the inputs are reached. For example, the sum of the errors introduced by each of the approximation adders S1 and S2 at nodes S1 and S2 is determined by the configuration of the adders.

**Findings.** Regarding Monte Carlo simulations and picture-based input data sets, research on various image-processing kernels has proven astonishingly accurate estimates. It has made it possible for speedier and more in-depth explorations of the error propagation that is produced by approximation calculations.

### 3.3 A Machine Learning Based Approximate Hardware Accelerator Assuring Quality and Dynamic Partial Reconfiguration (DPR)

The role of partial reconfiguration is somewhat like a microprocessor that can switch between jobs in the sense that PR allows the hardware resources on any device to be

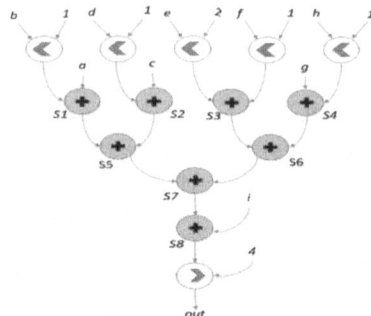

**Fig. 3.** DFG to represent a size 3 × 3 Gaussian kernel. Approximate adders potentially substitute the additions.

time-multiplexed. It enables the FPGA's utility to be significantly increased since there is no longer a requirement to completely re-configure and re-establish links. Moreover, it allows self-healing and adaptive systems that ultimately require less space to work. In [4], the researchers proposed approximate accelerators with hardware efficiency and sound quality that are suitable for implementation in FPGA-based ML algorithms along with other error-resilient applications. Deep Neural Networks (DNNs), which are a sub-domain of ML algorithms, are appropriate for error tolerance; however, these complex models have relatively colossal storage and computational requirements. Thus, an energy-efficient implementation of DNNs will have unlimited practical advantages. The suggested methodology [6] incorporated the advantages of approximation computing, DPR, and ML, which had a good influence on the area and power consumption. Moreover, researchers [6] introduced a novel design selector for an ML algorithm, i.e., a decision tree that continuously monitors the input data and readily calculates the most appropriate approx. design; in response, the selected approximate design is then partially re-configured into the FPGA while maintaining the entire error-tolerant application.

Figure 4 depicts the internal design for the approx. accelerator with 16 multipliers. The inputs, i.e., $A_j$ & $B_j$ while $j \geq 0$ & $\leq 16$, have 8-bit width. For the parallel execution, the proposed model utilizes the prevailing block RAM in Xilinx 7 series FPGAs, comprising 1,030 blocks of 36 Kbits.

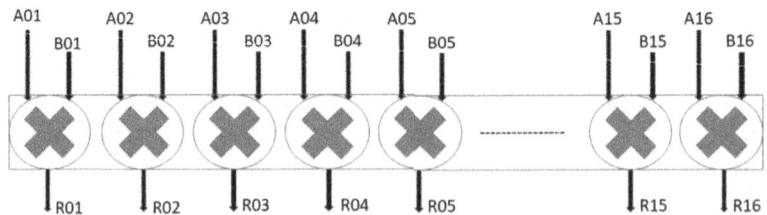

**Fig. 4.** An accelerator comprising 16 similar approx. multipliers.

**Findings.** The proposed design adaptation method was implemented around two thousand times while the target output quality (TOQ) was reached more than fifteen hundred times (PSNR used was greater than 30 dB). An overall accuracy of 81.82% was achieved.

### 3.4 Approx. Multiplier and HWA for Mobile Computing of DL Applications

The complexity and depth of a DNN rise exponentially as the number of perceptrons increases, thereby requiring a more significant number of arithmetic operations to train the network. Moreover, massive computing power and significant memory are also essential for saving the network settings, which include weights and corresponding losses. Research [5] offers an approximate radix-4 Booth multiplier and HWA for deploying DL applications on power-constrained mobile or edge computing devices. The workloads are accelerated by the proposed accelerator using approximate multiplier-based parallel processing components.

Multiplications consume 96% of the power used by MACs in a standard DNN, so reducing the power multipliers' use can considerably improve the HWA's energy efficiency. As seen in Fig. 5, the register adder, multiplier and truncation block are collectively called PE. The proposed accelerator mimics a large number of these PEs on the hardware built on the resources available on the examined FPGA fabric.

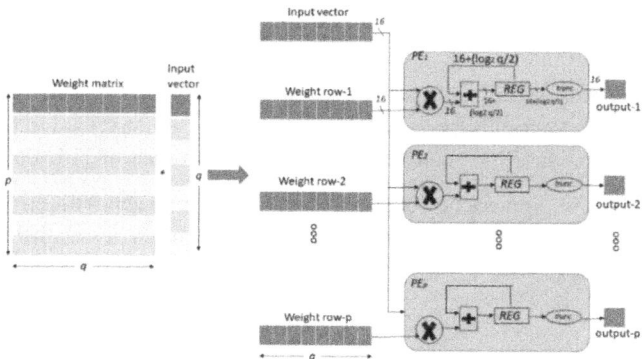

**Fig. 5.** Proposed accelerator architecture for the matrix multiplication operation.

**Findings.** The total time needed for MVM operation was cut by more than 85% for the weights of sizes [64 64] and [256 256], compared to the traditional architecture. The total number of clock cycles needed for MMM operation was decreased by 70%.

### 3.5 An Area-Efficient Consolidated Configurable Error Correction for Approximate Hardware Accelerators

Researchers presented effective Error Detection and Correction (EDC) implementations for approximative hardware accelerators in the cited study [6]. It was shown how to rectify errors that have accumulated from several additions using consolidated error correction (CEC) for cascaded adders. Only an AND gate is needed for error detection.

**Error Correction for Approximate HWA.** The majority of real-world applications use a network of adders as hardware accelerators to provide more intricate arithmetic data routes. A Consolidated Error Correction (CEC) circuit can be created by combining two approximate adders instead of separately for each one through simple changes to the proposed EC circuit. The circuit's area-on-chip is thereby decreased.

**Findings.** The proposed architecture was demonstrated as efficient in terms of the clock cycle and space requirement in comparison to the latest available designs (space requirement reduced by around 30% in CEC-8).

### 3.6 Fault-Tolerant Accelerators for Deep Neural Networks (DNN)

The performance of conventional Machine Learning (ML) methods has perhaps been surpassed by DNNs. For a variety of applications, including language translation and image and video recognition, they are the most appropriate option. These DNNs, however, have many parameters and require a lot of processing power to train and test. Therefore, designing specialized HWA for DNN implementation to enhance power and performance efficiency is becoming increasingly popular.

In [7], the challenge of developing error-tolerant HWA for DNN execution in high fault rate technologies is addressed by the researchers. The study put forth Fault-Aware Pruning (FAP), a method that demonstrates that a sizable percentage of a DNN's nodes can be trimmed without any effect on results. Beginning with the discovery that each weight in the DNN translates to precisely one MAC unit, as described in the section on "DNN Acceleration on TPU", comes the suggested fault-tolerant TPU design.

**Findings.** The novel approaches enable TPUs to function even with errors as high as 50% while experiencing a tolerable reduction in the accuracy of results/map (ranging from 0.1% for TIMIT to 1.7% for AlexNet). Both methods have no runtime performance overhead.

### 3.7 Multi-level Approximate Accelerator Synthesis Under Voltage Island Constraints

The circuit's latency and the quantity of critical paths are reduced via logical and algorithmic approximations [8]. Due to the fact that fewer routes are impacted by the voltage fall, VOS further reduces energy usage at the cost of a minor increase in error. The approximate accelerator synthesis idea proposed in [9] is built upon a collection of approximate arithmetic components. The approximation is applied in different layers. Figure 6 shows the proposed architecture for approx. accelerator synthesis. The proposed design of multi-layer approx. the accelerator is depicted in the Fig. 6.

**Findings.** The solutions offered by this architecture outperform single-level approaches for available benchmark and error bound. For instance, 5% error bound. For the Sobel, matrix multiplication, and DCT benchmarks, respectively, the proposed designs consume

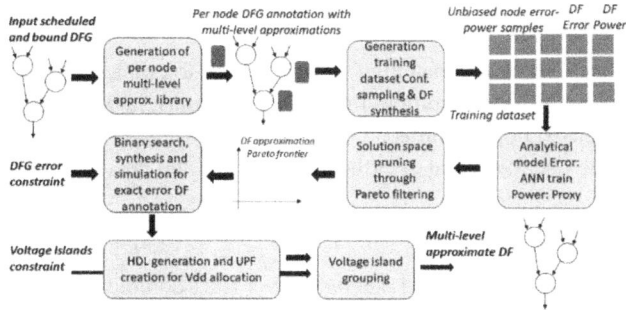

**Fig. 6.** The presented architecture for multi-level approx. accelerators.

61%, 40%, and 49% less power than the actual (non-approximate) designs when the island restriction is not followed.

### 3.8 Complexity Reduction of Fault-Tolerant System via Approximate Computing

The disciplines of DSP and image processing are where many applications utilizing hardware accelerators originate. These programmes have a rare capacity to tolerate specific output error levels. [10] suggests an automated process that will provide approx. Duplication With Compare (DWC) redundancy systems that are assured of producing accuracy within a specified maximum limits of error.

**Findings.** The proposed methodology was 28 times faster, on average than the exhaustive search in terms of required time, with the time increasing with the increase in FUs in the design.

### 3.9 Improving Power of DSP and CNN Hardware Accelerators Using Approximate Floating-Point Multipliers

Floating point (FP) arithmetic offers a more excellent range of values and higher accuracy for similar word length with a simplified programming approach, but at the same time, suffers from added hardware expense [11]. The work [12] discussed how the rising expense of floating-point multiplicators' hardware renders them unsuitable for embedded computing. An area/power efficient multiplier family called AFMU (Approximate Floating-point Multiplier) was introduced by researchers that employ two approximation methods in the resource-demanding mantissa multiplication and may be easily expanded to accommodate the setting of the approximation levels through gating signals.

**Findings.** According to the evaluation, AFMU produces energy gains between 3.6% and 53.5% for half-precision and 37.2% to 82% for single-precision, for mean relative errors of 0.5% to 3.33% and 0.1% to 2.20, respectively. This level of accuracy is accomplished while offering around 60–67% area and 57-6w% gains in power.

## 3.10 Approx. the Sum of Absolute Differences HW for FPGAs

A standard metric for block matching in many fault-tolerant systems is the sum of absolute differences (SAD) operation. In these applications, including stereo vision and video coding, the SAD operation is a commonly employed metric for block matching [13]; also, it is the operation that uses the greatest time and energy (1).

$$S = \left\{(-1)^{X_n} X\right\} + \left\{(-1)^{Y_n} Y - Y_n\right\} \tag{1}$$

where $X_n$ and $Y_n$ can either be 0 or 1, keeping $X_n = 1$, 2's complement of X is calculated, while keeping $Y_n = 1$, 1's complement of Y is calculated. The proposed adder/subtractor calculates the values of the two subtraction results for further addition.

**Findings.** The maximum and average errors of the demonstrated approx. SAD hardware is lower than those already described in the available literature. It utilizes up to 20% fewer LUTs and up to 38% less energy than the smallest approximation SAD.

## 3.11 MACISH: MAC Accelerators with Internal-Self-Healing

In comparison to conventional approximate computation approaches that limit errors, self-healing algorithms have shown to be a good compromise between quality and efficiency. Internal Self-Healing (ISH) is a ground-breaking methodology that researchers suggest in [14]. By enabling self-repairing within a system internally without needing a paired/parallel module, ISH opens the use of uneven data channels. For creating an approximative multiply-accumulate (xMAC), this ISH mechanism is used. According to Fig. 7 below, the multiplier is thought of as an approx. stage and the accumulator as a repairing stage.

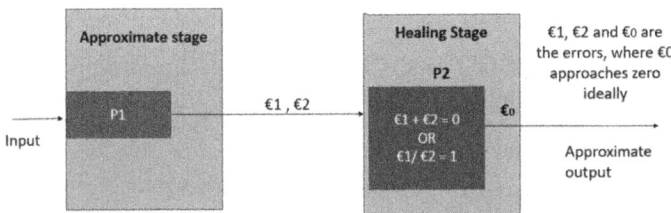

**Fig. 7.** Proposed ISH computing methodology

**Findings.** The presented ISH framework results in 55% better output for an iMac.

## 3.12 ENAP: An Efficient Number-Aware Pruning Technique of Approximate Configurations

[15] suggested using an effective number-aware pruning (ENAP) technique to choose the right configuration from several approximation units with distinct error characteristics in order to reduce resources while maintaining user-defined error tolerance.

**Findings.** Though not very significant, a compression rate of 0.0008% of search space, i.e., pruning, was demonstrated.

### 3.13 Approximate Computing Using Code Design in DNNs

In addition, coordinated software and hardware designs have been presented to produce effective, high-performing, and dedicated outputs using approximations. [16] proposed to integrate approximate circuits with DNN algorithms using the incremental network approximation (INA) technique with acceptable loss of accuracy. DNNs are encouraged to be fault tolerant by INA, which leads to greater trade-offs between accuracy and setup costs.

**Findings.** The approximate inference models that INA retrained caused reduction up to 80% at different hardware design levels, while mere decrease of 2% accuracy.

### 3.14 Increase in Approximation Requirement for DL Architectures

As elaborated in the reviewed works [15, 16], it becomes extremely challenging to deploy deep CNNs on resource-constrained edge devices with computational restraints. So, present researches have focused on approximating existing DL models, as much as possible. These approximations have reduced the FLOPS (floating-point operations per second) of existing DL architectures like VGG-16 and Resnet-50 by 77% and 47% respectively; with only a drop of 2% in accuracy [17]. Further researches in this domain have rendered significant and encouraging results.

## 4 Comparison Summary

Table 1. Comparison summary of research reviewed.

| Ref | Description of Research | Year | Results |
|---|---|---|---|
| [18] | Approximate Reconfigurable Hardware Accelerator (HWA) | 2017 | The average error was reduced from 54% to 10% |
| [19] | Approximate Accelerators Compiler-Driven | 2018 | Accurate results and Monte Carlo simulations for image data |

(*continued*)

**Table 1.** (*continued*)

| Ref | Description of Research | Year | Results |
|---|---|---|---|
| [4] | Approximate HWA–based on ML and DPR | 2021 | The accuracy of obtained results was 81.82% |
| [5] | Approx. multiplier and HW for edge computing of DL applications | 2021 | Timing of MVM & MMM reduced by 88% & 70%, respectively |
| [6] | Configurable Error Correction for Approx. HWA | 2016 | Space reduction of around 30% was shown |
| [7] | Fault-Tolerant Accelerators for DNN Execution | 2019 | Enables TPU operation even with error of 50% (AlexNet used) |
| [9] | Multi-Level Approx. Accelerator Synthesis Under Voltage Island Constraints | 2019 | Less power consumption of 61%, 40%, and 49% |
| [10] | Reducing the Complexity of Fault-Tolerant Systems Amenable to Approx. Computing | 2021 | In terms of speed, the proposed method was 28 times faster |
| [12] | Improving Power of DSP and CNN HW Using Approx. Floating-point Multipliers | 2021 | Power reduction of 57.4%, area up to 60.4% and power gains of 57.4% attained |
| [13] | Approx. The sum of Absolute Differences HW for FPGAs | 2021 | A reduction of 38% in power usage was demonstrated |
| [14] | Approx. MAC Accelerators design with Internal Self-Healing | 2019 | Around 55% improved output for equivalent-efficiency designs |
| [15] | Pruning Methodology for Design and Space Exploration | 2023 | A compression rate of 0.0008% was achieved |
| [16] | Approx. computing in DNN using code design | 2019 | Up to 80% reduction in hardware design level achieved |

## 5 Future Challenges

For future researches, various Deep Learning algorithms need to be examined for sound output and lower implementation costs. Approximate CNNs for already existing models like AlexNet, VGG-16 and Incetion-V3 may further be pruned and validated by layer-wise pruning of approximable neurons [20], similarly an extensive error-immune analysis of approximate CNNs [21] must also be looked into. Further, research can be focused on its applications like lightweight and low-cost aerial imaging solutions for small drones [22].

## 6 Conclusion

Design approx. implemented at the hardware level, such as approximate multipliers, is a feasible way to improve the power efficiency of FPGA-based fault-tolerant systems based on the studied proposed models. However, it calls for caution because, when applied to static approximate systems, a few approximate computing techniques can result in significant output inaccuracies, particularly for non-static inputs. In the reviewed research [3–17], different optimizations for data gathering, transporting, and storing have been proposed to enhance the data performance of systems. [19] and [4] provide accurate estimation results with regards to specific experimental set-ups; [6] provide significant area overhead reduction; [9, 12], and [13] provide noteworthy power requirement reduction; while [10] through the concept of asymmetric module redundancy significantly simplifies the resultant circuits. A novel design [7] enables TPUs to function even with errors around 50%, with minimum drops in results accuracy/mAP. Leveraging the efficiency of multi-level approximation [9] produces high-speed solutions that outperform single-level state-of-the-art approximate techniques.

## References

1. Rodrigues, G., Lima Kastensmidt, F., Bosio, A.: Survey on approximate computing and its intrinsic fault tolerance. Electronics **9**(4), 557 (2020). https://doi.org/10.3390/electronics9040557
2. Xu, Q., Mytkowicz, T., Kim, N.S.: Approximate computing: a survey. IEEE Des. Test **33**(1), 8–22 (2016). https://doi.org/10.1109/MDAT.2015.2505723
3. Liu, W., Gu, C., O'Neill, M., Qu, G., Montuschi, P., Lombardi, F.: Security in approximate computing and approximate computing for security: challenges and opportunities. Proc. IEEE **108**(12), 2214–2231 (2020). https://doi.org/10.1109/JPROC.2020.3030121
4. Masadeh, M., Elderhalli, Y., Hasan, O., Tahar, S.: A quality-assured approximate hardware accelerators–based on machine learning and dynamic partial reconfiguration. ACM J. Emerg. Technol. Comput. Syst. **17**(4), 1–19 (2021). https://doi.org/10.1145/3462329
5. Manikantta Reddy, K., Vasantha, M.H., Nithin Kumar, Y.B., Keshava Gopal, C., Dwivedi, D.: Quantization aware approximate multiplier and hardware accelerator for edge computing of deep learning applications. Integration **81**, 268–279 (2021). https://doi.org/10.1016/j.vlsi.2021.08.001
6. Mazahir, S., Hasan, O., Hafiz, R., Shafique, M., Henkel, J.: An area-efficient consolidated configurable error correction for approximate hardware accelerators. In: Proceedings of the 53rd Annual Design Automation Conference, Austin, Texas, pp. 1–6. ACM (2016). https://doi.org/10.1145/2897937.2897981
7. Zhang, J.J., Basu, K., Garg, S.: Fault-tolerant systolic array based accelerators for deep neural network execution. IEEE Des. Test **36**(5), 44–53 (2019). https://doi.org/10.1109/MDAT.2019.2915656
8. Lee, S., John, L.K., Gerstlauer, A.: High-level synthesis of approximate hardware under joint precision and voltage scaling. In: Design, Automation & Test in Europe Conference & Exhibition (DATE), Lausanne, Switzerland, pp. 187–192. IEEE (2017). https://doi.org/10.23919/DATE.2017.7926980
9. Zervakis, G., Xydis, S., Soudris, D., Pekmestzi, K.: Multi-level approximate accelerator synthesis under voltage island constraints. IEEE Trans. Circuits Syst. II Express Briefs **66**(4), 607–611 (2019). https://doi.org/10.1109/TCSII.2018.2869025
10. Zhu, Z., Schafer, B.C.: Reducing the complexity of fault-tolerant system amenable to approximate computing. In: 2021 IEEE International Symposium on Circuits and Systems (ISCAS), Daegu, Korea, pp. 1–5. IEEE (2021). https://doi.org/10.1109/ISCAS51556.2021.9401605
11. Yin, P., Wang, C., Liu, W., Swartzlander, E.E., Lombardi, F.: Designs of approximate floating-point multipliers with variable accuracy for error-tolerant applications. J. Signal Process. Syst. **90**(4), 641–654 (2018). https://doi.org/10.1007/s11265-017-1280-4

12. Leon, V., Paparouni, T., Petrongonas, E., Soudris, D., Pekmestzi, K.: Improving power of DSP and CNN hardware accelerators using approximate floating-point multipliers. ACM Trans. Embed. Comput. Syst. **20**(5), 1–21 (2021). https://doi.org/10.1145/3448980
13. Ahmad, W., Hamzaoglu, I.: An efficient approximate sum of absolute differences hardware for FPGAs. In: 2021 IEEE International Conference on Consumer Electronics (ICCE), Las Vegas, NV, USA, pp. 1–5. IEEE (2021). https://doi.org/10.1109/ICCE50685.2021.9427756
14. Gillani, G.A., Hanif, M.A., Verstoep, B., Gerez, S.H., Shafique, M., Kokkeler, A.B.J.: MACISH: designing approximate MAC accelerators with internal-self-healing. IEEE Access **7**, 77142–77160 (2019). https://doi.org/10.1109/ACCESS.2019.2920335
15. Dou, Y., Wang, C., Woods, R., Liu, W.: ENAP: an efficient number-aware pruning framework for design space exploration of approximate configurations. IEEE Trans. Circuits Syst. Regul. Pap. 1–12 (2023). https://doi.org/10.1109/TCSI.2023.3252483
16. Liu, Z., Jia, K., Liu, W., Wei, Q., Qiao, F., Yang, H.: INA: incremental network approximation algorithm for limited precision deep neural networks (2019)
17. Courbariaux, M., Hubara, I., Soudry, D., El-Yaniv, R., Bengio, Y.: Binarized neural networks: training deep neural networks with weights and activations constrained to $+1$ or $-1$. arXiv (2016). http://arxiv.org/abs/1602.02830. Accessed 09 May 2023
18. Xu, S., Schafer, B.C.: Approximate reconfigurable hardware accelerator: adapting the microarchitecture to dynamic workloads. In: 2017 IEEE International Conference on Computer Design (ICCD), Boston, MA, pp. 113–120. IEEE (2017). https://doi.org/10.1109/ICCD.2017.25
19. Castro-Godinez, J., Esser, S., Shafique, M., Pagani, S., Henkel, J.: Compiler-driven error analysis for designing approximate accelerators. In: 2018 Design, Automation & Test in Europe Conference & Exhibition (DATE), Dresden, Germany, pp. 1027–1032. IEEE (2018). https://doi.org/10.23919/DATE.2018.8342163
20. Gebregirogis, A., Tahoori, M.: Approximate learning and fault-tolerant mapping for energy-efficient neuromorphic systems. ACM Trans. Des. Autom. Electron. Syst. **26**(3), 1–23 (2021). https://doi.org/10.1145/3436491
21. Siddique, A., Hoque, K.A.: Exposing reliability degradation and mitigation in approximate DNNs under permanent faults. IEEE Trans. Very Large Scale Integr. VLSI Syst. **31**(4), 555–566 (2023). https://doi.org/10.1109/TVLSI.2023.3238907
22. Nomani, T., Mohsin, M., Pervaiz, Z., Shafique, M.: XUAVs: towards efficient approximate computing for UAVs—low power approximate adders with single LUT delay for FPGA-based aerial imaging optimization. IEEE Access **8**, 102982–102996 (2020). https://doi.org/10.1109/ACCESS.2020.2998957

# Deep Learning Based Multi Focus Image Fusion

Muhammad Ahmed[✉], Arfan Jaffer, and Natasha Ali

Superior University Lahore, Lahore, Pakistan
ahmadkahloon@superior.edu.pk

**Abstract.** Activity level measurement and fusion rule are crucial factors in image fusion. Existing fusion methods often employ local filters and elaborate rules to measure activity levels and compare clarity information of source images, resulting in a clarity/focus map. This map contains integrated clarity information, which is significant for various image fusion tasks such as multi-focus image fusion and multi-modal image fusion. However, achieving satisfactory fusion performance with these methods is challenging. This research addresses this challenge through a deep learning approach, aiming to learn a direct mapping between source images and the focus map. To accomplish this, a deep convolutional neural network (CNN) is employed, trained using high-quality image patches and their blurred versions to encode the mapping. The key innovation lies in jointly generating the activity level measurement and fusion rule through the learned CNN model, overcoming the difficulties faced by existing fusion methods. This paper primarily proposes a novel multi-focus image fusion method based on this idea. Experimental results demonstrate that the proposed method achieves state-of-the-art fusion performance in terms of visual quality and objective assessment. The computational speed of the proposed method using parallel computing is sufficiently fast for practical usage. Additionally, the potential of the learned CNN model for other image fusion tasks is briefly exhibited in the experiments.

**Keywords:** Image Fusion · Deep Learning · CNN

## 1 Introduction

In the domain of digital photography, capturing an image where all objects are in focus poses a challenge for imaging devices such as digital single-lens reflex cameras. Typically, when using a specific focal setting of the optical lens, only objects within the depth-of-field (DOF) appear sharp in the photograph, while others may appear blurred. To address this issue, the technique of multi-focus image fusion has been developed, which involves merging multiple images of the same scene taken with different focal settings. This technique falls within the broader field of image fusion and finds application in tasks like visible-infrared image fusion and multi-modal medical image fusion. Consequently, the study of multi-focus image fusion holds a twofold significance and remains an active topic within the image processing community [1].

Over the years, various methods for image fusion have been proposed, broadly classified into two categories: transform domain methods and spatial domain methods [1].

Transform domain fusion methods, particularly those based on multi-scale transform (MST) theories, have been widely utilized in image fusion for more than three decades. One of the pioneering MST-based methods is the Laplacian pyramid (LP)-based fusion method [2]. Since then, numerous MST-based image fusion methods have emerged, including the morphological pyramid (MP)-based method [3], the discrete wavelet transform (DWT)-based method [4], the dual-tree complex wavelet transform (DTCWT)-based method [5], and the non-subsampled contourlet transform (NSCT)-based method [6]. These methods share a common framework consisting of decomposition, fusion, and reconstruction steps [7]. The fundamental assumption of MST-based methods is that the activity level of source images can be measured through the decomposed coefficients in a selected transform domain. Additionally, significant efforts have been devoted to designing fusion rules for merging decomposed coefficients [8–11].

Recent advancements have introduced a new branch of transform domain fusion methods [12–16]. In contrast to the aforementioned MST-based methods, these approaches transform images into a single-scale feature domain using advanced signal representation theories like independent component analysis (ICA) and sparse representation (SR). Typically, these methods employ the sliding window technique to achieve an approximate shift-invariant fusion process. The key challenge lies in identifying an effective feature domain for measuring the activity level. For example, the SR-based method [13], which is a representative approach in this category, transforms source image patches into the sparse domain and utilizes the L1-norm of sparse coefficients as the activity level measurement.

Early spatial domain methods often adopt a block-based fusion strategy, where source images are decomposed into blocks, and each pair of blocks is fused based on a designed activity level measurement, such as spatial frequency and sum-modified Laplacian [17]. The choice of block size significantly impacts the quality of fusion results. From the initial manually fixed block sizes [18, 19], improved versions have been proposed, including the adaptive block-based method that uses the differential evolution algorithm to determine an optimal block size [20], as well as quad-tree-based methods that adaptively divide images into blocks of varying sizes according to the image content [21, 22]. Another category of spatial domain methods is based on image segmentation, sharing the concept of block-based methods but heavily relying on segmentation accuracy for fusion quality [23, 24]. Recent years have witnessed the introduction of novel pixel-based spatial domain methods [25–31] that leverage gradient information and have achieved state-of-the-art results in multi-focus image fusion. These methods often employ complex fusion schemes to calculate activity level measurements. It is worth noting that both transform domain and spatial domain image fusion methods consider activity level measurement and fusion rule as critical factors. In most existing methods, these factors are addressed separately and designed manually [32].

In the field of image fusion, activity level measurement and fusion rule are crucial factors for both transform domain and spatial domain methods. Existing fusion methods often address these issues separately and rely on manual design [32]. However, recent approaches have become increasingly complex in their attempts to improve image fusion. For example, MST-based methods have introduced new transform domains [33, 34] and fusion rules [9–11], while SR-based methods have incorporated new sparse models and complex fusion rules [35–37]. Similarly, block-based methods have proposed new focus measures [21, 22], and pixel-based methods have introduced novel activity level measurements and intricate fusion schemes [26–30]. These works, all published within the last five years, highlight the importance of elaborate activity level measurements and fusion rules, but manual design remains challenging due to the difficulty of considering all necessary factors.

To address this issue, this paper presents a deep learning approach for image fusion, specifically focusing on multi-focus image fusion in the spatial domain. The proposed method utilizes a deep convolutional neural network (CNN) [38] trained on high-quality image patches and their blurred versions to learn a direct mapping between source images and a focus map. The focus map represents pixel-level clarity information obtained by comparing the activity level measures of the source images. The main innovation lies in jointly generating the activity level measurement and fusion rule through CNN learning, which overcomes the limitations of existing fusion methods.

The proposed method demonstrates reliable results, as the focus map obtained from the CNN can be verified using simple consistency techniques, leading to high-quality fusion outcomes. Furthermore, the computational speed of the method is fast enough for practical usage, thanks to parallel computing. Finally, the potential of the learned CNN model for other image fusion tasks, such as visible-infrared image fusion, medical image fusion, and multi-exposure image fusion, is briefly discussed.

It is worth noting that this paper represents the first application of a convolutional neural network to an image fusion task. While a similar work by Li et al. [19] presented a fusion method based on artificial neural networks, significant differences exist between their method and ours. In [19], focus measures are calculated separately, and a three-layer network acts as a classifier for fusion rule design, requiring patch-by-patch fusion. In contrast, our CNN model simultaneously performs activity level measurement and fusion rule design using the original image content as input. This approach allows for deeper networks compared to the "shallow" network used in [19]. Furthermore, with the increasing popularity of GPU parallel computation, computational speed is no longer a concern for CNN-based fusion. Additionally, the convolutional nature of CNNs enables the input of source images as a whole, further improving computational efficiency [39].

## 2 CNN Model for Image Fusion

### 2.1 CNN

CNN, or Convolutional Neural Network, is a deep learning model that aims to learn a hierarchical feature representation mechanism for signal and image data, capturing different levels of abstraction [40]. It is a trainable multi-stage feed-forward artificial neural network, where each stage consists of feature maps representing different levels of abstraction for features. Neurons within these feature maps are responsible for computing specific units or coefficients. CNNs employ operations like linear convolution, non-linear activation, and spatial pooling to connect feature maps across stages. The fundamental architectural ideas behind CNNs are local receptive fields, shared weights, and sub-sampling [38].

The concept of local receptive fields implies that neurons at a particular stage are only connected to a few spatially neighboring neurons from the previous stage, resembling the mechanism observed in the visual cortex of mammals. This means that CNNs perform local convolutional operations on input neurons, in contrast to the fully-connected mechanism used in traditional multilayer perceptrons. The idea of shared weights suggests that the weights of a convolutional kernel are invariant across the feature maps within a specific stage. Combining these two ideas significantly reduces the number of weights that need to be trained. Mathematically, given the i-th input feature map (x_i) and j-th output feature map (y_j) of a convolutional layer, the 3D convolution and non-linear ReLU activation [41] in CNNs are expressed jointly,

$$y^j = max(0, b^j + \sum_i k^{ij} * x^i), \quad (1)$$

With k_ij representing the convolutional kernel between x_i and y_j, and b_j denoting the bias. The symbol "*" denotes the convolutional operation. When there are M input maps and N output maps, this layer will contain N 3D kernels of size d × d × M (d × d denotes the size of local receptive fields), each associated with a bias term.

The third idea, sub-sampling or pooling, is used to reduce the dimensionality of the data. Max-pooling and average-pooling are common pooling operations employed in CNNs. For instance, the max-pooling operation can be defined as follows:

$$y^i_{r,c} = \max_{0 \leq m,n < s} \left\{ x^i_{r.s+m, c.s+n} \right\}, \quad (2)$$

The neuron y_i^(r,c) located at position (r,c) in the i-th output map of a max-pooling layer is assigned the maximal value within a local region of size s × s in the i-th input map x_i. By integrating these three ideas, convolutional networks can acquire important invariances regarding translation and scale to some extent.

One landmark success in CNNs was achieved by Krizhevsky et al. [42], who proposed a CNN model for image classification. Over the past three years, CNNs have been successfully applied to various computer vision tasks, spanning from high-level tasks like face detection [43], face recognition [44], semantic segmentation [45], super-resolution [46], and patch similarity comparison [47] to low-level tasks. CNN-based methods have consistently outperformed conventional approaches in their respective domains, owing to advancements in powerful GPUs, effective training techniques, and the availability of large-scale image datasets. These factors have also contributed to the advancements made in this study.

## 2.2 CNNs for Image Fusion

### 2.2.1 Feasibility

As mentioned previously, the generation of a focus map in image fusion can be considered as a classification problem [19]. In this context, the activity level measurement serves as a form of feature extraction, while the fusion rule plays a role similar to a classifier used in general classification tasks. Therefore, it is theoretically viable to utilize CNNs for image fusion. The CNN architecture employed for visual classification is an end-to-end framework [38], where the input is an image and the output is a label vector indicating the probability for each category. Within the network, several convolutional layers (followed by non-linear layers like ReLU, which are not explicitly mentioned later) and max-pooling layers are present, along with fully-connected layers. The convolutional and max-pooling layers are commonly considered as the feature extraction component, while the fully-connected layers at the output end are associated with the classification part.

This perspective can be further clarified from an implementation standpoint. In many existing fusion methods, whether in the spatial or transform domain, activity level measurement is often realized through the design of local filters for extracting high-frequency details. For transform domain fusion methods, the images or image patches are typically represented using a set of pre-designed bases like wavelets or trained dictionary atoms. From an image processing perspective, this is equivalent to convolving them with those bases [46]. For example, discrete wavelet transform implementation relies on filtering. Similarly, in spatial domain fusion methods, many activity level measurements are based on high-pass spatial filtering. Moreover, the fusion rule, which determines the weight assignment strategy for different source images based on the calculated activity level measures, can also be expressed in a filtering-based form. Considering that the fundamental operation in a CNN model is convolution (with the fully-connected operation viewed as convolution with a kernel size equal to the spatial size of the input data [45]), it is practically feasible to apply CNNs to image fusion.

### 2.2.2 Superiority

The superiority of CNN-based fusion methods over existing approaches, akin to visual object classification applications, can be attributed to two main factors. Firstly, it circumvents the challenge of manually designing complex activity level measurements and fusion rules by shifting the focus towards network architecture design. With the availability of user-friendly CNN platforms like Caffe [48] and MatConvNet [49], researchers find it more convenient to implement network designs. Secondly, and more importantly, the CNN-based approach allows for the joint generation of activity level measurements and fusion rules through learning a CNN model. The learned outcome can be regarded as an "optimal" solution to some extent, and thus is likely to be more effective than manually designed alternatives. Consequently, CNN-based methods have a significant potential to generate fusion results of higher quality compared to conventional approaches.

## 3 The Proposed Method

### 3.1 Overview

In this section, we provide a detailed explanation of our CNN-based multi-focus image fusion method. The algorithm's schematic diagram is depicted in Fig. 1. Our focus in this study primarily revolves around scenarios involving two pre-registered source images. However, for situations with more than two multi-focus images, they can be fused sequentially, one by one. The method consists of four key steps: focus detection, initial segmentation, consistency verification, and fusion. In the focus detection step, the two source images are inputted into a pre-trained CNN model, resulting in a score map that encapsulates focus information from the source images. Each coefficient in the score map represents the focus property of corresponding patch pairs from the two images. Next, the score map is used to generate a focus map of the same size as the source images by averaging the overlapping patches. Subsequently, the focus map is segmented into a binary map using a threshold of 0.5 in the second step. The binary segmented map is then refined in the third step through two popular consistency verification strategies: small region removal and guided image filtering [50], producing the final decision map. Finally, in the last step, the fused image is obtained by employing a pixel-wise weighted-average strategy with the final decision map.

### 3.2 Network Design

In this study, the problem of multi-focus image fusion is approached as a two-class classification task. Our objective is to train a Convolutional Neural Network (CNN) that can output a scalar value between 0 and 1. Specifically, the network should produce a value close to 1 when one image patch (pA) is in focus while the other patch (pB) is defocused, and a value close to 0 when pB is in focus while pA is defocused. This scalar output represents the focus property of the patch pair. To achieve this, we utilize a large number of training examples consisting of patch pairs from the same scene. A positive example is defined when pA is clearer than pB (label set to 1), and a negative example is defined when pB is clearer than pA (label set to 0).

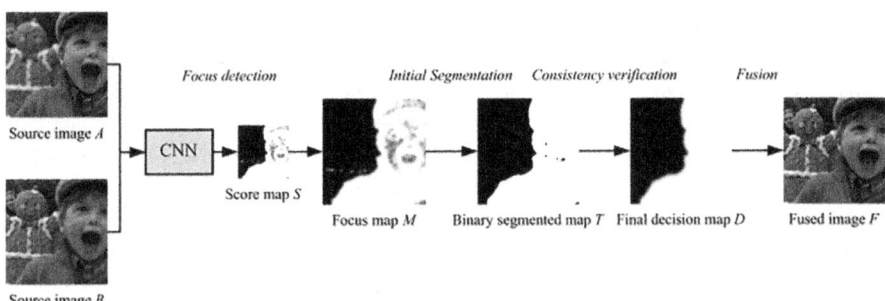

**Fig. 1.** Schematic diagram of the proposed CNN-based multi-focus image fusion algorithm. Data courtesy of M. Nejati [30].

To handle source images of arbitrary size, we explore two approaches. The first approach involves dividing the images into overlapping patches using a sliding-window technique and feeding each patch pair into the network individually. However, this method can be computationally expensive due to the extensive overlap and repeated calculations. The second approach is to input the entire source images into the network without patch division, generating a dense prediction map directly. This approach requires converting the fully-connected layers into convolutional layers by reshaping the parameters. The advantage of this approach is that it allows the network to process source images of any size as a whole, resulting in a score map where each coefficient represents the focus property of a patch pair. The patch size used in training matches the size of the training examples.

Regarding the CNN model, three types of networks are presented in [47]: siamese, pseudo-siamese, and 2-channel. The siamese network and pseudo-siamese network have two branches with the same architecture, differing in weight sharing. The 2-channel network concatenates the two patches as a 2-channel image input. Any solution from the siamese or pseudo-siamese network can be reshaped into the 2-channel format, providing more flexibility. In this work, the siamese network is chosen as the CNN model for two reasons. Firstly, it aligns well with image fusion tasks as the approach of feature extraction and activity level measurement is identical for both source images. Secondly, the siamese network tends to be easier to train due to its smaller solution space compared to the other two types.

Another crucial aspect in network design is the selection of input patch size. While a larger patch size (e.g., 32 × 32) generally improves classification accuracy by capturing more image content, it can lead to block artifacts when multiple max-pooling layers are involved. Conversely, using only one max-pooling layer can result in a large CNN model size due to increased weights in the fully-connected layers. Furthermore, a patch size of 32 × 32 is not always optimal for multi-focus image fusion as it may encompass both focused and defocused regions, causing undesired results at the boundary regions. Based on considerations and experiments, a patch size of 16 × 16 is set for this study.

The CNN model used in the proposed fusion algorithm consists of three convolutional layers and one max-pooling layer in each branch. The kernel size for convolutional layers is set to 3 × 3, and the stride is 1. The max-pooling layer has a kernel size and stride of 2 × 2. The 256 feature maps obtained from each branch are concatenated and fully connected to a 256-dimensional feature vector. The network output is a 2-dimensional vector that is passed through a 2-way softmax layer, producing a probability distribution over the two classes. During the test/fusion process, the fully-connected layers are converted into convolutional layers, allowing the network to handle source images of arbitrary size and generate a dense score map.

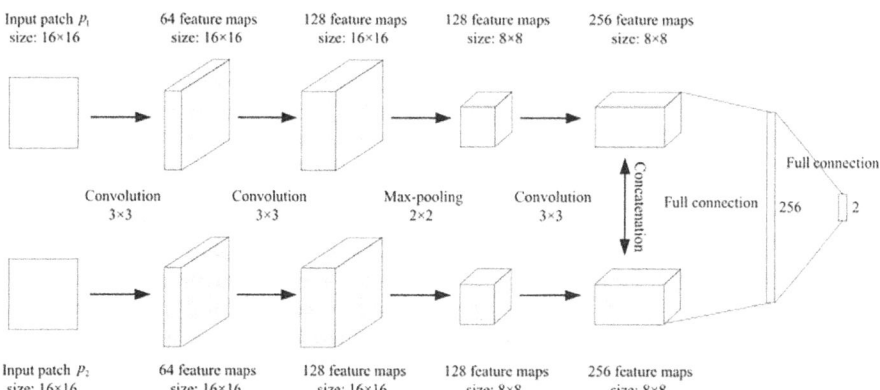

**Fig. 2.** The CNN model used in the proposed fusion algorithm. Please notice that the spatial size marked in the figure just indicates the training process. In the test/fusion

In summary, this work approaches multi-focus image fusion as a two-class classification problem using a CNN. The network is trained on patch pairs to learn the focus property, and two approaches are considered for handling source images of varying sizes. The siamese network is chosen as the CNN model due to its natural alignment with image fusion tasks and ease of training. A patch size of 16 × 16 is selected to balance accuracy and boundary effects. The CNN model architecture includes convolutional and max-pooling layers, and the output is a score map indicating the focus property of patch pairs in source images (Fig. 3).

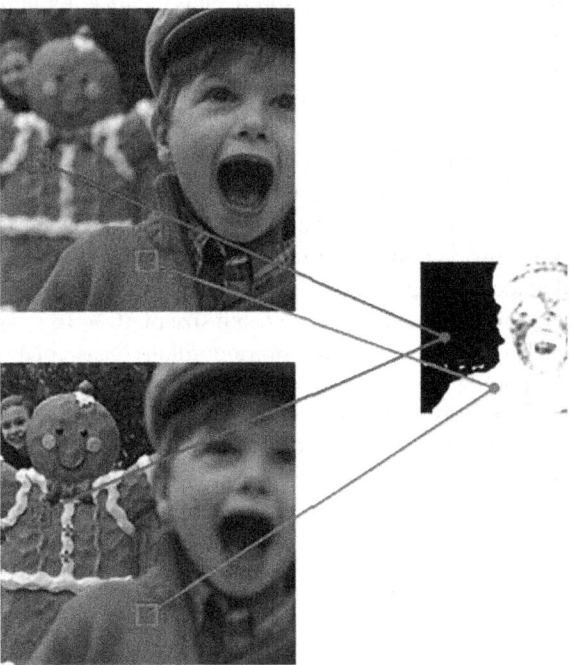

**Fig. 3.** The correspondence between the source images and the obtained score map

### 3.3 Training

The training examples for this study are generated from the ILSVRC 2012 validation image set, which consists of 500,000 high-quality natural images from the ImageNet dataset. Each image is converted to grayscale, and five blurred versions are created using Gaussian filtering with a standard deviation of 2 and a cutoff of 7 × 7. The first blurred image is obtained by applying the Gaussian filter to the original clear image, and subsequent blurred images are obtained by filtering the previous blurred image.

For each blurred image and the original image, 20 pairs of patches with a size of 16 × 16 are randomly sampled. The patches from the original image must have a variance larger than a threshold (e.g., 25). In total, 1,000,000 pairs of patches are obtained from the dataset, using around 10,000 images. A pair of clear and blurred patches is defined as a positive example (label set to 1) when the first branch receives the clear patch (p1) and the second branch receives the blurred patch (p2). Conversely, it is defined as a negative example (label set to 0) when p1 is the blurred patch and p2 is the clear patch. This results in a training set with 1,000,000 positive examples and 1,000,000 negative examples.

The network is trained using the softmax loss function, which is commonly used in CNN-based classification tasks. Stochastic gradient descent (SGD) is employed to minimize the loss function, with a batch size of 128. The momentum and weight decay are set to 0.9 and 0.0005, respectively. The learning rate is initially set to 0.001 and manually reduced by a factor of 10 when the loss reaches a stable state. The training is performed using the Caffe deep learning framework, initializing the weights of each convolutional layer with the Xavier algorithm and biases with zeros.

$$v_{i+1}=0.9. \; v_i - 0.0005.\alpha. \; w_i - \alpha . \frac{\partial L}{\partial w_i}, W_{i+1}=w_{i+1}=w_i+v_{i+1}. \tag{3}$$

The training process consists of approximately 10 epochs with around 2 million training examples. The learning rate is dropped once during training. It is worth noting that while the training examples could be sampled from a real multi-focus image dataset, the authors experimentally verified that using artificially created examples through Gaussian filtering yields comparable classification accuracies. Additionally, using artificially created examples allows for easier extension of the learned CNN model to other types of image fusion tasks, such as multi-modal or multi-exposure image fusion (Fig. 4).

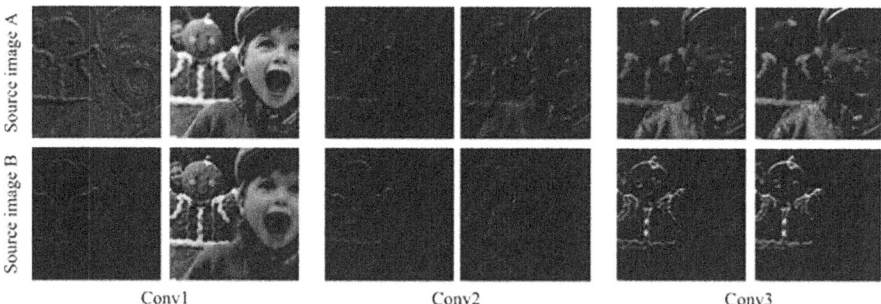

**Fig. 4.** Some representative output feature maps of the each convolutional layer. "conv1", "conv2" and "conv3" denote the first, second and third convolutional layer, respectively.

Representative feature maps from each convolutional layer of the learned CNN model are provided to gain insights. The feature maps capture high-frequency information, spatial details, and gradient orientations as the layers progress. The final output of the CNN model is a score map that accurately represents the focus information of different source images.

In summary, the training examples are generated from the ILSVRC 2012 validation image set using Gaussian filtering. Positive and negative examples are defined based on pairs of clear and blurred patches. The CNN model is trained using the softmax loss function and SGD, and the learned model demonstrates the ability to handle defocus blur effectively. The artificially created training set allows for generalization to other types of image fusion tasks, and the representative feature maps provide insights into the learned CNN model's behavior.

### 3.4 Detailed Fusion Scheme

#### 3.4.1 Focus Detection

The proposed fusion algorithm utilizes two source images, denoted as A and B. If the source images are in color, they are first converted to grayscale. The grayscale versions of A and B are represented as ^A and ^B, respectively. When the source images are already in grayscale, ^A is equal to A and ^B is equal to B.

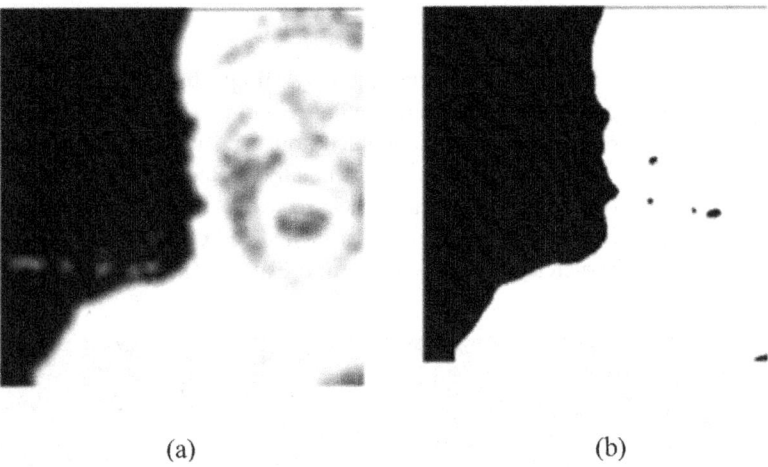

**Fig. 5.** Initial segmentation. (a) Focus map (b) binary segmentation map

The fusion process involves obtaining a score map, denoted as S, by inputting ^A and ^B into the trained CNN model. Each coefficient in S represents the focus property of a pair of patches with a size of $16 \times 16$ in the source images. The value of each coefficient in S ranges from 0 to 1, indicating the level of focus for the corresponding patch in either ^A or ^B. A value closer to 1 or 0 indicates higher focus, while a value closer to 0.5 represents a relatively plain region. The patches corresponding to neighboring coefficients in S overlap with a stride of two pixels.

To generate a focus map, denoted as M, with the same size as the source images, the value of each coefficient in S is assigned to all the pixels within its corresponding patch in M. The overlapping pixels are averaged. The resulting focus map accurately depicts the focus information. In regions with abundant details, the values tend to be close to 1 (white) or 0 (black), while plain regions exhibit values close to 0.5 (gray).

### 3.4.2 Initial Segmentation

In order to retain valuable information, the focus map M undergoes further processing. Similar to many spatial domain multi-focus image fusion methods, we employ the commonly used "choose-max" strategy to process M. This involves applying a fixed threshold of 0.5 to segment M into a binary map T, aligning with the classification principle of the trained CNN model. Specifically, the focus map is segmented as follows:

$$T(x, y) = \begin{cases} 1, & M(x, y) > 0.5 \\ 0, & \text{otherwise} \end{cases}, \qquad (4)$$

The resulting binary map is depicted in Fig. 5(b). It is important to note the optical illusion in the focus map shown in Fig. 5(a), where gray regions appear darker than their actual intensity against a white background, and brighter than their actual intensity against a black background. Despite this illusion, it can be observed that almost all the gray pixels in the focus map are correctly classified. This demonstrates the precise performance of the learned CNN model, even for plain regions in the source images.

*Consistency Verification:*

The binary segmented map shown in Fig. 5(b) may contain some misclassified pixels,

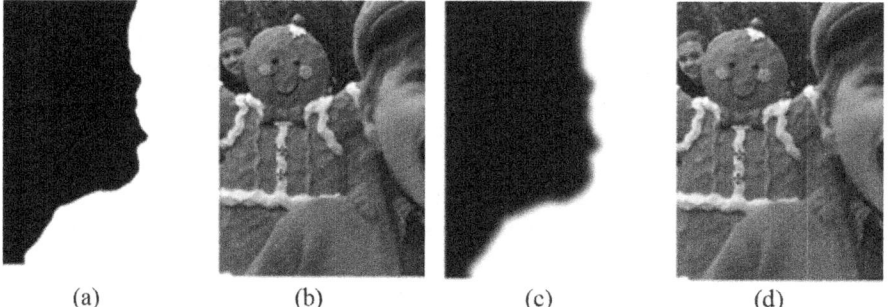

**Fig. 6.** Consistency verification and fusion. (a) Initial decision map (b) Initial fused image (c) final decision map (d) fused image

which can be easily eliminated using a small region removal strategy. This strategy involves reversing the regions in the binary map that are smaller than a predetermined area threshold. It is worth noting that in rare cases, the source images may have very small holes. In such situations, users have the option to manually adjust the threshold, even setting it to zero, which means the region removal strategy is not applied. In the upcoming section, we will demonstrate that the binary classification results already achieve high accuracy. For this study, the area threshold is universally set to 0.01 × H × W, where H and W represent the height and width of each source image, respectively.

Figure 6(a) presents the initial decision map obtained after implementing this strategy. However, some undesirable artifacts can be observed around the boundaries between focused and defocused regions in the fused image produced using the initial decision map with the weighted-average rule, as depicted in Fig. 6(b). To address this, similar to [30], we leverage the guided filter to enhance the quality of the initial decision map.

The guided filter is an efficient edge-preserving filter that transfers structural information from a guidance image to the filtering result of the input image. In our approach, the initial fused image serves as the guidance image to guide the filtering of the initial decision map. The guided filtering algorithm involves two free parameters: the local window radius r and the regularization parameter ε. In our experiments, we set r to 8 and ε to 0.1. Figure 6(c) illustrates the filtering result of the initial decision map depicted in Fig. 6(b).

## 4 Experiments

### 4.1 Experimental Settings

To evaluate the effectiveness of our proposed CNN-based fusion method, we conducted experiments using a dataset comprising 40 pairs of multi-focus images. Out of these pairs, 20 are commonly used in multi-focus image fusion research, while the remaining 20 pairs are sourced from the publicly available "Lytro" dataset [53]. In Fig. 7, a subset of the test image set is showcased, with the first two rows presenting eight traditional image pairs and the last two rows displaying ten image pairs from the new dataset.

To benchmark our fusion method, we compared it with six representative multi-focus image fusion methods: the non-subsampled contourlet transform (NSCT)-based method [6], the sparse representation (SR)-based method [13], the NSCT-SR-based method [11], the guided filtering (GF)-based method [25], the multi-scale weighted gradient (MWG)-based method [27], and the dense SIFT (DSIFT)-based method [29]. Among these methods, the NSCT-based, SR-based, and NSCT-SR-based methods fall under the transform domain category. The NSCT-based method has demonstrated superiority over most MST-based methods in multi-focus image fusion [54]. The SR-based method, utilizing the sliding window technique, presents advantages over conventional MST-based methods. The NSCT-SR-based fusion method, a recent introduction, addresses the individual drawbacks of the NSCT-based and SR-based methods.

The GF-based, MWG-based, and DSIFT-based methods are all spatial domain methods proposed in recent times, featuring elaborately designed fusion schemes that are widely recognized for generating state-of-the-art results in multi-focus image fusion. In our experiments, the NSCT-based, SR-based, and NSCT-SR-based methods were implemented using our MST-SR fusion toolbox, which is available online [55], with the relevant parameters set to the recommended values outlined in the related publications. The free parameters of the GF-based, MWG-based, and DSIFT-based methods were set to their default values as reported in the respective publications. MATLAB implementations of these three fusion methods are also available online [55–57].

Objective evaluation plays a crucial role in image fusion, as the performance of a fusion method is primarily assessed using quantitative scores obtained from multiple metrics [58]. In recent years, various fusion metrics have been proposed, and they can be classified into four groups: information theory-based metrics, image feature-based metrics, image structural similarity-based metrics, and human perception-based metrics, as summarized in a comprehensive survey by Liu et al. [59]. In this study, we selected one metric from each category to facilitate a comprehensive evaluation. The four chosen metrics are as follows:

1. Normalized mutual information (QMI) [60], which measures the amount of mutual information between the fused image and the source images.
2. Gradient-based metric (QG), also known as QAB/F [61], which assesses the degree of spatial details injected into the fused image from the source images.
3. Structural similarity-based metric (QY) proposed by Yang et al. [62], which quantifies the amount of preserved structural information in the fused image.
4. Human perception-based metric (QCB) proposed by Chen and Blum [63], which takes into account the key features in the human visual system.

For each of these four metrics, a higher value indicates better fusion performance.

### 4.2 Experimental Results and Discussions

#### 4.2.1 Commutativity Verification

In image fusion, commutativity is a fundamental rule stating that the order of source images does not affect the fusion result. However, in the designed network, the presence of fully-connected layers raises concerns about the validity of commutativity. When the source images are switched, the outputs of the fully-connected layers may not switch accordingly, compromising commutativity. Fortunately, a training technique employed in Sect. 3.3 ensures approximate commutativity at a high level, making the fusion algorithm insensitive to the order of the input images. To verify this point, we conducted experiments with all 40 pairs of source images using two possible input orders, resulting in two sets of fusion results.

**Fig. 7.** A portion of multi-focus test images used in our experiments.

We assessed commutativity using both the score map and the final fused image. For each pair of score maps generated from the same source images, we performed pixel-wise summation. Ideally, the sum value at each pixel should be 1 if commutativity is valid. To verify this, we calculated the average value over all pixels in the sum map. The mean and standard deviation of these average values for all 40 examples were 1.001468 and 0.001873, respectively. We also employed the Structural Similarity Index (SSIM)

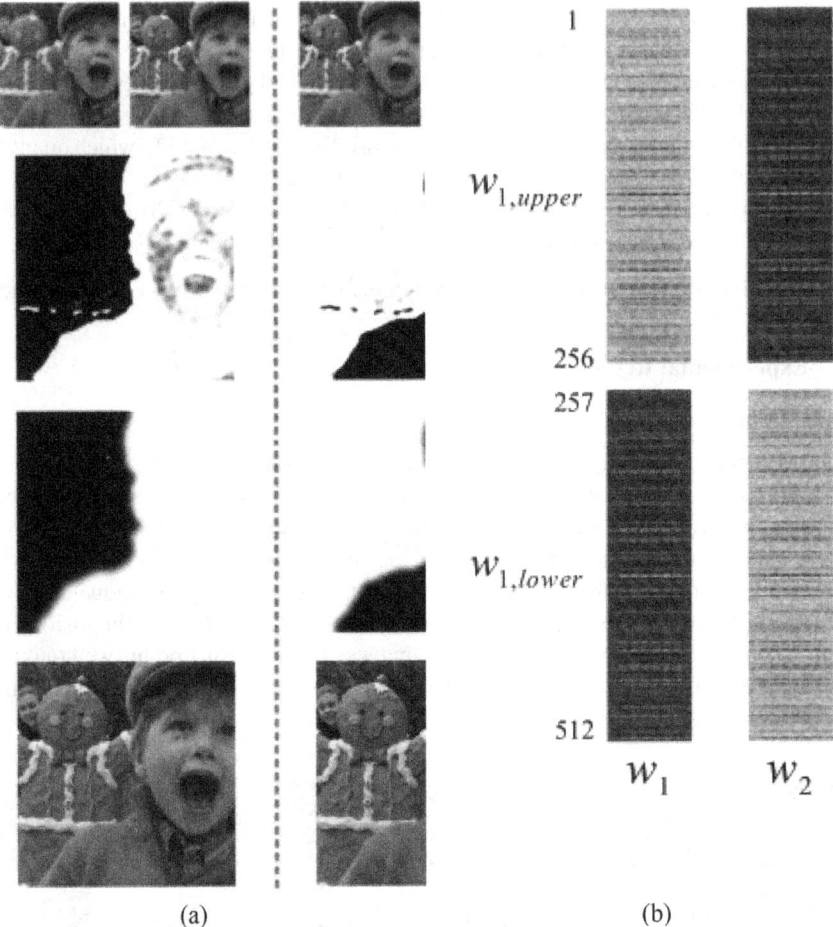

**Fig. 8.** Commutativity verification of the proposed algorithm. (a) A fusion example with two different input orders for source images. (b) the illustration of weight vectors

to measure the similarity between the fused images of the same source image pairs. A perfect SSIM score is 1, indicating identical images. The mean and standard deviation of the SSIM scores for all 40 examples were 0.999964 and 0.00161, respectively. These results demonstrate that the proposed method exhibits almost ideal commutativity. Figure 8(a) presents an example of this verification, showing fusion results with two different input orders for source images. The second, third, and fourth rows display the score maps, decision maps, and fused images, respectively, clearly indicating the validity of commutativity (Fig. 9).

To further illustrate these results, we simplified the analysis using a slight CNN model. We removed the first fully-connected layer from the network, directly connecting the 512 feature maps after concatenation to a 2-dimensional output vector. We trained this slight model using the same approach as the original model. In Fig. 8(b), we represent

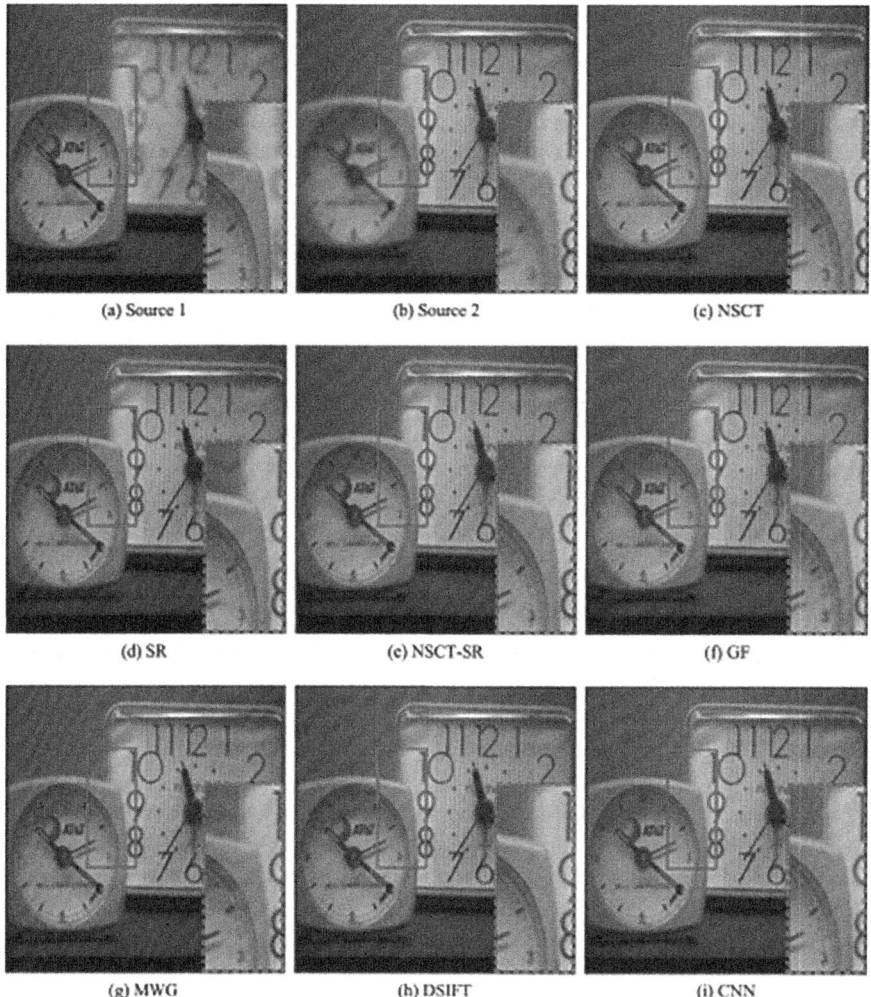

**Fig. 9.** The "clock" source image pair and their fused images obtained with different fusion methods

the weight vectors connected to the upper and lower neurons, denoted as w1 and w2, respectively, in a matrix form of size 512 × 64, divided into two equal-sized parts: an upper part and a lower part. This division is meaningful as the 512 feature maps are concatenated from two branches. By examining the upper and lower parts of the weight vectors (w1, upper, w1, lower, w2, upper, and w2, lower), we can investigate the conditions for valid commutativity. Let vA and vB represent the output feature maps of two corresponding source image patches sA and sB, respectively. Experimentally, we found that the biases of both neurons are very close to 0. When sA is input into the first branch and sB into the second branch, the outputs of the upper and lower neurons are V11 = wT1, upper vA + wT1, lower vB and V12 = wT2, upper vA + wT2, lower vB, respectively. Conversely, when sA is input into the second branch and sB into the first branch, the outputs of the upper and lower neurons are V21 = wT1, upper vB + wT1, lower vA and V22 = wT2, upper vB + wT2, lower vA, respectively. It is evident that if w1, upper = w2, lower and w1, lower = w2, upper, then V11 = V22 and V12 = V21, indicating valid commutativity. Figure 8(b) demonstrates the normalized weight vectors after division, showing that the above condition is well satisfied. Quantitative results further support this observation. The analysis approach is similar for the original network with two fully-connected layers, allowing for a quantitative explanation of the results obtained from the commutative experiments. The reason behind the satisfaction of the aforementioned condition can be attributed to the construction of training examples. Positive and negative examples are simultaneously obtained by switching the order of a clear patch and its blurred version, as explained in Sect. 3.3. The ground truth outputs for positive and negative examples are [1 0]T and [0 1]T, respectively, which satisfy commutativity. Consequently, the final learned weights are constrained by this property. In conclusion, we have demonstrated and explained the commutativity of the proposed fusion algorithm, alleviating concerns regarding the order of the source images in practical usage.

### 4.2.2 Comparison with Other Fusion Methods

In our research, we conducted a comparative analysis of different fusion methods based on visual perception. We used two example image pairs to demonstrate the differences among these methods. The fusion results were evaluated by examining magnified regions around the boundaries between focused and defocused areas, and by calculating the normalized difference images.

The results showed that the transform domain methods, such as NSCT-based and SR-based methods, exhibited undesirable artifacts and lower fusion quality in certain regions. The GF-based method had overall high quality but suffered from slight blurring in specific areas. The MWG-based method performed well in misregistered regions but had lower fusion quality in boundary regions. The DSIFT-based method captured details effectively but had artifacts around object edges.

Our proposed CNN-based method performed well in both boundary regions and misregistered regions, achieving the highest visual quality among all methods. It produced natural effects and outperformed other methods in terms of fusion quality, especially in capturing details and maintaining natural boundaries.

To further evaluate the performance objectively, we calculated scores based on four fusion metrics for each method. The DSIFT-based method and our proposed CNN-based method consistently outperformed the other methods across all metrics. The proposed method showed advantages over the DSIFT-based method in terms of average scores and achieved the first place more frequently in each metric.

However, it is important to note that the metric Q MI, which measures global statistical similarity, favored simple averaging methods over multi-scale transform-based fusion algorithms. We conducted a separate test using weighted average fusion and found that the weighted average methods obtained lower scores compared to the fusion methods. This highlights the need to consider Q MI together with other metrics.

# Deep Learning Based Multi Focus Image Fusion

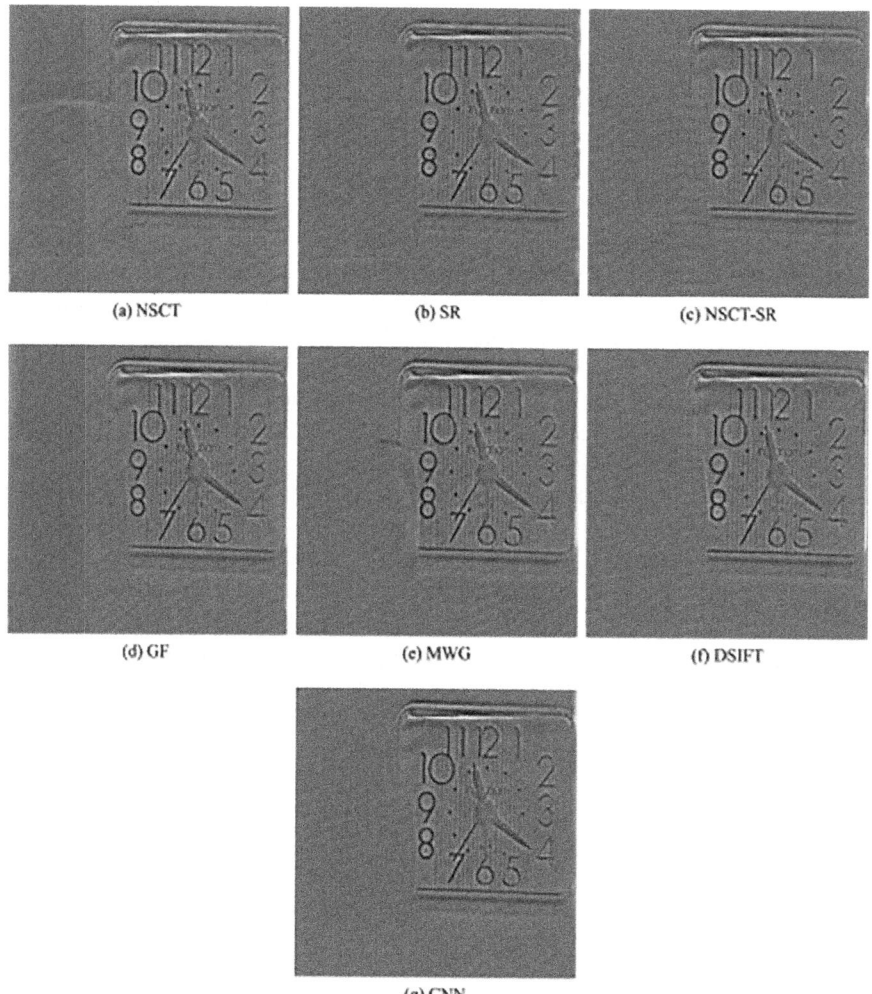

**Fig. 10.** The different image between each fused image in Fig. 10(c)–(i) and the source image in Fig. 10(a)

**Table 1.** Objective assessment of different fusion methods.

| Metrics | NSCT | SR | NSCT-SR | GF | MWG | DSIFT | CNN |
|---|---|---|---|---|---|---|---|
| $Q_{MI}$ | 0.9015(0,0) | 1.0798(0,2) | 1.0854(0,2) | 1.0632(0,0) | 1.0836(1,1) | **1.1884**(37,3) | 1.1455(2,32) |
| $Q_G$ | 0.7239(0,0) | 0.7397(1,1) | 0.7417(0,3) | 0.7456(2,4) | 0.7309(0,0) | 0.7489(14,21) | **0.7497**(23,11) |
| $Q_Y$ | 0.9502(0,0) | 0.9615(0,1) | 0.9643(1,0) | 0.9751(0,2) | 0.9811(3,5) | 0.9852(8,25) | **0.9865**(28,7) |
| $Q_{CB}$ | 0.7355(0,0) | 0.7596(1,0) | 0.7723(0,1) | 0.7768(0,1) | 0.7704(1,1) | 0.7948(7,31) | **0.7968**(31,6) |

In conclusion, based on subjective visual quality assessments and objective evaluation metrics, our proposed CNN-based fusion method demonstrated superior performance compared to other methods, establishing it as a state-of-the-art approach in multi-focus image fusion.

### 4.2.3 Intermediate Results of the Proposed Method

To demonstrate the CNN model's effectiveness in multi-focus image fusion, Fig. 13 presents the intermediate results of eight pairs of source images. In Sect. 3.4, we introduced our fusion algorithm, which employs a binary segmentation approach to obtain a binary segmented map using a threshold of 0.5. This approach aligns with the "choose-max" strategy commonly used in multi-focus image fusion [18–22, 24–27, 29, 30]. Hence, the binary segmented map serves as the actual output of our CNN model for multi-focus image fusion. The second column of Fig. 13 illustrates highly accurate segmented maps with correct classification of most pixels, demonstrating the CNN model's robust capability. However, there are two identified limitations concerning the binary segmented maps. First, a few pixels are occasionally misclassified, resulting in small regions or holes in the segmented maps. These misclassified pixels usually exist in plain regions where the distinction between two source images is minimal. Among the eight pairs of images, this situation occurs in six of them, except for the "golf" and "statue" set. Although the proportion of these misclassified pixels is small, and they typically appear in plain regions, their impact on the fusion result is negligible. Nonetheless, we apply a small region removal strategy to rectify these pixels. The third column of Fig. 13 presents the initial decision map obtained after this correction.

**Table 2.** The average objective assessment of the proposed fusion method with and without using consistency verification (CV) techniques.

| Method | $Q_{MI}$ | $Q_G$ | $Q_Y$ | $Q_{CB}$ |
|---|---|---|---|---|
| without CV | 1.1934 | 0.7494 | 0.9859 | 0.796 |
| with CV | 1.1455 | 0.7497 | 0.9865 | 0.7968 |

Second, the boundaries between focused and defocused regions often exhibit slight blocking artifacts. Addressing this issue is more crucial as the fusion quality around the boundaries is more important. Fortunately, edge-preserving filtering provides a suitable solution. The fourth column of Fig. 13 displays the fused images using the initial decision map. Compared to the first limitation, this aspect requires more urgent attention due to its impact on the fusion quality. By utilizing the guided filter, the final decision maps shown in the fifth column of Fig. 13 exhibit more natural boundary regions, leading to high visual quality of the fused results depicted in the last column of Fig. 13. In summary, we employ two time-efficient consistency verification approaches, namely small region removal/filtering and guided filtering, to refine the binary classification result. Consistency verification techniques have played an essential role in image fusion since the 1990s [4]. Commonly used approaches for consistency verification in image fusion methods involve various image filtering techniques, such as majority filtering [4, 18, 19], median filtering [26], morphological filtering [22], small region filtering [22, 29], edge-preserving filtering (e.g., bilateral filtering [66] and guided filtering [25]), and more. These techniques, known as conventional post-processing techniques, are simple and widely employed in image fusion for many years. Recent multi-focus image fusion methods tend to incorporate advanced post-processing techniques, including image matting [26], feature matching [29], and Markov Random Field (MRF)-based regularization [30], to achieve further improvements and pursue state-of-the-art performance. Due to the high focus detection accuracy of the CNN model, our fusion algorithm does not require complicated post-processing techniques. Table 2 presents the objective performance of the initial fused images and the final fused images using four fusion metrics. The average scores on the 40 source image pairs are provided. It can be observed that applying the consistency verification techniques slightly increases the scores for QG, QY, and QCB. The situation regarding metric QMI aligns with the analysis in Sect. 4.2.2. Furthermore, considering the information in Table 1 and Table 2 together, we observe that even the CNN-based method without using consistency verification techniques outperforms all other fusion methods across all four metrics. This finding further confirms the effectiveness of CNN for image fusion.

**Table 3.** The number of parameters in each convolutional/fully connected layer of our CNN model.

| Layer | conv1 | conv2 | conv3 | fc1 | fc2 | Sum |
|---|---|---|---|---|---|---|
| Number | 640 | 73856 | 295168 | 8388864 | 514 | 8759042 |

**Table 4.** The average objective assessment of the proposed fusion method using original and reduced models.

| Model | $Q_{MI}$ | $Q_G$ | $Q_Y$ | $Q_{CB}$ |
|---|---|---|---|---|
| Original | 1.1455 | 0.7497 | 0.9865 | 0.7968 |
| Slight | 1.1443 | 0.7482 | 0.9856 | 0.7955 |

**Table 5.** The average running time of the proposed fusion method using original and reduced CNN models for two source images of size 520 × 520 (Unit: seconds).

| Model | Parallel part | Serial part | Total |
|---|---|---|---|
| Original | 0.66 | 0.12 | 0.78 |
| Slight | 0.21 | 0.12 | 0.33 |

Of course, by incorporating advanced post-processing techniques as mentioned earlier, the fusion quality could be further improved.

## Memory Consumption and Computational Efficiency

Table 3 lists the number of parameters (weights and biases) in each convolutional/fully-connected layer of our CNN model shown in Fig. 2. The layers are named conv1, conv2, conv3, fc1, and fc2. Considering that each parameter occupies 4 bytes as a single-precision floating-point variable, the CNN model's physical memory size is 35,036,168 bytes (approximately 33.4 MB). The fc1 layer accounts for the largest percentage (approximately 95.8%) of the total parameters. To significantly reduce memory consumption, we propose removing the fc1 layer, connecting the 512 feature maps obtained by the conv3 layer directly to a 2-dimensional output vector. By doing so, the number of parameters in the remaining fully-connected layer is 65,538 (calculated as $512 \times 8 \times 8 \times 2 + 2$), resulting in a total of 435,202 parameters. Consequently, the reduced model occupies only about 1.66 MB, which is less than one twentieth of the original model size. To evaluate the effectiveness of the reduced model in multi-focus image fusion, we replace the original model with it while keeping the other parts of the proposed algorithm unchanged. Table 4 presents the average objective assessment of the proposed fusion method using the original and reduced models for eight source image pairs. The performance of the reduced model is slightly inferior to that of the original model, but the difference is negligible. This result highlights the high flexibility in CNN model design, where the network used in this work represents just one feasible approach. The proposed CNN-based image fusion algorithm is implemented in C++ by utilizing the interfaces provided by Caffe for forward propagation through the network. The GPU mode is employed, resulting in two parts: a parallel part and a serial part. The parallel part involves the procedure of passing source images through the network using Caffe interfaces to obtain the score map, while the serial part encompasses the subsequent steps starting from the score map. The hardware configurations used in our experiments include an NVIDIA GeForce GTX TITAN Black GPU, an Intel Core i7-4790k CPU, and 16 GB RAM. Table 5 presents the average running time of the proposed fusion method using the original and reduced CNN models for source images of size $520 \times 520$. The times for the parallel and serial parts are provided separately. It can be observed that the computing time for the proposed fusion method with the original model is less than one second, indicating sufficient speed for practical usage. The computational efficiency using the reduced model is more than two times higher than when using the original model, with the parallel part alone experiencing a three-fold increase.

### 4.3 Extension to Other-Type Image Fusion Issues

To demonstrate the versatility of the CNN model, we extend its application to two other types of image fusion: multi-modal image fusion and multi-exposure image fusion. These fusion issues have their own unique characteristics and require different approaches. For multi-modal image fusion, we utilize a fusion framework based on Laplacian pyramid (LP) and Gaussian pyramid (GP), which is commonly used in this field due to its consistency with human visual perception. The CNN model's focus map is used as a weight map to indicate the activity level of pixels. During the fusion process, the source images are decomposed into Laplacian pyramids, and the weight maps are decomposed into Gaussian pyramids. At each decomposition level, the weighted average fusion rule is applied to merge the information from the source images, and the fused image is obtained through LP reconstruction.

In the case of multi-exposure image fusion, exposure quality is a crucial factor. We adopt a simple threshold-based quality measure to generate the weight map for exposure quality, while the CNN model's focus map serves as the weight map for contrast extraction. These two weight maps are multiplied to generate the final weight map. The same multi-scale fusion scheme based on LP and GP, as described earlier, is then employed to obtain the fused image.

Figure 14 showcases three fusion examples using the presented CNN-based methods. The first two columns depict the source images, while the third column displays the fused image. These examples cover multi-modal image fusion in both visible-infrared and medical domains. It is evident that the fused images successfully preserve important information from the source images. Similarly, the fusion quality of multi-exposure images is relatively high, as the fused image captures most spatial details without introducing undesirable artifacts.

Although the techniques applied to different image fusion issues may vary, they all share the core task of mapping the source images to the focus map using the CNN model. This mapping process involves measuring and comparing the activity levels, which are essential for the fusion rule. The subsequent techniques applied to the focus map can be selected or designed based on the specific characteristics of each fusion task. This approach allows us to leverage the value of conventional techniques from related fields, which we believe should not be disregarded. In this work, we have employed popular techniques for multi-focus image fusion and other fusion issues, but further studies following this path can be explored in the future.

## 5 Conclusion

This research paper introduces a novel approach to multi-focus image fusion by utilizing a deep convolutional neural network (CNN). The key innovation of our method lies in training a CNN model to directly map source images to the focus map. By doing so, the CNN model can simultaneously handle the measurement of activity levels and the fusion rule, thereby overcoming the challenges faced by existing fusion methods. The main contributions of this paper can be summarized as follows:

1. We pioneer the integration of CNNs into the field of image fusion and discuss the feasibility and advantages of employing CNNs for this task. To the best of our knowledge, this is the first application of CNNs in image fusion.
2. We propose a multi-focus image fusion method based on the CNN model. Through comprehensive experiments, we demonstrate that our proposed method achieves state-of-the-art results in terms of both visual quality and objective assessment.
3. We showcase the potential of the learned CNN model for addressing other types of image fusion issues, indicating its versatility and applicability beyond multi-focus fusion.
4. We provide recommendations for future research in the domain of CNN-based image fusion. We believe that CNNs have the potential to open up new avenues of investigation and offer a promising research approach in the field of image fusion.

## References

1. Stathaki, T.: Image Fusion: Algorithms and Applications. Academic Press (2008)
2. Burt, P., Adelson, E.: The Laplacian pyramid as a compact image code. IEEE Trans. Commun. **31**(4), 532–540 (1983)
3. Toet, A.: A morphological pyramidal image decomposition. Pattern Recognit. Lett. **9**(4), 255–261 (1989)
4. Li, H., Manjunath, B., Mitra, S.: Multisensor image fusion using the wavelet transform. Graph. Models Image Process. **57**(3), 235–245 (1995)
5. Lewis, J., O'Callaghan, R., Nikolov, S., Bull, D., Canagarajah, N.: Pixel-and regionbased image fusion with complex wavelets. Inf. Fusion **8**(2), 119–130 (2007)
6. Zhang, Q., Guo, B.: Multifocus image fusion using the nonsubsampled contourlet transform. Signal Process. **89**(7), 1334–1346 (2009)
7. Piella, G.: A general framework for multiresolution image fusion: from pixels to regions. Inf. Fusion **4**(4), 259–280 (2003)
8. Qu, X., Yan, J., Xiao, H., Zhu, Z.: Image fusion algorithm based on spatial frequency-motivated pulse coupled neural networks in nonsubsampled contourlet transform domain. Acta Autom. Sin. **34**(12), 1508–1514 (2008)
9. Tian, J., Chen, L.: Adaptive multi-focus image fusion using a wavelet-based statistical sharpness measure. Signal Process. **92**(9), 2137–2146 (2012)
10. Li, X., Li, H., Yu, Z., Kong, Y.: Multifocus image fusion scheme based on the multiscale curvature in nonsubsampled contourlet transform domain. Opt. Eng. **54**, 073115 (2015)
11. Liu, Y., Liu, S., Wang, Z.: A general framework for image fusion based on multi-scale transform and sparse representation. Inf. Fusion **24**(1), 147–164 (2015)
12. Mitianoudis, N., Stathaki, T.: Pixel-based and region-based image fusion schemes using ICA bases. Inf. Fusion **8**(2), 131–142 (2007)
13. Yang, B., Li, S.: Multifocus image fusion and restoration with sparse representation. IEEE Trans. Instrum. Meas. **59**(4), 884–892 (2010)
14. Liang, J., He, Y., Liu, D., Zeng, X.: Image fusion using higher order singular value decomposition. IEEE Trans. Image Process. **21**(5), 2898–2909 (2012)
15. Jiang, Y., Wang, M.: Image fusion with morphological component analysis. Inf. Fusion **18**(1), 107–118 (2014)
16. Liu, Z., Chai, Y., Yin, H., Zhou, J., Zhu, Z.: A novel multi-focus image fusion approach based on image decomposition. Inf. Fusion **35**, 102–116 (2017)
17. Huang, W., Jing, Z.: Evaluation of focus measures in multi-focus image fusion. Pattern Recognit. Lett. **28**(4), 493–500 (2007)
18. Li, S., Kwok, J., Wang, Y.: Combination of images with diverse focuses using the spatial frequency. Inf. Fusion **2**(3), 169–176 (2001)
19. Li, S., Kwok, J., Wang, Y.: Multifocus image fusion using artificial neural networks. Pattern Recognit. Lett. **23**(8), 985–997 (2002)
20. Aslantas, V., Kurban, R.: Fusion of multi-focus images using differential evolution algorithm. Expert Syst. Appl. **37**(12), 8861–8870 (2010)
21. De, I., Chanda, B.: Multi-focus image fusion using a morphology-based focus measure in a quad-tree structure. Inf. Fusion **14**(2), 136–146 (2013)
22. Bai, X., Zhang, Y., Zhou, F., Xue, B.: Quadtree-based multi-focus image fusion using a weighted focus-measure. Inf. Fusion **22**(1), 105–118 (2015)
23. Li, M., Cai, W., Tan, Z.: A region-based multi-sensor image fusion scheme using pulse-coupled neural network. Pattern Recognit. Lett. **27**(16), 1948–1956 (2006)
24. Li, S., Yang, B.: Multifocus image fusion using region segmentation and spatial frequency. Image Vis. Comput. **26**(7), 971–979 (2008)

25. Li, S., Kang, X., Hu, J.: Image fusion with guided filtering. IEEE Trans. Image Process. **22**(7), 2864–2875 (2013)
26. Li, S., Kang, X., Hu, J., Yang, B.: Image matting for fusion of multi-focus images in dynamic scenes. Inf. Fusion **14**(2), 147–162 (2013)
27. Zhou, Z., Li, S., Wang, B.: Multi-scale weighted gradient-based fusion for multi–focus images. Inf. Fusion **20**(1), 60–72 (2014)
28. Guo, D., Yan, J., Qu, X.: High quality multi-focus image fusion using self-similarity and depth information. Opt. Commun. **338**(1), 138–144 (2015)
29. Liu, Y., Liu, S., Wang, Z.: Multi-focus image fusion with dense sift. Inf. Fusion **23**(1), 139–155 (2015)
30. Nejati, M., Samavi, S., Shirani, S.: Multi-focus image fusion using dictionary-based sparse representation. Inf. Fusion **25**(1), 72–84 (2015)
31. Zhang, Y., Bai, X., Wang, T.: Boundary finding based multi-focus image fusion through multi-scale morphological focus-measure. Inf. Fusion **35**, 81–101 (2017)
32. Li, S., Kang, X., Fang, L., Hu, J., Yin, H.: Pixel-level image fusion: a survey of the state of the art. Inf. Fusion **33**, 100–112 (2017)
33. Gao, G., Xu, L., Feng, D.: Multi-focus image fusion based on non-subsampled shearlet transform. IET Image Process. **7**(6), 633–639 (2013)
34. Zhao, H., Shang, Z., Tang, Y., Fang, B.: Multi-focus image fusion based on the neighbor distance. Pattern Recognit. **46**(3), 1002–1011 (2013)
35. Yang, B., Li, S.: Pixel-level image fusion with simultaneous orthogonal matching pursuit. Inf. Fusion **13**(1), 10–19 (2012)
36. Yu, N., Qiu, T., Bi, F., Wang, A.: Image features extraction and fusion based on joint sparse representation. IEEE J. Sel. Top Signal Process. **5**(5), 1074–1082 (2011)
37. Liu, Y., Wang, Z.: Simultaneous image fusion and denosing with adaptive sparse representation. IET Image Process. **9**(5), 347–357 (2015)
38. LeCun, Y., Bottou, L., Bengio, Y., Haffner, P.: Gradient-based leaning applied to document recognition. Proc. IEEE **86**(11), 2278–2324 (1998)
39. Sermanet, P., Eigen, D., Zhang, X., Mathieu, M., Fergus, R., LeCun, Y.: Overfeat: integrated recognition, localizaton and detection using convolutional networks, pp. 1–16 (2014). arXiv: 1312.6229v4
40. https://en.wikipedia.org/wiki/Deep_learning
41. Nair, V., Hinton, G.: Rectified linear units improve restricted Boltzmann machines. In: Proceedings of 27th International Conference on Machine Learning, pp. 807–814 (2010)
42. Krizhevsky, A., Sutskever, I., Hinton, G.: ImageNet classification with deep convolutional neural networks. In: Advances in Neural Information Processing Systems, pp. 1097–1105 (2012)
43. Farfade, S., Saberian, M., Li, L.: Multi-view face detection using deep convolutional neural networks. In: Proceedings of the 5th ACM on International Conference on Multimedia Retrieval, pp. 643–650 (2015)
44. Sun, Y., Wang, X., Tang, X.: Deep learning face representation from predicting 10,000 classes. In: Proceedings of the IEEE Conference on Computer Vision and Pattern Recognition, pp. 1891–1898 (2014)
45. Long, J., Shelhamer, E., Darrell, T.: Fully convolutional networks for semantic segmentation. In: Proceedings of the IEEE Conference on Computer Vision and Pattern Recognition, pp. 3431–3440 (2015)
46. Dong, C., Loy, C., He, K., Tang, X.: Image super-resolution using deep convolutional networks. IEEE Trans. Pattern Anal. Mach. Intell. **38**(2), 295–307 (2016)
47. Zagoruyko, S., Komodakis, N.: Learning to compare image patches via convolutional neural networks. In: Proceedings of the IEEE Conference on Computer Vision and Pattern Recognition, pp. 4353–4361 (2015)

48. Jia, Y., et al.: Caffe: convolutional architecture for fast feature embedding. In: Proceedings of the ACM International Conference on Multimedia, pp. 675–678 (2014)
49. http://www.vlfeat.org/matconvnet/
50. He, K., Sun, J., Tang, X.: Guided image filtering. IEEE Trans. Pattern Anal. Mach. Intell. **35**(6), 1397–1409 (2013)
51. http://www.image-net.org/
52. Glorot, X., Bengio, Y.: Understanding the difficulty of training deep feedforward neural networks. In: International Conference on Artificial Intelligence and Statistics (2010)
53. http://mansournejati.ece.iut.ac.ir/content/lytro-multi-focus-dataset
54. Li, S., Yang, B., Hu, J.: Performance comparison of different multi-resolution transforms for image fusion. Inf. Fusion **12**(2), 74–84 (2011)
55. http://home.ustc.edu.cn/~liuyu1
56. http://xudongkang.weebly.com/index.html
57. https://github.com/lsauto/MWGF-Fusion
58. Petrovic, V., Dimitrijevic, V.: Focused pooling for image fusion evalution. Inf. Fusion **22**(1), 119–126 (2015)
59. Liu, Z., Blasch, E., Xue, Z., Zhao, J., Laganiere, R., Wu, W.: Objective assessment of multiresolution image fusion algorithms for context enhancement in night vision: a comparative study. IEEE Trans. Pattern Anal. Mach. Intell. **34**(1), 94–109 (2012)
60. Hossny, M., Nahavandi, S., Creighton, D.: Comments on information measure for performance of image fusion. Electron. Lett. **44**(18), 1066–1067 (2008)
61. Xydeas, C.S., Petrovic, V.S.: Objective image fusion performance measure. Electron. Lett. **36**(4), 308–309 (2000)
62. Yang, C., Zhang, J., Wang, X., Liu, X.: A novel similarity based quality metric for image fusion. Inf. Fusion **9**(2), 156–160 (2008)
63. Chen, Y., Blum, R.: A new automated quality assessment algorithm for image fusion. Image Vis. Comput. **27**(10), 1421–1432 (2009)
64. Wang, Z., Bovik, A., Sheikh, H., Simoncelli, E.: Image quality assessment: from error visibility to structural similarity. IEEE Trans. Image Process. **13**(4), 600–612 (2004)
65. Hossny, M., Nahavandi, S., Creighton, D., Bhatti, A.: Image fusion performance metric based on mutual information and entropy driven quadtree decomposition. Electron. Lett. **46**(18), 1266–1268 (2010)
66. Zhang, W., Cham, W.-K.: Gradient-directed multiexposure composition. IEEE Trans. Image Process. **21**(4), 2318–2323 (2012)
67. Mertens, T., Kautz, J., Reeth, F.V.: Exposure fusion. In: Proceedings of Pacific Graphics, pp. 382–390 (2007)

# SLR Based on Requirement Elicitation and Modeling in GSD

Aftab Rafique[1], Usman Ahmed Raza[2], Usman Nawaz[3(✉)], Namra Waheed[1], Maryam Kauser[1], Mariam Munsif Mir[4], and Rohail Shahzad[5]

[1] Department of Software Engineering and Information Technology, Foundation University, Rawalpindi Campus, Islamabad, Pakistan
[2] Faculty of Information Technology (FOIT), University of Central Punjab (UCP), Lahore, Pakistan
[3] Department of Information Technology, University of Gujrat, Gujrat, Pakistan
usmannawaz065@gmail.com
[4] NAMAL University, Mianwali, Pakistan
[5] Information Technology Department, Faculty of CS & IT, Superior University, Lahore, Pakistan

**Abstract.** Requirements elicitation, also known as requirements gathering, refers to the process of researching and discovering the necessary requirements for a system or software prior to development. This is typically accomplished through deep consultations with users, customers, and other stakeholders involved in the project. However, this process can be challenging in software development, as it is difficult to ensure that all necessary requirements are obtained simply by asking users what the system should or should not do. As a result, requirement elicitation has become a complex and risky phase of the requirement engineering process. In the context of global software development (GSD), requirement elicitation becomes even more difficult. This has been a topic of extensive research over the past decade, with a focus on identifying effective methods for analyzing and identifying evidence-based results related to requirement elicitation models. In this study, we conducted a systematic literature review (SLR) to achieve two main objectives: first, to analyze existing systematic reviews and identify evidence-based results related to requirement elicitation in GSD; and second, to identify proposed requirement elicitation models and evaluate their efficacy. The use of systematic reviews is an advanced methodology that comprehensively covers this field, and can be applied in the proposed scenario. Existing literature contains numerous elicitation models that fulfill different development artifacts, but our results indicate that the evidence is insufficient in quantity and immature. We require full evidence from all perspectives to make actionable and context-sensitive decisions that evaluate solutions with novelty from the existing literature. The quality of systematic reviews is superior to other existing methods in terms of searching, study selection, and data presentation. However, the analysis of systematic reviews and the use of evidence in the initial stages of the study is not in depth, and only presents the types of evidence that already exist. To achieve our desired results, systematic reviews (SLRs and Maps) should be evidence-based, with better quality for the synthesis of results in the case of requirement elicitation.

**Keywords:** Systematic Literature Review · Requirement Elicitation · Systematic Reviews · Global Software Development · Requirement Engineering

## 1 Introduction

Requirement engineering (RE) is a comprehensive platform for collecting, managing, and documenting software system requirements to ensure user satisfaction by fulfilling their actual needs. Requirement elicitation, which involves direct communication with software users to gather relevant information through various techniques, is a crucial phase in the software development life cycle (SDLC) [20]. The quality of software is heavily reliant on the proper gathering of requirements from end users. In global software development (GSD) environments, requirement elicitation becomes even more challenging due to differences in culture, language, and time zones among customers and vendors from different countries worldwide. Effective elicitation in GSD requires specific skills, such as proficiency in English, cross-cultural understanding, knowledge of computer-based communication modes and protocols, problem-solving, and teamwork [8, 9]. Various surveys and interviews have shown that prototyping, proposed scenarios, and interviews are the most efficient techniques for elicitation in GSD environments. Traditional methods like questionnaires and surveys are often insufficient for requirements collection in GSD. Collaborative methods like social intelligence for networked software and semantic web technology are better suited for GSD. Systematic reviews (SRs) are a type of literature review that systematically synthesizes and summarizes available evidence about a specific topic. SRs are essential for evidence-based software engineering to improve overall decision-making, including software development and maintenance. SRs can be classified as systematic literature reviews (SLRs) and systematic mapping studies (SMS). SLRs analyze and deduce complete available evidence obtained as targeted research questions while remaining unbiased and repeatable. Maps, on the other hand, generate a classification scheme and structure based on the frequency of publications for categories within the scheme. SLRs and Maps are based on secondary studies by reviewing extracted original research results and help to create the state of evidence. SLRs integrate present best-evaluated evidence from research and are executed through practical experience and human values. The critical step in this process is to evaluate evidence for its validity, impact, and applicability. Maps are based on a greater number of research papers and discuss research with wider topics in broad areas, including methods, tools, types of evidence-based research, and proposed solutions.

The critical step in this proposed process is to daringly evaluate evidence for its validity, impact, as well as applicability. "Map is a technique to generate a classification scheme and structure in the interest of software engineering field. The analysis of results focuses on frequencies of publications for categories within the scheme". When we compare an SLR with Map based studies, Maps are based on greater number of research papers and discuss research with wider topics in broad areas. It includes methods, tools, and types of evidence-based research with its suggested solution in the form of proposal solution or evaluation research. Here we consider that in Maps collection of empirical evidence and detailed analysis is needless to collect for reason being shallow data extraction. At present, SLRs and Maps have attained the level of widespread research methods and possess practically many similarities. We find no distinction while undergoing comparison between SLRs and Maps in current research and the way of their application. At present, tertiary studies based on SLRs and Maps have become an increasingly popular and common practice of SRs [9]. It summarizes existing and selected secondary studies required for a specific research topic. It consists of review based on selected secondary studies having feed of primary studies else, conceded out as a SLR. In software engineering, these tertiary studies are being conducted on three broad topics. Firstly, there exist studies with regard to SRs where generally a tertiary study has the ability to search entire SRs of desired and required topics in software engineering field and is extended later on. Secondly, the SR method itself, including synthesis, experiences motivation the nature of research questions, the use of SRs and quality assessment in SRs.

Thirdly, in SRs we find studies with regard to specific topics. These include aspects of global software engineering (GSD), risks in software development including requirements engineering and usable results, considered for practical teaching. There exist studies reporting upon experiences on conducting SRs with ample discussion of SR methodology. In the last three decades, requirements elicitation being integral part of requirement engineering remained exposed to a wide-ranging and extensive research. Here we considered the same as very important and endeavored to characterized and stress upon on a state-of-the art practicing more elaborately to the attain maximum through an SLR or a Map. We focused our aim at gathering all empirical evidence which is obtained from the results of research, results obtained through a tertiary study in the form of SR comprising SLRs and Maps in GSD environment. Despite numerous SRs addressing requirement elicitation in GSD, a comprehensive tertiary study focusing on characterizing these SRs has yet to be found. This SLRs based paper, we had made an endeavor to present publications including general characteristics of existing SRs in relation to requirement elicitation and requirement elicitation in GSD environment. Here, we are depicting an investigation by examining quality including evidence explained through primary studies assessed using selected SRs. In addition, we also present an overview of all elicited models including all supporting evidence extracted. All-out effort made for utilization of available guidelines to follow for research methodologies used and implemented in a tertiary study by authors during different research.

This paper is organized as follows: Sect. 2 describes literature review. Section 3 represents proposed research methodology consisting of research questions and research method, the extraction of full data we needed in relation to research questions is presented in Sect. 3, summary of answers made to research questions are proposed in Sect. 4, Sect. 5 illustrate discussion on study, its limitations and validity followed by conclusion at the end of proposed research work.

## 2 Literature Review

Requirement engineering (RE) is a broad field; a lot of research work has already been done in this particular field. Some of an important research articles are discussed thoroughly as follows: Researcher has proposed and recommended numerous steps for literature of systematic studies prioritizing search string in diverse databases or interpreting reference lists with regard to research studies [9].

Article [1] proposed an overview of the existing elicitation techniques. After studying these techniques, authors focused on applying these techniques in one particular area and examined the results. The aim of the proposed work was to select one technique from these particular techniques which is suitable in the proposed scenario. The accurate selection of an elicitation technique is very important for application development. The wrong selection of an elicitation technique will lead you towards a poor project. Therefore, authors focused on the accurate selection of an elicitation technique [2] to solve the existing problem in this particular field. After studying existing literature, a new elicitation technique is proposed to help programmers in the field of software engineering [3]. In this article [4], a new framework was established for software engineers in terms of an elicitation technique selection to overcome the challenges in the assigned projects. The proposed manuscript overcomes the challenges through the proposed technique. The distribution of persons to create an effective team for the solution of projects, the teamwork always outperforms work individually. Therefore, the distribution of individuals in team is proposed for projects is discussed in [5]. Moreover, a comprehensive study of existing literature in the form of survey was presented in [6], the survey was based the understanding an elicitation technique to select the most effective and suitable method in the field of requirement engineering. Furthermore, the feasibility of the system improvement, the analysis of an elicitation and more relevant activities are presented in [7]. After studying the literature based on elicitation techniques, the proposed methodology is suggested and discussed in section below.

## 3 Proposed Methodology

Study has been conducted as systematic literature review-based research papers relevant to study topic to understand and identify approaches, techniques, challenges, benefits, levels, barriers and attributes of software requirement elicitation. By Systematic Literature Review (SLR), we mean identification, evaluation, and interpretation of all research (forty-five research papers out of fifty-five papers) relevant to a particular research question or topic area (software reuse).

### 3.1 Research Questions

Research Question 1: Has the suitability and description of studies for the inclusion and exclusion criteria been verified?
Research Question 2. How have quality and evidence been explored and extracted in SRs with regard to primary studies?
Research Question 3. What is empirical evidence provided for elicitation techniques and modeling for RE in GSD as per SRs?
Research Question.4: Do studies clearly mention Software Requirement Elicitation modeling?
Research Question 5. What all requirement elicitation techniques have been discussed in general and Global Software Development (GSD) Environment?
Research Question 6. What are barriers in Software Requirement Elicitation in general and GSD environment?

In the proposed research work, the first query about research is the SRs characteristics that had been conducted about requirement elicitation to achieve an overall point of view of the SRs. We illustrate all available and selected publications of SRs. Practically, if we see SRs themselves analyze these studies with regard to terms and their types including an initial study emphasizing methodological quality of research found and depicted by topics. Application of SRs as research methodical tool have been examined by thorough and focused analysis, use of quality and extraction of evidence from primary studies in SRs sand has been addressed in second research question. The motivational factor is that it caters for multiple concerns at an early stage. It includes search, SR methodology, analysis, use of quality, evidence usually not catered for in primary studies with concern and extensiveness. It is essential for SRs to cuddle evidence-based requirement elicitation within software engineering. It engages our second research question and analysis obtained through this way lays essential basis for our third research question. Empirical evidence provided for elicitation techniques and modeling as elicitation models remains the focus of the fourth research question. The motive behind the decision is to carry out tertiary study for elicitation models instead of a specific SR there by getting a more precise overview throughout elicitation process by considering techniques used by researchers. Key activities of requirement elicitation and their processes highlighted in models are addressed third and fourth research questions. Fifth question comprehends all worthwhile elicitation techniques discussed and evaluated in reviews. The sixth research question tells us about known barriers and limitations with respect to requirement elicitation for RE in GSD in SRs. Brief answers have been made in Sect. 4.

### 3.2 Criteria for Selection of Studies

We established criteria to include research articles fulfilling deliberate inclusion criteria. The research paper was not included due to well-defined exclusion criteria. Articles having SR as individual element were included.

1) The inclusion criteria considered for SR:
    1.1 Articles indicating an SR on requirement elicitation.
    1.2 Articles mentioning requirement elicitation and requirement elicitation in GSD environment and having their topic with their synonyms.
    1.3 All articles published journals and conferences. Accepted in a workshop, peer-reviewed and technical reports including book chapters.
    1.4 All articles written in English.
2) The exclusion criteria considered:
    2.1 Thesis all types (Master's and doctoral theses).
    2.2 Articles published in all journals on active Beall's List.
    2.3 All informal literature reviews.
    2.4 All articles discussing SRs but without a report with results presented in original

SR.
2.5 Articles that were only related to teaching or education but did not report the results of an SR that had been conducted.
2.6 Literary material including editorials, detailed introductions, lengthy summaries of workshops etc. that all do not report an original SR.

### 3.3 Conduct of Search Process

We began our research by searching electronic databases for primary and relevant studies on requirement elicitation in GSD environment, including well-reputed journals, workshops, and conference proceedings such as the Software Elicitation Conferences. Our search utilized major keywords such as Requirement Elicitation, Requirement Elicitation GSD, Techniques of Elicitation, and Barriers of requirement elicitation, elicitation modeling, and alternative terms such as Requirement Gathering. Boolean AND & OR operators were used to create an initial pilot search string. We also reviewed titles of International Conference on EASE papers from 2000 to 2020 as a primary source for publishing SRs. The repositories used for our search were ACM Digital Library, Web of Science, IEEE Xplore, Science Direct, Springer, and Scopus.

The search process has been carried out in four phases. The first phase was selection of topic of SLR which was finalized in first week of October 2022. Phase 2 was carried out from the second week of October 2022 to 31 October 2020. Finalization of searches has been conducted from 1 November 2020 to 30 march 2023. Writing of draft commenced into effect from 1 March 2023. All four phases have been shown in Fig. 1. To support and enhance quality search for selection and identification of research papers under mentioned search strategies were also incorporated.

1. Snowballing Search:
   a. Backward searches (references)
   b. Forwarded searches (references)
4. Criteria based on Wohlin (2014) search.
5. Database searches.
6. Searches conducted manually

### 3.4 Update to Include the Most Recent Papers

The forward period of searches (Phase No 3 of Fig. 1) was led with a comparable convention than prior to cover the latest distributions. Initially, an information base pursuit was directed. A similar information base inquiry convention depicted above was followed, with an extra constraint to distribution years 2015–2023, and in the wake of applying, the incorporation and avoidance rules 26 new SRs were incorporated. The snowballing brought about just a single emphasis. Manual inquiries focused on the previously mentioned distribution scenes in 2015–2023; no new SRs were incorporated. Subsequently, the last arrangement of included SRs has – considers.

### 3.5 Quality Assessment

The quality assessments are based on a checklist of factors/questions that need to be evaluated in each study. For assessing studies, we defined the following quality assessment

**Table 1.** Literature Review

| ID | Years | Types | Specific or General S or G | Domain Engineering | Applied Eng | Research Tool | Incl Primary Study | Topics | Elicitation Model | Evidence Available |
|---|---|---|---|---|---|---|---|---|---|---|
| 1 | 2005 | Map | S | Y | Y | A | Yes | Requirements Elicitation | Yes | Evidence based |
| 2 | 2014 | SLR | G | Y | Y | RQ | Yes | Requirements Engineering | Yes | No |
| 3 | 2015 | Map | G | Y | N | – | Yes | a systematic literature review based on the maturity of the techniques | No | Evidence based |
| 4 | 2014 | SLR | G | Y | N | – | Yes | Selecting Requirement Elicitation | Yes | No |
| 5 | 2010 | Map | G | P | P | A | Yes | Prioritization and Decision Making | Yes | Evidence based |
| 6 | 2007 | Map | G | Y | P | – | Yes | Global Software Development | No | Evidence based |
| 7 | 2012 | SLR | G | Y | P | RQ | Yes | Requirements Engineering | Yes | No |
| 8 | 2014 | SLR | G | Y | P | – | Yes | A Systematic Approach for Requirement Elicitation | No | No |
| 9 | 2014 | Map | S | Y | P | – | Yes | Requirement Elicitation | No | Evidence based |
| 10 | 2009 | Map | G | P | P | RQ | Yes | Systematizing requirements elicitation | No | Evidence based |
| 11 | 2009 | Map | G | Y | P | – | Yes | Assessment of Requirement Elicitation | Yes | Evidence based |
| 12 | 2009 | SLR | S | Y | N | A | Yes | Procedural Model of Requirements Elicitation | No | No |
| 13 | 2011 | SLR | G | Y | P | – | Yes | Elicitation of attributes of low involvement products | No | No |

(*continued*)

**Table 1.** (*continued*)

| ID | Years | Types | Specific or General S or G | Domain Engineering | Applied Eng | Research Tool | Incl Primary Study | Topics | Elicitation Model | Evidence Available |
|---|---|---|---|---|---|---|---|---|---|---|
| 14 | 2011 | SLR | G | Y | P | – | Yes | On standardizing syntactic elicitation | Yes | No |
| 15 | 2011 | SLR | G | Y | P | RQ | Yes | Fuzzy multiple attribute decision making | Yes | No |
| 16 | 2011 | SLR | G | N | Y | – | Yes | Preference elicitation techniques for group recommender systems | Yes | No |
| 17 | 2014 | Map | S | Y | Y | – | Yes | The impact of preference elicitation techniques | No | Evidence based |
| 18 | 2014 | Map | S | Y | Y | RQ | Yes | feedback information about product use | Yes | Evidence based |
| 19 | 2015 | Map | G | Y | Y | – | Yes | Building SSPs for climate policy analysis | No | Evidence based |
| 20 |  | Map | S | N | P | A | Yes | Weighting-by choosing: a weight elicitation method for map overlays | No | Evidence based |
| 21 |  | SLR | S | P | P | A | Yes | Information world mapping | Yes | No |
| 22 |  | SLR | S | P | P | RQ | Yes | Survey on Requirement Elicitation Techniques | Yes | No |
| 23 |  | Map | G | P | Y | – | Yes | Requirements Elicitation and Elicitation Technique Selection | No | Evidence based |

(*continued*)

**Table 1.** (*continued*)

| ID | Years | Types | Specific or General S or G | Domain Engineering | Applied Eng | Research Tool | Incl Primary Study | Topics | Elicitation Model | Evidence Available |
|---|---|---|---|---|---|---|---|---|---|---|
| 24 | | SLR | S | P | Y | – | Yes | Procedural Model of Requirements Elicitation Techniques | No | No |
| 25 | | SLR | G | N | Y | – | Yes | Requirement Elicitation | No | No |
| 26 | | SLR | G | Y | N | RQ | Yes | A Framework for Requirement Elicitation | Yes | No |
| 27 | | Map | G | Y | P | RQ | Yes | Agile Methodology | No | Evidence based |
| 28 | | SLR | S | N | P | – | Yes | Requirement Elicitation | No | No |
| 29 | | SLR | G | P | N | A | Yes | Techniques for Requirements Elicitation | Yes | No |
| 30 | | SLR | G | P | N | – | Yes | Software Projects | Yes | No |
| 31 | 2009 | Map | G | | | | Yes | Empirical Evaluation of Software Requirements Specifications Techniques | No | Yes |
| 32 | 2011 | – | G | P | P | | Yes | Automated Requirements Elicitation for Global Software Development (GSD) Environment | Yes | Yes |
| 33 | 2018 | Map | G | P | P | A | Yes | A Systematic Mapping Study on Requirements Engineering in Software Ecosystems | Yes | Yes |

(*continued*)

**Table 1.** (*continued*)

| ID | Years | Types | Specific or General S or G | Domain Engineering | Applied Eng | Research Tool | Incl Primary Study | Topics | Elicitation Model | Evidence Available |
|---|---|---|---|---|---|---|---|---|---|---|
| 34 | 2013 | Survey | S | Y | Y | M | No | A Survey On Global Requirements Elicitation Issues And Proposed Research Framework | Yes | Yes |

questions with answers as Y for Yes if study fully covers the topic and other requires aspects of requirement elicitation and elicitation in GSD Environment, P for Partially described and N for no relevance:

QA1: Has the suitability and description of studies for the inclusion and exclusion criteria been verified?

QA2: Is search procedure for required studies has covered all aspects of existing available literature?

QA3: Did quality and validity of included studies have been ensured by reviewers?

QA4: Were the adequate definition of basic data of included studies ensured and considered?

QA5: Can the consistency of primary research being examined be traced back to the primary studies?

QA6: Is data extracted during search traceable to primary studies?

QA7: Is consistency and proof used in the results analyzed?

QA8: Does each study clarify requirement elicitation in general and in GSD Environment particularly?

Why these Quality Assessment Questions?

We scored questions as bellow:

QA1: The inclusion and exclusion criteria based on research questions and search strings, so that it became almost clear how studies were found.

    a. Studies fulfilling criteria = 29 (82%)
    b. Studies partially fulfilling criteria = 6 (18%)
    c. Studies not fulfilling criteria = 0 (0%)

QA2: The completeness of the literature search (Google Search, Quasi-Gold Method, Automatic Search, Manual Search, Covered Secondary Studies, and Covered Primary Studies)

    a. Studies fulfilling criteria = 26 (74%)
    b. Studies partially fulfilling criteria = 9 (35%)
    c. Studies not fulfilling criteria = 0 (0%)

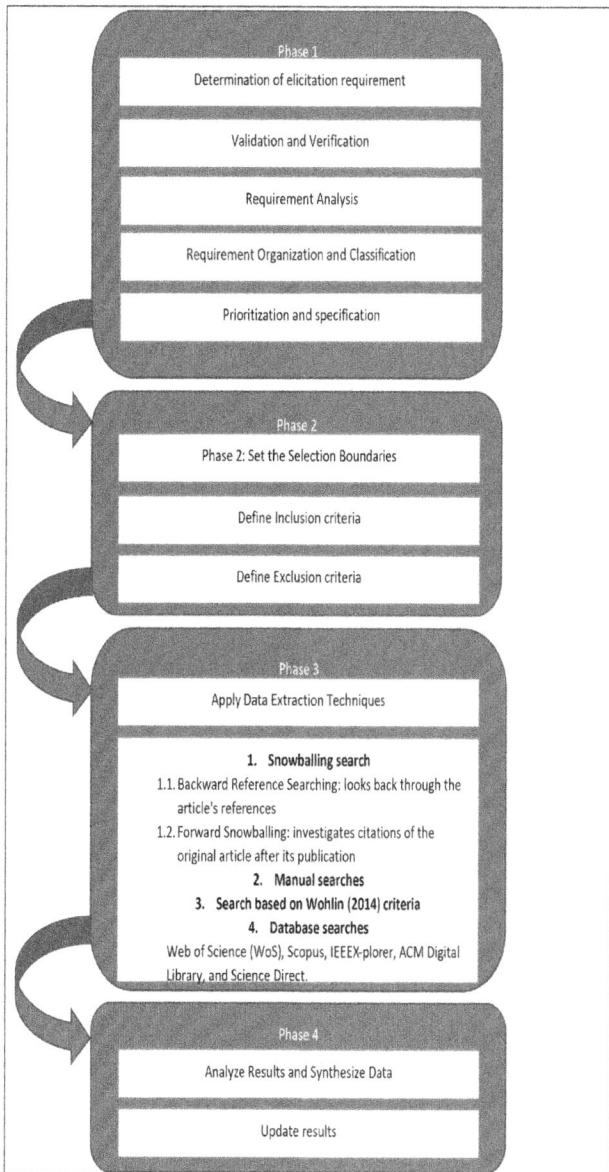

**Fig. 1.** Research Methodology

QA3: The quality assessment based on applied research methods, evidence and as per inclusion criteria of the primary studies.

a. Studies fulfilling criteria = 11 (31%)
b. Studies partially fulfilling criteria = 17 (48%)
c. Studies not fulfilling criteria = 7 (20%)

QA 4: The basic data of the primary studies.

  a. Studies fulfilling criteria = 23 (65%)
  b. Studies partially fulfilling criteria = 9 (26%)
  c. Studies not fulfilling criteria = 3 (9%)

QA5: The quality traceability of the primary studies

  a. Studies fulfilling criteria = 12 (34%)
  b. Studies partially fulfilling criteria = 19 (54%)
  c. Studies not fulfilling criteria = 4 (11%)

QA 6: Data extracted during search traceable to primary studies:

  a. Studies fulfilling criteria = 32 (91%)
  b. Studies partially fulfilling criteria = 2 (5%)
  c. Studies not fulfilling criteria = 1 (2%)

QA7: The use of evidence or quality in findings

  a. Studies fulfilling criteria = 27 (77%)
  b. Studies partially fulfilling criteria = 5 (14.5%)
  c. Studies not fulfilling criteria = 3 (8.5%)

QA8: Following studies has covered requirement elicitation and elicitation in GSD environment:

  a. Studies fulfilling criteria = 7 (20%)
  b. Studies partially fulfilling criteria = 19 (54%)
  c. Studies not fulfilling criteria = 9 (26%)

### 3.6 Quality Matrix for Selected Research Papers

Assessment of selected research studies is placed below in matrix form bases on studies and questions along with response as Yes, Partial and No.

## 4 Results and Discussion

This section summarizes the results of our study.

### 4.1 Search Results

At first, 252 papers were searched. As per constraints of supervisor and applying the including and excluding criteria 42 research studies emerged as desired papers. On further scrutiny of introduction and conclusion of the theses paper and resultantly 37 papers remained. 2 were further excluded. The process is shown below. Further details of selected papers are evaluated in Table 1 given below: Above graph indicates 80% coverage of QA-1 as yes. In QA-2 74% as yes, 26% each as partial and no. For QA-3, 30% yes, 48% Partial and 22% No. In QA-4,65% yes, 26% partial and 9% No. In in QA 5: Reliability of the primary studies remains yes 34%, 54% as partial and 11% as

No. QA-6 91% Yes, 5% Partial and 4% No. QA7: Studies fulfilling criteria is 77% yes, 14.5% as partial and 8.5% as no. QA8: studies fulfilling criteria as yes are 20%, partial are 54% and 26% are no.

### 4.2 Discussion on Results

Research Question 1: Do SRs included fulfill complete required criteria for this study?.

Research Question 2. How have quality and evidence been explored and extracted in SRs with regard to primary studies? Calculated in Table 2. Research Question.3. What is empirical evidence provided for elicitation techniques and modeling for RE in GSD as per SRs? All 35 studies cover the aspect in one way or the other. Research Question.4 Do studies clearly mention Software Requirement Elicitation modeling? Answer. 19 studies mention modeling. Research Question 5. What all requirement elicitation techniques have been discussed in general and Global Software Development (GSD) Environment?

Answer. Following are key elicitation techniques:

**Elicitation Techniques.** Two broad and main but different ways of extracting desired information to solve problems. The first one is direct while the second is indirect approach.

**Direct Approach.** It has the purpose of enhancing understandability of problems of the system in use currently. It enumerates interviews, case study and prototyping. Mentioned tools carry out comprehensive analysis of total procedure in hand to be done. Increases correct and genuine data on subject. Moreover, domain experts become able reasonably coherent and willing to share information (E. Burge, 2009).

**Indirect Approach.** Indirect methods have hindrance in direct articulation to access and obtain information. In this regard questioners and documents analysis presents fine examples it clears ambiguities thorough use of figures and statistics. In it a large quantity of data can be gathered from analyzing the documents. The results are manageable and easy to conclude decision.

These techniques with regard to elicitation are:

a. **Interview.** It consists of asking the domain expert questions about the domain of interest. It is about how they perform their assigned tasks. Types include unstructured, semi structured, and structured. Surety of success of an interview session is dependent on the questions asked and the ability of the expert to 136 Meghna Verma et al. articulate their knowledge. Models can be built interactively with the expert especially if there are software tools available for model creation" (E.Burge, 2009).

b. **Questionnaires.** "Questionnaires are very important technique in requirement elicitation techniques, questionnaires help to get the information from many peoples, and analyst can gather opinions from two ways: to get statistical evidence for an assumption, or to gather opinions and suggestions.

c. **Observation.** "In Observation methods, the knowledge engineer observes the expert performing a task. This prevents the knowledge engineer from inadvertently interfering in the process but does not provide any insight into why decisions are made" (E. Burge, 2009).

**Table 2.** Quality Matrix

| Studies | QA-1 | QA-2 | QA-3 | QA-4 | QA-5 | QA-6 | QA-7 | QA-8 |
|---|---|---|---|---|---|---|---|---|
| S-1 | Yes | Yes | Yes | Yes | Yes | Yes | Yes | Partial |
| S-2 | Yes | Yes | Yes | Yes | Partial | Yes | Yes | Partial |
| S-3 | Yes | Yes | Yes | Yes | Yes | Yes | Yes | N |
| S-4 | Yes | Partial | Yes | Yes | Yes | Yes | Yes | Partial |
| S-5 | Yes | Yes | Yes | Yes | N | Yes | Yes | Partial |
| S-6 | Yes | Yes | Yes | Yes | Partial | Yes | Yes | Partial |
| S-7 | Yes | Partial | Yes | Yes | Yes | Yes | Yes | N |
| S-8 | Yes | Yes | Yes | Yes | N | Yes | Yes | Partial |
| S-9 | Yes | Yes | Yes | Yes | Yes | Yes | Yes | Partial |
| RS-10 | Partial | Partial | Partial | Partial | Partial | Yes | Partial | N |
| S-11 | Yes | Yes | Yes | Yes | Yes | Yes | Yes | Partial |
| S-12 | Yes | Yes | Yes | Yes | Yes | Yes | Yes | N |
| S-13 | Partial | Partial | Partial | Partial | Partial | Partial | Partial | Partial |
| S-14 | Yes | Yes | Yes | Yes | Yes | Yes | Yes | N |
| S-15 | Yes | Yes | Yes | Yes | P | Yes | Yes | Partial |
| S-16 | Yes | Yes | Yes | Yes | Yes | Yes | Yes | Partial |
| S-17 | Yes | Yes | Yes | Yes | Yes | Yes | Yes | N |
| S-18 | P | P | P | P | P | P | P | P |
| S-19 | Y | Y | Y | Y | Y | Y | Y | P |
| S-20 | Y | Y | Y | Y | Y | Y | Y | N |
| S-21 | P | P | P | P | P | Y | P | P |
| S-22 | Yes | Yes | Y | Y | Y | Y | Y | P |
| S-23 | Yes | Yes | Y | Y | P | Y | Y | N |
| S-24 | Yes | Yes | Y | Y | Y | Y | Y | P |
| S-25 | P | P | P | P | P | N | P | P |
| S-26 | Y | Y | Y | Y | N | Y | Y | P |
| S-27 | Y | Y | Y | Y | Y | Y | Y | P |
| S-28 | P | P | P | P | P | P | P | N |
| S-29 | Y | Y | Y | Y | Y | Y | Y | Y |
| S-30 | Y | Y | Y | Y | P | Y | Y | Y |
| S-31 | Y | Y | Y | Y | Y | Y | Y | Y |
| S-32 | Y | Y | Y | Y | P | Y | Y | Y |

(*continued*)

**Table 2.** (*continued*)

| Studies | QA-1 | QA-2 | QA-3 | QA-4 | QA-5 | QA-6 | QA-7 | QA-8 |
|---------|------|------|------|------|------|------|------|------|
| S-33 | Y | Y | Y | Y | Y | Y | Y | Y |
| S-34 | Y | Y | Y | Y | N | Y | Y | Y |
| S-35 | Y | P | Y | Y | Y | Y | Y | Y |

d. **Documents Analysis** "Document analysis involves gathering information from existing documentation. It may or may not involve interaction with a human expert to confirm or add to this information" (E. Burge, 2009). It's an indirect method and varies depending on available documents and interaction with experts. After getting help from manuals of existing system, gathering of information about existing system along with its functions that can be analyzed that how it works and how it can perform different functions. "Document analysis involves gathering information from existing documentation. May or may not involve interaction with a human expert to confirm or add to this information" (E. Burge, 2009).

e. **Prototyping.** Prototyping has been used for elicitation where there is a great deal of uncertainty about the requirements, or where early feedback from stakeholders is required (Davis, Systematic Review of Requirement Elicitation Techniques 137 1992).

   i. Prototyping is the process to build the model about the system
   ii. Prototypes help the system designers to build the information system according to the requirements and easy to manipulate for end users.
   iii. Prototyping is an iterative process, and it is part of the analysis phase of system development life cycle. It can extend the information collection process because prototyping can convert the basic things
   iv. With the help of prototyping we can get feedback from the users; users can see facilities and provide the response and then system analysts can evaluate the response and modify existing requirements as well as developing new ones. Prototyping saves the cost and ambiguous work (Lauesen, 2004).

Research Question 6. What are barriers in Software Requirement Elicitation in general and GSD environment? In RE, elicitation of requirement proves to be the foremost step and helps analysts to acquire knowledge from relevance to specific concerning problem domain. This effort is utilized for the production of formal specifications of software being developed. During this process, challenges/ barrier is encountered as discussed below:

a. Understanding of larger and complicated software systems. Understanding requirements and their elicitation becomes an uphill task due to two aspects mentioned below:

   i. Large project takes along big constraints with regard to security (size, large number of users more vulnerability).

ii. Implantation of huge functionality. So, requirement elicitation of a complex system contains many of those requirements which remain unclear and extremely difficult during implementation phase.
b. Issue of undefined system and software boundaries. This proves to be a serious issue as no defined set of implementation requirements can be accomplished due to customers and stakeholders. Stakeholders slip to indulge into inclusion of unrelated and unnecessary functions those undermine important ones. It results in extremely large implementation cost beyond allocated budget.
c. Unclear Requirements and needs of customers and stakeholders. Customers and stakeholders can be unsure and unclear about wishing their software due to far-reaching list of functionalities. This occurs due to shallow idea about their needs without considering its implementation part.
d. Contradictory requirements. Strong possibility exists where demands, wishes and needs of different stakeholders in a particular project which contradict. Implementation of one affects the other. Cases also been seen an individual stakeholder might pose two incompatible requirements insisting for their implementation.
e. Changing requirements. Due to successive and excessive interaction (interviews or reviews) of stakeholders and customers, a strong possibility of change in requirement occurs while eliciting. These prove to be also gathered changed from initial draft. Although this seems better proves an uphill task in most cases.
f. Occurrence of Non-Overlapping of Partitioned System. In an effort in reduction of complexity of large and complex system, small modules and selected functionalities are divided among separate teams. This partitioning does not suffice and there is need to ensure non-overlapping and independence made.
g. Validation and Traceability. Validation and Traceability of elicited requirements is another uphill task. Cross-checking of selected and listed software requirements well before commencement of implementation part is very important. Forward and backward traceability needs to be ensured.
h. Identification of Critical Requirements. The most important set of requirements vital for the software system must be implemented as a priority and at all costs.
i. Proper documentation, proper meeting time and budget constraints. Ensuring proper documentation is an inherent challenge, especially in case of changing requirements. The time and budget constraints too need to be handled carefully and systematically.

## 5 Conclusion

SRs proved over the years a strongly established, widely adopted and effective research methodology. All Studies in the form of SLRs and Maps discussed on the paper provide the same knowledge area. Both of these need to be distinguishable providing expected knowledge area. It has been observed that requirement elicitation is the backbone of requirement engineering. It is the foremost process towards creativity and provides the basis of developing any software. Requirement elicitation acts as a deal of fact-finding, obtaining information and extracting correct requirements. We also conclude that correct and wisely utilized Requirement elicitation techniques prove important one and key to success for development of software and systems. It is depicted that no single technique proves to fulfill all requirement in case of elicitation. Elicitation depends on how effectively techniques are used as per expectation of stakeholder to meet their demands. We found in this investigation that most of works analyzed obstructions of requirement elicitation especially in GSD Environment and finding solution in this particular area can be a subject of a future work.

## References

1. Sharma, S., Pandey, S.K.: Revisiting requirements elicitation techniques. Int. J. Comput. Appl. **75**(12) (2013)
2. Elijah, J., Mishra, A., Udo, E.M.C., Abdulganiyu, A., Musa, A.: Survey on requirement elicitation techniques: it's effect on software engineering (2017)
3. Al-Zawahreh, H., Almakadmeh, K.: Procedural model of requirements elicitation techniques. In: Proceedings of the International Conference on Intelligent Information Processing, Security and Advanced Communication, pp. 1–6 (2015)
4. Singh, V., Sankhwar, S., Pandey, D.: A framework for requirement elicitation. Glob. J. Multidisc. Stud. **2**(2), 1–7 (2014)
5. Lloyd, W.J., Rosson, M.B., Arthur, J.D.: Effectiveness of elicitation techniques in distributed requirements engineering. In: Proceedings IEEE Joint International Conference on Requirements Engineering, pp. 311–318. IEEE (2002)
6. Zowghi, D., Coulin, C.: Requirements elicitation: a survey of techniques, approaches, and tools. In: Engineering and Managing Software Requirements, pp. 19–46. Springer, Heidelberg (2005)
7. Gunda, S.G.: Requirements engineering elicitation techniques (2008)
8. Effort estimation in global software development: a systematic literature review
9. Systematic literature studies: database searches vs. backward snowballing
10. Dieste, O., Grimán, A., Juristo, N.: Developing search strategies for detecting relevant experiments. Empirical Softw. Eng. **14**(5), 513–539 (2009). https://doi.org/10.1007/s10664-008-9091-7
11. Dybå, T., Dingsøyr, T.: Strength of evidence in systematic reviews in software engineering. In: ESEM, pp. 178–187 (2008)
12. Dybå, T., Kitchenham, B., Jørgensen, M.: Evidence-based software engineering for practitioners. IEEE Softw. **22**(1), 58–65 (2005). https://doi.org/10.1109/MS.2005
13. Easterbrook, S., Singer, J., Storey, M.-A., Damian, D.: Selecting empirical methods for software engineering research. In: Guide to Advanced Empirical Software Engineering, pp. 285–311. Springer (2008)
14. Galster, M., Weyns, D., Tofan, D., Michalik, B., Avgeriou, P.: Variability in software systems—a systematic literature review. IEEE Trans. Softw. Eng. **40**(3), 282–306 (2014). https://doi.org/10.1109/TSE.2013.56
15. Hanssen, G., Smite, D., Moe, N.: Signs of agile trends in global software engineering research: a tertiary study. In: International Conference on Global Software Engineering Workshop, pp. 17–23 (2023). https://doi.org/10.1109/ICGSE-W.2011.12
16. Haugen, O., Wasowski, A., Czarnecki, K.: CVL: common variability language. Empirical Softw. Eng. **16**(3), 365–395 (2013)
17. Jalali, S., Wohlin, C.: Systematic literature studies: database searches vs. backward snowballing. In: International Symposium on Empirical Software Engineering and Measurement, pp. 29–38 (2022)
18. Kang, K., Cohen, S., Hess, J., Novak, W., Peterson, A.: Feature-oriented domain analysis (FODA) feasibility study. Technical report, CMU/SEI-90-TR-21, ADA 235785. Software Engineering Institute (1990)

19. Kitchenham, B.: Procedures for performing systematic reviews. Technical report, Keele University Technical Report TR/SE-0401 and NICTA Technical Report 040 0 011T.1 (2004)
20. Kitchenham, B.: Guidelines for performing systematic literature reviews in software engineering. Technical report, EBSE-2007-01 version 2.3, Keele University (2007)
21. Gupta, V.: Requirement engineering challenges for social sector software development: insights from multiple case studies. Digit. Gov. Res. Pract. **2**(4), 1–13 (2021)
22. ABET Engineering Accreditation Commission: Criteria for accrediting engineering programs, 2018–2019 (2018)
23. Abran, A., Bourque, P., Tripp, L.L.: Guide to the Software Engineering Body of Knowledge (SWEBOK(R)): Version 3.0, 1st edn. IEEE Computer Society Press, Washington, DC (2004)
24. Adam, S., Doerr, J., Eisenbarth, M.: Lessons learned from best practice-oriented process improvement in requirements engineering—a glance into current industrial RE application. In: Fourth International Workshop on Requirements Engineering Education and Training, pp. 1–5 (2009)
25. Al-Ani, B., Yusop, N.: Role-playing, group work and other ambitious teaching methods in a large requirements engineering course. In: Proceedings of 11th IEEE International Conference and Workshop on the Engineering of Computer-Based Systems, pp. 299–306 (2004)
26. Alami, D., Dalpiaz, F.: A gamified tutorial for learning about security requirements engineering. In: Proceedings of IEEE 25th International Requirements Engineering Conference (RE), pp. 418–423 (2017)
27. Alexander, M., Beatty, J.: Effective design and use of requirements engineering training games. In: Proceedings of Seventh IEEE International Workshop on Requirements Engineering Education and Training (REET) (2008)
28. Anil, G.R., Moiz, S.A.: A holistic rubric for assessment of software requirements specification. In: Proceedings of 5th National Conference on E-Learning and E-Learning Technologies (ELELTECH) (2017)
29. Armarego, J., Minor, O.: Studio learning of requirements: towards aligning teaching to practitioner needs. In: REET 2005 (1st International Workshop on RE Education and Training). REET (2005)
30. Auriol, G., Baron, C., Fourniols, J.-Y.: Teaching requirements skills within the context of a physical engineering project. In: Proceedings of Seventh IEEE International Workshop on Requirements Engineering Education and Training (REET) (2008)
31. Babiceanu, R.F.: A software and systems integration framework for teaching requirements engineering. In: 2014 Proceedings of 121st ASEE Annual Conference and Exposition (2014)
32. Bano, M., Zowghi, D., Ferrari, A., Spoletini, P.: Inspectors academy: pedagogical design for requirements inspection training. In: 2020 IEEE 28th International Requirements Engineering Conference (RE), pp. 215–226 (2020)
33. Bano, M., Zowghi, D., Ferrari, A., Spoletini, P., Donati, B.: Learning from mistakes: an empirical study of elicitation interviews performed by novices. In: Proceedings of IEEE 26th International Requirements Engineering Conference (RE), pp. 182–193 (2018)
34. Bano, M., Zowghi, D., Ferrari, A., Spoletini, P., Donati, B.: Teaching requirements elicitation interviews: an empirical study of learning from mistakes. Requir. Eng. **24**(3), 259–289 (2019)
35. Barnes, R.J., Gause, D.C., Way, E.C.: Teaching the unknown and the unknowable in requirements engineering education. In: Proceedings of Seventh IEEE International Workshop on Requirements Engineering Education and Training (REET) (2008)
36. Bennaceur, A., Lockerbie, J., Horkoff, J.: On the learnability of i*: experiences from a new teacher. In: 1st International iStar Teaching Workshop (iStarT 2015), vol. 1370, pp. 43–48 (2015)

37. Berkling, K., Geisser, M., Hildenbrand, T., Rothlauf, F.: Offshore software development: transferring research findings into the classroom. In: Lecture Notes in Computer Science (Including Subseries Lecture Notes in Artificial Intelligence and Lecture Notes in Bioinformatics). LNCS, vol. 4716, pp. 1–18 (2007)
38. Berre, A.J., Huang, S., Murad, H., Alibakhsh, H.: Teaching modelling for requirements engineering and model-driven software development courses. Comput. Sci. Educ. **28**(1), 42–64 (2018)
39. Berry, D.M., Kaplan, C.S.: Planned programming problem gotchas as lessons in requirements engineering. In: Proceedings of 5th International Workshop on Requirements Engineering Education and Training, pp. 20–25 (2010)
40. Bhowmik, T., Niu, N., Reese, D.: Students vs. professionals in assisted requirements tracing: how could we train our students? In: Proceedings of 121st ASEE Annual Conference and Exposition (2014)
41. Bourque, P., Fairley, R.E.: Guide to the Software Engineering Body of Knowledge (SWEBOK(R)): Version 3.0, 3rd edn. IEEE Computer Society Press, Washington, DC (2014)
42. Brings, J., Daun, M., Kempe, M., Weyer, T.: On different search methods for systematic literature reviews and maps: experiences from a literature search on validation and verification of emergent behavior. In: Proceedings of the 22nd International Conference on Evaluation and Assessment in Software Engineering 2018, pp. 35–45 (2018)
43. Bubenko, J.A.: Challenges in requirements engineering. In: Proceedings of 1995 IEEE International Symposium on Requirements Engineering (RE 1995), pp. 160–162 (1995)
44. Callele, D., Makaroff, D.: Teaching requirements engineering to an unsuspecting audience. SIGCSE Bull **38**(1), 433–437 (2006)
45. Cico, O., Jaccheri, L., Nguyen-Duc, A., Zhang, H.: Exploring the intersection between software industry and software engineering education—a systematic mapping of software engineering trends. J. Syst. Softw. **172**, 110736 (2020)
46. Cockburn, A., Dragicevic, P., Besançon, L., Gutwin, C.: Threats of a replication crisis in empirical computer science. Commun. ACM **63**(8), 70–79 (2020)
47. Fuji, T.: Finding competitive advantage in requirements analysis education. In: 13th IEEE International Conference on Requirements Engineering (RE 2005), pp. 493–494 (2005)
48. Gabrysiak, G., Giese, H., Seibel, A.: Why should i help you to teach requirements engineering? In: 2011 6th International Workshop on Requirements Engineering Education and Training, pp. 9–13 (2011)
49. Gabrysiak, G., Giese, H., Seibel, A., Neumann, S.: Teaching requirements engineering with virtual stakeholders without software engineering knowledge. In: Proceedings of 5th International Workshop on Requirements Engineering Education and Training, pp. 36–45 (2010)
50. Gabrysiak, G., Hebig, R., Pirl, L., Giese, H.: Cooperating with a non-governmental organization to teach gathering and implementation of requirements. In: 2013 26th International Conference on Software Engineering Education and Training (CSEE T), pp. 11–20 (2013)
51. Garbers, B., Periyasamy, K.: A light-weight tool for teaching the development and evaluation of requirements documents. In: Annual Conference of American Society of Engineering Education (ASEE) (2006)
52. Garcia, I., Pacheco, C., León, A., Calvo-Manzano, J.A.: Experiences of using a game for improving learning in software requirements elicitation. Comput. Appl. Eng. Educ. **27**(1), 249–265 (2019)
53. García, I., Pacheco, C., León, A., Calvo-Manzano, J.A.: A serious game for teaching the fundamentals of ISO/IEC/IEEE 29148 systems and software engineering—lifecycle processes—requirements engineering at undergraduate level. Comput. Stand. Interfaces **67**, 103377 (2020)

54. Garousi, V., Mesbah, A., Betin-Can, A., Mirshokraie, S.: A systematic mapping study of web application testing. Inf. Softw. Technol. **55**(8), 1374–1396 (2013)
55. Gary, K.A.: Contextual requirements experiences within the software enterprise. In: Proceedings of Fourth International Workshop on Requirements Engineering Education and Training, pp. 12–19 (2009)
56. Gibson, J.P.: Formal requirements engineering: learning from the students. In: Proceedings 2000 Australian Software Engineering Conference, pp. 171–180 (2000)
57. Glinz, M.: Improving the quality of requirements with scenarios (2000)
58. Glinz, M.: Standard glossary for the certified professional for requirements engineering (CPRE) studies and exam v2.0.0. Technical report, International Requirements Engineering Board e.V. (2020)
59. Glinz, M., Fricker, S.A.: On shared understanding in software engineering: an essay. Comput. Sci. Res. Dev. **30**(3), 363–376 (2015)
60. Goldsmith, R.F.: BAs will falter until they learn to discover REAL, business requirements. In: Proceedings of Fourth International Workshop on Requirements Engineering Education and Training (REET 2009), pp. 6–11 (2009)
61. Gotel, O., Kulkarni, V., Say, M., Scharff, C., Sunetnanta, T.: Distributing responsibilities to engineer better requirements: leveraging knowledge and perspectives for students to learn a key skill. In: Fourth International Workshop on Requirements Engineering Education and Training, pp. 28–37 (2009)
62. Gotel, O.C.Z., Morris, S.J.: Case-based stories for traceability education and training. In: Proceedings of Seventh IEEE International Workshop on Requirements Engineering Education and Training (REET), pp. 1–8 (2012)
63. Hagel, G., Müller-Amthor, M., Landes, D., Sedelmaier, Y.: Involving customers in requirements engineering education: mind the goals! In: Proceedings of 3rd European Conference of Software Engineering Education (ECSEE), pp. 113–121 (2018)
64. Hasson, P., Cooper, S.: A case study involving the use of Z to aid requirements specification in the software engineering course. In: Proceedings of 17th Conference on Software Engineering Education and Training, vol. 17, pp. 84–89 (2004)
65. Heimbürger, A., Isomöttönen, V.: Infographics as a reflective assignment method in requirements engineering e-course? In: 2019 IEEE Frontiers in Education Conference (FIE), pp. 1–5 (2019)
66. Hertz, K., Spoletini, P.: Are requirements engineering courses covering what industry needs? A preliminary analysis of the United States situation. In: IEEE 8th International Workshop on Requirements Engineering Education and Training (REET), pp. 20–23 (2018)
67. Hmelo-Silver, C.E.: Problem-based learning: what and how do students learn? Educ. Psychol. Rev. **16**, 235–266 (2004)
68. Horkoff, J.: Observational studies of new i* users: challenges and recommendations. In: 1st International iStar Teaching Workshop (iStarT 2015), vol. 1370, pp. 13–18 (2015)
69. Horkoff, J.: The influence of agile methods on requirements engineering courses. In: Proceedings of IEEE 8th International Workshop on Requirements Engineering Education and Training (REET), pp. 11–19 (2018)
70. Huijs, C., Sikkel, K., Wieringa, R.: Mission 2 solution: requirements engineering education as central theme in the BIT programme (2005)
71. Iacob, C., Faily, S.: Using extreme characters to teach requirements engineering. In: Proceedings of IEEE 30th Conference on Software Engineering Education and Training (CSEE&T), pp. 107–111 (2017)
72. Ibrahim, Z., Soo, M.C., Soo, M.T., Aris, H.: Design and development of a serious game for the teaching of requirements elicitation and analysis. In: 2019 IEEE International Conference on Engineering, Technology and Education (TALE), pp. 1–8 (2019)

73. Idri, A., Ouhbi, S., Fernández-Alemán, J.L., Toval, A.: A survey of requirements engineering education. In: Proceedings of the 2012 IEEE Global Engineering Education Conference (EDUCON), pp. 1–5 (2012)
74. IEEE: IEEE standard for conceptual modeling language syntax and semantics for IDEF1X/Sub 97/ (IDEF/Sub Object/). IEEE Std 1320.2-1998 (1998)
75. IEEE: IEEE standard for software quality assurance processes. IEEE Std 730-2014 (Revision of IEEE Std 730-2002), pp 1–138 (2014)
76. IEEE & ACM JTFCC, Software Engineering: Curriculum guidelines for undergraduate degree programs in software engineering. Technical report, IEEE & ACM; The Joint Task Force on Computing Curriula (2004)
77. IREB: Certified professional for requirements engineering foundation level syllabus v3.0.1. Technical report, International Requirements Engineering Board e.V. (2020)
78. ISO/IEC: ISO/IEC 15474-1:2002 information technology—CDIF framework—part 1: overview (2002)
79. ISO/IEC: ISO/IEC 14102:2008 information technology—guideline for the evaluation and selection of CASE tools (2008)
80. ISO/IEC: ISO/IEC 10746-2:2009 information technology—open distributed processing—reference model: foundations (2009)
81. Jagielska, D., Wernick, P., Wood, M., Bennett, S.: How natural is natural language?: how well do computer science students write use cases? In: Companion to the 21st ACM SIGPLAN Symposium on Object-Oriented Programming Systems, Languages, and Applications, vol. 2006, pp. 914–924 (2006)
82. Jamaludin, N.A.A., Sahibuddin, S., Hidayat, N.H.: Challenges of a project-based learning approach towards requirement engineering. Int. J. Comput. Appl. **50**(3), 66–71 (2012)
83. Jiang, Y., Li, M., He, Z., Zhao, C.: Nine steps to shorten the distance between requirement theory and practice. In: First International Workshop on Education Technology and Computer Science, vol. 3, pp. 694–698 (2009)
84. Kakeshita, T., Yamashita, S.: A requirement management education support tool for requirement elicitation process of REBOK. In: 3rd International Conference on Applied Computing and Information Technology/2nd International Conference on Computational Science and Intelligence, pp. 40–45 (2015)
85. Keller, K., Neubauer, A., Brings, J., Daun, M.: Tool-support to foster model-based requirements engineering for cyber physical systems. In: Modellierung (Workshops), vol. 2060, pp. 47–56 (2018)
86. Kilicay-Ergin, N., Laplante, P.A.: An online graduate requirements engineering course. IEEE Trans. Educ. **56**(2), 208–216 (2013)
87. Kitchenham, B., Brereton, P.: A systematic review of systematic review process research in software engineering. Inf. Softw. Technol. **55**(12), 2049–2075 (2013)
88. Klapholtz, D., McDonald, J., Pyster, A.: The graduate software engineering reference curriculum (GSwERC). In: 2009 22nd Conference on Software Engineering Education and Training, pp. 290–291 (2009)
89. Knauss, E., Schneider, K., Stapel, K.: A game for taking requirements engineering more seriously. In: 2008 Third International Workshop on Multimedia and Enjoyable Requirements Engineering—Beyond Mere Descriptions and with More Fun and Games, pp. 22–26 (2008)
90. Koch, M., Landes, D.: Making means-end-maps workable for recommending teaching methods. In: Proceedings of Eighth International i* Workshop, vol. 1402, pp. 85–90 (2015)
91. Kramer, J.: Abstraction—is it teachable? 'The devil is in the detail'. In: 16th Conference on Software Engineering Education and Training, p. 32 (2003)
92. Kurkovsky, S., Ludi, S., Clark, L.: Active learning with LEGO for software requirements. In: Proceedings of the 50th ACM Technical Symposium on Computer Science Education, SIGCSE 2019, pp. 218–224. Association for Computing Machinery, New York (2020)

93. Laiq, M., Dieste, O.: Chatbot-based interview simulator: a feasible approach to train novice requirements engineers. In: 2020 10th International Workshop on Requirements Engineering Education and Training (REET), pp. 1–8 (2020)
94. Lami, G.: Teaching requirements engineering in the small: an under-graduate course experience. In: Proceedings of the 1st International Workshop on Requirements Engineering Education and Training (REET) (2005)
95. Lavallee, M., Robillard, P.-N., Mirsalari, R.: Performing systematic literature reviews with novices: an iterative approach. IEEE Trans. Educ. **57**(3), 175–181 (2013)
96. Liang, P., De Graaf, O.: Experiences of using role playing and wiki in requirements engineering course projects. In: Proceedings of 18th International IEEE Requirements Engineering Conference, pp. 1–6 (2010)
97. Lima, T., Campos, B., Santos, R., Werner, C.: UbiRE: a game for teaching requirements in the context of ubiquitous systems. In: Proceedings of XXXVIII Conferencia Latinoamericana En Informatica (CLEI) (2012)
98. Liu, L., Jin, Z.: Balancing academic and industrial needs in RE courses. In: Requirements Engineering Education and Training 2008 (2008)

# An Efficient Machine Learning Technique for Prediction of Cardiovascular Disease

Rida Nawaz(✉)

Superior University, Lahore, Pakistan
usmannawaz065@gmail.com

## 1 Introduction

Cardiovascular disease (CVD), a chronic and debilitating disease characterized by heart and blood vessel problems, is the leading cause of premature death and long-term disability worldwide today. Therefore, current CVD care is primarily focused on prevention. CVD has a slow onset and a long trial period, so it is often detected early. In recent years, an increasing number of CVD prevention and control guidelines have advocated the use of CVD risk prediction models to identify high-risk groups who may benefit from early intervention to reduce CVD risk [1, 2]. An electrocardiogram (ECG), blood pressure, cholesterol, blood sugar, and auscultation are performed prior to diagnosing cardiovascular disease. Machine learning is used to solve difficult problems across a range of disciplines. Cardiovascular disease is extremely complex and treatment requires extra care. Machine learning classification is used to detect cardiovascular disease [3]. Demographics, clinical history, symptoms, diagnosis, prescription, and therapy are all collected when a patient enters a hospital. Health Information Systems (HIS) are crucial because they give decision-making data. Thus, data science combines machine learning, statistics, and database systems that can be used to identify trends in large datasets. According to the Ministry of Health, cardiovascular disease is the leading cause of death globally, killing around 19 million people each year [4, 5].

The disease progresses so rapidly that there is not enough time to cure it. One of the most effective ways to detect heart problems is echo. Echocardiography, or echo, is a non-invasive treatment that uses vibrations to create images of the heart. This test determines the size and shape of the heart and the function of its cells and veins [6]. Machine learning and deep learning are terms used to describe a set of methods that allow computers to discover patterns and make decisions based on information. Discover new treatment targets, improve modeling of care pathways, and help us deliver faster information and high-quality, precise care [7]. As high-performance computers and machine learning algorithms that can handle difficult tasks become more widespread (such as artificial intelligence and reinforcement techniques), clinical interest in using these techniques in research and therapy has increased [8]. In this article, we discuss the pros and cons of the current use of machine learning in cardiovascular medicine. Diagnosing this condition is a difficult process. It must be diagnosed carefully and correctly. In some areas, the limited skills and lack of medical professionals put their patients at risk. It is usually diagnosed based on the intuition of a specialist. Various data mining techniques have been used to help clinicians diagnose heart disease. Naive Bayes, Decision Trees, and Neural Networks are the most commonly used classification algorithms. Clinical diagnosis is seen as an important but challenging process that needs to be performed accurately and quickly. It would be very beneficial to automate this process. Unfortunately, not all physicians are competent in all specialties, and there are shortages in some areas.

The majority of the writers in data mining classifications approaches offered for the prediction of heart disease, however the prediction system did not take uncertainty in the data measure into account. So, in order to reduce ambiguity and uncertainty, we tried a fuzzy approach by introducing a membership function to the classifier. The fuzzy K-NN predictor results are intriguing in nature for eliminating redundant and irrelevant features and improving classifier performance when compared to other classifiers of supervised and un-supervised learning methods in data mining [9, 10] (Fig. 1).

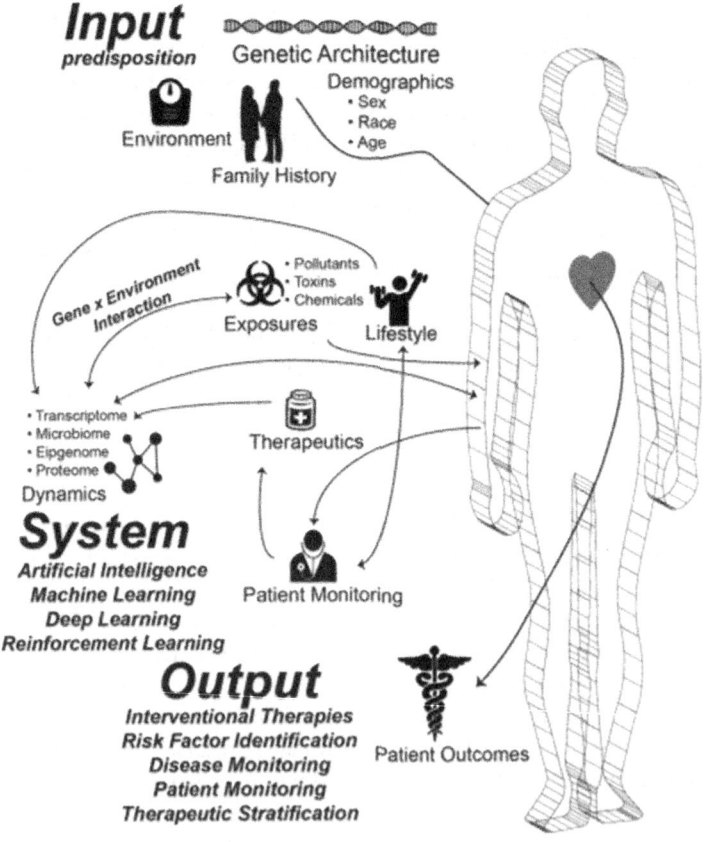

**Fig. 1.** Genetic Architecture Demographics

## 2   Literature Review

Heart disease is a major public health problem in today's culture. Traditional approaches are incapable of assessing the massive amount of medical data created by health care technologies in 2018. Data mining is used to enhance processes by discovering patterns and characteristics in massive amounts of complicated data. The most well-known data mining activities include recommendation systems, classification techniques, classification, clustering, prediction, and sequential patterns. Many research studies have been carried out to forecast cardiac ailments using various data mining algorithms based on feature selection techniques in order to obtain exact classification using the optimal feature set. Several research on the diagnosis of cardiovascular disease have been conducted. They investigated several data mining technologies for diagnosis and identified varying probabilities for each choice.

The number of patients with cardiovascular disease is growing exponentially. Researchers use a range of methods and algorithms to predict cardiovascular disease. Various data mining techniques have been used to help healthcare professionals diagnose heart disease. The most commonly used focus on classification: Naive Bayes, Decision Trees, and Neural Networks. Heart disease is more frequent in women after menopause and in men over the age of 40, and the majority of heart attack deaths occur in those over the age of 65. Men are more likely than women to suffer a heart attack, and they have them at a younger age [11]. Several research focusing on cardiovascular disease diagnosis have been published too far. These studies used various methods to the problem and produced classification accuracies of 78% or higher. Diagnosis of heart disease depends on clinical and morbid data. Heart disease prediction systems help medical professionals predict the status of heart disease based on a patient's clinical data. Researchers apply various data mining techniques to help medical professionals improve accuracy. Neural Networks, Naive Bayes, Genetic Algorithms, Decision Trees, Cluster Classification, Support Vector Machines (SVM) are some of the techniques used here [12]. The research focuses on employing higher-order harmonics to characterize coronary artery disease using ECG data. K-Nearest Neighbor and Decision Tree are used in the article. The accuracy calculated by these methods is 98.17% and 98.99%, etc. Data mining is another name for Knowledge Discovery (KDD) in Databases. The term KDD comes from the field of artificial intelligence (AI) research. The goal of data mining is to find important patterns and relationships. This is done by analyzing data patterns. It also supports by providing information about various user expectations or applications.

The severity of the patient's heart disease Determined through a series of data mining Neural Networks. Coronary heart disease is a difficult idea, and how therefore, it should be treated with caution. Also failed early detection of the disease can have serious consequences for the heart and even death [13]. An important part of the human body is the heart. All Blood is pumped by the heart to every part of the body the body and through this blood oxygen and other nutrients supply the body. Other organs of the body can stop works properly when the heart isn't working properly. The same goes for the care of the heart and other organs a challenge [14]. Any traditional CVD risk assessment model implicit assumptions about any risk factors associated with CVD outcomes in a linear fashion. Such models tend to oversimplify complex relationships, including multiple risk factors with nonlinear interactions [15]. CVD is a group of heart and blood vessel disorders, including Coronary heart disease, cerebrovascular disease, rheumatism Diseases and other conditions [6]. In application Decision Trees, Logistic Regression, SVM and Other algorithms for predicting early heart disease. These risk models are developed by Rapid Miner and WEKA tools have been tested for accuracy, precision, Sensitivity and specificity & although different methods and Algorithm used to best predict heart disease Accuracy of the latest research; however, some operations are less efficient. Our research focuses on identifying significant risks for non-invasive heart disease by using different feature selection techniques and attributes Classification algorithm. The result obtained measure demonstrate how to use these techniques effectively medical area.

## 3 Methodology

This study discusses the importance of feature selection in properly classifying cardiovascular disease. This paper discusses recommended methods, including dataset design, data preprocessing, machine learning, classifiers, feature evaluators, and performance evaluation. The purpose is to build a classification model using the provided dataset. The information is provided by the Cardio-Vascular Medicine domain. The purpose is to identify whether a patient is in danger. Because we're dealing with if/then classification, the model will be binary, also known as a 0 or 1 classification modality (binary classifier).

The study's effectiveness will be determined by how effectively a model properly classifies people as at risk. Multiple models will be created and analyzed to see which results best correspond with the goals of the organization. With the exception of Random and ID, all components will be employed in this attempt. This is due to the fact that, while the qualities are important for showing information on patients and their scores, they are incompatible with the overall goal and are so eliminated.

## 4 Phase of Data Modeling

### 4.1 Logistic Regression

When the classification objective is binary, Logistic Regression is a useful model to utilize, as explained in the module. It was employed since Linear Regression is ineffective for this purpose while Logistic Regression is. Linear SVC is a linear model based on SVM.

### 4.2 Neural Network

My latest model is a neural network, which I chose because it can be tweaked and updated to improve accuracy. It is advantageous to be able to modify the learning level of the model, and the parameters can be adjusted to achieve the desired output sooner or later. It works in the same way as the human brain and is very useful for problem solving. The input and output of each model are the same. Each model is trained and then cross-validated to use the train/test split method. Each model is trained on X and then tested on Y, where X is the data and Y is the target. Multiple iterations are used to train the algorithm. Some of the examined models had few network parameters that could be changed, but in this case several strategies were employed to obtain the best results, followed by cross-validation with the same hyper parameters. Before analyzing the accuracy measures, I cross-validated using 10-fold cross-validation to ensure that the accuracy achieved was reasonable. Thereafter, compare the accuracy indicated by the train/test split. Cross-validation is used to determine whether the data split is uniform and reflects the entire dataset used, and whether the model generalizes.

### 4.3 Phase of Evaluation

This is where all the findings are collated and evaluated. Because the six models were developed and trained using the same train/test split, it was critical to determine which model performed better and in which areas one model outperformed the other, even if the performance appeared to be the same. The commercial goal of these models is to achieve high accuracy while maintaining a low number of false negatives, which would indicate that a patient is classified as risk-free, when in fact, relevant to the medical profession, it is extremely detrimental. I have used various datasets and classification reports to determine how well the model is working and the best of all possibilities. The program is on schedule; there are some small items to check, such as: B. Visualization part, but the project time frame follows the CRISP-DM technique. In the evaluation section of this report, a progress evaluation is performed to see if there is anything that might mislead the established conclusions, and all results for each model are checked (Table 1).

**Table 1.** Heart Disease Prediction Dataset

| Sr # No | Features | Description | Value |
|---|---|---|---|
| 1 | Age | Years count | Continue |
| 2 | Figure | Ma/Fe | Male = 1, Female = 0 |
| 3 | Cpt | Chest Pain Types | 1 = classic angina<br>2 = Atypical angina<br>3 = Non-Angina Bread<br>4 = Asymptomatic |
| 4 | Rbp | Blood pressure checking in resting mode(mm/Hg) | Continue |
| 5 | Scholes | Serum cholesterol(mg/dl) | Continue |
| 6 | Fb | Blood sugar in fasting | $1 \geq 110$ mg/dl<br>$0 \geq$ mg/dl |
| 7 | Reselectg | Electrocardiographic results in resting mode | 0 = normal<br>1 = ST wave abnormality<br>2 = Left ventricular hypertrophy |

(*continued*)

**Table 1.** (*continued*)

| Sr # No | Features | Description | Value |
|---|---|---|---|
| 8 | Thalac | Achieved maximum heart rate | continue |
| 9 | Exeng | Do exercise included angina | 1 = yes<br>0 = no |
| 10 | Sloseg | The peak exercise segment of the slope | 1 = increase<br>2 = flat<br>3 = Slope down |
| 11 | Thale | Thalium scan | 4 = usually<br>7 = Fixed detection<br>8 = Reversible defect |
| 12 | Cf | Fluoroscopically stained number of major blood vessels | (1–5) |

## 5 Results

| Naïve Bayes | Accuracy: 90% | | Prediction |
|---|---|---|---|
| Observed | | Positive | Negative |
| | Positive | 300 | 3 |
| | Negative | 50 | 110 |

The result of Naïve Bayes accuracy, prediction and observation are between 1 to 300 positive and negative prediction data set.

| Naive Bayes Classification Report | Precision-Sensitivity | Recall-Specificity | P1 Score |
|---|---|---|---|
| Risk | 78% | 67% | 75% |
| Non Risk | 98% | 99.2% | 90% |

The Naïve Bayes classification report presents the precision-sensitivity, recall-specificity and P1 Score gives 60% to 99.2% accuracy (Fig. 2).

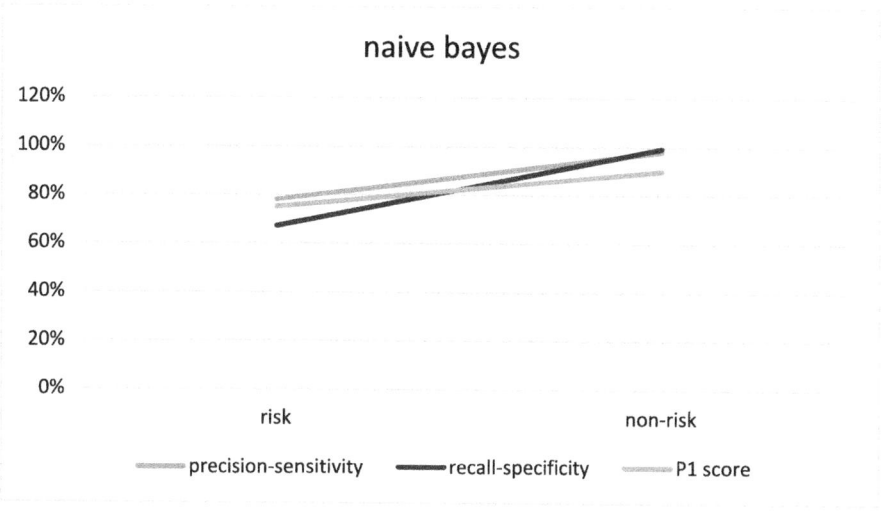

**Fig. 2.** Naïve Bayes

| LinearSVC | Accuracy: 98% | | Prediction |
|---|---|---|---|
| Observed | | Positive | Negative |
| | Positive | 300 | 3 |
| | Negative | 50 | 110 |

The result of Naïve Bayes accuracy, prediction and observation are between 1 to 300 positive and negative prediction data set.

| Linear-SVC Classification Report | Precision Sensitivity | Recall Specificity | P1 Score |
|---|---|---|---|
| Risk | 87% | 63% | 67% |
| Non Risk | 89% | 99.6% | 90.2% |

The Linear-SVC classification report presents the precision-sensitivity, recall-specificity and P1 Score gives 63% to 99.6% accuracy (Fig. 3).

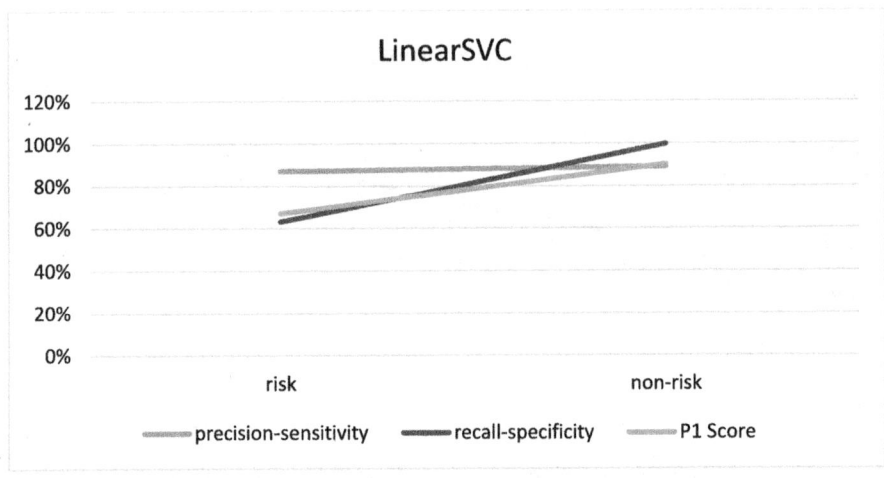

**Fig. 3.** Linear-SVC progress

| K-Nearest Neighbors | Accuracy: 98% | | Prediction |
|---|---|---|---|
| Observed | | Positive | Negative |
| | Positive | 295 | 8 |
| | Negative | 8 | 140 |

The result of Naïve Bayes accuracy, prediction and observation are between 1 to 295 positive and negative prediction data set.

| K-Nearest Neighbors Classification Report | Precision Sensitivity | Recall Specificity | P1 Score |
|---|---|---|---|
| Risk | 95% | 95% | 95% |
| Non Risk | 98.5% | 98.5% | 98.5% |

The Linear-SVC classification report presents the precision-sensitivity, recall-specificity and P1 Score gives 95% to 98.5% accuracy (Fig. 4).

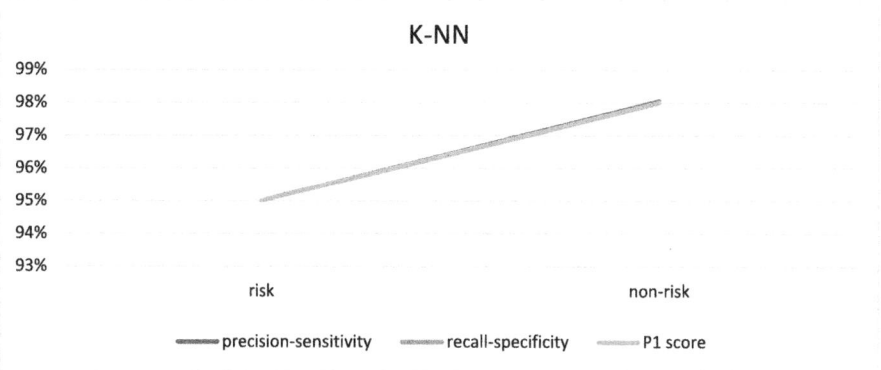

**Fig. 4.** K-NN progress

| Logistic-Regression | Accuracy: 98% | | Prediction |
|---|---|---|---|
| Observed | | Positive | Negative |
| | Positive | 296 | 5 |
| | Negative | 7 | 139 |

The result of Naïve Bayes accuracy, prediction and observation are between 1 to 296 positive and negative prediction data set.

| Logistic-Regression Classification Report | Precision Sensitivity | Recall Specificity | P1 Score |
|---|---|---|---|
| Risk | 95% | 96% | 97% |
| Non Risk | 98% | 98% | 98% |

The Naïve Bayes classification report presents the precision-sensitivity, recall-specificity and P1 Score gives 90% to 98% accuracy (Fig. 5).

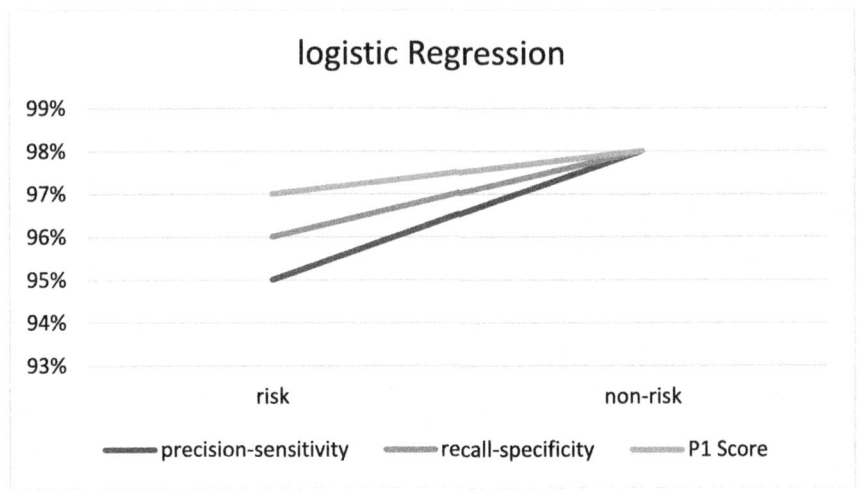

**Fig. 5.** Logistic regression progress

| Decision Tree | Accuracy: 98% | | Prediction |
| --- | --- | --- | --- |
| Observed | | Positive | Negative |
| | Positive | 300 | 7 |
| | Negative | 4 | 141 |

The result of Naïve Bayes accuracy, prediction and observation are between 1 to 300 positive and negative prediction data set.

| Decision-Tree Classification Report | Precision Sensitivity | Recall Specificity | P1 Score |
| --- | --- | --- | --- |
| Risk | 95% | 92% | 90% |
| Non Risk | 98% | 98.5% | 98% |

The Naïve Bayes classification report presents the precision-sensitivity, recall-specificity and P1 Score gives 90% to 98.5% accuracy (Fig. 6).

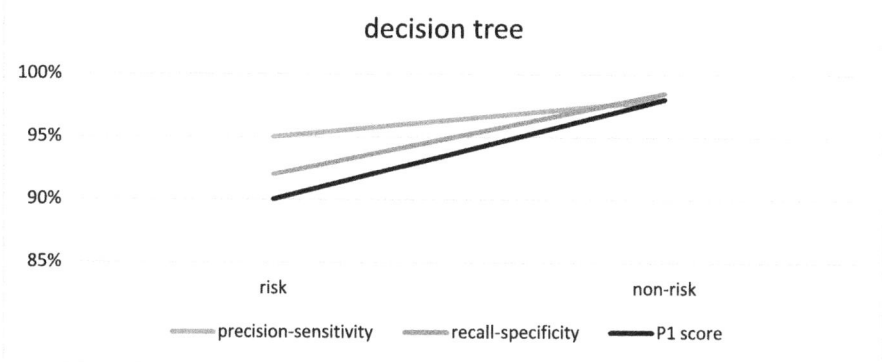

**Fig. 6.** Decision tree progress

| Neural Network | Accuracy: 99% | | Prediction |
|---|---|---|---|
| Observed | | Positive | Negative |
| | Positive | 298 | 3 |
| | Negative | 2 | 138 |

The result of Naïve Bayes accuracy, prediction and observation are between 1 to 298 positive and negative prediction data set.

| Neural-Network Classification Report | Precision Sensitivity | Recall Specificity | P1 Score |
|---|---|---|---|
| Risk | 8% | 5% | 9% |
| Non Risk | 92% | 95% | 91% |

The Naïve Bayes classification report presents the precision-sensitivity, recall-specificity and P1 Score gives 8% to 95% accuracy (Fig. 7).

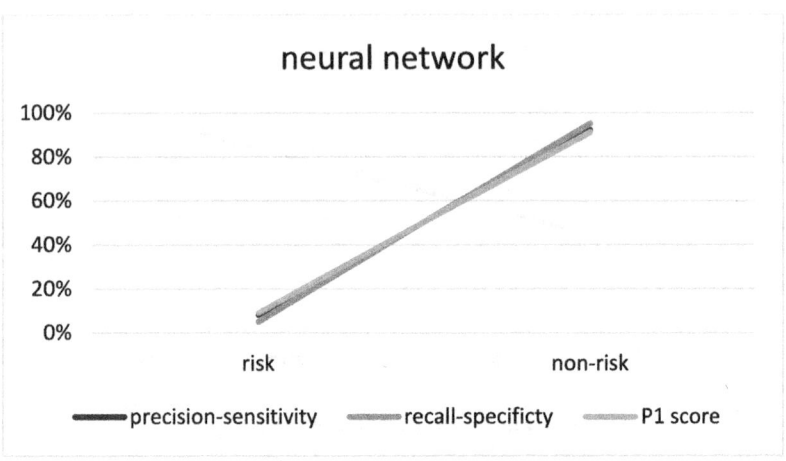

**Fig. 7.** Neural network progress

## 6 Conclusion

I checked each model's accuracy score, cross-validation performance, sensitivity score, and confusion matrix to determine the best model. The only model I've found that fails this purpose is Nave Bayes because of its lack of accuracy and weakness in classifying Type I errors, which can be fatal when the model is later used in a real-world setting. If the overall goal is to classify Type I errors, the results will indicate which model is the best fit. Looking at all six confusion matrices reveals two models that excel in this area. Considering the model accuracy, the model matching degree is very good, most of the accuracy is above 96%. It would be a mistake to treat any model with these flaws as a bad model. The problem is that only one model is allowed to be implemented later, so there must be a choice, which is why neural networks are considered the best in this regard. For risk classification, the neural network achieved 98% rounding accuracy (99% cross-validation), 97% accuracy, and only 3 out of 450 samples in the test dataset had a class I imprecision. The final selection is based not only on the score, but also on the degrees of freedom of hyper parameter variation available to the neural network. Predicting heart disease is one of the most difficult problems in medicine. Finding out what's causing this takes a lot of time and effort, especially for doctors and other healthcare professionals. Various methods are used in this work, including LR, ANN, SVM, etc., to predict heart disease. The CRISP-DM method was used for verification. These four methods were used in comparative studies. To evaluate the performance of the model, datasets from Beant Kaur, Hungary, Chitra, and Mohan, as well as the UCI Kaggle dataset for Cardiology were used. For the UCI Kaggle datasets of Hungary, Chitra and Mohan, and Cardiovascular Disease, the Extreme Multilayer Perceptron Classifier with

NN provided the highest and nearly identical accuracies of 95% and 98%, respectively. Extreme K-NN boosted classifier with NN is the best hyper parameter for test accuracy. The results were compared with previous cardiac prediction studies. The study had four participants. Four different algorithms are used to tune, train and test the algorithm. Neural networks, logistic regression, and K nearest neighbors are examples of models. Support for vector machine enhancements with and without hyper parameter tuning techniques. Their accuracy is compared with that of existing methods. Adjusting the settings of LR using the NN search test resulted in an accuracy of 99%. The boosted classifier K-NN with NN has the best test accuracy of the four methods at 99%. Without NN, the test accuracy of Extreme Gradient Boosting Classifier is 98%. In the future we plan to improve the model so that it can be used with different feature selection strategies. Another possibility is to combine NN with K-NN. The fundamental purpose of this study is to extend previous work by developing a new and unique modeling approach and using this model in a relevant and simple way in practical situations.

## References

1. Pathan, M.S., Nag, A., Pathan, M.M., Dev, S.: Analyzing the impact of feature selection on the accuracy of heart disease prediction. arXiv http://arxiv.org/abs/2206.03239 (2022). Accessed 06 Nov 2022
2. Pathan, et al.: Analyzing the impact of feature selection on the a.pdf (2022)
3. Chowdary, G.J.: Effective prediction of cardiovascular disease using cluster of machine learning algorithms. J. Crit. Rev. **7**(18), 11 (2020)
4. Taneja: Heart disease prediction system using data mining techniques, vol. 6, p. 10 (2013)
5. Mohan, S., Thirumalai, C., Srivastava, G.: Effective heart disease prediction using hybrid machine learning techniques. IEEE Access **7**, 81542–81554 (2019). https://doi.org/10.1109/ACCESS.2019.2923707
6. Martins, B., Ferreira, D., Neto, C., Abelha, A., Machado, J.: Data mining for cardiovascular disease prediction. J. Med. Syst. **45**(1), 6 (2021). https://doi.org/10.1007/s10916-020-01682-8
7. Wu, C.M., Badshah, M., Bhagwat, V.: Heart disease prediction using data mining techniques. In: Proceedings of the 2019 2nd International Conference on Data Science and Information Technology, Seoul Republic of Korea, pp. 7–11 (2019). https://doi.org/10.1145/3352411.3352413
8. Sitar-T, D.-A., Sitar-T, A.-V.: Overview on how data mining tools may support cardiovascular disease prediction (8), 7 (2010)
9. Krishnaiah, V., Narsimha, G., Subhash Chandra, N.: Heart disease prediction system using data mining technique by fuzzy K-NN approach. In: Satapathy, S.C., Govardhan, A., Srujan Raju, K., Mandal, J.K. (eds.) Emerging ICT for Bridging the Future - Proceedings of the 49th Annual Convention of the Computer Society of India (CSI) Volume 1, pp. 371–384. Springer, Cham (2015). https://doi.org/10.1007/978-3-319-13728-5_42
10. Chaithra, N., Madhu, B.: Classification models on cardiovascular disease prediction using data mining techniques. J. Biodivers. Endanger. Species **09**(03) (2018). https://doi.org/10.4172/2329-9517.1000348
11. Kiruthika Devi, S., Krishnapriya, S., Kalita, D.: Prediction of heart disease using data mining techniques. Indian J. Sci. Technol. **9**(39) (2016). https://doi.org/10.17485/ijst/2016/v9i39/102078

12. Raju, C., Philipsy, E., Chacko, S., Padma Suresh, L., Deepa Rajan, S.: A survey on predicting heart disease using data mining techniques. In: 2018 Conference on Emerging Devices and Smart Systems (ICEDSS), Tiruchengode, pp. 253–255 (2018). https://doi.org/10.1109/ICEDSS.2018.8544333
13. Ahmad, G.N., Fatima, H., Ullah, S., Salah Saidi, A., Imdadullah: Efficient medical diagnosis of human heart diseases using machine learning techniques with and without GridSearchCV. IEEE Access **10**, 80151–80173 (2022). https://doi.org/10.1109/ACCESS.2022.3165792
14. Katarya, R., Meena, S.K.: Machine learning techniques for heart disease prediction: a comparative study and analysis. Health Technol. **11**(1), 87–97 (2021). https://doi.org/10.1007/s12553-020-00505-7
15. Pal, M., Parija, S., Panda, G., Dhama, K., Mohapatra, R.K.: Risk prediction of cardiovascular disease using machine learning classifiers. Open Med. **17**(1), 1100–1113 (2022). https://doi.org/10.1515/med-2022-0508

# Analysis and Development of Kids' Cell Activities Monitoring App

Umme Tehreem[1], Muhammad Waseem Iqbal[2(✉)], Khalid Hamid[3], and Muhammad Mohsin Saeed[3]

[1] Department CS&IT, Superior University Lahore, Lahore 54000, Pakistan
[2] Department of Software Engineering, Superior University, Lahore 54000, Pakistan
waseem.iqbal@superior.edu.pk
[3] Department of Computer Science, Superior University Lahore, Lahore 54000, Pakistan

**Abstract.** Due to the COVID-19 lockdown, everything did go online so online education and business tools got very useful and vital, although those tools need improvements and innovation. The use of online applications for the educational purpose made it easy to keep things going for learning, smoothly. But the excessive use of technology for educational purposes comes up with many issues, particularly the negative use of technology instead of learning and a lot of bad habits as well. To counter this issue parents, need to digitally track and monitor the activities of their children. A lot of monitoring applications are available but the desired vigilance is not possible with the available applications. That's why in this research a Kids Monitoring App is designed and developed with all the features that make it happen for the parents to efficiently monitor all the activities of their children without disturbing any educational operation.

**Keywords:** COVID-19 · Social Media · Children screen time · location tracking · Online learning

## 1 Introduction

Screen Media Use, for example, sitting in front of the TV, playing computer games, and drawing in with web-based entertainment, has been related to the consideration and conduct issues, mental postponement, rest issues, and stoutness. Proposed foundations for the connection between time spent utilizing screen media and youngsters' weight records incorporate the supplanting of actual work with screen use and the advancement of unfortunate food sources in ads, which may adversely influence kids' food inclinations and dietary admission. A new methodical survey and meta-examination showed that both screen media access and use in the room were related to lacking rest amount and unfortunate rest quality. Given the physical and mental well-being outcomes brought about by corpulence and unfortunate rest and the universality of cell phones, expanding screen media use is a disturbing pattern [6–10]. Be that as it may, screen media use can likewise make critical positive impacts and can be properly consolidated to improve kid advancement, as well as filling in as an essential method of learning and improvement for young youngsters [17]. The review examines the connection between nurturing practices and youngsters' screen time following the Coronavirus flare-up. It was noticed that 68% of the moms didn't work, and 40.2% of the dads had moved to an adaptable work plan due to the Coronavirus pandemic. The review uncovered that 89.6% of the families had laid out guidelines connected with screen time and that the screening season of the offspring of 71.7% of the families had seen an increment, adding up to $6.42 \pm 3.07$ h/day. Orientation, age, family pay, mother's work status, family principles about screen time, and conflicting nurturing rehearses were characterized as huge indicators in the youngsters' screen time model made for the review [9]. The strategy of this paper is enlivened by Value-Sensitive Design (VSD) to concentrate on the upsides of the creator and client partners towards such functionalities. Other than the planning group of an internet-based diversion stage, we included guardians with somewhere around one kid matured 4 to 10 to investigate their qualities connected with the job of guardians in small kids' media use. As far as we could know, no exploration in the domain of CCI has unequivocally managed such a thought of points of view. The commitment of this study is the detailing of plan rules for functionalities that bear the cost of parental admittance to kids' internet-based conceivable outcomes to play, learn and mingle [13, 15].

## 2 Literature Review

Children's activities observing applications are turning out to be better known as innovation headways and keep on being incorporated into our regular routines. Guardians are progressively utilizing these applications to watch out for their youngsters' internet-based exercises, areas, and different angles. This writing audit plans to give an outline of the current examination of children's exercises observing applications, their viability, and moral worries [1–5].

### 2.1 Viability of Children's Exercises Checking Applications

A few examinations have researched the viability of children's exercise checking applications in forestalling cyberbullying and online hunters. A review directed by Hinduja and Patchin (2018) observed that parental checking of virtual entertainment and online exercises was related to a lower probability of cyberbullying exploitation. Essentially, a concentrate by Sticca and Perren (2013) found that parental control programming can be viable in decreasing the probability of online badgering [5]. In any case, not all investigations have discovered that children's exercise checking applications are successful. A concentrate by Van Sanctum Broeck et al. (2021) found that while observing applications can furnish guardians with data about their kids' internet-based conduct, they may not be guaranteed to forestall dangerous web-based conduct.

## 2.2 Moral Worries [7]

The utilization of children's exercises and observing applications additionally raises moral worries. One concern is the expected infringement of kids' security privileges. A concentrate by Livingstone et al. (2020) found that kids might feel that their protection is being attacked when their folks use observing applications to follow their web-based exercises [1]. Another moral concern is the potential for youngsters' exercises observing applications to make trust issues among guardians and kids. A concentrate by Coyne et al. (2020) found that kids might feel that their folks have zero faith in them when they use checking applications to follow their exercises.

Generally, the current exploration proposes that children's exercise checking applications can be compelling in forestalling cyberbullying and online hunters, yet their viability may not be widespread. Also, the utilization of these applications raises moral worries, for example, possible infringement of youngsters' protection freedoms and trust issues among guardians and kids. It is critical to painstakingly consider these worries before utilizing a children's exercise checking application and to have open correspondence with kids about the purposes behind utilizing such an application [2, 10].

## 3 Methodology

Fostering a Children's Exercises Checking Application includes following a particular strategy that incorporates a few phases. This strategy incorporates different advances, for example, prerequisites gathering, planning, execution, testing, and arrangement. In this segment, we will examine the philosophy of fostering Children's Exercises by Checking Applications exhaustively.

### 3.1 Necessities Get-Together

The most important phase in fostering a Children's Exercises Checking Application is to accumulate necessities. This includes distinguishing the objectives and targets of the application, as well as the elements and functionalities it ought to have. The necessities gathering stage ought to likewise include recognizing the interest group and their particular requirements and assumptions.

### 3.2 Plan

When the necessities are accumulated, the following stage is to plan the application. The planning stage includes making a visual portrayal of the application's UI, route, and other key highlights. This stage likewise includes making an information model that characterizes the design of the information that will be put away and overseen by the application.

## 3.3 Execution

After the planning stage, the application advancement group continues toward the execution stage. This stage includes composing the code and building the application as per the plan determinations. The execution stage likewise includes coordinating different parts and functionalities of the application, like the UI, data set, and backend administrations.

## 3.4 Testing

Once the application is carried out, the testing stage starts. This stage includes testing the application for usefulness, ease of use, and execution. The testing stage incorporates unit testing, joining testing, and client acknowledgment testing.

## 3.5 Organization

After the testing stage, the application is prepared for the organization. The sending stage includes introducing the application on the objective stage, like the Apple Application Store or Google Play Store. This stage likewise includes designing the application for different gadgets and stages, for example, cell phones and tablets. Fostering a Children's Exercises Checking Application requires following a particular strategy that includes a few phases, including prerequisites gathering, planning, execution, testing, and organization. It is vital to follow an organized procedure to guarantee that the application is grown proficiently and really and meets the necessities of the main interest group. At the end evaluate the app by performance-based ANOVA analysis [18–23].

## 3.6 Available Methodology

Most present-day software development processes can be enigmatically depicted as Agile Development Methodology, Waterfall Development Methodology, Rapid Application Development Methodology, Dev Ops Deployment Methodology, etc. There are the following methodologies:

- Agile method
- Crystal Methods
- Dynamic Systems Development Model
- Incremental Model
- Feature Driven Development
- Joint Application Development
- Learn Development
- Rapid Application Development
- Rational Unified Process
- Spiral
- System Development Life Cycle
- Waterfall

## 3.7 Functional Requirements

(See Table 1).

Table 1. Functional Requirements

| No | Requirement | Description |
|---|---|---|
| FR1 | Sign up (parent) | The parent will create a new account. The following information will be needed:<br>• New child name<br>• Email<br>• Password<br>• Re type password |
| FR2 | Register (child) | Create a new account by registering a child by using these steps:<br>• Category(child)<br>• Child name<br>• E-Mail(same as parent)<br>• Password(same as parent) |
| FR3 | Log in (parent) | • Log in as parent by using these steps:<br>• Email<br>• Password |
| FR4 | Select child | Select the child name we added while creating the child's account |
| FR5 | Location | Check location by clicking on the location button but the condition is the GPS and the Location must be on at child side |

# 4 Experimentation

- **Stakeholder:**
- *Parent*
- *Children*

  • Children's Age group: 5–13 years

## 4.1 Application Features

**Parent**
A person who is responsible for monitoring the other person's (child) phone's activities.

- Can check location
- Can get call log
- Can get messages
- Can record voice
- Can monitor key logs
- Can get photo (front/back) etc. (Fig. 1)

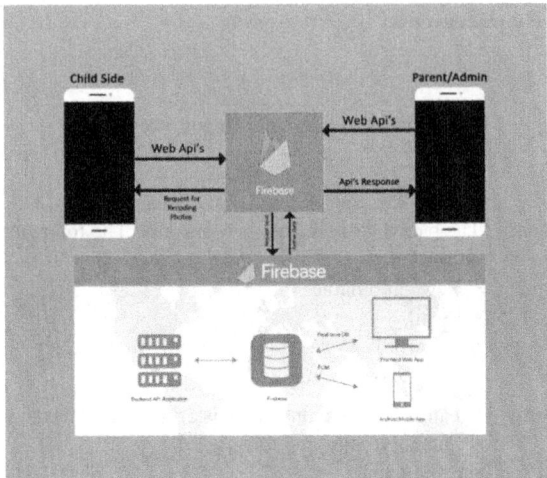

**Fig. 1.** Architecture Diagram

**Fig. 2.** High level Use Case Diagram

## 4.2 High-Level Use Case Diagram

A use case diagram is a graphic depiction of the interactions among the elements of a system. A use case is a methodology used in system analysis to identify system requirements (Fig. 2).

# 5 Results and Analysis

## 5.1 Use Case

**UC Number:** 1.1
**UC Name:** sign up
**Functional Requirement No:** FR1
**Primary Actors/Stakeholders:** user (parent)
**Secondary Actors/Stakeholders:** user (child)
**Description:** To get admin authentication and logged, the users will be prompted to login with their account information before they log in as child.
**Preconditions:** The user must have valid account.
**Main Success Scenario (MSS):**

1. The user connects to the system.
2. The user must select its category (parent).
3. The user enters his/her e-mail and password.
4. The system validates the e-mail and password.
5. The system determines the user's role.
6. The system create the users account.

**Alternative Scenario:**

1. Invalid account user or password
2. Account disabled by multiple attempts.

**Post conditions:**

1. The parent will log in to the system
2. The parent has access to the functions of the system

## 5.2 UC Number: 2

**UC Name:** log in (child)
**Functional Requirement No:** FR2
**Primary Actors/Stakeholders:** user (parent)
**Secondary Actors/Stakeholders:** user (child)
**Description:** After the selection of category the child will be logged in by using the same mail ID and password as parent.
**Preconditions:** The user must be login with his/her parent ID and password.
**Main Success Scenario (MSS):**

1. The user connects to the application.

2. They allow on all 8 permission while installation.
3. After the installation the user will be registered successfully.
4. The application displays a list of user (child) to the parent and they can select for track any one.

**Alternative Scenario:** Invalid ID or password
**Post conditions:** The user will log in to the application

### 5.3 UC Number: 3

**UC Name: log in (parent)**
**Functional Requirement No**: FR3
**Primary Actors/Stakeholders:** user (parent)
**Secondary Actors/Stakeholders:** user
**Description**: The user connect to the system by using correct ID and password.
**Preconditions:** The user must use valid ID and password.
**Main Success Scenario (MSS):**

1. The parent connects to the application and receive all the data against his/her child.
2. After the confirmation the task will be assigned successfully.
3. The application sends the information's to parent against the user.
4. The application displays a status of user i.e.: online, location, notifications etc.

**Alternative Scenario:** Incomplete user description
**Conditions:**

1. The admin will log in to the application
2. The admin has access to the functions of the application and can get all data related to the permission provided by child account.

### 5.4 UC Number: 4

**UC Name:** select child
**Functional Requirement No**: FR4
**Primary Actors/Stakeholders:** user (parent)
**Secondary Actors/Stakeholders:** user
**Description:** the parent will select the desired child.
**Preconditions:** The user must be login with his/her account.
**Main Success Scenario (MSS):** The user connects to desired child.
**Post conditions:** The parent will get the desired data related to that selected child.

### 5.5 Test Scenario

**Test Case ID:** 01
**Test Case Name:** log in as a child
**Test Priority:** High
**Preconditions:**

1. The user must be new to the system

Analysis and Development of Kids' Cell Activities Monitoring App    413

**Table 2.** Test case log in (as a child)

| SN | Action | Input | Expected Outcome | Actual Outcome | Test Application | Test Result | Test Comments |
|---|---|---|---|---|---|---|---|
| 1 | Select category, join as: child email, password | Category: child Email: Goldengold367@gmail.com Password: ******** | Home Page | Home Page | Cell phone | PASS | Log in Successfully |
| 2 | All fields are empty | Image Name: Phone Email: Password: Category: Address: | Login action Failed | Please Fill all required fields | Cell phone | fail | Log in unsuccessful |

2. The user do not have already an account

**Post conditions:** The user will not have access to the functions (Table 2).

**Test Case ID:** 02
**Test Case Name:** allow permissions
**Priority:** High
**Preconditions:** Email and password should be correct (Table 3).

**Table 3.** Test case of a task (allow permissions)

| SN | Action | Input | Expected Outcome | Actual Outcome | Test Application | Test Result | Test Comments |
|---|---|---|---|---|---|---|---|
| 1 | Allow permissions | Click on allow after reading all text | Allow permissions | Permissions allowed | Cell phone | PASS | Location has been showed |

**Test Case ID:** 03
**Test Case Name:** hide app
**Priority:** High
**Preconditions:** All permissions are allowed (Table 4).

**Test Case ID:** 04
**Test Case Name:** sign up as a parent

**Table 4.** Test case of hiding app.

| SN | Action | Input | Expected Outcome | Actual Outcome | Test Application | Test Result | Test Comments |
|---|---|---|---|---|---|---|---|
| 1 | Hide app | Click on hide app | App is hidden | App got hidden | Cell phone | PASS | App has been hidden |

**Test Priority:** High
**Preconditions:** must have registered child with parent's mail ID
**Post conditions:** The user will have access to the functions (Table 5).

**Table 5.** Test Case sign up (as a Parent)

| SN | Action | Input | Expected Outcome | Actual Outcome | Test Application | Test Result | Test Comments |
|---|---|---|---|---|---|---|---|
| 1 | select category, join as: Parent email, password | Category: parent Email: Goldengold367@gmail.com Password: ******** | Home Page | Home Page | Cell Phone | PASS | Sign up successfully |
| 2 | All fields are empty | Category: Email: Password: | Sign up Failed | Please Fill all required fields | Cell Phone | fail | Sign up unsuccessful |

### 5.6 Evaluation of the App

(See Table 6 and Figs. 3, 4, 5).
    Fit Statistics

| Std. Dev. | 0.0845 | $R^2$ | 0.9780 |
|---|---|---|---|
| Mean | 7.81 | Adjusted $R^2$ | 0.9725 |
| C.V. % | 1.08 | Predicted $R^2$ | NA[(1)] |
|  |  | Adeq Precision | 57.8828 |

Coefficients in Terms of Coded Factors

**Table 6.** Research Design Response 1: Usability

| Source | Sum of Squares | df | Mean Square | F-value | p-value | |
|---|---|---|---|---|---|---|
| Model | 15.23 | 12 | 1.27 | 177.87 | <0.0001 | significant |
| A-Input (Easiness) | 1.274E-07 | 1 | 1.274E-07 | 0.0000 | 0.9966 | |
| B-Test Application (Operability) | 0.0000 | 1 | 0.0000 | 0.0000 | 1.0000 | |
| C-Number of Actions (Cognative Load) | 0.0002 | 1 | 0.0002 | 0.0266 | 0.8712 | |
| D-6. Test Results (Effectiveness) | 7.342E-06 | 1 | 7.342E-06 | 0.0010 | 0.9745 | |
| E-7. Test Comments (Satisfaction) | 2.929E-06 | 1 | 2.929E-06 | 0.0004 | 0.9839 | |
| F-4. Actual Outcome (Actual Efficiency) | 0.0000 | 1 | 0.0000 | 0.0028 | 0.9581 | |
| G-3. Expected Outcome (Learnability) | 1.072E-06 | 1 | 1.072E-06 | 0.0002 | 0.9903 | |
| AB | 0.0000 | 1 | 0.0000 | 0.0000 | 1.0000 | |
| AC | 7.745E-08 | 1 | 7.745E-08 | 0.0000 | 0.9974 | |
| AD | 0.0001 | 1 | 0.0001 | 0.0106 | 0.9185 | |
| AE | 7.359E-06 | 1 | 7.359E-06 | 0.0010 | 0.9745 | |
| AF | 9.373E-07 | 1 | 9.373E-07 | 0.0001 | 0.9909 | |
| Pure Error | 0.3424 | 48 | 0.0071 | | | |
| Cor Total | 15.57 | 60 | | | | |

The **Model F-value** of 177.87 implies the model is significant.
**P-values** less than 0.0500 indicate model terms are significant.

| Factor | Coefficient Estimate | df | Standard Error | 95% CI Low | 95% CI High | VIF |
|---|---|---|---|---|---|---|
| Intercept | 7.68 | 1 | 13.99 | −20.45 | 35.82 | |
| A-Input (Easiness) | −0.2479 | 1 | 58.66 | −118.19 | 117.69 | 3.453E+06 |
| B-Test Application (Operability) | 7.535E−10 | 1 | 33.83 | −68.01 | 68.01 | 39480.82 |

*(continued)*

(continued)

| Factor | Coefficient Estimate | df | Standard Error | 95% CI Low | 95% CI High | VIF |
|---|---|---|---|---|---|---|
| C-Number of Actions (Cognative Load) | −1.62 | 1 | 9.95 | −21.63 | 18.38 | 80607.35 |
| D-6. Test Results (Effectiveness) | 0.6017 | 1 | 18.76 | −37.11 | 38.31 | 3.439E+05 |
| E-7. Test Comments (Satisfaction) | 0.7873 | 1 | 38.85 | −77.33 | 78.90 | 9.621E+05 |
| F-4. Actual Outcome (Actual Efficiency) | 1.13 | 1 | 21.39 | −41.87 | 44.13 | 4.408E+05 |
| G-3. Expected Outcome (Learnability) | 0.1712 | 1 | 13.96 | −27.91 | 28.25 | 54693.72 |
| AB | 4.228E−09 | 1 | 189.75 | −381.52 | 381.52 | 3.829E+06 |
| AC | 0.7782 | 1 | 236.16 | −474.05 | 475.60 | 6.972E+06 |
| AD | −1.84 | 1 | 17.88 | −37.79 | 34.11 | 42074.59 |
| AE | 4.58 | 1 | 142.45 | −281.83 | 290.99 | 3.293E+06 |
| AF | 1.40 | 1 | 122.33 | −244.55 | 247.35 | 9.287E+06 |

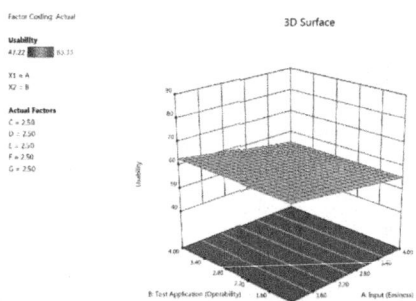

**Fig. 3.** As figure shows that apps is easy to work and operatable and has high usability

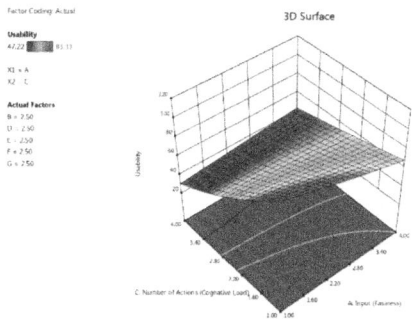

**Fig. 4.** As figure that very few tasks have more number actions and increase cognitive which effect the usability inversely

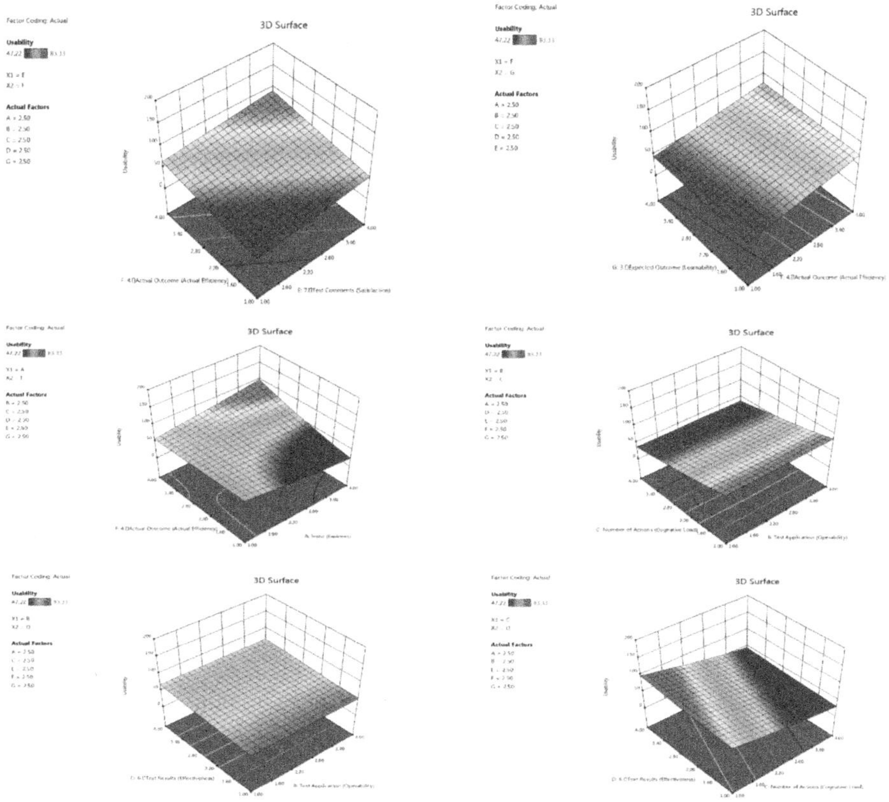

**Fig. 5.** Effect of Attributes on Usability

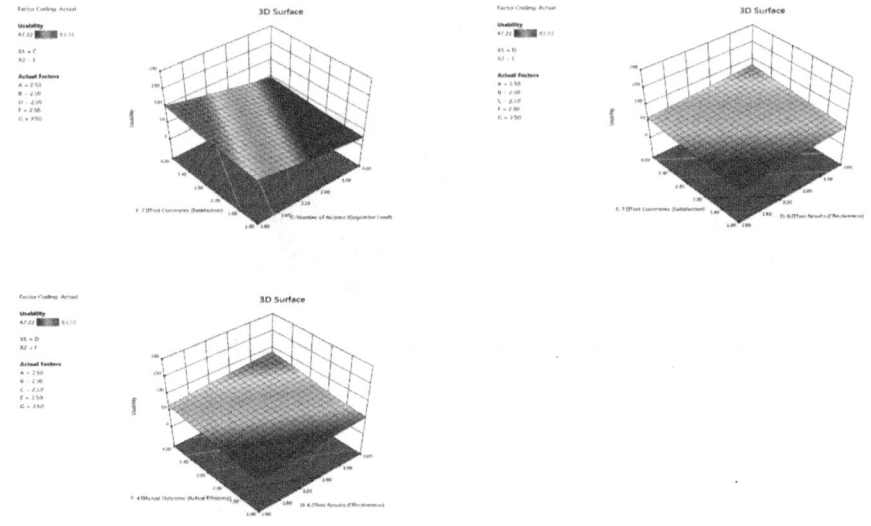

**Fig. 5.** (*continued*)

## 6 Conclusion and Future Work

This software documentation explains the whole processes and phases for the development of the application. Requirements are not told by the primary client. It is a final year project for graduation level, so requirements are gathered by the supervisor and based on team members' ideas. These requirements are categorized into functional and non-functional requirements. Then these requirements and aspects related to these requirements are represented in graphical and pictorial manners. As it is an Android-based application so it is important to create its functionality in a relevant manner. The team use xml for designing front-end designs. Designing phase also included DB designs and process designs. After designing, the team moves toward a new phase of development and coding. A team required great skills and experience in this phase, they used JAVA and its framework Ionic for the development of this system. This phase covered the development of the front end, DB, Web API and Back end. All this phase was completed in android studio. After the development of the system, another important thing is testing is also done by the team. They have done both unit testing and system testing. Now the system is working. After that performance-based usability evaluation of the app was done with the help of seven usability heuristics. This evaluation is done with 97% accuracy and usability with all attributes is up to 83.33%first time which is quite good just after the development.

## References

1. Ahmed, F., Phillips, M., Phillips, S., Kim, K.Y.: Comparative study of seamless asset location and tracking technologies. Procedia Manuf. **51**, 1138–1145 (2020)

2. Alelyani, T., Ghosh, A.K., Moralez, L., Guha, S., Wisniewski, P.: Examining parent versus child reviews of parental control apps on Google play. In: International Conference on Human-Computer Interaction, pp. 3–21. Springer, Cham (2019)
3. Brito, R., Dias, P.: "Which apps are good for my children?": How the parents of young children select apps. Int. J. Child-Comput. Interact. **26**, 100188 (2020)
4. Broekman, F.L., Piotrowski, J.T., Beentjes, H.W., Valkenburg, P.M.: A parental perspective on apps for young children. Comput. Hum. Behav. **63**, 142–151 (2016)
5. Bry, L.J., Chou, T., Miguel, E., Comer, J.S.: Consumer smartphone apps marketed for child and adolescent anxiety: a systematic review and content analysis. Behav. Ther. **49**(2), 249–261 (2018)
6. Dong, C., Cao, S., Li, H.: Young children's online learning during COVID-19 pandemic: Chinese parents' beliefs and attitudes. Child Youth Serv. Rev. **118**, 105440 (2018)
7. Eyimaya, A.O., Irmak, A.Y.: Relationship between parenting practices and children's screen time during the COVID-19 Pandemic in Turkey. J. Pediatr. Nurs. **56**, 24–29 (2021)
8. Gold, J.: Screen-Smart Parenting: How to Find Balance and Benefit in Your Child's Use of Social Media, Apps, and Digital Devices. Guilford Publications (2014)
9. Kesten, J.M., Sebire, S.J., Turner, K.M., Stewart-Brown, S., Bentley, G., Jago, R.: Associations between rule-based parenting practices and child screen viewing: a cross-sectional study. Prev. Med. Rep. **2**, 84–89 (2015)
10. Kuriakose, P., Greenlee, G.M., Heaton, L.J., Khosravi, R., Tressel, W., Bollen, A.M.: The assessment of rapid palatal expansion using a remote monitoring software. J. World Fed. Orthodontists **8**(4), 165–170 (2019)
11. Li, M., Xue, H., Wang, W., Wang, Y.: Parental expectations and child screen and academic sedentary behaviors in China. Am. J. Prev. Med. **52**(5), 680–689 (2017)
12. Adigwe, I., Van Der Walt, T.: Parental mediation of online media activities of children in Nigeria: a parent-child approach. Comput. Hum. Behav. Rep. **2**, 100041 (2020)
13. Monteiro, A.F.C., Miranda-Pinto, M., Osório, A.J.: Using mobile apps to promote children and youth online safety: a literature review (2017)
14. Azis, N.N.N., Chew, F.L.M., Rosland, S.F., Ramlee, A., Che-Hamzah, J.: Parents' performance using the AAPOS vision screening app to test visual acuity in Malaysian preschoolers. J. Am. Assoc. Pediatr. Ophthalmol. Strabismus **23**(5), 268-e1 (2019)
15. Wood, C.T., et al.: Concordance of child and parent reports of children's screen media use. Acad. Pediatr. **19**(5), 529–533 (2019)
16. Hamid, K., Iqbal, M.W., Muhammad, H., Fuzail, Z., Nazir, Z.: ANOVA based usability evaluation of kid's mobile apps empowered learning process. Qingdao Daxue Xuebao Gongcheng Jishuban J. Qingdao Univ. Eng. Technol. Ed. **41**, 142–169 (2022). https://doi.org/10.17605/OSF.IO/7FNZG
17. Riasat, H., Akram, S., Aqeel, M., Iqbal, M.W., Hamid, K., Rafiq, S.: Enhancing software quality through usability experience and HCI design principles **42**, 46–75 (2023). https://doi.org/10.17605/OSF.IO/MFE45
18. Hussain, D., Rafiq, S., Haseeb, U., Hamid, K., Iqbal, M.W., Aqeel, M.: HCI empowered automobiles performance by reducing carbon-monoxide **41**, 526–539 (2022). https://doi.org/10.17605/OSF.IO/S5X2D
19. Hamid, K., Muhammad, H., Iqbal, M.W., Nazir, A., Shazab, B., Muneeza, H.: ML-based meta model evaluation of mobile apps empowered usability of disables. Tianjin Daxue Xuebao Ziran Kexue Yu Gongcheng Jishu Ban J. Tianjin Univ. Sci. Technol. **56**, 50–68 (2023)
20. Hamid, K., Muhammad, H., Iqbal, M.W., Bukhari, S., Nazir, A., Bhatti, S.: ML-based usability evaluation of educational mobile apps for grown-ups and adults. Jilin Daxue Xuebao Gongxueban J. Jilin Univ. Eng. Technol. Ed. **41**, 352–370 (2022). https://doi.org/10.17605/OSF.IO/YJ2E5

21. Hamid, K., Iqbal, M.W., Nazir, Z., Muhammad, H., Fuzail, Z.: Usability empowered by user's adaptive features in smart phones: the rsm approach. Tianjin Daxue Xuebao Ziran Kexue Yu Gongcheng Jishu Ban J. Tianjin Univ. Sci. Technol. **55**, 285–304 (2022). https://doi.org/10.17605/OSF.IO/6RUZ5
22. Hamid, K., Iqbal, M.W., Muhammad, H.A.B., Fuzail, Z., Ghafoor, Z.T., Ahmad, S.: Usability evaluation of mobile banking applications in digital business as emerging economy, p. 250 (2022). https://doi.org/10.22937/IJCSNS.2022.22.2.32
23. Muhammad, H.A.B., Hamid, K., Iqbal, M.W., Khurram, S., Shahzad, F.M., Shaheryar, M.: Usability impact of adaptive culture in smart phones, 1 (2022)

# Author Index

## A

Abbasi, Waseem   I-73, I-239, II-330
Abdullah, Sanya   I-250
Abid, Mian   II-171
Afzal, Hamza   II-395
Ahmad, Muhammad   II-298
Ahmed, Masroor   II-1
Ahmed, Muhammad   I-345
Ahmed, Yawar   I-160
Ahsan,   II-128
Ahsan, Muhammad Junaid   II-191
Ain, Noor Ul   I-116
Akbar, Muhammad Hussain   I-324, II-21
Akhtar, Adnan   II-223
Akram, Sheeraz   I-324, II-21
Ali, Abid   II-108
Ali, Muddassar   I-130
Ali, Muhammad   II-405
Ali, Natasha   I-345
Ali, Rasikh   I-250
Almufareh, Maram Fahaad   I-181
AlWakid, Ghadah Naif   I-332
Amir, Muhammad   I-239
Anwar, Saeed   II-298
Anwar, Syed Muhammad   II-350
Aqeel, Muhammad   I-37
Arif, M.   II-128
Arif, Muhammad   II-93, II-149, II-339
Arshad, Hasna   II-61
Asaf, Muhammad   I-160
Ashiq, Masood   II-108
Ashraf, Abrar   II-287, II-362, II-380
Ashraf, Mohsin   I-228
Ashraf, Muhammad   I-193, I-206, I-332
Aslam, Muhammad   II-260
Assam, Muhammad   II-61

## B

Bhatti, Anam Maqsood   II-75

Bhatti, Sohail Masood   II-191
Bibi, Amina   I-11
Bilal, Afshan   II-298
Bqa, Rabranea   I-1
Bukhari, Faisal   I-24, I-116
Butt, Muhammad Adil   II-205
Butt, Umair Muneer   I-57

## D

Din, Irfan Ud   II-249
din, Irfan Ud   II-380
Din, Irfan ud   II-395

## E

Ejazulghaffar, Muhammad   II-93
Elahi, Ihsan   I-105

## F

Faraz, Hassan   I-250
Fareed, Asim   I-51
Farhat, Tayyaba   I-250
Farooq, Asif   I-228
Farooq, Umar   I-181
Faryal, Mehak   I-151
Fatima, Anam   II-191
Fatima, Noroze   II-128

## G

Ghadi, Yazeed Yasin   I-73
Ghafoor, Hafiz Yasir   II-171

## H

Hamid, Khalid   I-37, I-405
Hamza, M. Ameer   II-287
Haque, Ehtisham Ul   II-330
Hasan, Muhammad Zulkifl   II-1, II-298
Hassan, Ahmed   II-93
Hassan, Bilal   I-264
Hassan, Muhammad   II-322

## H

Humayun, Mamoona I-181, I-332
Hussain, Abida II-149
Hussain, Majid I-51, I-88, I-97, I-105, I-174, II-239, II-322, II-372
Hussain, Moodser I-300
Hussain, Muhammad Anwar I-219
Hussain, Muhammad Zunnurain II-1, II-298

## I

Ibrar, Muhammad I-51
Ilyas, M. Saad Bin II-205
Imran, Ali II-128
Imran, Syed Muhammad Ali II-149
Imtiaz, Ahsan I-11, II-395
Imtiaz, Muhammad Talha II-339
Iqbal, Adeel I-151
Iqbal, Amna I-174, II-239
Iqbal, Junaid II-108
Iqbal, Muhammad Junaid I-160
Iqbal, Muhammad Saqlain I-160
Iqbal, Muhammad Tassawar II-287
Iqbal, Muhammad Waseem I-37, I-130, I-300, I-308, I-405, II-75, II-191, II-223, II-287
Iqbal, Muhammad I-73, I-239
Iqbal, Waheed I-24, I-116
Iqbal, Waseem II-47
Irfan, Danish I-130, II-287, II-415
Irfan, Hafiz Muhammad II-223
Irfan, Roha I-300
Irshad, Muhammad Ahmad I-308
Islam, Atika I-24
Izhar, Muhammad II-171

## J

Jabbar, Taimoor Hassan I-300
Jaffar, Arfan I-324, II-21, II-47, II-93, II-149
Jaffer, Arfan I-345
Jahangir, Rashid II-171
Jameel, Muhammad I-300
Jamshaid, Amir II-223
Javed, Mannan I-206
Joseph, Sylvester II-287

## K

Kahloon, Ch Zubair I-324, II-21
Kauser, Maryam I-369
Khalid, Aleena II-249

Khalid, Humaira I-57
Khalil, Hisham II-362
Khaliq, Rida I-57
Khan, Farrukh Aslam I-181, I-193, I-206
Khan, Hamayun II-249, II-380
Khan, Javed Ali II-61
khan, Muhammad Bilal I-228
Khan, Muhammad Farhan I-151
Khan, Muhammad Imran I-151
Khan, Muhammad Irtaza I-228
Khan, Saif Ur Rehman II-271
Khan, Shehzad II-271
Khushi, Hafiz Muhammad Tayyab II-149
Kyinat, Samra II-141

## L

Lateef, Anam I-105

## M

Mabood, Nouman I-193
Masood, Sohail I-324, II-21, II-141
Masood, Tehreem II-405
Mazhar, Anas II-223
Mazhar, Sana I-308
Mazhar, Tehseen I-73, I-239
Meer, Ayaz Ahmad I-264
Mehmood, Danish I-181
Mir, Mariam Munsif I-369
Mubarak, Zaima II-1
Munawar, Munazzah I-51
Mushtaq, Muhammad Yousaf II-223
Mustafa, Hamza II-29
Mustafa, Hirra II-362

## N

Nadeem Jabbar, C. H. I-264
Nadeem, Muhammad Umer II-298
Nasim, Fawad I-324, II-21
Nauman, Nasir II-362
Naveed, Touheed II-1
Nawaz, Rida I-391
Nawaz, Usman I-160, I-369, II-108
Naz, Ammerha II-405
Naz, Amna II-249
Nazar, Muhammad Zeeshan II-298
Niaz, Muhammad Ahmad II-223
Noor, Misbah I-37
Nosheen, Summaira II-298

## Q

Qamar, Hafiza Iqra I-97
Qamar, Usman II-339
Qureshi, Ali Moiz II-1
Qureshi, Samia Asloob I-1

## R

Rafique, Aftab I-369
Rafique, Furqan II-108
Raheel, Muhammad I-130
Rana, Mehak II-372
Rasheed, Maryam II-191
Raza, Asaf II-61
Raza, Asif II-271
Raza, Saim I-174
Raza, Usman Ahmed I-160, I-228, I-369, II-108
Rehman, Ateeq Ur I-73, I-239
Rehman, Attique Ur II-260
Rehman, Faisal I-160, II-108
Rehmat, Nadia I-250
Rezaei, Saeid I-151
Riaz, Muhammad Danish II-339
Riaz, Muhammad Qasim II-339
Riaz, Samra II-350

## S

Saeed, Muhammad Mohsin I-405
Saeed, Uzair I-88, I-97, I-105, II-322, II-372
Saghir, Aqib I-264
Sahar, Sadia II-287, II-380
Sahi, Salman Ahmad I-264
Sajid, Omer I-1
Sajjad, Muhammad Umar II-339
Saleem, Maryam II-191
Salim, Kinza I-151
Sami, Mohsin I-228
Sanamaqbool, I-88
Sarwar, Nadeem II-1
Shafeeq, Muhammad Farrukh I-88
Shah, Syed Faisal Abbas I-239
Shah, Syed Yaqub II-61
Shahzad, Danish II-47
Shahzad, Inzamam II-271
Shahzad, Muhammad Khurram I-219

Shahzad, Rohail I-369
Sharif, Hanan II-108
Shehzad, Danish I-11, II-128
Siddique, Imran II-75
Siddiqui, Adeel Ahmad II-1
Sohail, Muhammad I-151
Soomro, Imtiaz Ali II-205
Sulaiman, Sarina I-219

## T

Tariq, Ammara I-160
Tariq, Iqra II-205
Tariq, Khizar II-1
Tariq, Muhammad Imran II-249, II-380
Tariq, Noshina I-181, I-193, I-206
Tehreem, Umme I-405

## U

Uallah, Naeem II-61
Ullah, Abaid II-308
Ullah, Kainat Azmat II-108
Ullah, Muhammad Farhat I-300
Umar, Muhammad II-239
Usman Bilal, M. II-415

## W

Waheed, Namra I-369
Waqas, Sahibzada M. I-332
Waseem Iqbal, M. II-415

## Y

Yaqub, Muhammad Atif II-298
Yasir, Siddiqui Muhammad I-264
Younas, Sana I-57

## Z

Zafar, Hina I-174, II-239
Zafar, Kashif II-29
Zafar, Muhammad Haseeb II-260
Zahra, Syeda Aqsa II-380
Zainab, II-249
Zakwan, Muhammad I-332
Zia, Saira I-37
Zubair, Muhammad II-141, II-171

Made in the USA
Monee, IL
03 May 2026

49438497R00249